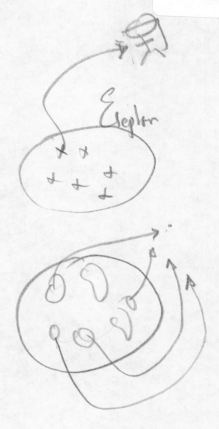

Elephant

W
DE
G

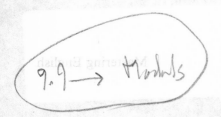

9.9 → Models

Mastering English

An Advanced Grammar for Non-native and Native Speakers

by
Carl Bache
Niels Davidsen-Nielsen

Mouton de Gruyter
Berlin · New York 1997

Mouton de Gruyter (formerly Mouton, The Hague)
is a Division of Walter de Gruyter & Co., Berlin.

Library of Congress Cataloging-in-Publication Data

Bache, Carl, 1953–
    Mastering English : an advanced grammar for non-native
and native speakers / Carl Bache ; Niels Davidsen-Nielsen.
        p.   cm. − (Topics in English linguistics ; 22)
    Includes bibliographical references and index.
    ISBN 3-11-015535-4 (alk. paper)
    ISBN 3-11-015536-2 (pbk)
    1. English language − Grammar.   I. Davidsen-Nielsen,
Niels. II. Title. III. Series.
PE1106.B27 1997 ;
428.2'4−dc21   97-23493
                                          CIP

Die Deutsche Bibliothek − Cataloging-in-Publication Data

Bache, Carl:
Mastering English : an advanced grammar for non-native and
native speakers / Carl Bache ; Niels Davidsen-Nielsen. − Berlin ;
New York : Mouton de Gruyter, 1997
    ISBN 3-11-015536-2
NE: GT

Printing: WB-Druck GmbH, Rieden am Forggensee.
Binding: Lüderitz & Bauer, Berlin.
Cover Design: Christopher Schneider, Berlin.
Printed in Germany.

Acknowledgements

In 1993, the Danish Research Council for the Humanities launched five foreign-language grammar projects. In being commissioned to write the grammar of English in this programme, we were largely relieved from our teaching duties. In addition to being sponsored by the research council, this book has received financial support from Odense University (on the recommendation of Fritz Larsen and Carl-Erik Lindberg), the Copenhagen Business School, Ingeniør N. M. Knudsens Fond and from Ib and Elise Bache. For all this generous support we would like to offer our sincere thanks.

Peter Harder (Copenhagen University) and Fritz Larsen (Odense University) have been our readers during the entire project and have provided us with extremely helpful and perceptive criticism. We are also grateful to Alex Klinge (Copenhagen Business School), Leo Hoye (Odense University) and Henning Kirkegaard (Odense University) for proposing a number of highly constructive revisions. Without the liberal assistance of these five scholars the task of completing this book would have been harder and the result poorer. Needless to say none of these persons can in any way be held responsible for remaining errors and obscurities in the text.

We would also like to thank our colleagues in the parallel grammar projects on French, German, Italian and Russian for commenting critically on selected topics in our grammar, presented at a series of very inspiring cross-linguistic symposia.

In our project we have been fortunate enough to have Christian Heyde Petersen (Odense University) as our research assistant. One of his various tasks was to compile the subject index. We would also like to thank Stefan B. Andersen (Odense University Press), Kjeld V. Sørensen, Jørn Erik Wennerstrøm and Elsebeth Jensen (Odense University Computer Service Centre) for technical assistance. For assistance received in the late phases of the work our thanks go to Anne Marie Køllgaard (Copenhagen Business School) for proofreading the entire manuscript and completing the subject index, and to Eva Bang and Mimi Swiatecka (students at the Copenhagen Business School) for helping out with the word index.

Our grammar has been tried out on students of English at Odense University and at the Copenhagen Business School, not only by ourselves but also by Alex Klinge, Christian Heyde Petersen and Marianne Stølen. Our thanks are due to these colleagues and to our students (particularly Stefan Mogensen) for providing a great deal of valuable feedback.

When in doubt about the acceptability of our examples we have conferred with native speakers of English, in particular John Murphy (Copenhagen Business School), John Dienhart, Leo Hoye, Sharon Millar, Tom Pettitt (Odense University) and Penny Rosier and Phil Staines (Sydney). Our thanks go to these colleagues as well for responding orally – with patience and apparent interest – to questions posed over a long period, often at inconvenient hours.

Copenhagen and Odense, April 1997

Carl Bache & Niels Davidsen-Nielsen

Contents

Chapter 7: The simple sentence   191

Chapter 8: The complex sentence   **253**

Part III

Chapter 9: Verbals   **277**

PART I

1. Preliminaries

1.1. Goals and framework

This grammar is aimed at native and non-native students of English in university and other tertiary education. At the same time, however, it is sufficiently extensive, thorough and detailed to serve as a source of reference for professional linguists and teachers of English. In order that it can be used not only as an advanced *textbook* but also as a *reference book*, specific topics are as far as possible dealt with separately and exhaustively. In this respect the present book differs from a number of other recent grammars of English.

The grammar itself is not explicitly contrastive and therefore not limited to a specific group of non-native students of English. It does, however, pay special attention to characteristic features of English which are more acutely felt by non-native than by native speakers of English, and in this sense it is implicitly contrastive. For example, more attention is given to constituent order – an important problem area for virtually all non-native speakers of English – than in most other grammars of English of comparable size.

The present book is not written within the framework of any particular linguistic theory (e.g. Functional Grammar or Chomskyan Generative Grammar). Such a theoretical attachment would isolate us from too many readers. In order to achieve the goals stated above we have been largely *eclectic* in our descriptive approach, though not in a random fashion. Our guiding principle will be a strict *form/function distinction* as it applies at all levels to the constituents of the sentence. In this respect the syntactic framework adopted here is largely the same as that presented in Bache, Davenport, Dienhart and Larsen 1993. The structure of the present grammar is thus determined by considerations of how to describe forms and functions most appropriately at all constituent levels in English.

1.2. Organization

The description of English grammar given in this book is divided into three parts. In *Part I* we offer an introduction to syntax (chapter 2), present the descriptive framework, i.e. the form/function distinction at all levels of analysis from sentence to word (chapter 3), and develop the sentence analysis system to cope with complex syntactic issues, such as stacking, ellipsis, zero constituents, complex predicators and the relationship between sentence type and pragmatic utterance function (chapter 4).

Part II describes basic syntactic characteristics in English: constituent order (including inversion, discontinuity and the position and order of optional adverbials) in chapter 5; coordination and subordination (including a discussion of determination, complementation and modification) in chapter 6; the simple sentence (including a discussion of situation types and participant roles, voice, negation and concord) in chapter 7; and the complex sentence (including a formal and functional classification of subordinate clauses) in chapter 8.

Part III is devoted to group structure and word classes. It discusses verbs and verb groups (chapter 9), nouns and noun groups (chapter 10), pronouns and pronoun groups (chapter 11), adjectives/adverbs and adjective/adverb groups (chapter 12). In this part of the book categories such as gender, number, tense, aspect, mood and comparison are investigated.

Though the book is structured according to *form*, it is characterized by a strong element of *function*. A great deal of attention will be given to syntactic functions such as subject, object, predicator, etc. and head-dependent relationships, to semantic functions such as agent, affected, instrument, etc. and to pragmatic functions such as topic and comment. However, our book is not a grammar of functions in the sense that it selects as its point of departure a number of major communicative functions such as 'referring to people and things', 'giving information about people and things', 'expressing time' and 'expressing manner and place' (cf. e.g. *Collins Cobuild English Grammar* from 1990 and Downing & Locke 1992).

Consideration will also be given to *information structure*, and in this connection the role played by stress and intonation and by textual factors outside the sentence influencing its syntax will be taken into account. As a very important function of the ordering of sentence constituents is to signal the way in which a message is organized into information units, information structure plays an important role in our account of constituent order in chapter 5 and of voice in section 7.4.

1.3. Data

The approach taken to data in this book is non-positivist and instrumental. We thus regard data as a means rather than an end: a means to secure analytical breadth and precision as well as illustrative exemplification. Our approach to grammar is not corpus-driven, and we do not see it as our task to provide an exhaustive description of one or more corpora. Our examples are derived from a number of sources: from modern British and American written texts (newspapers, magazines, fiction, etc.), from other grammars of English (including descriptions based on corpora of spoken and written English), from dictionaries and from introspection. Some of our examples are thus not 'real'. In those cases where we have invented examples, we have used our own intuitions about acceptability. When in doubt, however, we have conferred with native speakers of English. Sometimes we have also found it useful to modify authentic examples, thereby producing semi-authentic examples. In those cases where our examples are from dictionaries or from other books on English grammar we have indicated their source. In the remaining cases we have not regarded the benefit and interest to the reader of being informed about the source of each individual example as sufficiently great to necessitate an indication of sources (in the text and in the bibliography), which is both time- and space-consuming. Perceptive readers will recognize the following authors as being among our favourite literary sources: Martin Amis, Julian Barnes, A. S. Byatt, Len Deighton, John Irving, P. D. James, John le Carré, Timothy Mo and Isaac Singer.

The view held on data in this book is that the examples should be the ones that are relevant to a description of English grammar in all its aspects and that it does not matter whether they are derived from corpora, authentic texts, elicitation or introspection as long as they are relevant. Although corpora constitute a highly valuable source of material, and although access to corpora has been shown to reveal aspects of English grammar which have not been captured before, we do not think that a description of English grammar should proceed from authentic examples exclusively, for in that case relevant data may be excluded.

1.4. Varieties of English

All languages are characterized by variation. Some varieties are *user-related* and associated with language users living in a particular region or belonging to a particular class. But besides such regional and social dialects there are also varieties which are associated with special functions and which are *use-related*. Such variation is to do with field of discourse (e.g. law, business, science) or communicative situation (e.g. formal or informal) and differs from regional and social variation in being transient. Under use-related variation we can also include the difference between spoken and written language. There are other types of variation as well, for example according to sex and age, but the major types of variation may be said to be determined by region, social group, style (function, situation/participants) and medium (spoken/written).

English is the most widely used language in the world. It is used by at least 750 million people in addition to being the mother tongue of about 350 million people. In countries like India, Nigeria, Kenya and Singapore it is a *second language*, and is used for administration, education and broadcasting. It is therefore hardly surprising that it is characterized by a great deal of variation. Today its regional varieties differ from each other primarily with respect to pronunciation and vocabulary. While Australian English, for example, can be identified by a collection of pronunciation features (one of which concerns the pronunciation of the diphthong in words like *Australia* and *mate* as /æɪ/) and specific words and word meanings (for example *red-back*, a particular kind of spider, and *scrub* 'poor vegetation'), its grammar is remarkably similar to that of other regional varieties, particularly British English. Variation according to field of discourse primarily is to do with vocabulary. Legal English, for example, makes use of special legal terms and archaic expressions such as *aforesaid, aforementioned* and *hereinafter*. On the other hand its syntax, though tending to be rather complex, does not differ significantly from that of other varieties. Predominantly social varieties such as Cockney (the English used by working-class Londoners) and Black English (used by some US citizens of African background) have many special features of pronunciation and also many special words. But here there are also several grammatical features which are not shared by other varieties of English.

1.5. Standard English

The term 'Standard English' is widely used but is by no means easy to define. While it may be difficult to speak of a standard language as a whole, it is much less problematic to characterize some specific features as standard (e.g. the ending -*s* in the 3rd person singular form of English verbs: *she wants*) and other specific features as non-standard (e.g. the absence of the -*s* ending in such a form). A large number of those features which are considered standard in English today are derived from the Middle English dialect spoken in the East Midlands which became predominant as the official form of the language and was therefore the one preferred in writing and printing.

'Standard English' is used to describe the variety which is today most widely accepted and understood either within an English-speaking country (for example Standard American English) or throughout the English-speaking world (Standard General English, understood as a supra-regional language, or 'standard of standards'). Linguists tend to agree that Standard English is most easily identified in print (irrespective of pronunciation, which varies considerably from place to place), that it is the variety used by most newsreaders on radio and television networks (BBC, CBS, NBC, ABC, CBC, etc.) and that it relates to social class and level of education (see McArthur 1992, on which sections 1.4, 1.5 and 1.6 of this chapter are largely based). It is the written form used by all educated British writers in neutral or formal style. As Standard British English is remarkably similar to that of other national standards, for example the American, Australian and Canadian standards, it has been claimed to be the written form used by writers of English throughout the world. It is the English we find, for example, in the *New York Times*, the *Independent*, the *Toronto Globe and Mail* and the *Sydney Morning Herald* and which is described in *Webster's Third New International Dictionary* and the *Oxford English Dictionary*. This 'monocentric' view, according to which English has a (British) core and a periphery, has been challenged by some scholars, however, who hold that English has become 'pluricentric' and that it is therefore more correct to speak of 'Englishes' than of 'English'.

In this book we describe the grammar of Standard British English (BrE). Owing to the grammatical similarity between the different national standards this description will apply very largely to other national standards as well. As American English (AmE) is particularly important with respect to range and number of speakers, we shall, however, account for specific differences between BrE and AmE in the course of our description. We shall also pay attention to the difference between spoken and written English and describe grammatical features which are characteristic of spoken English.

1.6. Grammatical variation

The most important regional varieties of English are American, Australian, British, Canadian, Caribbean, Indian, Irish, New Zealand, Scottish and South African English. Regional subvarieties occur as well, as exemplified by Northern British English and by the American dialects spoken in Eastern New England and the South. Social subvarieties of a regional variety can be illustrated by the occurrence in Indian English of three levels: the acrolect (educated Indian English), the basilect (pidginized varieties) and the intermediate mesolect. Among the predominantly social varieties Cockney, Black English and Chicano English (the English used by speakers of Mexican heritage in the US Southwest) are particularly noteworthy. As pointed out in section 1.5, the grammatical differences between these regional and social varieties will not be systematically accounted for in this book. What we shall do instead here is to illustrate grammatical variation by looking briefly at a few selected grammatical features (all of which will be dealt with more extensively in subsequent chapters).

In BrE the *present perfect* (e.g. *has signed*) and the *simple past* (e.g. *signed*) are both used to describe events that precede the moment of speaking, but they differ in perspective. The former presents a past time event as having implications about what is true of the moment of speech, e.g. *She has signed the letter*. The latter presents a past event as something which has no such implications and which is in this sense over and done with, e.g. *She signed the letter*. The two verb forms are used in basically the same way in e.g. Australian, New Zealand, Scottish and South African English as in BrE. In AmE, however, the simple past is often used where the present perfect is used in other varieties, for example – addressing a child about to go to bed – in *Did you brush your teeth?*, where a very recent past event is referred to. Other examples illustrating this American use of the past are *Did the children come home yet?* and *You already told me*. In Indian English (the mesolect), on the other hand, the present perfect is often used under conditions where the simple past is used in other varieties of English, for example in a sentence like *He has bought the car yesterday*.

The so-called *progressive* construction – which consists of a form of *be* followed by a present participle, as in *She was reading* – is used to present an event as an ongoing process. In most varieties of English this construction is ruled out if the verb is meant to be 'stative', i.e. meant to express a relational state of affairs (e.g. *contain*) or inactive perception or cognition (e.g. *hear*, *know*). In some varieties, however, there are fewer restrictions on what verbs can be used in the progressive. In Scottish English we find progressive examples with stative verbs like *He was thinking he'd get paid twice* and in Indian English (the mesolect) examples like *Lily is having two books* (these examples and the ones given below in this section are quoted from McArthur 1992). In other varieties of English, progressive meaning is reinforced by a special word: in Black English this is *steady*, as illustrated by *We be steady rappin'*, and in South African English it is *busy*, as in *We were busy waiting for him*. In Black English progressive meaning can also be expressed by *steady* exclusively, as in *They be high steady*.

Thirdly, some varieties differ from others with respect to *modal verbs*. In AmE, *shall* and *ought* are rarely used outside formal style. In Scottish English there are several nonconformist uses of the modals: *shall* and *may* tend not to be used in informal speech, *must* is not used to express compulsion (for which *have to* or *have got to* are used) and *need* and *dare* are not used as auxiliaries but as main verbs exclusively, as in *He didn't need to do that* (not *He needn't do that*) and *She doesn't dare to talk back* (not *She daren't talk back*). This last property is shared by Black English as well.

As appears from these examples, many varieties of English stand out in that they differ grammatically from Standard British English.

1.7. Variation according to medium

There is in many languages a good deal of variation according to *medium*: the grammar of the *written* variety often differs significantly from that of the *spoken* variety. The extent to which speech and writing differ varies from language to language: in e.g. Arabic there are different standardized varieties for the two media and the relationship between them is tenuous (a situation referred to as 'diglossia'), while in English speech and writing are felt to be predominantly stylistic variants.

Before describing some of the characteristics of these variants, it is important to make a distinction between *medium* and *channel of communication* (cf. Lyons 1981: 18). Speech and writing are best understood as different media serving different communicative purposes in different contexts, as distinct from the actual (oral or written) channel of communication. Thus speech is used in e.g. everyday conversation while writing is used in e.g. newspapers. Usually writing is delivered 'in writing' and speech is actually spoken. But this is not necessarily so: we can speak the way we write (e.g. when we read aloud), and we can write, more or less, the way we speak (e.g. in e-mail and in dialogues in a novel). Despite such cases where we mix medium and channel of communication, the fact remains that speech and writing are often structurally and functionally different varieties of language, each facilitated (and restricted) by its usual channel of communication. Thus, for example, in speech we may rely heavily on *prosody* (intonation and stress) and *para-linguistic* means (such as e.g. voice quality, gestures, eye-contact, smiles, frowns, yawns, etc.) to get our message across. In writing, we are left with a number of conventional symbols for organizing our message: full stops, commas, question marks, exclamation marks, bold face, capitals, etc., not to mention the choice between handwriting and typing/printing. On the other hand, speech is more transient (unless, of course, someone makes a specific point of recording it), and it is more difficult to edit than written language, which is usually the product of relatively careful planning and drafting, and which always leaves you with a record of the communicative event. The communicative interaction between the participants of a speech situation is more immediate and complex than when writing is involved.

In terms of more specifically grammatical features, spoken and written English differ in a number of important ways. Characteristically, writing, unlike speech, is lexically very economical and, at the same time, dense: written sentences generally contain fewer (partially or wholly) 'redundant' words but more 'heavily loaded' words than spoken utterances. A feature that adds to the density of writing is the greater complexity of some of the units that make up the sentence, especially the so-called noun groups (cf. section

3.3.1), which tend to be longer and to contain more levels of structure than in speech. Conversely, speech has greater density or complexity in the organization of clauses (in terms of what is usually referred to as 'coordination' and 'subordination', cf. sections 3.3.3 to 3.3.5). These differences are borne out very nicely by examples like the following (from Halliday 1985) where the a-variants are typical instances of written language and the b-variants of spoken language:

(1a)   Investment in a rail facility implies a long-term commitment.

(1b)   If you invest in a rail facility, this implies that you are going to be committed for a long term.

(2a)   The growth of attachment between infant and mother signals the first step in the development of a child's capacity to discriminate amongst people.

(2b)   When an infant and its mother start to grow attached to each other, this is a sign that the child is beginning to discriminate amongst people.

Note also that the a-examples of writing are fairly *static* in their presentation of the message, whereas the b-examples of speech are much more *dynamic*. When information is crammed into a few complex units (as in (2a)), what we refer to becomes rather fixed, factual and unchanging. But when basically the same information is spread over a number of clauses (as in (2b)), we get a clearer sense of the activities and processes involved: there are more verbs and consequently a clearer time sequence emerges.

Apart from the very general differences between speech and writing mentioned so far, there are numerous more specific differences pertaining to the grammar of English. Let us mention a few of these. In *written* English, an adverbial (i.e. a sentence function which is not a subject, predicator, object or complement, see section 3.2.9) is frequently realized as an *-ing* participle clause or an *-ed* participle clause:

(3)   *Giving him a light*, I set fire to his moustache.

(4)   *Her oration finished*, she breathed heavily with an overflow of indignation.

While this type of realization is not an exclusive property of the written medium, it is found less frequently in spoken than in written English.

Secondly, the so-called *subjunctive* is typical of written English:

(5)   Whatever *be* the reason, we cannot tolerate his disloyalty.

(6)   Grafton would have rung if the plane *weren't* on its way.

In informal spoken BrE, these subjunctive forms would be replaced by *may be* (placed after *reason*) in (5) and by *wasn't* in (6).

In sentences like *We must put some flesh on your bones* and *I just saw a show on television* where there is both an object (*some flesh* and *a show*, respectively) and an adverbial (*on your bones* and *on television*, respectively), the former typically precedes the latter. Sometimes, however, this ordering may be reversed (as we shall return to in section 5.3.10). This can be illustrated by the following examples in which the adverbial is placed before the object:

(7)   I just saw [on television] [how some Indian people started a shop and put the old grocery on the corner out of business].

(8)   Hello, my name is Penny Rogers. I bought [some time ago] [a PowerBook 180]. I can't get the internal modem to work and would like to have someone look at it.

This ordering is found in both writing and speech, but often for different reasons: in writing it is the result of careful planning and involves consideration of e.g. weight as in example (7), where the object is very long and hence preferred at the end of the sentence to prevent it from unduly delaying the occurrence of the adverbial. In speech the ordering of the adverbial before the object is often the result of lack of planning, or rather, planning on the spur of the moment: the order of the units here reflects the order in which the speaker thinks of what to say rather than any strict grammatical principle.

As a final example of a grammatical feature which is typical of written English, it is the case that in English the verb, or 'predicator', may be placed before the subject if an adverbial is fronted to give prominence to it or to establish *narrative continuity* (see section 5.3.6 on so-called full inversion after a fronted adverbial):

(9)   On the walls were pictures of half-naked women and colourful landscapes.

(10)   On the doorstep sat women nursing their babies and gossiping.

This ordering is virtually only found in written English. In spoken English *there* would be used as a 'provisional subject' in (9), and in (10) the predicator *sat* would be placed after the subject.

In *spoken English* we find utterances of the following kind:

(11)   What a load of rubbish!

(12)   Mind if I smoke?

Such 'elliptical' constructions and 'non-sentences' abound in both speech and writing but often for different reasons. In speech, the dropping of redundant words or constructions is the result of a reliance on the immediate context and part of the easy-going flow of the conversation and the smooth turn-taking of the participants. In writing, such 'telegraphic style' is used to *catch the receiver's attention* (e.g. headlines, road-signs, chapter headings, titles, warnings, neon commercials) or *to arrange the message in a clear, systematic, comprehensible manner* (timetables, recipes, shopping lists, bank statements, television programmes, sports results, etc.). In writing, unlike speech, catching the receiver's attention cannot be done prosodically or through the use of gesture, etc.

Another characteristic feature of spoken English is the frequent occurrence of so-called 'comment clauses' – i.e. clauses like *you know*, *I take it*, *generally speaking* and *to be honest* which serve to add a parenthetic comment to another clause, as in *I don't think you'll pass, to be honest*. In speech it is especially stereotyped comment clauses like the ones just mentioned that are frequent. Comment clauses which are less idiomatic, and which require more planning, for example *(This is a serious mistake,) he will undoubtedly have realized by now*, are not typical of the spoken medium.

So-called *conditional* utterances are typically marked by *if* or *unless*, as illustrated by *If you do that again I'll strangle you* and *Unless you shut up I'll strangle you*. But they can also be expressed by an *imperative* construction followed by a statement introduced by *and* or *or*:

(13)   Do that again and I'll strangle you.

(14)   Shut up or I'll strangle you.

What the speaker expresses in these examples is an intention to inflict injury on the addressee if a certain behaviour continues or unless a certain behaviour is discontinued. This way of signalling a conditional threat is typically restricted to spoken English.

As a final illustration of a grammatical feature which is characteristic of spoken English, we can mention examples of 'dislocation' (cf. section 4.5):

(15)   He's an utter nitwit, *that boyfriend of yours*.

(16)   *Your brother George*, I've never understood why he didn't resign.

Here the identity of the person referred to is established by a noun group which is either added as an amplifying tag (as in (15)) or prefixed to the sentence (as in (16)).

In closing this section we should point out that differences between spoken and written English like the ones illustrated in this section are also largely characteristic of *formal vs. informal English*, whether written or spoken. Such differences thus characterize not only variation according to medium but also variation according to *style*. Many of the grammatical features which are typical of spoken English are found also in informal written English, for example private letters or memos. Conversely, many of the features characterizing written English are found also in so-called edited speech, for example lectures and political speeches, where medium and channel of communication are conventionally mixed.

1.8. English for Special Purposes

When describing variation it is customary to distinguish between Language for General Purposes (LGP) and Language for Special Purposes (LSP). LSP refers to varieties used by practitioners of a profession in their work (see Kragh 1991). As pointed out in section 1.4, variation according to field of discourse (law, business, science, technology, etc.) is use-related in the sense that it involves switching to a variety which the occasion demands. But as a variety of this sort is typically used by practitioners of a special profession, i.e. by specialists who have gone through a professional socialization process which is partly linguistic, it is in fact user-related as well. Legal language is typically used by members of the legal profession, scientific language by scientists, economic language by economists, and so on.

LSP is primarily characterized by its vocabulary, i.e. by special terms employed by a profession, such as *lien, liability, habeas corpus, statutory* and *aforesaid* in legal English. But it is also characterized by features of grammar which are particularly frequent. While some of these are typical of formal (vs. informal) and written (vs. spoken) English as well, others are largely restricted to a special professional variant.

English for Special Purposes (ESP) tends to be rich in *complex noun groups*. This can be illustrated by groups like *the FT-SE 100 Index of shares in Britain's leading companies* (business) and *the issues of breach of statutory duty and common law negligence in respect of the council's exercise of its power under the Act* (law). When realizing an object, such complex noun groups will often necessitate the reversal with an adverbial mentioned in section 1.7. In the following example the adverbial *on local authorities* in the clause beginning with *to* has been moved forward because of the length of the object noun group (the part of the sentence stretching from *any* to *statute*):

(1)   There was a considerable reluctance on the part of the courts to impose [on local authorities] [any liability for breach of statutory duty other than that expressly imposed in the statute].

The complexity of noun groups is often due to a string of words occurring before the noun constituting the nucleus, or head, of the construction. In its frequent use of such *heavy premodification* in noun groups ESP differs from English for General Purposes (EGP). In scientific English we find noun groups like *inertial confinement fusion, near-zero explosive yields* and *the first full digital image model of Mars*, in which the head nouns are *fusion, yields* and *model*. In business English heavy premodification can be illustrated by *global gross domestic product, International Business Machines' year-end results* and *purchasing power parity exchange rates*, where the head nouns are *product, results* and *rates*. In legal English we find heavily premodified nouns too, for example in *the Nurseries and Child Minders Regulation Act 1948*. Owing to its general condensation and the way in which its noun groups tend to be packed with information, LSP is sometimes informally referred to as 'agglomerese'.

As LSP is typically used to describe and direct, whereas emotive and social uses are not normally involved, it must aim at being clear, concise, objective and reliable. Such pragmatic requirements affect grammatical choices. Descriptive and directive technical texts, for example, have been shown to contain many passive constructions where the preferred verb form is in the present, and many compound nouns and adjectives which have been derived from clauses (see Munck 1991). In English this can be illustrated by an example like the following (quoted from McArthur 1992: 1026):

(2)   Three modes of operation are required: voice-activated mode (VOX), press-to-talk (PTT) and call.

Here the choice of the passive contributes to making the message objective (impersonal), its present form to making it general (what is described is valid at all times), and the use of compounds to making it concise. Conversion of clauses into compound words for the sake of brevity can be further illustrated by examples like *quick-drying (ink), quick-action (reversing gear), rapid-hardening (cement), diesel-powered (engine)* and *self-raising (flour)*. It can also be noted that in order to avoid ambiguity, the second of two noun groups referring to the same entity is sometimes not replaced by a pronoun as it typically is in EGP.

In legal English the modal verb *shall* is used with third-person subjects to denote what is legally mandatory:

(3)   The tenant *shall* quietly possess and enjoy the premises during the tenancy without any interference from the landlord.

This usage is not found in current EGP, nor in other types of ESP. While there are thus features of grammar which are restricted to (a variety of) ESP, the grammatical differences between ESP and EGP are nearly always quantitative rather than qualitative. We find the same features of grammar in both varieties, but the frequency with which they occur is often markedly different. As we saw in section 1.7, this is also largely the case with varieties engendered by differences in medium.

2. An introduction to syntax

2.1. The word

As native speakers of a language, and very often also as learners of a foreign language, we have an intuitive knowledge of that language, including its syntax and the basic units of its grammar. Thus, for a start, we all have a pretty good idea of what a *word* is. To realize this, we only have to consider the following passage, where we have eliminated any indication of word boundaries (such as, typically, an empty space between words):

(1)   thepolicemanlookedatthembothhesniffedthatwastheuncooperativeattitudeyou
       mightexpectfromafamilythatencouragedtheirdaughtertogoaroundwithyanksan
       dthesewerewelltodopeoplenotworkingclasssuchlaxattitudesoffendedhimhe'd
       makesurethatnodaughterofhiskeptcompanywithforeignsoldiers

Once we recover from the initial confusion of having to decipher such a muddled, uninviting passage, we can all find the individual words of the original text:

(2)   The policeman looked at them both. He sniffed. That was the uncooperative
       attitude you might expect from a family that encouraged their daughter to go
       around with Yanks. And these were well-to-do people, not working class.
       Such lax attitudes offended him. He'd make sure that no daughter of his kept
       company with foreign soldiers.

There are, admittedly, occasional problems: is *well-to-do* one or three words? Is *He'd* one or two words? But apart from such nitpicking, we are perfectly capable of identifying the words of any language familiar to us. In writing, word boundaries are signalled by blanks or by punctuation marks. In speech, they are often, though not always, signalled by factors such as the exact onset of stress (as in *see the 'meat* vs. *see them 'eat*) and/or the variant of speech sound selected (as in *keeps ticking* vs. *keep sticking*, where the /t/ is aspirated (i.e. pronounced with a puff of air) when it is a word-initial sound as in the former case). We all know how to signal and interpret word boundaries in both writing and speech, if only intuitively. And yet, amazingly, it is very difficult to define what a word is.

Obviously, *meaning* is somehow involved: *policeman* means one thing, *family* another. But what is the meaning of *the* and *of*? Clearly, these words mean something but their meaning is not as immediately transparent as the meaning of *policeman* and *family*, which express relatively concrete entities (more specifically, persons). And why is it that *the* and *policeman* are two words in English but only one word in, for example, Danish (namely *politimanden*, where the ending *-en* corresponds to the English *the*)? Such frivolity is not reserved for Danish and other foreign languages but is a regular feature of English, too, as we see in the word *uncooperative*, where *un* is only part of a word despite the fact that it has an independently identifiable meaning. Another example is, once again, *policeman*: why is *policeman* one word but both *police force* and *police constable* two? Similarly, why are there two separate words in *class struggle* but only one in *classroom*, which is normally identified as a *compound* word (i.e. a unit of elements which function independently elsewhere)? We are forced to conclude that words cannot be defined simply as 'units of meaning'.

In the language user's conception of words, *convention* seems to be an all-important factor. This, however, should not prevent us from trying to describe the words in English (for which the technical term *lexicon* is often used) with reference to any regular pattern applying to them. As a first step towards such a description, grammarians refer to the smallest meaningful units of language as *morphemes* whether or not they are independent words. In this sense *un-* in *uncooperative*, *police-* and *-man* in *policeman*, *work-* and *-ing* in *working*, and even *-s* in *attitudes* and *-ed* in *encouraged* are morphemes. *The, him, of, to, that* etc. are both morphemes and words. They are *free* morphemes in contrast to *un-, -s, -ing, -ed*, etc., which are *bound* morphemes. This means that a word consists of one or more morphemes. The precise identification of words is then to a large extent a question of conventional rules of *morphology*, i.e. rules describing the structure of words in terms of morphemes. There is little consistency across languages in the morphology of words: as we have seen, the meaning of definiteness is in English typically expressed by an independent word, the definite article *the*, whereas in Danish it is typically expressed by a word-internal bound morpheme. Sometimes principles seem to vary even within one and the same language (as in the case of English *policeman* vs. *police force*). Note also that while definiteness in English is expressed by means of an independent word, meanings pertaining to, say, number (singular or plural) and tense (present or past) are fully *grammaticalized* in that they are expressed by word-internal bound morphemes, more specifically by *inflections*. Our intuitive knowledge of the words of a language includes the knowledge of what is conventionally expresssed by means of individual words and what is conventionally grammaticalized at the morphological level.

One important characteristic of words is that they are *basic syntactic units*, i.e. the building blocks of larger language constructions, and thus have a high degree of *stability* and *cohesion*. Words are stable in the sense that – unlike many higher-level syntactic constructions such as the sentence – they do not allow rearrangement of their constituent parts. Nor do they allow internal separation. For example, as language users we are not free to organize the morphemes in words as we please. We have to say *childishness*, not **nessishchild*, **ishchildness*, etc. With higher-level constructions there is often a certain variability: we can say either *the sickening unresolvable mess* or *the unresolvable sickening mess* (with little or no difference of meaning) and we can say both *Bob kissed Gina* and *Gina kissed Bob* (although here there is a marked difference of meaning). Note also that normally words are internally inseparable. Thus while we are often free to separate independent words like *the* and *policeman* in a construction like *the policeman* by inserting an adjective, as in *the young policeman*, we cannot separate the individual parts of *the* or *policeman* and still retain their status as single words. In speech, words are also coherent in the sense that we can insert pauses (*uh, uhm*, etc.) *between* words but not usually *within* words (cf. Bolinger 1975: 119). Thus in an unsure and hesitant manner we might say:

(3a)   The *uhm* policeman *uh* got *uhm* confused.

But we are unlikely to say:

(3b)   The po-*uh*-liceman got con-*uh*-fused.

Stability and cohesion may be important clues in the identification of word boundaries. But they tell us little about what a word really is or about why the principles of word formation differ between languages and even within languages.

The interesting fact is that despite the problem of formulating a water-tight definition of the word, we all have an intuitive knowledge of what a word is. That knowledge comprises in part an awareness of morphemes as units of meaning, in part the recognition of largely conventional rules of how morphemes combine to make up the units that we know as words.

2.2. The sentence

Grammar is not just the study of words and their morphological structure but also of how words combine to make up larger units, such as *sentences*. Like words, sentences are notoriously difficult to define rigidly and objectively. And yet we all have an intuitive knowledge of what a sentence is (cf. Bolinger 1975: 156). To appreciate this, we only have to look at a passage where we have left out all the conventional markers of sentence boundaries (such as punctuation and capitalization of initial letters after full stops):

(1)   Victoria shuddered once again she realized that her father was trying to protect her and she loved him for it and if she admitted to knowing Vince Madigan the next question must inevitably be and what was this American's

    relationship with Mrs Hardcastle and then more questions I don't recognize
    him she said softly

Although this passage is a fairly complicated text with both internal and
external dialogue, it is easy to guess at its division into sentences:

(2)   Victoria shuddered. Once again she realized that her father was trying to
        protect her and she loved him for it. And if she admitted to knowing Vince
        Madigan, the next question must inevitably be, 'And what was this
        American's relationship with Mrs Hardcastle?' And then more questions. 'I
        don't recognize him,' she said softly.

Many people will even discover that there are alternative ways of dividing
this text into sentences. Thus *Once again* could equally well belong to the
first sentence: *Victoria shuddered once again. She realized* ... Similarly, *and
she loved him for it* might be a separate sentence: *She realized that her father
was trying to protect her. And she loved him for it.* But no-one would suggest
that *Once again she* is a separate sentence. Nor would we allow the long
sentence *And if she admitted to knowing ... Mrs Hardcastle?* to be broken
into two independent sentences *And if she admitted to knowing Vince
Madigan* and *The next question must .... Mrs Hardcastle*, despite the fact that
both contain a verb. While the second part could conceivably function as a
sentence on its own, the first part is clearly incomplete. It cannot stand alone.
According to conventional wisdom, the two parts are *clauses* within the
same sentence.

    In speech, clause and sentence boundaries are typically signalled and
interpreted in terms of *tone groups* ending with a special *intonational
contour*: e.g. a rise (to signal, say, the end of a question or the continuation
from one clause to another) or a fall (to signal, say, the end of a sentence). To
get a sense of such intonational signals, one can try reading out the passage
above with the different segmentations proposed.

    Though we have to recognize *And then more questions* as an independent
unit, many would hesitate to call it a sentence. It is somehow unfinished,
lacking a verbal component such as *(And then more questions) would follow*.
Similar problems arise with short units of text like:

(3)   No!
(4)   After him.
(5)   My turn?

Typically such units are complete utterances (cf. Bache *et al.* 1993: 183ff).
But are they sentences? Although they are perfectly acceptable in both
speech and writing (in writing as a substitute for a spoken utterance), we
hesitate to accept them as sentences. It would help considerably if we treated
them as somehow short forms of 'proper' sentences like the following:

(6)   I say no!
(7)   I want you to go after him.
(8)   Is it my turn?

But such 'full constructions' are often cumbersome and not entirely natural or appropriate in context and therefore should not be taken as 'more proper' than those in (3) to (5). We have to accept that not all utterances are sentences. Many linguists make a systematic distinction between 'sentence' as a theoretical unit (defined by grammar) and 'utterance' as a physical unit (a matter of speech production), cf. e.g. Lyons 1995: 32ff. On this view some utterances can be analysed in terms of sentences but utterances do not 'consist of' sentences.

Some grammarians have suggested that a sentence is a unit of grammar expressing a 'complete thought' or a 'complete event'. But surely such definitions are too imprecise to be of much use. Is the thought or event expressed in *Victoria shuddered* any more complete than those expressed by examples (3) to (5), which are not full sentences? Or is it more complete than that expressed by the non-sentential clause *And if she admitted to knowing Vince Madigan*? Or than that expressed by *And then more questions*?

What all this amounts to is that although we have intuitions about what a sentence is, and though we are perfectly capable of dividing a text into the appropriate orthographical or intonational units typically reflecting sentence or utterance boundaries, it is by no means obvious how actually to define a sentence. We usually expect a sentence to contain at least a verbal component and some other unit, but as we have seen, there are complications. Sometimes textual units which do not meet this requirement are treated like sentences in terms of punctuation or intonation, or in terms of their independence as acts of communication. Furthermore, there is a complex relationship between clause and sentence. Somehow, clauses are like sentences in normally requiring a verbal component and some other unit. So what is the difference between the two? In a sense the distinction between clause and sentence is very similar to that between morpheme and word. A sentence seems to consist of one or more clauses the way a word consists of one or more morphemes. Sometimes a clause is also a sentence (and thus resembles free morphemes which are independent words), sometimes a clause is simply too incomplete or dependent to serve as a sentence in its own right (and thus resembles bound morphemes, which never occur independently). While it is possible to consider words to be the basic units of syntax, the building blocks of larger units, sentences can be viewed as the maximal autonomous units permitting syntactic analysis. Sentences and their internal arrangement of words are the *domain of syntax*.

2.3. Grammatical structure

Our intuitions about language are not restricted to the mere identification of possible words and sentences but include the organization of words within sentences, i.e. the *grammatical structure* of sentences. Consider the following example:

(1)   John kissed the little old woman who owns that shaggy dog.

We doubt that our readers have ever seen a sentence completely identical to (1). And yet no one has any difficulty in recognizing it as a grammatical construction in English. In other words, there is an appropriate organization of the eleven words in the sentence: they are all used in the right place, at the right time. We know the individual words and their meaning, and somehow we know the kind of relationship they enter into. To appreciate that this organization of words, the *structure* of the sentence, is not random, we only need to change the order of its *constituent* words:

(2)   old the kissed dog shaggy who John woman little that owns.

Although we have exactly the same words here as in (1), (2) is completely ungrammatical. It has become a list of unrelated words.

If we consider the possible ways of arranging the eleven different words of (1) and (2) in a linear sequence, it is in fact a small miracle that – almost without thinking about it – we hit on the *grammatical* sequence in (1). There are, to be exact, 39,916,800 different ways of combining eleven different elements in a sequence (1 x 2 x 3 x 4 x 5 x 6 x 7 x 8 x 9 x 10 x 11). Some of these many alternatives to (1) are of course perfectly grammatical:

(3)   John kissed the old woman who owns that shaggy little dog.

(4)   John kissed the little woman who owns that shaggy old dog.

(5)   John kissed the woman who owns that shaggy little old dog.

Stretching our imagination a little we may even accept sequences like the following:

(6)   The shaggy little dog who owns that old woman kissed John.

(7)   The old woman who owns little John kissed that shaggy dog.

(8)   John owns the old woman who kissed that shaggy little dog.

These sequences are all grammatical (in the sense that the words enter acceptable, recognizable syntactic relationships), but their meaning may differ from our conception of what constitutes the normal state of affairs in the world (Can a dog own a woman? Can a human being own another human being?) and thus challenge us to think of contexts where it would be appropriate to use such sentences.

But even if we allow for a little stretching of our imagination, there are at the very most, maybe about a hundred possible sentences containing the eleven words in (1). There are millions of unacceptable ones. And yet we all have a fairly impressive ability to spot the very few grammatical sentences and reject all the ungrammatical sequences. This ability presupposes an intuitive knowledge of the possible syntactic relationships between words. In other words, we have an intuitive knowledge of grammatical structure.

2.4. Linearity and the principle of proximity

Let us have a closer look at our intuitive knowledge of grammatical structure. As we have already seen, language is necessarily *linear* in the sense that one constituent unit (a speech sound or a letter, a morpheme, a word, a group of words, a clause, a sentence) always follows another. In speech language takes *time*, and in writing it takes up *space*. Grammatical structure is basically a means by which language comes to terms with, and makes the best of, this basic condition.

Strictly from the point of view of linearity alone, we would expect a sequence of elements to be either *random*, with no discernible patterns in the organization of the elements, or *progressively* related, each element receiving its rank according to its position in the list (in terms of, for example, increasing or decreasing 'importance' or 'priority', or according to some convention, such as 'alphabetical order'). In human language we see both these main types of linear organization. A telephone directory is a good, if fairly artificial, example of progressive linearity, and so is counting. But alphabetical and numerical order is also exploited in many natural expressions, such as:

(1)   Gina got many *A's and B's* in her finals.
(2)   You are a nice chap but you will have to watch your *P's and Q's*.
(3)   Jim and Roger came in *first and second*, respectively.
(4)   They arrived in *twos and threes*.
(5)   He bought *ten or twelve* good books.

In a phrase like *Ladies and Gentlemen*, etiquette dictates a certain priority. Progressive linearity is also present in constructions like:

(6)   Gina is a competent, even brilliant, scientist.

which reflects an increase of the intensity with which *Gina* is described.

Random linearity may be present in constructions like the following:

(7a)   *Alex, Stephanie and Roger* went sailing this morning.
(7b)   *Roger, Stephanie and Alex* went sailing this morning.

(7c)   *Stephanie, Alex and Roger* went sailing this morning.

etc.

(8a)   She almost enjoyed the *warm stale sweet* air.

(8b)   She almost enjoyed the *warm sweet stale* air.

(8c)   She almost enjoyed the *stale sweet warm* air.

etc.

However, the basic randomness of the italicized constructions may be reduced by considerations of rhythm or by contextual factors.

There is a different, more general, derived sense in which linearity is important in the organization of language: since *simultaneity* of expression is excluded, we can predict that, in compensation, elements that somehow 'belong together' will be placed as closely together in the sequence as possible. Thus, in examples (7a-c), *Alex, Roger* and *Stephanie* belong together (in that they all took part in the event expressed by the rest of the sentence, i.e. they all went sailing) but since we cannot express them simultaneously they are instead placed as closely together as possible. The same applies to *sweet, stale* and *warm* in examples (8a-c): they belong together because they perform the same function in the sentence, namely that of describing *air*. As they cannot be expressed simultaneously but are forced into a sequence, they are at least placed closely together. Given the condition of linearity, it is thus in a sense *natural* that words that belong together should be placed together in the sequence of words making up the sentence. In this way we can say that the necessary linearity in the organization of language leads to the principle of *proximity*.

2.5. Constituency

Grammatical structure imposes an organization on the elements of the string which is neither progressive nor random. In doing this, grammatical structure usually exploits the principle of proximity to create groupings of words that belong together. Let us consider the following short version of example (1) in section 2.3:

(1)   John kissed the little old woman.

In this sentence, the word *the* is not in a random position relative to the other words, nor does it receive any rank according to its place in a progression of elements. Rather it is part of a grammatical structure in which it relates more closely to *woman* than to *John, kissed, little* or *old*. At first blush the order of words in this example seems to violate the principle of proximity: *woman* is further away from *the* than *John, kissed, little* and *old*. But on closer examination, it appears that *the, little, old* and *woman* all belong together in a group (according to the principle of proximity) and as such enter a 'joint' relationship with *kissed* and *John* at a higher level. The sentence describes an instance of kissing (expressed by *kissed*) in which there are two participants: one who performs the kissing (*John*) and one who receives the kiss (*the little old woman*). There is thus an indication that the sentence can be divided into three parts or *constituents*: [John], [kissed] and [the little old woman]. The interpretation of [the little old woman] as a group of words belonging together is supported by the fact that if we want to move one of the words relative to [John] and [kissed] and preserve the meaning of the three individual parts of the sentence, we normally have to move them all:

(2)   The little old woman kissed John.

(3)   *Woman kissed John the little old.

Another interesting feature that suggests that [the little old woman] is an integrated unit is that we can replace it by one word representing the whole group and that we can use it as the answer to a question about the identity of the person John kissed:

(4)   John kissed her.

(5)   - 'Who did John kiss?'
       - 'The little old woman.'

The grouping of words together which share a function is often referred to as *constituency*. Structure in language can be described in terms of constituency: complex language units (like the sentence) consist of a number of constituents which, in turn, may consist of lower-level constituents. Language structure is thus multilayered or *hierarchic*.

Despite the strong tendency for proximity in language, this principle may be overridden by other considerations. Compare the following two sentences:

(6a)   Sarah is painting her house.

(6b)   Is Sarah painting her house?

Example (6a) expresses an activity in progress (*is painting*) enacted by someone (*Sarah*) and involving an object (*her house*). It thus seems reasonable to divide the sentence into the following parts: [Sarah], [is painting] and [her house]. That *is* and *painting* form a group seems intuitively right. Nevertheless it is possible to move one of the words without moving the other, as in example (6b), where *is* is moved up in front of *Sarah*. The physical separation of the two words does not in any way impair the sense that they belong together in a group, as a constituent. The 'broken relationship' seems closely related to the communicative difference between the two examples: the first sentence is a *statement*, the second is a *question*.

It thus seems that *communicative function* is a factor which may override the principle of proximity. The term usually applied to a 'broken relationship' in language is *discontinuity*: in the second example, *Is* and *painting* form a discontinuous group to serve a specific communicative purpose.

Syntax deals with the relationship between the units of a sentence, more specifically the various constituency groupings (continuous as well as discontinuous) that the units enter. Like morphology, syntax is part of our intuitive linguistic knowledge.

2.6. Linguistic creativity and ambiguity

Our intuitive knowledge of syntax is not restricted to an ability to *recognize* various word order patterns when we see them: we all know how to use them whenever we engage actively in communication. Thus, as has been emphasized by proponents of a particularly influential school of grammatical thought, Generative Grammar, we all possess the ability to understand and produce *new* sentences, sentences which have never been uttered or written before, simply by using the familiar patterns of syntax and the lexicon, i.e. the words of the language. Some of the examples discussed in the preceding sections are examples of this kind: not many native speakers of English are likely to have come across them before. In this technical sense, language is *creative*: although it contains a finite number of building blocks (the words in the lexicon), the rules for their legitimate combination are such that an infinite number of sentences can be produced. Maximal flexibility in matching expression and meaning is thus ensured.

Another example of the open-endedness of language is the lack of *isomorphism*, i.e. the lack of a one-to-one relationship, between the units of language and the items of the world that we discuss and refer to, using language. One fairly trivial but instructive example of this is the fact that most nouns can be used to refer to more than just one particular item in the 'real world': in appropriate contexts an expression like *the car* can be used about any car, not just one car. Furthermore, *car* is so general in meaning that it appropriately covers a fascinating range of past, present and future vehicles. The units of language can be said to have a *generic* potential.

Yet another aspect of language, related to linguistic creativity, and which involves syntax more directly, is the principled diversity of meaning we sometimes encounter in a single expression. That *ambiguity* is indeed an important factor in language becomes evident when we consider examples like the following (taken from Bache 1985b: 56; Chomsky 1957: 88; Lyons 1968: 249; Schibsbye 1970: 30, Wells 1947: section 3; and others), which have been the object of much attention in the linguistic debate:

(1)   Old men and women are invited to the party.
(2)   Flying planes can be dangerous.
(3)   She wants to marry a Norwegian who is rich.
(4)   He left his wife to deal with the creditors.
(5)   The girl found a book on Main Street.

In some of these sentences, the ambiguity is more obvious than in others. But most of us will eventually recognize the different meanings potentially expressed in these examples.

In *Old men and women are invited to the party*, the expression [Old men and women] refers either to a group of old men and old women or to a group of old men and of women of any age (young and old alike), depending on whether we interpret the adjective *old* as a modifier of *men and women* or of *men* alone.

In *Flying planes can be dangerous*, [*Flying planes*] is either a word-like nominal expression for aeroplanes with primary stress on the first word (like *police force*) or it is a clause-like expression with primary stress on the second word referring to instances of the activity of flying a plane. The ambiguity arises because the normal concord rules are neutralized in *can*: when *Flying planes* is a word-like nominal expression it takes the plural (as in e.g. *Flying planes are dangerous*); when it is a clause-like construction on a par with *to fly a plane*, it takes the singular (as in e.g. *Flying planes is dangerous*).

The example *She wants to marry a Norwegian who is rich* shows that there are sometimes different interpretations of referring expressions: either [a Norwegian who is rich] refers to a particular person (e.g. Knut Flo from Oslo) or it refers to anyone who qualifies as a rich Norwegian, i.e. any member of the class of rich Norwegians.

In *He left his wife to deal with the creditors*, the person referred to by *He* either lets his wife deal with the creditors (i.e. *his wife* is the agent of *to deal*) or he leaves his wife with the purpose of dealing with the creditors himself (i.e. *He* is the agent not only of *left* but also of *to deal*).

Finally, in *The girl found a book on Main Street*, the girl either found a book about Main Street, or it was on Main Street, of all places, that she found a book. Either *on Main Street* is part of a more complex construction *a book on Main Street*, in which it describes the subject matter of the book involved, or it is a more independent construction describing the location where the girl found the book.

Characteristically, as we have seen, the different interpretations of all the examples described above are tied to different syntactic patterns (i.e. alternative relationships between the units involved) or different uses of the units making up the sentence. The recognition of ambiguity in such cases is thus a sign that we have a fairly advanced, if 'only' intuitive, knowledge of syntax and grammar.

2.7. Competence and performance

In the preceding sections we have established the fact that the speakers of a language have a high degree of linguistic sensitivity and informal knowledge of their own language. In other words, they have what is often referred to as *linguistic competence*. Not only are they capable of identifying grammatical units like words and sentences, they also recognize complex syntactic patterns and attach appropriate meanings to them, as witnessed in cases of ambiguity. Most important of all, they know how to put their intuitive knowledge to use whenever they engage in communication. More technically speaking, they know how to turn their linguistic competence into actual linguistic *performance*. The fact that few speakers of a language are capable of describing their language skills and of defining the relevant units and patterns of language in a rigid, principled manner should not make us underestimate their competence. Language is in this respect similar to activities like walking or riding a bike: we are very competent at doing these things without thinking about how we do them. And most of us would be hard put to describe all the exact movements involved in these activities in a principled, scientific manner.

The intuitive knowledge speakers have of a language comprises much more than a knowledge of its formal properties, i.e. linguistic competence. Intuitively, we know not only how linguistic expressions are structured but also how to *use them appropriately* in different contexts or situations and in relation to our communicative intentions. For example, speakers of English know how to be formal or informal in their verbal interaction with other speakers. They also know how to describe events as located in time, how to elicit information, how to refer to things and persons, and so on. In short, they have a knowledge of how to do things with linguistic structures. The overall intuitive knowledge that speakers have of a language and of how to use it in context is called their *communicative competence*. Though communicative competence is largely to do with language in use, it is still possible to regard it in terms of 'knowledge of language' and keep it clearly apart from performance; for there is obviously a difference between what speakers are capable of doing verbally and what they actually do in a given situation (see Dik 1989: 5).

Once we have accounted for the structural properties of a well-formed sentence, we have to consider in what context it is appropriately uttered.

When describing a language we are therefore concerned not only with syntactically and semantically well-formed sentences but also with the appropriateness of sentences in a given context. For example, the near-equivalent sentences *You must make your payment by May 31st* and *Your payment must be made by May 31st* are both syntactically and semantically well-formed, but in some contexts only the passive sentence is appropriate, in others only the active. To account for a native speaker's choice of one rather than the other, we need the concept of communicative competence, which combines linguistic competence with context.

2.8. Syntagmatic and paradigmatic relations

In this section, we shall draw attention to a specific example of the kind of knowledge that native speakers of a language seem to have, an important aspect of their linguistic and communicative competence, the knowledge of *paradigms* or *choice relations*.

As we have already pointed out, language is of necessity linear but has syntactic structure imposed on it which exploits and overrides the linearity. Consider a sentence like the following:

(1)   Sally teaches grammar.

This sentence has a relatively simple syntactic structure involving the *horizontal* relationship between the constituents [Sally], [teaches] and [grammar]. According to the rules of English grammar, we interpret the sentence as a statement to the effect that Sally is the one who teaches and grammar is the subject taught. From a cross-linguistic, universal point of view, there is no necessary single arrangement of constituents to express this particular piece of information. In other languages, it may well have to be expressed through a different arrangement of the constituents making up the sentence, corresponding to, for example, *Teaches Sally grammar* or *Sally grammar teaches*, which are ungrammatical in English. The kind of horizontal relationship that can be established between the constituents of a sentence is often referred to as *syntagmatic*.

Each of the constituents in the syntagmatic relationship in *Sally teaches grammar* might have been more complex, thus adding to the overall complexity of the sentence:

(2)   The young woman is teaching English grammar.

To go from the first sentence to the second we replace [Sally] by [The young woman], [teaches] by [is teaching] and [grammar] by [English grammar]. The basic structure of the two sentences is the same. Further complexity is of course possible:

(3)   The very beautiful young black American woman that you met at the pub last night could have been teaching advanced English grammar.

In this sentence, there are again three main constituents corresponding to those in the two first examples: [The very beautiful young black American woman that you met at the pub last night], [could have been teaching] and [advanced English grammar]. This means that despite the verbosity of this example, its basic structure is like that of *Sally teaches grammar*: there are three main constituents only.

The structural similarity of the three examples discussed above shows that although language is linear, thus calling for the syntagmatic, horizontal arrangement of the constituents in the sequence that we recognize as a syntactic structure, there is at the same time a *vertical* dimension to language. A sentence is not just a sequence of elements or units which enter some sort of horizontal relationship. Rather, a sentence contains a number of *slots* which may be filled in different ways for different communicative purposes. Thus, at one level, the three examples contain the same number of slots, namely three, but these slots are filled with constructions of different length and complexity. The constructions which are possible in a particular slot (e.g. [teaches], [is teaching] and [could have been teaching]) enter a choice relation: they are all candidates for a particular function at a particular point, and the choice of one excludes the others. The relationship between the possible constructions in a particular slot is often referred to as *paradigmatic*.

The implication of all this is that the linearity of language should be viewed in terms of a sequence of slots, each an important hallmark, at which the language user has a choice of expression. Language is both syntagmatic and paradigmatic.

Sometimes the choice of expression for a given slot is a choice of one lexical item rather than another:

(1)   Sally teaches *grammar*.

(1')   Sally teaches *physics*.

The paradigmatic choice between *grammar* and *physics* in the frame [Sally teaches _____] is a purely lexical choice, with no implication for the other constituents of the sentence, and therefore not terribly interesting from a grammatical point of view. Other paradigmatic choices involve grammar:

(1a)   Sally *teaches* grammar.

(1b)   Sally *is teaching* grammar.

(1c)   Sally *taught* grammar.
        etc.

The choice of verb form in a frame like [Sally ____ grammar], where a number of different forms of the verb *teach* are possible, must be accounted for. A grammar of English must provide answers to questions like 'Why is *teaches* but not *teach* all right in that particular frame?', 'What is the difference between *teaches* and *taught*?' 'Or between *teaches* and *is teaching*?' etc. Such questions concern inflectional morphology and competing syntactic constructions.

It is also important to specify in our grammar what *types of construction* are possible in particular slots. As we have seen, instead of a name in the first slot ([Sally]), we may have a group of words ([The young woman] and [The very beautiful young .... last night], respectively), but we cannot normally have a clause:

(4)   *That Sally is very competent teaches grammar.

In other frames, clauses as well as names and groups of words are perfectly possible in the initial slot of the sentence:

(5a)   *Sally* surprised Jack.
(5b)   *The young woman* surprised Jack.
(5c)   *That Sally is very competent* surprised Jack.

It is important to realize that the two *dimensions of language*, the syntagmatic and the paradigmatic, are closely interrelated. Thus the choice of a particular construction to fill a particular slot may well affect later choices of constructions (and, conversely, the choice of a construction may be made in anticipation of choices one wants to make later on). Consider the following pair of sentences:

(6a)   The young *woman teaches* physics.
(6b)   The young *women teach* physics.

Here the choice of the singular noun *woman* in the initial major constituent necessitates the choice of *teaches* rather than *teach* as the second constituent. By comparison, the choice of the plural noun *women* in the initial major constituent leads the speaker to choose *teach* rather than *teaches* later on in the sequence. The term grammar should be interpreted in a broad sense covering both the paradigmatic and syntagmatic dimension.

In conclusion, the intuitive knowledge that native speakers have, their competence, includes knowledge not only of the syntagmatic dimension of language but also of the paradigmatic dimension. As with the other aspects of native speaker intuition dealt with in the preceding sections, it is difficult to describe one's knowledge of language in a precise, appropriate and objective manner. The aim of this grammar is to provide such a description of

English. What we have set out to do is not simply to teach you, our readers, grammar, because in the sense discussed in the preceding sections you know a lot of grammar already. What we want to do is rather to offer the tools, the terminology and the insights necessary for making your knowledge more explicit.

2.9. Recapitulation

In this introduction to syntax we have shown that speakers of a language have a high degree of linguistic competence: they have an intuitive, implicit knowledge of the basic units of grammar and the various relationships these enter into. This linguistic competence includes intuitions about syntax (the principles of linearity and proximity as well as the principle of constituency which arises from and overrides the two other principles) and of grammatically conditioned ambiguity. Part of the linguistic competence of language users is also a knowledge of paradigmatic choice relations in language. Despite this highly developed competence, most speakers are unable to describe their language skills appropriately. They may be able to identify words and sentences but they cannot define these units. They easily recognize grammatical strings of words in contrast to ungrammatical ones, possible paradigmatic choices in contrast to impossible ones, as well as grammatically conditioned ambiguity. And above all, they know how to use language appropriately: they have communicative competence. But again, if prompted, most people would fail to offer an appropriate account of why and how they do these things. Thus, when we speak of 'learning the grammar of a language', it is not simply a question of acquiring new knowledge but also a question of becoming more conscious of something that we know intuitively already. Even to the foreign learner in need of getting 'all the facts of the language' right, the process of learning grammar to some extent involves getting intuitive linguistic and communicative knowledge turned into explicit conscious knowledge.

In order to teach (native as well as non-native) speakers of English the grammar of the language, we need to turn the intuitive linguistic and communicative competence that native speakers of English have into an explicit one. Against this background, the aim of the present grammar is to offer an appropriate descriptive apparatus and to present the relevant rules of competence that native speakers of English employ when they engage in linguistic performance, i.e. in actual communication.

3. Elementary sentence analysis

3.1. The basic form and function approach

As a first step towards establishing an appropriate descriptive apparatus for the grammar, we shall introduce a fairly elementary approach to the description of the constituents making up sentences. The specific aim of this is to provide the grammar with a common framework and terminology.

3.1.1. Form and function

We draw a basic distinction between the *form* and the *function* of constituents, which applies to all levels of description. We have already touched on this distinction. In our discussion of paradigmatic choice relations in section 2.8 above, we noted that different types of construction may fill a particular slot in a sentence. Thus, as we saw, [Sally], [The young woman] and [That Sally is very competent] are all possible choices in the empty slot in the frame [_____ surprised Jack]. Another way of formulating this insight is to say that different forms may assume the same function in a sentence: [Sally], [The young woman] and [That Sally is very competent] are different forms but may perform the same syntactic function relative to *surprised Jack*.

3.1.2. Sentence functions

The main slots for which there is a choice of form in a sentence frame are called *sentence functions*. We recognize five basic sentence functions:

S	=	subject
P	=	predicator
O	=	object
C	=	complement
A	=	adverbial

We employ two different techniques in our structural representations: *linear analyses* and *tree diagrams*. The two techniques are notational variants, i.e. different ways of showing the same structure. In a linear analysis (which is convenient for simple or partial analyses in run-on texts), we use square brackets to indicate the beginning and the end of constituents, each bracket tagged with the appropriate label of analysis. In a simple sentence like *Sarah laughed*, we can identify two sentence functions: a subject (*Sarah*) and a predicator (*laughed*). The linear analysis looks like this: ^{S}[Sarah] ^{P}[laughed].

The tree diagram, which is a conventional form of syntactic representation, provides an accessible overview of complex analyses. Using the label 'Sent' for sentence, we can draw the following tree diagram for *Sarah laughed*:

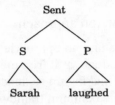

The lines slanting downwards from Sent indicate a 'consist-of relationship': Sent consists of S and P. We use triangles to indicate that our analysis of *Sarah* and *laughed* is incomplete: we have not assigned the appropriate form labels yet. Before we do so, let us first look at some more examples of the five sentence functions:

(1)   The old man wrote a long letter.
        S[The old man] P[wrote] O[a long letter]

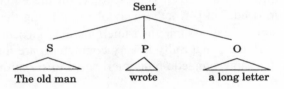

(2)   He was writing very slowly.
        S[He] P[was writing] A[very slowly]

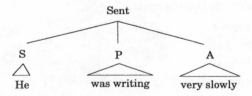

(3)   The letter was unbearably long.
        S[The letter] P[was] C[unbearably long]

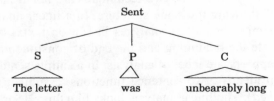

3.1.3. Four form types

There are four different form types capable of assuming sentence functions:

w	=	single word
g	=	group of words
cu	=	compound unit
cl	=	clause

For example, in *Sarah laughed*, both the subject and the predicator are single words: ^S[Sarah] ^P[laughed]. In *The old man wrote a long letter*, the subject and the object are groups of words, the predicator a single word: ^S[The old man] ^P[wrote] ^O[a long letter]. All four types of form are present in an example like *That Helen left the party so early had bothered Jack and Jill immensely*: the subject [That Helen left the party so early] is a clause; the predicator [had bothered] is a group; the object [Jack and Jill] is a compound unit with two elements linked together, or coordinated; and, finally, the adverbial [immensely] is a single word.

Notice that we use lower case letters for forms, capital letters being reserved for functions. Separating the two by a colon (:) we have a convention for describing both the function and the form of a constituent:

S:cl	[That Helen left the party so early]
P:g	[had bothered]
O:cu	[Jack and Jill]
A:w	[immensely]

The *colon convention* is used mainly for simple or partial analyses in run-on texts. For more complex structures displayed in tree-diagrams, we use a *function-over-form convention*:

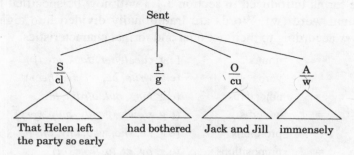

The function-over-form convention is used to indicate that a sentence constituent has a function 'upwards in the tree' in relation to the other constituents of the sentence, while internally it is a construction of a certain form type to be further analysed 'downwards in the tree' (unless of course it is a single word, permitting no further syntactic analysis).

Here are some more examples:

(1)   She had promised that they would come.

S:w[She] P:g[had promised] O:cl[that they would come]

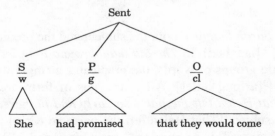

(2)   The farmers laughed and danced until morning arrived.

S:g[The farmers] P:cu[laughed and danced] A:cl[until morning arrived]

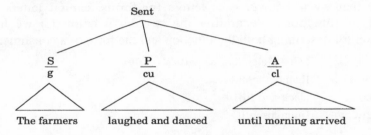

3.1.4. Word classes

One of the forms introduced in section 3.1.3 will now be specified further: the individual word (w). Words are traditionally divided into eight main *word classes* according to their notional and formal characteristics:

n	=	nouns	(e.g. *car, letter, Jack, idea*)
v	=	verbs	(e.g. *write, be, receive, hear*)
adj	=	adjectives	(e.g. *long, old, afraid, big*)
adv	=	adverbs	(e.g. *slowly, gently, duly, very*)
pro	=	pronouns	(e.g. *he, she, who, any, this*)
prep	=	prepositions	(e.g. *by, at, to, from, in*)
conj	=	conjunctions	(e.g. *that, because, although*)
art	=	articles	(*the, a, an*)

Nouns typically express things or persons. In doing so they are often combined with articles and inflected for the expression of number (e.g. *the car* vs. *the cars*) and the genitive case (e.g. *Jack* vs. *Jack's*).

Verbs typically express actions (e.g. 'writing') or states (e.g. 'being') and inflect for tense and aspect (e.g. *write* vs. *wrote*), person and number (e.g. *write* vs. *writes*).

Adjectives typically express qualities in relation to (pro)nouns (e.g. *a long letter / Jack is old*) and often allow comparison (e.g. *longer, longest / more afraid, most afraid*).

Adverbs typically express qualities in relation to verbs (e.g. *Jack moved slowly*), adjectives (e.g. *very big*), other adverbs (e.g. *so gently*), or the rest of the clause (e.g. *Fortunately, everybody was saved*). Adverbs are often derived from adjectives by means of the suffix *-ly*: e.g. *slow → slowly, gentle → gently*. Like many adjectives, many adverbs allow comparison (e.g. *more slowly, most slowly*).

Pronouns are a rather heterogeneous word class, comprising personal pronouns (*I, me; you; he, him; she, her; it*, etc.), possessive pronouns (*my, mine; your, yours*, etc.), reflexive pronouns (*myself, yourself, herself*, etc.), demonstrative pronouns (*that, those, this, these*), interrogative and relative pronouns (e.g. *who, which, what*) and indefinite pronouns (*some, something, any, anybody, no, nothing, every, everyone, all, (n)either, both*, etc.).

Prepositions express relations (often spatial relations) between constituents. They typically do so by relating a noun or group (e.g. *the table*) to another noun or group (e.g. *the book*) as in *the book on the table*, or to some action or state (*The book was placed on the table / The book is on the table*).

Conjunctions also express relations between constituents. They do so either by combining constituents at the same level (e.g. *cars and books, clever but arrogant*) or by placing one clause (e.g. *He didn't support her*) at a lower level in relation to another clause (e.g. *I said that he didn't support her*).

Articles typically combine with nouns to express definiteness (e.g. *the car, the idea*) or indefiniteness (e.g. *a car, an idea*).

To the eight main word classes we may add *intj* (interjections like *huh, ouch, well, oh, wow*, etc.) and *num* (numerals like *five, hundreds, 1993, tenth, twenty-first*, etc.). The infinitive marker *to* is special: like many adverbs it is obviously related to verbs; like auxiliary verbs such as *may, can, will*, etc., it is placed in front of verbs (and thus in fact also resembles the articles, which always precede nouns); like the conjunction *that* it seems void of meaning; and formally it looks like the preposition *to*. We treat it separately, as a word in its own right, and use the abbreviation *infm* to mark it in our analyses.

Each word class will be dealt with more elaborately in later chapters. At this point we shall merely point to certain important facts relating to the

division of words into classes: (i) the identification of word-class membership; (ii) the distinction between words as lexical items and words in use; and
(iii)   *open word classes* vs. *closed word classes.*

A) The identification of word-class membership. It is often difficult to
classify a word in isolation from its linguistic context. Many words are of
course easily identifiable as members of one, and only one, word class:
policeman is always a noun, *eliminate* is always a verb, *the* always an article,
always always an adverb, etc. But there are also cases where we have to rely
on the context to reveal the function of the word before we can classify it.
Put differently, there are cases where word-class membership cannot be
determined independently of function. For example, *blow* is a noun in *It was
a hard blow to him,* but a verb in *The referee may blow his whistle any time
now. Early* is an adjective in *He took an early train* but an adverb in *He left
the party very early. Down* is particularly versatile: it is an adverb in *The ship
went down,* a preposition in *Sally was walking confidently down the street,* an
adjective in *He is in one of his down periods at the moment,* a verb in *He
could down a pint of beer in twelve seconds.* It may even be used as a noun
in the plural, as in *He has his ups and downs,* or with a completely different
meaning, as in *The pillow was full of soft down.*
    As can be seen, it is necessary to distinguish, on the one hand, between
completely different words with the same form, and, on the other, between
different uses of what basically appears to be the same word. Thus it would
be sensible to say that *down* with the meaning 'first, soft feathers of young
birds' and *down* with a directional meaning are two different but *homonym-
ous* words, i.e. different words which happen to have the same manifestation
form. But then, what about the different uses of *down* with directional
meaning mentioned above: are they to be considered separate words? It
seems most appropriate to recognize the various functional realizations of
directional *down* as word-class distinct items (adverb, preposition, adjective,
etc.). In practice, then, we treat them as distinct but very closely related
words.

B) The distinction between words as lexical items and words in use.
Consider now the problem posed by the following examples:

(1)   We all *love* Sally.

(2)   Richard probably *loves* her more than the rest of us.

(3)   Even bad-tempered, old Graham *loved* her once.

(4)   As for myself, I cannot help *loving* her, too.

What we see here is formal (inflectional) variation of an item which does not
result in a change of word class. Though formally distinct, *love, loves, loved*

and *loving* 'belong' to the same word, or lexical item, the verb *love*. This means that we have to distinguish between a word in isolation – the base form as it appears in a dictionary – and its inflectional manifestation form in actual speech or writing. Henceforth we shall use capital letters when we want to emphasize the status of a word as a base form and italics when we want to emphasize the status of a word as a realized manifestion form: *love*, *loves*, *loved* and *loving* are manifestation forms of the base form LOVE. We use this convention in connection with verbs, nouns, adjectives and adverbs.

C) *Open word classes* vs. *closed word classes*. Of the eight main word classes listed above, the first four (nouns, verbs, adjectives and adverbs) are open word classes whereas the last four (pronouns, prepositions, conjunctions and articles) are closed classes. Numerals and interjections are open classes, while the infinitive marker is unique and thus does not fit into the open/closed distinction at all.

Open and closed word classes can be distinguished in several different ways. While open word classes have indefinitely many members, closed word classes have relatively few members. While open word classes have a fairly relaxed 'membership policy', admitting new members whenever there is a need for them, closed word classes rarely allow any change. Thus we often get new nouns (for example, as the result of new technology: LASER, VIDEO, SOFTWARE, etc.) but the classes of prepositions and articles stay the same for a very long period of time.

Members of open word classes typically have one or more independently identifiable meanings, and there is no necessary semantic relationship between the meaning of one member of a class and another member of the same class. Thus, simply by looking at nouns like POLICEMAN and STORY we get a clear sense of their meaning. At the same time there seems to be no obvious semantic relationship between them. Members of open word classes are used by the speaker to instruct the hearer to think of things, events, qualities, etc. that the speaker wants to talk about. By contrast, members of closed word classes seem to have little independent meaning: they are grammatical *function words*, assuming their meaning in relation to other words. For example, in isolation it makes little sense to discuss the meaning of, say, the definite article *the*, the conjunction *that*, the relative pronoun *which* and even the preposition *at*. In appropriate linguistic contexts, however, these words assist open-class words in forming coherent sentences and utterances. The presence of e.g. the definite article in the context of a singular noun typically ensures a reading of the noun as a word which refers to a specific, identifiable entity. Unlike open-class words, closed-class words often enter a tight network of functional interdependencies and relationships.

Thus, the function of the definite article is largely complementary to that of the indefinite article: together they share a *functional domain*. The same is true of the other closed word classes, though of course there are more members and therefore more complex networks and systems.

3.1.5. Simple complete analyses

We are now in a position to offer complete analyses of sentences consisting of one-word constituents, like the following (note that in such cases we no longer need the triangle convention):

(1)   John left her yesterday.
       S:n[John] P:v[left] O:pro[her] A:adv[yesterday]

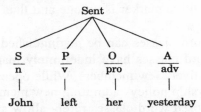

(2)   Predictably, everybody liked chocolate.
       A:adv[Predictably] S:pro[everybody] P:v[liked] O:n[chocolate]

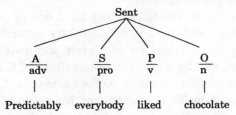

For sentences which contain complex constituents we still use the triangle convention to indicate that further analysis is possible:

(3)   Marion said it was just as well she had gone.
       S:n[Marion] P:v[said] O:cl[it was just as well she had gone]

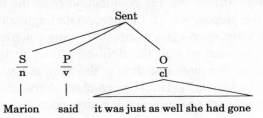

3.1.6. Discontinuity

As pointed out in section 2.4, there is a strong tendency in language for constituents which belong together to be positioned together. However, this principle of proximity is violated under well-defined conditions (see section 5.6 below). In both our linear analyses and our tree diagrams, the resulting discontinuity is marked by hyphens in the following way:

(1)   Ildiko *did* not *send* the letter last night.

   S:n[Ildiko] P:g-[did] A:adv[not] -P:g[send] O:g[the letter] A:g[last night]

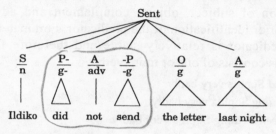

(2)   *Have* they ever *met* Francis?

   P:g-[Have] S:pro[they] A:adv[ever] -P:g[met] O:n[Francis]

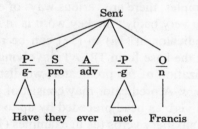

In these examples, right-hyphenation (i.e. hyphenation *after* a label, such as P:g- in example (1)) indicates a discontinuous relationship between the unit it represents in the tree (*did*) and a unit in the *subsequent* linguistic context (*send*), identically labelled but with left-hyphenation (i.e. a hyphen *before* the label, such as -P:g in example (1)).

Notice that only one hyphen is used for each part of the discontinuous constituent in our linear analyses, representing both discontinuous form and discontinuous function (e.g. 'P:g-' for *Have* in example (2)), whereas in our tree diagrams two hyphens are used, one for the form label (e.g. 'g-') and one for the function label (e.g. 'P-'). It is also important to notice that although each part of a discontinuous constituent may consist only of one word, as in all of the examples above, we have not yet reached word level in our analysis. The internal relationship of the parts that have been separated remains to be specified, exactly as in continuous constituents.

Having introduced the main sentence functions and the main types of form manifesting them, as well as the convention for marking discontinuity, we now turn to each of the functions S, P, O, A and C.

3.2. Sentence functions and sentence structures

3.2.1. The predicator

The identification of subject, object, complement and adverbial often depends on the prior identification of the predicator. Fortunately the form of the sentence predicator is relatively stable and therefore fairly easy to identify. It always consists of one or more verbs:

(1a)   Jack *treated* Sophia very badly.
(1b)   Jack *is treating* Sophia very badly.
(1c)   Jack *has been treating* Sophia very badly.
(1d)   Jack *may have been treating* Sophia very badly.
(1e)   ?Sophia *may have been being treated* very badly by Jack.

As we see in these examples, there are various ways of expressing a situation of 'Jack treating Sophia very badly': the key word is in each case TREAT. In fact, the italicized predicator in (1a) to (1e) can be regarded as different manifestation forms of the base form TREAT, involving one or more words. To describe the organization of the predicator, we distinguish between *full verbs* and *auxiliary verbs*. A predicator may consist of just a full verb (as in example (1a)) or a full verb as head preceded by up to three (in exceptional cases: four) dependent auxiliary verbs (as in examples (1b) to (1e)).

The difference between a full verb and an auxiliary is normally one of semantic weight: full verbs have independently identifiable lexical meanings whereas auxiliaries have functional characteristics like closed-class items (articles, prepositions, pronouns and conjunctions), relating to and modifying full verbs. Formally, the two types of verb can be distinguished in terms of linear position: in predicators where both are present, the last verb is almost always the full verb and the others are auxiliaries (we disregard cases of inversion like *Also killed in the shootout were three teenagers from the Bronx*, see section 5.3.7). If one wants to test whether a verb is a full verb or an auxiliary, one can convert a statement containing the verb into a '*yes-no* question' (i.e. a question of the type which tries to elicit either a yes or a no for an answer). If the verb readily precedes the subject it is an auxiliary whereas if it cannot precede the subject it is a full verb:

(2a)   Rob *was having* a nightmare.

(2b)   *Was* Rob *having* a nightmare?

(3a)   He *can run* a mile in six minutes.

(3b)   *Can* he *run* a mile in six minutes?

(4a)   Steven *finished* his cheeseburger.

(4b)   **Finished* Steven his cheeseburger?

(5a)   Cathy *kept* laughing.

(5b)   **Kept* Cathy laughing?

In examples (2) and (3) BE and CAN are shown to be auxiliaries. In (4) and (5) FINISH and KEPT are shown to be full verbs. To form a *yes-no* question from a statement containing a full verb we have to use *DO-support*:

(4c)   *Did* Steven *finish* his cheeseburger?

(5c)   *Did* Cathy *keep* laughing?

In such cases DO is an auxiliary.

Note that three verbs, BE, HAVE and DO, are special in that they function sometimes as auxiliaries and sometimes as full verbs. In the latter case they may stand alone in the predicator:

(6a)   Jack *is* now fully awake.

(7a)   The old dancer *has* fond memories of Paris.

(8a)   Her parents *did* nothing to change her mind.

The three verbs form a small closed class of so-called *primary verbs*. When functioning as a full verb, BE regularly precedes the subject in *yes-no* questions; HAVE occasionally allows this position in formal BrE; DO always takes DO-insertion:

(6b)   *Is* Jack now fully awake?

(7b)   *Has* the old dancer fond memories of Paris?

(7c)   *Does* the old dancer *have* fond memories of Paris?

(8b)   *Did* her parents *do* nothing to change her mind?

The following central *modal verbs* always function as auxiliaries: *can, could, may, might, shall, should, will, would, must*. Note that they have no base form, only a fixed present and past form. There can never be more than one central modal auxiliary in a predicator. In strings of auxiliaries, the others are typically forms of the primary verbs BE and HAVE.

A predicator is *finite* if it contains a finite verb. A predicator is nonfinite if all the verbs in it are nonfinite. A finite predicator may contain up to three (occasionally four) nonfinite verbs in addition to the finite verb. The distinction between finite and nonfinite hinges on the presence or absence of present/past marking: a finite verb is either formally present or formally past whereas a nonfinite verb belongs to one of the following three form types:

(i) infinitives (with or without the infinitive marker): *(to) break, (to) think, (to) worry*, etc.;

(ii) present participles (*breaking, thinking, worrying*, etc.);

(iii) past participles (*broken, thought, worried*, etc.).

In the following examples, all the predicators (marked in square brackets) are finite, containing a finite verb (in italics):

(9)   Jack and Jill [*take*] a walk every morning.

(10)   Jack [*takes*] things as they come.

(11)   Jack and Jill [*have* taken] their stand on the issue.

(12)   Both of them [*could* have been taking] the book to the library.

All the non-italicized verbs in these finite predicators (i.e. *taking, taken, have, been*) are nonfinite by themselves. The same is true of *take* when it is an infinitive, not a present form, as in the following examples:

(13)   To *take* a walk would be foolish.

In a string of verbs in a finite predicator, it is the first verb (the first auxiliary) which is finite. This verb is often referred to as the *operator*. To form *yes-no* questions there is subject-operator inversion, often referred to as *partial inversion* because only a part of the predicator is moved, cf. examples (2) and (3) above; for discussion see section 5.3 below.

Note finally that there can be only one full verb in a predicator. In examples like the following the second full verb is thus by definition outside the sentence predicator:

(14)   My old friend [decided] *to leave* the party.

(15)   His girlfriend [stopped] *singing*.

In these examples, *to leave* and *singing* are part of, or fully constitute, the object rather than belong to the predicator (see section 4.3.4).

Let us summarize the defining characteristics of the sentence predicator:

(i) A sentence predicator is always finite, containing a finite verb, showing formal present/past marking.

(ii) A predicator contains one, and only one, full verb. In a predicator group, the full verb always assumes head function.

(iii) Apart from the full verb, a predicator may contain up to three (occasionally four) dependent auxiliary verbs (a modal auxiliary and/or one or more forms of the primary verbs BE, HAVE and DO).

3.2.2. The subject

Once the predicator of a sentence has been found, it is usually fairly simple to locate also the subject. Typically, the subject expresses the person or thing which the predicator says, or predicates, something about. The subject is thus the *topic* of statements, whereas the predicator is part of what is being stated about the subject, the *comment* made about the subject. We can find the subject by asking 'Who or what' immediately followed by the predicator, i.e. 'Who or what P?' The answer to that question is the subject. Consider:

(1)   The parish *vibrated* with gossip the next day.

(2)   It *was* a terrible shock to Mummy and Daddy.

(3)   Daphne *had enjoyed* the illicit character of our relationship.

To find the subject in (1) to (3) we simply ask the question 'Who or what P?':

(1')   Who or what *vibrated*?   *The parish* (did)

(2')   Who or what *was*?   *It* (was)

(3')   Who or what *had enjoyed*?   *Daphne* (had)

While this fairly simple test applies to the vast majority of sentences, there are instances where it does not really make sense to ask 'Who or what P?':

(4)   It *was raining* cats and dogs.

(4')   Who or what was raining?   **It*

More formally, the subject displays a number of defining characteristics:

(i) The subject typically precedes the predicator in simple statements (as we see in examples (1) to (4)).

(ii) The subject is always placed between the operator and the rest of the predicator in *yes-no* questions, immediately following the operator (if the predicator is a primary verb it also immediately precedes the subject):

(1a)   *Did* the parish *vibrate* with gossip the next day?

(2a)   *Was* it a terrible shock to Mummy and Daddy?

(3a)   *Had* Daphne *enjoyed* the illicit character of our relationship?

(4a)   *Was* it *raining* cats and dogs?

(iii) Like the predicator, but unlike any other constituent, the subject is always obligatorily present in sentences expressing statements. This means that minimal sentences expressing statements contain S and P only:

(5)   John left.

(6)   The last glimmer of hope evaporated.

(iv) There is *concord* between subject and predicator, i.e. agreement between these constituents in terms of *number* and *person*. With one exception (see below), subject-predicator concord is restricted to the present form of the finite verb: if the subject is in the singular third person (i.e. *he*, *she*, *it*, or anything potentially represented by these pronouns), the verb takes the suffix *-(e)s*, otherwise it appears in its base form:

(7a)   I *take* it easy.
(7b)   She *takes* it easy.
(8a)   The young woman *teaches* English grammar.
(8b)   The young women *teach* English grammar.

The verb BE is especially expressive with respect to concord, being the only verb showing concord in the past form and showing three person distinctions in the present form:

(9a)   I *am* better now than I *was*.
(9b)   You/We/They *are* better now than you/we/they *were*.
(9c)   He/She/It *is* better now than he/she/it *was*.
(10)   The book/books *was/were* far too expensive.

(v) With pronouns to which the distinction between the subjective and objective case applies (e.g. *I/me, he/him, she/her, we/us, they/them*), the subjective case is used when the pronoun functions as the subject of a finite predicator (see e.g. (7a-b) and (9a-c)).

(vi) Subjects, but not objects, complements or adverbials can be represented by a pronoun in a so-called *tag question*:

(11)   {Bob} gave them extra work, didn't *he*?
(12)   {You and I} know better, don't *we*?

In some sentences there are *two* subjects, a provisional subject (Sp) and a real subject (Sr). Only *it* and *there* may function as provisional subject:

(13)   It was obvious that he disliked her.
       Sp:pro[It] P:v[was] C:adj[obvious] Sr:cl[that he disliked her]

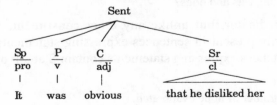

(14)   There were five books on the table.

Sp:pro[There] P:v[were] Sr:g[five books] A:g[on the table]

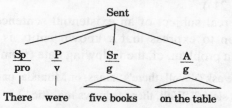

In such examples, the provisional subject is semantically very light: it functions as a grammatical prop word in subject position, merely representing the real subject, which – for reasons to be discussed later – has been postponed. In the case of *it*, it is usually possible to move the real subject back to subject position, and in the case of *there* this is occasionally possible:

(15a)   It was obvious that he disliked her.

(15b)   That he disliked her was obvious.

(16a)   There were five books on the table.

(16b)   Five books were on the table.

Note that in sentences with *it* as the provisional subject, the real subject is *extraposed* in the sense that it is placed at the end of the sentence, outside the actual sentence structure, and can sometimes be deleted without this affecting the grammaticality of the sentence (as in (15a): *It was obvious*). By contrast, the real subject in sentences with *there* as provisional subject is more closely integrated in the overall sentence structure: it is often followed by other constituents and it cannot be deleted.

   There is used as provisional subject in so-called *existential* sentences, i.e. sentences expressing that something or someone exists somewhere. Existential sentences are always *intransitive* (i.e. 'object-less', cf. sections 3.2.3 and 3.2.5 below). The real subject is in such sentences typically *indefinite* (e.g. *a book, books, some books, no book, something, somebody, nothing*) rather than definite (e.g. *the book, these books, John's books, that one, Bill, my parents*, etc.). The predicator is usually realized by a form of BE, by a modal verb + *be*, or by SEEM, APPEAR, HAPPEN or TEND followed by *to be*:

(17)   There *were* several students in the library.

(18)   There *could be* more than one kind of complexity.

(19)   There *seemed to be* no one left to talk to.

Other verbs are possible in existential sentences:

(20)   There *remained* a few unsolved problems.

(21)   There *emerged* in him a peculiar sense of affection for her.

Such constructions are fairly formal and the verbs are always semantically light, denoting either something stative (as in (20)) or the transition or arrival of something (as in (21)).

Occasionally the real subject of an existential sentence is realized by a definite construction to express that a known entity is an example or a possible solution to a problem, cf. the following data (from Swan 1995: 591):

(22)   'Who could we ask?' 'Well, there's James, or Miranda, or Ann, or Sue, ...'

(23)   'Where can he sleep?' 'Well, there's always the attic.'

It and *there* as provisional subjects should be distinguished from *it* and *there* with referential meaning. *It* and *there* with referential meaning relate to an entity (object, place, etc.) in the 'external world' or in the preceding text:

(24)   It came towards me with a fierce snarl.
        S:pro[It] P:v[came] A:g[towards me] A:g[with a fierce snarl]

(25)   There I finally found the letter.
        A:pro[There] S:pro[I] A:adv[finally] P:v[found] O:g[the letter]

In example (24), *It* obviously refers to something, e.g. an animal, in the (linguistic and/or extralinguistic) context. In (25), *There* refers to the place – contextually familiar to the speaker and hearer – where the letter was found (e.g. 'I opened the top drawer and *there* I finally found the letter').

Occasionally we find cases of *it* used as a non-referential grammatical prop word, i.e. with little or no meaning, as the *only* subject in a sentence (especially in expressions about weather conditions, time and distance):

(26)   *It* was raining again.
        S:pro[It] P:g[was raining] A:adv[again]

(27)   *It* was getting late.
        S:pro[It] P:g[was getting] C:adj[late]

(28)   *It* is a long way to Fitzroy Crossing.
        S:pro[It] P:v[is] C:g[a long way to Fitzroy Crossing]

We employ the abbreviation 'S' whenever there is only one subject, whether it is a grammatical prop word or a full referring expression. The abbreviations 'Sp' and 'Sr' are used only when there are two subjects.

3.2.3. Basic sentence structures

There are not only different types of subject but also different types of object and complement. These relate closely to the nature of the predicator. In the following, we shall therefore offer a subclassification of predicators allowing for the relevant distinctions pertaining to objects and complements.

Predicators can be divided into three main classes: *intransitive, transitive* and *copula*. An intransitive predicator is a predicator which takes no object or complement. Some intransitive predicators take an obligatory adverbial and/or a number of optional adverbials:

(1)   (Again) Richard *was sleeping* (heavily) (in the room next door).
       A:adv[Again] S:n[Richard] P:g[was sleeping] A:adv[heavily] A:g[in the room next door]

(2)   Jessica *was* in London.
       S:n[Jessica] P:v[was] A:g[in London]

Disregarding the possible occurrence of optional adverbials, we can represent the possible basic sentence structures in statements with intransitive predicators in this way:

    S P
    S P A

A transitive predicator is a predicator which takes an object:

(3)   Richard *kissed* Jessica.
       S:n[Richard] P:v[kissed] O:n[Jessica]

(4)   The naughty boy *teased* his parents at all times.
       S:g[The naughty boy] P:v[teased] O:g[his parents] A:g[at all times]

Transitive predicators are thus associated with the following basic structure:

    S P O

A copula predicator is a predicator which takes a complement:

(5)   Marion *is* such a nice person.
       S:n[Marion] P:v[is] C:g[such a nice person]

(6)   They *looked* so unhappy when I met them in Paris.
       S:pro[They] P:v[looked] C:g[so unhappy] A:cl[when I met them in Paris]

Copula predicators are thus associated with the following basic structure:

    S P C

It is important to note that many verbs may serve in more than one of these basic types of predicator. Consider the following examples:

(7a)   James *smoked* an expensive cigar after dinner.

(7b)   Richard never *smoked*.

(8a)   Sally *was reading* the newspaper when I got back.

(8b)   Marion *was reading* while Tom did the dishes.

(9a)   She *got* pretty mad at me.

(9b)   I *got* little reward for my efforts.

In examples (7a) and (8a), *smoked* and *was reading* are transitive, taking an object (*an expensive cigar* and *the newspaper*, respectively). In the corresponding b-examples, these predicators are intransitive. In example (9a), *got* is a copula predicator followed by a complement (*pretty mad at me*). In (9b), *got* is a transitive predicator taking an object (*little reward*).

3.2.4. More sentence structures

In addition to the basic sentence structures identified in section 3.2.3 above, there are a number of more complex structures which need to be introduced in this section. Consider, first of all, the following sentences containing two objects, a direct object (Od) and an indirect object (Oi):

(1)   John gave the little girl a new doll.
       S:n[John] P:v[gave] Oi:g[the little girl] Od:g[a new doll]

(2)   I bought my wife a new fur coat.
       S:pro[I] P:v[bought] Oi:g[my wife] Od:g[a new fur coat]

In our sentence analysis we use the abbreviation O if there is only one object present in a sentence, reserving Od and Oi for sentences with two objects. Predicators taking one object only are called *monotransitive*, those taking two objects are called *ditransitive*. In monotransitive constructions, the object is typically, though not inevitably, a direct rather than an indirect object. In ditransitive statements, the indirect object normally precedes the direct object:

S P Oi Od

Sometimes we find combinations of an object and a complement, or an object and an obligatory adverbial, following the predicator (we return to the distinction between obligatory and optional adverbials in section 3.2.9). Predicators in such constructions are called *complex-transitive*. In complex-transitive constructions, a complement is called an *object complement* (Co), because it refers back to the object rather than to the subject:

(3)   We painted the wall yellow.
       S:pro[We] P:v[painted] O:g[the wall] Co:adj[yellow]

(4)   Actually, the staff elected Miss Johnson dean.
       A:adv[Actually] S:g[the staff] P:v[elected] O:g[Miss Johnson] Co:n[dean]

The kind of complement that refers back to the subject in S P C structures is often referred to more specifically as *subject complement* (Cs) in terminological contrast to object complement.

Here are some examples of complex-transitive combinations of an object and an obligatory adverbial:

(5a)   My father put the book on the shelf.
       S:g[My father] P:v[put] O:g[the book] A:g[on the shelf]
(5b)   *My father put the book.
(6a)   I slipped the key into the lock.
       S:pro[I] P:v[slipped] O:g[the key] A:g[into the lock]
(6b)   *I slipped the key.

Complex-transitive predicators thus yield two different types of structure:

$$S \; P \; O \; Co$$
$$S \; P \; O \; A$$

These sentence structures are obviously related to the copula S P C structure and the intransitive S P A structure, respectively.

Before looking more closely at how objects, complements and adverbials are identified, let us summarize the typical sentence structures in statements:

S P	(intransitive predicator)
S P A	(intransitive predicator)
S P O	(monotransitive predicator)
S P Cs	(copula predicator)
S P Oi Od	(ditransitive predicator)
S P O Co	(complex-transitive predicator)
S P O A	(complex-transitive predicator)

For discussion of the position of optional adverbials, see sections 3.2.9 and 5.5.

3.2.5. The direct object

In this section we take a closer look at transitivity and the identification of direct objects. The term 'transitive' implies both 'relation between entities' and 'direction'. The nature of the relation established in a transitive construction is expressed by the predicator and involves the constituents subject and object(s). In section 3.2.2, we saw that the subject is commonly the topic of simple statements. To this *pragmatic* function (i.e. general communicative function) we can add one of a number of more specific semantic functions that constituents may have in relation to the action or situation expressed by the predicator. Typically, the subject has the role of *agent*, i.e. it is the participant performing the action expressed by the predicator. By contrast, the direct object (which like the predicator is considered to be part of the comment made about the subject) is typically the participant *affected* by the action expressed by the predicator, i.e. thing or person towards which/whom the action is directed. We get a sense of these roles or meanings when we consider examples like the following:

(1)   Harris moved the bike.
        S:n[Harris] P:v[moved] O:g[the bike]

(2)   The little girl kissed the shaggy dog.
        S:g[The little girl] P:v[kissed] O:g[the shaggy dog]

(3)   They hit Sally on the head.
        S:pro[They] P:v[hit] O:n[Sally] A:g[on the head]

In these examples, the subjects are agents performing the actions of 'moving', 'kissing' and 'hitting', respectively. The objects are affected by these actions: the bike gets moved, the shaggy dog gets kissed and Sally gets hit. That both subjects and direct objects may express many other semantic functions is evident in examples like (4) to (6):

(4)   This bottle contains cold tea.
        S:g[This bottle] P:v[contains] O:g[cold tea]

(5)   I saw her very clearly.
        S:pro[I] P:v[saw] O:pro[her] A:g[very clearly]

(6)   Max has received detailed reports.
        S:n[Max] P:g[has received] O:g[detailed reports]

A more detailed description of the various meanings and roles attached to subjects and direct objects can be found in section 7.3.

From the typical semantic function of *affected* in a transitive relation we can derive a simple question test for identifying direct objects similar to the one we devised in section 3.2.2 for identifying subjects: the direct object in a sentence may serve as an appropriate answer to the question 'Who(m) or what' followed by the relevant partially inverted S P construction. This test is in fact general enough to apply to all types of direct object, irrespective of the semantic function assigned to the object. Thus, applying it to examples (1) to (6) above, we get the following appropriate answers:

(1')   Who(m) or what did Harris move?   *The bike*

(2')   Who(m) or what did the little girl kiss?   *The shaggy dog*

(3')   Who(m) or what did they hit?   *Sally*

(4')   Who(m) or what does this bottle contain?   *Cold tea*

(5')   Who(m) or what did I see?   *Her*
(6')   Who(m) or what has Max received?   *Detailed reports*

There are a number of formal characteristics of direct objects:

(i) The direct object usually follows immediately after the predicator in monotransitive statements, as in examples (1) to (6).

(ii) The direct object in a monotransitive *active* construction may often, though not always, serve as the subject in an intransitive *passive* construction. The active/passive distinction is a *voice* distinction relating to information structure (i.e. the way information is presented) and the assignment of focus to constituents. Almost all the examples offered so far have been active. Passive counterparts to active sentences are formed by assigning subject function to the direct (sometimes indirect) object of the active sentence and by changing the active predicator into a passive one consisting of a form of BE followed by the *past participle* of the full verb of the active predicator. The original subject may be expressed by an adverbial *by*-group:

(7a)   Jack's secretary typed Bill's letters.
        S:g[Jack's secretary] P:v[typed] O:g[Bill's letters]
(7b)   Bill's letters were typed by Jack's secretary.
        S:g[Bill's letters] P:g[were typed] A:g[by Jack's secretary]
(8a)   The terrorists blindfolded everybody.
(8b)   Everybody was blindfolded (by the terrorists).

(iii) With pronouns to which the distinction between the subjective and objective case applies (e.g. *I/me, he/him, she/her, we/us, they/them*), the objective case is used when the pronoun functions as direct object:

(9)   She remembered *him* for his good manners.
        S:pro[she] P:v[remembered] O:pro[him] A:g[for his good manners]
(10)   They saw *us* from a mile off.

In some sentences there are *two* direct objects, a provisional direct object (Op) and an extraposed real direct object (Or). Only *it* may serve as provisional direct object:

(11)   I take it that he will not be present.

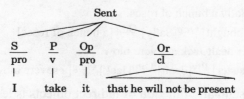

(12)   They found it difficult to work with him.

S:pro[They] P:v[found] Op:pro[it] Co:adj[difficult] Or:cl[to work with him]

The provisional direct object functions as a grammatical prop word in object position (immediately after the predicator), representing the extraposed real object. An extraposed real object is always a clause. It is not usually possible to move the extraposed object to normal object position:

(13a)   I made it clear to her that I accept no nonsense.

(13b)   *I made that I accept no nonsense clear to her.

It as a provisional direct object should be distinguished from *it* as a real direct object with referential meaning:

(14)   They took it (= e.g. his loyalty) for granted.

S:pro[They] P:v[took] O:pro[it] A:g[for granted]

In this example, *it* refers back to something mentioned in the previous discourse: *They never questioned his loyalty. I think they took it for granted.*

Occasionally, in more or less fixed expressions, we find *it* used as a non-referential grammatical prop word, i.e. with little or no meaning, as the only object in a sentence:

(15)   They hit *it* off together.

S:pro[They] P:v[hit] O:pro[it] A:adv[off] A:adv[together]

(16)   I like *it* here.

S:pro[I] P:v[like] O:pro[it] A:adv[here]

In our sentence analysis we employ the abbreviation 'O' whenever there is only one object (typically a direct object), whether it is a grammatical prop word or a full referring expression. 'Op' requires the presence of 'Or', and vice versa. Similarly 'Od' requires the presence of 'Oi', and vice versa.

3.2.6. The indirect object

An indirect object typically expresses the participant *benefiting* or *suffering* from the situation or action expressed by the combination of subject, predicator and direct object. The semantic function assigned to the indirect object is called *beneficiary*:

(1)   Fred bought Sally a bunch of roses.

S:n[Fred] P:v[bought] Oi:n[Sally] Od:g[a bunch of roses]

(2)   Her little sister dealt Jack a severe blow.

S:g[Her little sister] P:v[dealt] Oi:n[Jack] Od:g[a severe blow]

But sometimes the semantic function of indirect objects is less concrete:

(3)   My wife gave going to France a good deal of thought.

$^{S:g}$[My wife] $^{P:v}$[gave] $^{Oi:cl}$[going to France] $^{Od:g}$[a good deal of thought]

In addition to the semantic clue, there are a number of other characteristics of indirect objects which help us identify them:

(i) The indirect object usually appears immediately after the predicator and immediately before the direct object, as in (1) to (3). There is, especially in BrE, an exception to this rule: when functioning as direct objects, *it* and *them* are sometimes seen to precede pronominal indirect objects:

(4)   I gave it him.

$^{S:pro}$[I] $^{P:v}$[gave] $^{Od:pro}$[it] $^{Oi:pro}$[him]

A third option is often chosen here to avoid ambiguity or confusion: an expression containing an adverbial *to*-phrase instead of an indirect object, as in *I gave it to him*.

(ii) Related to this last point is the general paraphrase relation between ditransitive constructions and monotransitive (or complex transitive) constructions containing an adverbial *to*- or *for*-phrase:

(5a)   They offered the old man a new job.

$^{S:pro}$[They] $^{P:v}$[offered] $^{Oi:g}$[the old man] $^{Od:g}$[a new job]

(5b)   They offered a new job *to the old man*.

$^{S:pro}$[They] $^{P:v}$[offered] $^{Od:g}$[a new job] $^{A:g}$[to the old man]

(6a)   My mother has baked us a chocolate cake.

(6b)   My mother has baked a chocolate cake *for us*.

(iii) Like the direct object, the indirect object may often serve as the subject in a corresponding passive construction. Thus, to a ditransitive construction, we often find two alternative corresponding passive constructions, one – much the commoner – with the active indirect object as the passive subject and one with the active direct object as the passive subject:

(7a)   Jack gave Sally a silver ring.

$^{S:n}$[Jack] $^{P:v}$[gave] $^{Oi:n}$[Sally] $^{Od:g}$[a silver ring]

(7b)   Sally was given a silver ring (by Jack).

$^{S:n}$[Sally] $^{P:g}$[was given] $^{O:g}$[a silver ring] ($^{A:g}$[by Jack])

(7c)   A silver ring was given Sally (by Jack).

$^{S:g}$[A silver ring] $^{P:g}$[was given] $^{O:n}$[Sally] ($^{A:g}$[by Jack])

When the active direct object becomes the passive subject, there is a preference for expressing the beneficiary in an adverbial *to*- or *for*-phrase:

(7d)   A silver ring was given *to Sally* (by Jack).

(iv) With pronouns to which the distinction between the subjective and objective case applies (e.g. *I/me, he/him, she/her, we/us, they/them*), the objective case is used when the pronoun functions as indirect object:

(8)   Granny was reading *them* a chapter.

(9)   Mr Smith ordered *me* a new radio.

Note finally that from ditransitive constructions we can typically only derive monotransitive constructions with the direct object:

(10a)   Billy gave his brother a penknife.

(10b)   Billy gave a penknife.

(10c)   *Billy gave his brother.

With a few verbs, however, either the direct object or the indirect object in a transitive construction may function as the sole object in a monotransitive construction, cf. the following examples with TEACH:

(11a)   The young man taught us linguistics.

(11b)   The young man taught linguistics.

(11c)   The young man taught us.

Note that in clauses with TELL or TEACH, clausal direct objects require the presence of an indirect object:

(12a)   The young man taught us how to fix a lock.

(12b)   *The young man taught how to fix a lock.

(13a)   Jack told us that he missed his brother.

(13b)   *Jack told that he missed his brother.

In our sentence analysis we only use the labels Od and Oi in ditransitive constructions. In monotransitive constructions, we always use O, irrespective of the potential function of the constituent in ditransitive constructions.

3.2.7. The subject complement

A subject complement (for which we use the abbreviation 'Cs' or simply 'C') expresses further information about the referent of the form realizing the subject of the sentence:

(1)   This is a misfortune.
       S:pro[This] P:v[is] C:g[a misfortune]

(2)   Jack became my best friend.
       S:n[Jack] P:v[became] C:g[my best friend]

(3)   My brother looks very intelligent.
       S:g[My brother] P:v[looks] C:g[very intelligent]

(4)　　My sister often gets more upset than Jack.

S:g[My sister] A:adv[often] P:v[gets] C:g[more upset than Jack]

In examples (1) and (2), there is identity between the subject and the complement, the complement offering a (different) description of the thing or person referred to by the subject *This* or *Jack*, respectively. In examples (3) and (4), the complement simply assigns a quality to the subject, that of being 'very intelligent' and 'more upset than Jack', respectively.

One diagnostic feature of the complement function is that – unlike subjects, objects and adverbials – it can almost always be realized by an adjective or adjectival construction (such as *very intelligent* and *more upset than Jack* in examples (3) and (4), respectively). Like subjects and objects, complements are however often realized by nominal constructions. But when a complement is realized by a nominal construction (as in examples (1) and (2)) one way of deciding that it is indeed a complement rather than, say, an object is to see if it can be replaced by an adjectival construction without this affecting the acceptability of the sentence:

(1')　　This is *unfortunate*.

(2')　　Jack became *very friendly*.

Exceptions to this diagnostic feature are rare:

(5a)　　Stephen made (= became) a fine soldier.

(5b)　　*Stephen made very brave.

The verbs serving as copula predicators fall into two groups: the *stative* 'BE' family and the *dynamic* 'BECOME' family. The members of the 'BE' family express 'identity' or '(possible) current possession of quality or characteristic feature' (e.g. BE, REMAIN, APPEAR, FEEL, LOOK, PROVE, SEEM, SOUND, STAY, TASTE). Here are some more examples:

(6)　　She *remained* silent.

(7)　　The decision *appeared* all wrong to me.

(8)　　The directors simply *proved* far too inefficient.

(9)　　That *sounds* good to me.

(10)　　The cheese *tasted* sour.

The members of the 'BECOME' family express change and are resultative in meaning (e.g. BECOME, GET, FALL, TURN, GO, GROW, RUN and SPRING, particularly in set phrases). Here are some more examples:

(11)　　Within a week my mother *fell* seriously ill.

(12)　　Our teacher eventually *went* raving mad.

(13)　　I *grew* quite fond of her despite our differences.

(14)   The river *was running* dry.

(15)   The lock *sprang* open.

The descriptive meaning associated with S P C constructions can sometimes also be expressed by intransitive constructions with adverbials; compare:

(16)   She was happy.

S:pro[She] P:v[was] C:adj[happy]

(17)   She was in high spirits.

S:pro[She] P:v[was] A:g[in high spirits]

The approach adopted in such cases is to distinguish between adverbial and complement on the basis of *form*: when the descriptive attribute is realized by a preposition group (like *in high spirits*), it is an adverbial; when it is realized by an adjective (like *happy*), it is a complement. This approach is consistent with the way we distinguish between adverbial and indirect object in sentences involving a beneficiary like *I gave the book to John* vs. *I gave John the book*: in the former example, *to John* is an adverbial, in the latter, the noun *John* is an indirect object.

Note finally that many verbs functioning as copula predicators may serve also as transitive and/or intransitive predicators:

(18)   He *proved* the point by singing the ballad himself.

(19)   My mother *fell* and hurt her knee badly.

(20)   We *grow* oranges in our garden.

3.2.8. The object complement

Object complements (for which we use the abbreviation 'Co') express further information about the referent of the object of the sentence:

(1)   We painted the wall *white*.

S:pro[We] P:v[painted] O:g[the wall] Co:adj[white]

(2)   They drove Stephen *mad*.

(3)   Jack considered Jane *his closest friend*.

In these examples there is a close relationship between the object and the object complement very similar to the one between subject and subject complement in S P C constructions: in (1) the wall becomes white; in (2) Stephen gets mad; and in (3) Jane is Jack's closest friend. In other words, there is in each case an implied S P Cs construction. Interestingly S P O Co constructions are actually turned into S P Cs constructions in the passive voice. Thus corresponding to (1) to (3) we get the following:

(1')   The wall was painted white.

S:g[The wall] P:g[was painted] C:adj[white]

(2')   Stephen was driven mad.

(3')   Jane was considered his closest friend.

Note that object complements, like subject complements, are realized by nominal constructions or adjectival constructions. As with subject complements, the option of being realized by an adjectival construction is a fairly reliable diagnostic feature; but there are striking exceptions:

(4)   His fellow students elected him *president / *dutiful*.

(5)   The Vice-Chancellor appointed Bill *dean of the humanities / *responsible*.

The stative/dynamic distinction applies also to the relation between object and object complement. Thus in examples (1), (2), (4) and (5) above, the relation is dynamic whereas in (3) the relation is stative. Here are some more examples of a stative relation between object and object complement:

(6)   The directors found *him qualified*.

(7)   She always called *me uncle*.

The kind of relation which exists between object and object complement may be expressed by other types of construction, notably S P O A constructions:

(8)   Many people regard *Jack as an eccentric*.

S:g[Many people] P:v[regard] O:n[Jack] A:g[as an eccentric]

(9)   The professor took her *for a native speaker of English*.

3.2.9. Adverbials

Traditionally, the adverbial is regarded as the *default* sentence function in the sense that it characterizes any function at sentence level that is *not* a subject, predicator, object or complement. Here are some examples:

(1)   The Ford went *into the East Sector just after midnight*.

S:g[The Ford] P:v[went] A:g[into the East Sector] A:g[just after midnight]

(2)   *Unfortunately*, his leg was broken *in three places*.

A:adv[Unfortunately] S:g[his leg] P:g[was broken] A:g[in three places]

(3)   *As casually as she could*, she told me *about it*.

A:g[As casually as she could] S:pro[she] P:v[told] O:pro[me] A:g[about it]

(4)   *Really*, he *never even* met this woman, *because he never got out of prison*.

A:adv[Really] S:pro[he] A:adv[never] A:adv[even] P:v[met] O:g[this woman]
A:cl[because he never got out of prison]

By looking at examples like these we get a sense of the price we pay for treating the adverbial as a default function: it is far more heterogeneous in its range of roles than the other sentence functions. It is in fact so heterogeneous that it is difficult, if not impossible, to define it positively with any degree of precision. There are, however, a number of noteworthy general features characterizing adverbials: optionality, mobility, multiplicity, functional and semantic diversity.

Though adverbials participate as obligatory functions in the intransitive S P A structure type (e.g. *Jack was in London*) and the complex-transitive S P O A structure type (e.g. *Sally put the book on the table*), they are often far more peripheral to sentence structure than the other functions: they typically occur as syntactically optional constituents. Thus most of the adverbials in sentences (1) to (4) above could in fact be left out without this affecting either basic sentence structure or acceptability:

(1')   The Ford went into the East Sector.

(2')   His leg was broken.

(3')   She told me.

(4')   He met this woman.

Syntactic optionality should not be mistaken for semantic optionality: when we leave out syntactically optional adverbials, the meaning of the sentence is often radically changed. Thus in (4') the basic meaning of (4) is completely reversed. In the other examples, the adverbials offer additional information without which the sentences 'merely' lose specificity.

That adverbials are often mobile (in the sense that they may freely appear in more than one position in a sentence) can be ascertained in an example like the following:

(5a)   *One night* the couple returned from a party in a gay mood.

(5b)   The couple *one night* returned from a party in a gay mood.

(5c)   The couple returned *one night* from a party in a gay mood.

(5d)   The couple returned from a party *one night* in a gay mood.

(5e)   The couple returned from a party in a gay mood *one night*.

Basically these variant sentences mean the same thing but differ slightly in terms of the focus of each constituent, i.e. in terms of the speaker's presentation of the information. However, we do not want to imply that anything goes with respect to the position of adverbials. There are restrictions:

(6a)   *With diligence* she has completed the play.

(6b)   *She *with diligence* has completed the play.

(6c)   ?She has *with diligence* completed the play.

(6d)   ?She has completed *with diligence* the play.

(6e)   She has completed the play *with diligence*.

Sometimes the change of position has obvious semantic repercussions:

(7a)   *Clearly* Bill saw Jane.

(7b)   Bill saw Jane *clearly*.

(8a)   *Quite frankly*, Jack told me about all this.

(8b)   Jack told me about all this *quite frankly*.

In example (7a) what is clear is the fact that *Bill saw Jane* (i.e. it was clear to the speaker that Bill saw Jane), whereas in (7b) what is clear is Bill's visual experience of Jane. In (8a), *Quite frankly* is the speaker's comment on the rest of the sentence ('I am telling you this quite frankly'), whereas in (8b) this adverbial describes the manner in which *Jack told me about all this*. In other words, in the a-examples the adverbials are speaker-oriented and thus strictly outside the scope of the message conveyed, whereas in the b-examples they are fully integrated in the message, modifying the meaning of the predicator in terms of the manner in which the situation referred to is carried out.

With optional adverbials (unlike other functions), we get an impressive multiplicity of occurrence within the sentence. Instead of simply saying:

(9a)   Jack left the room.

we might say:

(9b)   [1]*Well,* [2]*to tell the truth,* [3]*last Monday,* [4]*without really meaning any harm,* Jack [5]*curiously enough* [6]*once again* [7]*quietly* left the room [8]*for a few minutes,* [9]*without locking the door,* [10]*in order to catch a glimpse of her.*

Exactly how many optional adverbials we can get in a sentence seems more a question of stylistic consideration than of grammatical principle, but even in elegant speech or writing it is not unusual to have several.

This multiplicity of occurrence is clearly related to the functional and semantic diversity of adverbials. It is impossible to give a complete survey of the many uses and meanings of adverbials, but again there are certain noteworthy characteristics.

Adverbials serve at least three main communicatively significant subfunctions, traditionally referred to as *adjunct*, *disjunct* and *conjunct*. An adjunct is fairly closely integrated in the sentence structure, typically relating closely to the predicator and somehow modifying or specifying its meaning. Adjuncts are commonly used to express 'negation', 'time', 'place' (including 'source' and 'direction'), 'manner', 'instrument', 'reason', 'purpose', 'condition', 'degree', etc., as in the following examples:

(10)   Owen did *not* believe in an afterlife.

(11)   I intend to leave for Rome *tomorrow*.

(12)   *In the distance* he heard the screeching tyres of a car.

(13)   Ursula chuckled *hoarsely* at her own choice of expletive.

(14)   He opened the lock *with a small pen-knife*.

(15)   Walter left the party *because he was angry with Enid*.

(16)   He rushed after her *to explain what had happened*.

(17)   I will do it *if you will*.

(18)   I *fully* agree that we ought to get rid of the vice dean.

As is evident in these examples, an adverbial serving as an adjunct is clearly a sentence function on a par with the subject, the predicator, the object etc., despite its frequent syntactic dispensability. By contrast, an adverbial serving as a disjunct takes on a broader scope in that it relates to the rest of the sentence and not just narrowly to the predicator. Disjuncts are commonly used to convey the speaker's or writer's comment on the information expressed by the rest of the sentence or on the style or form of the expression itself, as in the following examples:

(19)   James is *undoubtedly* a talented piano player.

(20)   *Fortunately*, Iris was not swept up in the Women's Liberation movement.

(21)   She *stupidly* tried to steer me off the subject of money.

(22)   Henry went to prison, *believe it or not*.

(23)   *Strictly speaking*, she should have reported the incident.

(24)   *Quite honestly*, I do not want you to leave Hawaii yet.

As we see, disjuncts concern the external relationship between the speaker or writer and the sentence and are thus more peripheral to sentence structure than adjuncts, which concern the internal relationship between sentence functions. Conjuncts are like disjuncts in being peripheral to sentence structure but differ from them in expressing a relationship between the sentence and its linguistic or non-linguistic context (thus often assuming a conjunction-like function). Typically, conjuncts serve to relate the sentence in which they occur to a previous sentence or to knowledge or experience shared by the speaker and listener, or they are used as discourse initiators:

(25)   He was beginning to feel better disposed towards Margaret. *All the same*, he would never allow John near her.

(26)   The rule seems to apply convincingly to all the Type A cases reviewed so far. *However*, there are important exceptions in the Type B material.

(27)   My wife is very busy this evening. *Nevertheless* she is likely to go to bed very early.

(28)   *So* how are you these days, Sally?

(29)   *Well*, it feels good to be outside Makai Manor for a change.

(30)   *In the first place,* I never wanted to get involved. *Secondly,* I do not like
being bossed around.

Like the other sentence functions, adverbials will be dealt with more thoroughly at a later stage (see especially section 5.5).

3.3. The internal structure of complex forms

3.3.1. The group

As we have seen, sentence functions may be realized by four different form
types: a word, a group, a compound unit or a clause. Of these, only the word
requires no further syntactic treatment. The other three forms are syntactically complex and must therefore be examined with respect to their internal
structure. In this and the following sections we shall deal with the internal
structure of complex forms.

A group always consists of a *head* (abbreviated as H) and one or more
dependents (abbreviated as DEP):

(1)   may have been held
DEP[may] DEP[have] DEP[been] H[held]

(2)   an extravagant party
DEP[an] DEP[extravagant] H[party]

(3)   interestingly enough
H[interestingly] DEP[enough]

(4)   in her honour
H[in] DEP[her honour]

Groups are subclassified according to the form realizing the head. Here is a
list of the most common kinds of group with a single word as head:

Verb groups have a verb as head:

(5)   might have been *dancing*
DEP[might] DEP[have] DEP[been] H[dancing]

Noun groups have a noun as head:

(6)   the sad *result* of the affair
DEP[the] DEP[sad] H[result] DEP[of the affair]

Pronoun groups have a pronoun as head:

(7)   *everyone* I know
H[everyone] DEP[I know]

Adjective groups have an adjective as head:

(8)   extremely *miserable*
       DEP[extremely] H[miserable]

Adverb groups have an adverb as head:

(9)   very beautifully
       DEP[very] H[beautifully]

Preposition groups have a preposition as head:

(10)   *to* a small town
        H[to] DEP[a small town]

The head of a group is normally an *obligatory characterizing* element without which the group would have been some *other* kind of group, or simply ungrammatical. Dependents are *obligatory or optional noncharacterizing* elements. In principle, both heads and dependents may be realized by all four types of form (the word, the group, the compound unit, the clause), but there are many restrictions applying to the individual kinds of group. Note that in our notational system we do not mark groups according to type (e.g. 'ng' for noun group): such information is redundant because it can be read off directly from the form of the head at the next level below. Examples:

(11)   S:g[the pilot] (left the party early)
        DEP:art[the] H:n[pilot]

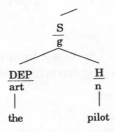

(12)   (She is meeting) O:g[someone you do not know]
        H:pro[someone] DEP:cl[you do not know]

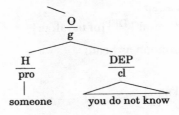

(13)   (We had) ᴼ:ᵍ[quite a party]
        ᴰᴱᴾ:ᵃᵈᵛ[quite] ᴴ:ᵍ[a party]

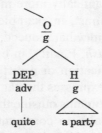

(14)   ˢ:ᵍ[His telling his wife about it] (does not help us much)
        ᴰᴱᴾ:ᵖʳᵒ[His] ᴴ:ᶜˡ[telling his wife about it]

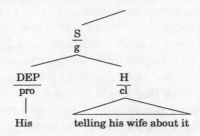

In examples (11) and (12) we have a noun group and a pronoun group, respectively. In (13) we have a 'group group' (i.e. a group with a group as head) and in (14) we have a 'clause group' (i.e. a group with a clause as head).

There is no simple head-dependent relationship characterizing all the different groups that we have examined. By marking heads and dependents we simply indicate that there is *some* relationship rather than a particular kind of relationship, the only common factor being the obligatory, characterizing nature of the head. Compare:

(15a)   ᴰᴱᴾ:ᵃᵈʲ[clever] ᴴ:ⁿ[girls]
(15b)   ᴰᴱᴾ:ᵃʳᵗ[the] ᴴ:ⁿ[girls]

In (15a) the dependent adjective *clever* 'modifies' the head *girls* by attributing a quality to the indefinite plural referent of the noun. In (15b) the dependent definite article *the* 'determines' the head, i.e. helps establish the referent of *girls* as a definite specific group of girls. Thus, the head-dependent relationship in the two examples is very different. Consider also examples like:

(16)   ᴰᴱᴾ:ᵛ[may] ᴴ:ᵛ[leave]
(17)   ᴴ:ᵖʳᵒ[anything] ᴰᴱᴾ:ᵃᵈʲ[British]
(18)   ᴴ:ᵖʳᵉᵖ[to] ᴰᴱᴾ:ᵍ[his girlfriend]

In example (16) the head-dependent relationship is not unlike that in (15a) in that the dependent modal verb *may* seems to modify the head verb *leave*. In both cases, the head seems semantically more independent and thus weightier than the dependent. By contrast, in example (17) the pronominal head *anything* seems semantically somewhat reduced, giving way to the meaning of the dependent adjective *British*. Finally, in example (18), it makes little sense to speak of either modification or a difference of semantic weight. Rather, the head preposition *to* expresses the nature of the relationship of the dependent *his girlfriend* to constituents outside the group.

It is necessary at this point also to comment briefly on the distinction between groups and single words. With the exception of preposition groups, groups can be viewed as *expansions* of single words (cf. e.g. Halliday 1994: 179ff). For example, the noun group *the water* is an expansion of the single noun *water*, the adjective group *very honest* is an expansion of the single adjective *honest*, and so forth. Often single words and groups are used in the same way (e.g. with the same syntactic function, as in <u>She</u> was <u>honest</u> / <u>Her sister</u> was <u>very honest</u>) and display very similar grammatical features (e.g. *cars* and *the cars*, which are both plural expressions). Another way of formulating this fact is to say that single verbs, nouns, pronouns, adjectives and adverbs exhibit a strong potential for being the head of a group. Given this close relationship between single words and groups, it is often convenient to be able to refer to both form types with a single label. In traditional grammar there was a strong word-orientation: grammarians talked about e.g. *nouns*, often implying also noun groups. In modern linguistics, there is a tendency to focus more on the group level: grammarians now often talk about e.g. *noun groups* (or 'noun phrases'), implying also single nouns. In addition to these practices, which are difficult to avoid completely, we shall operate with the following explicit cover terms:

verbal	=	verb group *or* single verb
nominal	=	noun group *or* single noun
pronominal	=	pronoun group *or* single pronoun
adjectival	=	adjective group *or* single adjective
adverbal	=	adverb group *or* single adverb

These cover terms are to be understood as *form* terms, not *function* terms.

Many grammarians go one step further and conflate nominal and pronominal constituents in one broad category of 'nominals', the reason being that the two types of constituent are very closely related, both functionally and referentially. While not disputing the soundness of this approach in principle, it is practical nonetheless to retain the term 'pronominal' and deal with nominals and pronominals separately (in chapters 10 and 11, respectively).

3.3.2. The preposition group

As we have seen, the preposition group is special: it is not an expansion of a single word and the relationship between H and DEP is different from that in other groups. The preposition group is always *binary*, i.e. it consists of two parts only, a head and one dependent. The dependent is traditionally referred to as the 'prepositional complement'. The complement may be realized by a nominal, a pronominal, a compound unit, or a nonfinite *-ing* clause:

(1)   (The clever girls objected) A:g[to the proposal]
       H:prep[to] DEP:g[the proposal]

(2)   (No, I haven't heard) A:g[from her]
       H:prep[from] DEP:pro[her]

(3)   (Richard flew) A:g[to Rome and Athens]
       H:prep[to] DEP:cu[Rome and Athens]

(4)   A:g[By leaving so early] (he offended my wife)
       H:prep[By] DEP:cl[leaving so early]

The complement may also be realized by an interrogative clause (as in (5)) or by a so-called independent relative clause (as in (6)), cf. sections 8.3 and 11.3.3 [B.c]):

(5)   I was wondering about *which doll to give her*.

(6)   You can give this book to *whoever wants to read it*.

Colloquially, finite clauses are used after *How about*:

(7)   How about I take Jenny to her music lesson?

Apart from examples like (5) to (7), finite clauses and nonfinite infinitive or past participle clauses cannot serve as prepositional complements.

Cases like the following present a slight complication:

(8a)   *Before midnight*, all the guests had disappeared.
(8b)   *Before he left*, he thanked me profusely.
(9a)   *After breakfast*, everyone joined the game.
(9b)   *After she arrived*, everyone seemed far more relaxed.

In the a-examples we seem to have straightforward examples of prepositional groups. In the b-examples, the status of *Before* and *After* is more debatable. They seem to have the same meaning as in the a-examples. But since prepositions are in general incapable of taking finite clauses as their complements (e.g. **By he left so early he offended my wife*), it seems more reasonable to analyse *before* and *after* in examples like (8b) and (9b) as subordinating conjunctions (like e.g. *when* in *When he left, he thanked me* *profusely / *When midnight, all the guests had disappeared*). In other words, we consider items like *before* and *after* to be in a grey zone between prepositions and conjunctions. For practical reasons we shall treat them as prepositions when they are followed by (pro)nominals or present participle clauses and as conjunctions when they are followed by finite clauses.

Another, very similar problem is provided by the following examples:

(10)   She told him nothing *except that Robert would soon join them.*

(11)   The case was very complicated *in that so many firms were involved.*

While some grammarians treat *except* and *in* as exceptions to the rule that prepositions cannot take finite *that*-clauses (cf. e.g. Schibsbye 1970: 189), others regard the sequences *except that* and *in that* as complex subordinators on a par with *as if, in case* and *in order to* (cf. Quirk et al. 1985: 998).

Preposition groups typically have either adverbial function at clause level (as in example (12)) or dependent function in (pro)nominal groups (as in example (13)):

(12)   *On Jack's advice* she will fly *to Rome.*

(13)   Someone *from our office* tapes the constant stream *of interviews she gives.*

The relationship between H and DEP in a preposition group is such that both constituents are in fact more independent than in other groups. Note in this connection the following points:

(i) The prepositional complement is occasionally capable of serving as the subject of a passive construction, leaving the prepositional head 'stranded' (cf. also sections 4.3.2 and 7.4.3):

(14a)   Someone has slept *in that bed.*

(14b)   *That bed* has been slept *in.*

(15a)   We must fight *for freedom.*

(15b)   *Freedom* must be fought *for.*

In the b-examples the prepositional complements of the a-examples have undergone a functional transformation and become syntactic subjects.

(ii) The prepositional complement is often separated from the head preposition, thus realizing a *discontinuous* group:

(16a)   You can draw water *from this well.*

(16b)   *This well* you can draw water *from.*

In such examples, the prepositional complement does not undergo a functional transformation but keeps its dependent status (for further discussion, see section 5.6.4).

(iii) The prepositional complement may by itself undergo *relativization*, i.e. be represented by a relative pronoun:

(17a)   The professor referred *to this passage*.

(17b)   This is the passage *to which* the professor referred.

(17c)   This is the passage *which/that* the professor referred *to*.

In connection with relativization of the complement the preposition group may be realized either as a continuous or discontinuous group, as in (17b) and (17c) respectively.

(iv) The prepositional head may grow more closely related to a preceding verb, forming a so-called 'prepositional verb' (cf. section 4.3.2):

(18)   Alfred's wife always *stood by* Jack.

      (i.e. 'Alfred's wife always supported Jack')

(19)   Miranda *waited on* the Wilson family.

      (i.e. 'Miranda served the Wilson family')

If the preposition is here analysed as part of the predicator, the 'prepositional complement' (*Jack* and *the Wilson family*, respectively) assumes direct object function.

It is important to note that many grammarians hesitate to speak of a head-dependent relationship at all in the preposition group, arguing that the relationship between the preposition and the prepositional complement is more like the interdependent relationship between sentence constituents (such as S and P or P and O), in that the two parts are normally both obligatory and, though functionally different, seem equally important in status. Preposition groups are thus in a sense more clause-like than group-like and can be viewed as a kind of 'contracted clause' (cf. Halliday 1994: 212ff). Note in this connection constructions like *concerning your application* (cf. *about your application*), where the present participle serves as a preposition-like item in a construction which basically seems to involve a P O structure. In the sentence analysis system proposed here, however, constituents consisting of a preposition and its complement are classified as *groups* with the preposition as head because, like the heads of other groups, the preposition is the characterizing element which distinguishes it from other groupings of words. At the same time, however, we recognize the fact that in preposition groups the relationship between H and DEP is of a special kind (for further discussion, see section 6.3.3 below).

Some grammarians hold that preposition groups are really noun groups with the noun or nominal construction as head rather than the preposition, the argument being that the preposition is a function word just like e.g. the definite article in traditional noun groups. A possible counter-argument is that a noun group with a definite determiner as dependent may still be a noun group if we leave the definite article out, and it may still assume the same kind of function in the immediate linguistic context (e.g. *The clever girls objected to the proposal* vs. *Clever girls objected to the proposal*, where both the initial constituents are clearly noun groups and both serve as the subject of the sentence). But a preposition group ceases to be a preposition group if we leave out the preposition, and what is left of the construction is usually incapable of functioning like the original construction in the linguistic context (e.g. *I went to Paris* → **I went Paris*). Moreover, in a preposition group, it is the preposition, not the prepositional complement, which is the formally stable element in the construction, the prepositional complement being potentially realized by a number of different forms (cf. examples (1) to (7) above).

3.3.3. The compound unit

Like groups, compound units may realize sentence functions:

(1) $^{S:cu}$[Rolf and Werner] (were devious devils)

(2)   (Bernard was) $^{C:cu}$[angry but calm]

(3)   (He gave) $^{Oi:cu}$[Tessa or Fiona] $^{Od:cu}$[guns and bullets] $^{A:cu}$[in London and in Berlin]

A compound unit typically consists of two or more *conjoints* (abbreviated as CJT) bound together by a *coordinator* (abbreviated as CO). Thus the internal functional structure of the examples above looks like this:

(4) ^{CJT}[Rolf] ^{CO}[and] ^{CJT}[Werner]
       ^{CJT}[angry] ^{CO}[but] ^{CJT}[calm]
       etc.

Conjoints may be realized by any of the four types of form (word, group, compound unit, clause); coordinators are realized by conjunctions:

(5)   Wendy and Kim (sat round the kitchen table).

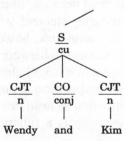

(6)   (They saw) your daughter and my son (at the party).

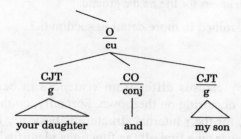

(7)   (The two winning teams were) Walter and Sally and Peter and Helen.

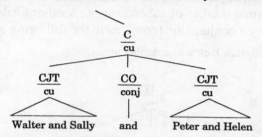

(8)   (I thought) that Jack had already left and that Helen would be coming to see me.

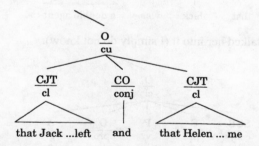

The examples listed above are all examples of *linked* coordination, where the conjoints are explicitly connected by a coordinator. Sometimes we get *unlinked* coordination, where there is no overt coordinator (as in example (9a)), but where a coordinator could be inserted (as in example (9b)):

(9a)   Who blew *the landing party, the coordinates, the beach, the time?*

(9b)   Who blew *the landing party, the coordinates, the beach and the time?*

In linked coordination of more than two conjoints, usually only the last two conjoints are separated by a coordinator (as in example (9b)). However, all the conjoints may be separated, as in examples like the following where there is emphasis on each of the conjoints:

(10)   It was only too easy to mistake our tortuous structures of *codenames and symbols and cutouts* for life on the ground.

Coordination is examined in more detail in section 6.2.

3.3.4. The clause

Functionally, many clauses differ from sentences in being bound, i.e. in being incapable of occurring on their own. Formally, on the other hand, they are like sentences, for their internal structure is basically identical with that of sentences. In clauses we find all the functions identified at sentence level: subjects, predicators, objects, complements and adverbials. In addition, there is sometimes a formal marker of subordination, a subordinator (abbreviated as SUB) realized by a conjunction (conj), as in the following examples:

(1)   (They figured) that Jack was a double agent.

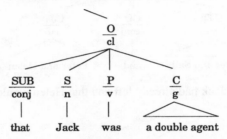

(2)   Whether he talked her into it (I simply do not know).

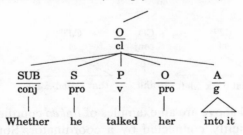

Like sentence functions, clause functions may be realized by single words, groups, compound units or clauses:

(3)   (Richard suspected) that Jack would tell Ursula and me if he got the chance.

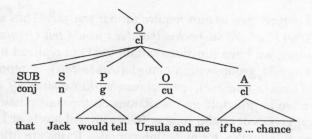

It is customary to distinguish between *main clauses* and *subordinate clauses* (henceforth referred to as *subclauses*). The main clause corresponds to the whole sentence, including subclauses. Subclauses function within main clauses, either by assuming a clause function (as in the examples above) or by assuming some lower-level function (e.g. as a dependent in a group or a conjoint in a compound unit). A further distinction which is sometimes useful is that between *main clause* and *matrix clause*. The term matrix clause is used about a superordinate clause minus its subclause (especially if the subclause functions as object or adverbial in the main clause). In the examples above, the matrix clauses are *They figured*, *I simply do not know* and *Richard suspected*, respectively.

An important difference between main clauses and subclauses is that while main clauses (and sentences) are finite, containing a finite predicator, subclauses are often nonfinite, containing an infinitive or participle as predicator (cf. section 3.2.1). Here are some examples of nonfinite subclauses:

(4)   *To see her* is *to love her*.

(5)   *Having finished my homework*, I went out.

A clause consists of at least two clause functions. As we have seen, there is almost always a predicator in a clause. But the presence of a predicator is not actually criterial for the definition of clauses. Occasionally we come across 'predicator-less' clauses, i.e. clauses where the predicator (and sometimes also other clause functions) is implied, and where the remaining constituents can only be analysed appropriately in terms of clause functions (cf. section 8.8):

(6)   (I am sure he will help you,) $^{A:cl}$[if necessary]
         $^{SUB:conj}$[if] $^{C:adj}$[necessary]

3.3.5. Embedding

In many of the examples cited in the preceding sections we have seen that the complex forms (groups, compound units, clauses) realizing sentence functions contain internal functions which themselves are sometimes realized by complex forms, which then in turn require further analysis. Thus in example (3) in section 3.3.4 (*Richard suspected that Jack would tell Ursula and me if he got the chance*), we have functions within the O:cl realized by all three complex form types: group-within-clause (*would tell*), compound unit-within-clause (*Ursula and me*), and clause-within-clause (*if he got the chance*). There are in principle no restrictions on the constellation of form types within form types or on the number of constituent levels in a sentence:

Constellations of complex forms within complex forms are often referred to as *embedding*. The phenomenon that language in principle permits infinite embedding is referred to as *recursiveness* because the rules of embedding may recur at any constituent level. Since embedded constituents are of the same form types as non-embedded constituents we can simply describe embedded constituents the way we do non-embedded constituents, as in the analysis of example (1) below, and we thus already have the full system for describing sentences irrespective of length and complexity.

(1)   Jack knew a young doctor who graduated from a university, where ...

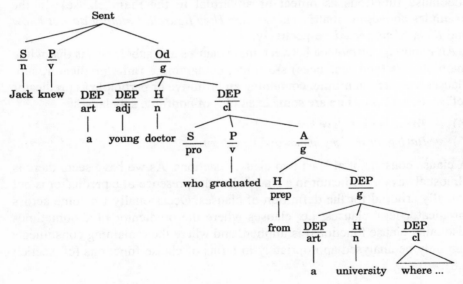

4. Advanced sentence analysis

4.1. Stacking

4.1.1. Form stacks

We shall now examine a number of more complex syntactic issues and show possible ways of dealing with them. The problem that we turn to first concerns the nature of syntactic relations and their representation. So far we have represented constituents hierarchically in terms of a consist-of relationship without concern for the more precise nature of the relationship between individual constituents on the same level of analysis. For example, in a subject noun group such as the following:

(1) $^{S:g}$[The beautiful little flower which she gave him] (was pink)

a simple consist-of analysis yields:

(2a)

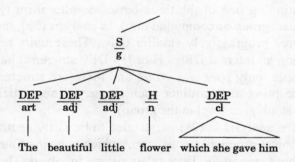

In this representation, the dependents are not only placed on the same level in relation to each other but they are placed on the same level as the head of the group. Thus the analysis does not reveal that the dependent article *determines* the head while the dependent adjectives *modify* the head, or that, somehow, the head is a more important constituent than the dependents, except through the fact that it is symbolized as H. Structurally, they are given the same status. Notice also that the configuration is identical to that assigned to sentence and clause constituents (subject, predicator, object, etc.), despite the fact that very different relationships are involved here. Our intuition about these different relationships is not reflected directly in the structuring of constituents (but only to some extent in the terms used: e.g. 'dependent article' vs. 'dependent adjective' vs. 'head noun'). For this reason it is often tempting to offer a more detailed hierarchical structure, as in:

(2b)

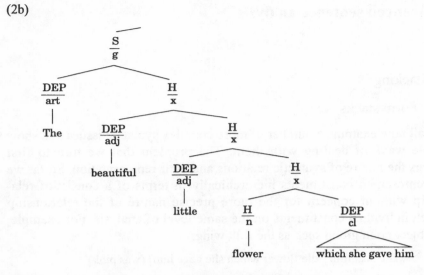

The form 'x' here represents what we refer to as a *form stack*. A form stack is a collection of constituents belonging together in one way or another without obviously constituting one of the three basic complex form types already introduced (clause, group or compound unit). In analysis (2b), the form stack x represents three progressively smaller units. These units resemble 'full groups' (in having an internal DEP - H or H - DEP structure) but are, in this particular example, only *part of a group* and therefore structurally limited (e.g. by not accepting a determiner such as the definite article, which is already present at a higher level in the group).

By contrast, the analysis in (2a) is intended to be fairly neutral: it simply describes the subject group as a constituent which contains four dependents and a head without stating the finer relationships involved. The analysis in (2b) makes a stronger claim: not only are there four dependents and a head in the subject group, they are related in terms of progressive subordination.

The motivation for sometimes choosing the more elaborate representation in (2b) instead of the more neutral one in (2a) is the desire to show certain important relationships or linguistic phenomena. We cannot say that the analysis in (2b) is *better* or *more correct* than that in (2a); but being more detailed, the analysis in (2b) may serve the purpose of showing something about the subject group which is not captured in the analysis in (2a). What (2b) may serve to reflect is the intuition that the dependents do not modify the head independently. For example, it could be argued that *beautiful* does not simply modify *flower* but *little flower which she gave him*, and that *The* determines everything which follows it, not just *flower*.

It is important to note that even the more elaborate structure in (2b) does not reveal everything there is to say about *The beautiful little flower which she gave him*. For example, there is a sense in which the definite article *The* is more closely related with the dependent clause *which she gave him* than with the other constituents. The definite article and the dependent clause could be seen to jointly determine *flower*: the clause is intended to provide information which is familiar to the listener, thus helping him or her to identify the referent of *flower*. In other words, the clause has a specifying function and thus in fact warrants the use of the definite article. There is no simple or natural way of showing this kind of relationship in a tree diagram. While obviously useful as a framework for discussion and as a first approximation to the structure of a sentence, constituent structure (as displayed in e.g. tree diagrams) has its limitations.

The use of form stacks in examples like (2b) is an attempt to attune our sentence analysis to some of our intuitions about constituent structure. It does not, however, enable us to show all the grammatical facts.

4.1.2. Function stacks: predicates and predications

As we have seen, it is sometimes useful to operate with form stacks to represent a collection of constituents somehow belonging together without constituting one of the complex form types already established in our system: clause, group or compound unit. But it is also sometimes useful to operate with *function stacks*. A function stack, for which we use the abbreviation 'X', is a collection of constituents somehow belonging together without constituting one of the functions already established in our analysis (subject, predicator, object, etc.; head, dependent, conjoint, coordinator). One such function stack which many grammarians operate with is the so-called *predicate*, which contains the predicator plus subsequent sentence or clause functions (such as objects, complements and adverbials, but not subjects), as in the following example:

(1)   Barbara seized a plate.

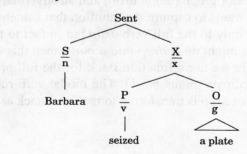

The predicate stack here includes the predicator and the object. By placing these two functions in a function stack, we can indicate that together they express some comment about the subject of the sentence (see section 3.2.2 on the topic/comment distinction). Note that the form stack which realizes the predicate stack is here similar to a 'full clause' (in the sense that it can be analysed in terms of clause functions like P and O) but cannot be said to be a clause in its own right: it is only *part of a clause* and therefore structurally limited (e.g. by not allowing a subject, which is already present at a higher level in the clause as a whole). In this respect, the form stack is here like the form stacks in example (2b) in section 4.1.1, which were not groups in their own right.

While stacking is an optional refinement in cases like (1), it is difficult to avoid in examples of *coordinated* predicates:

(2)   Barbara seized a plate and gave it to Jack.

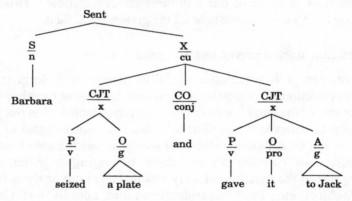

The predicate is only one of a number of useful stacks. Consider the following example (discussed in Bache *et al.* 1993: 93f):

(3)   He might drop into a bar.

This example could be analysed in a neutral way as consisting of a subject pronoun (*He*), a predicator group (*might drop*) and an adverbial group (*into a bar*). However, if one wants to capture the intuition that somehow the modal verb *might* relates not only to the full verb *drop* but in fact to the rest of the predicate (cf. 'What he might do is *drop into a bar*'), then this can be shown in a tree diagram where we use a function stack for the full predicate and a form stack for the predicate minus *might*. The modal verb retains its DEP status but the H status of *drop* is transferred to the form stack as a whole:

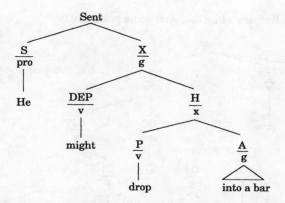

Again, while stacking is an optional refinement in simple cases like (3), it is difficult to avoid in examples involving coordination:

(4)   He might drop into a bar and down some liquor.

What we see coordinated here are not predicates but rather predicates minus the operator. The stack consisting of a predicate minus its operator is sometimes referred to as the *predication*. In *He might drop into a bar and down some liquor*, two predications are coordinated: *drop into a bar* and *down some liquor*. The stack convention allows us to illustrate the relationships involved:

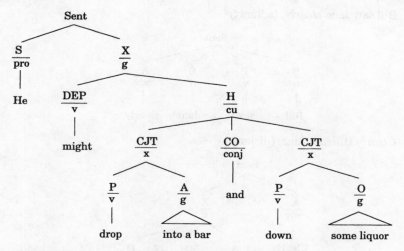

Stacking is also useful in examples like the following:

(5)   Jack gave Barbara a kiss and Ann some good advice.

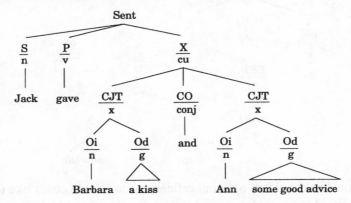

In this example, in which – for simplicity's sake – we do not operate with a predicate stack, the function stack X represents a unit for which we have no other name (not even a traditional one like 'predicate' or 'predication'). The form stack x contains in each conjoint an indirect and a direct object. For further discussion of complex coordination, see section 6.2.3.

The stack convention also allows us to show the difference in clausal integration between adjuncts, on the one hand, and disjuncts and conjuncts on the other (cf. section 3.2.9):

(6)   Bill saw Jane *clearly*. (adjunct)

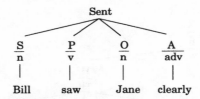

(7)   *Clearly* Bill saw Jane. (disjunct)

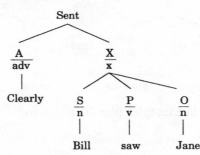

(8)   Bill saw Jane, *anyway*. (conjunct)

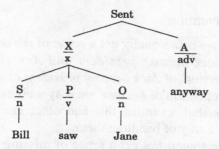

As these tree diagrams show, adjuncts are closely integrated constituents at clause level, while disjuncts and conjuncts are more peripheral: they relate to the rest of the sentence as a unit. The relative closeness of the constituents in this unit is captured by analysing them as belonging together in a stack.

4.1.3. A final comment on stacking

Tree diagram configurations of the kind employed in our sentence analysis allow us to show a consist-of relationship between constituents but do not reveal the nature of the relationship between constituents at the same level. In part this can be remedied by using well-defined terms for the forms and functions of constituents. Another useful technique is to use form and function stacks. These allow us to place constituents at different levels of analysis according to how closely related they seem to be. Stacks are especially useful in the analysis of progressive subordination and of co-ordination of complex units which do not clearly belong to the basic form and function types with which we operate. A stack is used whenever we have such a functionally or formally 'unusual' constituent.

As we have seen, there are in some examples several alternative analyses. This is hardly surprising: in sentence analysis we attempt to map our intuitions about language structure in a principled manner, and there is inevitably an element of interpretation which makes the analysis subject to an evaluation in terms of what is possible or not possible (or what is appropriate or inappropriate), rather than what is right or wrong. There is, moreover, an element of analytic purpose: to some extent our choice of structural representation in any given case depends on what we want to show about language, and on our hypotheses about language. Finally, even with the sophistication provided by the stacking technique, constituent structure does not reveal all the relevant grammatical facts.

4.2. Missing constituents, ellipsis and pro-forms

4.2.1. The zero convention

In sentence analysis, we occasionally get a sense of *missing constituents*. An example of this is: *Jack became president and Ann vice-president*. This sentence is a 'short version' of *Jack became president and Ann became vice-president*. To avoid repetition of *became* we may well use the short version. In the following, we shall examine this and other cases of missing constituents and propose a way of handling them.

The reason why we sometimes get a sense of missing constituents is that we have certain expectations as to the well-formedness of constructions. These expectations are based on general, typical ways of matching meaning with expression. Thus, normally, to convey the meaning 'Ann became vice-president' we have to say just that: *Ann became vice-president*. When in a specific linguistic context (such as *Jack became president and* ...) the meaning of this construction is conveyed by the shorter expression *Ann vice-president*, we sense that the predicator of the 'normal' expression, *became*, is somehow missing from the second half of the sentence. When a constituent 'goes missing' in this way it is customary to talk of *ellipsis*. Ellipsis is a common device for abbreviating sentences and serves to avoid redundancy.

One way to deal with ellipsis in our sentence analysis is to incorporate the appropriate *function* label in the 'place' of the missing constituent and to have the function 'realized' by a 'zero form' (represented by 'Ø') to indicate the lack of formal expression. This approach allows us to treat the sequence *Ann vice-president* as a clause consisting of a subject noun (*Ann*), a predicator that is missing ('Ø') and a complement noun (*vice-president*):

(1)   Jack became president and Ann vice-president.

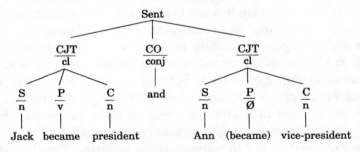

Here are some other examples of missing forms:

(2)   We parked Ildiko's car behind Sandor's.

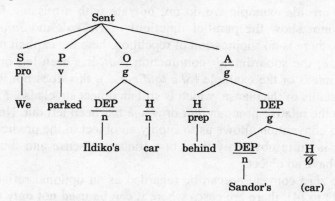

(3)   She told me she wanted to return.

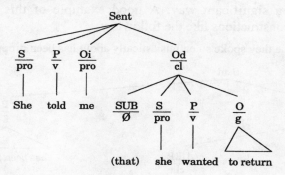

(4)   Francis never received the letter Ildiko sent from Rome.

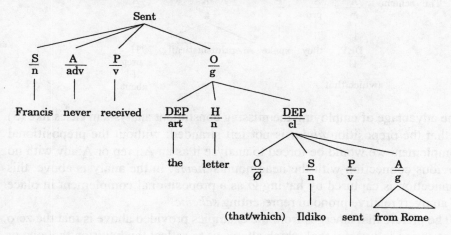

In example (2), the speaker again suppresses repetition of a constituent (*car*). Note that if in this example we do not operate with a missing form, the analysis cannot show the parallel functions of *Ildiko's* and *Sandor's*. In example (3), there is no suppression of repetition: here the explicit marker of the subclause, the subordinator conjunction *that*, has been left out. In the linguistic context of the example (*She told me ...*), this does not, however, change the status of the clause, which is still an object subclause. Finally, in example (4) the relative pronoun *that* or *which* has been left out. Notice here that the zero convention allows us to supply an object to the predicator verb *sent*, which is quite obviously used in a transitive sense and thus can be expected to have an object.

While the zero convention can be regarded as an optional refinement in examples (1) to (4), there are cases where it can be used not only to reflect our intuition that something is missing but to clarify the analysis of the overt constituents in a significant way. A good example of this is found in 'discontinuous' constructions like the following:

(5)   The scheme they spoke so enthusiastically about has been dropped.

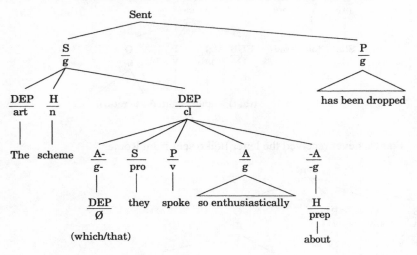

The advantage of employing the missing constituent analysis in cases like (5) is that the preposition *about* is not left stranded: without the prepositional complement we would be forced to analyse it as an A:prep or A:adv with no obvious connection with the head noun *scheme*. In the analysis above, this connection is captured by having Ø as a prepositional complement in place of an overt relative pronoun representing *scheme*.

The picture that emerges from the examples provided above is that the zero convention is a useful tool which allows us to reflect the intuition that one or more constituents are missing. In each case the missing constituent can be retrieved without this resulting in a change of the meaning or of the overall syntactic organization of the sentence. And in some cases the use of a zero constituent in the place where the missing form is felt to belong helps to clarify the relations between the constituents of the sentence.

4.2.2. Types of ellipsis

In the examples discussed in section 4.2.1, missing forms can be explained in terms of 'economy of expression' within the sentence: we can retrieve the missing forms by looking at other constituents in the same sentence. Thus, in *Jack became president and Ann Ø vice-president* the missing predicator in the second conjoint is retrievable from *became* in the first conjoint. And in *She liked the story Ø I told them about Jack*, the missing form *that* or *which* has to be an appropriate relative pronoun representing *story*. In some cases, the retrievability of a constituent is dependent on our grammatical know-ledge of the relationships between the constituents in the sentence rather than on the presence of a particular constituent. An example of this is *She told me Ø she wanted to return*, where the SUB:conj *that* is retrievable on the basis of the subordinate status of the clause *she wanted to return* in relation to the clause *She told me*. Similarly, in examples like the following:

(1)   Serves you right.
(2)   Anything the matter?

the hearer is capable of inferring the missing words too, not because of the linguistic or situational context but because he knows that the utterances are in free variation with *It serves you right* and *Is anything the matter?* All the examples of missing forms discussed so far display ellipsis with *intra-sentential* retrievability, or 'intrasentential ellipsis' for short.

In addition to intrasentential ellipsis we often come across missing forms that can only be retrieved from outside the sentence, either from the linguistic context, i.e. from other sentences, or from the situational context in which the communication takes place. Consider the following examples:

(3)   Speaker A: Bill came at eight.
      Speaker B: Susan already at seven.
(4)   Speaker A: I thought you were in a biology department.
      Speaker B: I was.

We can argue here that the predicator *came* in (3) and the adverbial *in a biology department* in (4) have been omitted. In both (3) and (4) the missing constituent is easily recoverable from the preceding linguistic context. What we find here is thus *extrasentential* ellipsis, i.e. ellipsis with extrasentential retrievability. Such ellipsis is not restricted to examples of communicative turn-taking:

(5)   Quite frankly, I left this morning. Ø Couldn't stand the noise.

The missing subject can be retrieved as *I* from the preceding sentence.

In some cases the part omitted from a simple sentence is not recoverable from the linguistic context but from the *situational context* (see Greenbaum and Quirk 1990: 256f):

(6)   Told you so.
(7)   See you later.

In the absence of a clarifying linguistic context we cannot be sure whether it is *I* and *I'll* or *We* and *We'll* which are missing. In a specific situational context, however, the hearer will often be able to determine precisely what is missing, so in examples of this type it seems warranted to operate with *situational* ellipsis.

Ellipsis can be described as *anaphoric, cataphoric* or *nontextual* according to how we retrieve the missing form(s). Retrievability which depends on the presence of some constituent in the linguistic (intra- or extrasentential) context rather than simply on our grammatical knowledge, is typically *anaphoric*: the position of the missing element is *after* the position of the constituent that allows us to retrieve the missing element. Examples like *Jack became president and Ann Ø vice-president* and *Quite frankly, I left this morning. Ø Couldn't stand the noise* display anaphoric ellipsis. Cataphoric ellipsis is rare. Arguably we have it in examples like *Jack's Ø is a beautiful voice* and *She handed me the red Ø and the yellow box*. Nontextual ellipsis can be illustrated by (6) and (7) above, as well as examples like e.g. *She told me Ø she wanted to return.*

Ellipsis can be further described in terms of the position in the clause of the missing constituent(s). In examples like *Ø Serves you right* and *Ø Couldn't stand the noise*, we have *initial* ellipsis. The omitted element(s) here would typically have constituted the prehead of a tone group, i.e. would have been pronounced without stress and pitch prominence. This lack of prosodic prominence reflects their paucity of information value and sheds light on their susceptibility to ellipsis. In constructions like *Jack became president and Ann Ø vice-president* and *Susan Ø already at seven*, we have *medial* ellipsis. Medial ellipsis is typically the result of the suppressed repetition. Finally, it can be argued that we have *terminal* ellipsis in examples like *I was Ø* and *We parked Ildiko's car behind Sandor's Ø*. In this position, too, ellipsis is usually the result of suppressed repetition.

4.2.3. Pro-forms

Ellipsis is not the only way of achieving economy of expression. Consider the following examples:

(1)   {My little sister} saw *herself* in the mirror.
(2)   They arrested {Jeremy Soames}, *who* was on his honeymoon.
(3)   When {Jill's mother} asked for {a new film for the camera}, I gave *her one*.

The italicized constituents in these examples are *pro-forms*, more specifically *pronouns*, representing other constituents in the sentences, viz. those appearing in curly brackets. In (1) the reflexive pronoun *herself* represents *My little sister*, in (2) the relative pronoun *who* represents *Jeremy Soames*, and in (3) the personal pronoun *her* represents *Jill's mother* and the indefinite pronoun *one* represents *a new film for the camera*. In all four cases, the pronouns are light constituents standing proxy for heavier constituents in the linguistic context. Like ellipsis, the use of pro-forms secures economy of expression: rather than repeating a heavy constituent we use a light pro-form.

Most pro-forms present no difficulty with respect to sentence analysis. In the examples above, each pronoun assumes an easily identifiable function: *herself* is O:pro, *who* is S:pro, *her* is Oi:pro and *one* is Od:pro.

Certain pro-forms may represent larger chunks of material in the linguistic context:

(4)   He's a friendly dog called Poulidor, but {he's now got so old that he's gone stone deaf}. Both Oliver and I find *this* terribly sad.
(5)   Deny *it* though he might, {he dumped his wife in Paris}.

In these examples, the pro-forms represent a whole clause, *this* anaphorically and *it* cataphorically. Again the analysis is fairly straightforward: both pro-forms are O:pro. There is a tradition for treating items like *this* and *it* as *pronouns* even in cases where they represent larger constituents, such as clauses.

Sometimes pro-forms represent less clearly identifiable constituents:

(6)   He may decide to join us next week, but I don't think *so*.
(7)   Speaker A: Will he join us next week?
        Speaker B: I hope *not*.

In (6) the adverb *so* represents the preceding clause but with an appropriate change of operator: ... *but I don't think <u>he will join us next week</u>*. In (7), the adverb *not* represents the whole of the preceding clause but changes it into a negative statement: ... *I hope <u>he will not join us next week</u>*. The proposed analysis of both items is O:adv.

Consider next the following examples:

(8)   I would like to go to Rome. *So would* my wife.

(9)   He cannot withdraw at this point. *Nor can* she.

(10)   My father didn't like Jenny, and *neither did* my mother.

Here we have complex pro-forms consisting of an adverb (*so, neither, nor*) plus an operator (either a repeated operator or a form of D O). In each example, the combination as a whole represents a *predicate stack*:

(8')   ... My wife *would like to go to Rome too.*

(9')   ... She *cannot withdraw at this point, either.*

(10')   ... and my mother *didn't like Jenny, either.*

The analysis of such examples is not entirely straightforward. In each case, the adverb stands proxy for a *predication stack*, i.e. a predicate minus the operator (e.g. *like to go to Rome too*). We therefore propose to analyse the combination of the operator and the adverb in the same way as we analysed the combination of an operator and a full predication in section 4.1.2, i.e. in terms of a DEP - H relationship within a predicate stack:

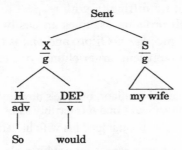

Finally it may be noted that it is not always easy to decide whether an example shows ellipsis or the use of proforms:

(11)   For years he wanted to *win the race* and he finally *did.*

(12)   Speaker A: *Will* he *propose marriage to her*?
       Speaker B: Well, he *may.*

In these examples, the operator (*did, may*) either serves as a pro-form representing a whole predicate (*won the race* and *may propose marriage to her*) or is left stranded after ellipsis of the predication (*win the race, propose marriage to her*). Similarly, in an example like *We parked Ildiko's car behind Sandor's* (cf. section 4.2.1), an alternative to saying that there is ellipsis of *car* after *Sandor's* is to regard *Sandor's* as a pro-form for *Sandor's car*.

4.3. Complex predicators

4.3.1. Phrasal verbs

So far, all the predicators we have looked at have consisted of verbs only. In this and the following sections we shall deal with predicators that are somewhat more complex in that they consist not only of verbs but also of items from other word classes. These items have become so closely related with the full verb that they are felt to make up an integrated unit of expression with it. We turn first to predicators in which the full verb is fused with a following adverb, the so-called 'phrasal verb':

(1)   Thor *turned down* the generous offer.

(2)   Julia *called up* Simon.

(3)   Cassandra *gave in* eventually.

We analyse the predicators in examples like (1) to (3) as consisting of phrasal verbs because in each case the verb and the following adverb are felt to constitute a formal and semantic unit. To appreciate the close relationship between the adverb and the full verb in a phrasal construction, we can compare example (1) to the following:

(4)   Thor *turned down* the street.

(5)   Thor *went down* to Melbourne the other day.

In example (4), *turned* has the fairly concrete meaning of 'changing direction' (unlike *turned* in example (1), which seems to derive a new, more abstract meaning in the phrasal construction) and *down* is clearly a preposition relating to *the street*, indicating 'direction' and 'path'. In example (5), *down* can be viewed as an adverb functioning separately as an adverbial specifying the direction of the event expressed by *went*. In both instances *down* is felt to be much more independent of the full verb than in example (1).

The combination of a verb and an adverb in a phrasal construction can usually be replaced by a simple verb with a similar, or identical meaning:

(1')   Thor *rejected* the generous offer.

(2')   Julia *phoned* Simon.

(3')   Cassandra *surrendered* eventually.

In the clearest cases of phrasal predicators, the verb and the adverb are thus fused semantically: the meaning is not simply a composite of the meaning of the verb and the meaning of the adverb but rather derived in a fairly unpredictable way. Neither verb nor adverb seems to retain the meaning they usually have when used more independently. As we see in examples (1) to (3), *up*, *down* and *in* have lost their concrete spatial or directional meaning;

and the relationship between *call* and *phone*, *turn* and *reject*, and *give* and *surrender* is very tenuous.

There are several characteristic features of adverbs in phrasal verbs: a) they are typically drawn from a fairly small set of mono- or disyllabic adverbs (ABOUT, ACROSS, DOWN, IN, OFF, ON, OUT, OVER, UP, etc.); b) outside the phrasal construction they have general locative (spatial or directional) meaning; c) they are capable of serving also as prepositions (e.g. *up the chimney*, *down the street*, *in a bad mood*); and d) they receive primary stress. Because of their subordinate, dependent status in phrasal constructions they are often referred to as 'particles'.

One syntactic characteristic of adverbs in phrasal predicators is that, unlike many other adverbs, their position is relatively fixed. In intransitive phrasal predicators, the adverb always immediately follows the full verb (as in example (3) above). In transitive constructions with a direct object which is not realized by a pronoun, the adverb may occur before or after the object with no difference of meaning:

(1a)   Thor *turned down* the generous offer.

(1b)   Thor *turned* the generous offer *down*.

In pre-object position the full verb and the adverb are generally inseparable in the sense that no other constituent may intervene:

(1c)   *Thor *turned again down* the generous offer.

If the object is an unstressed pronoun, the adverb follows the object:

(1d)   Thor *turned* it *down*.

(1e)   *Thor *turned down* it.

In intransitive constructions and in transitive constructions with the adverb in post-object position, the adverb bears the nuclear tone if it is the last word of the sentence.

Transitive phrasal constructions allow of pronominal question form with *who* or *what* like other S P O constructions (see section 3.2.5 on the identification of objects):

(1f)   What *did* Thor *turn down*?

It is not always possible to distinguish rigidly between phrasal predicators (as in e.g. example (1)) and non-phrasal predicators (as in e.g. examples (4) and (5)). Consider the following examples:

(6)   The children *put on* the gumboots.

(7)   Francis *took away* the little silver box.

(8)   Cassandra *knelt down*.

In these examples, the full verbs *put, took* and *knelt* retain much more of their independent meaning than the full verbs in the other phrasal constructions reviewed in this section; in addition, the adverbs *on, away* and *down* have a clearly locative meaning. Yet the transitive examples (6) to (8) conform very nicely to the rule of adverb mobility applying to phrasal predicators, e.g.:

(6a)   The children *put* the gumboots *on*.

(6b)   The children *put* them *on*.

(6c)   *The children *put on* them.

In the intransitive construction in example (8) (*Cassandra knelt down*), although the verb and the adverb retain their independent meaning as in clearly non-phrasal constructions, there is a close relationship between them: the locative meaning of *down* is somehow integrated in the meaning of *knelt*. We cannot, for example, say *Julia knelt up/away/across*, etc. In this respect *knelt down* is different from *went down* in example (5) (*Thor went down to Melbourne the other day*): it is quite possible to say *Thor went up/away/across* etc.

There is thus a gradation of constructions from very clear cases of phrasal fusion between verb and adverb to very clear cases of verb and adverb functioning independently. In between these two extreme end-points there are constructions which conform to some but not all of the criteria.

It is not easy to offer a fully satisfactory *syntactic* analysis of phrasal verbs, simply because the phenomenon involved is primarily to do with lexicalization. But since in English this kind of lexicalization does not lead to a formal fusion at word level, we are forced to try to cater for it syntactically. The simplest, but also most unsatisfactory, way of analysing sentences with phrasal predicators is to disregard the phrasal nature of the verb and adverb:

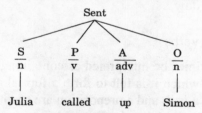

If we want to reflect the phrasal combination of the verb and the adverb in our analysis, this can be done by including the adverb as a dependent in the predicator:

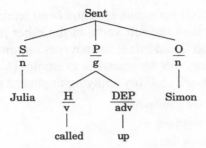

If one wants to show the close relationship between verb and adverb while at the same time keeping the predicator 'pure' (i.e. strictly for verbs only), e.g. for identificatory purposes (see section 3.2.1), one alternative is to use the stack convention, delaying the assignment of sentence functions:

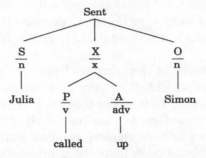

To each of the possible analyses of phrasal predicators there is a discontinuous counterpart for cases with the adverb in post-object position. We leave it to the reader to work out what they look like! As always, the choice of analysis among competing options very much depends on exactly what you want to show and how.

4.3.2. Prepositional verbs

Predicators can sometimes be interpreted as containing a full verb followed by a preposition with which it is felt to form a formal and/or semantic unit. Such combinations of a verb and a preposition are traditionally referred to as 'prepositional verbs'. In the following examples it is possible to analyse the predicator in such terms:

(1)   Miranda *waited on* the Wilson family.

(2)   Alfred's wife always *stood by* Jack.

(3)   Stephen *took after* his father.

These can be compared with clauses where an ordinary predicator is clearly followed by an adverbial realized by a prepositional phrase:

(4)   Miranda *waited* on the corner.

(5)   Alfred's wife always *stood* by the fireplace.

(6)   This is what Stephen *took* after his divorce.

Notice that in these examples the full verb and the preposition have compatible but fairly independent meanings. By contrast, the predicator and the preposition are semantically fused in examples (1) to (3) and could be replaced by single verbs with little difference of meaning:

(1')   Miranda *served* the Wilson family.

(2')   Alfred's wife always *supported* Jack.

(3')   Stephen *resembled* his father.

Unlike phrasal predicators, prepositional predicators are always transitive, taking a direct object. This object is sometimes referred to as a 'prepositional object' to indicate that, despite the analysis of the preposition as belonging to the predicator, there is still a close relationship between it and the following constituent. Like 'ordinary' S P O constructions, sentences with prepositional predicators allow pronominal question forms with *who* or *what* (see section 3.2.5 on the identification of direct objects):

(1a)   Who(m) *did* Miranda *wait on*?

(2a)   Who(m) *did* Alfred's wife always *stand by*?

(3a)   Who(m) *did* Stephen *take after*?

This obviously lends credence to the analysis of such combinations as prepositional predicators in S P O constructions: unlike the analysis of phrasal verbs, the analysis of prepositional verbs affects the function of the following constituent. If we treat the preposition as a part of the predicator (the 'prepositional predicator' analysis), the following constituent is an object. But if we treat the preposition as outside the predicator (the 'simple predicator' analysis), the following constituent is a dependent in an adverbial preposition group. The fact that pronominal question form with WHO is possible in the examples above indicates that we have an S P O structure rather than an S P A structure.

Unlike adverbs in phrasal constructions, prepositions in prepositional predicators are normally unstressed and constitute the tail of the tone group if in clause-final position (e.g. *Who did Miranda `wait on*, where nuclear stress is symbolized by a preceding accent mark). And while adverbs in transitive phrasal constructions may occur in post-object position (if the object is not pronominal), prepositions are fixed in pre-object position:

(1b)   *Miranda *waited* the Wilson family *on*.

Another difference between phrasal and prepositional predicators is that it is possible to separate the preposition from the verb even when the two are closely fused semantically, either by inserting an adverbial between the two or by forming a *wh*-question fronting both the preposition and the pronominalized prepositional object:

(1c)   Miranda *waited* diligently *on* the Wilson family.

(1d)   *On* whom *did* Miranda *wait*?

In some cases the verb and the preposition may be separated by another object, which arguably yields *ditransitive* prepositional predicators:

(7a)   The incident *reminded* me *of* her warning.

(8a)   Her stepparents *deprived* her *of* her childhood.

(9a)   The countess *supplied* him *with* opium.

The verb and the preposition form a continuous group in passive constructions with the non-prepositional object of the active construction as subject:

(7b)   I *was reminded of* her warning.

(8b)   She *was deprived of* her childhood.

(9b)   He *was supplied with* opium.

Pronominal question forms with *who* or *what* are possible (cf. section 3.2.5 on the identification of objects):

(7c)   What *did* the incident *remind* me *of*? (her warning)

(8c)   What *did* her stepparents *deprive* her *of*? (her childhood)

(9c)   What *did* the countess *supply* him *with*? (opium)

As with phrasal predicators (see section 4.3.1 above), it is very difficult to distinguish rigidly between prepositional predicators and predicators followed by a prepositional group realizing a separate adverbial at clause level. There is a clear gradation in the degree of semantic fusion between verb and preposition: at one end of the scale both verb and preposition seem to lose their independent meaning, forming a tightly knit unit with a derived, more or less unpredictable, meaning (as in examples (1) to (3) above). At the other end of the scale, we find examples where the preposition and its complement quite obviously function together as an adverbial (as in examples (4) to (6)). In between these two end-points, there are cases where there seems to be a relatively close link between verb and preposition but little actual semantic fusion, both constituents largely retaining their 'original' meaning. This is true not only of the 'ditransitive' constructions offered above but also of many 'monotransitive' constructions:

(10)   Julia often *looked at* the picture.

(11)   As always, I *dealt with* his request at once.

(12)   My parents *did* not exactly *approve of* this decision.

Here *looked*, *dealt* and *approve* mean exactly what they say and the prepositions *at*, *with* and *of* are relational in meaning as we would expect them to be
when serving as heads in preposition groups. Semantically, there is thus
perhaps little motivation for treating the predicators in these examples as
comprising the preposition: they could simply be classified as S P A constructions (where the A is realized by a preposition group) rather than S P O
constructions (where the preposition is a part of the P). Yet, in each case, the
preposition is regularly associated with the verb (i.e. verb and preposition
usually 'go together') and together they often have nearly the same meaning
as non-prepositional predicators:

(10')   Julia often *saw* the picture.

(11')   As always, I *treated* his request at once.

(12')   My parents *did* not exactly *like* this decision.

Possibly the best argument for analysing (10) to (12) in terms of prepositional predicators is that they can be passivized like other S P O
constructions:

(10a)   The picture *was* often *looked at*.

(11a)   As always, his request *was dealt with* at once.

(12a)   This decision *was* not *approved of*.

Here the 'prepositional object' (strictly: the dependent in the adverbial
preposition group) in each of the examples in (10) to (12) has become the
subject of a corresponding passive sentence and thus behaves like an object
in an ordinary S P O sentence. Notice that unless we analyse the preposition
as a part of the predicator, it is left 'stranded' by passivization, its dependent
having assumed subjecthood, i.e. an independent function. A stranded
preposition is obviously difficult to analyse. But if we have the preposition
instead as a part of the predicator, it can be fully accounted for. The only
problem with this argument is that passivization, as well as the stranding of
prepositions, is possible in cases that we would not normally think of as even
remotely involving prepositional predicators:

(13a)   Alice slept in the bed.

(13b)   The bed was slept in (by Alice).

In such constructions, 'subjectivization' of a prepositional dependent seems to
be possible only when it is affected by the situation expressed by the
predicator (cf. *The problem was gone into* / **The tunnel was gone into*).
Again we are forced to conclude that language is at times very elusive: we

cannot always capture its structure in a revealing way by applying absolute criteria to what is in reality a gradation. It is important to recognize the fuzziness of distinctions that become apparent in a rigid analysis.

Before concluding this section, we shall look at the various ways in which we can use our sentence analysis system to show a close relationship between verb and preposition. As with phrasal verbs, it is not easy to offer an entirely satisfactory *syntactic* analysis of prepositional verbs, simply because the phenomenon involved is primarily of a lexical nature. But again we are forced to provide a syntactic representation: the lexical-like fusion between verb and preposition does not lead to a formal fusion at word level.

There are two obvious competing analyses of clauses involving some sort of relationship between a verb and a preposition: a) a basic one in which the preposition is not syntactically recognized as part of the predicator but rather is the head of an adverbial group containing the following constituent as a dependent (the 'simple predicator' analysis); b) one in which the preposition is recognized syntactically as part of the predicator, viz. as a dependent preposition, which leaves the following constituent as an object rather than as a dependent in an adverbial group (the prepositional predicator analysis):

(14a)

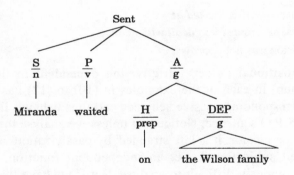

(14b)

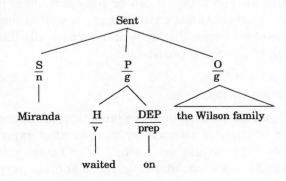

The analysis in (14a) is in keeping with the simplest possible analysis of phrasal predicators mentioned in section 4.3.1. The only advantage of this 'basic' analysis is that we keep the predicator 'pure' by only accepting verbs as internal constituents (full verbs and auxiliary verbs) and by allowing no dependents to the right of the head verb. In this way we gain a high degree of internal consistency in predicators and make them more unambiguously identifiable. The disadvantage is that we inevitably create 'external' complexity in the sense that we make it more difficult to analyse adequately what is left outside the predicator. For example, by making no syntactic difference between *Miranda waited on the Wilson family* and *Miranda waited on the corner*, we obscure the fact that, intuitively, the relations between the constituents of these two sentences are very different, something that should be reflected in our analysis.

If we choose the analysis in (14b), we may get more complex predicators (by allowing non-verbal elements as internal constituents and by accepting dependents to the right of the head verb). But the analysis enables us to capture the difference between prepositional predicators and S P A constructions. One other advantage of the analysis in (14b) is that we avoid stranding the preposition in passive counterparts (such as *The Wilson family was waited on*).

If we adopt the prepositional predicator analysis (as in (14b)) and want to carry it through consistently, we are, on the other hand, forced to accept a number of discontinuous constructions, e.g.:

(9c)   What *did* the countess *supply* him *with*? (O P- S -P- O -P)

In this example, we might have assigned indirect object status to *him* and direct object status to *What*. But in other ditransitive constructions with a prepositional predicator, the assignment of direct and indirect object status is more problematic (e.g. in *She confined her remarks to the matter of income tax*). We therefore propose simply to leave the second object as an implicit prepositional object.

Again, the choice of representational form is really a question of exactly what one wants to show, and thus involves an element of subjectivity.

4.3.3. Phrasal-prepositional verbs

Sometimes there is fusion between a verb and both an adverb and a preposition, as in the following examples:

(1)   Cassandra *looked down on* the nurses.
(2)   She *came up with* a solution in no time.
(3)   He no longer *put up with* her whims.

The order of constituents in such constructions is always: verb + adverb + preposition, reflecting the different degrees of separability in phrasal predicators and prepositional predicators, respectively. To qualify as a phrasal-prepositional verb, there should be some fusion between all three elements with a new derived meaning; compare examples (1) to (3) with the following, where the adverb and the preposition are more independent of the verb, and all three elements actually retain their original lexical meaning:

(4)   From the tower one could *look* down on the roof of Julia's house.

(5)   After a couple of minutes the diver *came* up with an interesting shell.

(6)   Did you read the notice he *put* up with yellow tape?

Notice also that phrasal-prepositional predicators can often be replaced by a single verb with little or no difference of meaning:

(1')   Cassandra *despised* the nurses.

(2')   She *found* a solution in no time.

(3')   He no longer *tolerated* her whims.

Arguably, the examples like the following involve 'ditransitive' phrasal-prepositional constructions:

(7)   Stephen always *took* her infidelity *out on* me.

(8)   They *put* her behaviour *down to* lack of confidence.

Both 'monotransitive' and 'ditransitive' phrasal-prepositional constructions pass the *wh*-question test for objecthood like ordinary S P O constructions:

(1a)   Who *did* Cassandra *look down on*?

(8a)   What *did* they *put* her behaviour *down to*?

It is, of course, always possible to represent phrasal-prepositional constructions in terms of separate, non-integrated functions, in which case both *She came up with a solution* and *The diver came up with an interesting shell* are interpreted as consisting of a subject, a predicator and two adverbials (the first realized by an adverb, the second by a prepositional group). If one wants to recognize a syntactic difference between phrasal-prepositional predicators and simple predicators, the simplest way of doing so is to have both the adverb and the preposition as dependents within the predicators:

(9)   His father *had walked out on* his mother.

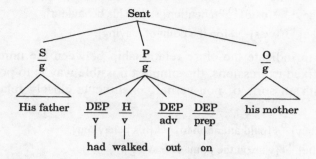

(10)   They *let* her brother *in on* their plans.

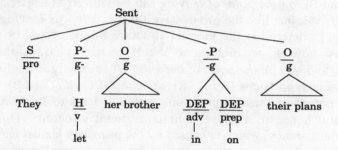

As with 'ditransitive prepositional predicators', the assignment of direct and indirect object is not entirely unproblematic in 'ditransitive phrasal-prepositional constructions'. We therefore leave the first object as an ordinary, unspecified object as in a monotransitive construction, and the second object as an implicit prepositional object.

4.3.4. Other complex predicators

A number of expressions, largely of an idiomatic nature, seem to involve other combinations of words in predicators. Here are some of them:

v + adj	e.g. CUT *short,* FORCE *open,* PUT *straight,* RUB *dry,* BREAK *even;*
v + n (+ prep)	e.g. TAKE *place,* BRING *home,* MAKE *amends (for),* GIVE *offence (to),* PAY *heed (to),* PAY *attention (to),* TAKE *care (of),* LOSE *touch (with),* CATCH *sight of,* GIVE *rise to;*
v + v (+ prep)	e.g. MAKE *do with,* GET *rid of,* HAVE *done with,* BE *going to;*
others	BE *on the point of,* BE *about to.*

In many of these cases it is possible simply to ignore the semantic fusion:

(1a)   S:pro[They] P:v[paid] O:n[attention] A:g[to his behaviour].

(2a)   S:pro[She] P:v[was] A:g[on the point of leaving].

If one wants to indicate the close relationship between the units of these more or less fixed expressions, the simplest possible way is to populate the predicator with all sorts of non-verbal constituents closely related to the lexical verb:

(1b)   S:pro[They] P:g[paid attention to] O:g[his behaviour].

(2b)   S:pro[She] P:g[was on the point of leaving].

Semantically these analyses make good sense: PAY *attention to* corresponds to HEED and BE *on the point of leaving* can be viewed as a special form of the verb LEAVE, just like the progressive form in *She was leaving*. But it is problematic to determine the internal structure of such fixed or idiomatic expressions: how do we determine the H - DEP relationships in *paid attention to* and *was on the point of leaving*? What exactly is the head of the construction in expressions like MAKE *do with*, GET *rid of* and BE *going to*? The fixed nature of these expressions makes it hard to think of internal relations and hence to analyse their constituent structure. This lack of syntactic transparency, which is caused by the primarily lexical nature of the phenomena involved, naturally opens up for a large number of competing analyses, none of which is completely satisfactory.

Rather than pursuing the problem posed by fixed expressions, we shall close this section with an observation on certain v + v (... + v) constructions which pose a special problem of analysis. Consider the following examples:

(3)   They *wanted to leave* the party early.

(4)   Rosemary *remembered posting* the letter.

(5)   Jack *tried to stop smoking*.

In these examples, we have strings of two or three verbs. Though it is tempting to treat them as complex predicators, there are good reasons why they should be analysed in terms of single-verb predicators (*wanted / remembered / tried*) followed by clausal objects (*to leave the party early / posting the letter / to stop smoking*): all the verbs are full verbs according to the definition provided in section 3.2.1 rather than combinations of auxiliaries and full verbs; also, whatever follows the first verb can be identified as an object in the *wh*-question test for objecthood:

(3a)   What did they want?   (To leave the party early)

(4a)   What did Rosemary remember?   (Posting the letter)

(5a)   What did Jack try?   (To stop smoking)

Notice finally that the single-verb predicator analysis captures the similarity between the examples in (3) to (5) and examples containing the same predicator verbs but (pro)nominal objects:

(3b)   They wanted *it*.

(4b)   Rosemary remembered *the whole thing*.

(5b)   Jack tried *something else*.

In these examples we would not hesitate to treat *wanted, remembered* and *tried* as predicators in their own right.

4.4. The top of the tree

4.4.1. Exit Sent

In this and the following sections we shall reconsider the top label *Sent* in our analysis and replace it by a set of more revealing form and function terms. As we saw in section 2.2, native speakers of a language may have strong intuitions about what a sentence is and may be perfectly capable of dividing a text into appropriate orthographical or intonational units. Nevertheless, it is very difficult to define exactly what a sentence is. One of the problems is that, even in writing, which is often considered the medium susceptible of analysis in terms of sentences, punctuation is a very unreliable criterion. Thus, as noted in section 2.2, we find units which we hesitate to call sentences but which we treat like sentences punctuationwise:

(1)   Spain.

(2)   What?

(3)   Good God!

In (1), *Spain* may, for example, be the answer to a question like *Where do you come from?* In (2), we have possibly one of the most basic questions of all in the form of just one word. And in (3), we have an exclamation, i.e. a speaker's emotional reaction to some event, in the form of a simple two-word group. The units in (1) to (3) are perhaps more characteristic of speech or written representations of dialogue than actual written language. But even in writing which is not meant to represent dialogue we often find units of text which are not sentences in any obvious sense:

(4)   An Introduction to English Sentence Analysis.

(5)   Fragile.

(6)   Bureaucratic battle over commas and spelling.

Here we have, respectively, a group serving as the title of a book, a one-word label on e.g. goods to be transported, and a group serving as a news headline.

Obviously we want to be able to handle cases like (1) to (6) in our sentence analysis system. To that end we need to revise the starting point of our analysis, the *Sent* label. So far *Sent*, which is neutral with respect to the form-function distinction (which we insist on at all other levels of constituency), has been a convenient cover term for the kind of language unit we wanted to analyse. But when confronted with a richer variety of speech and writing it proves inadequate. It is inadequate from a *formal* point of view because it signals the presence of a clausal structure, which is often simply not there. As we have seen in (1) to (6), there are units of speech and writing which do not fit into this form of structure but seem rather to be single words or groups. *Sent* is also *functionally* inadequate because it does not allow us to distinguish between the various functions that sentences and other independent units seem to adopt in a larger context. Such functions, which can be identified in both speech and writing, are not syntactic but *communicative* functions, or 'speech acts', such as e.g. *questions* or *statements*. So what we want instead of *Sent* is a form-function distinction allowing a broad range of both forms and functions.

4.4.2. Communicative functions

It is perfectly reasonable to begin by asking if communicative functions are at all like the functions identified at lower levels of analysis (such as subject, subordinator, head, etc.). At first blush they seem to be radically different: while lower-level, grammatical functions seem to indicate relationships *between constituents*, communicative functions like 'statement' and 'question' indicate a relationship *between language and situation* (in a broad sense). For example, a question indicates that the speaker (or writer) wants to obtain some information from the listener (or reader). However, there is some similarity between lower-level functions and communicative functions in that the language form to be assigned a function is related 'externally' to 'the next level up'. For example, a subject is a function at clause level, a dependent is a function at group level, and so forth. Such functions characterize external relations of the constituents: a subject is a subject in relation to a predicator, a dependent is a dependent in relation to a head, and so forth. In a sense these lower-level functions *license* the occurrence of constituents within higher-level clauses and groups. When we reach a complete unit with a communicative function like a sentence (or a group or individual word, as in examples (1) to (6) in section 4.4.1), there may or may not be a next level up in terms of a higher-level formal unit, i.e. there may or may not be a larger text within which the unit is a part. But in either case, it is always possible to identify an external function of the unit in relation to the *context* within which it occurs. This function justifies the occurrence of the unit in the larger context (textual or non-textual), i.e. it is a communicative function characterizing the speech act (or act of writing) producing the unit. It is in this sense that a communicative function of a language unit is like a lower-level syntactic function: it characterizes an external relation to 'the next level up' and thus licenses the occurrence of the unit. The difference is that while the next level up for a lower-level function is always textual and within the bounds of grammar, for a communicative function it is the (textual or non-textual) context within which it occurs and strictly outside the bounds of grammar.

The communicative function of a language unit is often referred to as *the illocutionary value* of the unit. There is no obvious limit to the number of such values that might be identified in speech and writing if one wants a very fine-grained analysis. However, we shall here closely follow the tradition of operating with four: statements (STA), questions (QUE), directives (DIR) and exclamations (EXC). These four main illocutionary values, or speech acts, will often, but not always, be marked differently in the internal syntactic organization of the language unit or in its intonational properties:

STA (= statement): unit which gives information

(1)   James left Brisbane yesterday.
(2)   In London.
(3)   John and Sarah.
(4)   Yes.

QUE (= question): unit which seeks information

(5)   Will you join me tonight?
(6)   From whom?
(7)   When and where?
(8)   Why?

DIR (= directive): unit which instructs the receiver to perform some action

(9)   Listen to me.
(10) After him!
(11) Smile and be happy!
(12) Down!

EXC (= exclamation): unit which indicates emotional reaction (surprise, disapproval, pleasure, etc.)

(13) She can't mean that!
(14) Good Lord!

(15)   Blood and sand!

(16)   Wow!

Three other illocutionary values are obviously important but somewhat more specialized and mostly restricted to formal expression:

PER (= performative): unit which actually performs the situation stated. Performatives usually contain a 'performative verb' (e.g. PROMISE, SWEAR, SENTENCE) in the present tense and a first person (singular or plural) agent.

(17)   I (hereby) pronounce you man and wife.

(18)   We (hereby) promise to support James.

OPT (= optative): (from a Latin word meaning 'choose, wish') unit which expresses a wish or a benediction/malediction. Optatives often involve a fixed expression and/or the subjunctive in English (cf. section 9.8.3).

(19)   If only I were you.

(20)   Would that he was here.

(21)   I wish that you loved me.

(22)   God save the Queen.

(23)   May you rot in hell.

CON (= condition): unit which expresses a condition which must be met for some situation or event to come about. In English, conditions are often expressed in subclauses initiated by conjunctions like IF and UNLESS, or by the subjunctive *were* and/or inversion:

(24)   *If you trust her*, I'll let her in.

(25)   *Unless you sober up*, you will fail the test.

(26)   *Were this to happen*, he would be in serious trouble.

(27)   *Had I known this*, I would have helped her these last few weeks.

The terms used for illocutionary values should not be confused with the terms used for the form of sentences typically used to express illocutionary values. Thus a *statement* often, but not always, takes the form of a *declarative* sentence and a *question* often, but not always, takes the form of an *interrogative* sentence. Similarly, there is no necessary relationship between *directives* and *imperative* sentences and between *exclamations* and *exclamatory* sentences.

It is also important to note that the illocutionary values introduced above do not constitute an exhaustive list. Nor are they meant to be clear-cut categories allowing a rigid classification of language units. Rather, they are main types of speech acts into which language units will fit more or less comfortably. The broad categories of communicative functions listed above may in fact vary in strength and intensity from language unit to language unit, and they may blend with each other and with other illocutionary values. It is useful to think of the speech acts as end points on *interacting illocutionary dimensions* along which language units may be placed differently according to illocutionary force. Consider e.g. *questions*. Questions can be asked more or less explicitly, with more or less subtlety, according to the form employed; compare:

(28a)   Did John write this book?

(28b)   John did not write this book, did he?

(28c)   John wrote this book, didn't he?

(28d)   John wrote this book, did he?

(28e)   John wrote this book?

(28f)   I do not know if John wrote this book.

(28g)   John wrote this book. ('Actually I do not know, it is my tentative guess, correct me if I am wrong, am I right so far?')

Though all of these (even (28f,g)) may be construed as questions and, in appropriate contexts, should be classified as such, the illocutionary force with which the speaker or writer puts the question varies along the STA-QUE dimension, with the a-example as the most directly inquisitive, the f- and g-examples as very nearly pure statements and the others as different blends of statement and question.

That the illocutionary dimensions are interrelated is also clear from the following examples:

(29a)   Close the window.

(29b)   Close the window, will you?

(29c)   Do you mind closing the window?

(29d)   Could you possibly close the window?

(29e)   Gee, it is cold in here!

(29f)   According to the building regulation, this window should remain closed at all times.

(29g)   The window is open.

All of these can be construed as directives, but like the questions in (28), some are more subtle than others. The different illocutionary force can be described in terms of the different locations of the expressions on the various dimensions. The two imperatives in (29a,b) are fairly explicit directives. The a-example is the most unambiguous DIR case of the set. The b-example is slightly modified by the interrogative tag *will you?* and thus placed on the DIR-QUE dimension but fairly close to the DIR end. The *yes-no* questions in (29c,d) both express a request beyond a simple *yes-* or *no*-answer and must be placed on the DIR-QUE dimension, too. The e-example has the form of an exclamation and expresses a fairly indirect request: it is left to the listener to conclude that the closing of the window is desired by the speaker. The example must be placed on the DIR-EXC dimension. The last two examples belong on the DIR-STA dimension: they have the typical form of statements but clearly may be spoken in order to make the hearer close the window.

The varying degrees of illocutionary force should not prevent us from carrying out a rough classification into the main types of speech acts. Thus, in appropriate contexts, all the examples in (29) should be assigned the function label DIR. The interesting point that emerges when we review examples like (29a) to (29g) is that there is a subtle interplay between function and form. For example, an imperative sentence has more illocutionary force as a DIR than an interrogative or a declarative sentence.

4.4.3. The forms of communicative functions

There are two major points to make in connection with the form of speech acts. The first point concerns the general form that speech acts may take. Usually *any speech act may take any form*: clause, group, compound unit or single word. The second point concerns the type of sentence involved in cases where the speech act takes the form of a clause (rather than group, compound unit or single word). As we have seen, there is no necessary relationship between speech act and type of sentence (declarative, interrogative, imperative, etc.). Let us first examine the general form of speech acts.

When we introduced the four main types of speech act (statement, question, directive and exclamation) in section 4.4.2, we were careful to offer four examples of each: a clause, a group, a compound unit and a single word. Here is the full analysis of some of the examples from section 4.4.2 with the *Sent* label replaced by the appropriate function:form specification.

(1)   James left Brisbane yesterday.

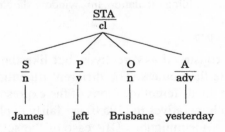

(6)   From whom?

(11)   Smile and be happy!

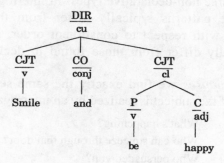

(16)   Wow!

With regard to the type of sentence involved just in case a speech act is realized by a clause, it is possible to subspecify the clause label (e.g. 'decl' = declarative clause, 'inter' = interrogative clause, etc.). On the other hand, such subspecification of the clause label is largely redundant, just as a subspecification of groups as noun groups, verb groups, preposition groups, etc. is largely redundant. The type of clause can in most cases be read off directly from the syntax or other features of the analysis. Thus, for example, there is typically subject-operator inversion in interrogative clauses (except when an interrogative pronoun is subject, as in *Who painted this wall?*). So unless one wants to call special attention to the type of clause, there is little motivation for complicating the clause label.

We want to emphasize the fact that communicative functions signal a link between sentence and 'larger context' and are hence a subject worthy of attention in the analysis of larger texts and of utterances in context (as carried out in 'text linguistics', 'discourse analysis' and 'functional linguistics'). In this grammar, however, we are primarily interested in the *forms* adopted by communicative functions (clauses, groups, compound units, single words) and their internal structure. Apart from our discussion above showing how a communicative link can be established in our 'sentence analysis', we shall have little to say about communicative functions except when they are relevant for strictly 'sentence-internal', grammatical phenomena.

4.4.4. Non-declarative clauses

As in declarative clauses (cf. section 3.2.4), there are certain regular syntactic patterns in all the three non-declarative types. In interrogative and exclamatory clauses these patterns typically differ from the ones found in declarative clauses with respect to constituent order, and in imperative clauses they typically differ from those found in declarative clauses in lacking subjects.

In *interrogative clauses* we find exactly the same seven patterns as in declarative clauses if the subject is realized by an interrogative *wh*-word:

S P	What's happening?
S P A	Who can squeeze through that door?
S P O	Who persuaded you?
S P C	Who is your source?
S P O O	Who will do me this favour?
S P O C	Who would call Quayle clever?
S P O A	Whatever put that idea into your head?

In *wh*-interrogative clauses in which the opening *w h*-word or *wh*-construction does not realize the subject there is change of constituent order: subject-operator inversion, often accompanied by discontinuity. What we find in such clauses are patterns like A P- S -P (*Why did you leave?*), O P- S -P (*What do you mean?*) and C P S (*What good is your assistance?*).

In *yes-no* interrogative clauses there is always inversion:

P- S -P	Is your attitude changing?
P- S -P A	Can you squeeze through that door?
P- S -P O	Must you insult me?
P- S -P C	Did they prove uncooperative?
P- S -P O O	Could you do me a favour?
P- S -P O C	May I call you darling?
P- S -P O A	Did you put it in the boot of the car?

In this interrogative subtype there is typically discontinuity as well, as illustrated by the examples. Note, however, the patterns P S A and P S C in clauses with BE as the only verb like *Is he in Paris?* and *Is she a doctor?*

In *imperative clauses*, which are typically subjectless, we find the following six syntactic patterns:

P A	Stay here.
P O	Shut the door.
P C	Be good.
P O O	Give me your keys.
P O C	Knock him unconscious.
P O A	Put it on the shelf.

Note that one-word imperatives like *Smile* are analysed simply as DIR:v. In imperative clauses with an overt subject all seven patterns are possible, as in other clause types, for in addition to patterns with adverbials, complements and objects we find the pattern S P here: *You listen! You behave!*, etc.

In *exclamatory clauses* the following patterns are all possible:

S P	What a big crowd turned up!
A S P	How beautifully she sings!
O S P	What a load of rubbish you're saying!
C S P	How delightful it is!
A S P O	How confidently you work the machine!
A S P O O	How professionally you gave them help!
A S P O C	How gently you call me silly!

Some of these patterns are undoubtedly rare – particularly the first one and the last one – but all of them are grammatically well-formed.

4.4.5. Block language

So far it has been fairly unproblematical to assign a regular form (single word, g, cu or cl) to complete examples like *Spain / An Introduction to English Sentence Analysis / Jim and Jenny / Pushed to the edge*. But there are sometimes more complex cases of what is sometimes referred to as *block language* (headlines, captions, advertisements, notices, telegrams, etc.):

(1)   Bad Days at the Bourse.
(2)   Alarm bells over nuclear near-misses.
(3)   One More Essential for the Overnight Case.

In such examples we usually cannot operate with ellipsis, for there is often no way of knowing precisely what is missing, if anything (i.e. there is no unique retrievability, cf. section 4.2). The only thing we can say about (1) to (3) is that the elements [at the Bourse], [over nuclear near-misses] and [for the Overnight Case] have adverbial *or* group-internal dependent function (cf.

Bache et al. 1993: 192ff). If we interpret them as dependents, the whole utterance can be assigned group status. If, however, we interpret them as adverbials, there is no obvious way of determining whether the remainder of the utterances should be construed as complements, subjects or objects. One possible solution to this problem is to extend the notion of function stack to cases where we cannot decide among several established functions, e.g.:

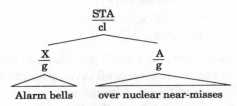

4.5. Vocatives, interjections and dislocation

Simple sentences may be expanded by vocatives. In languages where syntactic functions are expressed by case forms (e.g. subject: nominative, object: accusative, indirect object: dative), the term vocative refers to the case taken by a noun when it is used in the function of an *address*. This can be illustrated by a Latin example like *Et tu, Brute!* 'You too, Brutus!', in which the inflectional ending *-e* signals the vocative.

In English an address is expressed not inflectionally but syntactically, phonologically and by word class: a proper or common noun or a noun group is placed initially, medially or finally and is pronounced as a separate tone unit in the first of these positions and without prosodic prominence as the tail – or part of the tail – of a tone unit in the last two positions:

(1)   Brenda, I could do with a glass of sherry.

(2)   We are certainly, sir, treating the death as suspicious.

(3)   You must trust me, my darling.

A vocative may also be realized by the personal pronoun *you* or by a group containing this word. Except in informal expressions like *you guys* and *you chaps*, this type of address is usually rude:

(4)   You (there), I need some service right away.

In those cases where several people are addressed, furthermore, the pronouns *all*, *everybody*, *everyone* may be used, and if the speaker wishes to catch the attention of any member of a group, he can use *somebody* or *someone*:

(5)   Clap your hands, everybody.

(6)   Answer the phone, somebody.

Vocatives have a number of different subfunctions. In the first place, they may be used to initiate an act of communication, and when used for this purpose they are naturally enough placed initially. Secondly, it is common practice for speakers to ensure that this act of communication is continued by interspersing their text with references to the listener. Thirdly, vocatives have various emotive functions. Their use has an implicitly positive effect which has been described as 'stroking', but they may also be descriptively positive (*darling, dearest John*, etc.) or negative (*clumsy clot, you idiot*, etc.). Finally, vocatives may signal respect for the addressee and often be required by rules of etiquette (*Your Majesty, Mr President, professor, sir*).

A problem which has to be considered is how vocatives should be classified grammatically. As they behave like sentence adverbials positionally and prosodically and have no text-connective function, one possibility is to classify them as *disjuncts*. But pragmatically they differ from disjuncts in being used to express meanings like the ones just mentioned and not to convey the speaker's comment on the information expressed by the rest of the sentence or by the style of the expression itself. And formally they differ from disjuncts in being realized not by adverbs but by (pro)nominals. For these reasons we shall therefore here consider a vocative a special subtype of adverbial. Like disjuncts and conjuncts, vocatives have a peripheral status in the sentence. This can be shown by using the stack convention (cf. section 4.1). For example, (3) can be analysed in the following way:

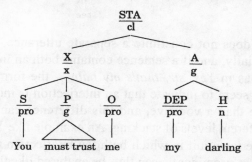

This analysis is supported by the fact that vocatives are prosodically non-prominent in medial and final position.

In some respects, vocatives are similar to *interjections*, i.e. to the class of words which includes emotive words like *oh, ugh, mm*, etc. and which is here assumed to include also 'reaction signals' like *yes, no, well* and greetings like *hi* and *hello*. Traditionally, interjections are defined as words which do not enter into syntactic relations, and in many cases they do indeed constitute separate utterances. If the interjection is pronounced with falling intonation and is separated from the following by a pause, examples like *Oh! I see* and

Yes! I know must be analysed as a sequence of two utterances with EXC realized by an interjection followed by STA realized by a clause:

But interjections may also be pronounced in the same tone unit as the following clause, and in that case they typically constitute the prehead – or part of the prehead – of the tone unit, i.e. are pronounced without pitch prominence and are prosodically connected with what follows. In writing, this is indicated by a comma: *Oh, I see / Yes, I know*. As an utterance is generally assumed to be preceded and followed by silence, it seems problematic to assume that examples like these constitute a sequence of utterances. An alternative is to assume that the interjection is a peripheral adverbial and that the other constituents form a stack:

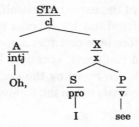

If an interjection does not constitute a separate utterance, it is practically always placed initially, and if a sentence contains both an initial interjection and a vocative – as in *Yes, sir, that's my baby* – the former precedes the latter. This would seem to indicate that an interjection is more peripheral to sentence structure than a vocative, and this difference can be captured by operating with different levels of stacking. An example like *Yes, I know, sir* – pronounced as one tone unit in which both the interjection and the vocative are prosodically non-prominent – can thus be analysed like this:

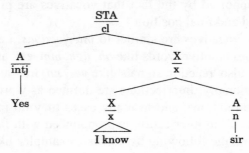

In imperative sentences it is sometimes difficult to separate vocatives from *subjects*. The reason for this is that imperative sentences are inherently vocative, either expressing or, more typically, assuming a second person singular or plural subject *you*, representing the listener(s) or reader(s). The difficulty of distinguishing between imperative subjects and vocatives can be illustrated by the following examples, which are pronounced as one tone unit, and in which the initial constituent is prosodically prominent:

(7)   Everybody clap your hands.

(8)   John and Peter stand over there.

Traditionally, such sentences are held to contain third person subjects, but as they are synonymous with sentences with final vocatives (*Clap your hands, everybody*, etc.), we assume that what we find here are not subjects but vocatives. These vocatives differ from other initial vocatives in being pronounced not as a separate tone unit but as an integrated part of a tone unit spanning the entire sentence. On this interpretation, the subject of imperative sentences is always implied or explicit *you*, cf. the presence of the possessive form *your* in (7) and the possibility of adding tag questions with *you*:

(9)   Somebody answer the phone, will you?

In informal speech a noun group which does not constitute the comment is sometimes *dislocated* to the periphery of a sentence and replaced by a corresponding pronoun (see Quirk et al. 1985: 1416ff). In examples with *right*-dislocation, the final noun group is normally pronounced without prosodic prominence as the tail – or part of the tail – of a tone unit:

(10)   *She*'s an excellent pianist, *your sister-in-law*.

(11)   I can't stand *him, that friend of yours*.

In such sentences – which are characteristic of unplanned discourse – the noun group tag amplifies the message and serves to ensure that the entity referred to by the pronoun is correctly identified by the hearer. *Left*-dislocation is less common:

(12)   *Your sister-in-law, she*'s an excellent pianist.

(13)   *That friend of yours*, I simply can't stand *him*.

Here the initial noun group is normally pronounced as a separate tone unit and serves to establish the identity of the entity referred to right away and to emphasize what constitutes the topic of the sentence. The peripheral syntactic status of a dislocated noun group – like that of a vocative – can be captured by means of stacking. For example, (12) can be analysed like this:

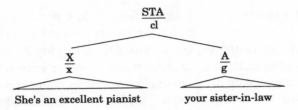

Not only noun groups but also single proper nouns may be dislocated, as illustrated by *He's a decent sort of bloke, Jonathan* and *Jonathan, he's a decent sort of bloke*. As a dislocated extra identifier is usually pronounced like a vocative, the function of a proper noun as one or the other usually has to be determined by the hearer on the basis of the linguistic or situational context. However, the speaker can make the identifying function unambiguously clear by pronouncing a final proper noun as a separate tone unit (*He is a `decent sort of bloke/ `Jonathan*) and an initial proper noun as the stressed beginning of a tone unit spanning the entire sentence (*'Jonathan he is a `decent sort of bloke*).

4.6. A final word on advanced sentence analysis

In the preceding sections we have seen a number of construction types which challenge any simplistic view of language. As the possible analyses of a particular phenomenon multiply (as they do in cases involving e.g. stacking, missing constituents and complex predicators), we get a sense not only of a subjective element of purpose in sentence analysis but also of the complexity and subtlety of language structure. It is important to realize that an appreciation of language structure may be arrived at by applying a descriptive apparatus in a consistent manner even if it reflects an incomplete knowledge of language and even if it seems to impose too rigid a system on the data. Whenever our descriptive tools fail to cope adequately with data, we may conclude that we have encountered still another aspect of language that we do not fully understand yet but which we may come to understand a little better if we try to incorporate it in our model. It is in this spirit we want our readers to use our sentence analysis system: as an instrument to approach language, as a framework for talking about the things we think we understand and as a means of identifying areas where there are interesting problems we do not yet know quite how to tackle. There is, of course, often a practical problem of choosing one out of a number of possible alternative analyses. Our advice here is that, unless one chooses to focus on a particular area of interest (say, in order to develop some hypothesis or test some analytic tool against a broader range of data), one should make one's sentence analysis as simple as possible.

PART II

5. Constituent order

5.1. Introduction

Constituent order is more rigid in English than in many other languages, e.g. Italian, Greek, Spanish and Russian. As we saw in section 3.2.4 above, in *declarative sentences* with obligatory constituents only, the following orderings are so common that they may be regarded as constituting the *norm*:

Structure	Examples
S P	Nothing happened.
S P A	He squeezed between two motor-cars.
S P O	You must persuade her.
S P Cs	She proved surprisingly uncooperative.
S P Oi Od	You do me a very great honour.
S P O Co	He had knocked two opponents totally senseless.
S P O A	We must put some flesh on your bones.

Since these constructions are regarded as the norm, other orderings are usually described in terms of *mobility* or *movement* (such as *fronting* and *inversion*). Consider, for example, the A S P O sequence in:

(1)   On the table he put the book.

Here the adverbial is regarded as having moved from the designated A position of the regular S P O A structure to a position before the subject for reasons of style or focus, for example.

The picture of English sentence structure is, however, not complete unless we consider the role also of optional adverbials. In our discussion of adverbials in section 3.2.9, we saw that there were very few general restrictions on the position of optional adverbials and that an adverbial is often equally happy in a number of different positions in a sentence. In declarative sentences, the adverbial is in fact the most *mobile* constituent.

By contrast, the other clause functions (subject, predicator, objects and complements) are more firmly fixed in their designated positions in the structures listed above. But principled deviation does occur. Like adverbials, for example, objects and complements may, under certain conditions, be placed in sentence-initial position. In reply to a question like *What do you see?*, for example, a speaker may say *That I will tell you another time*, i.e. he may place the direct object initially (Od S P Oi A). Fronting of a complement can be illustrated by an example like *Waddle his name is* (C S P). Another important deviation from the norm is the relative positions of S and P in sentences like *Here comes Bill* and *Did you see her again?*

When constituent order is compared across languages, what is compared is the 'favourite' order found in each language. While the favourite order of predicator, subject and object is S P O in a large number of languages including English, it is S O P in many other languages (e.g. Turkish, Japanese), and in a third group of languages it is P S O (e.g. Arabic, Hebrew).

When constituent order is discussed within a particular language, such as English, it is done so in terms of the norm identified in declarative sentences and deviation from this norm. Central questions which have to be considered are 'What does constituent order signal communicatively?' and 'What are the conditions under which the normal constituent order is changed?'

5.2. Functions of constituent order

5.2.1. Grammatical relations

Constituent order performs a number of different functions. One is *to signal grammatical relations*. Consider the following example (which refers to the historical situation right after the Napoleonic wars):

(1)   England gave Sweden Norway. (S P Oi Od)

Here the subject, object and indirect object are identified through constituent order exclusively. When confronted with it, the hearer will therefore understand England to be the agent, Sweden the beneficiary and Norway the affected country. If we change the order of the three nouns while retaining the predicator in the second position, the locations of the subject, object and indirect object will remain unaffected. The subject will still be in the first position, the direct object in the last position and the indirect object in the last but one. This implies that reversal of the last two words, for example, will be taken by the hearer to mean that it was Sweden which was given to Norway. One among several interacting principles of constituent order is that of *functional stability*: constituents with the same syntactic function tend to be placed in the same position (cf. Dik 1989: 343). We can therefore speak of a characteristic subject position, a characteristic object position and so on.

5.2.2. Illocutionary value

Another function of constituent order is to give information about the *illocutionary value of an utterance*, i.e. about the speech act it is used to perform. As we saw in section 4.4.2, four basic speech acts can be distinguished: statement, question, directive and exclamation. Recall that, roughly speaking, statements give information to the listener, questions seek information from the listener, directives instruct the listener to perform an action and exclamations tell the listener that the speaker reacts emotionally with surprise, disapproval, pleasure, etc. In section 4.4.4, these basic illocutions were found to be relevant to the question of constituent order. All languages appear to have special sentence structures associated with statements, questions and directives (declarative, interrogative and imperative sentences respectively), and many languages have a special sentence structure for exclamations as well (exclamatory sentences). Although there is a far from necessary relationship between illocutionary value and sentence form, the association between form and function is strong enough for the form to serve as a general signal of the function. In other words, when we use a declarative sentence it can in general be interpreted as a signal of the illocutionary value of statement; and so forth.

If we restrict our attention to transitive sentences, the difference between the sentence types can be symbolized and illustrated like this:

declarative:	S P O	You must learn grammar.
yes-no interrogative:	P- S -P O	Must you learn grammar?
wh-interrogative:	O P- S -P	What must you learn?
	S P O	Who must learn grammar?
exclamatory:	O S P	What you must learn!
imperative:	P O	Learn grammar.

In very general terms we can say that the constituent order P- S -P will guide the listener towards the illocutionary value 'question'. The order O S P where O is realized by *What* will guide the listener towards 'exclamation', and P O alone will make him expect the illocutionary value to be 'directive'. S P O is the typical order found in declarative sentences, but it is also found in imperative sentences with a subject and in *wh*-interrogative sentences in which the subject contains the interrogative word. Though most likely to signal 'statement', this constituent order is therefore a more unreliable guide to illocutionary value than the others.

5.2.3. Information structure

A third function of constituent order is to *signal information structure*, i.e. the way in which a message is organized into information units. The organization of a message often reflects a division between *given information*, i.e. what is assumed to be known to the hearer, and *new information*. Normally the speaker will proceed from what he assumes to be known (the *topic* or *theme*) to what he assumes to be new (the *comment* or *rheme*). This can be illustrated by an example like *The letter on the desk is from your mother*, in which the information contained in the first part (the subject noun group *The letter on the desk*) is assumed and that contained in the second part (the predicate stack *is from your mother*) is new and at the centre of the speaker's communicative interest. The general tendency towards placing new and particularly important information at the end of the sentence is called the principle of *end-focus*.

The use of *passive vs. active voice* in English is largely determined by the way the speaker wishes to organize his message in terms of given and new information. In an active example like *Arsenal beat Tottenham*, the speaker's point of departure is *Arsenal* while the rest of the sentence is at the centre of his communicative interest. In the passive equivalent *Tottenham were beaten by Arsenal*, on the other hand, it is *Tottenham* which constitutes the point of departure. Though the basic meaning is the same in these two sentences, the presentation is different in terms of given, new and focus. In this respect the passive sentence is similar to an active sentence like *Tottenham lost to Arsenal*. In passive sentences the initial constituent tends not only to express given information but also to have a connective function in the text:

(1)   This was on a rotation of six days a week at the restaurant with one off (Thursday). *That day* was spent in recuperation on his back on the sofa, generally with open eyes, for his feet ached after the hours of standing.

Here the subject noun group *That day* refers back to the day off referred to in the preceding sentence.

In order to *highlight part of a message*, the speaker may place a sentence constituent in a special position, i.e. he may for this purpose deviate from the typical orderings described above. For example, he may place an object or a complement in the initial position of a declarative sentence. Such placement of a constituent in marked first position is called *fronting*:

(2)   *That story* I will tell you another time. (Od S P Oi A)

(3)   *Chris Waddle* his name is. (C S P)

In moving an object or complement from its usual position to the initial position, the speaker gives *prominence* to this part of the message, i.e. he instructs the listener to pay special attention to it. Highlighting by means of fronting is particularly common if the speaker can in this way simultaneously establish direct linkage with the preceding part of a conversation or of his own message. This illustrates that the position of a constituent is dependent not only on factors within the sentence in which it occurs but also largely on the relation between that constituent and the preceding text.

(4)   Speaker A: What do you see?

        Speaker B: *That* I will tell you another time.

While fronting of objects and complements is relatively rare in declarative sentences, adverbials are frequently placed in initial position to give prominence to them and to link them to the preceding text:

(5)   Lo' s room contained his iron bed and one chair, over which he had thrown his black trousers and a shirt. *In a corner of the room* was a gas ring, a kettle and a single glass. (A P S)

Part of a message may be highlighted not only through fronting but also by means of *postponement*. One example of this is extraposition of the subject (cf. section 3.2.2):

(6)   It worries me *that the children have not returned*. (Sp P O Sr)

(7)   It would be awkward *to go now*. (Sp P C Sr)

Not only subjects but also objects may be postponed to give them special prominence:

(8)   The court pronounced not guilty *a black man*. (S P Co O)

(9)   The court pronounced not guilty *the woman who had been charged with the murder*. (S P Co O)

In English as in other languages there is a preference for constituents to occur in an order of increasing heaviness. This is called the principle of increasing complexity, or of *end-weight*.

Object postponement may also involve extraposition (cf. section 3.2.5):

(10)   I find it a challenge *writing this report*. (S P Op Co Or)

Informationally, the type of highlighting obtained by postponement is not the same as that obtained by fronting. By means of fronting the speaker informs the hearer that the element thus moved constitutes the *topic* (or *theme*), i.e. the entity about which something is said (see section 3.2.2). By means of postponement, on the other hand, he informs the hearer that the element thus moved is at the *focus* of his communicative interest. For these reasons highlighting by means of fronting is termed *topicalization* (or *thematization*) while highlighting by means of postponement is termed *focalization*.

To recapitulate: constituent order is used to signal syntactic functions (subject, object, etc.), to give information about the speech act an utterance performs (statement, question, directive, exclamation) and to signal how a message is structured informationally (what is highlighted through topicalization or focalization).

5.3. Inversion

5.3.1. Preliminaries

The term inversion (from Latin *inversio/inversionis* 'turning around') is used in grammar to refer to a reversal of syntactic constituents. This may be illustrated by an interrogative sentence like *Was it disappointing?*, in which the predicator precedes the subject. The order P S may here be seen as a result of a syntactic change which reverses the order S P found in a declarative sentence like *It was disappointing*. Inversion in its broad sense, it should be pointed out, refers not only to reversal of subject and predicator (or operator). In *The court pronounced not guilty the woman who had been charged with the murder*, the order Co O may be seen as a reversal of the normal order O Co found in an example like *The court pronounced the woman not guilty*. In *She placed on the topmost shelf her entire collection of grammar books*, similarly, the order A O may be seen as a reversal of the normal order O A found in *She placed her books on the topmost shelf*. Furthermore, inversion operates not only on the level of sentence structure but also on the level of group structure. For example, the ordering of an example like *He had no patience with problems hypothetical* may be regarded as a reversal of the ordering in *He had no patience with hypothetical problems*. In descriptions of English grammar, however, the term inversion usually refers to reversal of subject and (part of the) predicator, to which we now turn.

5.3.2. Full and partial subject-predicator inversion

Depending on whether it is the entire predicator or only part of it (the operator) which changes places with the subject we distinguish between *full inversion* and *partial inversion*. Full inversion, which is often optional, can be illustrated by the following example with the sentence structure A P S:

(1)   In rhyme and rhythm resides a certain magic power.

Partial inversion, which is usually obligatory, is found in the next example, which has the sentence structure A P- S -P O A:

(2)   Only with difficulty had Lily explained her conduct to her parents.

As is apparent, only the first of the two verbs realizing the predicator – the operator – is here inverted with the subject. If there are more verbs than two in a predicator group, it is the first of these only (the operator) which changes places with the subject. For this reason partial inversion is often referred to as 'subject-operator inversion':

(3)   Only with difficulty *could* Lily *have explained* her conduct to her parents.

In those cases where a sentence without inversion has a predicator which is realized by a single verb, the corresponding sentence with partial inversion requires DO-support (cf. section 3.2.1):

(4)   Only after a while *did* he *notice* that his mother was crying.

As will be recalled from section 3.2.1, special rules apply to the primary verbs BE and HAVE: sometimes they behave like full verbs, sometimes like operators. If the predicator is realized by the verb BE there is in interrogative sentences no DO-support. For example, the sentence with inversion which corresponds to *He is comfortable* is not **Does he be comfortable?* but *Is he comfortable?* What we find here therefore looks like full inversion in that it is the entire predicator which is moved. Nevertheless, we shall treat reversal of a subject and a form of BE under partial inversion in those cases where subject-operator inversion occurs generally. We shall thus treat an example like *Are you comfortable?* together with *Have you been comfortable?* and *Never was I so deeply in love* together with *Never have I been so deeply in love*. On the other hand, the reversal of a subject and a form of BE found in examples like *Here is the milkman?* and *On the walls were pictures of half-naked women and colourful landscapes* will be dealt with under full inversion, i.e. together with *Here comes the milkman* and *On the walls hung pictures of half-naked women and colourful landscapes*, because it occurs under those conditions where this subtype of inversion occurs generally.

In BrE, there is not invariably DO-support in inverted sentences if the predicator is realized by the verb HAVE. This can be illustrated by an example like *Have you any doubt about his guilt?* As in the case of sentences with BE, for example *Are you in doubt about his guilt?*, we shall treat this type of reversal under partial, subject-operator inversion, in spite of the fact that it is the entire predicator which is moved. The reason for this is once again that reversal of a subject and a form of HAVE is found under those conditions where this obligatory subtype of inversion occurs generally. We shall accordingly treat examples of the type *Have you any doubt about his guilt?* together with the less formal and more common varieties *Do you have any doubt about his guilt?* and *Have you got any doubt about his guilt?*

Partial inversion is used under two well-defined conditions. In the first place it serves to signal *illocutionary value*, most importantly to perform the speech act of posing a question. Secondly, it is used in those cases where a sentence contains a *special opening constituent*, most importantly a negative or restrictive opener.

5.3.3. Partial inversion with illocutionary value

The most important role played by partial inversion in English is to pose a *question* by way of forming an interrogative sentence. As illustrated by the following examples, it is by this means that a speaker typically elicits information from the listener about a *yes-no* relationship:

(1)   Could you live without me?
(2)   Have you liked me for a long time?
(3)   Did they let him go?
(4)   Are you sure I can't fix you a sandwich?

Yes-no questions, it should be added, can also have straight constituent order and be signalled by other means. In spoken English this normally requires that they are uttered with rising intonation. The following examples are thus usually pronounced with a final upward tonal contour:

(5)   So you never had a chance to talk to him again?
(6)   And you made up your mind to come and see me first?

In English (unlike spoken French, for example) partial inversion is the general rule in *yes-no* questions, however. It is found also in *tag questions*, i.e. in questions where a construction with inversion of the type *isn't it, has he*, usually consisting of an operator and a personal pronoun, is added to a non-interrogative sentence:

(7)   This is the tendency, isn't it?
(8)   You didn't feel very well, did you?

Partial inversion is also found in *wh*-interrogative clauses and here typically performs the function of posing a *wh-question*. In contrast to *yes-no* questions, however, *wh*-questions are signalled as such not only by inversion but also by a special question word. If this realizes the subject or part of the subject, there is straight subject-operator order (e.g. *What happened?*) and the illocutionary value is signalled by the *wh*-word exclusively. On the other hand, *wh*-words occur also in statements (for example *I'll say what I mean*) and in exclamations, so they do not in themselves signal the speech act of posing a question either. In examples like the following, the difference between question and exclamation is signalled exclusively by the ordering of subject and operator:

(9a)   How can you say that?
(9b)   How you can say that!
(10a)   What sounds can you make?
(10b)   What sounds you can make!

Partial inversion in *wh*-interrogative clauses can be illustrated by the following examples:

(11)   What do you mean, the police?
(12)   Why are you always making such a fuss about your brother?
(13)   How could you go to bed with somebody you didn't love?
(14)   Which way should we go?

The optative speech act of expressing a *wish* – or a malediction – can in English be performed in several ways, some of which do not involve inversion. For example, a speaker may for this purpose use the performative verb WISH (after the personal pronoun *I* functioning as subject) or the performative opener *If only*. This can be illustrated by *I wish / If only the performance would begin soon*. He may also, though this strategy is much rarer, express a wish by means of the subjunctive mood (cf. section 9.8). Wishes signalled in this way are frozen expressions, of which some have straight constituent order and others take inversion:

(15)   God save the Queen.
(16)   Heaven forbid.
(17)   Long live Trotsky.
(18)   Suffice it to say that your essay is unsatisfactory.
(19)   So be it.

Wishes and maledictions, however, can also be expressed by sentences in which the verb MAY occurs, and in this case there is partial inversion:

(20)   Please may it have been instantly.
(21)   May she rot in hell.

That inversion is crucial here appears from the fact that utterances with MAY in which the order of constituents is straight, e.g. *She may rot in hell*, are not used to express a wish but a statement.

As the use of utterances with inversion and MAY for the expression of wishes is rare, this particular type of inversion with illocutionary value is of rather minor importance.

Finally, to anticipate section 5.4 on constituent order in subclauses, there may be partial inversion in the subclause of a complex sentence which indicates *conditional commitment* on the part of the speaker. In English, conditional sentences are normally signalled by *if* or *unless* and less commonly by words or word groups such as *supposing, in case* and *assuming (that)*. In formal style, however, they can also be signalled by partial inversion (with *had, should* or *were* as operator):

(22)   *Had* I known this, I would never have accepted the offer.

(23)   *Should* he do that, I will crucify him.

(24)   The total output would be much worse *were* it not for the winter crop.

What the speaker indicates by inversion here is that the subclause performs the function of laying down a condition, typically hypothetical, on which the state of affairs described in the matrix clause is dependent.

Before leaving partial inversion with illocutionary value, we should mention that this constituent order is sometimes also found in directives and exclamations. As illustrated by *Don't you let him force you back*, this is the constituent order we find in negative imperative sentences with an expressed subject. And as illustrated by *Isn't she lovely!* (pronounced with falling intonation) there is, of course, inversion in *yes-no* interrogative sentences not only if they function as questions but also as exclamations.

5.3.4. Partial inversion caused by an initial constituent

There is partial inversion in sentences beginning with a negative or restrictive constituent other than the subject. This constituent may often be regarded as fronted and is in most cases an adverbial:

(1)   Nowhere are the effects of these policies more evident than in Denmark.

(2)   Under no circumstances must you leave the room.

(3)   Rarely have I set eyes on such a stunning beauty.

(4)   Not another pound will you get from me. (fronted negative object)

(5)   Only after a while did he notice that his mother was crying.

(6)   Hardly a word did he utter. (fronted restrictive object)

If a negative word does not apply to the entire sentence but only locally to the constituent in which it occurs, there is straight subject-predicator order:

(7)   Not long ago my grandmother turned eighty.

In examples of this type with local negation the sentence as a whole expresses a positive statement (note that *Not long ago* could be replaced by *Recently*). In such cases, where the event described by the part of the sentence following the negative opener is true irrespective of this opener, partial inversion is not used. Attention should also be drawn to examples without inversion of the following type:

(8a)   Only last month we could cope with the increase in demand.

Here the initial adverbial is not really restrictive but has a temporal meaning which can be captured by the paraphrase 'as late as last month'. If the word group *only last month* does have restrictive meaning, i.e. if it means 'last month and no others', it will trigger inversion:

(8b)   Only last month could we cope with the increase in demand.

In spoken English, partial inversion after a negative opener is particularly common in clauses beginning with one of the pro-forms NEITHER and NOR (cf. section 4.2.3). Examples of inversion after NEITHER:

(9)   I didn't turn up and neither did my wife.

(10)   Speaker A: I can't swim.   Speaker B: Neither can I.

If we compare these with *I didn't turn up and my wife didn't turn up either* and *I can't swim either*, it seems reasonable to assume that *n't ... either* is fronted in the contracted shape of *neither* to underline its connective function and that the main verb is dropped because it is redundant in the context. Inversion in clauses with NOR can be exemplified by a dialogue like

(11)   Speaker A: I don't like her. Speaker B: Nor do I.

Partial inversion after NOR in a full sentence is characteristic of formal style:

(12)   I have never procrastinated. Nor do I intend to start doing so now.

Initial placement of a negative or restrictive constituent clearly involves information structure, for it is motivated by a wish to topicalize this part of the message. For example, a sentence like *Never have I heard such nonsense* differs from *I have never heard such nonsense* in that it topicalizes a constituent with negative meaning through placement in the initial position. What is created by this constituent order is often a *double focus*: the negative constituent is highlighted through placement in the initial position (topicalization of *Never*) and another constituent is highlighted by occupying the final position (focalization of *nonsense*), which according to the principle of *end-focus* is typically reserved for new information.

While initial placement of a negative or restrictive constituent relates to information structure, the inversion which accompanies it cannot plausibly be explained in this way as well. A double focus could just as well be created with straight order as with inversion, for example by the order in an ungrammatical sentence like **Never I have heard such nonsense*. As the initial constituent pulls the first part of the predicate into the position before the subject, this type of subject-predicator reversal may be characterized as *attraction inversion* (see Hartvigson & Kvistgaard Jakobsen 1974: 25) Historically it reflects a stage of the English language when inversion after all kinds of initial constituents other than the subject was the general rule.

We now turn to partial inversion in sentences beginning with the adverb SO or SUCH. In examples of the following type, SO/SUCH is part of a discontinuous complex constituent – object, complement or adverbial – which ends in a correlative *that*-clause (i.e. a clause regularly accompanying SO/SUCH but separated from it by other linguistic material):

(13)   *So much* did he eat *that he was almost sick.* (O- P- S -P -O)

(14)   *Such* was the heat *that she was unable to finish the recital.* (C- P S -C)

Through partial fronting, the premodifier *So* and the head *much* in (13) have been separated from the postmodifying *that*-clause. In (14) it is the pronominal head *Such* that has been separated from its dependent clause through partial fronting. In both examples the effect is one of double focus. If no fronting takes place, as in *He ate so much that he was almost sick*, the complex constituent introduced by SO/SUCH only has end-focus. But in the partially fronted variations of such sentences both the postmodifying *that*-clause and the head word of the fronted constituent are highlighted.

In spoken English, partial inversion triggered by the pro-form SO is particularly frequent in clauses of the same type as those mentioned above beginning with NEITHER or NOR (cf. also section 4.2.3):

(15)   I turned up and so did my wife.

(16)   Speaker A: I can swim.   Speaker B: So can I.

Such sentences may be compared with sentences without inversion and pro-forms like *I turned up and my wife turned up too* and *I can swim too*. Note that the adverb *so* is not here a marker of degree but means 'also'.

In *formal* style, attraction inversion is also found in comparative sub-clauses with the subordinator conjunction *as* or *than*:

(17)   Crabs were fresh and plentiful in the market at the moment, white vegetable was good, as were Holland beans.

(18)   Alice knew Peter far better than did most of her classmates.

In such constructions, the operator serves as a pro-form representing a full predicate (P C or P O).

Before leaving partial inversion caused by an initial constituent, we should point out that it is sometimes also found after other openers than the ones mentioned above, for example WELL in the sense of 'fully' and RATHER:

(19)   Well do I know that you hate me.

(20)   Much rather would I be dead.

As a manner adjunct THUS is particularly versatile as an opener: it allows both partial and full inversion with little or no difference of meaning:

(21)   Thus did a lovely evening end. / Thus ended a lovely evening.

5.3.5. Full inversion and information structure

While partial inversion is used to signal illocutionary value, or is mechanically triggered once the speaker (for reasons of information structure) has chosen to place a negative or restrictive constituent initially, full inversion is a matter of *information structure*. As pointed out in section 5.2.3, a speaker may move a constituent to a special position to give prominence to it. If he moves an object, complement or adverbial to initial position, he may in this way establish linkage with the preceding part of the text, i.e. such a constituent is not only highlighted through fronting (i.e. topicalized) but also acquires a connective function. When such fronting is called for in S P O, S P C and S P A sentences, the predicator will come to occupy the final position – and thus get end-focus – if it is not fronted as well by being moved to the position before the subject. As illustrated by *That story I don't believe*, end-focus on the predicator is by no means ruled out in sentences with topicalization. But in sentences with fronted adverbials of certain types – particularly adverbials of place – it tends to be avoided. This can be illustrated by an example like *In the middle of the room stood a table* (A P S), in which the predicator and the subject normally cannot change places.

While inversion in connection with fronting of an adverbial appears to be due primarily to a tendency to avoid end-focus on the predicator, it may be supported by the principle of end-weight. For example, this principle would be badly violated if the fronting of an adverbial in a sentence like *A vat of boiling water stood in the middle of the room* were to be unaccompanied by subject-predicator inversion. If the structure of this sentence is changed from S P A not just to A S P but to A P S, however, the resulting sentence is as well balanced as the one with normal S P A order: *In the middle of the room stood a vat of boiling water* has just as much end-weight as *A vat of boiling water stood in the middle of the room*.

If a place adverbial can be fronted without resulting in final placement of the predicator, and without throwing the sentence off balance, inversion does not take place, or is not obligatory:

(1)   In the distance a sunlit range of mountains could be seen very clearly.
(2)   On the doorstep women sat nursing their babies and gossiping.
        (On the doorstep sat women nursing their babies and gossiping.)

Generally speaking, fronting of adverbials (and of complements and objects as well) is usually *un*accompanied by inversion, and in this respect English differs from e.g. German, Dutch and the Scandinavian languages. This is illustrated by the next examples, in which inversion would be impossible:

(3)   After the birth of their son, Lily had been unable to cope with all the housework.

(4)   On this occasion the young engineer capitulated without a struggle.

In the few cases where complements and objects are fronted, full inversion is decidedly rare. After fronted adverbials, however, it is not uncommon, particularly in literary language.

5.3.6. Full inversion after a fronted adverbial

The following examples illustrate inversion accompanying fronting of an obligatory adverbial:

(1)   On the walls were pictures of half-naked women and colourful landscapes.

(2)   At his side sat a black Alsatian dog.

(3)   On street corners appeared posters with long lists of executed persons.

(4)   In rhyme and rhythm resides a certain magic power.

In these examples fronting serves the purpose of establishing *narrative continuity*. In all of them, it will be observed, fronting unaccompanied by inversion would result in structures which to a higher or lower degree – and in most cases flagrantly – would violate the principle of end-weight. As illustrated by the examples, it is typically fronting of *adverbials of place* which is accompanied by inversion. Fronting of adverbials of time, however, may also necessitate inversion, for instance in *Now comes the time we've been waiting for so long*. The verbs occurring in sentences with fronted adverbials and inversion are typically BE and other intransitives such as APPEAR, HANG, LIE, SIT and STAND. Potentially transitive verbs (such as SEE) are only possible in such sentences if the construction as a whole is intransitive. This can be illustrated by a passive example like *In the distance could be seen a sunlit range of mountains*, which has the intransitive structure A P S. This example also demonstrates that the predicator which changes places with the subject may be realized by a complex verb group.

In ordinary, informal speech, full inversion after a fronted adverbial is not very common. We find it in short intransitive sentences beginning with one of the adverbs of place HERE and THERE:

(5)   Here comes the bus.

(6)   There goes the last bus.

There may also be inversion in intransitive sentences beginning with one of the directional adverbs DOWN, UP, IN and OUT. Such a fronted adverb may realize an independent adverbial:

(7)   Out darted a mouse.

However, it may also realize the second part of a phrasal predicator:

(8)   Up went the prices once again.

As appears from the examples, the verbs occurring after HERE, THERE and directional adverbs in sentences with inversion typically express *movement*: COME, DART, FALL, FLY, GO, JUMP, etc.

The common factor in all the examples with a fronted adverbial and inversion is intransitiveness. While fronting of adverbials accompanied by inversion in literary language usually serves the purpose of establishing narrative continuity, fronting in examples like the ones just given from informal spoken language does not usually have this specific function but creates a more vivid impression.

5.3.7. Full inversion after a fronted participial predication stack

A special form of inversion – related to the one found after fronted adverbials – is found in sentences where *a present or past participle* is moved from a complex predicator to the initial position together with an adverbial (or with more adverbials than one) which accompanies it. Such fronting of predication stacks is characteristic of literary language. Instead of writing *The Curry Mahal was sandwiched between the Chinese restaurants*, for example, an author may write *Sandwiched between the Chinese restaurants was the Curry Mahal*. Here are some more examples:

(1)   *Standing around in the shops were* heavily bearded men in long gaberdine coats, wearing thick boots.

(2)   *Heaped on a lectern near the window were* religious books and sheets of paper covered with writing.

In sentences of this type, not only has the order of the subject and the predicator been reversed but also that of the two constituents in the complex predicator. The fronted adverbial and verb typically indicate *location* and *posture* respectively. In moving participle + adverbial(s) to the front of the sentence, the writer gives prominence to this part of the message, particularly to the state described by the initial verb. If he fronts only the locative adverbial(s), it is only this part of the message which is highlighted. For example, the meaning of *heaped* is not emphasized in an example like:

(3)   On a lectern near the window were heaped religious books and sheets of paper covered with writing.

It should be pointed out that predicators which potentially describe dynamic situations such as HEAP, LAY, etc. describe stative situations exclusively if the participle is fronted. Out of context an example like *Religious books were heaped on a lectern near the window* is potentially ambiguous in that the situation it describes can be either a stable state of affairs or involve a change. In *Heaped on a lectern near the window were religious books*, on the other hand, the situation referred to can only be understood to be stative. In addition to having a highlighting function, participle + adverbial fronting may thus be chosen to avoid ambiguity.

Fronting of a present participle in sentences with full inversion is found also in cases where it is not an adverbial but an object which accompanies it:

(4)   Awaiting *them* were a tray of sandwiches, two bottles of wine, the director in uniform, and, to top it all off, an exceptionally beautiful girl.

(5)   Filling *the chamber* was a grand plan of the City of Willows, metaphor of that legendary matrix of Hung heroes.

In examples of this type, the subject is heavy and the rest of the sentence light. One way in which the speaker can observe the principle of end-weight is therefore to front part of the predicator together with the object.

Sentences with fronted participles of the type exemplified above often vary with less 'literary' sentences in which *there* is used as provisional subject (and in which there is therefore not inversion):

(6)   Heaped on a lectern near the window *there* were religious books and sheets of paper covered with writing.

As this 'existential *there'* is normally used to introduce new entities into the discourse (cf. section 3.2.2), the possibility of using it in sentences with fronted participles demonstrates that the information expressed by the heavy structure realizing the subject is new. On the other hand, the elements fronted here do not necessarily specify given information or have the cohesive function that initial constituents often have. What they typically do is *set the scene* for the state of affairs described by the rest of the sentence.

Sentences with inversion and fronted participles are also common in news reporting. Here the fronted constituents usually do have cohesive function and refer to given information:

(7)   Also killed in the shoot-out were three teenagers from the Bronx.

The analysis of a fronted participle as part of the predicator is not the only one which presents itself. The participle and the construction which is fronted together with it might instead be analysed as an adverbial (in the case of a present participle construction) or as a complement (in the case of a past participle construction). In support of such an alternative analysis it may be argued that sentences like the following are possible, in which the finite verb is not a form of BE:

(8)   Awaiting them *stood* a group of heavily armed soldiers. (A P S)

(9)   Heaped on a lectern near the window *lay* religious books and sheets of paper covered with writing. (C P S)

As such sentences are syntactically closely related to sentences in which the finite verb is a form of BE, and as the connection between BE and a fronted participle appears to be looser than that between BE and a following participle, the analysis in sentences with BE of a fronted participle construction as an adverbial or a complement cannot be ruled out as an alternative.

5.3.8. Full inversion after a fronted subject complement

In the relatively few cases where a subject complement is fronted in English, the ordering of subject and predicator may be straight or inverted. The former has already been illustrated by the example *Waddle his name is*. If a subject is heavy, however, inversion is possible in order for the principle of end-weight to be observed:

(1)   Strange indeed was her urge to tell everybody what she thought of them.

Inversion after a fronted complement is chiefly found in clauses with BE, and where the complement refers to given information and is realized by a *comparative* construction which refers to a preceding part of the text:

(2)   A course in trigonometry may be useful enough, but far more useful would be a refresher course in elementary maths.
(3)   Grammar is undoubtedly relevant, but equally relevant are recent approaches to language learning.

In selecting the constituent order C P S in the second clause of such compound sentences, the speaker accomplishes three things: he gives prominence to the part of the message covered by the group realizing the complement, he establishes a direct link to the preceding clause and he observes the principle of end-weight.

5.3.9. Full inversion after a fronted object

Objects are rarely placed initially in English. As pointed out in section 5.2.2, this placement is found in *wh*-interrogatives of the type *What must you learn?* where the interrogative pronoun realizes the object. And as mentioned in section 5.2.3, an object may be fronted in a declarative sentence if the speaker wishes to highlight the part of the message its realization spans: *That story I will tell you another time*. Such fronting, which is unaccompanied by inversion, usually also has a cohesive function, as in the following example, where the fronted object pronoun *This* refers back to the preceding clause:

(1)   He knew what he liked and Lily didn't conform to the specifications. *This* he knew with a certainty as absolute as his knowledge that the food he served from the 'tourist' menu was rubbish.

Fronting of objects accompanied by inversion is chiefly limited to *reporting clauses*, in which a verb of saying in the simple present or past tense takes the clause quoted as its direct object (O P S):

(2)   'Eh?' said the driver.

(3)   'I didn't hear anything,' answered the woman's voice.

In examples like these, inversion, though not obligatory, is chosen in order to observe the principle of *end-weight*. If a reporting clause contains an adverbial, this principle can be observed without changing the normal ordering of subject and predicator (O S P A):

(4)   'We are going to visit a different town,' their driver announced cheerfully.

The order of subject and predicator is also straight if the reporting clause contains an indirect object (Od S P Oi):

(5)   'That's your father in the car, Son,' Lily informed him.

If the subject of a reporting clause is a personal pronoun, which is even lighter than a verb of saying, there is naturally enough no inversion:

(6)   'This is madness,' he said.

In earlier stages of English, inversion of pronoun and verb of saying was common, and thus has an archaic, poetic or even comical ring to it:

(7)   "Tis madness,' quoth he.

This order is very occasionally used in modern English in narrative contexts with the predicator and pronominal subject of the reporting clause in pre-object position ('initial reporting clauses'):

(8)   Says he: 'Sit down. My God, you are glistening like an apple!' Says she: 'Well, I'd rather not, you see, I'm fed up with your condescending manners.'

The effect here is to emphasize the conversational turn-taking, with a more clearly felt contrast between the interlocutors.

In everyday conversation, inversion is not uncommon in cases like:

(9)   Speaker A: 'Jack can do it.'
       Speaker B: 'Says who!'

(10)   Speaker A: 'John's wife can run a mile in four minutes.'
       Speaker B: 'Yeah, says he!'

In both cases the pronoun is fully stressed, and the construction conveys a tone of disbelief or contempt.

Finally, both inversion and straight order are used in reporting clauses whose subject is realized by a proper noun and in which there is no adverbial or indirect object:

(11)   'I am no coward!' declared Xavier / Xavier declared.

If there is no object fronting, i.e. if the reporting clause is placed initially, the ordering of subject and predicator is straight:

(12)   Then Jane said, 'Don't be angry with me, I beg you!' (A S P O)

In journalism, however, there is occasionally inversion in initial reporting clauses, in accordance with the principle of end-weight:

(13)   Explained Clay Mulford, the national group's general counsel: 'We don't want to be held responsible for every action they take.' (P S O)

The conditions under which subject and predicator are inverted in English are summarized in *table 1*.

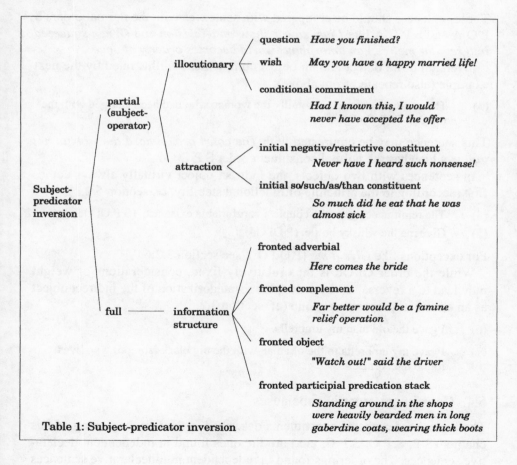

Table 1: Subject-predicator inversion

5.3.10. Inversion of other sentence constituents

As pointed out in section 5.3.1, inversion may be understood to refer not only to reversal of subject and predicator but also to reversal of other sentence constituents. In nearly all cases such re-orderings can be explained as caused by the principle of *end-weight*.

Inversion of an adverbial and an object or complement can be illustrated by the following examples (the first of which is repeated from above):

(1)   I just saw on television how some Indian people started a shop and put the old grocery on the corner out of business. (S A P A O)

(2)   When squeezed into regular metres, an amorphous world becomes at once orderly, lucid, clear and beautiful. (A S P A C)

These sentences should be compared with sentences with the normal orders S P O A and S P C A like *I just saw a show on television* and *(When squeezed into regular metres,) an amorphous world becomes orderly at once.*

Inversion of an object and an object complement is illustrated by the next example (also repeated from above):

(3)   The court pronounced not guilty the woman who had been charged with the murder. (S P Co O)

This sentence may be contrasted with *The court pronounced the woman not guilty*, which has the normal constituent order S P O Co.

In sentences with two objects, the indirect object virtually always comes first (according to the principle of functional stability, cf. section 5.2.1):

(4)   The remittances gave the couple a comfortable existence. (S P Oi Od)

(5)   Give me the whisky bottle. (P Oi Od)

For exceptions like *Give it me* (P Od Oi), see section 3.2.6.

While the order Oi Od is thus relatively fixed, considerations of weight may lead to a reversal of the order plus recategorization of the indirect object as an adverbial preposition group (cf. section 3.2.6):

(6)   I gave the old man my umbrella.

(7)   I gave my umbrella to the old man with the big black labrador who lives round the corner.

5.4. Constituent order in subclauses

The typical orderings of constituents described at the very beginning of this chapter (S P, S P O, S P C, etc.) are the ones found in independent declarative sentences. The orderings found in independent non-declarative sentences – interrogative, exclamatory, imperative – were described in sections 4.4.4

and 5.2.2. We must now take a look at constituent order in subclauses. Before going into specific details, we can state as a very general rule that in subclauses a *wh*-constituent occupies the initial position irrespective of its syntactic function. This can be illustrated by the following examples in which the *wh*-constituent does not realize a subject:

(1)   The house *which I've bought* is beyond repair. (relative)
(2)   I can't hear *what you're saying*. (interrogative)
(3)   I remember *what a mistake I made*. (exclamatory)

5.4.1. Relative clauses

In relative clauses we find initial, relativized objects or complements:

(1)   The honour *(which) you do me* is too great. (Od S P Oi)
(2)   The man *(that) you do this honour* is my uncle. (Oi S P Od)
(3)   He is not the man *(that) he was*. (C S P)

As appears from the bracketing, the pronoun realizing an object or complement may be omitted in restrictive relative clauses. In such cases O or C is assumed to be realized by 'zero' (cf. section 4.2). In so-called non-restrictive relative clauses, which do not restrict the reference of the preceding noun or noun group but offer additional information, initial objects and complements (as well as subjects and prepositional complements) are always realized by overt pronouns. This can be illustrated by examples like *Susan, who(m) you met last night, has been promoted to sergeant* and *He behaved like a child of twelve, which evidently he still felt himself to be*.

If a relative pronoun functions as complement in a preposition group realizing an adverbial, it is placed at the beginning of the clause, either preceded by the preposition or followed by it at the very end of the clause:

(4)   I called the editor *to whom you posted the manuscript*. (A S P O)
(5)   I called the editor *(who(m)/that) you posted the manuscript to*. (A- S P O -A)

As appears, a relative pronoun realizing a prepositional complement may be omitted in restrictive clauses if the preposition is placed finally.

In those relative clauses which we term *independent* because they do not function as dependent in a group but perform an independent clause function, we also find objects, complements and adverbials in initial position:

(6)   They believed *what I told them*. (Od S P Oi)
(7)   That's exactly *what it is*. (C S P)
(8)   Home is *where you needn't mask your feelings*. (A S P O)

5.4.2. Interrogative clauses

In subordinate *wh-interrogative clauses*, we find the same constituent order as in relative clauses. Objects, complements and adverbials realized by a *wh-*word are placed initially as they are also in main-clause *wh-*interrogative sentences, for example *What are you doing these days?*, *What was the source of her sorrow?* and *Where do you live?* (see section 5.2.2 above). But in subordinate *wh-*clauses the order of subject and predicator is straight:

(1)   I fail to see *what you mean.* (O S P)

(2)   Tell me *what your name is.* (C S P)

(3)   I don't understand *how you can say that.* (A S P O)

If an interrogative pronoun is complement in a preposition group, it is placed at the beginning of the clause, preceded by the preposition or followed by it at the end of the clause:

(4)   I would like to know *to whom* I should post the manuscript. (A S P O)

(5)   I would like to know *who(m)* I should post the manuscript *to.* (A- S P O -A)

In subordinate *yes-no interrogative clauses*, which begin with one of the subordinating conjunctions *if* or *whether*, there is no fronting of objects, complements or adverbials, nor is there inversion of subject and operator as in main-clause *yes-no* questions (see section 5.2.2 above):

(6)   He asks *if we think the weather will stay fine.* (SUB S P O)

(7)   I wonder *whether I hurt her feelings.* (SUB S P O)

5.4.3. Exclamatory clauses

In subordinate *exclamatory clauses*, the order of constituents is the same as in main-clause exclamatory sentences (see sections 4.4.4 and 5.2.2 above):

(1)   It is impressive *how confidently you work the machine.* (A S P O)

(2)   I remember *what a silly mistake I made on that occasion.* (O S P A)

As the order of subject and predicator is straight in subordinate *wh-*interrogative clauses, subordinate exclamatory and interrogative clauses have the same constituent order and therefore cannot be distinguished formally. For example, a sentence like *I told them how confidently Miss Tang worked the machine* is ambiguous. If it means 'I told them that Miss Tang worked the machine with surprising confidence', the subclause is exclamatory. But if it means 'I informed them about the degree of confidence with which Miss Tang worked the machine', it is interrogative. In spoken language the difference is signalled prosodically. If the subclause is intended by the speaker to be exclamatory, the word *confidently* will be pronounced with strong stress and the rest of the clause with weak stress and low pitch. If it is meant to be interrogative, on the other hand, not only *confidently* but also the words *Tang, worked* and *machine* will be given prosodic prominence.

5.4.4. Other finite, nonfinite and verbless clauses

In other subclauses, constituent order in English (unlike that in many other languages) is basically the same as in declarative sentences. In *finite* subclauses we find the same structures as the ones listed at the very outset of this chapter, apart from the fact that there is often an initial subordinator:

(1)   *If you had phoned me* I could have warned her. (SUB S P O)

(2)   I guess *she is Catholic*. (S P C)

(3)   It is unlikely *that anything could happen to Maggie*. (SUB S P A)

First, as noted in sections 5.3.3 and 5.3.4, there is sometimes partial inversion in subclauses to signal conditional commitment (e.g. *Had I known this, I would never have accepted the offer*) or as a result of attraction to a clause-initial constituent (e.g. *Alice is far more intelligent than are most of her classmates*).

Occasionally, in so-called *concessive clauses* with one of the conjunctions *as, if, that*, or *though*, we find fronting of a complement (as in example (4)) or a full predication stack (as in example (5)). The fronted element(s) appear(s) to the left of the subordinating conjunction:

(4)   *Confused* though he is, he manages beautifully. (cf. Though he is confused, he manages beautifully.)

(5)   I knew it for an aspect of my inheritance that I could never root out, *deny it* though I might. (cf. ..., though I might deny it.)

In these examples, the fronted constituent receives more prominence than in the corresponding non-inverted constructions.

In *nonfinite* subclauses we may also find the same constituents and orderings as in declarative sentences:

(6)   The case was closed by *the defendant paying the fine*. (S P O)

(7)   *Her oration finished*, she breathed heavily with an overflow of indignation. (S P)

(8)   I want *Gerard to become a schoolteacher*. (S P C)

(9)   She felt *the earth shake violently*. (S P A)

Typically, however, nonfinite clauses contain fewer constituents than finite clauses. If the subject of the nonfinite verb form is understood to be identical with the subject of the predicator in the matrix clause, it is not expressed:

(10)   After *shaking everyone's hand,* the young lady nodded to several youths standing behind huge reflectors. (P O)

(11)   You must try *to see things in perspective.* (P O A)

In so-called *verbless clauses,* i.e. clauses without a predicator, the only constituents found are subordinators, subjects, complements and adverbials:

(12)   With *Peter on vacation,* there is not much we can do. (S A)

(13)   *Although invariably polite,* she was disliked by many. (SUB A C)

While the conjunction *although* in example (13) is a subordinator linking the verbless clause to the matrix clause, *with* in example (12) is interpreted as a preposition which takes the verbless clause *Peter on vacation* as its complement. It is therefore completely outside this clause and functions as head of an adverbial preposition group.

5.5. Position and order of adverbials

In this chapter we have so far been concerned with the position and order of obligatory sentence functions, especially in terms of deviation from the basic sentence structures defined in sections 3.2.3-4. We shall now examine the position and order of optional adverbials, i.e. the one major function type not included in our list of sentence structures. As will be recalled (from section 3.2.9), optional adverbials are not restricted to one particular position in the clause (which raises the question of what positions they may occupy), and sometimes more than one adverbial may in fact be placed in the 'same' position relative to other clause functions (which raises the question of relative ordering of adverbials). Below we shall deal with these questions.

5.5.1. Main positions in finite clauses

In finite clauses we distinguish *three* main positions: initial (I), medial (M) and terminal (T), as in the following examples:

(1)   *Quite frankly,* she gave him every excuse.

(2)   Owen *substantially* improved my abilities as a student.

(3)   The Voice had not been idle *for the summer*.

Each of these main positions needs closer examination.

5.5.2. Initial position

I-position is always *before* the subject (or the predicator plus subject in inverted constructions) but *after* conjunctions, if any:

(1)   *Quite frankly,* did she give him any excuse?

(2)   I admire her because, *quite frankly*, she gave him every excuse.

(3)   He loved her and, *quite frankly*, she gave him every excuse.

Initial adverbials may occur after a *fronted* constituent (e.g. an object):

(4)   This solution, *obviously*, she would never accept.

In relative subclauses, initial adverbials follow the relative constituent if it realizes a clause function other than subject (e.g. object):

(5)   He drew a lesson from it which, *in his heart*, he had long understood.

5.5.3. Medial position

Any adverbial which follows the subject but precedes the head verb of the predicator is said to be in M-position. This definition accommodates several more specific M-positions:

Pre-M operator **central-M** aux2 **post-M^1** aux3 **post-M^2** ... H:v

The following examples illustrate these different M-positions:

(1)   Owen *substantially* `did improve my abilities as a student.

(2)   Owen had *substantially* improved my abilities as a student.

(3)   Owen may have *substantially* improved my abilities as a student.

(4)   Owen's abilities may have been *substantially* improved, too.

Note that the adverbials are not in fact restricted to one *specific* M-position: in each example the adverbial could be moved to at least one other M-position without this affecting the acceptability of the construction (e.g. *Owen may substantially have improved my abilities as a student* as a possible alternative to (3)).

In example (1), the adverbial is in pre-M position *after* the subject and *before* the first auxiliary, the operator, on whose presence in the clause a pre-M adverbial is dependent. This position is often marked in BrE and requires primary stress on the operator. In AmE, pre-M position is often unmarked (see below).

In example (2), the adverbial is in central-M position: it is the unmarked M-position after the subject and the operator, if any, and before any other auxiliaries. Thus in both *Owen substantially improved my abilities* ... and *Owen had substantially improved my abilities* the adverbial is said to be in central-M position. In the first example, the distinction between pre-M and central-M is neutralized but since the position of the adverbial is as unmarked as in the second example, we classify it as central-M. The most frequent type of adverbial, the clause negator NOT, always appears in central-M position:

(5)   Owen did *not* improve my abilities as a student.

(6)   Owen could *not* improve my abilities as a student.

In negative interrogative constructions, NOT is contracted across the subject to pre-subject position in spoken and informal written English; compare:

(7)   Had*n't* Owen improved my abilities as a student?

(8)   Had Owen *not* improved my abilities as a student?

Moving on to examples (3) and (4), we find that they illustrate two different post-M positions: post-M^1 after the second auxiliary in a string and post-M^2 after the third auxiliary in a string. Post-M^2 is relevant only after the past participle of BE in passive and progressive constructions (as in example (4) and e.g. *Owen may have been actively trying to undermine her authority*).

What all the four different M-positions seem to share is immediate 'contact' with the predicator somewhere *before* the head verb. There is an exception to this, involving the primary verb BE:

(9)   She is *always* happy.

(10)   Keith was *clearly* a man of the world.

The adverbials in these examples are classified as central-M adverbials. BE being an operator in such examples (cf. section 3.2.1), we expect central-M adverbials to follow it rather than precede it. This means that the following constructions, which are marked in BrE (unlike AmE) and require primary stress on the primary verb, illustrate pre-M position:

(11)   Jane *never* `was fond of her sister.

Note also that, in negative constructions, *not* follows rather than precedes BE (which supports the characterization of the position as central-M):

(12)   She is *not* happy.

Although it is possible to find similar examples with HAVE followed by *not* (e.g. *We haven't the time*), as a primary verb it usually behaves like an ordinary full verb with respect to the position of adverbials:

(13)   Keith *never* had what it took to be a murderer.

(14)   Kathy *obviously* had other ideas.

Pre-M position is common in elliptical clauses with an operator representing a full predicate:

(15)   I miss you, darling, I *really* do.

(16)   You know that I fancy you, I *always* have.

Post-M^2 is statistically rare. This position is relevant in passive and progressive constructions, where, typically, manner and degree adjuncts in

M-position immediately precede the head verb, to which it is closely related semantically, irrespective of the number of auxiliaries:

(17)   She was *seriously* crippled by the blow. (central-M)
(18)   She may be *secretly* supporting their cause. (post-M^1)
(19)   He may not have been *completely* recovering from the accident. (post-M^2)

The precise M-position assigned to such adjuncts thus depends on the number of auxiliaries.

5.5.4. Terminal position

Turning now to T-position, we observe first of all that it is the position of obligatory adverbials in S P A and S P O A constructions:

(1)   Last week I stayed *with my parents*.
(2)   She reluctantly stood the figure *on a stool*.

T-position is also the position of optional adverbials which follow objects, complements and obligatory adverbials, or intransitive predicators:

(3)   She gave me a quick kiss *on the cheek*.
(4)   Her parents got very upset *when they saw us together*.
(5)   I put the gun in my pocket *as casually as I could*.
(6)   He smoked *incessantly*.

In transitive and complex-transitive constructions we sometimes encounter cases where the optional adverbial follows the predicator (and hence is not in M-position) but immediately precedes an object or obligatory adverbial:

(7)   Many subscribers to NLLT experienced *four times a year* excitement of a sort that the arrival of a scholarly journal in one's mailbox rarely occasions.
(8)   I put the gun *casually* in my pocket.

The position taken up by the italicized adverbials in these examples is called pre-T. Pre-T is the position after P but before other obligatory constituents.

   In clauses with both a provisional and a real subject, the real subject normally follows adverbials in T-position if the provisional subject is realized by *it*:

(9)   It worried me *immensely* that Jack did not get in touch.

If the provisional subject is realized by *there*, the real subject is more tightly integrated in the clause structure (cf. section 3.2.2) and usually precedes adverbials in T-position:

(10)   There will be two loaded guns *in the top drawer*.

As with O A sequences (see above), considerations of weight (and semantic clarity) may force an adverbial into pre-T position:

(11)   There once lay, *in the valley*, a large boulder, reputedly the first chunk of America to be touched by the Pilgrims' feet.

Similarly, adverbials which most naturally occur in central-M position are sometimes placed in pre-T position, as in the following cases involving copula verbs and subject complements:

(12)   His parents seemed *often* very dependent on his support.

(13)   Jack became *only very rarely* this angry with his wife and children.

Pre-T position is thus primarily to be thought of as a more marked alternative position where adverbials with a potential for straight T-position or some M-position are sometimes placed (see further sections 5.5.8 and 5.5.11 below).

5.5.5. Overview of positions in finite clauses

Let us briefly summarize the seven different positions in which we find adverbials:

I	*Quite frankly*, she gave him every excuse.
pre-M	Owen *substantially* `did improve my abilities as a student.
central-M	Owen *substantially* improved my abilities as a student.
	Owen had *substantially* improved my abilities as a student.
post-M^1	Owen may have *substantially* improved my abilities as a student.
post-M^2	Owen's abilities may have been *substantially* improved, too.
pre-T	I put the gun *casually* in my pocket.
T	She gave me a quick kiss *on the cheek*.

5.5.6. Positions in nonfinite clauses

In nonfinite clauses: a) adverbials do not occur in genuine I-position; b) the distinction between pre-M and central-M is neutralized because there is no operator (operators being always finite, cf. section 3.2.1); c) pre-T and T are parallel to pre-T and T in finite clauses (e.g. *Having put the gun* <u>*casually*</u> *in my pocket, I opened the window* and *She reassured me by giving me a quick kiss* <u>*on the cheek*</u>).

Although superficially adverbials do occur initially in nonfinite clauses, they never actually co-occur with a subject:

(1)   *Always* feeling guilty, she mostly kept to herself.

(2)   *Obviously* having difficulty reading the book, he decided to watch television instead.

The italicized adverbials here correspond to central-M adverbials in finite clauses containing a subject:

(3)   She was *always* feeling guilty.

(4)   He was *obviously* having difficulty reading the book.

When a subject is present in a nonfinite clause, it precedes such adverbials:

(5)   Sarah *always* feeling guilty, I did not want to tell her what had happened.

(6)   We all felt depressed, Jack *obviously* having difficulty reading the book.

Moreover, for clausal negation, NOT immediately *precedes* the first verb in the predicator, even BE:

(7)   *Not* feeling guilty, she never hesitated to call on them.

(8)   *Not* being happy with this decision, he quit.

It is therefore more appropriate to classify the adverbials in all these examples as M-adverbials, more specifically as central-M adverbials, than to classify them as I-adverbials.

The second characteristic feature of adverbial positions in nonfinite clauses is the absence of a distinction between pre-M and central-M adverbials. By definition, pre-M adverbials are adverbials that precede the operator. Since there is no operator in nonfinite clauses, there can be no pre-M adverbials, either. However, on analogy with finite predicators, adverbials are often placed after the *first* auxiliary in nonfinite predicators. We thus find unmarked adverbials both before and after the first auxiliary of a nonfinite predicator – even in BrE; compare the following examples:

(9a)   With Jack *always* being so honest, we endanger the whole operation.

(9b)   With Jack being *always* so honest, we endanger the whole operation.

We classify *always* in the a-example as a central-M adverbial and *always* in the b-example as a post-M[1] adverbial, but the difference between the two positions is not as clearly felt as in finite clauses.

There is in nonfinite predicators normally a maximum of two auxiliaries, the second of which is always the past participle of BE. Like post-M[2] in finite clauses, post-M[2] in nonfinite clauses is relevant only in passive or progressive constructions:

(10)   Having been *repeatedly* counteracted by his superiors, he decided to quit.

(11)   To have been *deliberately* misrepresenting things in this way, she must have been mentally deranged.

To complete the picture, there is a special M-position in nonfinite predicators between infinitive marker and infinitive. An adverbial in this position creates the so-called *split infinitive* (for discussion, see e.g. Quirk *et al.* 1985: 496ff):

(12)   For me to *suddenly* resign my job is unthinkable.

(13)   She has tried to *consciously* stop worrying.

The split infinitive is felt by many to be not only marked but in fact un-acceptable. Despite widespread prejudice against it, this construction type is by no means rare. In some cases, as in (13) above, it even serves the purpose of making the meaning more precise and unambiguous; compare (13) to the following examples with continuous *to*-infinitive constructions (cf. Quirk et al. 1985: 497):

(13')   She has tried *consciously* to stop worrying.

(13")   She has tried to stop *consciously* worrying.

5.5.7. Factors governing the distribution of adverbials

There are few hard-and-fast rules for the distribution of adverbials in the positions defined in sections 5.5.1-6 above. The fact that many adverbials are mobile often makes it impossible to predict the exact location of a particular adverbial in a particular clause. Thus, except for the negation NOT and a few other adverbs (typically adverbs of degree and frequency) such as ALWAYS, EVER, OFTEN, NEVER, RARELY, REALLY, HARDLY (which are nearly always located in central-M position in BrE), it is more appropriate to speak of certain factors contributing to the speaker/writer's location of adverbials. Though T-position is for many adverbials (especially obligatory adverbials and long optional adverbials) the most natural, unmarked position, there is a great deal of variation. In the following sections we shall look briefly at some of the most important factors contributing to this variation. They are: 1. the form and relative weight of the adverbial; 2. (con)textual cohesion; 3. the scope of the adverbial; 4. semantic clarity; 5. stylistic considerations.

5.5.8. Position, form and relative weight

The form of the adverbial is the major factor determining the position it assumes in the clause. Statistical analyses have shown that *long* adverbials (clauses and long groups) tend to occur in I- and especially T-position (in accordance with the principle of end-weight) rather than in M-position:

(1)   *Knowing that Keith would be elsewhere*, I staked out the Black Cross.

(2)   One of the black guys was staring at me *with either affection or contempt*.

Short adverbials (adverbs and small groups) are more evenly distributed in the three main positions:

(3)   I cried all the time, *actually*.

(4)   *Actually* I cried all the time.

(5)   I *actually* cried all the time.

Within the range of different M-positions, even short adverbials are relatively rare in pre-M and especially post-M.

M-position is especially rare for weighty adverbials if the subject is an unstressed personal pronoun. Thus while we find:

(6)   Guy, *feeling no closer to life than to death*, pressed on.

we do not find:

(7)   *I, *knowing that Keith would be elsewhere*, staked out the Black Cross.

Long parenthetical adverbials occasionally occur in M-position:

(8)   Keith, *in my mind*, blew all his chances.

(9)   Nicola Six, *he confided to all who cared to listen*, sang in the church choir.

In constructions with complex predicators such adverbials assume pre-M position, even in BrE:

(6')   Guy, *feeling no closer to life than to death*, was pressing on.

(8')   Keith, *in my mind*, had blown all his chances.

As already indicated in section 5.5.4, considerations of weight may lead to adverbials in pre-T position, preceding direct objects:

(10)   She drank two cups of black coffee and tasted *with hunger* the black tobacco of a French cigarette.

(11)   How do I know, *for instance*, that Keith works as a cheat?

Such ordering is especially frequent when the object contains a dependent clause. Even if the adverbial is actually weightier than the object, we usually get A O rather than O A in such cases:

(12)   She thought, absolutely wrongly and with characteristic lack of imagination, that they loved her for her mind.

In the passive counterpart to a ditransitive construction, the adverbial *by*-phrase will typically appear in pre-T position if the direct object is a clause or lengthy group:

(13)   Keith was told *by various magistrates* that he had a 'poor character'.

5.5.9. Position and (con)textual cohesion

As noted above, T-position is for many adverbials the most unmarked position, i.e. the position they take up unless there is some reason for taking up a different position. (Con)textual cohesion (i.e. the binding together of sentences in a coherent text or, in speech, the use of utterances in particular contexts) is one such reason for appearing in I-position rather than T-position. As with other clause functions, adverbials appearing initially either receive special highlighting (as a fronted constituent) or establish a link to the context or preceding text, thus forming part of what is 'given' (cf. section 5.2.3). In sections 5.3.4 and 5.3.6 we dealt with cases involving fronting of adverbials accompanied by partial and full inversion, respectively. However, adverbials may appear in I-position to receive highlighting without this resulting in inversion. Thus instead of simply saying e.g.:

(1a)   You are going to have a smashing time in Copenhagen.

we may put more focus on the adverbial *in Copenhagen* by saying:

(1b)   In Copenhagen you are going to have a smashing time.

The subtle difference between the two examples can be formulated in this way: in the first example, the information contained in the adverbial *in Copenhagen* forms part of the prediction expressed by the clause as a whole, whereas in the second example, this information forms part of a given *background* to the prediction even if it does not link up explicitly with the preceding context. It is this background effect of initial adverbials that explains why many adverbials in I-position do in fact link up very nicely with the preceding context, as in the following examples:

(2)   Sometimes, when he stumbled into her bedsit in the small hours, Analiese was alone. *On other occasions* he surprised her in bed with famous people.

(3)   When Analiese gave herself to you, she would give herself utterly, and probably wouldn't ring the house. *In this last particular alone*, appearances were deceptive.

In many such examples the link to the preceding context is created specifically by anaphoric pronouns (such as the demonstratives *this* and *that* and referential *it*) or other definite expressions.

Not surprisingly, I-position is thus the 'natural' (but not the only) position for adverbials serving more particularly as *conjuncts* (cf. section 3.2.9):

(4)   *Besides*, Keith generally preferred short girls.

(5)   *To conclude*, I'll never have dealings with Intercom again.

5.5.10. Position and scope

By the 'scope' of an adverbial is meant the extent of its semantic relations to other constituents or to the context. The scope of an adverbial may be just one other constituent, typically the predicator, as in:

(1)   He walked *briskly* down the road.

or it may be a whole sentence:

(2)　*To tell the truth*, he was limping when he got up off the basketball court.

There is in language a general tendency for the scope of constituents to be determined by their position: the earlier they occur in the linear sequence the broader their scope. There is thus a narrowing of scope as we move from left to right in a clause or sentence, according to what is sometimes referred to as the *principle of linear modification* (Bolinger 1952, for discussion see Johansson & Lysvåg 1991, vol. II: 240ff). The varying scope of adverbials is very nicely demonstrated by comparing examples which differ with respect to the position of the adverbial:

(3a)　*Clearly* he saw her.

(3b)　He saw her *clearly*.

(4a)　*Quite frankly* he told me about the affair.

(4b)　He told me *quite frankly* about the affair.

Here the adverbials in the a-examples are disjuncts with sentential scope ('It was clear that he saw her' and 'I am telling you quite frankly that he told me about the affair'), while the adverbials in the b-examples are likely to be interpreted as manner adjuncts with predicator scope. As in these examples, adverbials in I-position tend to have wider scope than adverbials in M- or T-position. Thus disjuncts (such as initial *To tell the truth*, *Clearly* and *Quite frankly* in the examples above) and conjuncts (see examples in section 5.5.9) are frequently in I-position (or M-position), while adjuncts relating more narrowly to the predicator or the predication are frequently in M- or T-position. The difference of scope is, however, also seen in adverbials of the same kind (see Johansson and Lysvåg 1987, vol. II: 241), as in the following example where a place adjunct is placed in I- and T-position, respectively:

(5)　*Outside in the street* we could see the car. (i.e. 'we were in the street')

(6)　We could see the car *outside in the street*. (i.e. 'the car was in the street')

When disjuncts with sentence scope are placed in T-position, they are felt to be more detached from the rest of the clause, like an afterthought:

(7)　I wasn't worrying, *for Christ's sake*.

(8)　She fell for the old trick, *obviously*.

In such cases the adverbial is always separated by the rest of the clause by an intonation boundary, if emphatic and stressed.

　A few conjuncts appear in T-position, especially in short sentences:

(9)　I didn't want to go *anyway*.

(10)　She wouldn't sleep with him, *though*.

5.5.11. Position and semantic clarity

In any communication, a very basic consideration on the part of the speaker or writer is to make sure that constituents which are intended to belong together semantically are placed in such a way that they are recognized by the listener or reader as actually belonging together. Thus, for example, if we wish to communicate the information that someone decided to study art and that this decision was made in Paris (to use an example from Johansson & Lysvåg 1991, vol. II: 241), (1a) is more appropriate than (1b):

(1a)   In Paris he decided to study art.

(1b)   He decided to study art in Paris.

Example (1b) is likely to be interpreted to mean that the studying of art was to take place in Paris: *in Paris* seems to locate the 'studying' rather than the 'decision-taking'. But strictly speaking, (1b) could mean the same as (1a) and is thus ambiguous. Syntactically, the difference between the two readings of the (1b) hinges on whether or not *in Paris* belongs as an adverbial to the object clause *to study art*. In (1a), the adverbial is unambiguously a matrix clause function. To ensure an unambiguous reading, the speaker or writer may thus decide to place the adverbial in I-position.

In transitive constructions where we normally expect the order O A, the form and weight of the object may lead to a reversal of this order (see sections 5.5.4 and 5.5.8). But semantic clarity is also an important consideration in such constructions (cf. Quirk *et al.* 1985: 499, Dienhart 1992: 122f):

(2)   She herself interviewed *with hurtful disdain* the student I had turned down.

(3)   He urged *secretly* that she be dismissed.

(4)   He hoped *fervently* to be applauded.

In these examples, the only alternative to pre-T position, if we want to preserve the intended meaning, is M- or I-position, not T-position, which would drastically change the meaning of the sentence.

The distribution of adverbials within the range of M-positions is sometimes governed by considerations of semantic clarity (cf. Quirk *et al.* 1985: 494):

(5a)   She hadn't *really* delighted her audience.

(5b)   She *really* hadn't delighted her audience.

(6a)   They have *seriously* considered him for the post.

(6b)   They *seriously* have considered him for the post.

The italicized adverbials here function as disjuncts in pre-M position and as degree or manner adjuncts in central-M.

5.5.12. Position and style

While other clause functions are relatively fixed in the basic sentence structures (cf. sections 3.2.3-4 and 5.1), optional adverbials often move around more freely and thus lend themselves to stylistic variation. For example, in a string of S P O constructions, the monotony of the initial S in this basic sentence structure can be broken by placing adverbials in different positions relative to S. Thus, instead of letting the adverbials take up unmarked M- or T-position, as in:

(1a)   She slowed her pace *with obvious deliberation*. She *briskly* removed her hat and the black clip that secured her chignon. She shook out her hair *with a roll of her throat*.

we could let some of them occupy I-position to create a little variation:

(1b)   She slowed her pace *with obvious deliberation*. *Briskly* she removed her hat and the black clip that secured her chignon. *With a roll of her throat* she shook out her hair.

The effect of this operation is to tie the sentences more closely together in a more balanced and easy-going flow of narration.

Another stylistic factor is *avoidance of heavy adverbial clusters*. There is a natural tendency for adverbial clustering in T-position in accordance with the general principle of end-weight. However, the possibility of placing adverbials in other positions makes it possible to avoid too heavy clusters in one position and to create more evenly balanced constructions:

(2)   *On the fifth day* the sun burst through *again inexorably*.

(3)   *In excellent fettle, in the pink or the blue of boyish good health during their absence*, Marmaduke sickened *dramatically within a few hours of their return*.

Avoidance of clustering in a particular M-position may lead to utilization of different M-positions; compare:

(4a)   The key-note address was *certainly elegantly* delivered by David.

(4b)   The key-note address *certainly* was *elegantly* delivered by David.

In negative clauses, where NOT occupies central-M position, disjuncts may be shifted into pre-M position:

(5)   She *probably* has *not* seen David yet.

(6)   Keith *obviously* will *not* listen to you.

Marked, or unexpected, adverbial position may be a device characteristically employed by authors to create a certain effect, mood or atmosphere in a novel, as arguably in the following constructions containing adverbials in pre-T position (for discussion, see Dienhart 1992: 123ff):

(7)   He crumpled some bread in a bowl and poured *over it* hot milk.

(8)   On Sunday he got up early and took *from the suitcase* his serge suit.

5.5.13. Relative position of adverbials

When adverbials appear in clusters, as they frequently do at I-position (for extensive backgrounding) and especially at T-position (in accordance with the general principle of end-weight), the question of sequential order becomes relevant. Again there are no hard-and-fast rules but rather a number of general tendencies. These tendencies can be described in terms of some of the factors governing the position of adverbials reviewed above: form of realization, relative weight, scope, semantic and stylistic considerations. Often the order is determined by the interaction of several of these factors.

A) Order and form/relative weight. There is a tendency for short adverbials to precede long adverbials. Single words thus often precede groups, and groups often precede clauses:

(1)   They were walking [arm in arm] [towards the café where they had taken to having their mid-morning snack].

(2)   [In excellent fettle], [in the pink or the blue of boyish good health during their absence], Marmaduke sickened [dramatically] [within a few hours of their return].

(3)   [Twenty minutes later], [as he strode back up the beach], the wind threw everything it had at him.

Identity of form is often avoided in clusters of adverbials (cf. Quirk *et al.* 1985: 649):

(4)   ?*Finally probably only* John will be chosen.

(5)   ?I kissed her *on the cheek on the plane*.

B) Scope. From the point of view of scope and the principle of linear modification, we would expect the sequence disjuncts-conjuncts-adjuncts (e.g. adjuncts of time, place and manner) in I-position. A sequence of all three types is possible but cumbersome (cf. Quirk *et al.* 1985: 651):

(6)   [Unfortunately], [however], [last night] the old lady declined to see me.

Disjuncts tend to precede adjuncts in I-position but inversion is possible – especially if the disjunct serves as a parenthetical insertion; compare:

(7a)   [To be quite honest], [last night] he vowed never to see her again.

(7b)   [Last night], [to be quite honest], he vowed never to see her again.

There is more vacillation in sequences containing both a conjunct and an adjunct:

(8a)   [However], [last night], he vowed never to see her again.

(8b)   [Last night], [however], he vowed never to see her again.

In T-position adjuncts generally precede conjuncts and disjuncts (which are often felt to be added as parenthetical afterthoughts):

(9)   Keith left the pub [a bit later], [unfortunately].

(10)   Trish called her [twice], [probably].

Sequences of all three types of adverbial (adjunct-conjunct-disjunct) are possible in T-position but rare:

(11)   She didn't like him [much] [anyway], [to be frank].

In a sequence of adjuncts in T-position, those with narrow predicator scope precede those with broader predication or sentence scope:

(12)   Hope kissed him [passionately] [on the cheek].

(13)   Keith will react [violently] [if we press him too hard].

C) Semantic considerations. Closely related to the question of scope is the question of semantic content. Adverbials in clusters often supplement each other progressively so that each new adverbial in the sequence offers further elaboration, determination or specification:

(14)   [On the front passenger seat], [under the elegant rag of a white silk scarf], lies a heavy car-tool.

(15)   [Right from the start], [from the moment that her thoughts began to be consecutive], Nicola knew two strange things.

Sometimes, adverbials seem to be in a completely random order, simply enumerating different aspects:

(16)   A couple of mornings a month, [stiff with pride], [deafened with aspirin], [reckless with Bloody Marys], Nicola would adumbrate serious reform.

(17)   [Feeling neither vigour nor its opposite], [feeling no closer to life than to death], [feeling thirty-five], Guy pressed on.

Time and place adjuncts are occasionally followed by adverbial clauses either relating some event to the time/place expressed by the adjunct or bringing the plot or narration forward:

(18)   I'd been standing under the sign saying TAXIS [for about a half-hour] [when the royal-blue Cavalier made its second circuit and pulled up at the bay].

(19)   Keith pondered and agonized [for several days] [before filling in the section marked HOBBIES].

There is a general tendency for time and place adjuncts to precede adjuncts expressing circumstance, purpose or contingency:

(20)   He had entered the competition [some months ago] [on the advice of various friends and admirers].

(21)   The boulder had to be moved [closer to the shore], [in order to satisfy expectations of how history ought to happen].

Many grammarians have noted that we often find the sequence manner-place-time-others (cf. e.g. Steller & Sørensen 1974: 105; Preisler 1992: 60):

(22)   She played [beautifully] [at the concert] [last night] [even if she hadn't had time to practice].

There is great vacillation, however:

(23)   He whispered the same words [at night] [in the hotel] [with that strange accent of his].

(24)   He called her [at three o'clock in the morning] [from the Black Cross].

In M-position time and frequency adjuncts usually precede manner adjuncts:

(25)   He had [never] [knowingly] drunk a glass of wine.

(26)   She had [often] [secretly] admired Keith.

In T-position after predicators expressing motion, short manner adjuncts tend to precede adjuncts expressing place or direction:

(27)   Keith rose [steadily] [towards the very crest of his new profession].

(28)   She walked [evenly] [to the back].

Similarly short manner adjuncts tend to precede obligatory adverbials:

(29)   I put the gun [casually] [in my pocket].

Note also the position of the short manner adjuncts in the following cases:

(30)   I think [with shame] *of my contorted little crib in Hell's Kitchen.*

(31)   I was looking [with dread] *at the blood on your hands.*

(32)   Keith dealt [angrily] *with her application.*

The italicized constructions are either independent adverbials or part of a transitive construction involving a discontinuous prepositional verb (THINK *of*, LOOK *at*, DEAL *with*) followed by a direct object (see section 4.3.2).

5.6. Discontinuity

It has been pointed out earlier that the forms realizing a constituent tend to stay together rather than to be interrupted by other constituents but that this principle is often defeated by other principles (illocutionary value, highlighting, increasing complexity). In the following sections we shall examine the types of discontinuity found in English and the conditions under which discontinuity occurs.

5.6.1. Discontinuous clauses

Arguably we have discontinuous clauses in cases like:

(1)   *John*, I think, *never returned to Ireland.*
(2)   *This*, he claimed, *was caused by the inefficient handling of young criminals*.

These sentences contain parenthetical 'matrix clauses' with verbs of conviction or communication. It is tempting to analyse such sentences in terms of discontinuous *object* clauses, as in e.g.:

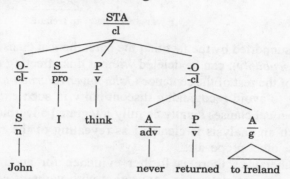

This proposal reflects our interpretation of the discontinuous clause as somehow the 'logical' object of the verb of conviction or communication. By adopting this analysis we capture the obvious relationship between such examples and continuous alternative expressions like:

(1')   I think (that) John never returned to Ireland.
(2')   He claimed (that) this was caused by the inefficient handling of young criminals.

In these examples, it seems, the only possible analysis of the italicized part is O:cl. Note, however, that there is a significant difference between the two sets of examples: unlike the continuous object clauses, the discontinuous ones cannot be supplied with an explicit marker of subordination (e.g. *That John, I think, never returned to Ireland*). Thus while the status of the clause as a subclause is clear in the continuous examples, it is at least questionable in the discontinuous examples. Another, related problem with the proposed analysis of the discontinuous cases is that it does not reflect the parenthetical status of the 'matrix'.

If we want to reflect the parenthetical nature of the 'matrix', this can be done by assigning to it instead the status of dependent, adverbial clause in relation to the rest of the sentence, which accordingly is analysed as a discontinuous clausal function stack:

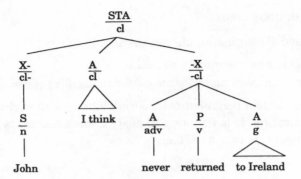

This analysis is supported by the fact that the parenthetical clause, like many adverbials (e.g. *probably*), can be deleted without this affecting the status or grammaticality of the rest of the sentence (*John never returned to Ireland*).

The only way to avoid recognizing discontinuity in such examples is to treat the parenthetical clauses simply as fully integrated adverbials (like e.g. *never*). But such an analysis is clearly less revealing of the relationships involved than the other proposals.

In relative subclauses there is further evidence for an interpretation involving discontinuous clauses in connection with verbs of conviction or communication. Consider the following examples:

(3)   The house that you told me Jack built last year is now put up for sale.

(4)   The passage which he thought he had referred me to had been removed.

The discontinuity is here caused by the relativization and fronting of an object or prepositional complement, as in the last example, where we have two discontinuities (a clause and a preposition group):

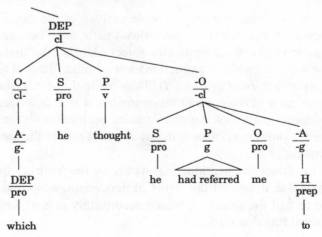

Unless clearly marked as parenthetical (by means of intonation or e.g. commas: *The passage which, he thought, he had referred me to ...*), the subject and predicator are here not as readily interpreted as parenthetical as in main clauses and therefore should not be assigned adverbial status.

In interrogative sentences, we get discontinuous clauses in cases like:

(5)   When did you say he would arrive?

(6)   Why did he say she left her husband?

(7)   How did you say she packed the suitcase?

Such sentences are strictly ambiguous: the question relates either to the first predicator or to the second, i.e. 'when did you say' or 'when would he arrive'; 'why did he say' or 'why did she leave her husband'; 'how did you say' (e.g. angrily or impatiently) or 'how did she pack the suitcase'. If the question relates to the first predicator, there is no clausal discontinuity:

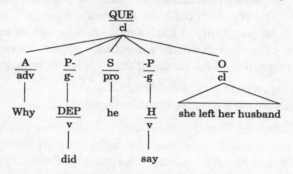

If, however, the question relates to the second predicator (i.e. if the underlying question is 'why did she leave her husband?', rather than 'why did he say anything about it?'), we have a discontinuous clause:

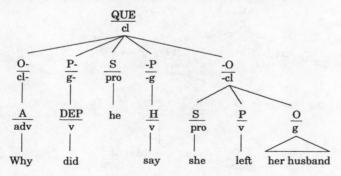

The interesting feature of such interrogative sentences is that the question word (e.g. *why*) triggers (or attracts) subject-operator inversion in the matrix clause, not the subclause, no matter which of them it relates to semantically.

Thus, even when the interpretation is such that we assume an underlying question 'why did she leave her husband' rather than 'why did he say anything about it?', we do not actually say *Why he said did she leave her husband*. This, however, fits nicely with the lack of subject-operator inversion in corresponding continuous interrogative subclauses:

(8)   Did he say *why she left her husband*?

Having discussed discontinuous finite clauses, we turn now to discontinuous nonfinite clauses. Corresponding to cases with verbs of conviction or communication like *John, I think, never returned to Ireland*, we get nonfinite clauses with a fronted, topicalized constituent of the following type:

(9)   *Linda* he believed *to be less innocent than Jim*.

This sentence is derived from *He believed Linda to be less innocent than Jim*. Notice that the subject-predicator sequence *he believed* cannot here be interpreted as parenthetical: **Linda, he believed, to be less innocent than Jim*. There is thus no possibility of analysing *he believed* as an adverbial.

Topicalization of a constituent in a nonfinite object clause may cause discontinuity, irrespective of the nature of the verb in the finite predicator:

(10)   This vase I want you to sell to the Americans.

(11)   The old lady they saw climbing the stairs with difficulty.

Such examples (derived from *I want you to sell this vase to the Americans* and *They saw the old lady climbing the stairs with difficulty*) are fairly marked. Embedded in relative clauses, however, where such topicalization is inbuilt, as it were, we find unmarked cases:

(12)   You won't like the essay *which* you wanted *me to submit*.

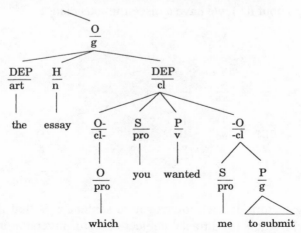

As pointed out in section 5.2.3, part of a message may be *postponed* in order to highlight it and achieve end-weight. This was illustrated by an example like *It worries me that the children have not returned* (Sp P O Sr), in which the clause realizing the subject is replaced by the substitute form *it* and moved to the end of the sentence. Extraposition, however, is not the only way in which end-focus and end-weight can be achieved. Instead of moving an entire subject clause to the end of the sentence it is possible to divide it and place the part of it following its subject in final position. This happens with *to*-infinitive clauses:

(13)   *He* is believed *to be guilty*.
(14)   *She* is known *to behave rather badly*.
(15)   *I* happen *to know him well*.
(16)   *John* seems *to take his job too much to heart*.
(17)   *Alfred* appears *to be hungry*.
(18)   *His explanation* was hard *to believe*.

Such discontinuity (traditionally referred to as 'nominative with infinitive') is found in passive sentences (such as (13) and (14)) with verbs like ALLOW, BELIEVE, EXPECT, FIND, HOLD (in the sense of 'consider'), KNOW, SUPPOSE and THINK, in active sentences (such as (15) to (17)) with verbs like APPEAR, HAPPEN, SEEM and in sentences with complements (such as (18)) realized by adjectives (or adjective groups) like DIFFICULT, HARD, EASY, SIMPLE. While extraposition of an entire subject clause is largely optional (compare examples like *It would be awkward to go now* and *To go now would be awkward*), final placement of the predicator and any following constituents of *to*-infinitive clauses is obligatory in examples like the ones given above. For instance, structures like **He to be guilty is believed* and **Alfred to be hungry appears* are ungrammatical.

While end-focus and end-weight are achieved both by means of extraposition and by means of discontinuity, the latter strategy serves the additional purpose of highlighting one of the functions of the subclause, e.g. the subject, through placement initially in the sentence. For example, the speaker gives more prominence to *Alfred* in choosing *Alfred appears to be hungry* than *It appears that Alfred is hungry*.

It is not entirely self-evident that it is the entire *to*-infinitive clause which functions as subject in the type of examples discussed here, and that discontinuity is thus in fact involved. It would not be far-fetched to assume instead that it is the (pro)nominal element preceding the finite verb which functions as subject, i.e. that the subject of an example like *She is known to behave rather badly* is realized by the pronoun *She* exclusively. In favour of such an analysis it could be argued that the subject of a nonfinite clause normally takes the objective case (as in *I want him to go*) and that this is not the case here. Furthermore, there is concord of number and person, not between the *to*-infinitive clause and the finite verb but between the initial element and the finite verb. The type of construction we find is *I happen to know him well*, not **I/Me happens to know him well*, and as subject clauses count as 3rd person singular for concord, this is an argument against a clausal subject analysis. Thirdly, it is clearly the (pro)noun alone, not the combination of the (pro)noun and infinitive construction which constitutes the topic of the utterance.

Semantically, however, it is clearly the state of affairs described by the entire *to*-infinitive clause which is specified by the finite verb. In *He is believed to be guilty*, for example, it is not 'he' but 'he to be guilty' that is believed. In favour of a clausal subject analysis it may be argued syntactically that there are closely related structures in which it is rather obviously the entire clause which functions as a sentence constituent. Corresponding to the passive sentences there are often active sentences in which a continuous TO-infinitive clause functions as the object ('accusative with infinitive'):

(13')   The judge believes *him to be guilty*.

(14')   We know *her to behave rather badly*.

Corresponding to the active sentences, similarly, there are sentences with extraposition in which a continuous *that*-clause functions as the real subject:

(15')   It (so) happens that I know him well.

(16')   It seems that John takes his job too much to heart.

(17')   It appears that Alfred is hungry.

For these reasons a clausal subject analysis is here preferred to a non-clausal one. That the subject of the discontinuous *to*-infinitive clause takes the subjective rather than the objective case and determines the number and person of the finite verb is assumed to be due to the special condition that it appears in the position normally reserved for the subject of finite verbs. The choice of the subjective rather than the objective case seems to be motivated by position rather than function.

Since it looks as if the subject of the subclause has been 'raised' into the matrix clause – note that it displays the defining subject characteristics A through D mentioned in section 3.2.2 – the term *subject raising* is used by many grammarians in their account of sentences of the type discussed in this section.

Discontinuity is occasionally also found in passive sentences in which the predicator of the subject clause is an *-ing* participle, compare:

(19)   *The girl* was heard *screaming*.

(19')   They heard *the girl screaming*.

As the goal against which the event described by *heard* is directed appears to be the event described by *the girl screaming* rather than the person referred to by *the girl*, it is reasonable to assume that the object is here clausal. In this analysis, the subject of the corresponding passive sentence may be assumed to be the discontinuous *-ing* participle clause *The girl ... screaming*.

5.6.2. Discontinuous verb groups

Verb groups are very frequently discontinuous. In the first place this is the case in all *interrogative sentences* except *yes-no* questions with BE as main verb, *wh*-questions in which the interrogative pronoun realizes (part of) the subject and tag questions (in which the main verb is ellipted):

(1)   *Did* she ever *spend* the money I gave her?

(2)   *Isn*'t there *supposed* to be a reading here in about twenty minutes?

(3)   How *would* you *suggest* that I get in touch with her?

Discontinuous verb groups are found also in *negative sentences*, in which the operator is separated from the rest of the verb group by the negative adverb NOT, and in sentences where other *adverbials* are placed after the operator:

(4)   You *have*n't *missed* much.

(5)   Other than the title, I *do*n't *know* a thing about your book.

(6)   I*'ve* never *trusted* hand squashers.

(7)   I*'m* only *joking*.

A much less important source of discontinuity is the *fronting of predication stacks* (cf. section 5.3.7):

(8)   [*Standing* around in the shops] *were* heavily bearded men with long gaberdine coats, wearing thick boots.

Finally, verb groups can be viewed as discontinuous in cases like the following, which involve complex predicators (cf. section 4.3):

(9)   Mary *called* the man *up*.

(10)   Miranda *waited* diligently *on* the Wilson family.

(11)   They *put* her behaviour *down to* lack of confidence.

5.6.3. Discontinuous noun and pronoun groups

While premodifiers are hardly ever separated from their heads in noun groups, postmodifiers are sometimes postponed in order to observe the principles of end-focus and end-weight, i.e. for reasons of *information structure*. Since postmodifying clauses are typically longer and heavier than postmodifying groups, it is mainly clausal postmodifiers which are separated from their head noun or pronoun. As illustrated by the following examples, these may be so-called elaborative *that*-clauses (cf. section 10.1.3), relative clauses, *-ing* participle clauses and *to*-infinitive clauses:

(1)   *The rumour* spread *that the King had been beheaded.*

(2)   Peter met *a girl/someone* last night *who lives in Tasmania.*

(3)   I saw *a woman* yesterday *carrying a dead baby in her arms.*

(4)   *The time* has come *to evict the squatters from our premises.*

In (1) and (4) the subject noun (or pronoun) group is so long and heavy and the rest of the sentence (the part realizing the predicator) so short and light that the principle of increasing complexity would be grossly violated if the postmodifying clauses were not postponed, i.e. these sentences would be completely off balance without discontinuity. In (2) and (3), on the other hand, discontinuity could be avoided without throwing the sentence off balance by moving the adverbial to the initial position, e.g. *Last night Peter met a girl/someone who lives in Tasmania*. But if the speaker does not wish to give prominence to this part of the message, and if Peter constitutes his communicative point of departure (the topic, see section 3.2.2), such fronting would run counter to his communicative intentions.

Like postmodifying clauses, postmodifying groups may be separated from their head noun/pronoun in order to achieve end-focus or for reasons of end-weight. As appears from the next examples, both preposition groups and nominal modifiers may be postponed in this way:

(5)   *The entire crew/Everybody* was drowned *except the captain of the ship.*

(6)   *What business* is that *of his*?

(7)   I pressed the trigger and *a hole* appeared in his forehead *the size of a quarter.*

Postponed preposition groups often denote exception and begin with *except, but, save, excluding* or *apart from*.

Not only clauses and groups but also single words may be separated from the noun/pronoun they postmodify. For example, emphatic *self*-forms (*himself, herself,* etc.) can readily be moved from the position right after the noun to the end of the sentence to achieve end-focus:

(8)   *Helen/She* told me the sad news *herself.*

(9)   *The boys/They* have often made that mistake *themselves.*

The degree of emphasis provided by the *self*-form decreases with distance from the (pro)noun it postmodifies, compare:

(10a)   *John/He himself* read the book several times.

(10b)   *John/He* read the book *himself* several times.

(10c)   *John/He* read the book several times *himself.*

The first of these examples, where there is no discontinuity, is the most emphatic, and the third example, where the distance between head and dependent is the greatest, is the least emphatic (unless the pronoun is pronounced with very heavy stress).

Like *self*-forms, the quantifying indefinite pronouns *all*, *both* and *each* can be separated from their head noun to give prominence to them:

(11)   *The students* have *all* understood what you are driving at.

(12)   *My brothers* have *both* understood what you are driving at.

(13)   *My brothers* have *each* taken a big apple.

In these examples, *all* and *both* are separated from their head through postponement to the position after the operator of the verb group (compare *All the students / Both my brothers*). In the example with *each*, the only corresponding continuous construction is a pronoun group (*Each of my brothers/*Each my brothers*) or a singular noun group (*Each brother*). Interestingly enough, the separate position typically occupied by these quantifiers is the *adverbial* central-M position (i.e. between S and P if P is realized by a full verb, or after the operator if P is complex or realized by the primary verb BE; cf. section 5.5.3):

(14)   The students (probably) *all* understood what you are driving at.

(15)   The students may *all* have understood what you are driving at.

(16)   The students were *all* interested in what you are driving at.

Note that *each*, unlike *all* and *both*, allows adverbial T-position:

(17)   My brothers took a big apple *each.*

The possibility of inserting *probably* between *The students* and *all* in the first example shows that the pronoun does not simply behave like a post-modifying dependent in a continuous subject group.

On the evidence provided by examples (14) to (17), a possible alternative to an analysis in terms of discontinuity is to interpret *all*, *both* and *each* when separated from their heads as *adverbials.*

In pronoun groups we find the same positions for *all*, *both* and *each* as in noun groups:

(18)   *They* (probably) *all* understood what you are driving at.

(19)   *We* have *both* understood what you are driving at.

(20)   *They* have *each* taken a big apple.

(21)   *They* have taken a big apple *each.*

Notice that continuous constructions (as in *All the boys, Both my brothers*, etc.) are not possible with pronominal heads. The only option for the speaker is to promote the dependent pronoun to head in a pronoun group; compare:

(22a)   **All they* understand what you are driving at.

(22b)   *All of them* understand what you are driving at.

(23a)   **Both we* understand what you are driving at.

(23b)   *Both of us* understand what you are driving at.

In all the constructions with *all*, *both* and *each* discussed here, the function of these pronouns is to provide a further specification of the quantification of the head noun/pronoun. An alternative way of offering such specification, especially in spoken or informal English, is right-dislocation, i.e. a kind of delayed *apposition*, where a parenthetical dependent construction is used which is capable of replacing the head:

(24)   *The boys* left the party, *both of them*.
       (cf. Both of them left the party)

(25)   *They* understood what you are driving at, *all of them*.
       (cf. All of them understood what you are driving at)

In this way, *both* and *all* can receive end-focus like *each* (cf. *The boys took a big apple each*). Unlike most other cases of appositional dependents, continuity is only possible if the head of the construction is a pronoun rather than a noun, or if the apposition is clearly marked as parenthetical:

(26a)   *They both of them* left the party.

(26b)   **The boys both of them* left the party.

(26c)   *The boys – both of them –* left the party.

(27a)   *They all of them* understood what you are driving at.

(27b)   **The students all of them* understood what you are driving at.

(27c)   *The students – all of them –* understood what you are driving at.

Again it is possible to view the quantifying expression as an adverbial rather than as a dependent in a discontinuous group.

Leaving quantifying dependent pronouns aside, we turn finally to cases of *internal discontinuity* in noun groups:

(28)   The discovery in 1929 of penicillin has saved millions of lives.

While the subject noun group is not interrupted by another constituent here, the normal order *the discovery of penicillin in 1929* has been changed to give end-focus – in the first of the two tone groups which this utterance is divided into at normal speech tempo – to the word *penicillin*. In noun groups of this type, the two dependents are not coordinated. What we find here is *subordination*, for while *of penicillin* is a dependent of *discovery* only, *in*

1929 is a dependent of *the discovery of penicillin*. This is shown in the following tree diagram:

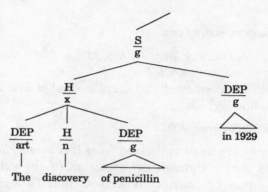

This order reflects the normal S P O A order in the clause underlying the nominalization: *Someone discovered penicillin in 1929*. If the dependent preposition group in the head stack *the discovery of penicillin* is moved to the position after *in 1929*, this head noun group is realized discontinuously. This is shown in the next tree diagram. Communicatively, the effect of such internal discontinuity is the same as that of many instances of external discontinuity. In either case a part of a message is given extra prominence through postponement.

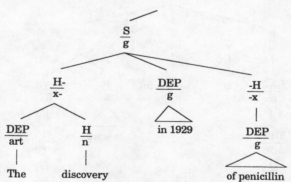

5.6.4. Discontinuous preposition groups

In *wh*-questions and relative clauses, the *wh*-complement of a preposition often leaves the preposition behind at the end of the clause when it is fronted to clause-initial position:

(1)   *What* did you do that *for*?

(2)   My computer, *which* I've had a lot of trouble *with*, is up for sale.

In independent declarative sentences, preposition groups may be realized discontinuously if the speaker wishes to topicalize the referent of the complement:

(3)   *This well* you draw water *from.*

For examples like *Democracy must be fought <u>for</u> every day* containing a stranded preposition, see section 4.3.2.

Finally, it should be mentioned that there is double discontinuity in an example like the following:

(4)   *Kiri* is wonderful *to work with.*

This sentence may be regarded as derived from *It is wonderful to work with Kiri*, which in its turn – through extraposition of the subordinate T O-infinitive clause – may be considered derived from *To work with Kiri is wonderful*. The communicative purpose it serves is to topicalize *Kiri*, and this is done by moving the complement of the preposition group realizing the adverbial in the subclause into sentence-initial position (where it ousts the substitute form *it*). As a result of this fronting both the subject clause and the adverbial preposition group are realized discontinuously, the former as *Kiri ... to work with* and the latter as *Kiri ... with*.

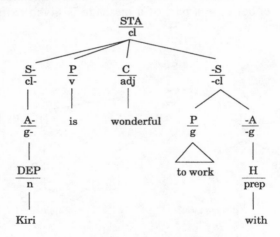

5.6.5. Discontinuous adjective and adverb groups

Adjective and adverb groups are often realized discontinuously in *comparative constructions*. We shall therefore begin this section by examining some of the basic facts of adjective and adverb comparison in English. We operate with three members of the category of comparison: *positive*, *comparative* and *superlative*. There are two types of formal expression: *morphological* (or *inflectional*, or *synthetic*) comparison and *syntactic* (or *analytic*) comparison. The following table summarizes the possibilities:

	Positive	Comparative	Superlative
Morphological comparison	tall	taller	tallest
	early	earlier	earliest
Syntactic comparison	beautiful	more beautiful	most beautiful
	wisely	more wisely	most wisely

A maximal comparative construction consists of three parts: a *comparative element*, an adjective or adverb, and *a comparative basis*. The comparative element is either realized morphologically as an inflection of the adjective or adverb (*-er, -est*) or syntactically as a separate word (the adverbs *more/less* or *most/least*). The comparative basis is the standard on the basis of which the comparison is expressed. This is typically realized as a *than*-construction in the comparative degree and an *of*-construction in the comparative or superlative degree:

(1)   Sally is taller *than I am/than me*.
(2)   Mary danced more beautifully *than Jane (did)*.
(3)   John is the brighter *of the two*.
(4)   Sam worked the most diligently *of them all*.

The sentence analysis of morphologically compared adjectives or adverbs is straightforward:

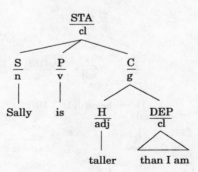

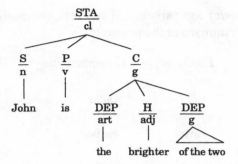

While the *of*-construction is always considered a group, the *than*-construction may sometimes be interpreted as a clause with *than* as SUB:conj (e.g. *than I am*) or as a group with *than* as H:prep (e.g. *than me*).

The sentence analysis of syntactically compared adjectives or adverbs is more complicated and may well involve discontinuity. In constructions like *Sally is more beautiful than Jane* and *Jane danced more beautifully than Sally*, we might simply treat the comparative element (*more*) and the comparative basis (the *than*-construction) as separate dependents of the head adjective or adverb. But there are two alternatives. The first alternative is to group the comparative element and the adjective or adverb together as a H:g followed by the *than*-constructions as a DEP:g or DEP:cl. This solution is parallel to constructions with morphologically compared adjectives and adverbs (i.e. where the comparative element is morphologically 'grouped with' the adjective or adverb). The second alternative is to treat the comparative element and the constructions expressing the comparative basis as a discontinuous dependent of the head adjective or adverb; e.g.:

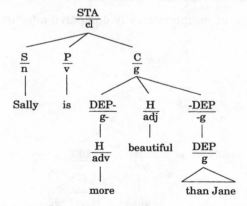

A similar analysis could be postulated for superlative constructions like *Sam worked the most diligently of them all* with *the most ... of them all* as a discontinuous dependent of the head adverb *diligently*.

An argument in favour of treating the construction expressing the comparative basis as a dependent of the comparative element rather than of the head adjective or adverb is that it provides a specification of the comparative element. Furthermore, its occurrence is more directly dependent on the occurrence of the comparative element. Thus we cannot say e.g. *Sally is beautiful than Jane* or *Sam worked diligently of them all*. And if we leave out the construction expressing the comparative basis, its meaning is implied only if the comparative element is present. Thus *Sally is more beautiful* implies e.g. *than Jane* whereas *Sally is beautiful* does not. It therefore seems reasonable to assume that there is a close relationship between the comparative element and the construction expressing the comparative basis, and an obvious way to reflect this in our analysis is to treat them as grouped together in a discontinuous constituent.

Another kind of discontinuity occurs in comparative constructions when another clause function – usually an adverbial – intervenes between the adjective or adverb and the construction expressing the comparative basis:

(5)   Sally is *calmer* now *than she was yesterday*. (S P C- A -C)

(6)   Mary danced *more beautifully* last night *than ever before*. (S P A- A -A)

In the first example the adjective group realizing the subject complement is split into two parts by an adverbial, and in the second the adverb group realizing the adverbial (of manner) is split by another adverbial (of time). These discontinuities are motivated by considerations of end-weight and end-focus, i.e. they are to do with information structure.

If a comparative adjective group containing a comparative basis modifies a noun, it is often realized discontinuously:

(7)   Sally is a *calmer* woman *than she was last year*.

If sufficiently weighty, such constructions may be realized as a continuous postmodifier in relation to the noun:

(8)   Sally is a woman *noticeably far more considerate than Mary*.

We also find discontinuous adverb groups modifying adjectives:

(9)   John is *better* prepared *than his sister*.

Not only comparative forms but also superlative forms may be interpreted as discontinuous in examples like the following:

(10)   Peter has the *strongest* will *of them all*.

(11)   This is the *least dramatic* anecdote *of the ones I've heard*.

In such cases, however, the status of the definite article is problematic: does it go with the superlative form or with the noun?

When the comparative basis is an OF-construction we sometimes find topic-alization of this construction with obvious discontinuity as a result:

(12)   *Of all the boys* Peter was by far *the brightest.*

(13)   *Of the two teams* Norwich were *the more efficient.*

We also find discontinuity in constructions expressing comparison which are neither comparative nor superlative:

(14)   Sally is *as calm* now *as she was yesterday.* (C:g)

(15)   Mary danced *so beautifully* last night *that people began to cry.* (A:g)

(16)   The person who called me was *too busy* at the time *to answer my questions over the phone.* (C:g)

(17)   *So ardently* had he been preaching the efficacy of prayer *that he now silently invoked the name of Diana for every desire that passed through his head.* (A:g)

In examples (14) to (16), the construction expressing comparison is realized discontinuously with an intervening adverbial. In (17) the head and premodifier of the italicized adverb group have been fronted in order to highlight that part of the message, and as the adverbial begins with *so* this fronting is accompanied by partial inversion (see section 5.3.4). In all four examples, the discontinuity is clearly due to factors of weight and balance.

Discontinuous adjective groups are not only found in comparative constructions. Adjective groups containing heads like *comparable (to ...)*, *different (from ...)*, *difficult (to ...)*, *easy (to ...)*, *opposite (to ...)*, *(im)possible (for, to ...)*, *preliminary (to ...)*, *similar (to ...)* and *suitable (for ...)* are often realized discontinuously:

(18)   It falls into a *different* category *from the rest.*

(19)   I don't imagine she was an *easy* person *to live with.*

(20)   This was only a *preliminary* little gathering *to the one planned for the autumn.*

Considerations of weight and end-focus may lead to continuous post-modification instead:

(21)   It falls into a category *very different from the rest.*

(22)   I don't imagine she was a person *in any way easy to live with.*

(23)   This was only a little gathering *supposedly preliminary to the one planned for the autumn.*

6. Coordination and subordination

In this chapter, we shall examine two major syntactic relations more closely than we have done so far: coordination and subordination. We begin by recapitulating some of the basic facts about these two relations (see also sections 3.3.3 to 3.3.5).

6.1. Introduction

In English, as in other languages, linguistic units can be *linked* in two different ways: *subordination* and *coordination*, as shown in the following examples, in which the units linked together are clauses:

(1)   I'll tell him that you called.

(2)   His hair was rumpled and he wore a raincoat over his pyjamas.

In (1) the two clauses have a different syntactic status: the second is embedded in the first, as a realization of its direct object. Subordination is here signalled by the subordinating conjunction *that*. In (2) the two clauses have the same syntactic status. Neither is subordinated to the other and embedding is not involved. Coordination is here signalled by the coordinating conjunction *and*.

Coordination and subordination apply not only to clauses but also to groups. The following examples illustrate subordination in groups:

(3)   I have *formidable enemies* in the Literature Division.

(4)   It's all *quite friendly*.

(5)   He helped an old lady *across the street*.

In the italicized groups in (3) and (4) the dependents *formidable* and *quite* are subordinate to the heads *enemies* and *friendly*, respectively. We also operate with subordination in preposition groups. Thus in (5) the preposition *across* is analysed as head and the prepositional complement *the street* as subordinate dependent (cf. section 3.3.2).

Coordination of words and groups can be illustrated by:

(6)   *Henry and Charles* were talking only yesterday about how *brusque and boorish* he's become. (noun + noun, adjective + adjective)

(7)   I never thought I'd be surprised at anything he *did or said*, but *he and I* had a very odd conversation the other day. (verb + verb, pronoun + pronoun)

(8)   Did your album sell *over or under* 10,000 copies? (preposition + preposition)

(9)   On his side there were *flower arrangements and corny get-well cards*. (noun groups)

(10)   This is *very unfortunate and acutely embarrassing*. (adjective groups)

(11)   What he *has said or may have done* in the past need not concern us at this stage. (verb groups)

As is apparent from these examples, it is frequently words of the same class which are coordinated. In an example like *Jim and I*, we have coordination of words from closely related word classes (nouns and pronouns).

So far we have looked at examples of *binary coordination* or *binary subordination*, i.e. examples with a relation between two linguistic units only. But in both coordination and subordination the number of linguistic units linked together need not be restricted to two. The following examples illustrate *multiple coordination*:

(12)   On our return we were *cold and hungry and exhausted*.

(13)   The woman had earlier drunk what one witness called a "lethal cocktail" of *cider, vodka and Drambuie*.

(14)   Would you like *port or Madeira or claret?*

(15)   I *waited and worried and hoped and prayed*.

In sentences with the coordinating conjunctions *and* and *or* there is in principle no limit to the number of conjoints that may be joined together. In such sentences – where the conjunction is commonly 'understood' except between the last two conjoints – coordination is thus *recursive*: we can go on adding conjoints. Nothing in the structure of English prevents this, but in actual communication the speaker will generally avoid taxing the patience and memory of the listener with immoderate multiple coordination.

Multiple subordination is illustrated by the next examples:

(16)   In *very great poetry* the music often comes through even when one doesn't know the language.

(17)   *Anything overtly religious* filled him with pagan alarm.

In (16) the head of the italicized noun group is *poetry*, and the dependent is the adjective group *very great* in which *great* functions as head and the adverb *very* as dependent. In (17), we have a pronoun group with *Anything* as head and *overtly religious* as a dependent group consisting of *religious* as head adjective and *overtly* as dependent adverb.

As in the case of coordination with *and* and *or*, there is in principle no end to the amount of subordination which can be used in English sentences, i.e. subordination is *recursive*. Here as well, however, massive multiple linking will tend to be avoided in order to prevent monotony and difficulty of understanding due to memory limitations (cf. e.g. *the cat on the mat in the kitchen in the house by the river that ...*), see also section 3.3.5.

6.2. Coordination

6.2.1. Coordination and ellipsis

In coordination it is sometimes the case that one or more words are left out from one of the conjoints. Such ellipsis can be illustrated by the following example (see also section 4.2):

(1)   Tanner is our dean and Stopford our bursar.

As linguistic units joined together in coordination are normally formally similar, we assume that the verb *is* has been omitted between *Stopford* and *our bursar* and that it is therefore clauses which are coordinated:

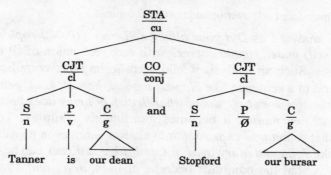

Once ellipsis has been recognized in some cases of coordination, we must decide under what conditions such a zero-analysis is warranted. Consider:

(2)   Henry is very brusque and boorish.

Here there is no need to postulate ellipsis as in (1), for the conjoined units are syntactically alike, both with respect to form and function:

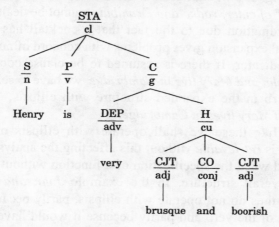

It would not be unnatural to assume, however, that the adverb *very* has been omitted between *and* and *boorish*. If this analysis is chosen, it is adjective groups rather than adjectives which are coordinated. But the example can be expanded even more:

(2')   Henry is very brusque and (Henry is very) boorish.

If such an analysis with three zeros is adopted, the conjoints are neither adjectives nor adjective groups but clauses. The question which has to be considered is now how much ellipsis we should recognize in coordination?

If we adopt a strategy of *maximal expansion*, we end up in a situation where coordination involves only clauses. An example like:

(3)   Did your album sell over or under 10,000 copies?

will then be analysed as *Did your album sell over (10,000 copies) or (did your album sell) under 10,000 copies?* with zero realization of all the words in parentheses. Such an analysis would seem to be more complicated than necessary, and in a sentence like *He was a good, honest, kind, gentle bobby doing what the Met does best, doing what British policing does best, working with his local community*, it becomes inordinately complex. To this we should add that sometimes expansion into clauses is not even possible. While a sentence like *John and Mary lived in Cambridge last year* can be expanded in such a way that the conjoints become clauses, *John and Mary met in Cambridge last year* cannot, for when used intransitively MEET is a reciprocal verb requiring reference to at least two persons. So while we can say *John lived in Cambridge* we cannot say *John met in Cambridge*. For the same reason we cannot operate with ellipsis and clausal coordination in a sentence like *John and Mary are very much alike* with a reciprocal adjective. Note also that e.g. *The woman had earlier drunk what one witness called a "lethal cocktail" of cider, vodka and Drambuie* cannot be dealt with in terms of clausal coordination due to the fact that a cocktail has to be mixed. Finally, maximal expansion gives problems with concord of number between subject and predicator. If there is assumed to be clause coordination in a sentence like *John and Mary live in Cambridge*, we have to select a different form of the verb in the expanded structure with ellipsis: *John (live̲s̲ in Cambridge) and Mary live̲s̲ in Cambridge.*

For reasons like these we shall operate with ellipsis only when the "missing form" is *retrievable* without this affecting the analysis of the other constituents and when the specification of a function without an overt form *clarifies* the overall structure. In the example *John and Mary live in Cambridge* we thus do not operate with ellipsis, partly because this would affect the form of the verb and partly because it would have no clarifying effect. Nor is there assumed to be ellipsis in example (2) above (*Henry is very brusque and boorish*). On the other hand we do recognize ellipsis in an example like (1) (*Tanner is our dean and Stopford our bursar*). Here the conditions just mentioned are met. If we did not operate with a missing form (*is*), the conjoints of the coordinate structure would be syntactically dissimilar. Note also that the second conjoint cannot stand for the whole. While we can say *Tanner is our dean*, we cannot say *Stopford our bursar.

6.2.2. What can be coordinated?

In section 6.1 we showed that clauses may be coordinated with clauses, groups with groups and words with words. Often, however, we find examples of what looks like *mixed coordination*:

(1)   No doubt they think it *aristocratic and very grand.*

(2)   What he *said or may have done* on that occasion need not concern us now.

What we find here is coordination of a word and a group, i.e. of formally different units. Nevertheless, the conjoints are formally similar in the sense that the head word of the group belongs to the same class as the single word: in (1) we have adjectivals and in (2) we have verbals (cf. section 3.3.1 on the use of these form terms). Furthermore, the conjoints are *functionally equivalent*, not only in the obvious sense of being both conjoints but, more significantly, by being each capable of assuming the same function as the compound unit as a whole. In (1) either of the conjoints may thus by itself realize the object complement and in (2) either of the conjoints may by itself realize the predicator in the subject clause. Even in cases where the conjoints of a compound unit cannot single-handedly assume the function of the unit as a whole (as in e.g. *John and Mary met in Cambridge*), the conjoints are felt to be functionally of exactly the same status.

So far, then, the conjoints of a coordinated structure are functionally identical and formally similar. But they may also be formally dissimilar:

(3)   She played the sonata *expertly and with great spirit.*

(4)   This will not explain *the fundamental magic of his personality or why I still have an overwhelming wish to see him.*

In (3) the conjoints are realized by an adverb and a preposition group and in (4) by a noun group and a clause. In order to avoid coordination of unmatching entities, some grammarians might prefer to operate with ellipsis and clausal coordination here. Though formally different, however, the conjoints are functionally identical: in (3) either of the conjoints is capable of realizing the adverbial by itself, and in (4) either of the conjoints is capable of realizing the object by itself. For this reason we shall therefore operate here with formally mixed coordination rather than ellipsis. If we assumed instead that there was clausal coordination, the 'missing forms' would be retrievable without this affecting the analysis of the other constituents, but the resulting expressions would be very cumbersome and there would be little clarification of structure.

We also find coordination of stretches of speech which are neither words nor groups nor clauses:

(5)   My sister *lives in Norwich and works for the council.*

(6)   He might *drop into a bar and down some liquor.*

In example (5) we have coordination of predicates and in example (6) we have coordination of predications. In section 4.1, we introduced the notion of stacking to cope with such examples. Would it be more reasonable to analyse them in terms of clause coordination? Such an analysis would yield:

(5')   My sister lives in Norwich and (my sister) works for the council.

(6')   He might drop into a bar and (he might) down some liquor.

Intuitively this solution is not very convincing, and in some cases it is not even feasible. In an example like the following with *both-and* it is simply not possible to insert the 'missing' words, for this correlative conjunction (to be discussed in section 6.2.4 below) cannot link finite clauses:

(7)   This solution both satisfies our staff and placates our students.

Here we cannot insert *this solution* after *and*:

(7')   *This solution both satisfies our staff and (this solution) placates our
        students.

For this reason we assume that in some cases the conjoints of a coordinated structure are stacks of constituents, i.e. collections of constituents somehow belonging together without constituting any of the basic grammatical form or function types recognized in this book.

Our approach to coordination is thus to recognize ellipsis but to operate with it very sparingly. In those cases where the conjoints are formally non-equivalent but functionally identical in the sense discussed here, as in examples of the type illustrated by (1) through (4), ellipsis is not recognized. Nor is there assumed to be ellipsis in examples like (5) to (7), where the units joined together are not words, groups or clauses but stacks. On the other hand we do recognize ellipsis in examples of the type *Tanner is our dean and Stopford our bursar* and *John likes apples and Bob cherries.* As pointed out in section 6.2.1, the second conjoint could not stand for the whole here, and there is therefore no viable alternative to an analysis by which the predicator has been omitted and both the conjoints are clauses. In short, only in those cases where one conjoint differs from the other in not being able to stand for the whole is coordination assumed to involve ellipsis.

Finally we should point out that the conjoints of a coordinated structure are nearly always *semantically similar*. For clauses to be coordinated they must have a common theme, as in *His hair was rumpled and he wore a raincoat over his pyjamas* (note that an example like *His hair was rumpled and he lived in Cambridge* challenges us to think of a context where 'rumpled hair' and 'living in Cambridge' are thematically related). In example (1) (*No doubt they think it aristocratic and very grand*), the semantic function of either conjoint is to describe an attribute – or characterization – of the referent of the object pronoun *it*. In an example like (3) (*She played the sonata expertly and with great spirit*), where a word and a group are coordinated, the semantic function of either conjoint is to describe the manner in which the sonata was played. Occasionally, however, we come across coordination of semantically incongruous units. This can be illustrated by the following example (see Matthews (1981: 213), by whose work this chapter is influenced):

(8)   He left in a Rolls Royce and a bad temper.

Here the semantic roles of the conjoints are markedly different. Together with the preposition the former describes the means by which the person referred to left and the latter the state in which he left. Such coordinations are exceptional, though, and often characteristic of humorous style. This being so, we can round off this section by stating that the units which can be coordinated always have the same function, nearly always express the same type of meaning and frequently have the same form.

6.2.3. Types of coordination

As pointed out in section 3.3.3, there are two types of coordination depending on whether the coordinator is present or understood: *linked* and *unlinked*. The following example illustrates three instances of linked coordination:

(1)   I never thought I'd be surprised at anything he did or said, but he and I had a
        very odd conversation the other day.

Linked coordination is clearly the normal state of affairs. In those cases where the conjoints of a compound unit are adjectives, adjective groups, adverbs or adverb groups, however, coordination is not infrequently unlinked. The next examples illustrate unlinked coordination of adjectives:

(2)   He was speaking in a low, urgent voice.
(3)   Reason is always apparent to the discerning eye. But luck? It is invisible,
        erratic, angelic.

In unlinked coordination the missing coordinator practically always corresponds to *and*. In tree diagrams and linear analyses such an understood *and* could be represented by the symbol Ø, but this would be redundant.

In linked multiple coordination there is typically only one overt coordinator (see section 3.3.3). Its position is between the last two conjoints:

(4)   They found Guzman vain, garrulous and excessively concerned about his health.

(5)   Would you like port, claret or Madeira?

While *and* and *or* may thus be omitted between the first conjoints in a series, and while *and* may be omitted altogether as in examples (2) and (3), the coordinator *but* is never omitted from a coordinated construction.

Besides being linked or unlinked, coordination can be divided into two types depending on whether the order of the conjoints is *reversible* or *irreversible*. In coordination, unlike subordination, the units joined together have the same syntactic status, and it is therefore not surprising that they can sometimes be interchanged with little or no difference of meaning:

(6a)   Stopford is deaf to Tanner's indignation and Wilson tends to ignore Cook's accusations.

(6b)   Wilson tends to ignore Cook's accusations and Stopford is deaf to Tanner's indignation.

Conjoints realized by words or groups are also frequently interchangeable. For example, the ordering of the prepositions is immaterial in an example like *Did your album sell over or under 10,000 copies?* In many cases, however, the order of the units joined together is fixed. In the first place, coordinated clauses cannot be interchanged if the second describes an event which is subsequent to or follows from that described by the first:

(7)   She slammed the door *and* Philip pulled out from the kerb with a short cry of rubber. ('and then')

(8)   I have forgotten my keys *and* there is nothing I can do to help you. ('and therefore')

Nor is reversal of order possible if the second clause of a compound unit contains a pro-form that refers back to a word in the first clause, or if there is ellipsis in the second clause:

(9)   The new constitution will enable Fujimori to stand for election in 1995, and *it* will give *him* the power to close congress again.

(10)   John likes apples and Bob cherries.

Like clauses, coordinated verbs or verb groups often describe successive events, cf. an example like *He came, saw and conquered*. Here the order of the conjoints is fixed as well. In those cases where other words or groups are joined together, the ordering of the units is in principle free. But reversal of the order in which such conjoints occur may be obstructed by the principle of end-weight mentioned in section 5.2.3. In an example like *This is sad and acutely embarrassing* the conjoints of the compound unit realizing the subject complement cannot be interchanged without throwing the sentence off balance. Furthermore, such a reversal would invite a reinterpretation of *acutely* as modifying both *embarrassing* and *sad*.

Coordination may be *recursive* or *non-recursive*. As pointed out in section 6.1, there is in principle no limit to the number of conjoints that may be joined together by *and* and *or*. Coordination with *but*, however, is non-recursive. Here the number of conjoints is always restricted to two, and structures of the type **I like claret but not port but Madeira* do not occur. In an example like *It wasn't cheap, it wasn't easy, but it's the best solution*, the understood coordinator between the first two clauses is *and*, not *but*:

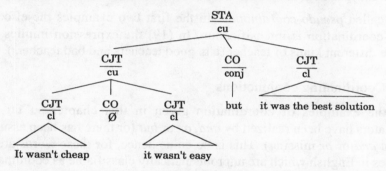

A distinction must also be drawn between *simple* and *complex* coordination. Simple coordination involves functionally unitary constituents: by itself each conjoint would serve only one clause or group function. Thus, in e.g. *My neighbour and his daughter laughed*, each of the conjoints might serve as the subject (*My neighbour laughed* and *His daughter laughed*). By contrast, in cases of complex coordination, each conjoint contains a form stack of constituents (see section 4.1.2) serving more than one function:

(11)   He gave *Barbara a kiss* and *Ann some good advice*.

(12)   Laurence called *my brother a fool* and *my sister a slut*.

(13)   *She sold* and *I bought* the house.

The conjoints in these examples are form stacks, each containing more than one function: indirect object + direct object (example (11)), object + object complement (example (12)), and subject + predicator (example (13)). By definition coordination of predicate stacks (as in *My sister lives in Norwich and works for the council*) and of predication stacks (as in *He might <u>drop into a bar and down some liquor</u>*) is also complex coordination.

Additional information is often added to a clause in the form of an appended construction consisting of a coordinator and a conjoint:

(14)   Barbara sings beautifully, *and Joan too.*

(15)   She is brilliant, *but not her husband.*

(16)   He has threatened to leave her, *or sue her parents.*

Such *appended coordination* typically involves elliptical clauses.

Note finally that we sometimes have coordination of completely identical constituents. In such constructions there is no notional coordination:

(17)   Jack became *more and more* upset.

(18)   They *talked and talked and talked.*

(19)   Well, you know, there are *teachers and teachers.*

This is called *pseudo-coordination*. In the first two examples the effect of pseudo-coordination is intensification. In (19) the expression implies that there are different kinds of teacher (e.g. good teachers and bad teachers).

6.2.4. Coordinating conjunctions

In all the examples of coordination given in this chapter so far, the coordinators have been realized by *and*, *or* or *but* (or there has been assumed to be an *and* or *or* missing). This is no coincidence, for these words are the only ones in English which are unproblematically classifiable as coordinating conjunctions. An important property by which they differ from other linkers is that they are *restricted to the position between the units they connect*. In this way they differ from subordinating conjunctions, which besides occupying the position initially in the second clause can also introduce the first of two linked clauses:

(1a)   The children want a holiday abroad, *whereas* we would rather stay at home.

(1b)   *Whereas* we would rather stay at home, the children want a holiday abroad.

(2a)   The children want a holiday abroad, *but* we would rather stay at home.

(2b)   **But* we would rather stay at home, the children want a holiday abroad.

In those cases where nouns or noun groups are connected, the three coordinating conjunctions differ from prepositions in the same way: *and*, *or* and *but* are fixed in the position between the conjoints, and immediately preceded and followed by them, while prepositions such as *with*, *in*, *on* and *by* can be placed in several positions together with their complements:

(3a)   Patton *and* his army sped northwards.

(3b)   *And* his army Patton sped northwards

(3c)   (*) Patton sped northwards *and* his army

(4a)   Patton *with* his army sped northwards.

(4b)   *With* his army Patton sped northwards.

(4c)   Patton sped northwards *with* his army.

Example (3c) is only acceptable if *and his army* is added as an appended afterthought and even then the example becomes much better if we add *too*: *Patton sped northwards, and his army too.*

Another property of *and*, *or* and *but* is that they cannot be preceded by a conjunction the way subordinators sometimes can, for example *whether* in a sentence like *I don't know where she is or whether she has received my telegram*. The three words also differ from other linkers in permitting ellipsis, for example in *Tanner is our dean and Stopford Ø our bursar*, *Tanner can be transferred or Stopford Ø fired* and *Tanner is highly qualified but Stopford Ø a less controversial choice*. There are only two ways in which the three coordinators differ from each other: unlike *and* and *or*, *but* cannot link more than two conjoints together and it cannot be omitted.

Some linking words are so similar to *and*, *or* and *but* that it would not seem unnatural to include them among the coordinating conjunctions. Among the clausal linkers the conjunction *for* comes particularly close to being a pure coordinator. It can only stand between the units it connects and it does not permit a preceding conjunction:

(5)   Injection is the most dangerous way of taking drugs, *for* the drug goes
        straight into the bloodstream.

Note, however, that ellipsis is not possible in clauses introduced by *for* the way it is in examples like the ones with *and. or* and *but* given above. For instance, the auxiliaries cannot be omitted in the second clause of *Stopford has been hired, for Tanner has been transferred* in spite of the fact that they are identical with the ones occurring in the first clause. Furthermore, the conjunction *for* differs from *and*, *or* and *but* in being a purely clausal linker. While *for* thus differs from the three prototypical coordinators, it is not clearly classifiable as a subordinator either. What this shows us is that the division of conjunctions into coordinators and subordinators is not clear-cut. There is a grey zone with conjunctions which in some ways behave like coordinators and in others like subordinators.

Another linker which resembles coordinating conjunctions is *as well as*, which appears to perform the same function as *and* in examples like *He is clever as well as determined* and *Henry as well as Charles objected*. When *as well as* links nouns and noun groups together in the subject position, however, the finite verb of a sentence in the present tense normally ends in *-s* if the first noun (group) is singular: *Henry as well as Charles objects*. In this way *as well as* differs from *and*: *Henry and Charles object*. In triggering singular rather than plural concord under these circumstances *as well as* behaves unlike a coordinator. In *Henry as well as Charles objects*, the word sequence *as well as* appears to subordinate *Charles* in relation to *Henry*.

Another group of words which resemble coordinating conjunctions are adverbs such as YET, SO, STILL and NOR:

(6)   He felt sorry for her *yet* at the same time relieved.

(7)   I was furious, *so* I didn't mince my words.

While these words are clearly linkers and behave like coordinators in being restricted to the position between the units they connect, they differ from *and*, *or* and *but* in that they can be preceded by a conjunction. We therefore assume that YET, SO, STILL and NOR are linkers which at the same time serve as adverbials (more specifically as conjuncts) within the clause they introduce.

Semantically, *and* is inclusive and non-contrastive, *but* inclusive and contrastive and *or* exclusive and disjunctive, as illustrated by respectively *clever and reasonable*, *clever but unreasonable* and *clever or stupid*. Besides having additive meaning, *and* sometimes appears to signify 'subsequent to' or 'following from', as in e.g. *He knocked three times and went in* and *She felt nervous and took a tranquillizer*. These meanings – which can be made explicit by inserting *then* or *therefore* after *and* – are not expressed by *and*, however, but are due to the conjoints, which describe temporally or causally related situations (and which are therefore irreversible). Similarly, *or* sometimes seems to signal a negative condition (*if not ... then*), for example in *You must put on winter woollies or you'll catch cold*. This meaning – which can be made explicit by inserting *else* after *or* – does not belong to *or* either, though, but is due to the conjoints, which describe conditionally related situations (and which are irreversible here as well). In order for *but* to be used, finally, the conjoints must be semantically contrastive, and (as pointed out in section 6.2.2) the conjoints of any coordinated structure must have a common theme. Both these conditions are met in *clever but unreasonable*, where the common theme is 'mental characteristics'.

There are three pairs of *correlative conjunctions*: *both ... and*, *either ... or* and *neither ... nor*:

(8)   He decided *both* to leave his wife *and* to sell his Porsche.

(9)   Baroness Thatcher is one of those politicians you *either* love *or* hate.

(10)   Women priests tend to be *neither* authoritarian *nor* submissive.

We suggest that correlative conjunctions are analysed in this way:

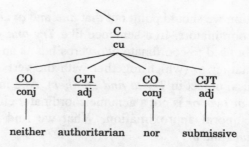

Both ... and and *either ... or* can be regarded as expansions of *and* and *or*, and like these they express inclusive and exclusive meaning respectively. They differ semantically from *and* and *or*, however, in that they give extra prominence to the individual conjoints, i.e. *both* and *either* underscore the bipartite nature of the following unit. Distributionally, *both ... and* differs from *and* in being unable to link finite clauses. For example we cannot say **Both his hair was rumpled and he wore a raincoat over his pyjamas* (compare example (2) in section 6.1 above). Otherwise there are no restrictions on the type of conjoints it can connect.

While *and* and *or* can link more than two conjoints, multiple coordination is not normally found if the conjunctions used are correlative. For example, sentences like *On our return I was both cold and hungry and exhausted* and *Would you like either port or Madeira or claret?* are unacceptable to most speakers. In the case of *either ... or* and *neither ... nor* multiple coordination cannot entirely be ruled out, though. This is apparent from the following authentic example:

(11)   Why did God bestow on *Homo sapiens* such an abundance of emotions?
        What is their biological function? Neither Plato nor Spinoza nor
        Schopenhauer could really answer this.

Unlike *and* and *or*, *but* is not matched by any pair of correlative conjunctions. However, it often combines with the adverb group *not only*:

(12)   Not only was he gifted with a marvellous voice, but he worked on it like a
        trouper all his life.

Here *Not only* functions as an adverbial in the first clause, and it is thus not the first part of a correlative conjunction. Semantically, the combination *not only ... but* is very similar to *both ... and*, for it has inclusive meaning and emphasizes the bipartite nature of the stretch of speech it applies to. But this emphasis is stronger than the one signalled by *both ... and*, and the state of affairs referred to by the second clause, group or word is presented as particularly noteworthy.

In closing this section we should point out that *and* and *or* are not in all cases used as genuine coordinators. In a sentence like *Try and find another*, for example, *and* is not used to coordinate two verbs but as an informal variant of the infinitive marker *to* (which together with the verb and the pronoun functions as a clausal object in *Try to find another*). And in an example like *Hang on a minute or two*, *or* is not a genuine coordinator either but is used to signal a rough temporal approximation. What we find here are special idiomatic uses of *and* and *or*.

6.3. Subordination

6.3.1. Introduction

As argued in chapter 4, constituent structure does not reveal everything there is to say about the relationship between constituents. Our sentence analysis system plots fairly crude consist-of relations but does not really specify the nature of the relationship between, say, a dependent article and a head noun, or between a predicator and a direct object, except by marking the constituents involved as precisely DEP, H, P and O, respectively. On the contrary, dependents and heads, as well as predicators and objects, are often placed at the *same* level in our analysis. While coordination is catered for explicitly in our system by the *compound unit* (with its coordinators and conjoints at the same level of analysis), subordination is often left implicit. Occasionally subordination between two constituents can be shown by placing them at *different* levels in our analysis. Thus, a subordinate clause is analysed at a *lower* level than the main clause within which it is embedded (see e.g. section 3.3.5). However, there is no obvious single configuration for showing subordination between units *within* a group, or *within* a clause.

Stacking (see section 4.1) is no solution to this problem. By definition, stacking is used to indicate that certain constituents are more closely related than others (e.g. in a predicate or in a complex group head). But it does not specify the nature of such closeness relations.

In the following sections we shall look at some of the main types of subordination between constituents, all of which elude our sentence analysis system.

6.3.2. Subordination at clause level

In many descriptions of English grammar some sentence constituents are assumed to be subordinate to others. Very commonly objects, complements and adverbials – but not subjects – are analysed as subordinate to the predicator. In an example like *She left the groceries on the kitchen table* the noun group realizing the object and the preposition group realizing the adverbial are thus considered subordinate to the verb realizing the predicator. In syntactic analyses, the predicator and its subordinate constituents are therefore often grouped together in a comprehensive predicate stack, the so-called *verb phrase*. Furthermore, it is common practice to speak of *verbal complementation*. This term refers to the way in which the action specified by the verb can be complemented – or filled out – by an object as in *kill the enemy*, a complement as in *seem right*, an adverbial as in *live in Cambridge*, and so on. While the units realizing objects, complements and adverbials are thus regarded as subordinate to the verb, the unit realizing the subject can hardly be considered coordinated with the verb. In coordination, typically, one conjoint must be able to stand for the whole, and this is obviously not the case in constructions like *John snores*. What we find here is neither a dependent relation as in subordination (e.g. *quite friendly*) nor an independent relation as in coordination (e.g. *tall and mighty*) but an *interdependent relation*. The unit realizing the subject is dependent on the unit realizing the predicator and vice versa. Traditionally, this relation has been termed *nexus* and characterized as more dynamic than dependent and independent relations. While a group like *the skating girls* can be likened to a still, a clause like *The girls are skating* can be likened to a film.

In some grammatical theories there is assumed to be subordination of a different sort between the sentence constituents. Here the verb is regarded as superordinate not only to the units realizing objects, complements and adverbials but also to the unit realizing the subject. This type of analysis is based on the assumption that the verb constitutes the pivotal part of the sentence. It is characteristic of so-called *valency grammar* (the term 'valency' being taken over from chemistry, where it refers to the combining properties of atoms), according to which the verb has one or more dependents, or valents. A verb like DISAPPEAR takes only one dependent (a subject) and is accordingly termed monovalent; KILL takes two (a subject and an object) and is termed bivalent; and GIVE takes three (a subject, an indirect object and a direct object) and is termed trivalent. This type of analysis is found in other versions of *dependency grammar* as well and also in the theory of *functional grammar*.

Accepting that the verb is the pivotal constituent of a clause (inviting description in terms of valency) is not strictly incompatible with the view that the actual relationship between subject and predicator is one of inter-dependence and that the actual relationship between predicator and object (or complement or adverbial) is one of complementation. This is the position adopted in this grammar.

6.3.3. Subordination at group level

In groups we find three main types of subordination, all of which can be illustrated by the following example:

(1)   By the time he left the Dean's room *the painful erosion of his self-respect* was almost complete.

In *the painful erosion of his self-respect* – in which the noun *erosion* functions as head – there are three dependents, realized by the article *the*, the adjective *painful* and the preposition group *of his self-respect*. The type of subordination realized by *the* is *determination*, that realized by *painful* is *modification*, and that realized by *of his self-respect* is *complementation*. In the example, *the* signals that the noun group has definite reference, *painful* adds descriptive meaning to the meaning of the head noun, and the preposition group *of his self-respect* completes this meaning, i.e. the action specified by the deverbal noun *erosion* (derived from *erode*) is 'filled out' by this group. Let us look more closely at these three main types of subordination.

A) Determination. In English, determination can be separated fairly clearly from modification and unproblematically from complementation, for while a determiner always precedes the head of a group (typically a noun group), the unit realizing a complementation always follows it (except in certain cases of inversion). The words which function as determiners are placed in the position before a premodifying adjective. They generally serve to signal what kind of reference a noun group has, for example definite as in *the girl* and indefinite as in *a girl*. The following forms are used as determiners (see section 10.3): the articles (*the, a/an*), the demonstrative pronouns (*this, that, these, those*), the possessive pronouns (*my, your*, etc.), genitives (*Peter's, boys', the shrewd politician's*, etc.), the *wh*-pronouns *what, which, whose* (whether interrogative or relative) and a number of indefinite pronouns (*another, any, each, either, every, neither, no, some*). In the following sentence there are four instances of determination:

(2)   If *this* lamentable speech was anything to go by, *his* statements must have raised *some* hackles on *the* back benches.

B) Complementation. While determination applies mainly to noun groups, the type of subordination termed *complementation* is more generally applicable, not only to noun groups (e.g. *need for expansion*), but also to adjective groups (*immune to criticism*), preposition groups (*across the street*) and adverb groups (*fortunately for me*). There is a close relationship between complementation at group level and complementation at clause level (see section 6.3.2 above), as is borne out by constructions like *We hesitate to accept your offer* (complementation at clause level), *We are hesitant to* *accept your offer* (complementation in adjective group) and *He noted our hesitancy to accept your offer* (complementation in noun group). Semantically, complementation contrasts with determination by *filling out* the meaning of the unit complemented. Thus *to accept your offer* fills out the meaning of *hesitant*. Typically, if we leave the complementation of a unit out, it can be assumed to be understood in the context, e.g. *We are hesitant* can only be used appropriately if it is clear from the context *with respect to what* we are hesitant.

While in most cases there is only one complement in a group, we occasionally do find examples with two or more complements such as *responsible [to the School] [for keeping the class in order]* and *his donation [of the money] [to the trust] [on Tuesday night]*. Note that if the head word is a nominalized verb (such as *donation* in the second example), each complement represents a clause function in a corresponding clause (cf. *He donated the money to the trust on Tuesday night*).

C) Modification. The third main type of subordination is called modification. As pointed out in section 3.3.1, the nature of the relationship between head and dependent is far from uniform. While a determiner typically serves to signal what kind of reference a noun group has and a complementation fills out the meaning specified by the word of which it is a dependent, broadly speaking a modifier *qualifies* the meaning of its head word, i.e. it attributes a property to the referent of this word. And unlike determination, which is restricted to the position before the head, and complementation, which is normally restricted to the position after the head, modification occurs both before and after the head. In groups like *depraved tastes, freely available* and *only rarely* there is *premodification* and in *a creature of habit, the woman I love* and *young to be a pilot* there is *postmodification*. Simultaneous pre- and postmodification is common as well and can be exemplified by a group like *the new police station that they built last year*. Unlike missing complementation, missing modification is not implied. For example, by saying *the woman* instead of *the woman I love*, the speaker does not imply *I love* but simply assumes that he has offered enough information for the hearer to know whom he is talking about.

D) Other types of subordination. A possible fourth type of subordination in groups is found in cases where two or more words make up a close unit for the expression of a single concept, as, for example, in HOUSE RULES, ˋDANCING MASTER (with primary stress on *dancing*, indicated by ˋˊ, as distinct from ˊDANCING ˋMASTER with primary stress on *master*), DOCTOR'S DEGREE (i.e. a particular kind of degree, not the degree attained by a particular doctor). We consider such examples to be cases of *complex* *lexicalization* or *lexical compounding*. Subordination is clearly present in lexicalization of this kind: in e.g. HOUSE RULES, *house* is subordinate to *rules* both semantically (because the expression refers to a certain kind of rules, not a certain kind of house) and syntactically (since the word *rules* rather than *house* dictates concord: *Our house rules are most reasonable*). Arguably, there is complex lexicalization involving subordination in complex predicators (phrasal verbs, prepositional verbs, etc.) such as GIVE *up* (= 'yield' or 'surrender'), WAIT *on* (= 'serve'), TAKE *place* (= 'happen'), etc. (cf. section 4.3). While subordination in complex lexicalization is 'to the left' in noun groups, it is 'to the right' in verb groups, where e.g. *up* in GIVE *up* must be considered the dependent if we want to preserve the status of the group as a *verb* group. Complex lexicalization is present also in the so-called complex prepositions: e.g. *out of* (cf. *into*), *because of, instead of, according to, due to, in view of, in spite of, for (the) sake of*, etc. But here internal head-dependent relationships are more difficult to determine and are best left unanalysed to indicate the idiomatic unity of the 'groups'.

An important subfunction in noun groups is *quantification* (see section 10.1.4). Quantification is syntactically less constrained than modification, determination and complementation: it is not associated with a particular kind of constituent. Quantification may affect the head noun directly (as in the singular/plural number distinction: *car/cars*). At the same time however, it may affect determiners (e.g. *this car/these cars/a car/some cars*) and modifiers (e.g. *numerous cars*). A number of words are recognized as 'quantifiers': e.g. *all, both, half, many, few, several*, etc.; multipliers (*double, twice, three times*, etc.); fractions (*two-thirds, one-fifth*, etc.), cardinal and ordinal numbers (*one, two, three, first, second, third*, etc.). Such quantifiers are clearly subordinate to the head noun but it is not entirely clear what kind of subordination is involved: most often they are simply treated as a special kind of determiner or as a special kind of modifier (for further discussion, see section 10.3.3).

Finally, as we saw in section 3.3.2, it is by no means obvious that there is subordination in *preposition groups*. Traditionally, in fact, a preposition is assumed always to be accompanied by an overt complement, and in many descriptions of English grammar there is accordingly said to be a relation of interdependence between preposition and complement. In this book, however, we take the view that the type of relation involved is dependence, i.e. that the complement is subordinate to the preposition. We also retain the traditional term 'complement' since the kind of relationship between preposition and complement is complementation rather than modification or determination: a prepositional complement 'fills out' the meaning of the preposition (compare *He helped an old lady across* and *He helped an old lady across the street*). As pointed out in section 3.3.2, in a preposition group the preposition is the head by virtue of being the *characterizing* element of the group without which the group would have been some other group. The prepositional complement, which may be realized by any form type (word, group, compound unit and (nonfinite) clause) without this affecting the status of the preposition group as a whole, is the dependent. Another argument in favour of this analysis is *government*: those English pronouns which have two case forms always select the objective case after a preposition. This can be illustrated by examples like *Give it to me*, *I've received a letter from them* and *She is a woman with whom age doesn't count*. Here the case of the pronoun realizing the complementation depends on the preceding preposition.

Subordination in groups will be further examined in the chapters on the individual groups.

6.4. Markers of clausal subordination

6.4.1. Subordinating conjunctions

When clauses are linked together, subordination is usually indicated by means of a connective word. One way in which this can be done is to use a subordinating conjunction, i.e. a word which does not realize any of the regular functions within the subclause (S, P, O, C, A) but constitutes a linking element. The commonest subordinating conjunction is *that*:

(1)   What is needed is *that* the two governments signal quite clearly *that* they are looking for a new beginning.

(2)   *That* she should do a thing like that is unbelievable.

(3)   My wife is most anxious *that* you should dine with us one evening.

In some contexts *that* can be omitted. This is particularly common when the clause it introduces realizes an object: *We always knew Ø this sort of thing went on*. But there may also be ellipsis where the subclause realizes an extraposed subject (*It is unbelievable Ø she should do a thing like that*), a subject complement (*The main thing is Ø the audience should be curious*) or adjective complementation (*I'm sure Ø this is just a misunderstanding*). In such cases, then, subordination is not overtly marked, but it can be recognized by the possibility of inserting *that*.

In *yes-no* interrogative clauses subordination is signalled by the conjunctions *if* and *whether*:

(4)   I wonder *if* he's got the qualifications for that job.

(5)   It is not known at the moment *if* the intruder had intended to burgle the flat.

(6)   Primary schools will be required to consider *whether* to offer sex education lessons.

(7)   I am uncertain *whether* we should go ahead as planned.

In English there is a fairly large class of conjunctions which are used to introduce *adverbial clauses*:

(8)   I know that the world has always been and will always remain *as* it is.

(9)   I will write it *if* somebody wants it.

(10)   The 80-year-old woman was attacked on her doorstep *when* she answered a knock on her door.

(11)   He wants Anglo-Catholics to be able to join the Roman Catholic Church *while* retaining an Anglican liturgy and identity.

The class of subordinating conjunctions introducing adverbial clauses also includes *after, before, because, once, since, (al)though, till, until, whenever, where, whereas, whereupon* and *whereever*. In British English, furthermore, *whilst* is used as a variant of *while*. Attention should also be drawn to *lest* and *like*, which are particularly common in American English, and which in British English are formal and informal respectively.

    As in the case of *that, if* and *whether*, we assume that the subordinator introducing an adverbial subclause does not realize a regular clause function within the clause it introduces but is a special peripheral element (SUB:conj). We thus analyse an example like *I will write it if somebody wants it* in the following way:

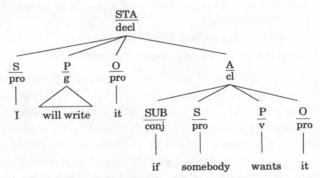

At first blush it is less obvious that the subordinators introducing adverbial clauses should be analysed as peripheral in the clause they introduce than in the case of *that* and of *if* and *whether* in interrogative subclauses. While *that* is semantically empty and *if* and *whether* have highly general meaning, subordinators like *after, because, before, once, since, when(ever)* and *where* are less evidently function words. It is tempting, therefore, to analyse them as realizations of an adverbial in the (adverbial) subclause they introduce rather than simply as subordinating conjunctions. However, if we consider sentences like the following more carefully it appears that this analysis is not tenable:

(12)   She got depressed *because* he left.

(13)   She got depressed *after* he left.

(14)   She got depressed *whenever* he left.

In these examples, it is surely not the situation referred to by the subclause (i.e. 'his leaving') that is explained (by *because*) or located temporally (by *after* and *whenever*) but the situation referred to by the matrix clause ('her getting depressed'). In other words the 'adverbial force' of *because*, *after* and *whenever* is directed towards the matrix predicator rather than the predicator in the subclause. This means that the content of such words ensures an adverbial interpretation of the subclause as a whole in relation to the matrix. There is no sense in which they can be said to function like adverbials within the subclause. The function they serve here is merely to *connect* the clause as a subclause in (adverbial) relation to the matrix and therefore they should be analysed as SUB:conj just like *that*, *if* and *whether*. The difference between all these conjunctions is simply the degree of semantic specificity with which the subclause is connected with the matrix.

6.4.2. Interrogative and relative pronouns

Subordination may also be marked by *interrogative or relative pronouns*. In this case the connective word is *integrated* in the subclause and realizes an object, a complement, an adverbial or part of such a constituent. The following examples illustrate interrogative pronouns in subclauses:

(1)   I've discovered *who* my real friends are. (C)

(2)   The police have no idea *whose* car it is. (part of C)

(3)   Tell me *which* you prefer. (O)

(4)   You're probably wondering for *what* specific reason I've resigned. (part of A)

Here subordination is signalled by the combination of the interrogative pronoun and the non-inverted S P order in the subclause. In the corresponding main clauses there is subject-operator inversion (e.g. *Whose car is it?* and *Which do you prefer?*). If the interrogative pronoun realizes the subject in the subclause, there is no formal marker of subordination, compare:

(5a)   I asked her *who* did it.

(5b)   Who did it?

In relative clauses the subordinating pronoun also realizes a syntactic function within the clause it links to the preceding noun, pronoun or clause.

Besides *who, whom, which* and *whose* the class of relatives includes the pronoun *that* and *Ø* (for missing relative):

(6)   He will be missed by all *who* knew him. (S)

(7)   Ian, *whom* I trusted with the money, has disappeared. (O)

(8)   She talked to the students *whose* parents had complained. (DEP in S:g)

(9)   This is the book *Ø/that/which* I talked to Jill about. (DEP in A:g)

In examples like *I did not like what I saw* and *What I want is to get on with the resolutions, what* is traditionally analysed as an 'independent relative pronoun' (cf. *I did not like that which I saw*) because it has no antecedent. Like the other relative pronouns it signals subordination but realizes a function in the subclause other than SUB.

In tree diagram analysis, subordination of interrogative or relative clauses is represented in the following way:

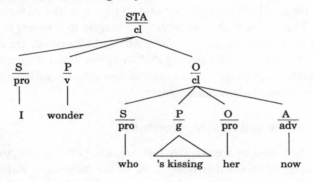

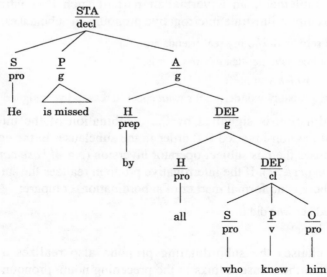

In other words, interrogative and relative pronouns are assigned functions like S, O, DEP, etc. rather than SUB, which is reserved for elements with a purely subordinating function.

In an example like *The village in which the murder was committed has been thrown into a turmoil* the adverbial of the subclause is realized by a preposition group which has a relative pronoun as its complementation. Here it would also be possible to use *where* instead of *in which*. Some grammarians therefore classify this word as a *relative adverb* and assume that it realizes an adverbial in the same way that *in which* does. Other words analysed as relative adverbs are *when, why* and *how* which may be considered replacements of *at which, for which* and *the way in which* respectively in examples like *That was the time when he entered the house, That is the reason why I called you* and *That is how she died*. If this analysis is accepted, it would not be unnatural to recognize *interrogative adverbs* as well. In e.g. *I wonder when/where/why the meeting is taking place* the wh-words could be considered replacements of *at what time, at what place* and *for what reason*, respectively. In e.g. *Do you know how I can get to Ely*, similarly, *how* could be considered a replacement of *in what way* or *by what means* and be assumed to realize an adverbial in the subclause. Note that unlike *when* as a subordinating conjunction (as in *She got depressed when he left*, cf. our discussion in section 6.4.1 above), *when* as an interrogative or relative adverb functions adverbially in the subclause. Thus in examples like *That was the time when he entered the house* and *I wonder when the meeting is taking place*, the meaning of *when* clearly relates to the situation expressed by the predicator in the subclause. In this connection it is interesting to note the difference between the following two (sets of) examples:

(10)   I wonder if/whether he's got the qualifications for this job.

(11)   I wonder when/where/why the meeting is taking place.

If the subclauses in these examples are turned into main clauses we get:

(10')   Has he got the qualifications for this job?

(11')   When/where/why is the meeting taking place?

The fact that *if* and *whether* are dropped but *when, where* and *why* are retained in main clauses indicates that the former are clearly to be analysed as SUB:conj in the corresponding subclause while the latter are clearly to be analysed as A:adv.

6.4.3. Complex subordinating conjunctions

Subordination can also be indicated by a *complex subordinating conjunction*, i.e. a linker consisting of more words than one:

(1)   You're as pale and drawn *as if* you just got out of a sickbed.

(2)   He smiles *as though* he knows the final truth and I can't stand that smirk.

(3)   The apartment isn't mine, and *even if* it was, I couldn't pay for it.

(4)   The police play with us like cats with mice. But *so long as* we remain on this side of the bars, we don't feel like being alone.

(5)   *As soon as* he leaves the house, I start looking up at the ceiling for a hook.

(6)   The diagnosis is made harder if a child's gifts go unnoticed for a while, *so that* frustration reduces his or her academic performance.

Other complex subordinators which are common in English include *in case*, *in (order) that*, *provided (that)* and *on condition (that)*. Like the ones illustrated by the examples above, we choose to interpret these as (complex) conjunctions, i.e. as peripheral elements in the subclause.

6.4.4. Correlative subordinators

According to some grammarians, English has not only correlative coordinators (*both ... and, either ... or* and *neither ... nor*, see section 6.2.4) but also *correlative subordinators*. The most natural candidates for membership of such a class are *if ... or* and *whether ... or*. In a sentence like *We must decide if/whether I should call him or you should write him* the object is realized by two subclauses the subordinate status of which might be said to be signalled by *if ... o r* or *whether ... or* as a unit. In favour of analysing *whether ... or* as a correlative coordinator it might be argued that when *whether* introduces a conditional-concessive clause, it is obligatorily accompanied by *or* and another such clause. This can be illustrated by an example like *I'm going whether you wish to come with me or prefer to stay here* from which the last five words cannot be omitted. The argument cannot be extended to all cases, though. For one thing, *if* cannot introduce a conditional-concessive clause. Further, when *whether* or *if* introduces an interrogative subclause, it need not be followed by *or* and another such subclause. From the first example given in this paragraph we could omit *or you should write him* without making the sentence ungrammatical. In such cases it would be natural to assume that subordination is signalled by *whether* or *if* exclusively and that *or* is an independent *co*ordinating conjunction, i.e. that correlative subordination is not involved. When *whether ... or* and *if ... or* are used, it is typically *stacks* of constituents which are linked together by *or*. If we employ the stack convention and assume that *or* realizes a coordinator, we can analyse an example like *I wonder if/whether she loves me or hates me* in the following way:

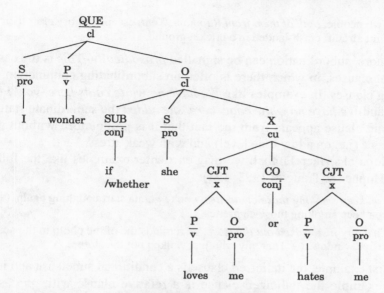

In favour of analysing *if* and *whether* as independent of *or*, it could be argued that they can also be followed by structures which are linked by the coordinating conjunctions *and* and *but*: *I wonder if/whether she loves me and hates me at the same time / I wonder if/whether she loves me but fears me.*

A subordinating conjunction often *correlates* with a following conjunct, though never obligatorily:

(1)   *If* a child's gifts go unnoticed, *then* the child will get frustrated and perform less well academically.

(2)   *Although* my Volvo is from 1985, it is *nevertheless* very reliable.

In examples of this type there is only one subordinator (the conjunction), but the meaning of the word realizing it is reinforced by the conjunct in the following clause.

6.4.5. Other markers of subordination

Subordination can also be signalled by *nonfinite verb forms* or by *zero-realization of a predicator*:

(1)   I watched *her cross the street.*

(2)   It is refreshing *to describe a major American company that is successful.*

(3)   Anyone *doing anything in computers* faces the formidable task of competing with IBM.

(4)   The objects of all that attention are elusive submarines, *widely believed to be Russian.*

(5)   Two people, *both of them from Rainham, Kent*, escaped injury after their light aircraft crash-landed in a cricket ground.

Furthermore, subordination can be signalled *prosodically*. This is the case in comment clauses, in which there is often no subordinating conjunction, and reporting clauses. In examples like *We have no white coats here, you'll have noticed* and *We have no white coats here, she added* the subordinate status of the second clause appears from the fact that it is pronounced without pitch prominence (i.e. on a low tone level) and with weak stress.

In colloquial spoken English we may encounter examples like the following (cf. Hopper & Traugott 1993: 173):

(6)   *You keep smoking those cigarettes*, you're gonna start coughing again. (= 'If you keep smoking those cigarettes, ...')

(7)   That guy *just walked out the store*, he reminds me of the photo in the post-office window. (= 'That guy who just walked out the store, ...')

In the first example, the italicized clause is a conditional subclause and in the second example the italicized clause is a relative clause with *guy* as the antecedent. In both cases, the subordination of these clauses is indicated prosodically through rising intonation. With falling intonation they would be interpreted as main clauses.

Finally, attention should be drawn to two minor markers of subordination, namely *inversion* in conditional clauses (see section 5.3.3) and the use of *what* and *how* in exclamatory subclauses:

(8)   Had he reached the balcony a moment earlier, he would have heard the rattle of the chain and the click of the bolts.

(9)   It surprised me what a boring lecturer he is.

(10)   I'm impressed how confidently you work the machine.

7. The simple sentence

7.1. Introduction: simple and complex sentences

Sentences are either *simple* or *complex*. A sentence is simple if it consists of one clause only:

(1)   The papers blew from my desk.
(2)   Marion is such a nice person.

A sentence is complex if it contains one or more *subclauses*:

(3)   If we are attacked we will defend ourselves.
(4)   Police believe that the shooter was a professional.

In this chapter we take a closer look at a number of issues relating to the simple sentence and its internal organization: referential properties (section 7.2), participant roles of clause functions (section 7.3), voice (section 7.4), polarity (section 7.5), subject-predicator concord (section 7.6) and other types of external concord (section 7.7). Much of the discussion here applies also to the complex sentence, which is examined in chapter 8. The reasons for dealing with the two types of sentence in different chapters are that simple sentences provide a convenient pedagogical descriptive basis and that complex sentences display a number of unique features which require separate treatment.

7.2. Referential properties: situations

Language allows us to talk about all the goings-on, dealings, emotions, perceptions, attitudes, etc. that are part of everyday human lives. With language we also identify things, and we classify, characterize and relate them. In this book, the term 'situation' is used as a cover term for the many different meanings that sentences express. For example, by saying *Jack fixed the old motorbike*, the speaker informs the hearer of an instance of 'fixing' (expressed by *fixed*) in which there are two participants: someone who does the fixing (*Jack*) and something that is affected by this, i.e. something that gets fixed (*the old motorbike*). These components make up a total meaning, a proposition expressing 'the *situation* of Jack fixing the old motorbike'.

7.2.1. Actionality: dynamic vs. stative situations

As human beings we conceive of the world and of all the situations taking place or existing in the world in terms of *differences* and *similarities*. For example, the situation expressed by a sentence like *The old man painted the wall* shares a number of features with the situation of 'Jack fixing the old motorbike': in both cases there is a participant doing something to another participant with a certain result (the motorbike gets fixed and the wall gets painted) and both situations endure over time before they reach a natural endpoint. For this reason it is tempting to say that they belong, at some level of classification, to the same *type of situation* despite the fact that they obviously differ with respect to all the more specific characteristics. Turning now to an example like *Ottawa is the capital of Canada*, we find that here there is no participant doing something to another participant. Nor is there any natural endpoint or result of an activity. Rather, the example expresses a *relation* between two (referentially identical) 'participants': one (*Ottawa*) is characterized in terms of the other (*the capital of Canada*). By looking at a large number of sentences, we discover that it is possible to classify the situations they express (real-world, hypothetical or fictional) in *situation types* on the basis of our conception of their differences and similarities.

The study of situations expressed by sentences is called the study of *actionality*. The different *types of situation* that we recognize are described in terms of the *action category*. Like other categories (such as *tense*, *aspect* and *mood*), the action category is very controversial: few linguists agree on exactly what situation types should be recognized, what they should be called and how they should be defined. In the following, we shall restrict ourselves to certain fundamental distinctions which are relevant to English grammar (such as the active/passive distinction and the use of the progressive verb form).

It is important to note that what we are doing here is to typologize *situations* referred to by sentences, not *sentences* referring to situations. Nor should the typology of situations offered below be confused with a typology of *verbs*. How exactly verbs are used in language expressions referring to situations is a topic dealt with in chapter 9 below.

The primary actional distinction is that between *dynamic* and *stative*. A dynamic situation requires a continual input of energy and typically involves change while a stative situation requires no input of energy and remains the same. A dynamic situation *happens* or *takes place* while a state *exists* or is *true* of someone or something. The situations of 'Jack fixing the old motorbike' and 'The old man painting the wall' are both dynamic whereas the situation of 'Ottawa being the capital of Canada' is stative.

7.2.2. Subtypes of dynamic situations

There is, strictly speaking, no end to the number of *subtypes* of dynamic and stative situations that may be identified for the action category. However, some subtypes are more important than others in the description of the English verb. Let us look first at the most important dynamic ones:

Punctual situations have little or no extension in time and hence no internal structure. The situation referred to by e.g. *He suddenly switched from Spanish to English* is punctual in this sense. Other examples: *She hit me hard on the nose / Stephen dropped the gun.* Beginnings and endings are also punctual situations, e.g. *He started running* and *He stopped talking.*

Telic situations are conceived of as durative (i.e. as having extension over time) leading up to and including a natural terminal point beyond which no further progression is possible or relevant, and without which the situation is not fully completed. The situations of 'Jack fixing the old motorbike' and 'The old man painting the wall' (described above), as well as the situation referred to by e.g. *The student wrote an article about the split infinitive*, are telic. The term 'telic' is based on Greek *télos* 'goal, end'.

Directed situations progress towards a natural terminal point but do not in fact include this point. The situation referred to by e.g. *Sally was building a small garden shed* is directed in this sense: the 'building' activity is directed towards a point of completion but this point is outside the situation expressed by the sentence, not inside as in the case of telic situations. Other examples: *The girl was catching up with the rest of us / He slowly approached the door / She tried to solve the problem.*

Self-contained situations are durative situations conceived of as not having, or being directed towards, any natural point of completion. In other words, they may be terminated at any time without this affecting their completeness. Self-contained situations are the least dynamic and the most stative of the dynamic situation types. Examples: *James and George were sailing along the coast / We were celebrating Stephanie's birthday at my uncle's place / We discussed their predicament at the last meeting.*

Iterative situations consist of a number of identical, or similar, consecutively realized subsituations. The situation referred to by *Jack was knocking at Sally's door* is thus complex: it consists of a number of knocks. Other examples: *Someone was tapping me on the shoulder / The telephone was ringing / Roger kept calling me.*

To fully understand the nature of actional subtypes, it is essential to make a distinction between 'the real world' and 'the world *as conceived by the speaker*', i.e. between objective facts and the subjective way that we think of these objective facts or choose to think of them in a particular context. Actional distinctions are to do with our conceptualization of the world rather than with the world itself. Thus, for example, the situation expressed by an example like *The bus stopped for a red light* is probably best classified as *punctual* from the point of view of the action category (because we tend to conceive of 'stopping' as a punctual situation), but, strictly speaking, it is not punctual in the real world (because here it involves braking and slowing down to a complete halt). Consider also:

(1)   Jack was reading the report when I got back last night.

(2)   Jack was reading when I got back last night.

Whether we choose to refer to a situation of 'reading' as directed (as in (1)) or as self-contained (as in (2)) may have very little to do with the objective reality of the situation, which may well be the same. What matters is what the speaker wishes to make of this situation in his message to the listener.

7.2.3. Subtypes of states

Stative situations, which are almost always *relations* of some sort, can be subclassified in this way:

Intensive relations. An intensive relation involves either a description of an entity in terms of another (for identificatory or classificatory purposes) or an assignment of a property to an entity (characterization). The situations referred to by *Ottawa is the capital of Canada* and *Victoria is beautiful* are both intensive relations. Other examples: *They were in high spirits / Joan is the small girl talking to Bob over there / She seemed very unhappy.*

Extensive relations. An extensive relation is a physical state, condition, location, position or possession obtaining for an entity. The situation referred to by e.g. *The village lies in a dark valley* is an extensive relation in which the village is specified with respect to location. The situation referred to by an example like *Ildiko has a red Mercedes Benz* is an extensive relation between a person and a thing in terms of possession. Other examples: *This factory belongs to Mr Hardcastle / The key is in the top drawer / This box contains all his private papers.*

Attitudes. An attitude is a psychological state (opinion, belief, love, hatred, liking, need, knowledge, supposition, etc.). The situation referred to by e.g. *George believes in God* is an attitude in this sense. Other examples: *I appreciate all her help / She hates all the fuss / Everybody knows the truth about Jim / Nobody likes me / They wanted it all.*

Perceptions. A perception is a sense relation (visual, auditory, etc.). The situation referred to by e.g. *I saw her clearly from my bedroom* is a perception, more specifically a visual sense relation. Other examples: *Charles heard her cries in the distance / She sensed a certain uneasiness on his part / I felt her damp hair against my skin*.

Habits. A habit is the product of a (dynamic or stative) situation occurring so regularly that it is conceived of as characteristic of someone or something. The situations referred to by e.g. *John teaches linguistics* and *Sally smokes* are not dynamic instances of teaching and smoking, respectively (though such instances are implied), but rather characterizations of John and Sally, cf. *John is a teacher of linguistics* and *Sally is a smoker*. The term 'habit' should be understood in a broad sense as including not only personal habits (like *Roger plays the guitar, Victoria would call me every day before breakfast*) but also 'universal truths' (e.g. *The sun rises in the east*) and 'ability' (e.g. *Vera speaks Italian*). Like iterativity, habituality is situationally complex, often implying a dynamic input.

Many verbs have a strong potential with respect to the specific values of the action category: thus verbs like HIT, DROP, CRASH, OPEN, SWITCH, SNATCH, START, STOP, etc. are often used as predicators in sentences referring to punctual situations and verbs like BELIEVE, SUPPOSE, ASSUME, PRESUME, KNOW, etc. are often used as predicators in sentences referring to attitudes. This has led many grammarians to talk about verb classes such as e.g. 'punctual verbs' and 'attitudinal verbs'. Such terminology is misleading. It is important to realize that there is seldom a one-to-one relationship between lexical verb and type of situation referred to. As we saw in the last section, the presence of a direct object after a verb like READ may turn a self-contained situation (*He was reading*) into a directed one (*He was reading the report*). Many verbs which regularly appear in sentences referring to dynamic situations can be used statively about habits; cf. *Roger was playing the guitar* (self-contained situation) vs. *Roger plays the guitar* (habit). And even verbs with a distinct potential for expressing punctual or otherwise dynamic situations can be used to express extensive relations, as in:

(1)   The cliffs *dropped* into the endless yellow sabre of the Chesil Bank.

(2)   The path *climbed* and *curved* slightly inward beside an ivy-grown stone wall. A little beyond them the real cliff *plunged* down to the beach.

Conversely, verbs with a strong stative potential like KNOW may occasionally be used dynamically, as in e.g. *Roger at once knew (= 'realized') what was wrong*. To cut a long story short: the action category allows us to classify situations, *not* verbs. Obviously the choice of a lexical verb is important for the type of situation referred to. But so are a number of other considerations: inflectional form (e.g. the progressive/nonprogressive distinction and the present/past distinction), syntactic relations (e.g. the presence or absence of a direct object) and the extralinguistic context in which the sentence is used.

7.3. Participant roles

7.3.1. Introduction: general roles

The study of the number and kinds of participants that may be associated with verbs is called the study of *valency*. Like the category of action, valency is a controversial subject: there is no generally accepted terminology, and few linguists agree on how many participant roles should be identified and exactly how they should be defined. Strictly speaking, it is possible to argue that every verb has its own participant roles: KILL (killer, victim); OWE (creditor, debt, debtor); etc. However, as with the action category, we examine a number of roles that are important to the grammar of English. Together with action, valency may contribute to a better understanding of the semantics of the basic sentence patterns.

First we draw a distinction between those participant roles which are involved in dynamic situations and those which are involved in stative situations. The typical dynamic situation involves a 'DOER' and a 'DONE-TO', i.e. someone /something bringing the situation about and someone or something passively affected by the situation. In *Jack fixed the old motorbike*, the subject *Jack* is the DOER and object *the old motorbike* is the DONE-TO (it gets fixed). In *The landslide killed the old man*, similarly, *the landslide* is the DOER and *the old man* is the DONE-TO (he gets killed). In addition to these very general primary participants, there are a number of relevant EXTRAS. For example, in *Roger teased the rat with a stick*, the subject *Roger* is the DOER, the object *the rat* is the DONE-TO (it gets teased) and the adverbial *with a stick* is an EXTRA, indicating more specifically the instrument with which Roger brings about the situation.

By contrast, the typical stative situation, being a relation rather than a going-on, involves a 'SPECIFIER' and a 'SPECIFIED'. A SPECIFIER determines the nature of the state (relation) in conjunction with the predicator, and a SPECIFIED is someone/something for whom/which the state exists or is true. In *Jack is in London*, *Jack* is SPECIFIED with respect to the locational SPECIFIER *in London*. In *The girl is exceptionally clever*, *the girl* is SPECIFIED with respect to the qualitative SPECIFIER *exceptionally clever*. Like dynamic situations, states may involve various

EXTRAS. For example, in *Jack was in London last week*, the adverbial *last week* is an EXTRA providing a temporal restriction of the extensive relation.

The very general roles proposed here are syntactically based in the following sense. In active declarative sentences, the DOER or the SPECIFIED always occupies subject position, the DONE-TO always occupies object position and the SPECIFIER always occupies object or complement position. Whatever functions as a subject in an active declarative sentence expressing a dynamic situation is thus conceived of as the DOER; whatever appears as the object in such sentences is conceived of as the DONE-TO; and so forth. Thus, even in a problematic example like *John received the telegram*, *John* is the DOER of the situation of receiving, and *the telegram* is the DONE-TO. In other words, our general participant roles reflect the semantic functions conceptually assigned at a very general level to the primary syntactic functions.

7.3.2. Specific roles

It is useful to operate also with a central system of specific roles based on the following two distinctions: *dynamic* vs. *stative* and *volitional* vs. *non-volitional*. The possible combinations of the values in these distinctions yield the following four more specific roles:

AGENT represents the volitional (typically human) instigator of a dynamic situation (cf. *Jack fixed the old motorbike*).

CAUSE represents the non-volitional (typically non-human) entity bringing about a dynamic situation (cf. *The landslide killed the old man*). Note that an example like *Sally ruined my marriage* is ambiguous, or simply vague, between an AGENT reading and a CAUSE reading of the subject noun.

CONTROLLER represents the volitional (typically human) participant for whom a state obtains for so long as the controller keeps it that way (e.g. *John keeps a gun in the cupboard / Sally wants some ice cream / Roger is in London / Mick Jones is a university professor / John teaches linguistics*).

HOLDER represents the non-volitional (typically but not inevitably non-human) participant for whom the state obtains (e.g. *The village lies in a dark valley / The jar contained some milk / Victoria is beautiful / The sun rises in the east*).

Schematically the central system of specific roles looks like this:

	Dynamic	*Stative*
Volitional	AGENT	CONTROLLER
Non-volitional	CAUSE	HOLDER

To this central system of specific roles we must add an important *default* role:

AFFECTED represents people or entities crucially involved in, or affected by, a dynamic situation (e.g. *Jack fixed <u>the old motorbike</u> / The old man painted <u>the wall</u> / Somebody had beat <u>him</u> up*) or passively forming part of the state description in extensive relations, attitudes, perceptions and habits (e.g. *John keeps <u>a gun</u> in the cupboard / Sally wants <u>some icecream</u> / I saw <u>her</u> clearly from my bedroom / Roger collects <u>stamps</u>*).

Two other specific roles are recognized by most grammarians:

BENEFICIARY represents people or entities for whose sake the dynamic situation is brought about (e.g. *Roger bought <u>Sally</u> an expensive necklace / Mother baked <u>us</u> a chocolate cake*).

INSTRUMENT represents entities or means (typically non-human) used to bring about a dynamic situation (e.g. *Roger peeled the potatoes <u>with his pocket-knife</u> / Sally travelled <u>by train</u>*).

In addition, it is often useful to extend the notion of 'participant role' to more general semantic meanings like the following:

ATTRIBUTE represents three stative subroles: characterization (as in *Victoria is <u>beautiful</u>*), identification (as in *Bill Clinton is <u>the fellow in the corner</u>*) and classification (as in *Mick Jones is <u>a university professor</u>*).

RESULT represents an entity created by the situation (as in *He dug <u>a hole</u>*) or a change of state (*She became <u>a raving lunatic</u> / He got <u>very upset</u>*).

PLACE represents a variety of spatial concepts, such as goal or 'place to' (*I went <u>to Rome</u>*), source or 'place from' (*He left <u>the mansion</u>*), 'path' (*She moved <u>along the corridor</u>*), location (*Jack was <u>in London</u>*), etc.

TIME represents a variety of temporal concepts, e.g. temporal location (*Jack was in London <u>last year</u>*), duration (*He read <u>for several hours</u>*), 'time as a resource' (*<u>Time</u> is running out / We spent <u>too much time</u> on the project*), etc.

CIRCUMSTANCE represents a variety of more specific meanings expressing the background, circumstance, setting etc. of the dynamic situation or some sentence-external relation (as in *He assembled the model <u>with great</u>*

care / *Quite honestly, I didn't even kiss her goodbye* / *On top of all this, she left her children* / *To my surprise, the jar contained milk only*).

7.3.3. Additional points

Note first that participant roles are sometimes ambiguous or vague. In examples like *He fell to the ground*, the subject could be interpreted as either DOER AGENT or DOER AFFECTED depending on whether or not the subject falls intentionally.

Secondly, participant roles may change according to the nature of the state specified by the lexical verb even if the reality of the situation remains more or less the same, which indicates that participant roles are often a question of the speaker's *presentation* of situations; compare:

(1a)   [Mr Wilson]CONTROLLER owns [this house]AFFECTED.

(1b)   [This house]HOLDER belongs to [Mr Wilson]AFFECTED.

In the first example, *Mr Wilson* is the SPECIFIED CONTROLLER of the 'state of owning' and *this house* is SPECIFIER AFFECTED. In the second example, the same reality is presented differently: with *This house* as the SPECIFIED HOLDER of the 'state of belonging to' and with *Mr. Wilson* as SPECIFIER AFFECTED.

It is important to emphasize that there are many alternative ways of handling the question of participant roles in English. We have tried not to make our system too fine-grained. Thus, for example we do not want to reflect the different degrees of 'affectedness' in units to which AFFECTED applies (cf. e.g. *Roger hurt Sally* and *Roger knows Sally*). Nor do we distinguish between participants truly benefiting from a situation (as in *Roger bought Sally an expensive necklace*) and e.g. 'victims' (as in *I'll give them hell* and *She told us a pack of lies*): in both cases we operate with the label BENEFICIARY.

On the other hand, unlike many other systems, we operate with two levels of role participation: the very general conceptual level associated with syntactic functions (DOER, DONE-TO, etc.) and the more specific level reflecting our knowledge of the nature of referents and their involvement in situations (AGENT, BENEFICIARY, INSTRUMENT, etc.).

This characteristic allows us to handle many cases of abstract and meta-phorical use of language. Consider, for example, the following sentences (cf. Lakoff and Johnson 1980: 33ff):

(2)   John attacked Sally.

(3)   His theory attacked the very notion of transformations.

(4)   Inflation attacked the foundation of our economy.

In all three cases, the direct object can be analysed unproblematically as AFFECTED irrespective of the various degrees of concreteness. The subject, however, is to be analysed very differently in the three examples: in (2) it is AGENT; in (3) it is INSTRUMENT (cf. <u>*With his theory*</u> *he attacked the very notion of transformations*); in (4) it may be interpreted variously as the CAUSE of the attack on the foundation of our economy, or as the RESULT of certain developments in our society which may affect the foundation of our economy, or as a CIRCUMSTANCE threatening our economy. In any case, the three subjects represent different degrees of abstractness: *John* is very concrete; *His theory* is more abstract but probably tied to some written exposition (e.g. a book or an article); and *Inflation* is – to most people – a very abstract concept, which may explain our difficulty in analysing it in precise participant terms. At the same time, however, all three subjects (even *inflation*) are DOERs at the more general level of analysis. A DOER is typically an AGENT (as in example (2)) but all sorts of other participants may serve as DOERs (as in examples (3) and (4)). The more a participant departs from our prototypical AGENT DOER by not being *human*, *volitional* and *concrete*, the more we feel that language is used metaphorically: theory and inflation are presented as if they were AGENTS. By thus relating the two levels of role participation, we may capture the more elusive examples of abstract and metaphorical use of language.

7.3.4. Formal links

In this section we briefly examine some of the ways in which valency can be usefully integrated in the grammatical description of English:

A) The S P pattern. There are in this pattern few restrictions on the role of the subject:

(1)   The architects of this affair apologised. (AGENT)

(2)   *The boat* capsized. (AFFECTED)

(3)   *All the guests* stayed on. (CONTROLLER)

(4)   *Little of the original fortress* remains. (HOLDER)

Note that there is often a correspondence between S P constructions like *Suddenly the rock moved* and S P O constructions like *Someone moved the rock*. In both cases, *the rock* is AFFECTED. The difference is that in the S P construction *the rock* is presented as the DOER whereas in the S P O construction, it is presented as the DONE-TO. In the passive counterpart to the S P O construction, *The rock was moved*, the noun group *the rock* is made the syntactic subject as in *The rock moved*, but unlike this active S P construction, it retains its analysis as DONE-TO. Similar trios of constructions are found with verbs like OPEN, CLOSE, SCAN, LOCK, etc. (e.g. *The gate opened / Someone opened the gate / The gate was opened*).

B) The S P A pattern. Syntactically there is a grey zone area between the S P pattern and the S P A pattern because it is not always easy to determine whether an adverbial is optional (as in *She was sleeping on the floor*) or obligatory (as in *She was in London*). And the S P A pattern shows the same range of semantic subject roles as the S P pattern. But while many different kinds of adverbial may be included optionally in the S P pattern (as in e.g. *She was sleeping when I got back / heavily / on the floor*), the adverbial in the S P A pattern is more restricted. Typically we find PLACE adverbials:

(5)   The Ford went *into the East Sector*.

(6)   Turkey will also stay *at arm's length*.

But also adverbials expressing TIME and ATTRIBUTE are possible:

(7)   His death came *at the worst possible time*.

(8)   She was *in high spirits*.

C) The S P C pattern. When examples of this pattern refer to stative situations we typically get HOLDER or CONTROLLER subjects and ATTRIBUTE complements (expressing characterization, classification, identification, or a combination of these):

(9)   The marriage appeared happy. ⎯

(10)   The banana plantation is a reservoir of rats. ⎯

(11)   Schmeichel is the goalkeeper. ⎯

In dynamic instances of the S P C pattern we typically get AFFECTED subjects and RESULT complements:

(12)   Marital breakdown became a commonplace consequence of unemployment.

(13)   She got pretty mad at me.

In dynamic examples like the following (discussed by Radden 1989: 459), the subject receives *double* role analysis as the result of monovalent intransitive verbs being used as divalent copula verbs:

(14)   He was born a slave.

(15)   He returned a new man.

In (14) the subject is both AFFECTED (in relation to the basically intransitive predicator) and HOLDER (in relation to the imposed complement ATTRIBUTE). In (15) the subject is both AGENT and HOLDER (or CONTROLLER). Note that there is a temporal link between the two role relations, cf. the following paraphrases:

(14')   *When* he was born, he was (already) a slave.

(15')   *When* he returned, he was a new man.

D) The S P O pattern. This pattern typically consists of AGENT subjects and AFFECTED objects:

(16)   This guy killed many people.

(17)   Police searched the MP's office.

But it is also the pattern used for the expression of many states with HOLDER or CONTROLLER subjects:

(18)   Two towers support the middle part of the bridge.

(19)   Roger plays the guitar.

With sentences referring to dynamic situations there is a lot of variation, especially in the case of the subject:

(20)   [He]^{AGENT} dug [a big hole]^{RESULT}.

(21)   [The report]^{INSTRUMENT} proved [his guilt]^{AFFECTED}.

(22)   [The wind]^{CAUSE} broke [all the windows]^{AFFECTED}.

In the following examples (from Radden 1989: 428) we find objects serving two semantic functions as the result of primarily intransitive verbs being used transitively:

(23)   The guard marched the prisoners (to the camp).

(24)   The lady is walking her spaniel (in the park).

While the subject in such examples is clearly AGENT (sometimes referred to as the 'primary agent') the object is both AFFECTED and AGENT (sometimes referred to as 'secondary agent').

E) The S P O O pattern. The subject is here typically AGENT or CAUSE, the indirect object BENEFICIARY and the direct object AFFECTED:

(25)   He may have told the Russians everything.

(26)   The book gave left-wingers a lot of inspiration.

A distinction must be made between BENEFICIARIES actually participating in the situation as DONE-TO on a par with the AFFECTED direct objects (as in (25) and (26)) and BENEFICIARIES not really participating in the situation but having the general role of EXTRAS, as in:

(27)   My mother baked *us* a chocolate cake.

(28)   Roger ordered *Stephen* a new radio.

F) The S P O A pattern. In this pattern the subject is typically AGENT, the object is AFFECTED and the adverbial is PLACE:

(29)   The robbers put her in the boot of their car.

(30)   She placed her grammar books on the topmost shelf.

But there is some variation, as we see in the following examples:

(31)   [Mr Major]^{AGENT} put [it]^{AFFECTED} [differently]^{CIRCUMSTANCE}.

(32)   [He]^{AGENT} offered [a beer]^{AFFECTED} [to me]^{BENEFICIARY}.

When the adverbial has the semantic function of ATTRIBUTE, the object receives double analysis:

(33)   [Clinton]^{AGENT} described [the case]$^{AFFECTED+HOLDER}$ [as serious]^{ATTRIBUTE}.

Here *the case* is affected in relation to the predicator but at the same time there is an intensive relation between *the case* and *as serious*. The analysis of *the case* as also HOLDER and of *as serious* as ATTRIBUTE captures this intensive relation.

G) The S P O C pattern. In this pattern there is a secondary, intensive relation between object and complement and this calls for a double analysis of the object in terms of role participation. When the main situation expressed is dynamic, the subject is prototypically AGENT or CAUSE, the object is *twice* AFFECTED and the complement is RESULT:

(34)   [Tyson]^{AGENT} knocked [Bruno]$^{AFFECTED+AFFECTED}$ [unconscious]^{RESULT}.

(35)   [He]^{AGENT} pronounced [us]$^{AFFECTED+AFFECTED}$ [man and wife]^{RESULT}.

The analysis of the object as AFFECTED+AFFECTED reflects the fact that it is affected both in relation to the situation expressed by P (in e.g. *Tyson knocked Bruno unconscious*, 'something happened to Bruno') and in relation to the implied change of state ('Bruno became unconscious').

    In some dynamic cases, the complement is more loosely attached to the proposition than in the examples above (in the sense that the sentences make perfectly good sense even if the complement is left out):

(36)   [Roger]^{AGENT} painted [the wall]$^{AFFECTED+AFFECTED}$ [blue]^{RESULT}.

Before concluding this section on formal links, let us briefly examine some additional points in relation to role participation.

H) Optional adverbials. Optional adverbials may express a wide range of semantic roles:

(37)   The bike was stolen [by the neighbour's boy]^{AGENT}.

(38)   She left early [because of her sick mother]^{CAUSE}.

(39)   Roger broke the window [with a hammer]^{INSTRUMENT}.

(40)   I talked to her [for several hours]^{TIME}.

(41)   [In Paris]^{PLACE} I told her my little secret.

To these can be added the default role CIRCUMSTANCE that covers a multitude of adverbial meanings (manner, degree, condition, background, intention, text-relation, speaker-relation).

I) Role suppression. There is in English a tendency for fusion between the predicator and one or more of the following constituents (cf. section 4.3 on complex predicators). In our discussion of the S P O C pattern we thus noted that there are varying degrees of attachment between the complement and the predicator: sometimes, as in *Tyson knocked Bruno unconscious*, there is interdependence, sometimes, as in *Roger painted the wall blue*, the complement seems much freer. When a constituent is very closely fused with the predicator, both constituents may lose some of their semantic independence. In turn, this may affect the assignment of semantic roles, not only to the fused constituent itself, but also to other constituents in the sentence. Consider first an example like the following:

(42)   I caught sight of her.

Here it would be counter-intuitive to assign a separate participant role to *sight*: Rather, it would be reasonable to analyse *caught sight of* as a complex predicator (= 'sighted') and simply analyse *her* as AFFECTED object.

The S P O and S P O O patterns are especially prone to fusion between predicator and direct object when the predicator is realized by semantically general verbs like GIVE, TAKE, DO, HAVE, MAKE. The effect on the S P O pattern is to make it 'semantically intransitive':

(43)   They had an argument. (cf. *They argued*)

(44)   She made a complaint. (cf. *She complained*)

The effect on the S P O O pattern is to turn it into a 'semantically mono-transitive' construction. GIVE is especially frequent in this pattern:

(45)   She gave her daughter a smack/nudge/bath/kiss. (cf. *She smacked/nudged/ bathed/kissed her daughter*)

(46)   I paid my mother a visit. (cf. *I visited my mother*)

As a result, the semantic function of the indirect object is in such cases not BENEFICIARY but AFFECTED.

Finally, mention should be made of cases where the predicator is realized by a lexical verb embodying an INSTRUMENT (cf. Radden 1989: 441f):

(47)   The assassin *knifed* the President.

(48)   I *spoon-fed* her daughter.

(49)   She *winked* humorously.

(50)   I *mouthed* the insult behind her back.

Many verbs imply the INSTRUMENT with which the situation referred to is usually brought about: e.g. GRAB, SMILE, WADE, STAB, SWEEP, etc.

7.4. Voice

7.4.1. Introduction

In English, a sentence in the passive voice is a sentence in which the realization of the predicator contains a form of the auxiliary BE followed by the *-ed* participle form of the main verb and in which the subject form prototypically performs the participant role DONE-TO (see section 7.3):

(1)   The county prosecutor was finally prodded into action.

The terms 'active' and 'passive' are based on the semantic function performed by the subject form in sentences describing dynamic situations. While this form denotes the active participant (DOER) in an active sentence like *Our boss will kill me*, it denotes the passive participant (DONE-TO) in a passive sentence like *Our boss was killed in a plane crash*.

In passive sentences the DOER may be specified by a prepositional *by*-group:

(2)   No public explanation or apology was made by the Hazelton police.

If this sentence is compared with the active sentence *The Hazelton police made no public explanation or apology*, we see that voice is to do with the way in which the forms referring to the participants involved in the situation described are syntactically related to the verb. In this sense voice is a category of the entire clause, and our account of it is therefore given in the present chapter on the simple sentence. But as voice also involves two different realizations of the predicator (e.g. *made* vs. *was made*), it is simultaneously a category of the verb group, and in this respect it resembles tense (e.g. *makes* vs. *made*).

Each of the four transitive patterns found in active declarative sentences (cf. section 3.2.4) has a passive counterpart. In the case of S P O, S P O Co and S P O A, the passive counterparts are S P (A), S P Cs (A) and S P A (A):

(3)   She might have been saved (by her fellow passengers).
(4)   He was ruled mentally unfit (by the judge).
(5)   They were placed on their backs (by the robbers).

A passive sentence containing a DOER *by*-group is roughly synonymous with the corresponding active sentence. For example, *He was ruled mentally unfit by the judge* has the same propositional meaning as *The judge ruled him mentally unfit*.

The passive counterpart of S P Oi Od is S P O (A):

(6)   The butler was given a reward (by the police).

As can be seen, it is the noun group realizing the *indirect* object of the corresponding active sentence which functions as subject. For some speakers of English it is also possible to select as subject form in a passive S P O (A) sentence a noun group which in the active sentence realizes the direct object:

(7)   A reward was given the butler (by the police).

This type of construction, however, is much rarer than *A reward was given to the butler (by the police)*.

A large majority of passive sentences do not contain a *by*-group, and this type of adverbial is practically never obligatory. Examples like *Elizabeth I was preceded by Henry VIII* and *Henry VIII was followed by Elizabeth I* are thus exceptional in that their final preposition group cannot be omitted.

Passive sentences may also contain complex predicators:

(8)   Her personal effects *had been parcelled out* to her sons after her death.

(9)   The restaurant was surprisingly crowded but they *were waited on* quickly.

(10)   This *must be taken care of* immediately.

In closing this section we should draw attention to passive sentences with complex predicators like the following (cf. van Ek & Robat 1984: 246f):

(11)   Great fun was made of his remark.

This sentence may be compared with *His remark was made fun of*, which behaves like (10) in that its subject is realized by the form which in the corresponding active sentence functions as object of the complex predicator: *People [made fun of] [his remark]*. If the noun of a complex predicator has a pre-head dependent (a quantifier or a modifier), as in *People [made great fun of] [his remark]*, however, it is this noun which together with its pre-head dependent realizes the subject of the passive sentence, as in (11). Other examples illustrating this difference are *You have been taken advantage of* and *Little advantage has been taken of this opportunity*.

7.4.2. Functions of the passive

The passive provides a systematic means of choosing another participant than DOER as starting-point for the message without departing from subject-first constituent order (see Johansson & Lysvåg 1986: 99 and section 7.3 above). It should be recalled that through fronting of objects, complements and adverbials we also select another participant than DOER as starting-point, as illustrated by *That story I will tell you another time, Chris Waddle his name is* and *Here comes the bus* respectively. But in such cases of fronting the preferred subject-first order is not retained.

In other words, the use of the passive vs. active voice in English is largely determined by the way the speaker wishes to organize his message, i.e. is to do with information structure. In a passive sentence like *Tottenham were beaten by Arsenal*, where the participant AFFECTED DONE-TO is placed initially, it is this participant (*Tottenham*) and not AGENT DOER (*Arsenal*) which constitutes the speaker's communicative point of departure.

A main reason for choosing the passive voice is thus *thematization* (or topicalization, see sections 3.2.2 and 5.2.3): a form performing the participant role DONE-TO is placed initially – where it realizes the subject – in order to make it the theme (or topic) of the message. The passive sentence *Tottenham were beaten by Arsenal* differs from the corresponding active sentence in that it is a statement 'about' Tottenham, not Arsenal. While the two sentences have the same propositional meaning and the same illocutionary force, they differ with respect to *thematic meaning*. Thematic meaning has been defined as "what is communicated by the way in which a speaker or writer organizes the message, in terms of ordering, focus and emphasis" (Leech 1981: 19) and shown primarily to involve choice between alternative syntactic constructions.

A second main reason for selecting the passive voice is *to avoid mentioning the DOER* participating in the situation described. This is illustrated by the following example, which simultaneously illustrates thematization in that it is a text 'about' a specific person:

(1)   Evander Jones is a war veteran, *was awarded* a Purple Heart, honorably *discharged* at the end of the war. Nine years ago he *was convicted* of first-degree murder in a drugstore holdup and *sentenced* to death.

By means of the passive the speaker is at liberty not to provide information which has to be provided in active sentences. As DOER is often unknown, irrelevant, unimportant or can be inferred from the linguistic or situational context, this makes the passive an extremely useful construction. In (1) it saves the sender the trouble of specifying who awarded Evander Jones a Purple Heart, discharged him, convicted him and sentenced him.

As pointed out in section 5.2.3, the organization of a message often reflects a division between *given and new information*, and the choice of the passive may also be due to a wish to proceed from given information:

(2)   The front of the station waggon was crushed like an accordion by a big boulder.

This principle obviously cannot apply to sentences containing new information only, as illustrated by *Residents have drawn up and signed a petition* and *A petition has been drawn up and signed by residents* in which there is no given material to proceed from.

The passive may also be selected to obtain *end-focus* or *end-weight*:

(3)   The last cup final was won by Newcastle.

(4)   The hearing was undercut by Edward's refusal to testify and Thiel's obvious reluctance to provide jurors with information.

In narrative, the passive may be selected in order to *retain the same subject* in successive clauses. In this way the presentation of new before given information is avoided. The selection of the passive here may also be connected with a wish to avoid mentioning the DOER or with the principle of end-weight:

(5)   He demanded to speak to her but was refused.

(6)   The case received a good deal of publicity locally and was taken up immediately by the state branch of the ACLU.

Finally it should be mentioned that passives may be motivated by a wish on the part of the speaker to *avoid self-reference* and come across impersonally:

(7)   Enough has been said above about the implications of the Faculty's announcement for the future of our Ph.D. programme.

In scientific English, where it is typically what happens which is of interest rather than who makes it happen, passive constructions (without DOER *by*-groups) tend to be more frequent than in other registers of English. This usage can be illustrated by the following example (quoted from *Collins Cobuild English Grammar* 1990: 404):

(8)   Food *is put* in jars, the jars and their contents *are heated* to a temperature which *is maintained* long enough to ensure that all bacteria, moulds and viruses *are destroyed*.

7.4.3. Extended use of the passive

As we have seen, the voice category involves a regular correspondence between a transitive construction with a DOER subject, an active predicator and a DONE-TO object and an intransitive construction with a DONE-TO subject, a passive predicator and an optional DOER *by*-group:

(1)   John caught the rat.

(2)   The rat was caught (by John).

The members of the voice category are thus typically alternative syntactic expressions of dynamic situations. In this section we examine two extensions of this basic model.

A) Sentences describing stative situations. The most important extension of the passive in English concerns sentences describing *stative situations*. Active transitive sentences of this kind are normally unmatched by passive sentences. This can be illustrated by the following examples:

(3)   Ildiko has a red Mercedes Benz. (extensive relation)
(4)   She hates all the fuss. (attitude)
(5)   I felt her damp hair against my skin. (perception)
(6)   Roger collects stamps. (habit)

As pointed out in section 7.2.3, stative situations are almost always *relations* of some sort, i.e. the general participant roles involved are not DOER and DONE-TO but SPECIFIED and SPECIFIER. Now, in a number of cases the passive may be extended to sentences describing stative situations and in which the subject form is AFFECTED SPECIFIER. The situational subtypes involved are *attitudes* and *perceptions*:

(7)   She is feared and resented for her outspokenness.
(8)   This rumour is widely believed.
(9)   She's been seen at night in neighbourhoods unsafe for solitary women.
(10)   A shot was heard in the dark.

A possible reason why such passive sentences are found is that the situations they describe are not entirely stative. For example, the situations described by (7) through (10) require a certain input of energy (see section 7.2.1), like those described by active sentences such as *People in the neighbourhood believe this rumour* (attitude) and *Several witnesses have seen her at that hour* (perception). But even where attitudes or perceptions are involved, the passive does not have free play, as illustrated by (4) and (5). This particularly goes for sentences describing attitudes. For example, *John believes the rumour* – in which the SPECIFIED is identified very precisely – can hardly be said to have a natural passive parallel. In sentences describing perceptions – and in which the SPECIFIED is identified precisely – the passive is sometimes acceptable and sometimes problematic or unacceptable. While e.g. *Sally was seen by John* can hardly be ruled out as an alternative to *John saw Sally*, a sentence like *John smelled the flowers* appears to be unmatched by any passive sentence.

The passive is particularly frequent in stative examples like the following:

(11)   They were assumed to be dead.
(12)   Andy was considered unfit for fight.
(13)   Clyde is known by everybody as a good swimmer.

In these examples, the constituent in subject position receives a double participant role analysis. In (11), which is a 'nominative with infinitive' (cf. section 5.6.1), *They* is not simply SPECIFIER AFFECTED in relation to the attitudinal state of 'assuming' but also, at a secondary level, SPECIFIED HOLDER of the ATTRIBUTE *dead* (cf. section 7.3). And in (12) and (13), *Andy* and *Clyde* receive a similar analysis.

Before proceeding to another passive extension, we should draw attention to sentences like *Her dress touched the ground*, which has no passive parallel, and *The intruders haven't touched the merchandise*, which is matched by *The merchandise hasn't been touched by the intruders* (see Huddleston 1984: 439). The first of these describes a stative situation of the subtype extensive relations, so here the passive is regularly ruled out. The second, on the other hand, describes a dynamic situation involving the participant roles DOER and DONE-TO, so here the passive is regularly permitted. What the examples show is that the same lexeme (TOUCH) may be used for the description of different situations. Other verbs behaving in this way are HAVE and POSSESS. Normally they are ruled out in passive constructions, but when used in sentences describing dynamic situations they are permitted, as illustrated by *Cheese can be had in the store across the street* and *He is possessed by demons*.

B) Sentences with 'stranded' prepositions. Another extended use of the passive can be illustrated by examples like the following:

(14)   The bed has been slept in.
(15)   Their house hasn't been lived in for a long time.

It seems most reasonable to assume that these examples do not contain prepositional predicators, i.e. predicators which in active sentences are followed by objects. There is no clear semantic fusion between verb and preposition, and the preposition is not the only one associated with the verb (cf. section 4.3.2). What we have here therefore appear to be passive sentences with a stranded preposition matched by *intransitive* active sentences. For example, the nearest active parallel of (14) is *Someone has slept in the bed*, which can only be classified as an S P A construction. In such cases, the subject of the passive sentence corresponds not to an object but to the prepositional complement in the adverbial of the active sentence.

7.4.4. Voice restrictions

So far we have established that transitive sentences in the active voice are often matched by intransitive sentences in the passive voice, and vice versa (e.g. *The cat chased the mouse : The mouse was chased by the cat*). Because of this highly regular pattern, it has often been assumed that there is a fixed, automatic correspondence between active and passive sentences. However, this view of the voice category is too simplistic. A number of important restrictions apply to both active and passive constructions.

A) Passives without corresponding actives. In the large majority of cases where a passive sentence contains no DOER *by*-group, there is no specific corresponding active sentence. In *The county prosecutor was finally prodded into action*, for example, we do not know what form the subject of the corresponding active sentence is realized by (*somebody? something? people in the community?*). The subject form may be recoverable from the *situational* context, but in very many instances it cannot be recovered from the *linguistic* context. In some cases, furthermore, it is virtually impossible to supply a corresponding active construction with a subject form at all: e.g. *Clyde was known locally as a very good swimmer*.

Passives without corresponding actives are also found where a small group of specific verbs are involved. For example, sentences with BE *born*, like *Shakespeare was born in 1564*, have no active parallels. When followed by *to*-infinitive constructions, similarly, SAY and SEE are passive only: while we can say e.g. *She is said to be very rich* and *She was seen to leave the house* (with discontinuously realized subject clauses, see section 5.6.1), we cannot say **They say her to be very rich* and **They saw her to leave the house* (though the latter becomes acceptable if the infinitive marker is removed). What we find here are nominative with infinitive passive sentences unmatched by accusative with infinitive active sentences (cf. section 5.6.1). Attention should also be drawn to nominative with infinitive constructions with BE *rumoured* and BE *reputed* like *She is rumoured to have shot him* and *He is reputed to be very rich*. Again there are no active counterparts and a *by*-group cannot be inserted. Finally it should be mentioned that a number of verbs are largely though not wholly restricted to passive sentences. This goes for ACCLAIM, SCHEDULE and phrasal verbs like BOWL *over* (in the sense of 'surprise') and TAKE *aback* (e.g. *Our next meeting is scheduled for Monday* and *I was completely taken aback by her behaviour*).

Consider next an example of the following type:

(1)   Princeton has been visited by Einstein.

Here there is no corresponding active sentence either, for **Einstein has visited Princeton* is normally unacceptable if pronounced with unmarked prosody, i.e. with nuclear stress on *Princeton*. The reason for this is that it would be a sentence 'about' Einstein, and in English the present perfect cannot normally be used if the subject form realizing the topic (or theme) refers to a deceased person. If *Einstein* is uttered with nuclear stress and *Princeton* with weak stress, the active sentence is acceptable, for by means of such marked prosody the speaker indicates that the former word constitutes the comment and the latter (part of) the topic.

B) Actives without corresponding passives. In the first place, restrictions on the passive may be of a *formal* nature. If an active sentence combines the progressive marker BE + *-ing* with a modal verb or/and the perfect marker HAVE + *-ed* – as in *The cat must be chasing the mouse, The cat has been chasing the mouse* and *The cat must have been chasing the mouse* – a corresponding passive sentence would contain two nonfinite forms of BE. Such a combination is decidedly rare: *?The mouse must be being chased by the cat, ?The mouse has been being chased by the cat, ?The mouse must have been being chased by the cat.* In those cases where the perfect occurs, it may be added, speakers nearly always match a progressive active sentence with a nonprogressive passive sentence, that is, they select e.g. *The mouse has been chased by the cat* and *The mouse must have been chased by the cat* instead of *The mouse has been being chased by the cat* and *The mouse must have been being chased by the cat.* Very occasionally, however, one does come across sentences with two nonfinite forms of BE and in some cases even sentences with four auxiliaries (see section 3.2.1 on the extreme rareness of this):

(2)   Not all instances of a given strategy *may be being used* to do politeness.

(3)   ... another £98m was paid direct by absent parents to their former parents. Much of that *could* well also *have been being paid* before April last year, Mr Field argued.

Though passive sentences with two nonfinite forms of BE thus cannot be ruled out, they are so infrequent that it is reasonable to speak of a restriction on the passive voice here. And particularly perfect progressive forms in the passive are very rare indeed.

With respect to *sentence type*, it should be mentioned that the passive occurs in declarative sentences, interrogative sentences (e.g. *Has a public apology been made?*) and exclamatory sentences (e.g. *How elegantly I'm received!*) but that it is heavily restricted in *imperative* sentences, which are typically exhortations to the addressee to act. Only in fixed expressions like *Please be seated* and in those cases where the hearer is ordered or advised to avoid becoming the target of an action, as in *Don't be taken in by that scoundrel,* do we find imperative sentences in the passive voice.

Constraints on the passive may also be due to the nature of the *object* of an active sentence (see e.g. Johansson & Lysvåg (1986: 103ff), who give a detailed account of such constraints). If the object is *cognate,* i.e. if the noun realizing its head is derived from the verb preceding it as in *live a good life* and *sleep the sleep of the just*, the passive voice is normally ruled out. Nor do fused P O constructions like *take a bath* and *have a smoke* have passive counterparts. Furthermore, if there is *coreference* between the subject and object forms, the passive voice is usually also excluded. For example, sentences with reflexive or reciprocal object pronouns like *He shot himself* and *We hate each other* have no passive counterparts. As reference is here made to the same person(s), there is no thematic reason why an alternative arrangement should be preferred.

Restrictions on the passive may also be due to the fact that the object of a transitive (complex) sentence is realized by a *clause*. As illustrated by e.g. *That he is clever is known by all his friends and colleagues* the passive is not impossible here. But most sentences with objects realized by finite clauses have no natural passive counterparts. Only by means of extraposition – which secures end-weight – is it possible to match an example like *The public believe that there will be an election* with a passive: *It is believed by the public that there will be an election* (see section 5.2.3 on extraposition and end-weight). In those cases where the object of an active sentence is realized by a *nonfinite* clause, the passive is heavily restricted too. For example, sentences like *I would like to visit you, I don't like interrupting you* and *I would like you to visit me* are unmatched by passive sentences.

In those cases where the predicator of an active sentence is realized by a *reciprocal verb*, such as MARRY, EQUAL, MEET and RESEMBLE, there is usually no corresponding passive sentence (see Huddleston 1984: 440). Here there is little need for the passive, for if the speaker wishes to thematize the entity referred to by the object form, all she needs to do is to interchange this form with the subject form. Instead of saying *John married/met/resembles Mary* she can simply say *Mary married/met/resembles John*. This thematic strategy is not available in a case like *John resembles a poodle* where the object form refers to a category. Note also examples like *Tyson has only been equalled by one fighter* and *Mary was met by John in the airport*, which illustrate that these verbs are not completely ruled out in passive sentences.

Attention should also be drawn to sentences which contain both a *negative element* and one or more so-called *nonassertive forms* (i.e. forms typically restricted to negative and interrogative sentences like *ever, any, either* and *yet*). For example, sentences like *The committee hasn't accomplished anything* and *She hasn't ever kissed anyone* are unmatched by passive sentences composed of the same words, as shown by the ungrammaticality of *Anything hasn't been accomplished by the committee* and *Anyone hasn't ever been kissed by her*. Here the nearest passive constructions are *Nothing has been accomplished by the committee* and *No one has ever been kissed by her*. We return to the ordering of negative elements and nonassertive forms in section 7.5 below.

Consider finally examples like the following:

(4a)   Many arrows didn't hit the target.

(5a)   We won't do the job.

Here it is easy enough to construct the following passive sentences:

(4b)   The target wasn't hit by many arrows.

(5b)   The job won't be done by us.

It will be noticed, however, that the *propositional meaning* of the passive sentences is different for each pair from that of the active sentences. In (4a) and (4b) this is due to the semantic effect of negation (cf. section 7.5 below): by means of (4a) – but not (4b) – the speaker may describe a situation where the target was in fact hit by many arrows, for example 50 out of 100. Though many missed, many others didn't. In (5a) and (5b) the difference in meaning is due to the *modal verb*. In (5a) *won't* means 'are unwilling to' or 'refuse to', but in (5b) it will in most situations be understood to signify a prediction of a future event. In other words, (un)willingness is not involved here.

7.4.5. Nonfinite passives, GET-passives and notional 'passives'

In complex sentences – which we have chosen to touch on occasionally to confine our discussion of the passive to one chapter – the predicator of a subordinate passive clause is often *nonfinite* (see section 3.2.1):

(1)   What the boy had done now – or failed to do – Lee hoped not *to be told*.

(2)   A few days after *being released* from jail he disappeared.

(3)   Nowhere in this place could she move among people who knew her without *being critically observed, assessed, commented upon*.

As appears from (1) through (3), nonfinite passive verb groups are either *infinitive* or *-ing participle* constructions and, in addition to *to be* + V + *-ed* and *being* + V + *-ed*, we also find the perfect forms *to have been* + V + *-ed* and *having been* + V + *-ed*.

Vacillation between passive and active occurs after the main verbs BE, NEED, DESERVE and WANT, as in *There is no time to lose/to be lost*, *It needs doing/to be done*, *She deserves punishing/to be punished* and *Your aspidistra wants watering/to be watered*. Note in this connection examples with REQUIRE and BEAR like *My car requires servicing* and *This does not bear repeating*; although the active form here also has passive meaning, only the active voice is possible.

In section 7.4.1 we stated that in passives the predicator is realized by a form of the auxiliary BE followed by an *-ed* participle form of the main verb. It should be added, though, that the predicator of a subordinate passive clause is sometimes realized by an *-ed* participle form exclusively:

(4)   Lydia knew herself *watched*.

(5)   We saw Denmark *beaten* by Spain.

This type of construction – in which *being* could be inserted at the beginning of the nonfinite predicator – is restricted to those cases where the finite predicator is realized by a small group of verbs, such as KNOW, SEE, WATCH, HEAR and WANT (see Huddleston 1984: 444). Attention should also be drawn to passives without BE like the following:

(6)   *Considered* unqualified for the job, she was asked to leave on the spot.

Note that *being* could be inserted here as well. Participle *-ed* clauses are not invariably passive, it should be added. For example, the subclause of a sentence like *Escaped from prison, the convict immediately contacted his old partners in crime* is clearly active (*Escaped* = *Having escaped*).

Another case in which BE is absent from a passive sentence occurs where it is a form of GET which precedes the *-ed* participle:

(7)   Dreyfus got hit on the head with a rake.

(8)   Denmark got beaten by Spain.

A GET-passive typically serves to express that the referent of the subject form passes from one state to another, as in *The thief got caught in the end*. This appears to be due to the meaning of GET, which has been described as "arrive at a resultant state" (Palmer 1987: 89). Consequently, there are many instances where GET cannot replace BE. While e.g. *Denmark were beaten by Spain* and *Denmark got beaten by Spain* are equally acceptable, the finite verb cannot be replaced by *got* in examples like *A public hearing was held* and *Through the spring they were often seen together in Yewville*.

GET-passives differ from BE-passives in that an element of initiative or responsibility is often ascribed to the referent of the subject form, as illustrated by *Malcolm got promoted/arrested* (see Huddleston 1984: 445). This obviously only applies to those cases where such a referent is human, but GET-passives like *The jug got broken* in which the referent of the subject form is non-human are relatively rare. Note in this connection the possibility of using GET-passives in the imperative: *Get lost! / Get (yourself) invited to the meeting* (cf. Halliday 1994: 76).

In some contexts, the GET-passive has the advantage over the BE-passive that it is unambiguous. In examples like *The jug got broken* and *They got married* it can only be dynamic situations which are described. On the other hand, *The jug was broken* and *They were married* can refer either to a dynamic situation or a state. In the former case they are passive S P sentences but in the latter they are active S P C sentences in which the complement is realized as an adjectival participle (see section 7.4.6 below).

In BrE, GET-passives are relatively infrequent and restricted to colloquial style. In AmE, according to Granger 1983: 235, they are becoming very common among young people, particularly males and blacks.

In section 7.4.2 we pointed out that the passive provides a systematic means of choosing another participant than DOER as starting-point for the message (thematization) and that it permits the speaker to avoid mentioning the DOER participating in the situation described. Instead of saying *Somebody opened the door* we can thus say *The door was opened*. A fairly large class of verbs also appear in *intransitive active* sentences: *The door opened*. As this is semantically similar to the (syntactic) passive, it is sometimes termed the *notional passive*. If *The door opened* is compared with *Somebody opened the door*, we see that conversion from transitive to intransitive is accompanied by thematization of *the door* and that *somebody* is not only gone but also incapable of appearing in a *by*-preposition group. As pointed out in section 7.3.4 [A], however, *The door opened* differs from *The door was opened* in that the participant chosen as starting-point for the message is not DONE-TO but DOER. By means of the intransitive construction the speaker presents the situation as if the subject is DOER while at the same time being aware that it cannot do this of its own accord. What is similar to the two constructions, though, is that there is no prepositional *by*-group and that the specific participant role performed by the subject is AFFECTED. Although the semantics of the two constructions is not the same, we are thus likely to understand them in terms of similar situations.

The verbs found in notionally 'passive' sentences will here be called *middle verbs*. Such verbs can take the same form as their object or subject, in transitive and intransitive sentences respectively. As the intransitive sentences involved are both (syntactically) active and passive, middle verbs involve *trios* of constructions, as illustrated by *Somebody opened the door*, *The door was opened* and *The door opened* (see section 7.3.4 [A]).

The intransitive use of middle verbs in examples like *The door won't lock*, *Sugar dissolves in water*, *The shop has closed* and *This stanza doesn't scan* is lexically restricted, but the class of middle verbs in English is by no means a small one (see *Collins Cobuild English Grammar* 1990: 155ff). In addition to verbs like OPEN, CLOSE, LOCK, BREAK, CRACK, SHATTER and WIDEN, there are verbs relating to cooking like BAKE, BOIL, COOK, FRY and ROAST (e.g. *The eggs are frying*) and verbs which combine with a few specific subject forms only, like FIRE, SHOW and SOUND (e.g. *The pistol fired, Her fatigue showed* and *The bugle sounded*). Some middle verbs are nearly always accompanied by *adverbials* (adjuncts), usually of manner:

(9)   Julia Roberts photographs well. (= is photogenic)

(10)   This loaf doesn't cut easily.

Note finally the use in BrE of BE *drowned* and BE *burned*:

(11)   Shelley was drowned.

(12)   The house was burnt down.

These are more or less synonymous with the now more frequent active middle-verb construction *Shelley drowned* and *The house burnt down*, i.e. without a sense of there being a suppressed agent: in both the active and the passive construction the subject is AFFECTED (by water or by fire). But there is also a truly passive interpretation possible in formally passive constructions with an overt or implied AGENT: *The kittens were drowned (by the two boys) / The palace was burnt down (by the rebels)* corresponding to *The two boys drowned the kittens / The rebels burnt the palace down*.

7.4.6. Passives vs. adjectival non-passives

In English it is often the case that a sentence containing a form of BE followed by an *-ed* participle is not passive but active:

(1)   I *am* not *accustomed* to being interrupted.

(2)   All these people are *educated* and very reliable.

(3)   My heart *was* so *swollen* with feeling I could not reply.

Here BE is not an auxiliary but a main verb, and the *-ed* participle form does not realize the main verb but (part of) the subject complement. The situations described are stative, and the participles are not verb forms but *adjectives* derived by lexical-morphological conversion of a verbal *-ed* form.

As pointed out in section 7.4.5, sentences like *The jug was broken* and *They were married* are ambiguous in that they can refer either to a dynamic situation or to a state. In the former case they are passive S P sentences and in the latter case active S P C sentences. In sentences like *The ship was sunk* and *His cheeks were sunken* (cf. Schibsbye 1970: 18) the difference between passive and active is signalled formally. Like *sunken*, the word *shaven* is exclusively used as an adjective, but here the other form *shaved* need not be passive when preceded by a form of BE. Out of context a sentence like *He was shaved* is ambiguous between a dynamic and a stative reading.

Adjectival *-ed* forms differ from passive participles in a number of ways (see e.g. Palmer 1987: 85f and van Ek & Robat 1984: 252):

(i) They may be used after verbs other than BE, such as SEEM and BECOME.

(ii) They accept intensifiers like VERY, RATHER, etc., the markers of comparison MORE and MOST and negative prefixes. (Non-gradable *-ed* forms like *married*, however, cannot normally be intensified or compared.)

(iii) They may be coordinated with a true adjective.

(iv) Insertion of ALREADY in sentences in which they occur does not necessitate the use of the perfect.

The sentence pattern encountered in an example like *The case is complicated* is thus S P C, not S P (see Palmer 1987: 86):

(i)   The case seems/is becoming complicated.

(ii)   The case is quite complicated.
       The case is more complicated than we expected.
       The case is uncomplicated.

(iii) The case is awkward and complicated.

(iv)   The case is already (quite) complicated.

On the other hand, a sentence like *Three of the passengers were saved* is passive, for here the *-ed* form has none of the properties listed in (i) through (iv), and the same goes for e.g. *Plans for an amnesty were complicated by renewed terrorism*. Note that insertion of ALREADY in these two examples would necessitate a change of *were* to *had been*.

While the distinction between passives and adjectival non-passives is basically clear, it should not be overlooked that borderline cases do exist and that a grey zone has to be reckoned with in this grammatical area as in so many others. In *The students were amused/annoyed/embarrassed by my dirty jokes*, for example, the existence of the corresponding active construction *My dirty jokes amused/annoyed/embarrassed the students* points towards a passive analysis. On the other hand, the possibility of replacing *were* by *seemed* and of premodifying the participle with an intensifying adverb, a comparative marker or a negative prefix (e.g. *quite amused/more amused than I'd expected/unamused*) seem to indicate that the *-ed* forms are adjectival non-passives instead. The presence of a *by*-group, it will be noted, is thus not a sure sign that the preceding *-ed* participle is passive (see e.g. Quirk et al. 1985: 169). This appears very clearly from an example like *The students were unamused by my dirty jokes*, which can only be analysed as an S P C sentence whose complement is realized by an adjective group. Note also that the head of the postmodifying preposition group could be realized by *at* instead of *by* with little or no change of meaning. Such prepositional variation can be further illustrated by *worried by/about, satisfied by/with* and *disappointed by/in/at/about /with*.

7.5. Polarity

7.5.1. Introduction

One of the optional adverbials that may expand the basic sentence patterns (cf. sections 3.2.4 and 3.2.9) is the negative adverb NOT:

(1)   Software is *not* like other intellectual property.

This example is a *negative* sentence. The distinction between positive and negative is one of *polarity*. Semantically, a negative sentence differs from a corresponding positive sentence in expressing that one or more of the conditions which must be satisfied in order for this positive sentence to be used appropriately are not satisfied. For a positive sentence like *Sanctions challenge vital interests* to be used appropriately, a number of conditions must be satisfied (see Huddleston 1984: 432). These conditions represent different layers of meaning: (i) Something challenges something, (ii) sanctions challenge something, (iii) something challenges interests, (iv) sanctions challenge interests, (v) something challenges vital interests, (vi) sanctions challenge vital interests. When the corresponding negative sentence *Sanctions don't challenge vital interests* is used, the speaker expresses that one or more of these conditions is not satisfied. If it is (ii), (iv) and (vi) which are not satisfied, this can be indicated by pronouncing the word *sanctions* with contrastive stress:

(2)   `Sanctions don't challenge vital interests.

If it is conditions (v) and (vi), on the other hand, this can be shown by placing the nuclear stress on the adjective *vital*:

(3)   Sanctions don't challenge `vital interests.

What is indicated prosodically in (2) and (3) is *focus of negation*, i.e. the place where the contrast of meaning expressed by the negation is located (the subpart of the sentence expressing the condition that is not satisfied). In (2), for example, it is only the referent of the subject noun which is at issue, not the truth of the rest of the sentence. This focus can be made explicit by using a so-called cleft sentence instead (cf. section 8.4):

(4)   It isn't sanctions that challenge vital interests.

Such a construction can naturally also be used in spoken English. In that case *sanctions* will still be pronounced with nuclear stress, so here the focus of negation is doubly marked.

Negative sentences can also be pronounced 'neutrally', i.e. with the nuclear stress on the last content word – e.g. *interests* in (4) – and without stress reduction in the preceding part of the sentence. In that case it is not specified exactly what condition or conditions are not satisfied, and it therefore becomes a matter for the hearer to work this out on the basis of the context.

Note finally that a negative sentence may be used as a *denial*, i.e. as a refusal to accept as a fact a previous statement. If speaker A says e.g. that *Sanctions challenge vital interests*, speaker B may deny this statement by a negative sentence in which *don't* is pronounced with nuclear stress:

(5)   Sanctions ˋdon't challenge vital interests.

The difference between denials and 'ordinary' negative statements sometimes sheds light on difficult examples. For instance, a sentence like *They don't owe me nothing* can in Standard English only be used as a denial of *They owe me nothing*, i.e. roughly in the sense 'They owe me something'. Outside Standard English, such an example can also be used as an ordinary negative statement, i.e. with the same meaning as *They don't owe me anything*.

7.5.2. Standard negation

In its 'standard' version, negation is signalled by placing NOT after the operator, as illustrated by *The cycle of death will not continue*. If there is no operator in the corresponding positive sentence, as in *Sanctions challenge vital interests*, the dummy operator DO is inserted before NOT in the negative sentence. In informal English the negative adverb is typically *contracted* with the preceding operator. In that case it is pronounced /nt/ and written *n't*:

(1)   They shouldn't blame us.

(2)   I didn't know much about Rwanda.

When contracted with CAN, it should be added, NOT can also be written as *not* and pronounced – without stress – as /nɒt/:

(3)   Without autonomy, we can't/cannot be a truly free and democratic society.

The only auxiliary which NOT may not be freely contracted with is MAY. The contracted form *mayn't* does not occur in AmE, and in BrE it is extremely rare.

In those cases where the predicator is realized by a form of the full verb BE or by a complex verb group in which the operator is a form of BE, HAVE or WILL, the negative adverb may thus be contracted with the preceding verb form like the modal auxiliaries and DO (compare examples (1) through (3)):

(4)   It isn't true.

(5)   She hasn't resigned yet.

(6)   He won't be missed much.

Here, however, there is another alternative: the finite verb may be contracted with the preceding subject realization instead (verb contraction instead of NOT-contraction). When this happens, NOT is obligatorily stressed:

(7)   It's 'not `true.
(8)   She's 'not re`signed yet.
(9)   He'll 'not be `missed much.

This type of contraction is particularly common if the subject is realized by a pronoun, but in the shape of *'s* BE and HAVE are often contracted with a subject nominal too, and informally WILL sometimes behaves that way as well:

(10)   The answer's not especially complicated.
(11)   Peter's not resigned yet.
(12)   Pete'll probably not accept the deal.

While DO and the modal auxiliaries (except WILL) permit only NOT-contraction, the verb form AM permits only verb contraction, as in *I'm not sorry* and *I'm not studying*. In non-standard English, particularly non-standard AmE, the contracted form *ain't* is used for *am, are, is* or *has/have* + NOT, for example in *I/she/you/they ain't sorry* and *I/she/you/they ain't finished yet*. Finally it should be mentioned that the contracted form *aren't* may be used in BrE not only with 2nd person singular or with plural subjects as in *You aren't the only survivor* and *They aren't here* but also with 1st person singular subjects. This use is restricted to negative questions, though, and is particularly common in tag questions: *I'm your wife, aren't I?*

7.5.3. Domain of negation

In examples with standard negation, the domain of negation is global in the sense that the unit affected semantically by NOT is the entire clause. Global negation as in *You can't come tomorrow* is analysed in the following way:

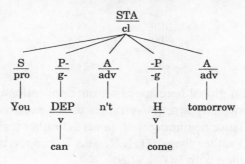

In order to separate global from non-global negation a number of criteria can be used (see Klima 1964 and Payne 1985: 198). It is a characteristic of a sentence with global negation that it permits:

(i) a positive rather than a negative tag question;

(ii) a coordinated clause beginning with (*and*) NEITHER rather than (*and*) SO or ending in EITHER rather than TOO;

(iii) a construction beginning with NOT EVEN.

According to these criteria a sentence like *You can't come tomorrow* with contraction has global negation:

(1)   You can't come tomorrow, can you?
(2)   You can't come tomorrow and neither can your wife.
(3)   You can't come tomorrow and your wife can't come either.
(4)   You can't come tomorrow, not even in tails.

If there is no contraction and NOT is pronounced with stress, the syntactic structure of the sentence may be the same (i.e. S P- A -P A), and apart from the degree of emphasis involved so may its meaning. However, *You can not come tomorrow* differs from *You can't come tomorrow* in being ambiguous, for it can be used either to express that the person addressed is 'not permitted to come' or that he is 'permitted not to come'. The latter meaning can be made clear by the addition of adverbials, as in *You can always not come tomorrow if you like*. Here the negation is not global but *local*. In sentence analysis this can be captured by using the stack convention (cf. section 4.1):

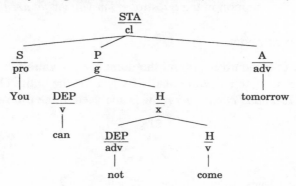

That negation is non-global here appears from application of the criteria: the clause can be followed by a negative rather than a positive tag question, or by a coordinated clause beginning with (*and*) SO rather than (*and*) NEITHER or ending in TOO rather than EITHER, and it cannot be followed by a construction beginning with NOT EVEN:

(5)   You can not come tomorrow, can't you?
(6)   You can not come tomorrow and so can your wife.
(7)   You can not come tomorrow and your wife (can not come) too.

Global and local negation are capable of cooccurring, for example in *You can't not come tomorrow* (= You are not at liberty to stay away tomorrow).

While the combination of global and local negation is stylistically marked here, it is natural in those cases where local negation is realized by a negative prefix, i.e. where negation operates within the boundaries of the word:

(8)   Gates doesn't address these matters *ir*reverently.
(9)   He isn't *un*happy about his work.

Global negation is not an exclusive property of standard negation. For example, we find it not only in a sentence like *The earthquake didn't cause any casualties* but also in a sentence without standard negation like *The earthquake caused no casualties*. That this is so appears from the fact that the second of these examples, like the first, selects a positive tag question, combines with NEITHER and EITHER instead of SO and TOO and permits a following NOT EVEN construction:

(10)   The earthquake caused no casualties, did it?
(11)   The earthquake caused no casualties and neither did the ensuing landslide.
(12)   The earthquake caused no casualties and the ensuing landslide caused no casualties either.
(13)   The earthquake caused no casualties, not even around the epicentre.

While *The earthquake caused no casualties* thus resembles *The earthquake didn't cause any casualties* in having global negation, it differs from it with respect to *syntactic field*, a subject which we now turn to.

7.5.4. Syntactic field of negation

While the domain of negation concerns the overall polarity of clauses, syntactic field concerns the syntactic material actually negated. In an example with global negation like *The earthquake caused no casualties*, the syntactic material negated is not the entire clause (as it is in all cases of standard negation) but only the *object*. Here, then, the syntactic field of negation is not clausal but *limited*. Negation of a sentence function, however, frequently leads to global negation, i.e. although the syntactic field of negation is limited, the speaker presents and the hearer understands such a sentence as negative as a whole.

As we saw in section 7.3, sentences describe situations with one or more participants. In an S P O O sentence like *They gave us the tickets* the participants involved are AGENT (the subject), BENEFICIARY (the indirect object) and AFFECTED (the direct object). Now if one of these sentence functions is negated, as it is in *None of them gave us the tickets*, *They gave none of us the tickets* and *They gave us no tickets*, a participant is eliminated. The situation described by the sentence as a whole therefore cannot materialize, i.e. no situation arises where somebody hands over something to somebody else. For that reason the hearer understands the sentence as a whole to be negative. That there is global negation here appears from application of the criteria, e.g. addition of a positive tag question:

(1)   None of them gave us the tickets, did they?
(2)   They gave none of us the tickets, did they?
(3)   They gave us no tickets, did they?

Limited syntactic field of negation involves not only subjects and objects but also complements and adverbials, e.g. *She is no one of importance* (*is she?*) and *At no point in the meeting did they tell us the truth* (*did they?*).

Negation of a complement or of an adverbial, it should be added, is not always accompanied by global negation. This can be illustrated by an S P C sentence like *Simpson pleads not guilty* and an S P O A sentence like *He'll fix your car in no time*. That the domain of negation is here local appears from application of the criteria. For example, both sentences select a negative tag question: *doesn't he? / won't he?*.

What we have shown in this section is that the syntactic field of negation is either clausal (as it always is in the case of standard negation) or limited (which it is if S, O, C or A is negated). In the former case the domain of negation is always global. In the latter case it is very frequently global too.

7.5.5. Negative sentences with global domain and limited field

Global domain combined with limited syntactic field is found in sentences with *negative or negated quantifiers and pronouns*, i.e. in sentences with *no*, *nothing*, *nobody*, *no one*, *none*, *neither* or words like *one*, *many*, *much*, *all* and *every* preceded by NOT:

(1)   A predawn earthquake in eastern Java caused *no* casualties or serious damage.
(2)   My mother noticed *nothing* of this.
(3)   *Nobody*'s perfect.
(4)   *Neither* of us said anything.
(5)   *Not one / Not many* of the students will pass the exam.
(6)   She is *no one* of importance.

The syntactic field of negation is here limited to subjects, objects or complements, but the sentences become globally negative all the same.

Occasionally global negation with negative quantifiers/pronouns is the only alternative. Thus, for example, *Nobody cares* is the negative counterpart of *Somebody cares* when *somebody* has non-specific reference (*Somebody doesn't care* being possible only if *Somebody* has specific rather than non-specific reference). In a number of idiomatic cases, furthermore, it is practically the only alternative, and in existential sentences and sentences with HAVE in the sense of 'possess' it tends to be preferred to standard negation (see Johansson and Lysvåg 1986: 241):

(7)   It's no wonder.

(8)   There's no claret in the decanter.

(9)   We have no cash.

Otherwise, the choice between negation with a negative quantifier/pronoun and standard negation is largely a matter of style. For example, the next two examples can both be used to express the same kind of negative statement. It should be added, though, that (11) differs from (10) in that it can also be used as a denial, a use which is not likely in the case of (10):

(10)   The earthquake caused no serious damage.

(11)   The earthquake did not cause any serious damage.

Global quantifier negation may cooccur with (global) standard negation:

(12)   Nobody didn't know the answer.

(13)   Not many of the students didn't pass the exam.

Here both the negative elements are operative, so although (12) and (13) as a whole are negative sentences – as application of the three criteria will show – their meanings are roughly similar to those of *Everybody knew the answer* and *Most of the students passed the exam*. This type of genuine 'double negation' is also found in an example like *They don't owe me nothing* (= 'They owe me something') and should be distinguished from the one found outside Standard English, where there is *negative concord* (as in e.g. Spanish) and where the extra negative adds nothing to the meaning of the sentence apart from emphasis (*They don't owe me nothing* = *They don't owe me anything*). As illustrated by *I didn't say nothing to nobody*, this type of semantically redundant negation may even be 'multiple'.

We also find global negation in sentences with negative/negated adverbs:

(14)   Alan Clark has *never* concealed his philandering ways.

(15)   That approach will get you *nowhere*.

(16)   *Not everywhere* are the effects of these policies noticeable.

In each example the syntactic field of negation is limited to the adverbial function. But the sentence as a whole becomes negative.

Among the negative adverbs we should perhaps include BARELY, HARD-LY, RARELY, SCARCELY and SELDOM. Formally, these words are not marked as negative by an initial /n/, but semantically they can be paraphrased as 'almost not' (BARELY, HARDLY, SCARCELY) or 'not often' (RARELY, SELDOM). The following examples illustrate a kind of 'global negation' expressed in this way:

(17)   I barely know her.

(18)   Bill Clinton's reflexive faith in their efficacy is hardly surprising.

(19)   She scarcely speaks a word of Danish.

In such examples, application of the tag question test and the NOT EVEN test does not yield a completely clear result. In all three examples we can add a positive tag (e.g. *do I?* in (17)), which indicates that they are negative sentences. At the same time, however, they seem to prefer an EVEN clause to a NOT EVEN clause (e.g. *even to her husband* in (19)), especially if there is little or no pause between the two clauses. If constituting a separate information unit, the NOT EVEN clause improves somewhat. Note finally that all three examples select a coordinated clause with NEITHER or EITHER instead of SO or TOO, so in this respect they are globally negative.

Before proceeding to non-global negation we must consider examples with LITTLE or FEW like the following:

(20)   The earthquake caused few casualties.

(21)   The earthquake caused little damage.

In some descriptions of English grammar such sentences are considered negative (unlike sentences with A FEW or A LITTLE). According to the tests used here, however, they appear to be positive. Sentences like (20) and (21) can be expanded with *and so did the ensuing landslide*, with *and the ensuing landslide caused few casualties / little damage too* or with *didn't it?* Furthermore, they cannot be followed by NOT EVEN constructions or clauses with NEITHER or EITHER, and the tag question will normally be *didn't it?*, indicating that the matrix clause is positive.

Semantically, LITTLE and FEW resemble BARELY, HARDLY, SCARCELY ('almost not') and RARELY, SELDOM ('not often') in having negative colouring ('not much', 'not many'). They also behave like these words with respect to inversion. As mentioned in section 5.3.4, there is inversion in sentences beginning with a negative or restrictive constituent other than the subject (if negation/restriction applies to the whole sentence). There is thus inversion in sentences beginning with explicitly negative words or with implicitly negative words like BARELY, HARDLY, etc. (as illustrated by *Hardly a word did he utter*). However, there is also inversion in sentences like the following beginning with LITTLE or FEW:

(22)   Little did John expect this move.

(23)   On few matters is our conception of the future this clear.

With respect to inversion, then, LITTLE and FEW behave like NEVER, NOWHERE, etc. and BARELY, RARELY, etc. Furthermore, it is sometimes difficult to apply the criteria to sentences beginning with these words. For example, (22) cannot readily be followed by either *and neither did his wife* or *and so did his wife*. It thus appears that sentences with LITTLE or FEW are not entirely determinate with respect to polarity, i.e. that there is a grey zone between clearly positive and clearly negative sentences. In this grey zone – though closer to the negative end of the scale – we should probably also place sentences with BARELY, RARELY, etc.

7.5.6. Local negation

The most obvious cases of local negation are those where a word begins with a *negative prefix* and where negation operates within the limits of the word. In a sentence with a negative prefix like the following there is thus no global negation:

(1)   These distinctions were virtually *non*existent before the mid-17th century.

As illustrated by the next example, however, a word beginning with a negative prefix may naturally also occur in a sentence with global negation:

(2)   This situation is not *a*typical.

As already shown, local negation outside the boundaries of the word may be expressed by NOT. This is common before adjectives or adverbs, particularly if these begin with a negative prefix:

(3)   Our new therapy is a not insignificant step in the right direction.

(4)   Not infrequently there is torrential rain on this part of the coast.

(5)   Simpson pleads not guilty.

(6)   Not long ago Marion turned eighty.

The domain of negation is also local in sentences like *I hope not* and *I'm afraid not* in which NOT realizes an object and the complementation of an adjective respectively and is used as an anaphor with clausal antecedent, for example in reply to a question like *Are Norway winning?*

Local negation with negative elements other than NOT or prefixes can be illustrated by examples like these:

(7)   We'll have your roof fixed in no time.

(8)   A hundred pounds for that room is nothing short of robbery.

(9)   She had a barely noticeable smile on her face.

The different types of negation examined so far are summarized and exemplified in table 1:

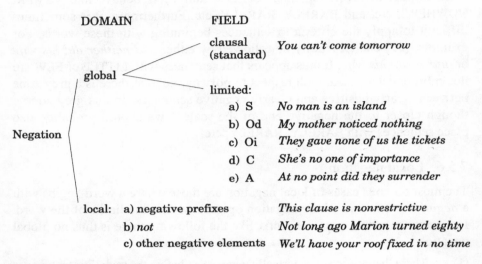

Table 1: Types of negation

7.5.7. Nonassertive forms

Some English words are typically restricted to occurring in negative sentences, interrogative sentences and conditional clauses, i.e. in constructions which do not express an assertion the way positive declarative sentences usually do. One such nonassertive form is EVER:

(1)   She hasn't ever made me happy.

(2)   Has she ever made you happy?

(3)   If I have ever made you happy I will not have lived in vain.

(4)   *She has ever made me happy.

EVER also occurs in comparative clauses, which resemble conditional clauses in not expressing an assertion in themselves:

(5)   She is making me happier than I have ever been before.

Forms typically limited to nonassertive contexts in English are *any*, complex pronouns and adverbs beginning with *any (anything, anybody, anyone, anywhere*), *either*, *ever*, *yet* and *at all*. The corresponding assertive forms are *some* (*something, somebody, someone, somewhere*), *too, sometimes* and *already* (*at all* having no obvious counterpart). For example, the assertive version of (1) is *She has sometimes made me happy*. In negative sentences, the use of nonassertive forms can be illustrated by the following examples:

(6)   My father had given no hint to her of *any* malaise.

(7)   To my surprise, I didn't see *anybody/anyone*.

(8)   My father has never liked bridge *either*.

(9)   The Prime Minister hasn't resigned *yet*.

(10)   They've done nothing *at all* about it.

As can be seen, nonassertive forms occur both in sentences with standard negation and sentences with other types of global negation. Sometimes we also find them in positive declarative sentences in which there are words with negative prefixes (local negation) or negative meaning:

(11)   We *disapprove* of *any* intervention in that area.

(12)   We *oppose any* intervention in that area.

The use of nonassertive forms in implicitly negative sentences with the adverbials BARELY, HARDLY, RARELY, SCARCELY, SELDOM is illustrated by the next examples:

(13)   They have *barely* settled down *yet*.

(14)   Bill Clinton's reflexive faith in their efficacy is *hardly* surprising *either*.

(15)   They *rarely* go *anywhere* outside Britain.

In all the examples given above, the nonassertive form follows the negative element. This order cannot be reversed. While we can say *She hasn't ever kissed anyone* we cannot say **She has ever kissed no one*.

With respect to assertive vs. nonassertive forms, LITTLE and FEW behave like explicitly and implicitly negative elements:

(16)   The earthquake caused *little* damage *anywhere*.

(17)   *Few* people have *ever* made me that happy.

ONLY, which resembles LITTLE and FEW as well as BARELY, HARDLY, etc. in having a negative hue ('with no others in the same class'), also combines with nonassertive forms:

(18)   *Only* my husband has *ever* made me that happy.

For further discussion of nonassertive forms and examples like *Anybody can do this* and *Did you see someone in the garden?*, the reader is referred to section 11.3.4 [A.f].

7.5.8. Semantic scope of negation

We have so far discussed the overall polarity of clauses in connection with negation (domain of negation) and the syntactic material actually negated (syntactic field of negation). In this section we take a closer look at what parts of a clause are affected *semantically* by negation (semantic *scope* of negation). Consider first examples like the following:

(1)   Fortunately the earthquake didn't cause casualties.

(2)   Fortunately the earthquake caused no casualties.

In both of these the domain of negation is global. On the other hand the two examples differ in that the syntactic field of negation is clausal in (1) and limited (to the object) in (2).

In order to give a full account of negation in these examples, it is not enough to account for domain and field: we must also specify that negation – though global – has no semantic influence over the part of the meaning referred to by *fortunately*. To cope with examples of this type we need the concept of *semantic scope*. The semantic scope of negation may be either *complete* or *incomplete*. While it is incomplete in examples like (1) and (2) in that the meaning described by *fortunately* is unaffected by negation, it is complete in examples like the next ones:

(3)   At first the earthquake didn't cause casualties.

(4)   At first the earthquake caused no casualties.

Here, then, the part of the meaning described by *at first* is inside the semantic scope of negation.

In an example like (2) the domain, syntactic field and semantic scope of negation are all different: the domain is the entire clause, the syntactic field is the object and the semantic scope is the part of the meaning described by everything except *fortunately*. While field is exclusively syntactic (involving the negation of syntactic entities like S, O and clause) and scope is exclusively semantic (involving the effect of negation on meaning), domain is both syntactic and semantic: it is established on syntactic criteria (cf. the tests mentioned in section 7.5.3) and relates to the clause; at the same time, however, it concerns the language user's conception of a sentence as negative or positive on the most general level.

In examples where the domain of negation is *local*, domain, syntactic field and semantic scope all go together. This can be illustrated by an example like 'Simpson pleads not *guilty*', which has local domain, limited field and incomplete scope.

In the case of *global* negation, the negative may have semantic scope over the entire simple sentence. This is true of (3) and (4) above and for an example like *Sanctions don't challenge vital interests*, which can be analysed semantically as [Not [sanctions challenge vital interests]]. That it is not just the subpart of meaning following *n't* that lies within the semantic scope of negation, but also the subject noun, is evident from the fact that the sentence may be produced with contrastive stress on *sanctions*, i.e. the focus of negation may be on this word (see section 7.5.1). Not infrequently, however, some of the semantic material encoded in a sentence with global negation falls outside the semantic scope of negation.

This is often the case with *adverbials* (as illustrated by examples (1) and (2)). In the first place, disjuncts and conjuncts always behave in this way:

(5)   Sanctions don't challenge vital interests, *unfortunately*.

(6)   Sanctions don't challenge vital interests, *however*.

These examples can be paraphrased 'Unfortunately/However it is not the case that sanctions challenge vital interests', i.e. they must be analysed semantically as [Unfortunately/However [not [sanctions challenge vital interests]]]. Adjuncts differ from disjuncts and conjuncts in that, more often than not, they fall within the semantic scope of negation. This is always the case with obligatory adjuncts:

(7)   Software is not *like other intellectual property*.

(8)   He didn't place the figures *in the right order*.

Optional adjuncts falling inside the scope of negation can be illustrated by:

(9)   *Without autonomy*, we cannot have a truly free and democratic society.

(10)   This bottle isn't labelled *very clearly*.

(11)   Nothing much had changed *in 1994*.

In some cases, however, optional adjuncts fall outside the semantic scope of negation. This is commonly the case with adverbials of reason or purpose:

(12)   *For those reasons*, I didn't write the book.

(13)   *With this objective in mind*, we have neglected none of the suggestions from our customers.

If such an adverbial is placed finally, it may also stand outside the semantic scope of negation. In an example like *I didn't write the book for those reasons*, the scope is the same as in (12) if the adjunct is pronounced without prosodic prominence:

(14)   I didn't write the `book for those reasons.

If the adjunct is pronounced with prosodic prominence, however, it is brought within the semantic scope of negation. Nuclear stress may be placed either on *reasons* or – contrastively – on *those*, and the tonal contour is typically falling-rising:

(15)   I didn't write the book for those ˅reasons.

(16)   I didn't write the book for ˅those reasons.

Whether an optional adjunct is inside or outside the semantic scope of negation may be signalled not only prosodically but also by constituent order. In an example like *I didn't kill him deliberately* where it follows the negative elements, the adjunct is inside the scope of negation. But in *Deliberately, I didn't kill him* and *I deliberately didn't kill him*, where the adjunct precedes the negative, the negative has no semantic influence over it.

If an adjunct is outside the semantic scope of negation, the sentence which remains if this adjunct is removed is entailed by the sentence in which it is retained (see Huddleston 1984: 429). What this means becomes clear when we look at an example like *I didn't kill him* which is entailed by *Deliberately, I didn't kill him* and *I deliberately didn't kill him*. On the other hand, it is not entailed by *I didn't kill him deliberately*, where the adjunct is inside the semantic scope of negation. What this sentence implies is that the person referred to by *him* was in fact killed. If in doubt about the role played by an optional adverbial with respect to scope of negation, we can thus use the test of entailment. This test will show the adjunct to be outside the scope of negation in examples like (12) and (13) (entailment) but inside the scope of negation in examples like (9) through (11) (no entailment).

In addition to adverbials, some *modal auxiliaries* may stand outside the semantic scope of negation. As illustrated by the following example, this goes for MAY used in the sense of 'be perhaps likely to':

(17)   She may not understand your decision.

This sentence can be paraphrased as 'It is possible that she won't understand your decision' and analysed as [Possible [not [she understand your decision]]]. If MAY is used in the sense of 'be allowed to', it normally stands inside the scope of negation. For example, a sentence like *You may not borrow my car* can be paraphrased as 'You are not permitted to borrow my car' and analysed semantically as [Not [permitted [you borrow my car]]]. But as illustrated by *This once you may not do the dishes*, used in the sense of 'I permit you to refrain from washing up', it may also stand outside the scope of negation: [Permitted [not [you wash up]]]. For further discussion of negation in connection with modal auxiliaries, see section 9.9.

Note finally examples with *indefinite quantified subjects* like the following:

(18)   Many arrows didn't hit the target.

(19)   Two goals weren't scored by Michael Laudrup.

There is a sense in which the subject is here excluded from the semantic scope of negation. Thus the fact that many arrows didn't hit the target does not exclude the possibility that many (other) arrows *did* hit the target. Similarly, the fact that two goals were not scored by Michael Laudrup does not exclude the possibility that Michael Laudrup *did* score two (other) goals.

Negation is without a doubt a highly complicated field of grammar. In tackling the analysis of negation in specific sentences, the following three-stage approach is recommended:

(i) Find out whether the domain of negation is global or local by using the criteria mentioned in section 7.5.3.

(ii) Then find out whether the syntactic field of negation is limited to a specific sentence function or is clausal.

(iii) Finally find out whether the semantic scope of negation is complete or incomplete by examining whether all the semantic material encoded in the sentence is influenced by negation or not.

When applied to a sentence like *Fortunately the earthquake caused no casualties*, this approach will demonstrate that the domain of negation is global, that the syntactic field of negation is limited to the object and that the semantic scope of negation is incomplete in that the meaning expressed by the first word is unaffected by negation.

Here is an overview of the possible combinations of domain, field and scope:

global domain	unlimited syntactic field	complete semantic scope	examples
+	+	+	*The earthquake didn't cause casualties*
+	+	-	*Fortunately the earthquake didn't cause casualties*
+	-	+	*The earthquake caused no casualties*
+	-	-	*Fortunately the earthquake caused no casualties*
-	-	-	*Simpson pleads not guilty*

Graphic representation:

The earthquake didn't cause casualties

```
scope   |_____|
field   |_____|
domain  |_____|
```

Fortunately the earthquake didn't cause casualties

```
scope        |_____|
field   |_____|
domain  |_____|
```

The earthquake caused no casualties

```
scope   |_____|
field                      |_____|
domain  |_____|
```

Fortunately the earthquake caused no casualties

```
scope        |_____|
field                           |_____|
domain  |_____|
```

Simpson pleads not guilty

```
scope              |_____|
field              |_____|
domain             |_____|
```

7.5.9. Non-declarative sentences

In *yes-no* interrogative sentences there is negation if the speaker's expectation with respect to positive-negative is not neutral but positive:

(1)   Isn't your attitude changing?

(2)   Didn't they prove uncooperative?

Here the speaker seeks information but at the same time expresses that he expects the state of affairs referred to to hold ('Tell me if I'm right in assuming that your attitude is changing/that they proved uncooperative'). In *wh*-interrogative sentences the speaker's assumption is always positive. A positive sentence like *Who persuaded you?* requests information about the identity of the person who performed an action the speaker assumes to have taken place ('Somebody persuaded you. Who was it?'). Here the negative counterpart *Who didn't persuade you?* is not very natural, but if it is made possible by contextualization it clearly does not refer to the same situation as the positive sentence. In some cases a *wh*-interrogative sentence has no negative counterpart, e.g. *Whatever put that idea into your head?* On the other hand, negative sentences with *why* are very common:

(3)   Why don't you live in London?

(4)   Why didn't it work?

Semantically, these sentences are obviously quite different from the corresponding positive sentences. While (3) can be paraphrased as 'Tell me the reason you don't live in London', a positive sentence like *Why do you live in London?* can be paraphrased as 'Tell me the reason you live in London'.

Negative imperative sentences are formed by placing *don't* before the main verb, also when this is BE:

(5)   Don't knock him unconscious.

(6)   Don't be afraid.

Note in passing that BE only accepts DO-support in negative imperatives like (6) and in emphatic imperatives like the following:

(7)   Do be nice to him.

A *you*-subject may be used in imperative sentences to add an element of e.g. displeasure. This is possible in negative imperative sentences as well:

(8)   Don't you knock him unconscious.

Here the presence of *you* makes the message come across as a threat.

Exclamatory sentences differ from other sentence types in not normally being capable of negation. For example *How beautiful she doesn't look!* is not grammatical in any context. On the other hand a negative exclamatory sentence like *How cleverly she doesn't stop speaking!* cannot be ruled out in a context where the person talked about tries to retain the upper hand in a debate. The illocutionary value 'exclamation' is often expressed by negative sentences, but these nearly always belong to other sentence types, particularly the interrogative one. This can be illustrated by examples like *Wasn't she lovely!* and *Isn't he English!*, the communicative function of which, despite the interrogative form, is not to seek information but to indicate an emotional reaction.

7.5.10. Emphasis and focus

The dummy operator DO is used not only in connection with negation and inversion but also to create emphasis:

(1)   Sanctions *do* challenge vital interests.

In this example the operator DO – pronounced with nuclear stress – is used to *emphasize* the truth of the sentence. What is emphasized in this way is the *entire statement*. If a speaker wishes to underline only individual parts of a sentence, he will do so by means of strong nuclear stress exclusively (see section 7.5.1 on focus of negation). For example, a sentence like *Jane speaks English correctly* may be emphasized not only as a whole by means of DO but also in part by *focussing* on a constituent prosodically, i.e. by pronouncing its realization with strong nuclear stress:

(2)   ˋJane speaks English correctly. (but not Tarzan)
(3)   Jane ˋspeaks English correctly. (but spells it incorrectly)
(4)   Jane speaks ˋEnglish correctly. (but not French)
(5)   Jane speaks English corˋrectly. (but not fluently)

In these examples the special attention given to an individual constituent by means of prosody is *contrastive* (so we speak of 'contrastive focus' here). When DO is used in positive declarative sentences, it is often used not only to emphasize the entire statement but simultaneously to express a contrast to the corresponding negative statement, i.e. a kind of 'denial in reverse':

(6)   A: Why didn't you own up?
       B: I ˋdid own up.

In using *Jane does speak English correctly* the speaker may express a contrast to something mentioned before too, but he can also use it for emphasis exclusively, for example to signal that Jane's command of English strikes him as remarkably impressive. The following examples with DO illustrate emphasis which is not necessarily contrastive:

(7)   Lucky girl! But I am relieved. I do worry, you know.
(8)   I won't be alone. But I do worry about you here in the flat.

Expansion by means of DO for the expression of emphasis is found not only in positive declarative sentences but also in positive imperative sentences:

(9)   Jane, do ask Harry to join us. (complex sentence)

When a speaker wishes to emphasize the entire statement expressed by a sentence in which the predicator is realized by a group with one or more auxiliaries, she will do so by pronouncing the operator with nuclear stress:

(10)   Accidents ˋwill happen.
(11)   A: Why haven't you owned up?
        B: I ˋhave owned up.

In emphatic sentences with or without DO the part following the operator is often contextually redundant and may therefore be *omitted* (see section 4.2.3 on ellipsis and pro-forms):

(12)   A: Why didn't you own up?

        B: I did.

(13)   A: You weren't expecting to do any work, were you?

        B: I was, actually.

As the auxiliary HAVE and the modal auxiliaries are used for the expression of time and modality respectively, sentences with these verbs are frequently used to draw attention to temporal contrasts or to contrasts between real and possible or desirable states of affairs (see Quirk et al. 1985: 1371f):

(14)   A: They are a handsome couple, aren't they?

        B: They *have* been, no doubt. A little past their best now, perhaps.

(15)   A: I'd like to treat us both.

        B: You *could*, of course.

(16)   A: Well, I think they enjoyed it.

        B: They *should* have done. It was not exactly an inexpensive evening.

In negative sentences, denial of the entire statement expressed by the corresponding positive sentences is emphasized by assigning nuclear stress either to NOT or – in the case of NOT-contraction – to the operator (see sections 7.5.1-2):

(17)   Jane does ˈnot speak English correctly.

(18)   Jane ˈdoesn't speak English correctly.

(19)   Jane can ˈnot speak English correctly.

(20)   Jane ˈcan't (or ˈcannot) speak English correctly.

Under neutral conditions nuclear stress falls on the last content word (as mentioned in section 7.5.1). In an example like (5) the prosodic prominence given to the word *correctly* therefore need not signal contrastive focus but may signal ordinary *end-focus* instead. In closing this section we should add that nuclear stress may also signal *corrective focus*. In an example like *She wound a bandage round my foot* pronounced with nuclear stress on the verb the speaker's purpose in selecting this prosodic pattern may be to correct a misunderstanding on the part of her interlocutor, for example to make it clear that the verb form she had used was not *bound*.

7.6. Subject-predicator concord

7.6.1. Introduction

By concord is understood agreement in form between different linguistic units. In noun groups like *this girl* and *these girls*, for example, the pronoun and the noun agree with respect to number: in the former both forms are singular and in the latter they are plural. Concord involves not only number but also other grammatical categories. In a sentence like *I'm sorry* there is agreement between the pronoun realizing the subject and the verb realizing the predicator not only with respect to number (singular) but also with respect to person (first). In a language like French there is concord of gender in noun groups like *un petit signe* 'a small sign' and *une petite clef* 'a small key'. Here the forms of the indefinite article and the adjective agree in being masculine in the first group and feminine in the second, due to the fact that the gender of *signe* is masculine and that of *clef* feminine. Though gender is not an inherent feature of nouns in English, a related kind of agreement is found in examples like *This is my son, who lives in London* and *This car, which is brand-new, belongs to Ann* where the choice of relative pronoun is determined by the personal vs. nonpersonal meaning of the preceding noun.

Concord may be *internal* in the sense that the co-occurrence restrictions it imposes involve the realization of group constituents (as in *this girl/these girls*) or *external* in that it involves the realization of sentence functions (e.g. of subject and predicator in *I'm sorry*).

7.6.2. The basic rule

In English there is agreement between subject and predicator when the latter contains a present form of a full verb or of one of the primary verbs BE, HAVE and DO. The *-s* form of the finite verb is used if the subject is realized by a singular nominal or third person singular pronominal:

(1)   France *has* always relished its "special role" in Africa.

(2)   She *does*n't know much about Rwanda.

(3)   This consideration *has* led France to play gendarme in Africa.

(4)   The stated objective *seems* laudable.

Otherwise the *-Ø* form of the verb is used:

(5)   France and England *have* always disagreed on this point.

(6)   They *do*n't know much about Rwanda.

(7)   These considerations *have* led France to play gendarme in Africa.

(8)   The stated objectives *seem* laudable.

This basic rule does not apply to sentences with modal auxiliaries (e.g. *The stated objective(s) may seem laudable*) or to sentences or clauses in the subjunctive mood (e.g. *Long live Prince Charles / I suggest he see a psychiatrist*). In those cases where the predicator is realized by a form of BE, on the other hand, concord involves not only the present form but also the past form: if the subject is realized by a singular nominal, the first person singular pronoun *I* or a third person singular pronominal, the verb form selected is *was* (e.g. *Escape was easier than before / My mother was concerned about her brother's health / I was clearly an embarrassment on that visit / Nothing of this was said to me*). Otherwise the form selected is *were*. In the present form of BE, furthermore, there are not two but three distinctions: *am* is selected if the subject realization is *I*, *is* if it is in the third person singular and *are* otherwise. In the following account of concord, *are* and *were* are to be regarded as the present and past -Ø form of BE.

Subject-predicator concord is largely a matter of *inflectional co-variation* (see Huddleston 1984: 241). If the nominal realizing the subject is in the singular, the verb adds the inflection *-s* (as illustrated by *My sister lives in Rome*). If the subject nominal is in the plural, however, and thus in regular cases marked by the inflection *-s* on the noun, no suffix is added to the verb (e.g. *My sisters live in Rome*). As the relation between noun form and verb form is thus of an automatic nature, it is not surprising that the meaning of the verb in sentences in the present form is highly *redundant* with respect to number. In an example like (4), for instance, the suffix *-s* only *reflects* the singular meaning of *objective* and thus adds very little to the meaning of the sentence (see Juul and Sørensen 1978: 13f). In (2), similarly, the suffix *-s* in *doesn't know* only reduplicates the meaning of *she* with respect to person and number. Verb inflection (*-s* vs. *-Ø*) is not invariably bleached, though. In sentences like *Counsel representing the payees expects a settlement* and *Counsel representing the payees expect a settlement*, it obviously makes a great difference that the suffix *-s* is present and absent respectively, for here the head of the subject group is realized by a noun which shows no inflectional difference between singular and plural.

Number is essentially a category of nouns and of pronouns (cf. distinctions like *book : books* and *this : these*), and person is essentially a category of pronouns (e.g. *I : you : it*). The reason we say that a verb is, for example, singular and third person is that the *-s* which accompanies it (e.g. *becomes / has become / is becoming*) is selected if the noun realizing the (head of the) subject (group) is in the singular (e.g. *tobacco / my sister*) or the pronoun realizing the (head of the) subject (group) is in the third person singular (e.g. *she / neither of us*).

Though the basic rule of concord is quite simple, concord problems arise for three main reasons (see Johansson and Lysvåg 1987: 346ff): 1) in some cases it is not obvious whether the form realizing the subject or head of the subject group is singular or plural; 2) syntactic concord may be overruled by so-called notional concord; 3) the rule of syntactic concord may be broken, particularly in long sentences, because there are nouns between the subject head noun and the predicator whose number differs from that of the subject realization (a side-tracking factor referred to as 'attraction').

7.6.3. Singular or plural subject realization?

Normally, the noun realizing the (head of the) subject (group) is marked inflectionally as singular or plural by means of *-s* and *-Ø* respectively. In some nouns, however, there is no such inflectional distinction. In order to determine whether the subject realization is in such cases singular or plural, it is helpful to look at determiners, certain pronouns and the noun realizing a subject complement or the head of a subject complement noun group. As shown in section 7.6.2, some nouns do not inflect for number. However, their number can often be determined as singular or plural in the linguistic context:

(1)   The *sheep ignore/ignores* the dogs.

(2)   *This/These sheep* will die soon.

(3)   The *sheep* will die unless you give *it/them* an injection.

(4)   Jane's *sheep* had been *an ideal pet*.

(5)   In the mist the *sheep* looked like *mole-hills*.

Under those conditions where the rule of concord does not apply, and where there are no number-revealing determiners, anaphoric pronouns, subject complement realizations, etc., the number of the subject noun can only be determined by looking at the larger linguistic context or the situational context (cf. Juul and Sørensen 1978: 55ff). An example illustrating this situation is *The sheep may die before the vet gets here*, which is ambiguous as it stands. Other nouns behaving like *sheep* are *counsel, craft, deer, cod, means, (gas)works, headquarters, series*, etc., see section 10.4.2 below.

Let us now investigate subject-predicator concord in a number of other cases where the subject realization is not clearly marked as either singular or plural:

A) Subjects realized by number-invariable nouns. In English some nouns are restricted with respect to singular/plural contrast. Such nouns, which are often referred to as number-invariable nouns because they are invariably singular *or* plural, are relevant in any discussion of subject-predicator concord. We distinguish the following general types (for more details, see section 10.4.3 on the number category):

(i) Nouns with 'plural form' used as singular nouns only, such as names of sciences and subjects like *mathematics* and *phonetics*, diseases like *measles* and *mumps*, of games like *billiards* and *darts*, and the individual mass noun *news*. These select the *-s* form of the verb.

(ii) Nouns with 'singular form' used as plural nouns only, such as nouns referring to a collection of entities like *cattle*, *police*, *clergy*, *livestock*, *vermin*, etc. These select the -Ø form of the verb.

(iii) Nouns with plural form only used as plural nouns, such as names of tools and articles of dress consisting of two parts like *scissors*, *shears*, *binoculars* and *jeans*, *tights*, *pyjamas* and some geographical proper nouns, for example, *the Andes*, *the Alps*, *the Hebrides*. These select the -Ø form of the verb. Note also nouns like *customs*, *contents*, *colours*, *pains*, etc., which have semantically distinct singular forms (*custom*, *content*, *colour*, *pain*).

(iv) Nouns with singular form only used as singular nouns, such as mass nouns like *anger*, *furniture*, *music*, *peace*, *poverty*, *resentment*, etc. and proper nouns (*John*, *Rome*, *Spain*, etc.). These select the *-s* form of the verb.

B) Subjects realized by compound units. If the conjoints are plural, the -Ø form is selected: *The boys and girls are now with their parents / The boys or the girls are on duty now*. If the conjunction is *and* and the conjoints are realized by singular nominals, the compound unit selects the -Ø form of the verb, i.e. counts as plural: *Bradbury and his partner bear a heavy responsibility*. If the conjunction is *or*, on the other hand, concord is usually determined by the last conjoint: *Bradbury or his partner bears a heavy responsibility / Bradbury or his partners are likely to want a settlement / His sisters or his father is to blame*. One exception to this rule is the expression *one or more* followed by an *of*-construction containing a plural noun, cf.: *One or more of these conditions has not been observed* vs. *One or more politicians have leaked information to the company*. Constructions with the correlative conjunctions *both ... and* and *either ... or* behave like constructions with *and* and *or* respectively, i.e. insertion of *both* in the first of the examples just given and of *either* in the second would not affect the choice of verb form. In those cases where one or both of the conjoints of a compound unit are realized by a singular pronoun, concord operates in the manner just outlined: there is plural concord if the conjunction is *and* (*She and Bradbury bear a heavy responsibility*) and singular concord if it is *or* (*She or Bradbury bears a heavy responsibility*).

The correlative conjunction *neither ... nor* is the negative counterpart of *both ... and* and has inclusive meaning. Nevertheless, a compound unit in which the conjoints are realized by singular words or groups has singular concord when coordinated by *neither ... nor*: *Neither Bradbury nor his partner bears a heavy responsibility*. In informal language plural concord cannot be ruled out here.

Special problems arise where the conjoints of a construction with the coordinators *or* and *either ... or* are realized by nominals or pronominals which differ with respect to number or person. In such cases there is some vacillation, but most commonly it is the -Ø form of the verb which is selected (see also section 7.6.5):

(6a)   (Either) the cabinet ministers or Major himself *refuse* to face reality.

(7a)   (Either) you or your partner *are* crazy.

However, there is sometimes 'attraction' to the last conjoint:

(6b)   (Either) the cabinet ministers or Major himself *refuses* to face reality.

(7b)   (Either) you or your partner *is* crazy.

Subject compound units with pronominal conjoints in different persons are often felt to be awkward. When they do occur, the -Ø form is normally used, though attraction to a third-person pronoun cannot be entirely ruled out:

(8a)   (Either) you or he *are* crazy.

(8b)   (Either) you or he *is* crazy.

(9a)   (Either) they or I *are* crazy.

(10)   (Either) she or I *are* crazy.

There is no attraction to a first-person pronoun:

(9b)   *(Either) they or I *am* crazy.

If the subject is realized by a group in which the noun is premodified by a coordinated adjective construction with *and*, the -Ø form of the verb is selected if the speaker has a plurality in mind:

(11)   Primary and secondary education *require* more skilled teachers.

If the speaker does not regard the situation in this way, however, she will select the -*s* form of the verb:

(12)   Secondary and tertiary education *needs* support from the government.

C) Subjects realized by clauses. In complex sentences the subject is sometimes realized by a finite or nonfinite clause. As already indicated, in such cases it is the -*s* form of the verb which is selected, i.e. clausal subjects count as singular:

(13)   That I have done a thing like that *bothers* me night and day.

(14)   To have done a thing like that *bothers* me night and day.

The singular nature of such clausal subjects appears from the fact that they can be replaced by the singular pronoun *it* (*It bothers me night and day*). An exception to this rule is constituted by independent relative clauses, i.e. clauses beginning with a *wh*-word which functions both as relative and antecedent (see sections 6.4.2 and 11.3.3), but then, their status as clauses rather than groups is not unproblematic. If *what* or *whatever* determines a plural noun in such a subject clause, the predicator of the matrix clause is always realized by the -Ø form of the verb:

(15)   What friends he has *live* abroad.

(16)   Whatever guests you invite *are* welcome.

In S P C sentences with a *what*-clause as subject and in which the complement is realized by a plural noun or noun group, there tends to be plural rather than singular subject-predicator concord:

(17)   What is required now *are (is)* food, drink and good company.

More generally, independent relative clauses resemble noun groups or pronoun groups. For example, *What friends he has* ... can be paraphrased as *The friends he has* ... or *Such friends as he has* ... and *What is required now* ... as *That which is required now* ... . It is therefore not surprising that such clauses behave differently from others with respect to concord.

    Another exception concerns subjects realized by discontinuous 'nominative with infinitive' clauses, i.e. constructions with raised subjects (see section 5.6.1). In sentences like *They are believed to be guilty* and *The children appear to be hungry* where the subject of the *to*-infinitive is realized by a plural form, it is the -Ø form of the finite verb which is selected in spite of the fact that its subject is realized clausally (*They* ... *to be guilty* / *The children* ... *to be hungry*).

D) Subjects realized by pronouns. If a subject is realized by an indefinite pronoun, there is in most cases singular concord. For example, *somebody*, *anybody*, *everybody*, *nobody* and the corresponding pronouns ending in *-one* select the *-s* form of the verb, as illustrated by *No one knows* and *Everybody loves somebody sometime*. Only in those cases where a pronoun from this group is postmodified by a preposition group in which the dependent is realized by a plural form do we occasionally find plural concord as a result of attraction (cf. section 7.6.5): *Nobody except members of the Conservative Party believe(s) this*. Pronouns like *one, each, something, anything* and *everything* naturally enough take singular concord, too.

Some indefinite pronouns behave differently, however. *Either* and *neither* prefer singular concord, for example in *(N)either seems qualified for the job*, but when postmodified by an *of*-group in which the dependent is realized by a plural construction, it is often the -Ø form of the verb which is selected, particularly in the case of *neither* (*Neither of the applicants seem qualified*). With non-textual reference to persons, *none* prefers plural concord, as in *None are so deaf as those that will not hear*. When postmodified by a preposition group containing a plural (pro)noun – as it typically is – *none* selects the -*s* form of the verb in formal BrE and the -Ø form in American and informal BrE. This is the case both when the pronoun group refers to persons (e.g. *None of the applicants seem(s) qualified*) and to a plurality of nonpersonal entities (e.g. *None of your suggestions seem(s) useful*). Under these conditions *some* and *all* always have plural concord (*Some/All of the applicants seem qualified*; *Some/All of your suggestions seem useful*), and when these pronouns realize a subject on their own, plural concord is obligatory in the case of personal reference too (*Some like it hot / All accept your proposal*). With reference to something non-countable *none*, *some* and *all* select the -*s* form, e.g. *Some (of the cheese) has been left in the fridge*. When *all* means 'everything' it takes the -*s* form, even if a plurality is implied (e.g. *All is lost now / All we need now is doctors*).

When realizing a subject, the interrogative pronouns *what*, *which* and *who* take singular concord if the speaker refers to a singular entity and plural concord if she refers to a plurality. This can be illustrated by examples like *What is your reason* vs. *What are your reasons? / Which (of the two books) is the more interesting* vs. *Which (of these books) are in stock? / Who is that girl over there? / Who are the girls over there?* When independent relative *what* is used as a subject in an independent relative clause (cf. section 11.3.3), it usually takes singular concord but may occasionally take plural concord if the speaker has a clear plurality in mind:

(18)   What *is (are)* required now are food, drink and good company.

A provisional subject realized by the personal pronoun *it* always selects the -*s* form of the verb, as in *It seems likely that they won't come* and *It seems advisable to accept their offer*. As the real subject in such cases is realized by a finite or nonfinite clause, and as clauses count as singular with respect to concord, this is hardly surprising. On the other hand, concord in sentences with a provisional subject realized by *there* is determined by the number of the form realizing the real subject. This can be illustrated by examples like *There's a fly in my soup* and *There are good reasons for this*. In colloquial language, however, there is singular concord also in those cases where the real subject is realized by a plural form (e.g. *There's many Danes who dislike*

European integration). If the real subject contains the expression *more than one* or the coordinator *both ... and* with a singular first conjoint, there is singular concord (despite the plurality of the real subject as a whole) even in formal language: *There is/*are more than <u>one reason</u> for this / In this construction there is/*are both an adverbial and an object.*

7.6.4. Notional concord

Syntactic subject-predicator concord is sometimes overruled by *notional concord*. This can be illustrated by the following examples:

(1)   The department *are* now in full agreement.

(2)   The first six months *was* spent in India.

In (1) the singular noun of the subject group combines with the plural form of BE in order to describe the referent of this noun group as a plurality, i.e. to focus on the separate members of a set rather than on the set as a unit. In (2), conversely, the plural noun of the subject group combines with the singular (past tense) form of BE in order to describe the referent of this group as a unit, i.e. as a temporal whole rather than six separate sections of time. In both examples there is thus *syntactic discord* but notional concord. What they illustrate is that English has a certain degree of freedom in interpreting the referent of a noun group as a unity or a plurality, irrespective of the grammatical number of the noun in this group.

Let us now turn to the specific conditions under which notional concord prevails and the rule of syntactic concord is breached.

A) Collective nouns. A noun like DEPARTMENT obviously inflects for number (*department : departments*), but when its singular form realizes the head of a subject group it does not invariably select the *-s* form of the verb. As illustrated by example (1), it may for semantic reasons select the *-Ø* form instead. DEPARTMENT is a so-called *collective noun*, i.e. a number-inflecting noun denoting a set of members and which in the singular is capable of combining not only with the *-s* form but also with the *-Ø* form. Other nouns belonging to this class are AUDIENCE, BAND, CHORUS, CLASS, COMMITTEE, COMPANY, CROWD, FAMILY, FIRM, GOVERN-MENT, HERD, JURY, MAJORITY, OPPOSITION, etc.

The Janus-like nature of a collective noun in the singular form is reflected not only in the form of the verb but also in the selection of coreferential pronouns, whether personal, possessive, reflexive or relative (e.g. *it* vs. *they*, *its* vs. *their*, *itself* vs. *themselves* and *which/that* vs. *who*). In the following examples with syntactic discord it is the forms of such pronouns indicating plural or – in the case of the relative – personal antecedent which have been selected together with the plural verb forms:

(3)   The orchestra are playing poorly tonight, for they haven't been rehearsing.

(4)   The committee are clearly pleased with their progress.

(5)   The jury seem to be disagreeing among themselves.

Sometimes the coreferential pronouns *they* and *their* are used instead of *it* and *its* even in those cases where a collective noun selects the *-s* form:

(6)   The company needs a new managing director for their Paris branch.

Conversely, the relative pronoun selected may be *which* or *that* rather than *who* in those cases where the collective noun group selects the -Ø form:

(7)   The crowd *which/that has* gathered at the entrance *keep* shouting slogans and throwing stones.

The 'good language' requires consistency across all the relevant elements in the sentence, but inconsistency (as in (6) and (7)) is by no means uncommon.

   In AmE, the *-s* form of the verb is practically always selected if the noun group contains a collective noun in the singular (see Preisler 1992: 163). The referent of such a noun group is thus not usually interpreted as a plurality in this variety of English. However, there may be conflict of number between a singular verb form and a following pronoun which has the same reference as the noun group:

(8)   The band is playing poorly tonight, aren't they?

In a weak sense, then, the Janus-like nature of collective nouns may show itself syntactically even in AmE.

   The collective singular vs. collective plural treatment of a collective noun is affected by certain syntactic factors. If such a noun combines with *singular determiners* like *a*, *this*, *that*, *(n)either* and *each*, it nearly always selects the *-s* form of the verb:

(9)   This commission recommends the abolition of entrance exams.

If a collective noun combines with number-neutral determiners like *the*, *my*, *your*, *Peter's*, on the other hand, the determiner does not prevent a collective plural interpretation of the referent. Secondly, the presence of a subject complement realized by a plural noun, or by a noun group in which the head is realized by a plural noun, rules out selection of the *-s* form of the verb, even in AmE:

(10)   The majority are members.

(11)   My family are early risers.

Proper nouns referring to companies, organizations, etc. like *Ford*, *Leyland* and *UNESCO* are, strictly speaking, not collective nouns in the sense described above as they do not inflect for number. However, in BrE, they resemble such nouns in permitting selection of the -Ø form of the verb for the purpose of expressing collective plural meaning (e.g. *Toyota have decided to launch yet another advertising campaign*). Singular names of sports teams very occasionally select the -*s* form of the verb, but in an overwhelming majority of cases they take plural concord, as in *Arsenal are playing Tottenham on Saturday* (in AmE only: *Arsenal is playing Tottenham on Saturday*). With respect to subject-predicator concord they therefore basically behave like the unmarked plural nouns CATTLE, POLICE, etc. discussed in section 7.6.3.

B) Plural expressions of quantity and measure. In example (2) above – *The first six months was spent in India* – we saw that there may be syntactic discord in order to obtain the *opposite* effect from the one obtained by combining a collective noun in the singular with the -Ø form of the verb. Here the rule of subject-predicator concord is breached in order to describe the referent of a plural noun group as a unit rather than as a plurality. This type of notional concord is found not only with plural nouns referring to time but also to other types of quantity or measure:

(12)   Three square miles of marsh *was* bought in 1995.
(13)   Two pints of milk *has* always been sufficient.

If the subject group begins with a singular determiner, it is nearly always the -*s* form of the verb which is selected, and if the sentence begins with a provisional subject realized by *there*, there is usually singular concord too (see Juul and Sørensen 1978: 100ff):

(14)   Another fifteen pounds *is* due tomorrow.
(15)   There'*s* two pints of milk in the fridge.

While plural expressions of quantity or measure very often select the -*s* form, the speaker may also prefer to focus on the separate members of the set referred to and thus observe the rule of syntactic concord:

(16)   The first six months *were* spent in India.
(17)   Two pints of milk *have* always been sufficient.

C) Plural proper nouns. As pointed out in section 7.6.3, geographical proper nouns in the plural form like *the Andes*, *the Alps* and *the Hebrides* select the -Ø form. With some geographical plural nouns, however, the speaker has a choice between the -Ø form and the -*s* form and can in this way focus on a set as a unit or on the separate members of a set. To these nouns belong *the Netherlands, the Midlands* and *Kew Gardens*. The combination of such nouns with the *-s* form and the -Ø form can be illustrated by the following examples (cf. Juul 1975: 260):

(18)   The Midlands *reflects* the same picture of poverty and misery.

(19)   The Midlands *attract* surprisingly many tourists.

The United States nearly always selects the *-s* form of the verb (except where one of its national sports teams is referred to) and so does *the United Nations.*

Titles of books, plays, etc. select the -s form of the verb if they are regarded as names, i.e. are used as proper nouns: *'The Three Musketeers' is undoubtedly Dumas' best known work / 'Ghosts' was produced last night at the National Theatre / My Canterbury Tales is on the table.* But if they are used to describe a literary production as consisting of a number of separate parts, it is usually the -Ø form of the verb which is selected: *The Canterbury Tales contain several bawdy stories.* Names of companies, institutions, etc. in the plural form behave like collective nouns with respect to subject-predicator concord: *British Airways expect(s) still more customers next year.*

D) Plural 'fact' expressions. We also find notional concord in:

(20)   Many cars on the roads *means* many traffic accidents.

If this sentence is compared with *Many cars on the roads are in bad repair*, it appears that something seems to be missing from the subject realization, for example *The presence of* ... . Behind the plural expression there appears to lie a singular concept which explains the selection of the *-s* form of the verb. Reference is made to a *fact* or *circumstance*, and the meaning of the plural subject expression can therefore be captured by the paraphrase 'The fact that there is/are x', i.e. by a noun group in which the head is realized by the singular form of FACT. Another possible paraphrase is 'That there is/are x', and as this is a clause, the selection of the *-s* form makes sense as well.

Plural 'fact' expressions are particularly common in sentences where the predicator is realized by MEAN (or related verbs like ENTAIL, IMPLY, INVOLVE), but we find it in sentences with other verbs as well:

(21)   High production costs *prevents* reasonable consumer prices.

E) Compound units with *and*. As mentioned in section 7.6.3 [B], a coordinated construction with *and* in which the conjoints are realized by singular nominals selects the -Ø form of the verb. In those cases where the referents of such a construction are regarded as constituting a unit, however, notional concord overrules syntactic concord:

(22)   Bed and breakfast *is* provided at fifteen pounds.

Notional concord of this type is found with coordinated noun groups referring to meals (*bacon and eggs, fish and chips*), drinks *(gin and tonic, whisky and soda, rum and cola)*, pubs (*the Spade and Becket, the Fox and Goose*) and with other established expressions such as *board and lodging, trial and error* and *the Stars and Stripes*. Names of companies, etc. (e.g. *Harland and Wolff)*, behave like collective nouns.

If a compound unit with *and* is used to refer to one person or thing only, it is naturally enough the -*s* form of the verb which is selected:

(23)   My colleague and friend, Ian Mackay, *has* just published another book.

7.6.5. Attraction

In section 7.6.3 [B], we noted attraction of verb form to the last conjoint in certain compound units (e.g. *You or your partner is crazy* instead of *You or your partner are crazy*). Similarly, in section 7.6.3 [D], we mentioned that pronouns like *no one, everybody, either, neither*, etc. are more likely to select the -Ø form if they are postmodified by a preposition group in which the dependent contains a plural noun than if they realize the subject on their own (recall the examples *Neither seems qualified for the job* and *Neither of the applicants seem qualified*). We speak of attraction when a form other than the one we would normally expect to determine concord exerts decisive influence on the form of the verb. Typically, in the case of subject groups, such a distracting form intervenes between the head of the subject and the predicator, and the longer the distance between the subject head and the predicator, the more likely it is that the speaker will let this form determine the form of the verb. In examples like the ones with pronouns already given, attraction can hardly be considered incorrect. But in an example like the following – which is characteristic of unplanned discourse and not uncommon – it is generally considered incorrect:

(1)   The situation in Bosnian mountain areas and forests now *seem* critical.

Attraction to a post-head dependent may also be exerted by a compound unit with *and* in which the conjoints are realized by singular nominals:

(2)   The systematic study of grammar, phonetics, semantics and linguistics *are* generally considered indispensable to university students of a foreign language.

It may also be a singular form which determines the choice of verb form in sentences where the subject is realized by a plural form:

(3)   He is one of those students who never *prepares* for class.

In the relative clause of this complex sentence the subject is realized by *who*, the antecedent of which is the plural form *students* and not *one of those students*, the head of which is the singular pronoun *one*. Though very frequent, this type of attraction is often considered incorrect too. Note that it is here a more distant word which 'attracts' the verb with respect to number. In order to appreciate the difference between a one-word antecedent immediately preceding the relative pronoun and one whose head word is separated from the pronoun by a postmodifying construction, it is useful to compare noun groups like:

(4)   clauses beginning with a *wh*-word which *functions* as object

(5)   clauses beginning with a *wh*-word which *have* the structure S P C

A third type of attraction is found in sentences in which a subject complement is realized by a plural form (see Juul and Sørensen (1978: 95), who cite the following example):

(6)   Markoff's material *were* 20,000 letters comprised in the first chapter and the first 16 sonnets of the second chapter ...

In S P C sentences it is regularly the subject which determines the choice of verb form (though the fossilized biblical expression *The wages of sin is death* may be noted). Attraction of the type illustrated by (6) is generally considered incorrect and is therefore 'fatal' too, like that illustrated by examples (1), (2) and (3).

7.7. Other types of external concord

In those cases where a subject complement is realized by a noun or noun group there is usually *subject - subject complement concord* of number:

(1)   However, *the latest setback* is *a further embarrassment* to the troubled economy.

(2)   *The banana plantation* is *a reservoir of rats.*

(3)   *The liaison* may even prove *a good career movement.*

(4)   *The warehouses and storerooms* are *perfect breeding grounds for rats.*

(5)   *The children* have become *good friends.*

(6)   *They* proved *very amusing companions.*

As in the case of subject-predicator concord, however, there are many exceptions to this syntactic rule. Here as well the semantic nature of the noun groups involved plays an important role (see Huddleston 1984: 187). An example like *Laurel and Hardy are an amusing pair* is perfectly natural, for 'an amusing pair' can obviously only be predicated of two entities, and Laurel and Hardy constitute a unit (though notional concord does not here, as in the case of *bed and breakfast*, etc., overrule syntactic subject-predicator concord). In *Laurel and Hardy are a good choice* the complement is realized by a noun group which is usually predicated of a single entity, so in this example discord of number can only be explained semantically as being due to the unitary conception of Laurel and Hardy. Altogether S P C sentences in which S is realized by a plural form and C by a singular form are not uncommon. While examples (5) and (6) could not be changed, the subject complement of example (4) could also have been realized by a singular noun group: *The warehouses and storerooms are a perfect breeding ground for rats*. Note also that while e.g. *(Both) Woody Allen and Clint Eastwood are good choices* – where the referents of the subject nouns can hardly be regarded as constituting a unit – is a more natural sentence than *(Both) Woody Allen and Clint Eastwood are a good choice*, the latter cannot be ruled out as ungrammatical (Huddleston 1984: 187).

While sentences in which S is realized by a plural form and C by a singular form are thus fairly common, the opposite kind of discord is practically never found. Apart from idiomatic expressions like *Thatcher is friends with Reagan* it only occurs in examples of the type illustrated by a sentence like *The policy I advocate is lower tariffs*.

In S P O C sentences there is usually *object - object complement concord* of number:

(7)   God has made *me a cripple*.
(8)   God has made *them cripples*.

Here as well, however, we find syntactic discord – in the shape of O realized by a plural and Co realized by a singular form:

(9)   This makes *Laurel and Hardy a good choice*.

Unlike a complement form, an object form selects its number independently of that of the subject form, as illustrated by examples like *That guy has killed my best friends* and *Those guys have killed my best friend*. Only in the case of the so-called *distributive plural* is there concord of number between S and O (for more details on the distributive plural, see section 10.4.6):

(10)   *The terrorists* lost *their lives*.
(11)   *Such clauses* rarely have *third person subjects*.

In these sentences – which should be compared with *The terrorist lost his life* and *Such a clause rarely has a third person subject* – the members of a set of entities denoted by one constituent form are matched one by one by those denoted by another form. This type of plural concord is found not only in S P O sentences but also where other constituents are involved. Examples illustrating this are *We complained about our wives* and *The students were shouting at the top of their voices* (S P A). In some cases it is possible either to focus on the one-by-one correspondence between the members of two sets or to refrain from doing so: *The monks bowed their head(s) in shame.* Where idiomatic expressions are involved, the rule of the distributive plural tends to be ignored: *The inspectors can't put their finger on the cause of trouble / The inspectors put their foot down.*

In S P O sentences like *She shot herself* and *They shot themselves* there is agreement of number, person and gender between the reflexive pronoun realizing the object and the subject form. This is not an instance of subject-object concord, however, but due to a more general rule that a pronoun agrees with its antecedent. This rule also explains the agreement found in examples like *She is not herself these days, They gave themselves a break, I'll pay for myself* and *We finished the job ourselves* where the reflexive pronouns realize a complement, an indirect object, a prepositional complementation and part of a subject respectively.

8. The complex sentence

8.1. Introduction

By a complex sentence we understand a sentence with one or more sub-clauses. There are two types of complex sentence: that in which one or more sentence functions have clausal realization (e.g. O:cl) and that in which this is not the case but where one or more *group constituents* are realized clausally. The latter type of complex sentence can be illustrated by:

(1)   The residents *living in the poorhouse* avoided her like a leper.
(2)   As soon *as he gave me that guitar* I forgot about piano.
(3)   The passengers were marshalled into *what appeared to be the arrivals hall*.
(4)   His *giving me this note* is an act of defiance.

In the first three examples, the italicized clause realizes the dependent of a group: a noun group in (1), an adverb group in (2) and a preposition group in (3). In example (4), the italicized clause realizes the head of a group determined by the dependent pronoun *His*. Complex sentences of the type exemplified by (1) through (4) will be dealt with in chapters 10 through 12 on word classes and groups.

In this chapter we examine complex sentences of the first type, i.e. sentences in which one or more sentence functions have clausal realization. We note, first of all, that the same *seven basic patterns* are found in complex sentences as in simple sentences:

S P	*To see her falling in love* hurts.
S P A	*Going abroad with her* was on the agenda.
S P C	The question is *whether she wants him back*.
S P O	We must assume *that elsewhere all hell is being let loose*.
S P O O	He gives *whoever turns up after office hours* a rough ride.
S P O A	Lucy spent that summer *writing letters of application*.
S P O C	We'll elect you *whatever you like*.

As we see in these examples, any of the sentence functions S, Od, Oi, Cs, Co and A (but not P) may have clausal realization.

We also very frequently find clausal realization of *optional adverbials*:

(5)   *As dusk fell*, the group's mood became more querulous.
(6)   *To be quite honest*, I hope they think we're travelling together.

Some complex sentences can be found which do not readily fit into one of the seven basic patterns. A case in point is sentences in which an indirect

directive is expressed by verbs like ADVISE, ASK, BEG, ENTREAT, PER-
SUADE, REMIND, REQUEST, TELL, URGE followed by a noun group + a *to*-
infinitive clause (see Quirk et al. 1985: 1215):

(7)   They persuaded the young man to see a psychiatrist.

It is not entirely obvious how such sentences should be analysed. An analysis
in terms of an S P O C structure seems excluded because there is no implied
S P C construction in the structure following the finite verb, as there is in an
ordinary S P O C sentence like *They made the young man their leader* (see
section 3.2.8). But should it then be classified as an S P O sentence or as an S
P O O sentence? If an S P O analysis is adopted, the problem arises that the
entity *affected* by the action expressed by P is not everything following the
finite verb, as it is in a S P O sentence like *They wanted <u>the young man to see
a psychiatrist</u>*, but *the young man* exclusively (see section 3.2.5 on the
identification of objects). Note also that the infinitive clause can be omitted
without changing the semantic relation between *persuaded* and *the young
man*. If (7) is analysed as an S P Oi Od sentence, we should expect *the young
man* to be a BENEFICIARY DONE-TO like the indirect object in an
ordinary S P O O sentence like *They gave the young man what money they
had*. Semantically, the role performed by *the young man* in (7) is instead
simultaneously AFFECTED DONE-TO and AGENT DOER. The problem
of classifying examples like (7) arises because two clausal structures overlap:

$$\text{cl}^1$$
$$\overline{\text{They persuaded} \quad {}_{\lfloor}\text{the young man}^{\rfloor} \quad \text{to see a psychiatrist}_{\rfloor}}$$
$$\text{cl}^2$$

Rather than assign examples of this type to one specific pattern, we suggest
that they belong in a grey zone between the S P O and the S P O O patterns.

8.2. Classification of subclauses

Formally, subclauses may be divided into *finite clauses*, *nonfinite clauses*
and *verbless clauses*. The most common types of finite clauses are *that*-
clauses, independent relative clauses and interrogative clauses:

(1)   She discovered *that they were listening with apparent interest.*

(2)   *What you said* kept me awake all night.

(3)   *Whether your plan will succeed* remains to be seen.

(4)   I've discovered *who my real friends are.*

As illustrated by (3) and (4), there are both *yes-no* interrogative subclauses
(signalled by *if* and *whether*) and *wh*-interrogative subclauses (signalled by

interrogative pronouns and WHEN, WHY, HOW). The subordinating conjunction is in some contexts omitted from *that*-clauses, particularly if the clause it introduces realizes an object (see also section 6.4.1).

Nonfinite clauses may be divided into *-ing participle clauses* (also referred to as present participle clauses), *-ed participle clauses* (or past participle clauses), *to-infinitive clauses* and *bare infinitive clauses*:

(5)   *Going home that evening,* I stopped at the chemist's for some razor blades.
(6)   The soldiers were impassive *unless challenged by the passengers.*
(7)   I was only trying *to forestall alarm and despondency.*
(8)   All I did was *ask them round for drinks.*

As illustrated by these examples, nonfinite clauses are usually subjectless, but all four types permit overt subjects:

(9)   *Our chairman being away on holiday,* there is nothing we can do right now.
(10)   *Dinner finished,* the fellows adjourned to the combination room.
(11)   I want *you to leave immediately.*
(12)   *Rather than he call her,* I prefer to tackle this problem myself.

As will appear below, *-ing* participle clauses and *to*-infinitive clauses are commoner than *-ed* participle clauses and particularly bare infinitive clauses.

Verbless clauses are nearly always adverbial and may or may not contain a subject form:

(13)   Ronald knelt down, *his hands behind his back.*
(14)   *Although invariably very considerate,* she strikes me as somewhat cold.

Note also the existence of examples like the following in which a verbless clause with adverbial properties could be viewed as a reduced 'nonrestrictive relative clause', i.e. a clause which provides further information about the person or entity it refers back to (cf. sections 10.1.4 and 11.3.3 [A]):

(15a)   George, *ready for action now,* stared at the intruder.
(15b)   George, *who was ready for action now,* stared at the intruder.

According to *syntactic function*, subclauses realizing sentence functions can be subdivided into subject clauses, direct object clauses, indirect object clauses, subject complement clauses, object complement clauses and adverbial clauses. The first five types are traditionally referred to as 'nominal clauses', because the sentence functions involved are typically realized by nominals. In our discussion below we select the functional classification of subclauses into these six types as our point of departure.

8.3. Subject clauses

Subjects realized by *finite* clauses can be illustrated by:

(1)   *That you dislike her* is obvious to everybody in the department. (*that*-clause)

(2)   *What you said* kept me awake all night. (independent relative clause)

(3)   *When you can help me* is what I want to know. (*wh*-interrogative clause)

(4)   *Whether she will recover* is still an open question. (*yes-no* interrogative clause)

In some cases it is difficult to tell whether a subject clause is realized by an independent relative clause or by a *wh*-interrogative clause (see Quirk et al. 1985: 1059ff). This is particularly the case if the *wh*-word involved is *what*. For example, a sentence like *What he said was unclear* is ambiguous in written English in that it can mean either 'That which he said was lacking in clarity' or 'I didn't get what he was trying to say'. In spoken English, we should add, this example is unambiguous, for here *what* is unstressed if the subject clause is relative and is pronounced with nuclear stress if the subject clause is interrogative. Syntactically, independent relative clauses realizing a subject differ from interrogative *wh*-clauses performing this sentence function in that they select the plural form of the verb if a noun determined by *what* is in the plural, thus behaving more like groups than clauses (see section 7.6.3 [C]):

(5)   *What enemies he has* have left the department.

(6)   *What enemies he has* is hard to tell.

Furthermore, independent relative clauses in which *what* determines a noun differ from interrogative *what*-clauses of this type in that they may be followed by *few* and *little*. For example, *few* can be inserted after *what* in (5) but not in (6), and *little* can be inserted after *what* in *What money he has will soon be spent* but not in *What money he has is hard to tell*. Semantically, interrogative *wh*-clauses differ from independent relative clauses in that they contain a gap of unknown information (Quirk et al. 1985: 1060).

As in the case of subject clauses, it is sometimes difficult to tell whether an *object clause* is realized by an independent relative clause or a *wh*-interrogative clause. For example, a sentence like *He asked me what I expected* (quoted from van Ek & Robat 1984: 47) is ambiguous – not only in written but also in spoken English – in that it can mean either 'He asked me that which I expected' or 'He asked me "What do you expect?"'.

In those cases where a subject is realized by a *nonfinite clause*, the subtypes of such clauses are *-ing* participle clauses and *to*-infinitive clauses:

(7)   *Getting on with things* is just what we can't do.

(8)   *To say that my heart isn't in it* would be the understatement of all time.

Continuous *to*-infinitive clauses with subject function do not have subjects. Arguably, discontinuous *to*-infinitive clauses have subjects in cases like the following (for discussion, see section 5.6.1):

(9)   *John* happened *to be around at the time.*
(10)   *Sally* is believed *to be guilty.*

In continuous *to*-infinitive clauses, an AGENT (or another participant with subject-potential in a corresponding finite clause) may be expressed by an initial adverbial group with the preposition *for* as head, compare:

(11a) *To step down now* would be frowned upon by everybody.
(11b) *For Rita/her to step down now* would be frowned upon by everybody.

That *For* is here a preposition rather than a conjunction appears from the fact that it comes and goes with the following (pro)nominal constituent and from the fact that the infinitive clause is already marked as subordinate by virtue of being nonfinite and therefore has no need for a semantically empty subordinator conjunction. Like the very similar *by*-group in passive constructions, the *for*-group is syntactically optional.

The next example illustrates subject realization by an *-ing* clause which has its own subject:

(12)   John/Him being Jewish makes no difference. (cf. Vestergaard 1985: 216)

This should be compared with *John's/His being Jewish makes no difference*, where the subject is not realized by a clause but by a group in which the dependent is realized by a genitive or possessive pronoun determiner (*John's/His*) and the head by the *-ing* participle clause *being Jewish* (cf. *John's/his Jewishness makes no difference*). As regards the use of these competing constructions in subject clauses, it should be mentioned that (i) possessive pronouns are usually preferred to personal pronouns, (ii) the genitive form is preferred to the uninflected nominal form, especially in formal style, unless the nominal has impersonal or inanimate reference (see section 10.3.8 on the genitive). It should be added that while the genitive is thus generally preferred to the uninflected form of a nominal in subject clauses, the opposite is the case in clauses realizing other sentence functions:

(13)   *John's being Jewish* makes no difference.
(14)   I remember *John telling me that joke.*

As pointed out in section 5.2.3, a subject is often moved from its neutral position to the end of the sentence for reasons of end-weight and/or end-focus. Such extraposition can be illustrated by the following examples in which the postponed subjects are realized by finite clauses:

(15)   It has been known *that there are groups out there that are willing to kill at random*.

(16)   It doesn't matter *who fired him*.

(17)   It's uncertain *when we can tackle this problem*.

(18)   It's still an open question *whether she will survive*.

With *that*-clauses, extraposition is the norm rather than the exception and may even be obligatory, for example in *It seems/appears that the house was set on fire*. Interrogative clauses of both types (*yes-no*; *wh-*) are also freely postponed, as illustrated by examples (16), (17) and (18), but extraposition of independent relative clauses is not common. If a sentence like *It was unclear what he said* is pronounced neutrally with nuclear stress on *said*, or if it is pronounced with contrastive nuclear stress on *what*, the subject clause will be understood to be interrogative ('I didn't get what he was trying to say'). Only if the entire subject clause is pronounced without prosodic prominence and the nuclear stress falls on *(un)clear*, can it be understood to be an independent relative clause ('That which he said was lacking in clarity').

Extraposed subject clauses may be nonfinite:

(19)   It frightens me *to think how vulnerable we are*.

(20)   It's splendid *seeing you back on form*.

While *to*-infinitive clauses are freely postponed, extraposition of *-ing* participle clauses is much rarer and is usually characteristic of informal style (van Ek & Robat 1984: 412). In e.g. *Getting on with things is just what we can't do*, postponement of the subject clause would have the effect of demoting the part of the message expressed by this clause to an explanatory appendage: *It's just what we can't do, getting on with things*. Such right-dislocation (cf. section 4.5) is not motivated by weight as it is in the case of extraposed clauses.

8.4. Cleft sentences

In this section we shall examine a special type of subject clause. Consider first a complex S P C sentence like the following in which the subject is realized by an independent relative clause beginning with *what*:

(1)   *What worries me* is the poor quality of your work.

If this is compared with the simple sentence *The increasingly poor quality of your work worries me*, we notice an important difference in information structure: the part of the message realizing the noun group is highlighted through final position (end-focus). Highlighting (combined with identification) can also be obtained in another way, however, namely by means of a so-called *cleft sentence*:

(2)   It is the poor quality of your work that worries me.

A cleft sentence is a sentence in which a constituent singled out for emphatic identification is placed between *it* + BE and a subclause realizing the remainder of the corresponding simple sentence. *It*, it should be added, has no reference outside the sentence, and in this way it differs from *it* used in superficially similar but noncleft sentences. In a noncleft sentence like *It is Mr Blake, who has just been appointed* – used in reply to e.g. *Who is your boss? – It* refers to *your boss* in the preceding question (see Nølke 1984: 73).

Sentences like (2) are called 'cleft' because they are divided into two parts. Typically, the second of these, the subclause, expresses given information and is pronounced without prosodic prominence, whereas the focalized element in the matrix clause (such as *the poor quality of your work* in (2)) expresses new information and is pronounced with nuclear stress.

By means of the cleft construction not only subjects but also objects and adverbials may be focalized, cf. the following cleft versions of *Russell met Keynes in Cambridge*:

(3)   It was Russell that/who met Keynes in Cambridge.
(4)   It was Keynes (that) Russell met in Cambridge.
(5)   It was in Cambridge (that) Russell met Keynes.

Prepositional complements may also be focalized, as shown by an example like *It is her last novel (that) I'm interested in*. Indirect objects, subject complements and object complements are rarely focalized by cleaving in English, but examples like *It's me you do a great honour* and *It's president of the board of directors he's become/they've elected him* can hardly be considered unacceptable. Predicators cannot be focalized by cleaving at all.

Cleft sentences are not declarative exclusively but may also be interrogative:

(6)   Is it the quality of his work that worries you?

Furthermore, cleft constructions may be subordinated:

(7)   I hope it isn't the quality of my work that worries you.

Cleft sentences are nearly always used for the same purpose, namely to signal an *identification*. In (3), for example, the person who met Keynes in Cambridge is identified as Russell. Another property shared by cleft sentences is that in addition to describing a situation they contain a *presupposition*, i.e. a proposition regarded as true by the speaker, which is both positive and negative (Vikner 1973 and Hansen, ms.). By uttering (3), for example, the speaker assumes not only that someone met Keynes in Cambridge but also that there was somebody else who did *not* do so. Any positive cleft sentence is thus matched by a negative cleft sentence. Conversely, any negative cleft sentence, for example *It wasn't me who did it*, is matched by a positive cleft sentence.

Sometimes the subclause is omitted from a cleft sentence. Such a *reduced cleft* is context-bound in that it can only be used if the subclause can be recovered from the context (see Nølke 1984: 74). For example, *It wasn't me* can be used instead of an unreduced cleft sentence in reply to a question like *Who broke the window?*

As a cleft sentence expresses an identification, it is obvious that the form focalized should permit such identification, i.e. it should refer to a person, a thing, a place, a cause, etc. (see Vikner 1973). A number of *restrictions* on the cleft construction can be explained in this way. For example, disjuncts like *possibly, fortunately, in all likelihood* and conjuncts like *nevertheless, though, anyhow* do not permit such referential identification and consequently cannot be focalized in clefts. If a subject or an object is realized by a clause (which describes a situation), cleaving is heavily restricted. For example, we cannot by means of cleaving focalize the object clause of a sentence like *He tried to concentrate upon rational assessment of the situation*. On the other hand, clausally realized adjuncts are frequently focalized by means of the cleft construction:

(8)   It is because you drink so much that I avoid your company.
(9)   It is only when you drink that I avoid you.

A number of restrictions on clefts can be explained semantically (see Hansen, ms.). For example, negative expressions like *nobody, nothing, nowhere, in no way* and *never* cannot be focalized as this would lead to a contradiction of the positive presupposition contained in the subclause. Thus **It is nobody that/who loves me* is not a possible cleft version of *Nobody loves me* because it contradicts the presupposition that somebody loves me. Similarly, indefinite expressions like *somebody, somewhere, anyone* and *anywhere* are incapable of being focalized in clefts, as illustrated by the unacceptability of e.g. **It is somebody who loves me* (cf. *Somebody loves me*). In this case the constraint is due to the fact that *somebody, somewhere*, etc. do not provide any identification because no option is eliminated. Note, however, that while e.g. **It is somewhere that you will find the gun* is unacceptable, this is not the case with *It is somewhere in here that you will find the gun*. The reason for this is that *somewhere* is postmodified restrictively by a preposition group which provides the necessary identification and contrasts with e.g. *out there*.

Let us turn now to the *syntactic* properties of cleft sentences. The subclause is usually analysed as a *restrictive relative clause* (cf. section 11.3.3 [A]), but it differs from regular clauses of this type in three ways:

(i) It may be added to a proper noun (e.g. *It is John that has resigned*).

(ii) There is often a preference for *that* or zero instead of *who* and *which*, except if it serves as subject.

(iii) It may be added to an adverbial clause, as in *It is only <u>when you drink</u> that I avoid you* (see Quirk et al. 1985: 1387).

In those cases where an adjunct is focalized, it is perhaps not immediately obvious whether *that* should be analysed as a relative or as a subordinating conjunction. On reflection, however, it seems clear that it has its own syntactic function inside the subclause and that this function is the same as that of the focalized element. In a sentence like *It was in Toronto that I met her*, *that* is thus a relative, and its function in the subclause is adverbial, like that of *in Toronto* in the matrix clause. If *that* is omitted, this analysis also applies to zero: *It was in Toronto Ø I met her*.

Having analysed the subclause of a cleft sentence as a special type of restrictive relative clause we must consider what its antecedent is and – more generally – how cleft sentences should be analysed syntactically. The analysis which comes to mind first is the straightforward one that the highlighted element is the antecedent and the subclause is a post-head dependent in a group realizing a subject complement. Like other relative clauses, the relative clause in a cleft construction shows concord relations with its antecedent:

(10)   It is my brother *who wants* to go on a holiday.
(11)   It is these books *which challenge* his views.

If this analysis is adopted, however, we run into serious difficulty. This can be illustrated by an example like *It was the vase that Agatha gave us* (quoted from Huddleston 1984: 461). In written English this is ambiguous, for it may represent not only a cleft sentence but also an ordinary uncleft sentence in which the subclause restricts the reference of the preceding noun ('It was the vase given to us by Agatha'). We would not want the same syntactic analysis for both. In the cleft version the subclause is more loosely connected with *the vase* than in the noncleft version, as shown by the fact that the focalized element can be fronted: *The vase it was that Agatha gave us*. This seems to indicate that the subclause is not part of the same constituent as the focalized element. In other words, the problem at hand is how to show that the

focalized element and the relative clause are at the same time closely related
and yet two separate constituents. One possibility is to employ stacking:

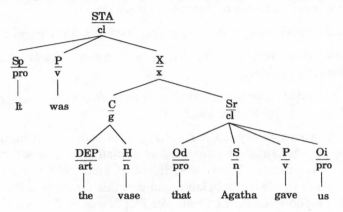

The closeness relation between the focal element and the relative clause is
here reflected by means of a form and function stack. The separate status of
the two constituents is then acknowledged at a lower level by assigning
different functions to them within the stack. The focal element, which
expresses new information and follows a form of BE, is assigned subject
complement status. The relative clause, which expresses given information,
is interpreted as a real subject in fixed position. The pronoun *It* is simply a
form word representing the information expressed by the relative clause (*It* =
'what Agatha gave us'). Note that this information could have been expressed
by an independent relative clause in normal subject position (e.g. *What
Agatha gave us was the vase*), but with unmarked end-focus on *the vase*.

In closing this section we return to examples with independent relative
clauses like the one just mentioned, as well as (1) above: *What worries me is
the increasingly poor quality of your work*. As these examples are closely
related to the simple noncleft sentences *Agatha gave us the vase* and *The
poor quality of your work worries me*, not only semantically but also
syntactically, they would seem to represent a second type of cleft sentence.
In many cases, however, sentences of this type are unmatched by simple
sentences, as illustrated by an example like *What went wrong was that the
valve was overheated* (cf. Huddleston 1984: 464). Note also the functional
diversity of the independent relative clause: in the examples discussed so far
it serves as subject, but often it might equally well serve as subject
complement instead, in which case it receives unmarked end-focus, e.g. *The
poor quality of your work is what worries me*. For these reasons we do not
classify them as cleft. Such sentences – traditionally termed *pseudo-cleft* –

may be regarded as a special case of sentences whose subject is realized by an independent relative clause with *what*.

Pseudo-cleft sentences differ from cleft sentences in that they make it possible for the entire predicate to be singled out for identification:

(12)   What she did was (to) tell me off in public.

If this sentence is compared with the simple sentence *She told me off in public*, we see that it is the entire predicate stack which is focalized by means of the finite proform of DO in the relative clause. Another characteristic of pseudo-cleft sentences is that the subject complement may be realized by a *clause*. Such a clause may be nonfinite, as in (12), or it may be finite:

(13)   What bothers us is that you take no interest in your work.

In truly cleft sentences a subject complement cannot be realized clausally, cf. the ungrammaticality of **It is that you take no interest in your work that bothers us*.

8.5. Object clauses

Object clauses realized by *finite* object clauses can be illustrated by the following examples:

(1)   Police believe *(that) the shooter was a professional.* (that-clause)
(2)   The child does *what society says he must.* (independent relative clause)
(3)   Keeping a nervous eye on passing traffic, many wondered out loud *which of them would be next.* (wh-interrogative clause)
(4)   I'll ask her *if she'll lend us the money.* (*yes-no* interrogative clause)

Objects may be realized by all four subtypes of nonfinite clauses, but *to*-infinitive clauses are particularly frequent:

(5)   I enjoy *travelling by train.*
(6)   I want *this reported to the police.*
(7)   We watched *the sun set behind the mountains.*
(8)   I don't want *to become a refugee for the rest of my life.*

Continuous *to*-infinitive object clauses may have their own subject (unlike corresponding subject clauses, cf. section 8.3):

(9)   I don't want *you to become a refugee for the rest of your life.*

Recall that a clausally realized object may be postponed to secure end-weight and that in those cases where there is a provisional object in the shape of *it*, object postponement involves extraposition (see sections 3.2.5 and 5.2.3):

(10)   I just saw on television *how some Indian people started a shop and put the old grocery on the corner out of business.* (S A P A O)

(11)   I find it a challenge *writing this report.* (S P Op Co Or)

Verbs vary considerably with respect to what forms of clausal complementation they take. For example, AVOID requires an *-ing* clause and ANSWER a *that*-clause:

(12)   I avoided drinking wine.
(*I avoided to drink wine / *I avoided that I drank wine)

(13)   She answered that she joined the party.
(*She answered to join the party / *She answered joining the party)

WANT may take an object *to*-infinitive clause, in some cases a participle clause, but not a *that*-clause:

(14a)   I want you to leave at once.
(*I want that you leave at once)

(14b)   I don't want you arriving late.

(14c)   I want it done now.

Other verbs that allow of more than one type of clausal complementation:

(15a)   I believe him (to be) guilty of murder.

(15b)   I believe that he is guilty of murder.

(16a)   She liked to swim in the morning.

(16b)   She liked swimming in the morning.

In these examples there is very little semantic difference between the options. In other cases, there is a clear difference of meaning:

(17a)   I remembered to post the letter. (= 'I did not neglect to post it')

(17b)   I remembered posting the letter. (= 'I looked back on the event')

(18a)   She tried to close the window (but it was stuck).

(18b)   She tried closing the window (but there was still too much noise coming from the street).

Note that different types of clausal complementation sometimes assume different sentence functions, resulting in an even clearer difference of meaning:

(19a)   Jack stopped to examine the results. (S P A)

(19b)   Jack stopped examining the results. (S P O)

(20a)   Sally went on to discuss the children. (S P A)

(20b)   Sally went on discussing the children. (S P O)

Finally, it should be mentioned that objects are realized clausally in (directly or indirectly) reported speech:

(21)   *'I'm no puritan,'* she answered.

(22)   She says (that) she would like another whisky.

For discussion, see sections 5.3.9. and 5.6.1.

8.6. Subject complement clauses

Subject complements can be realized by most clause types. The following examples illustrate realization by finite clauses:

(1)   The point is *that we are now involved*. (*that*-clause)
(2)   All I can think of is *what you said last night*. (independent relative clause)
(3)   My worry is *how you could do a thing like that*. (*wh*-interrogative clause)
(4)   The question is *whether she will recover*. (*yes-no* interrogative clause)

In subject complement *that*-clauses the subordinating conjunction cannot readily be omitted as it can if such a clause realizes an object.

Subject complements may also be realized by *-ing* participle clauses, *to*-infinitive clauses and – in very specific contexts – bare infinitive clauses:

(5)   The dividing line between a good and a bad politician is *knowing what can be achieved with the means at his disposal at any given time*.
(6)   My only aim in life is *to free my children*.
(7)   What she did was *(to) tell me off in public*.
(8)   All I did was *(to) ask them round for drinks*.

The realization of a subject complement by a bare infinitive clause typically requires the presence of a form of DO in the realization of the subject, either in an independent relative clause beginning with *what* (as in (7)) or in a postmodifying relative clause (as in (8)). In such examples, the subject complement may also be realized by a *to*-infinitive clause.

Present participle clauses realizing a subject complement may have an overt subject:

(9)   A crucial event was *Gascoigne being sent off for a professional foul*.

To-infinitive clauses realizing a subject complement do not have subjects (the same way that clauses of this type with subject function do not have subjects, see section 8.3). In an example like the next one, *for Rita* is a preposition group realizing an adverbial within the complement clause:

(10)   The only solution is *for Rita to step down*.

As appears, a complement *to*-infinitive clause may express an agent (or some other participant with subject potential) in an initial adverbial *for*-group.

8.7. Indirect object clauses and object complement clauses

In the case of indirect objects and object complements the possibilities of clausal realization are heavily restricted. Both can be realized clausally by an independent relative clause or by an *-ing* participle clause:

(1)   He gives *whoever turns up after office hours* a rough ride.

(2)   She gave *going to France* a good deal of thought.

(3)   You can paint the wall *what(ever) colour you like*.

(4)   I would call that *casting pearls before swine*.

Arguably, an object complement can be realized by an *-ed* participle clause:

(5)   I keep the will *hidden in my drawer*.

The analysis of this sentence poses a number of problems, but it seems most natural to assume that *the will* realizes an object and *hidden in my drawer* an object complement. Note that the semantic relationship between these two word sequences is of the same nature as that between *the will* and *safe* in an S P O C sentence like *I keep the will safe*. As *hidden* must be analysed as a passive participle rather than as an adjectival *-ed* form (see section 7.4.6), the object complement in (5) is realized by a clause in which *hidden* functions as predicator and *in my drawer* as adverbial.

8.8. Adverbial clauses

Adverbial clauses are extremely frequent and may be finite, nonfinite or verbless. Finite adverbial clauses are typically introduced by subordinating conjunctions (cf. section 6.4.1):

(1)   A glider pilot is in hospital with a fractured rib *after his aircraft crashed into an electricity pylon*.

(2)   I left my wife *because I realized that I had made an awful mistake*.

An adverbial may be realized by the following subtypes of nonfinite clause:

(3)   *Keeping a nervous eye on passing traffic*, many wondered out loud which of them would be next. (*-ing* participle clause)

(4)   The soldiers lounging at the entrance were impassive *unless challenged by the passengers*. (*-ed* participle clause)

(5)   The family enrolled in courses *to attain enlightenment*. (*to*-infinitive clause)

If *rather than* is interpreted as a complex conjunction (and not as an adverb followed by conjunction) on a par with *instead of*, the adverbial in the following example is realized by a bare infinitive clause:

(6)   *Rather than call her*, you should invite her over for lunch.

Realization of an adverbial by a *verbless* clause can be illustrated by:

(7)   *Although invariably very considerate,* she strikes me as somewhat cold.

Nonfinite and verbless clauses may also have their own subject (see section 8.2), typically in formal style:

(8)   *Our chairman being away on holiday,* there is nothing we can do right now.
(9)   *Dinner finished,* the fellows adjourned to the combination room.
(10)   Ronald knelt down, *his hands behind his back.*

A nonfinite or verbless adverbial clause which has its own subject and is not introduced by a subordinating conjunction is traditionally called an *absolute clause*. In this connection attention should also be drawn to so-called *supplementive clauses*, i.e. participial and verbless clauses without a subordinator like the ones occurring in examples such as *This passage is unclear, taken out of context* and *I slammed down the receiver, furious after a day of frustrations* (see Quirk et al. 1985: 1123ff). Such clauses – which may also have their own subject and thus be absolute – describe attendant circumstances the value of which (conditional, temporal, causal, etc.) has to be inferred from the context.

   In nonfinite or verbless adverbial clauses without an overt subject, the 'understood' subject form normally has the same reference as the subject form of the superordinate clause, as in (3) through (7). As illustrated by the next examples, however, this is not always so:

(11)   *Keeping a nervous eye on passing traffic,* it suddenly occurred to me that my own family might be next.
(12)   *Known primarily as the author of 'Changing Places' and 'Small World',* many consider Lodge a humourist and writer of campus novels.
(13)   *Taking his recent record into account,* Major appears to be the wrong man for the job.

In cases like these it is customary to speak of *unattached participles* (or 'dangling participles'). This term is not entirely appropriate, however. In (11), the hearer is able to attach the *-ing* participle clause to the words *me* and *my* in the matrix clause and infer that the understood subject of the subclause is *I* (*As I was keeping a nervous eye on passing traffic, it* ...). In (12), similarly, there is something to hang on to in the matrix clause, namely the object noun *Lodge*, so here as well the hearer is capable of inferring the understood subject of the subclause. In (13) there is no noun or pronoun in the matrix clause on the basis of which the subject form of the subclause can be inferred; but here the hearer will correctly assume that it is a pronoun with generic reference (*one, you* or *we*).

While (13) is unproblematical, and while (11) and (12) are acceptable to most speakers of English, an example like the following is unacceptable, or at least highly questionable:

(14)   *Known primarily as the author of 'Changing Places' and 'Small World'*, my brother considers Lodge a humourist and writer of campus novels.

What is wrong here is that the understood subject of the participle clause may by the hearer or reader be understood to have the same reference, not as the object *Lodge* in the superordinate clause but as the subject *my brother*. In this way (14) differs from (12), in which there is no risk that the understood subject of the participle clause may be assumed to have the same reference as the subject *many* in the superordinate clause.

An unattached participle is also found in an example like the next one (quoted from McArthur 1992: 753):

(15)   There, coasting comfortably down the attractive green coastline, the town of Malacca with its prominent hill was very evident.

As the matrix clause of this complex sentence describes a specific past situation, the addressee cannot here as in the case of (13) assume that the understood subject form of the subclause is a pronoun with generic reference. The intended subject form appears to be a pronoun with specific reference (*I, we* or *they*), and as there is nothing in the matrix clause from which such a pronoun can be inferred, the participle clause must be considered wholly unattached and unacceptable.

In general, an unattached adverbial clause is acceptable only if (i) it serves as a disjunct; or (ii) if the implied subject is the whole of the matrix clause; or (iii) if the implied subject is a generic pronoun or *it* as a prop word, as in the following three examples, respectively (cf. Greenbaum & Quirk 1990: 328):

(16)   *Putting it mildly*, you have caused us some inconvenience.

(17)   I'll tell you *if necessary*.

(18)   *When dining in the restaurant*, a jacket and tie are required.

In closing this section, we should point out that adverbial clauses may perform a variety of *semantic functions*. Some of these are illustrated in the following examples:

(19)   *When independent publications were finally legalized*, dozens of new titles sprang up. (TIME)

(20)   You can sit *where you like*. (PLACE)

(21)   I left my wife *because I realized I had made an awful mistake*. (REASON)

(22)   Shortly after the shooting, anonymous callers telephoned TV stations *to warn that more police officials would be harmed*. (PURPOSE)

(23)   *Though my car is quite old*, it's still in running order. (CONCESSION)
(24)   I slammed down the receiver, *furious after a day of frustrations*.
       (ATTENDANT CIRCUMSTANCE)
(25)   I'll write it *if somebody wants it*. (CONDITION)

8.9. Conditional clauses

One particularly important subtype of adverbial clause is the one expressing
a condition. As illustrated by the following examples, a conditional clause
realizes an adverbial in a conditional sentence:

(1)   *If we are attacked*, we will defend ourselves.
(2)   You will sleep better *if you get a new mattress*.

A conditional sentence consists of two parts, an *if*-clause (the protasis) and a
matrix clause (the apodosis). By means of such a sentence the speaker
informs the hearer that the situation described by the subclause is
hypothetical and that the truth of the situation described by the matrix clause
is dependent on that of the subclause.

Typically, the two situations described by a conditional sentence are linked
both *causally and temporally*. In examples like (1) and (2) the situation
described by the matrix clause is not only dependent on that described by the
subclause, it also follows it in time. When in such cases the predicator of the
subclause is realized by a present verb form, that of the matrix clause is
realized by the future verb form (as in the examples) or by a modal verb form
like MAY + V (as in *You may sleep better if you get a new mattress*).

In conditional sentences the predicator of the subclause may also be
realized by a *past* verb form without past time meaning. In that case the
condition which is laid down is not neutral as it is if the verb form of the
subclause stands in the present but is biassed towards a negative response.
While it is a completely open question whether the situation described by the
subclause of e.g. *If she asks him, he will be angry* turns out to materialize or
not, the event described by the subclause of an example like the next one is
presented as more unlikely to take place:

(3)   *If she asked him*, he would be angry.

In examples of this type the predicator of the matrix clause is realized by a
verb form in the past future (*would* + V) or by a complex verb form
beginning with a past modal form like *might* or *could* followed by an
infinitive (e.g. *If she asked him, he might be angry*).

Thirdly, the predicator of the subclause may be realized by a *past perfect*
verb form with past time meaning:

(4)   *If she had asked him*, he would have been angry.

In such cases – where the predicator of the matrix clause is realized by a verb form in the past future perfect (*would have* + V + *-ed*) or by a past modal form like *might* or *could* followed by a perfect infinitive – the condition laid down by the subclause is so strongly biassed towards a negative response that it may be considered practically closed. The reason for this is that the opportunity for the event described by the subclause is presented as having already passed. Conditional clauses in the past perfect like (4) are thus nearly always counterfactual.

Conditional clauses may begin with subordinators which are semantically or stylistically more specialized than *if*, such as *in case, supposing (that), assuming (that), on condition (that)* or *unless* (= *if not*):

(5)   *In case we are attacked*, we will defend ourselves.

(6)   *Unless we are attacked*, we will stay put.

The subordinator *if* may also introduce concessive adverbial clauses, which should be kept apart from conditional clauses. This can be illustrated by an example like *If he's poor, he's at least honest* (cf. Quirk et al. 1985: 1099), in which *if* is synonymous with *even if* and *even though* and the situation expressed by the subclause thus factual rather than hypothetical.

A conditional clause may be signalled not only by *if* or another subordinator but also by partial *inversion* (recall section 5.3.3):

(7)   *Should you change your mind about him*, I'll invite him too.

(8)   *Had he been convicted of theft*, he would have had to resign.

As pointed out above, the two situations described by a conditional sentence are typically linked not only causally but also temporally, as reflected in the fact that the verb form of the matrix clause typically refers to a stage which is posterior in time to that referred to by the verb form in the subclause (present - future / past - past future / past perfect - past future perfect). But there are also conditional sentences where the two situations are not in this way linked temporally and in which the verb form of the matrix clause is therefore not determined by that of the subclause. This type of conditional sentence can be illustrated by the following example where there is an implicational link between the two events but in which the event described by the matrix clause is not presented as subsequent to that described by the subclause:

(9)   *If quirkiness is what you crave*, there's no place to beat North Korea.

In examples of this type it is often natural to insert the adverb *then* in the sense of 'in that case' (not 'afterwards') at the beginning of the matrix clause.

In conditional sentences where the two events are unlinked temporally and in which it is a past form that realizes the predicator of the subclause, this verb form has past time meaning:

(10)   *If they purchased the House of Fraser with their own money*, then their funds are the taxable funds of United Kingdom residents.

(11)   But *if the assault was meant to intimidate authorities*, there were no signs of anyone backing off.

Conditional sentences are not declarative exclusively but may also be *interrogative*, *imperative* or *exclamatory*:

(12)   What happens *if the Queen turns out to be a foreigner*?

(13)   *If that's all you've got to say*, let's go home right away.

(14)   How wonderful it would be *if that's true*!

Attention should also be drawn to the existence of so-called *inferential conditional sentences*, in which the speaker on the basis of the evidence put forward in the subclause infers that the event described by the matrix clause has taken, is taking or will be taking place. An example of this type of conditional sentence is provided by (10) above, and it can be further illustrated by the following sentence:

(15)   *If today is Friday*, he is here already.

It has been pointed out (see Harder 1989, from which this example is quoted) that the use of *if* – or another marker of subordination – in a conditional sentence counts as an instruction to understand the proposition contained in the subclause as a hypothetical basis for the speaker's message in the matrix clause. This feature appears to be shared by all conditional sentences, i.e. whether the two events are temporally linked or not and whether the matrix clause is declarative or not.

8.10. Clausally realized disjuncts

As pointed out in section 4.1.2, disjuncts may be analysed as peripheral adverbials by means of the stack convention. There are three major types of clausally realized disjuncts: comment clauses, tag clauses and sentential relative clauses.

A) Comment clauses, which are particularly common in spoken English, add a parenthetic comment to the content of a superordinate clause, as in *That's outrageous, I agree.* They are typically markers of linguistic *interaction*, as shown by the fact that their subject is in most cases realized by a 1st or 2nd person pronoun (referring to the speaker and the hearer). Commonly occurring examples are *I'm sure, I'm afraid, I admit, I gather, I dare say* and *you see, you know, mind you, you must admit*. Comment clauses like these are syntactically incomplete in that they contain a transitive verb (e.g. KNOW) which is not followed by an object, or an adjective (e.g. SURE) which is unaccompanied by the complementation it usually requires else-where (see Quirk et al. 1985: 1113). Prosodically, comment clauses behave largely like vocatives (see section 4.5). When placed finally or medially, they are in most cases pronounced rapidly without prosodic prominence; but if the speaker considers their content worth emphasizing, they are pronounced as a separate tone unit. When placed initially, they are usually pronounced as a separate tone unit:

(1)   It's private, *you see.*

(2)   I do, *I'm afraid,* rather act on impulse.

(3)   *Mind you,* it isn't just embarrassment.

Many comment clauses are stereotyped fillers which are inserted into running speech in order to establish informal contact with the hearer. When the subject is realized by *I*, their function is to inform the hearer of the speaker's degree of certainty (e.g. *I know / I suppose*) or of his emotional attitude to the content of the matrix clause (e.g. *I'm happy/sorry to say*). When the subject is realized by *you*, the function of comment clauses is typically to catch or keep the hearer's attention or to request his agreement (e.g. *you see / you must admit*).

There are also comment clauses whose subject is not realized by *I* or *you*. The most important of these are *to*-infinitive clauses, *-ing* participle clauses and finite clauses introduced by *as*:

(4)   I don't know, *to be frank.*

(5)   There are 200 students in the auditorium, *roughly speaking.*

(6)   They're out, *as it happens.*

As, it should be added, may also introduce finite comment clauses which have *you* or *I* as their subject. This can be illustrated by examples like *as you know* and *as I've told you.* Similar examples with *if* are *If you see what I mean* and *If I may say so.*

B) Tag clauses. Like comment clauses, *tag clauses* are characteristic of spoken English and are markers of linguistic interaction. A tag clause consists of a subject pronoun preceded by a primary verb or modal auxiliary (*has she, did you, can't we, isn't it*, etc.). It is appended to (tagged on to) another clause, and this clause – the matrix clause – may be declarative, imperative or exclamatory:

(7)   This has been the tendency, hasn't it?

(8)   Shut the door, will you?

(9)   How well she sings, doesn't she!

The subject form of a tag clause is co-referential with that of the matrix clause (in imperative sentences with the understood subject form *you*), and in declarative and exclamatory sentences the finite verb form of the matrix clause is repeated in the tag clause or is replaced by a form of DO.

Tag clauses are also called *tag questions* because they signal a questioning attitude (like their nearest equivalents in French and German *n'est-ce-pas* and *nicht wahr*). When a tag is added to a declarative clause, the speaker simultaneously tells and asks the hearer the same thing. However, the questioning force of a tag varies with its intonation. If the tag is pronounced with rising intonation, the utterance in which it occurs is a more genuine request for information than if it is pronounced with falling intonation. In either case the speaker puts forward the view that the proposition contained in the matrix clause is true, but if the tag is rising he is less certain of this view than if it is falling:

(10)   She's a 'Roman `Catholic / ˌisn't she?

(11)   She's a 'Roman `Catholic / `isn't she?

A declarative sentence ending in a tag clause is thus closer to a pure question (e.g. *Is she a Roman Catholic?*) if the tag is pronounced with rising intonation than if it is pronounced with falling intonation. In the former case the speaker is genuinely invited to verify the truth of a statement, in the latter only to confirm what the speaker feels reasonably sure of (see Quirk at al. 1985: 811). In fact, the main function of a tag pronounced with falling intonation is not to request information but to make sure that the contact between speaker and hearer is retained.

Declarative sentences ending in tag clauses are normally characterized by *reversed polarity*: if the declarative sentence is positive, the tag is negative (as in *This has been the tendency, hasn't it?*), and if it is negative, the tag is positive (as in *This hasn't been the tendency, has it?*). However, both the declarative clause and the tag clause may be positive. In such cases – in which the tag is pronounced with rising intonation – the illocutionary force of the sentence is that of a pure question (see Nässlin 1984):

(12)   She's a 'Roman `Catholic / ˌis she?

What we find here is illocutionary conversion, i.e. the tag clause functions as an *illocutionary converter* (statement to question). The speaker is not really telling the hearer anything but only asks whether the content of the matrix clause is true or false.

Sentences like the following in which both the declarative clause and the tag clause are negative are rare:

(13)   She can't come, can't she?

In cases like this it would seem that the function of the tag is to challenge a view held by the hearer. For example, it would be natural for a speaker uttering (13) to continue his turn with an utterance like *Oh yes, she can.* Such a challenging attitude is occasionally also noticeable if a declarative clause and a tag clause are both positive. Thus an utterance like *You'd like it, would you?* may in some contexts function not as a genuine question (= *Would you like it?*) but as a remonstration against something intended by the hearer.

When a tag is added to an imperative clause, it is usually pronounced with rising intonation:

(14)   Shut the door, won't you?

(15)   Make up your mind, would you?

By means of such imperative sentences the speaker simultaneously instructs and asks the hearer to perform a certain action, i.e. the illocutionary value is here a mixture of a directive and a question. Note that only a limited number of tags can be added to an imperative clause: the subject is nearly always realized by *you* and the predicator by *will/would, can/could* or *shall/should*.

When a tag clause is added to an exclamatory clause, it is nearly always pronounced with falling intonation:

(16)   How `well she sings / `doesn't she!

Here the illocutionary value of the utterance is that of an exclamation in which there is a relatively weak admixture of a question. That it is the exclamatory function which dominates in such examples appears from the fact that the tag clause cannot readily be uttered with rising intonation.

C) Sentential relative clauses. A *sentential relative clause* refers back to the preceding clause, from which it is separated by intonation or – in written English – punctuation (comma or sometimes full stop). It nearly always begins with the relative pronoun *which*:

(17)   The twins don't look alike, which puzzles me.

(18)   The terrorists have claimed responsibility for the bomb blast, which is exactly what we've been expecting.

In such examples, *which* has demonstrative-like meaning (= 'and this').

The antecedent of a sentential relative clause need not be the entire preceding clause but may be limited to the predicate or predication of that clause:

(19)   She commutes between Boston and New York, which I wouldn't be able to stand.

(20)   She will commute between Boston and New York, which I wouldn't be able to stand.

The antecedent may also be a longer stretch of speech than the preceding clause. In the following example it is constituted not only by the clause immediately preceding *which* but also by the initial conditional sentence:

(21)   If you aren't registered to vote, then they can't pursue you for the poll tax – that is the received wisdom. Which left us with the possibility of one of the ripest political ironies.

The examples examined so far show *anaphoric* sentential relative constructions. Occasionally we come across *cataphoric* cases with *what*, as in the following examples where the two types are juxtaposed:

(22)   She was late, *which* was bad, but *what* was worse, she didn't apologize.

Which is used cataphorically after a coordinating conjunction from which it is separated by means of a comma or some other device clearly marking the relative clause as a parenthetical insertion, cf. also section 11.3.3 [B.c] and Schibsbye (1970: 253), who provides the following example:

(23)   Change of meaning may also be effected, by means of figurative language, or, *which* is a similar process, the use of a concrete term for an abstract conception.

Sentential relative clauses may also be introduced by *when* preceded by a preposition or – in formal style – by *whence* or *whereupon* (see Quirk et al. 1985: 1119f):

(24)   The price of bread rose sharply, since when many have found it difficult to make ends meet.

(25)   One of the pupils stabbed another, whereupon the headmaster immediately called the police.

In an example like *Margaret Thatcher is now a life Baroness, which everyone knows*, we can replace *which* with *as* with virtually no change of meaning. But unlike *which*, *as* is not generally used as a relative but as a conjunction. Note also that *as everyone knows* is positionally less restricted than *which everyone knows*: it could also be placed initially or medially. We therefore do not classify such an *as*-clause as a sentential relative clause but as a comment clause.

8.11. Polarity in complex sentences

In complex sentences negation may affect the matrix clause, the subclause or the entire sentence. These three possibilities are illustrated in the following examples:

(1)   Sanctions don't challenge vital interests, as it happens.

(2)   Police know that the shooter was not a professional.

(3)   I didn't write the book in order to make money.

In (1) the comment subclause realizes a disjunct and falls outside the semantic scope of negation (see section 7.5.8). In (2), conversely, it is only the object subclause which falls inside the scope of negation, i.e. this sentence can be analysed semantically as [Police know [not [the shooter was a professional]]]. In (3), finally, both the matrix clause and the adverbial subclause fall inside the scope of negation, i.e. negation is here biclausal: [Not [I wrote the book in order to make money]].

In some cases – particularly in informal style – negation is *transferred* (or *raised*) from a subclause where it belongs semantically to the matrix clause. The matrix clause verbs which permit such negative raising are verbs of opinion like BELIEVE, EXPECT, IMAGINE, SUPPOSE, THINK and verbs of perception like APPEAR, SEEM, FEEL/LOOK/SOUND *as if* (see Quirk et al. 1985: 1033):

(4a)   I don't believe/think it's raining any longer.

(5a)   I don't expect/imagine/suppose I'll pass the exam.

(6a)   They didn't appear/seem to be convinced by the argument.

(7a)   It doesn't look/sound as if Major knows the answer to this.

These examples should be compared with:

(4b)   I believe/think it's not raining any longer.

(5b)   I expect/imagine/suppose I won't pass the exam.

(6b)   They appeared/seemed not to be convinced by the argument.

(7b)   It looks/sounds as if Major doesn't know the answer to this.

in which the negative element is placed where it belongs semantically.

Complex sentences with transferred negation are practically synonymous with complex sentences in which the negative element is retained in the subclause. A sentence like *It doesn't look/sound as if Major knows the answer to this* has virtually the same meaning as *It looks/sounds as if Major doesn't know the answer to this*. If a difference in meaning can be detected, it involves the force of negation, which tends to be slightly weaker in sentences with raising (see Quirk et al. 1985: 1033).

PART III

9. Verbals

9.1. Introduction

As pointed out in section 3.3.1, we use the form term 'verbal' as a cover term for single verbs and verb groups. By a verb group we understand a group which has a full verb as its head, for example *may have been dancing*, in which *dancing* functions as head and the preceding words as dependents. In verb groups with premodification like this one, all the constituents are realized by verbs, i.e. by words that can typically be inflected for the present/past distinction (*dance/danced*, *have/had*, etc.). As pointed out in section 3.2.1, the verbs preceding the head of a verb group like *may have been dancing* are called *auxiliary verbs*. There may also be dependents after the head of a verb group, but only if the group realizes a complex predicator such as e.g. *The analysis <u>threw up</u> several surprises* (cf. section 4.3). Verbals usually function as predicators and may be *finite* or *nonfinite*. In finite verbals the first verb is inflected for the present/past distinction (cf. section 3.2.1). In nonfinite verbals a dependent preceding the head may be realized not only by a verb (as in *Having given him a light, I set fire to his moustache*) but also by the infinitive marker *to* (as in *To take a walk here would be foolish*).

Verbals typically describe *situations*, and in this respect they differ from e.g. nominals and pronominals, which typically express the participants involved in situations. In an example like *Our sales representative gave your husband the wrong tickets*, the verb *gave* is used to describe a past time situation where somebody hands over something to somebody and the three noun groups are used to specify the participant roles AGENT, BENEFI-CIARY, AFFECTED. While a sentence describes a situation and in so doing identifies the entities performing the participant roles involved, a verbal describes a situation without identifying these entities.

The type of situation described by a sentence is determined not only by its lexical verb but also by the inflectional form of this verb, by syntactic relations (e.g. the presence or absence of an object) and even by the extralinguistic context (cf. section 7.2.3). While an objectless sentence like *He was reading* describes a self-contained situation, a sentence with an object like *He was reading the report* describes a directed situation, i.e. a situation progressing toward a terminal point. In both sentences, to be sure, the verb group describes a dynamic situation, but the subtype of dynamic situation involved is presented in different ways.

The main communicative function of a verbal – to describe a situation – is composite in that it involves a number of lower-level communicative functions, such as locating a situation in time, presenting it as hypothetical rather than factual (e.g. *may know*) and presenting it as being in progress (e.g. *is drowning*). It can therefore be thought of in terms of a *functional domain*, by which we understand a general main function comprising a number of subfunctions. In this chapter we examine the ways in which verbals and their constituents occupy this domain, i.e. in what ways they enable the speaker to describe situations.

9.2. Verb forms

Most lexical verbs in English have four distinct forms: a base form, an *-s* form, an *-ing* form and an *-ed* form. A verb like FISH, for example, has the forms *fish*, *fishes*, *fishing*, *fished*. A lexical verb is considered morphologically *regular* if both the past form and the past participle form are formed by adding the suffix *-ed* to the base form.

In many irregular verbs the past participle form differs from the past form in ending in *-en*, as illustrated by verbs like TAKE (*took - taken*), BEAT (*beat - beaten*) and SHOW (*showed - shown/showed*). For this reason – and in order to have separate terms for the two forms – some grammarians refer to the past participle form as the *-en* form.

Irregular verbs may have five, four or three inflectional forms. This can be illustrated by respectively DRIVE (*drive - drives - driving - drove - driven*), HANG (*hang - hangs - hanging - hung (- hung)*) and PUT (*put - puts - putting (- put - put)*). The verb BE is idiosyncratic in having eight distinct forms (*be - am/are/is - being - was/were - been*). This proliferation is due to the fact that historically its forms are derived from three different roots.

There are about 200 irregular verbs in English, the exact number depending on whether verbs with prefixes such as OUTBID, OVERSLEEP and UNBIND are included in the list of irregular verbs or are excluded because the list contains the corresponding verbs without prefixes (BID, SLEEP, BIND, etc.). For an overview of the inflectional morphology of irregular verbs the reader is referred to good dictionaries of English, such as *Oxford Advanced Learner's Dictionary*.

Let us briefly consider what the different forms of a verb are used for. The *base form* is used in present indicative constructions (except in the 3rd person singular), imperative constructions, subjunctive constructions and infinitive constructions (for the terms 'indicative' and 'subjunctive', see section 9.8). Examples: *I wash my hands in Pears soap / Wash your hands / I insist that he wash his hands / I would like to wash my hands*. The *-s form* is used in 3rd person singular present indicative constructions (*He washes his hands in Pears soap*). The *-ing form* is used in progressive constructions and in participle constructions (*She is washing her hands / He hates washing his hands*). The *-ed form*, finally, is used partly for the expression of pastness, partly participially for the expression of the perfect and the passive. Examples: *I washed my hands this morning / I've washed my hands / The crops were washed away by the floods.*

The *-ing* suffix is pronounced /ɪŋ/ in both regular and irregular verbs, as illustrated by *drowning* /'draʊnɪŋ/ and *singing* /'sɪŋɪŋ/. In some regional and social varieties /ɪn/ and /ɪŋg/ are found as alternative pronunciations. The *-s* suffix is pronounced in three different ways, depending on the nature of the final sound segment in the base form:

(i) /ɪz/ (in some varieties /əz/) in verbs ending in a sibilant, i.e. in one of the consonants /s z ʃ ʒ tʃ dʒ/. Examples: *kisses, buzzes, wishes, rouges, watches, judges.*

(ii) /s/ in verbs ending in a voiceless non-sibilant, i.e. one of the consonants /p t k f θ/ (/h/ does not occur finally). Examples: *hops, bets, kicks, laughs, baths.*

(iii) /z/ otherwise, i.e. in verbs ending in a vowel or a voiced non-sibilant consonant. Examples: *sees, dies, goes / begs, sings, sells.*

These rules apply not only to regular verbs but also to irregular verbs (apart from the modal auxiliaries which do not accept an *-s* suffix and have only two forms, e.g. *can - could*). As can be seen, a supporting vowel is inserted in those cases where the sibilant suffix consonant is added to a base form ending in a sibilant consonant, i.e. to a closely related or identical sound. Otherwise the suffix consonant agrees with the preceding consonant with respect to voicing. In either case, the pronunciation of the suffix can readily be understood in terms of 'ease of articulation'. While it would be difficult to pronounce the final consonant clusters in e.g. /wɪʃs/, /betz/ and /begs/ – sound sequences which are ruled out by the phonotactic rules of English – it is much easier to pronounce e.g. /wɪʃɪz/, /bets/ and /begz/.

The *-ed* suffix is also pronounced in three different ways depending on the nature of the final sound segment in the base form:

(i) /ɪd/ (in some varieties /əd/) in verbs ending in an alveolar stop consonant, i.e. in /t/ or /d/. Examples: *heated, handed.*

(ii) /t/ in verbs ending in a voiceless consonant other than /t/. Examples: *stopped, watched, kicked, laughed, bathed* (in BrE in the sense of 'gave a bath to'), *kissed, wished.*

(iii) /d/ otherwise, i.e. in verbs ending in a vowel or a voiced consonant other than /d/. Examples: *kneed, died, glowed / begged, hanged, felled*.

As in the case of the *-s* suffix, the three pronunciations of the *-ed* suffix can readily be explained phonetically: a supporting vowel is inserted for ease of articulation if the final sound segment is of the same specific articulation type as the suffix consonant; otherwise the suffix consonant assimilates to the preceding sound with respect to voicing.

Orthographically, the *-s* suffix has a variant *-es*, which occurs if the base form of the verb ends in a sibilant or in a single written *o*, cf. examples like *wish/wishes* and *go/goes*. Conversely, the *-ed* suffix has a variant without *e* which occurs if the base form ends in the letter *e*, as illustrated by *knee/kneed, referee/refereed* and *please/pleased*.

Apart from this orthographic variation in the suffix, it should be noted that the addition of a suffix may bring about a change of spelling in the base form. If *-ing* is added to a verb ending in 'mute' *e*, this letter is usually dropped, cf. examples like *live/living* and *fake/faking*. As shown by e.g. *age/ageing* and *dye/dyeing*, however, there are exceptions to this orthographic rule. If *-ing* is added to a base form ending in *ie*, secondly, this letter sequence is replaced by *y*, as in *die/dying, lie/lying* and *tie/tying*. The spelling of a verb may also be affected by *-s* and *-ed*. If either of these suffixes is added to a base form ending in a *y* preceded by a consonant, this *y* is changed to *i(e)*, for example in *try/tries/tried* (but not in e.g. *play/plays/played* where *y* comes after a vowel letter).

A final consonant may also be *doubled* before *-ing* and *-ed*. This happens if the base form is monosyllabic and its final consonant is preceded by a vowel spelled with one letter, for example in *pat/patting/patted* (but not in e.g. *sweat/sweating/sweated*), and it also happens if the base form is polysyllabic and has stress on the last syllable, for example in *propel/propelling/propelled*. In BrE, but not usually in AmE, consonant doubling is further found in some polysyllabic verbs whose last syllable is unstressed and ends in *l* or *m*. Examples illustrating this are *travel/travelling/travelled* and *program/programming/programmed*. In polysyllabic words whose last syllable is unstressed and ends in *p* there is sometimes doubling but usually not (compare *worship/worshipping/worshipped* with *develop/developing/developed*). In a few verbs there is vacillating orthography, for example in *focus/focus(s)ing/focus(s)ed*. Finally it should be mentioned that if a base form ends in *c*, there is 'doubling' in the shape of *ck* (as in *panic/panicking/panicked*).

9.3. The external relations of verbals

Finite verbals always function as P:

(1)   He *had* always *loved* Rosemary.

but may in that capacity be coordinated, in which case they technically function as CJTs within the P function:

(2)   Roger *bought* and *sold* companies.

Nonfinite verbals also function as P and CJT within P:

(3)   *Having* always *loved* Rosemary, he moved to Falmer.
(4)   She let Roger *buy* and *sell* companies.

but they may assume other clause functions:

(5)   *To love* is more important than to work. (S)
(6)   To negotiate at this point would be *to surrender*. (C)
(7)   I do not want *to go*. (O)
(8)   He stopped *to smoke*. (A)

In the following examples the italicized verb serves as DEP:

(9)   By *leaving* he indicated his dissatisfaction with the negotiations.
(10)   There was a *dancing* girl on the stage.

Verbals realizing other functions than P still have P potential in full nonfinite clauses realizing the same functions in the main clause, e.g.:

(5')   *To love her* is more important than to work.
(8')   He stopped *to smoke a cigar*.
(9')   By *leaving the meeting* he indicated his dissatisfaction with the negotiations.

9.4. The internal structure of verb groups

In verb groups with more pre-head dependents than one, the order of auxiliaries is fixed and looks like this:

Modal	Perfect	Progressive	Passive
can			
may			
must	have	be	be
shall			
will			

This ordering can be illustrated by the following very rare example with four auxiliaries, repeated from section 7.4.4:

(1)   ... another £98 m was paid direct from absent parents to their former parents. Much of that *could* well also *have been being paid* before April last year, Mr Field argued.

Each auxiliary determines the inflectional form of the following verb. A modal is followed by a base form, perfect HAVE by an *-ed* form, progressive BE by an *-ing* form and passive BE by an *-ed* form: e.g. *may call, has called, is calling* and *is called*.

In *nonfinite* verb groups there are no modal auxiliaries, such auxiliaries having only finite forms. In *participial* verb groups we find the forms *having* + V + *-ed*, *being* + V + *-ed*, *having been* + V + *-ed* and *having been* + V + *-ing*. Examples (cf. Davidsen-Nielsen 1990: 153f):

(2)   Palme accused him of *having made* "contact with American spies".

(3)   The Navy conducted 2,000 patrols without *being spotted* by the Soviets.

(4)   Her arm was in a sling but showed no signs of *having been damaged*.

(5)   *Having been drinking* since last night I feel somewhat indisposed.

The absence of a non-perfect progressive participle construction is due to the fact that English does not allow two consecutive *-ing* forms (see Palmer 1987: 34). The occurrence of three auxiliaries cannot be ruled out entirely. But though an example like *Having been being pestered with phone calls all morning, I'm in a nasty mood* is not ungrammatical, it is much less likely to occur than a corresponding sentence without *being*.

In *infinitive* verb groups we find the forms *to have* + V + *-ed*, *to be* + V + *-ed*, *to be* + V + *-ing*, *to have been* + V + *-ed* and *to have been* + V + *-in*:

(6)   Roger was thought *to have resigned*.

(7)   John Paul was said *to be angered* by the editorial.

(8)   He appears *to be working for the Russians*.

(9)   The meeting seemed *to have been planned* by the CIA.

(10)   Linda appears *to have been walking* in the rain.

As in participial verb groups, the occurrence of three auxiliaries cannot be ruled out altogether. But though a constructed example like *I believe him to have been being operated on all morning* is not ungrammatical, it is so cumbersome that it is highly unlikely to occur.

Nonfinite verb groups realized by an infinitive verb group without *to* are found in sentences with *had better*, unless this modal idiom is analysed as an auxiliary. Examples illustrating this are *She'd better have finished the report soon* and *You'd better be studying hard when I return*.

9.5. Auxiliaries and their delimitation

Unlike a lexical verb, an auxiliary typically requires the presence of another verb. Auxiliaries are also called *grammatical verbs* because they perform the same kinds of function as verbal inflections, which are indisputably grammatical entities. For example, the work done by the auxiliary WILL in a sentence like *It will matter a great deal* resembles that done by the suffix *-ed* in *It mattered a great deal* in that it is used for the expression of time.

Auxiliaries form a closed system and are separated from lexical verbs by a combination of morphological, syntactic and semantic criteria. They are typically morphologically defective, they share a number of syntactic features, and semantically they differ from most lexical verbs in expressing highly general meanings, relating to tense, aspect, modality or voice.

The class of auxiliaries is commonly assumed to comprise primary HAVE, BE, DO and modal CAN, MAY, MUST, SHALL, WILL (see section 3.2.1). All the modals are morphologically defective: MUST has only one form and the rest only two (*can - could, may - might, shall - should, will - would*). When combined with another word, i.e. when used as an auxiliary, DO is morphologically defective too, for the forms *doing* and *done* are not used in this context. On the other hand, HAVE and BE have the same four and eight forms as when they are used as lexical verbs, as illustrated by *have called, has called, had called, having called* and *to be called, am called, are called, is called, was called, were called, (is) being called, (has) been called.*

Syntactically, auxiliaries differ from lexical verbs in requiring *no DO-support* in negative, interrogative and emphatically affirmative sentences (cf. sections 3.2.1, 7.5.2 and 7.5.10).

In the case of so-called 'code-constructions', i.e. in sentences with tag questions or similar constructions where the description of a situation is repeated, we observe the same difference:

(1)   They were laughing, weren't they?
(2)   They kept laughing, didn't they?
(3)   They were laughing and so was their teacher.
(4)   They kept laughing and so did their teacher.

Here DO serves as a pro-form (cf. section 4.2.3).

The syntactic properties of English auxiliaries just described are often referred to as the NICE-properties because they involve negation, inversion, code and emphatic affirmation (see Twaddell 1965 and Huddleston 1976). While these properties constitute a relatively practicable and reliable criterion for establishing a class of auxiliaries, it should not be overlooked that they are shared by BE and (partly) HAVE when these are used as lexical verbs (see section 3.2.1). Furthermore, a modal verb like OUGHT requires no DO-support in negative and interrogative sentences (e.g. *You oughtn't to have said that / Ought I to see a doctor?*), and in tag questions it is more often than not repeated (compare *We ought to go, oughtn't we?* with *We ought to go, shouldn't we?* and *We ought to go, hadn't we?*). In other cases of code, however, OUGHT is not normally repeated; for example, *You ought to go and so ought your wife* borders on unacceptability. Another reason why OUGHT can be excluded from the class of central auxiliaries is that it is not attached directly to the verb it modifies but obligatorily separated from it by *to*. In this respect it differs both from the central auxiliaries and from verbal inflections. In some descriptions of English, OUGHT is regarded as a *semi-auxiliary*, and so are USED TO, NEED and DARE in certain types of construction in nonassertive contexts. An 'ideal' auxiliary has all the NICE-properties and is accompanied by a nonfinite verb form while an 'ideal' lexical verb has none of the NICE-properties and is followed by non-verbal constituents only (except in examples of the type *He tried to escape* and *My sister enjoyed swimming*, where a verbal constituent serves as direct object). Between the end points of this auxiliary-lexical scale a number of intermediary types of auxiliary can be identified, the most important of which are semi-auxiliaries and the so-called catenatives, which we turn to below.

As semi-auxiliaries DARE and NEED show three characteristics (cf. Schibsbye 1970: 24f, 83f): a) there is no DO-support; b) the following infinitive is a bare infinitive; c) there is no third person singular *-s* in the present; compare *Dad need not be told* (where *need* is a semi-auxiliary with an association of 'requirement' attached to the circumstances) with *Dad does not need to be told* (where *need* is a full verb with an association of 'requirement' attached to the subject). Blends of the two uses are not unusual for DARE: e.g. *They do not dare ask for more money* (where there is DO-support but the following infinitive is bare) and *He dares not try to contact the authorities* (where DARE takes the third person singular *-s* suffix but is followed by the bare infinitive).

USED TO, which expresses past states or (discontinued) habits, cannot be ruled out as an auxiliary in negative and interrogative constructions (*He used not to work late hours / Used she to smoke?*), or even in tag questions (*They used not to smoke, use(d)n't they?*). More commonly, however, USED TO takes DO-support in constructions (*He didn't use to work late hours / Did she use to smoke? / They didn't use to smoke, did they?*). The 'd' is sometimes retained in writing (*... didn't used to ... / Did ... used to ...?*) though this is generally considered incorrect. USED TO always behaves like a full verb in other CODE constructions (e.g. *He used to smoke a pipe, and so did she*).

What we find in English is thus in fact a *scale* ranging from clear auxiliaries to clear lexical verbs. While a verb like MAY belongs to the former category and a verb like NEGOTIATE to the latter, verbs like OUGHT TO, NEED, DARE, USED TO, HAVE TO and BE TO occupy a borderline area between the two. Attention must also be drawn to so-called catenatives such as GET and KEEP, which behave like full verbs with respect to the NICE-properties but which may serve auxiliary-like functions in examples like *He got arrested* (cf. *He was arrested*) and *They kept laughing* (cf. *They were laughing*). In this grammar we prefer to operate with a small class of auxiliaries proper (BE, HAVE, DO, CAN, MAY, MUST, SHALL, WILL) and to analyse verbs like OUGHT, NEED, BE GOING TO, etc. as semi-auxiliaries and verbs like GET and KEEP as catenatives.

Even within the class of auxiliaries there are differences with respect to the degree to which they can be considered grammatical words. The modals have more lexical meaning than BE, HAVE and particularly DO (which is semantically empty). Morphologically, on the other hand, the primary auxiliaries are less defective than the modals. Within the class of modal auxiliaries there are differences as well, for the meaning of these is more general in some of their uses than in others (see section 9.9). For example, the meaning of MAY is more general in *The economy may get worse* (where the auxiliary is used to judge the probability of a situation) than in *May I come in?* (where it expresses permission).

We should point out that it would be possible to analyse WILL used for the expression of future time (e.g. in *The meeting will take place*) not as a modal auxiliary but as a primary auxiliary. The reason we have chosen not to do so is that WILL belongs in a paradigm with CAN, MAY, MUST, SHALL where it blocks out the occurrence of any of these verbs. As WILL in one of its senses is clearly a time marker, however, we return to this verb not only in section 9.9 on modality but also in section 9.6 on tense and aspect.

In closing this section we recapitulate that an auxiliary in English is a 'helping verb' which modifies another verb to which it may be directly attached (and usually is), that it expresses general meaning, that it is (typically) morphologically defective and that it requires no DO-support in sentences involving negation, inversion, code or emphatic affirmation.

9.6. Tense and aspect

9.6.1. Introduction

Tense and aspect are closely related categories in that both of them concern the presentation of situations. Tense is defined as grammatically expressed assignment to situations of 'location in time' and can be illustrated by examples like *Linda lives in Stockholm* and *Linda lived in Stockholm*. In using the inflection -*s* in the first of these, the speaker instructs the hearer to identify a situation that applies at the moment the utterance is made, and in using the inflection -*ed* in the second to identify a situation that applies before this moment. Aspect is defined as grammatically expressed assignment of 'situational focus' and can be illustrated by examples like *It was snowing in Stockholm* and *It snowed in Stockholm*. In using the auxiliary *was* and the inflectional ending *-ing* in the first of these, the speaker instructs the hearer to select an internal focus, i.e. to adopt an *in medias res* perspective and view the situation as unfolding. In using the simple verb form in the second example, the speaker instructs the hearer to select an external focus, i.e. to view the situation from without, as a complete unit.

In English, tense and aspect are tightly interwoven. We therefore treat them together and operate with a fused tense-aspect system. The meanings belonging to this system may be expressed by a verbal inflection, an auxiliary or a combination, as in *happened*, *will happen* and *has happened / was happening*, respectively.

The tense-aspect system in English involves four ordered choices:

1. present : past
2. future : nonfuture
3. perfect : nonperfect
4. progressive : nonprogressive

The first distinction is marked inflectionally (as in *happens : happened* and *has : had*) and is *deictic*. The term 'deixis' (a Greek word that means 'pointing') refers to those features of a language which are relative to the place and time of the utterance, and which can therefore only be properly understood in relation to the speech situation. Clear examples of deixis are locative adverbs like HERE and THERE and temporal adverbs like NOW and THEN (at the place/time of the speaker : not at the place/time of the speaker).

The other three distinctions are *relative* to the first, deictic one. The future is signalled by a form of non-volitional WILL and the nonfuture by the absence of this auxiliary, as in *will happen : happens* and *would happen : happened* (cf. Davidsen-Nielsen 1988). The perfect is signalled by a form of the auxiliary HAVE followed by an *-ed* verb form and the nonperfect by the absence of this combination, as illustrated by *has happened : happens* and *had happened : happened*. The progressive is signalled by a form of the auxiliary BE followed by an *-ing* participle and the nonprogressive by the absence of this combination, as illustrated by *is happening : happens* and *was happening : happened*.

As there are four binary distinctions, the speaker has at his disposal a total of sixteen tense-aspect forms: the present (*happens*), the past (*happened*), the present future (*will happen*), the past future *(would happen)*, the present perfect (*has happened*), the past perfect (*had happened*), the present future perfect (*will have happened*), the past future perfect *(would have happened)*, the present progressive (*is happening*), the past progressive (*was happening*), the present future progressive (*will be happening*), the past future progressive (*would be happening*), the present perfect progressive (*has been happening*), the past perfect progressive (*had been happening*), the present future perfect progressive (*will have been happening*) and the past future perfect progressive (*would have been happening*).

In our account of tense-aspect meanings we shall adopt a *functional-instructional* rather than a traditional referential point of view (see Harder (1996), by whose work this section is significantly influenced). In an example like *Arsenal scored a crucial goal* we prefer to say not that the past refers to a situation that precedes the moment this utterance is spoken, but rather that it instructs the hearer to identify a situation before this moment as that which the descriptive content applies to ('world-before-now'). In examples like *It smells awful* and *Wright passes the ball to Bergkamp*, similarly, we shall say not that the present refers to a situation that is simultaneous with the moment of speech but rather that it instructs the hearer to identify a situation at this moment as that which the descriptive content applies to ('world now'). In other words, we regard finite verb forms as forms that tell the hearer where to look, i.e. where to tag the descriptive content of a sentence on to the world.

9.6.2. Deictic forms: present and past

The present (e.g. *happens*) instructs the hearer to identify a situation as it is at the moment of speech ('world now') and the past (e.g. *happened*) to identify a situation as it was before this moment ('world-before-now'). Complex verb forms also instruct the hearer to identify a situation either as it is at the moment of speech (e.g. *will happen, has happened, is happening*) or as it was before the moment of speech (e.g. *would happen, had happened, was happening*). But here other instructions – which we return to in sections 9.6.3 to 9.6.6 – are given as well.

The use of the simple *past* can be illustrated by the following examples (cf. Davidsen-Nielsen 1990: 124):

(1)   A luxury jet yesterday *brought* Imelda Marcos to New York.
(2)   The election *got* off to a lacklustre start at a relatively low-key rally.
(3)   Nick Faldo, the British golfer, *won* the Volvo Masters in Sotogrande.

In using the past, the speaker signals that he has *a particular past time* in mind and assumes that the hearer is able to infer what this time is (see Elsness 1997). This particular time may be expressed by a temporal adverbial which functions as an *anchor* (the way *yesterday* does in example (1)). Otherwise it is expressed or implied by the wider linguistic context (e.g.

if *I hated it* comes after *I was in L. A. last week*) or implied by the situational context (as in *Did the postman bring any letters?*). A sentence in the past like *John understood* – unlike a sentence in the present like *John understands* – thus cannot be used appropriately unless the hearer is given a clue about the specific occasion on which the situation described took place. If unanchored past time needs to be expressed, the present perfect has to be used instead (as in *John has resigned*, see section 9.6.4).

Modal usage of the past will be dealt with in section 9.7, and the use of the past in indirect speech in section 9.6.13.

As pointed out in section 9.6.1, the *present* instructs the hearer to identify a situation at the moment of speech as that which the descriptive content applies to. If the situation referred to by a sentence in the present is *stative* (see section 7.2.1), it spans the moment of speech, and in such cases it is customary to speak of the *inclusive present*, as in the following examples expressing attitudes, intensive and extensive relations:

(4)   George *believes* in God.

(5)   She *hates* all the fuss.

(6)   They *are* in high spirits.

(7)   This factory *belongs* to Mr Hardcastle.

If a situation described by a sentence in the nonprogressive present belongs to the subtype of dynamic actionality termed *punctual*, it coincides with the moment of speech. This so-called *instantaneous present* is fairly restricted. As pointed out by Bache (1985a: 273f; 1986: 92), it is found in (broadcast) commentaries, demonstrations, special exclamatory sentences and performatives, i.e. constructions supplementing a visual experience and/or referring to highly regulated, ritualized or ordered events:

(8)   Wright *passes* the ball to Bergkamp.

(9)   I now *remove* the moss on top of the soil and *top* up the pot with compost.

(10)   Here *comes* the bride!

(11)   I *promise* to be back by ten.

Apart from such cases, dynamic situations taking place at the moment of speech require description by means of the present progressive (e.g. *Right at this moment Jack is writing an e-mail message to his boss*).

Inclusion and instantaneousness (where possible) are not properties of the present itself but of the actionality of the sentence. In uttering e.g. (4) the speaker instructs the hearer to identify a present-time situation of 'somebody believing in something', and as this situation is stative it will be understood to include the moment of speech. In uttering e.g. (8), the speaker instructs the hearer to identify a present time situation of 'somebody passing a ball to somebody else', and as this situation is dynamic, it will be understood to coincide with the moment of speech, i.e. be instantaneous.

The present is found also in sentences expressing habitual situations, including:

(i) *universal conditions* (eternal and mathematical truths, for example):

(12)   Water *boils* at 100 degrees centigrade.

(13)   Two and two *makes* four.

(14)   The sun *sets* in the west.

(ii) *personal habits*, i.e. constructions which describe a settled manner of human (or animal) behaviour:

(15)   Sally *buys* her clothes at Marks & Spencer's.

(16)   I *go* to bed at twelve o'clock.

(17)   She *cycles* to work.

(iii) *present ability*:

(18)   Evelyn *speaks* Russian.

(19)   Jim *runs* a mile in less than 6 minutes.

It should be remembered that the situation described by a personal habitual construction like (15) is not dynamic instances of buying – though such instances are implied – but rather a characterization of Sally (see section 7.2.3). Similarly, the situations described by the universal statement in (12) and the expression of present ability in (19) are not dynamic instances of boiling and running but rather characterizations of water and Jim.

The present virtually always counts as an instruction to the hearer to look at the world as it is now. Note that this is the case even in examples like:

(20)   The meeting *takes* place tomorrow.

(21)   Peter *tells* me you're going to the States.

Both these sentences instruct the hearer to identify a situation as it is now, the same way the semantically closely related sentences in the present future and the present perfect do (*The meeting will take place tomorrow / Peter has told me you're going to the States*). We return to the additional instructions signalled by such sentences in sections 9.6.3 and 9.6.4.

An apparent exception to the rule that the present counts as an instruction to identify a situation at the moment of speech is the so-called *dramatic present* (or historic present), i.e. a present used to make the description of a past situation more vivid:

(22)   We proceeded along the main road. Up the road we *enter* the courtyard of a rund-down palazzo.

In this example the present form *enter* is used atypically in that it seems to apply to the world as it was before now. But even here there is at the same time an element of 'world now', for in using the dramatic present the speaker "steps outside the frame of history, visualizing and representing what happened in the past as if it were present before his eyes" (Jespersen 1929: 258). In selecting the dramatic present the narrator eliminates the temporal distance between the chain of events described and his account of it.

9.6.3. Future forms

The *present future* can be illustrated by the following examples (quoted from Davidsen-Nielsen 1990: 117):

(1)   In a day or two – father – you *will feel* yourself again.

(2)   Oh dear ... whatever *will* the Bishop *say*?

(3)   You *will* not *get* such ham with the trappists.

The WILL found in present future forms differs from volitional WILL in expressing *time exclusively*. Unlike examples like (1) through (3), an example with volitional WILL like *I will gladly help you* expresses not only futurity but also willingness. Another property of present future WILL is that a sentence in which it occurs describes the real world *categorically*, though at a time that is still ahead. In this way non-volitional WILL differs from a modal auxiliary like MAY. While both *Peter may recover* and *Peter will recover* describe something as still unrealized, the real world is not spoken about categorically in the former sentence as it is in the latter. In using the present future the speaker talks about the future as if it were certain.

Futurity does not have a structural home of its own in English as it has in e.g. French (where it is expressed inflectionally, as in *Il signera* 'He'll sign') but is a squatter in the modal paradigm (see Harder 1996: 369). Nevertheless, it is both possible and appropriate to operate with a present future form in the shape of non-volitional WILL + V. Note in this connection that non-volitional WILL differs from volitional WILL not only semantically but also syntactically in occurring in passive sentences, progressive sentences and before HAVE + V + *-ed*:

(4)   I *will be brought* back in disgrace.

(5)   We*'ll be throwing* a party.

(6)   By this time tomorrow, I*'ll* no doubt *have finished* sorting out the first batch of replies.

Furthermore, WILL used for the expression of pure future differs from modal-volitional WILL in not normally occurring in conditional or temporal subclauses. In an example like *If you'll be patient for a few minutes more, I'll have finished* we thus find modal WILL in the subclause and future WILL in the matrix clause.

We choose to disregard the marginal realization of the present future by SHALL + V, for the purely temporal use of SHALL found in sentences with 1st person pronoun subjects is restricted to formal BrE and by now relatively rare. As appears from examples in which it is found, such as *I feel I shall never get over it* and *We shall never be as we were*, this SHALL can readily be replaced by WILL (see Davidsen-Nielsen 1990: 57).

Talking of the 'present future' (rather than merely the 'future') means that we see it as semantically complex, i.e. its meaning is 'It applies now that something is ahead'. Formally this can be expressed by the notation [Present [future [situation]]]; spelled out in terms of a complex instruction, it means that the hearer is instructed to tag the sentence on to present time ('world now') and then look ahead at a situation. Unlike the past, the present future does not require any expressed or implied anchor. Such an anchor is not necessary for a proper understanding of what is meant. While a past time anchor is required to understand a sentence like *She regretted the decision*, no future time anchor is necessary for the understanding of *She'll regret the decision*.

Semantically, the present future is closely related to BE *going to* + V. In a large number of cases the two constructions are used for the same purpose, i.e. to instruct the hearer to think of present time and then look ahead:

(7)   It*'ll be* very difficult.

(8)   It*'s going to be* very difficult.

While there is thus considerable overlap, there are also cases where only the present future or BE *going to* can be used. For example, a sentence like *It's going to rain* cannot be replaced by *It'll rain* if the situation described is one where dark clouds are gathering. This is due to the fact that a function of BE *going to* – but not of WILL – is to express future of present cause. Conversely, we find WILL but not normally BE *going to* in the matrix clause of a conditional sentence:

(9)   Unless something goes wrong, she*'ll have* a baby soon.

The reason why BE *going to* cannot very well be used here is that in expressing future of present cause *She's going to have a baby soon* means approximately 'She's several months pregnant', and this type of meaning obviously cannot be made dependent on a condition like that laid down by the subclause in (9).

The most important difference between the present future and BE *going to* + V concerns scope and degree of grammaticalization (see section 7.5.8 on the semantic scope of negation). Like French ALLER found in e.g. *Il va venir* 'He'll come', BE *going to* has not yet become fully grammaticalized and can therefore only be classified as a semi-auxiliary. This appears from the fact that it only shares some of the properties of central auxiliaries discussed in section 9.5. As for scope, BE *going to* has semantic influence over a smaller part of the meaning of a sentence than WILL. This can be illustrated by (10), which is exceptional in containing both WILL and BE *going to*:

(10)   She*'ll be going to have* a baby soon (unless she changes her lifestyle).

Semantically, this sentence must be analysed as [Will [be going to [she have a baby soon]]], i.e. WILL has semantic scope over the rest of the sentence including BE *going to*.

In accounting for the present future we also have to consider some cases where it competes with the simple present. In section 9.6.2 it was pointed out that a sentence in the present like *The meeting takes place tomorrow* is semantically closely related to a sentence in the present future like *The meeting will take place tomorrow*. In both examples the hearer is instructed to think of present time and then look ahead. In the former the additional instruction to look ahead is given lexically exclusively by means of *tomorrow* and in the latter both grammatically by WILL and lexically. While WILL instructs the hearer simply to look ahead, TOMORROW instructs him to look ahead to a specific point in time. In sentences of this type WILL is therefore largely redundant and could without communicative consequences be omitted. Nevertheless the use of the simple present in sentences signalling aheadness is not common. In simple sentences and in matrix clauses of complex sentences it is restricted to those cases where something planned and certain is involved and where there is a future time adverbial. Furthermore it usually requires that the actionality of the sentence is dynamic:

(11)   Mr Major *visits* Poland next week.

(12)   President Yeltsin *arrives* in India tomorrow for a weekend visit.

In subclauses, however, the simple present is the rule rather than the exception, particularly in conditional and temporal clauses:

(13)   You'll sleep better if you *get* a new mattress.

(14)   When my son *comes* home, we'll kill the fatted calf.

Here it may perhaps be assumed that WILL has semantic scope over the entire complex sentence.

Futurity can also be expressed by the verbal idiom BE *about to* and the modal semi-auxiliary BE *to*, and here as well more specific meanings are signalled than by WILL. The former is used to describe the imminent future, as in *She's about to join the navy*, and the latter can be used to describe a future event which has already been arranged, as in *There is to be a new hearing*.

Modal uses of the present future will be dealt with in section 9.7.

Let us turn now to the *past future*. If this form is used temporally, it instructs the hearer to think of a time in the world before now (i.e. to think of some past time) and then look ahead; in other words, its meaning is 'It applied then that something was ahead'. This use is found in *subclauses* of sentences with matrix clause verbs of thinking, believing, feeling or knowing (see Davidsen-Nielsen 1990: 139):

(15)   I expected it *would take* us three hours to reach the summit, but now I realize
        I was too optimistic.

Here *would take* instructs the hearer to think of some past time and then look ahead.

In indirect speech the past future is typically a so-called backshifted version of the present future. We return to indirect speech in section 9.6.13.

In *matrix clauses* the past future is common in *conditional sentences*, i.e. in examples like *If she asked him, he would be angry*. Here the matrix clause does not describe a past time situation but a hypothetical situation that is dependent on the truth of the situation described by the subclause and which is temporally ahead of this. The use of the past future in conditional sentences was dealt with in section 8.9 and will not be taken up again.

9.6.4. Perfect forms

In using the *present perfect* the speaker instructs the hearer to think of present time and then to look back at a situation. The former instruction is given by selecting a present form of HAVE and the latter by means of the *-ed* participle. The meaning of the perfect is thus 'It applies now that something is *anterior* in time'. This can be expressed by the notation [Present [anterior [situation]]]. Examples (cf. Davidsen-Nielsen 1990: 127):

(1)   I *haven't seen* Marilyn like that before.

(2)   It*'s become* part of the folklore.

(3)   I*'ve lived* in Copenhagen since 1958.

(4)   A Protestant paramilitary leader *has been given* a 19-year sentence.

As appears from e.g. (2) and (3), the present perfect implies either a present *result* or a present *continuation* of a previous situation. Normally the former is the case if the actionality of the sentence is dynamic and the latter if the actionality is stative.

Unlike the past, the present perfect does not require any expressed or implied anchor (although it may be present, as in (1) and (3)). Such an anchor is not necessary for a proper understanding of what is meant (for example by sentences like (2) and (4)). While a past time anchor is required to understand a sentence like *She regretted the decision*, no anchor is necessary for the understanding of *She's regretted the decision*.

The present perfect combines with *adverbials* which include the moment of speech, e.g. *up to now, so far, yet* and *since 1958*. Such adverbials do not normally combine with the simple past; but exceptions to this rule are found in AmE, as illustrated by *Did the children come home yet?* (BrE: *Have the children come home yet?*). On the other hand, the present perfect does not combine with adverbials which exclude the moment of speech, such as *yesterday*, *a year ago* and *the other day*. Adverbials of this type require the past, which in itself signals that the speaker has a particular past time in mind (see section 9.6.2). A third group of time adverbials which are neutral with respect to the temporal distinction just mentioned – e.g. *recently*, *today* and *this morning* – combine both with the present perfect and the simple past. When they are used in sentences in the past, the time described is divorced from the moment of speech. This can be illustrated by *I saw her this morning*, spoken in the late morning, afternoon or evening of the same day. In sentences where they combine with the present perfect, on the other hand, no such separation from the moment of speech is signalled. This can be illustrated by *I've seen her this morning*, normally spoken in the morning of the same day.

In many cases a past situation may equally naturally be described by a sentence in the present perfect and a sentence in the past. If the speaker's balance of focus inclines towards the present time result or continuation of this situation, he will use the present perfect, i.e. instruct the hearer to tag the situation on to present time and then look back on a situation. If the focus is on the past situation itself, on the other hand, he will select the past, i.e. instruct the hearer to identify a past time situation directly. This can be illustrated by *I have made that point in the telegram* and *I made that point in the telegram*.

In their relation to the present perfect and the past, the time adverbials ALWAYS, EVER and NEVER constitute a special case (see Davidsen-Nielsen 1990: 128f). As these words describe all-inclusive time, one would expect them to go with the present perfect rather than the past, for as already stated the use of the latter form signals that the speaker has a particular past time in mind. The expected combination is indeed found very frequently:

(5)   I *have* always *approved* of the honours system.

(6)   One of the best writers we*'ve* ever *had*.

(7)   I*'ve* *never* trusted hand-squashers.

However, the three adverbials are also common in sentences in the past. In some of these this is because the speaker does have a particular past time in mind, a fact which may be indicated by other time adverbials or which the hearer understands for non-linguistic reasons:

(8)   In my childhood I always *detested* celery.

(9)   *Did* you ever *meet* John Lennon?

(10)   Before the war she never *wrote* poems.

Here the present perfect could not be used. But ALWAYS, EVER and NEVER are sometimes also found in sentences in the past where there is no otherwise expressed or understood specific past time involved:

(11)   James *was* always a man of honour.

(12)   *Did* you ever *hear* of incest?

(13)   I never *saw* such a crowd.

Examples like these are exceptions to the rule that the past counts as an instruction to identify a situation as it was before the moment of speech, and express the same meaning as *James has always been a man of honour, Have you ever heard of incest?* and *I've never seen such a crowd.*

One reason why it is sensible to operate with an integrated tense-aspect category concerns the nature of the perfect. In being to do with temporal location (a past time situation), it may be analysed as part of a pure tense system (as it is by e.g. Huddleston 1995). But in simultaneously dealing with the way the speaker looks at the situation expressed (see Bache 1985a: 5ff, 124ff, 1995: 268ff), it may also be analysed as part of an aspect system (as it is by e.g. Quirk et al. 1985). It should also be pointed out that the perfect is tightly interwoven with the action category (see Bache 1994). In a resultative example like *Alex has turned off the telly*, the present time situation is *stative* (i.e. the telly is in a *state* of being off at the moment of speech) while the anterior situation is *dynamic* (more specifically *punctual*, see section 7.2.1). In a continuative example like *They've owned the house for many years*, on the other hand, both the present time situation and the anterior situation are stative.

In using the *past perfect* the speaker instructs the hearer to tag the sentence on to 'world-before-now' and look back on a previous situation. The first instruction is given by means of the past form *had* and the second by means of the *-ed* participle. The meaning of the past perfect is thus 'It applied at a past time that something was anterior in time'. This can be captured by the notation [Past [anterior [situation]]] and illustrated by examples like these:

(14)   When the second half began, Rush *had scored* two goals.

(15)   Well, I *had gone* off to church and everything was peaceful and still.

Here scoring two goals and going off to church are represented as anterior to the past time the hearer is instructed to reckon with.

The past perfect is common in *indirect speech* as a 'backshifted' version of the past or of the present perfect (cf. section 9.6.13). This can be illustrated by examples like *Linda told me she had gone to Egypt last year* and *Linda said she hadn't been to Egypt since 1990*, which should be compared with *I went to Egypt last year* and *I haven't been to Egypt since 1990*.

The past perfect competes with the simple past in clauses beginning with *after*, such as *After we (had) parked, I peeped through a flap in the tent and saw it all*. As *after* unequivocally places the situation described in the matrix clause as subsequent to that described by the subclause, the past perfect can here without loss of information be replaced by the simple past. A similar vacillation is found in matrix clauses containing an adverbial introduced by *before*: *I (had) read the novel before I visited my sister*.

Modal usage of the past perfect will be dealt with in section 9.7.

Perfect forms are also found in *nonfinite verb groups*:

(16)   It is better *to have loved* and *lost* than never *to have loved* at all.

(17)   Accusations of *having shirked* one's responsibilities are difficult to face.

Here the time the hearer is instructed to look back from is *unspecified*.

What is common to any perfect form is that the situation described is *anterior to a time of reckoning* (see Harder 1996: 382). The time of reckoning is at the moment of speech in examples (1) through (7), before the moment of speech in (14) and (15) and unspecified in (16) and (17).

Note finally perfect-like constructions like the following with BE rather than HAVE:

(18)   The guests *are gone*.

The difference between this sentence and an ordinary perfect (*The guests have gone*) is slight: (18) expresses pure stative meaning ('they are not here') whereas the example with HAVE expresses this state as a result of the prior situation of 'going'.

9.6.5. Future perfect forms

The meaning signalled by the *present future perfect* can be expressed by the notation [Present [future [anterior [situation]]]]. In using this form the speaker encodes a complex instruction that can be paraphrased: tag the sentence on to present time, look ahead to a future time, and then place the situation before that. In its bidirectionality the present future perfect is semantically quite complex, and not very frequent. It can be illustrated by the following examples:

(1) The committee *will have finished* its work on April 30th.

(2) If you could be patient for a few minutes more, I*'ll have finished*.

(3) By this time tomorrow, I*'ll* no doubt *have finished* sorting out the first batch of replies.

By means of the first of these sentences the speaker instructs the hearer that right now there is ahead of him a time in relation to which the committee's finishing of their work is anterior. Here the time from which the hearer is instructed to look back is specified by means of the adverbial *on April 30th*. Adverbials occurring in sentences in the present future perfect are often realized by preposition groups beginning with *before* or with *by* (which in its temporal use means 'not later than' and is therefore semantically close to *before*) and whose complement is realized by future time expressions like *tomorrow* and *next week*. As *before* and *by* signal anteriority and *tomorrow*, *next week*, etc. signal futurity, the prevalence of adverbials of this type in sentences in the present future perfect is hardly surprising.

In temporal subclauses, future anterior situations are expressed by the present perfect rather than by the present future perfect (cf. also section 9.6.3 on the use of present nonfuture forms about the future in temporal subclauses), compare:

(4) I*'ll have finished* when you come.

(5) When you *have finished* I'll leave.

These examples also show that the sequence of events depends not so much on the division of labour between the matrix clause and the subclause but on the verb forms chosen: in both examples the event expressed by the perfect form is presented as anterior to the event expressed by the nonperfect form.

The *past future perfect* has the semantic structure expressed in the formula [Past [future [anterior [situation]]]]. In using it, the speaker thus instructs the hearer to tag the sentence on to an identifiable past time, go ahead to a later time and then place the situation before that. The following examples (cf. Davidsen-Nielsen 1990: 141) illustrate the use of this form:

(6) I was convinced that she *would have finished* the book before the first of April.

(7) I was hoping his fit of rage *would have culminated* soon.

The use of the past future perfect in conditional sentences, e.g. *If she had asked him, he would have been angry*, was dealt with in section 8.9. Its use in indirect speech and its modal use will be dealt with in sections 9.6.13 and 9.7 respectively.

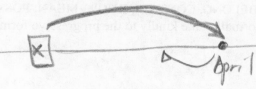

9.6.6. Progressive forms: introduction

As indicated by its name a progressive form serves the purpose of presenting a situation as being in progress, or unfolding, i.e. with an *internal focus*. In using a nonprogressive form, on the other hand, the speaker presents a situation as a fact, or a complete unit, i.e. with an external focus. This distinction, which is often described by grammarians in terms of the aspect category, can be illustrated by the following examples:

(1)   It *was raining* in Dublin.

(2)   It *rained* in Dublin.

While (1) describes only the middle phase of the situation involved, i.e. adopts an *in medias res* perspective excluding both the initial phase and the terminal phase, (2) describes the situation without concern for its internal phasal constituency. The difference between presenting a situation with an external focus (i.e. with a nonprogressive form) and presenting it with an internal focus (i.e. with a progressive form) represents the fourth choice in our integrated tense-aspect system in English (after present/past, future/non-future and perfect/nonperfect).

In accounting for progressive forms it is essential also to take *actionality* into consideration (see section 7.2). At the most general level it should be pointed out that the progressive is normally used only in sentences whose actionality is *dynamic*. That it is uncommon in sentences describing stative situations is not surprising, for progression entails an input of energy that characterizes dynamic but not stative actionality. For example, sentences like *Ottawa is the capital of Canada* (intensive), *The village lies in a dark valley* (extensive) and *George believes in God* (attitude) could not be changed to corresponding sentences in the progressive. Note secondly that though e.g. *My back aches* and *The wound itches* can be changed to *My back is aching* and *The wound is itching*, the situation described is no longer viewed as purely stative (perception) but as dynamic (self-contained). Attention should also be drawn to examples like *Sally was being silly* and *You're being pigheaded* where the main verb involved is BE. These differ from *Sally was silly* and *You're pigheaded* (both intensive) in describing a dynamic situation, i.e. *being* here means approximately 'acting' or 'behaving'. In such cases temporariness is expressed in addition to progression, and so it is in e.g. *Peter is/was living in London*, which differs from *Peter lives/lived in London* (extensive) in expressing non-permanent residence.

Certain verbs have a strong potential for expressing stative meaning, such as BELIEVE, BELONG, CONTAIN, KNOW, MEAN, POSSESS and OWN, and these do not normally take kindly to the progressive form:

(3)   He *possessed/*was possessing* a certain wildness.

(4)   This bottle *contains/*is containing* two pints of milk.

(5)   In those days I *knew/*was knowing* him well, of course.

When such verbs are used dynamically to denote progression or a change of state, they are of course compatible with the progressive form:

(6)   He said it with that smug look that *had been possessing* him lately.

(7)   The jug inexplicably seemed *to be containing* less water as the experiment progressed. (Lauridsen 1986: 21)

In using a progressive form the speaker instructs the hearer to tag the sentence on to a time (present, past, present + anterior, past + anterior, etc.) and then to look at a *progressing* situation which is *simultaneous* with it. The latter instruction is given by the *-ing* participle and the former by the remainder of the verb group (*is, was, has been, would be*, etc.). Examples:

(8)   The small figure *is moving* slowly along the fence.

(9)   I*'m speaking* not just from the pulpit but from experience.

(10)   The waitresses *were looking* at us.

(11)   You*'re turning* your back on people in need.

(12)   The Yucatec Mayan language *is disappearing* among the Mayan population.

(13)   I knew I *was making* a mistake.

In these examples the hearer is instructed to tag the sentence on to present time (8, 9, 11, 12) or a past time (10, 13) and then to view the situation as progressing simultaneously with it. And in an example like *You'll be turning your back on people in need*, the hearer is instructed to tag the sentence on to present time, look ahead to a future time and view the situation as progressing simultaneously with that (see section 9.6.3).

If the subtype of actionality is *self-contained* as in (8), (9) and (10), the situation progresses in a uniform way (see section 7.2.2). If it is *directed* as in (11), (12) and (13), on the other hand, the situation progresses towards a different state of affairs. This explains why sentences with directed actionality in the progressive may be used to describe a *future* (posterior) situation – usually under the control of the person referred to by the subject form – which is in preparation at the time identified by the form of BE:

(14a) Linda *is moving* to France tomorrow.

(14b) Linda *was moving* to France the following day.

In these examples the adverbial informs the hearer that the speaker has a situation ahead in mind; but even in the absence of such adverbials a sentence in the progressive may be used intentionally to describe a posterior situation which is in preparation at the time identified. Depending on the larger linguistic and/or situational context examples like *Linda is moving to France* and *Linda was moving to France* may thus describe a situation that is in progress at the time identified or which is ahead of it.

The subtype of dynamic situation described by a sentence in the progressive may not only be self-contained as in (8), (9) and (10) or directed as in (11), (12) and (13) but also *iterative*:

(15)   The telephone *is/was ringing*.

On the other hand the actionality of a sentence in the progressive cannot be *telic* for, as mentioned in section 7.2.2, telicness requires that a natural terminal point is included beyond which no further progression is possible. Such a terminal point is clearly not included in e.g. *Jack is/was fixing the old motorbike*. Nor can the actionality of a sentence in the progressive be punctual, for lack of extension in time is incompatible with progression. In e.g. *She is/was switching from Spanish to English* the situation described is therefore not punctual but directed.

There are cases where a situation may equally well be described by a progressive sentence and a nonprogressive sentence. This can be illustrated by the following examples (see Bache 1986):

(16a)   We *celebrated* Stephanie's birthday at my uncle's place.

(16b)   We *were celebrating* Stephanie's birthday at my uncle's place.

Here it is the same (self-contained) situation which is described but in slightly different ways (external vs. internal focus). Note in this connection verbs like STAND, SIT, LIE, HOLD, KEEP, OCCUPY, SLEEP, STAY, WAIT, WEAR. These verbs, which have a clear stative potential, are often used to refer to temporary posture or conditions: e.g. *He waited for her in the library / She wore her mother's wedding dress*. In connection with subjects referring to volitional agents more or less 'in command' of what is going on, such situations are in a grey zone between dynamic and stative and are therefore best classified as self-contained (i.e. the most stative of the dynamic subsituations). They often permit expression by both the progressive and nonprogressive verb forms with only a slight difference of aspectual meaning (cf. *He was waiting for her in the library / She was wearing her mother's wedding dress*).

In examples like the next ones, on the other hand, there is a marked semantic difference:

(17a)   Walter *moved* to the door.

(17b)   Walter *was moving* to the door.

Here again a situation is described with an external or with an internal focus (this is indeed the constant difference between the nonprogressive and the progressive). But in choosing the latter focus (example (17b)) the speaker eliminates the completion of the situation from the reference of the verbal, i.e. he describes a situation where the door is approached but not reached. As a result the situation is described not as telic – as it is in (17a), which indicates that the door was reached – but as directed. The difference between a progressive and a corresponding nonprogressive sentence is thus much stronger if there is a concomitant difference in actionality than if the actionality remains the same. Note in this connection that while (16a) is entailed by (16b) – i.e. the truth of (16a) follows from that of (16b) – (17a) is not entailed by (17b): if we *were celebrating* Stephanie's birthday it follows that we also *celebrated* it; but if Walter *was moving* to the door it does not follow that he also *moved* (all the way) to the door.

The choice between progressive and nonprogressive forms is basically *non-deictic* but like the choices involving the future and perfect forms it sometimes has deictic implications. In choosing the progressive (along with the present, nonfuture and nonperfect) in a sentence like *He's speaking like a professional*, the speaker relates the situation described more precisely to the present moment than in choosing the nonprogressive in *He speaks like a professional*: while the latter sentence describes a situation which applies generally, a habit, the former describes a dynamic situation taking place here and now, i.e. specifically at the time and place of the speaker.

As indicated at the beginning of this section, progressive forms are often assumed to differ from corresponding nonprogressive forms in terms of *aspect*, and one reason for that is undoubtedly that the choice between progressive and nonprogressive is basically non-deictic. However, like the perfect forms and the future forms, progressive forms are clearly governed by, and integrated with, the primary deictic choice between present and past. The four ordered choices in the English tense-aspect system (present/past, future/non-future, perfect/nonperfect and progressive/nonprogressive) represent a cline of temporal meaning. Only the first choice (present/past) involves pure deictic temporal meaning. The other choices express *relative time orientation* more independently of the deictic base provided by the moment of speech (see section 9.6.1), but as we have seen, they occasionally have deictic implications. The further away a choice is from the first choice, the weaker and the more sporadic these implications become, and the more other factors become important, such as actionality and aspect, which affect the perfect/nonperfect and especially the progressive/nonprogressive oppositions.

We conclude this section by offering an overview of some of the characteristic aspectual and actional meanings associated with pairs of nonprogressive and progressive forms:

Nonprogressive <-> Progressive

Aspect

external focus	<->	internal focus

Action			Examples
stative	<->	dynamic	*He speaks like a professional* *He is speaking like a professional*
punctual	<->	iterative	*A door slammed behind him* *A door was slamming behind him*
punctual	<->	directed	*She caught up with the others* *She was catching up with the others*
telic	<->	directed	*She built a new garden shed* *She was building a new garden shed*
self-contained	<->	self-contained	*They walked along the beach* *They were walking along the beach*

9.6.7. Present and past progressive forms

In using the present progressive the speaker instructs the hearer to think of present time and then look at a simultaneously progressing situation. The meaning of the present progressive is thus 'It applies now that a situation is simultaneous and in progress'. This can be expressed by the notation [Present [progressing [situation]]] and illustrated by an example like *Federal authorities are investigating allegations of currency violations*.

As pointed out in section 9.6.2, the simple present is often used to express habitual meaning (including universal conditions, personal habits and ability). In such cases the hearer is instructed to think of the world now but clearly not to view a dynamic situation as taking place simultaneously with the moment of speech. For this purpose the speaker must use the present progressive, and if he chooses to do so the habitual meaning disappears:

(1a)   The sun *sets* in the west.

(1b)   The sun *is setting* in the west.

(2a)   Evelyn *speaks* Russian.

(2b)   Evelyn *is speaking* Russian.

(3a)   Sally *buys* clothes at Marks & Spencer's.
(3b)   Sally *is buying* clothes at Marks & Spencer's.

If the simple present is replaced by the present progressive in a sentence describing a *personal habit*, as in (3a-b), there are two possibilities: either the habitual meaning disappears and a situation is presented as being in progress at the moment of speech, or the habitual meaning is retained but with the difference that it is a *temporary habit* which is now described. The special use of the present progressive for a temporary habit can be further exemplified by sentences like *I'm walking to work this week* and *She's sleeping away her days*. It should be added that the temporary implication of the habitual progressive may be cancelled by adverbials expressing all-inclusive time like ALWAYS and FOREVER, as illustrated by *She's always/forever asking silly questions*. In such cases annoyance is often expressed. Temporariness is a natural implication of progressive meaning and thus present also in most nonhabitual progressives.

In using the *past progressive*, the speaker instructs the hearer to tag the sentence on to a past time and then to look at a simultaneously progressing situation. The meaning of the past progressive is thus 'It applied at a past time that a situation was simultaneous and in progress'. This can be expressed by the notation [Past [progressing [situation]]] and illustrated by examples like the following:

(4)   I thought he *was* simply *babbling*, but suddenly he got up and left.
(5)   Since it *was snowing*, I went with her in the direction of the Praga Bridge.
(6)   Like the damned in hell, I *was being tossed* from fire to ice. (passive)

In complex sentences a past progressive form in one clause may have the effect of surrounding a situation described by a simple past form in another clause by a *temporal frame*:

(7)   When Mrs Moore *returned*, her husband *was painting* the view from their hotel window.
(8)   While I *was eating*, a new customer *entered* the restaurant.

Here the situation described by the matrix clause in (7) and the subclause in (8) are presented as being in progress at the time when the situations described by the subclause in (7) and the matrix clause in (8) took place. Note that if the nonprogressive had been used in the matrix clause of (7), the painting of the view would be subsequent to the return of Mrs Moore.

Though the framing effect of the past progressive is very common in complex sentences with temporal clauses, it is by no means a constant property in constructions with the subordinator *while*:

(9)   While I *was eating*, I *looked* at the other customers.

(10a)   While Minna *was being measured* for her clothes, I *looked* over her books.

Here the situations described by the matrix clauses are not framed by those described by the subclauses but are simultaneous with them and span the same stretch of time. In such cases it is also possible to use the past progressive in the matrix clause:

(10b)   While Minna *was being measured* for her clothes, I *was looking* over her books.

Semantically, the difference between (10a) and (10b) is slight and only involves a choice between a neutral external focus and a more marked internal focus. Note, however, that if the replacement of a nonprogressive by a progressive form affects the actionality of a sentence – which is not the case in (10a) and (10b), both of which describe self-contained situations – the difference between progressive and nonprogressive becomes quite clear:

(11a)   While Minna *was being measured* for her clothes, I *finished* my breakfast. (*finished* = punctual)

(11b)   While Minna *was being measured* for her clothes, I *was finishing* my breakfast. (*was finishing* = directed)

In closing this section we should point out that in *narration* the framing effect of the progressive typically serves the purpose of describing the *background frame* against which a number of consecutive events described by clauses in the simple past (or present) are recounted:

(12)   At twelve o'clock sharp I *left* my flat. The sun *was shining* and people *were sunning* themselves on benches in the park. I *unlocked* the car, *fastened* the seat belt, *started* the engine and *drove* to the first intersection. On the pavements pedestrians *were strolling* along. Suddenly an idea *occurred* to me.

Here each nonprogressive form makes the action advance in narrative time by introducing a new time focus. The progressive forms do not perform this function but are used to describe a situation that is simultaneous with that described by the preceding nonprogressive form.

9.6.8. Future progressive forms

In using the *present future progressive* the speaker instructs the hearer to tag the sentence on to present time, then look ahead to a future time and finally to look at a simultaneously progressing situation. This can be captured by the notation [Present [future [progressing [situation]]]] and illustrated by:

(1)   They *'ll be leaving* in half an hour.

(2)   You're right. But in the meantime we *'ll be travelling* by boat, and you can always jump off a boat.

In some situations the present future progressive may be preferred to the present future because WILL + V may out of context be ambiguous:

(3)   I'*ll keep* watch for you.

(4)   I'*ll be keeping* watch for you.

Here WILL in (3) may be either volitional or purely temporal, and only by means of the context is the hearer able to determine whether the communicative function of the sentence is a promise or a descriptive statement. In (4), on the other hand, WILL can only be understood to be purely temporal. The speaker pays a price for this type of 'disambiguation': she must instruct the hearer to look not only at a future situation but at a future situation as being in progress.

In using the *past future progressive* the speaker instructs the hearer to tag the sentence on to a past time, then look ahead to a posterior time and finally to look at a simultaneously progressing situation. This can be expressed by the notation [Past [future [progressing [situation]]]] and illustrated by:

(5)   I knew she *would be asking* payment for my meals.

In *indirect speech* the past future progressive is typically a backshifted version of the present future progressive (cf. section 9.6.13).

The past future progressive occurs in the matrix clause of *conditional sentences*, i.e. in examples of the type *I'd be wandering around alone if it weren't for Sonya*. Here the matrix clause does not describe a past time situation but a hypothetical situation (cf. section 8.9).

9.6.9. Perfect progressive forms

In using the *present perfect progressive*, the speaker instructs the hearer to tag the sentence on to present time, then look back at an anterior time and finally to look at a situation progressing simultaneously with the anterior-present period (i.e. towards present time). This can be captured by the notation [Present [anterior [progressing [situation]]]] and illustrated by:

(1)   *Has* Father *been talking* to you?

(2)   Minna, they tell me you'*ve been looking* for me.

(3)   She'll suspect I'*ve been telling* you things.

Like the present perfect, the present perfect progressive does not combine with adverbials which exclude the moment of speech, such as *yesterday*, *a year ago* and *the other day* (see section 9.6.4).

In using the *past perfect progressive* the speaker instructs the hearer to tag the sentence on to a past time, then look back at an anterior time and finally to look at a situation progressing simultaneously with the anterior-past period (i.e. towards the past time). This can be expressed by the notation [Past [anterior [progressing [situation]]]] and illustrated by examples like:

(4)   Then the thing I *had been dreading* happened.

(5)   One of the writers *had been hanging* around Edusha.

(6)   I could tell that she*'d been talking* for a long time.

Modal usage of the past perfect (progressive as well as nonprogressive) will be dealt with in section 9.7 and its use in indirect speech in section 9.6.13.

9.6.10. Future perfect progressive forms

These forms are semantically highly complex, so not surprisingly they are rarely encountered. The *present future perfect progressive* instructs the hearer to tag the sentence on to present time, then look ahead to a future time, then look back at an anterior time and finally look at a situation progressing simultaneously with the future-anterior situation (i.e. towards the future time). It can be formally represented as [Present [future [anterior [progressing [situation]]]]] and illustrated by:

(1)   The committee *will have been negotiating* the treaty for two months soon.

In using the *past future perfect progressive* the speaker instructs the hearer to tag the sentence on to a past time, then look ahead to a posterior time, then look back at an anterior time and finally look at a situation progressing simultaneously with the posterior-anterior period (i.e. towards the posterior time). This can be captured by the notation [Past [future [anterior [progressing [situation]]]]] and illustrated by:

(2)   I was convinced that she *would have been pondering* this problem all morning before doing anything about it.

9.6.11. Nonfinite progressive forms

In complex sentences, progressive forms are also found in nonfinite verb groups. Consider first examples in the *nonfinite perfect progressive* like the following:

(1)   *Having been drinking* whisky since Friday, I feel somewhat indisposed.

(2)   He seemed *to have been drinking*.

Here the verb groups in italics instruct the hearer to look back at an anterior time and then to look at a simultaneously progressing situation. As the time the hearer is instructed to look back from is neither present nor past but *unspecified* (see section 9.6.4), the appropriate formula in examples of this type is [Anterior [progressing [situation]]]. Note, however, that an instruction to tag the sentence on to present or past time which applies to the complex sentence as a whole is given by means of the finite verb forms (*feel* vs. *seemed*). If the speaker wishes to instruct the hearer to tag the sentence on to present or past time by means of the verb groups in the subclause, he must do so by choosing sentences with finite subclauses like *As I have been drinking whisky since Friday, I feel somewhat indisposed* (synonymous with (1)) and *It seemed that he had been drinking* (synonymous with (2)).

Consider secondly examples in the nonfinite nonperfect progressive like the following:

(3)   He seems *to be handling* the affair very well.

(4)   He seemed *to be handling* the affair very well.

Here the nonfinite verb forms instruct the hearer to look at a progressing situation without specifying what time the situation is simultaneous with. Again it is only by means of the finite verb that the hearer is able to figure out whether he should think of present time (*seem*) or of a past time (*seemed*). In this case, therefore, simultaneity is only involved *indirectly*. If the speaker wishes to instruct the hearer to think of present time or a past time by means of the verb group in the subclause, he must do so by selecting sentences with finite subclauses like *It seems as if he's handling the affair very well* (synonymous with (3)) and *It seemed as if he was handling the affair very well* (synonymous with (4)).

Attention should also be drawn to examples where simultaneity remains an unrealized potential meaning even in the context of the matrix verb:

(5)   *To be drowning* is/was said to be a hallucinatory experience.

Here *any* time may in principle serve as a basis for the orientation of the progressive as simultaneous.

Note finally that after certain verbs of perception (such as SEE and HEAR) there is an opposition between bare infinitive and present participle constructions which is semantically very similar to the distinction between progressive and nonprogressive forms:

(6)   I heard a small child *cry/crying* next door.

(7)   She saw them *laugh/laughing* together.

Here the difference is primarily one of external focus (the infinitive) vs. internal focus (the present participle).

9.6.12. Recapitulation

We can now recapitulate the standard notations and semantic instructions for the sixteen forms expressing relative time in the English tense-aspect system.

Instructions generally:

Present:	tag on to world-now (general present time)
Past:	tag on to world-before-now (past time)
Future:	look ahead (future time, posteriority)
Perfect:	look back (anteriority)
Progressive:	look here (simultaneous progression)

Instructions specifically (as applied to the verb HAPPEN):

1. The present   *happens*
    [Present [situation]]

    Tag a situation of 'happening' on to world-now.

2. The past   *happened*
    [Past [situation]]

    Tag a situation of 'happening' on to world-before-now.

3. The present future   *will happen*
    [Present [future [situation]]]

    Tag on to world-now and then look ahead to a situation of 'happening'.

4. The past future   *would happen*
    [Past [future [situation]]]

    Tag on to world-before-now and then look ahead to a situation of
    'happening'.

5. The present perfect   *has happened*
    [Present [anterior [situation]]]

    Tag on to world-now and then look back at a situation of 'happening'.

6. The past perfect   *had happened*
    [Past [anterior [situation]]]

    Tag on to world-before-now and then look back at a situation of 'happening'.

7. The present future perfect   *will have happened*
    [Present [future [anterior [situation]]]]

    Tag on to world-now, then look ahead to a future time and finally look back
    at a situation of 'happening'.

8. The past future perfect   *would have happened*
    [Past [future [anterior [situation]]]]

    Tag on to world-before-now, then look ahead to a posterior time and finally
    look back at a situation of 'happening'.

9. The present progressive   *is happening*
    [Present [progressing [situation]]]

    Tag on to world-now and then look here at a simultaneously progressing
    situation of 'happening'.

10.   The past progressive   *was happening*
      [Past [progressing [situation]]]

      Tag on to world-before-now and then look here at a simultaneously progressing situation of 'happening'.

11.   The present future progressive   *will be happening*
      [Present [future [progressing [situation]]]]

      Tag on to world-now, then look ahead to a future time and finally look here at a simultaneously progressing situation of 'happening'.

12.   The past future progressive   *would be happening*
      [Past [future [progressing [situation]]]]

      Tag on to world-before-now, then look ahead to a posterior time and finally look here at a simultaneously progressing situation of 'happening'.

13.   The present perfect progressive   *has been happening*
      [Present [anterior [progressing [situation]]]]

      Tag on to world-now, then look back at an anterior time and finally look at a situation of 'happening' progressing simultaneously with the anterior–present period (i.e. towards present time).

14.   The past perfect progressive   *had been happening*
      [Past [anterior [progressing [situation]]]]

      Tag on to world-before-now, then look back at an anterior time and finally look at a situation of 'happening' progressing simultaneously with the anterior–past period (i.e. towards the past time).

15.   The present future perfect progressive   *will have been happening*
      [Present [future [anterior [progressing [situation]]]]]

      Tag on to world-now, then look ahead to a future time, then look back at an anterior time and finally look at a situation of 'happening' progressing simultaneously with the future–anterior period (i.e. towards the future time).

16.   The past future perfect progressive   *would have been happening*
      [Past [future [anterior [progressing [situation]]]]]

      Tag on to world-before-now, then look ahead to a posterior time, then look back at an anterior time and finally look at a situation of 'happening' progressing simultaneously with the posterior–anterior period (i.e. towards the posterior time).

It is important to remember that this list contains instructions reflecting the *basic* semantics of the tense-aspect system. As we have seen, specific constructions may express derived meanings and/or have special uses, depending on actional and aspectual properties. The English tense-aspect system can also be represented by means of a tree diagram:

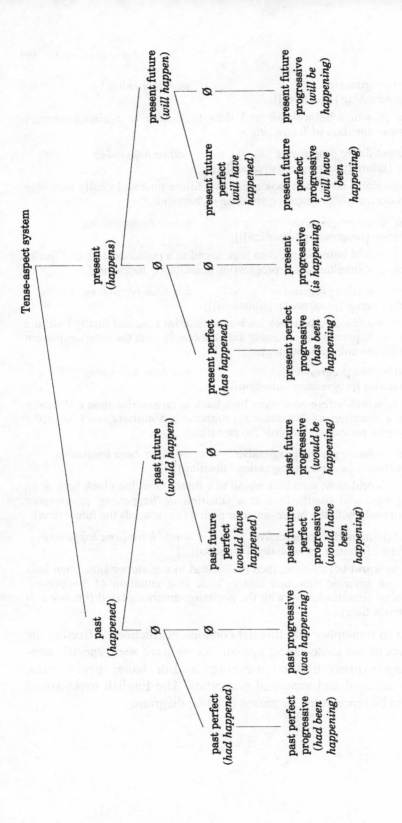

Tense-aspect system

past
(happened)

present
(happens)

past perfect
(had happened)

past progressive
(was happening)

Ø

past future
(would happen)

present perfect
(has happened)

present progressive
(is happening)

present future
(will happen)

past perfect
progressive
(had been
happening)

Ø

past future
perfect
(would have
happened)

past future
progressive
(would be
happening)

present perfect
progressive
(has been
happening)

present future
perfect
(will have
happened)

present future
progressive
(will be
happening)

Ø

past future
perfect
progressive
(would have
been
happening)

present future
perfect
progressive
(will have
been
happening)

This shows that the first choice is between the present and the past, the second choice between future and nonfuture, the third choice between perfect and nonperfect and the fourth choice between the progressive and the nonprogressive (the choice of nonfuture, nonperfect and nonprogressive is symbolized by Ø).

There is a *deictic cline* in the diagram: the lower you go, the less deixis alone motivates the choice of verb form. At the same time other factors become more relevant in the description, such as aspectual meaning, which affects the perfect and especially the progressive forms (i.e. the third and fourth choices, respectively) (see also section 9.6.4).

Note that [progressing] can *only* be the fourth choice. If it was assumed to be the third, the non-progressive perfect forms could not be produced (*has happened, had happened, will have happened, would have happened*). If it were assumed to be the second choice, none of the eight perfect forms could be produced.

Note finally that the proposed ordering of the four choices reflects the ordering of auxiliaries in verb groups (see section 9.4). The first auxiliary is present or past (*will/would, has/had, is/was*), and future WILL precedes perfect HAVE, which in turn precedes progressive BE.

9.6.13. Tense-aspect in indirect speech

By indirect speech we understand the reporting of what an original speaker said. This is normally accompanied by changes of tense-aspect, person and other deictic elements (such as place references and demonstratives), as in:

(1)   Peter said that his commanding officer *would regard* that as cowardice.

If this sentence is compared with its direct speech counterpart *Peter said, "My commanding officer will regard this as cowardice"*, it can be seen that the past future form *would regard* is a *backshifted* version of *will regard*. Here the past future does not necessarily instruct the hearer to look ahead from some past time, i.e. it does not necessarily have its normal temporal meaning (cf. *Peter said that his commanding officer would regard that as cowardice, and he may be right*).

Backshifting in indirect speech is not obligatory, as demonstrated by the acceptability of *Peter said that his commanding officer will regard this as cowardice*. But it is more neutral than lack of backshifting, so if a verb of saying is in the past, the verbs in the following subclauses are normally past forms too (past, past perfect, past future or past future perfect), as in *She said she agreed with those who had suggested to reschedule the meeting*. This so-called *consecutio temporum principle* operates in conditional sentences too, though in such sentences it is rarely refrained from and not restricted to concord of past forms.

In indirect speech a past form in a subclause following a matrix clause with a verb of saying in the past may or may not be a backshifted form. This can be illustrated by the following examples (which like several others in this section are cited from Davidsen-Nielsen 1990: 147ff):

(2)   Your wife said you didn't smoke but I see you do.

(3)   Your wife said you didn't smoke when you were a teenager.

In (2), unlike (3), *didn't smoke* is a backshifted version of *doesn't smoke*.

Optional backshifting in indirect speech in English affects the first tense-aspect choice (present vs. past). If the original construction contained a present form, the possible backshifts can be summed up in this way:

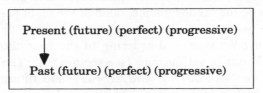

Present (future) (perfect) (progressive)

Past (future) (perfect) (progressive)

This system yields the following specific shifts:

Present	→	Past
Present perfect	→	Past perfect
Present future perfect	→	Past future perfect
Present future progressive	→	Past future progressive
etc.		

These shifts can be illustrated by the following examples:

(4)   The counsellor said that blood was thicker than water.

(5)   Mary said she hadn't been to the States since 1972.

(6)   He said he would have finished sorting out the first batch of replies next Friday.

(7)   The contractor told me they would be working again next week.

If the original construction contained a past form, the possible backshifts can be summed up in this way:

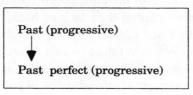

Past (progressive)

Past perfect (progressive)

This system yields the following specific shifts:

Past	$\rightarrow$	Past perfect
Past progressive	$\rightarrow$	Past perfect progressive

These two shifts can be illustrated by the following examples:

(8)   Mary told me she had gone to California last year.

(9)   Jim claimed that he had been staying at the Park Lodge over Christmas.

In indirect speech a past perfect form may thus represent either a backshifted past form or a backshifted present perfect, and the hearer has to work out which of the two types of backshifting is involved. In (5) and (8) the temporal adverbials (*since 1972* vs. *last year*) provide an answer to this question. In (9), on the other hand, there is no such clue, so here the hearer must decide whether it is a past progressive or a present perfect progressive which has been backshifted by taking the wider linguistic context or the situational context into consideration: the original statement could be either *'I was staying at the Park Lodge over Christmas'* or *'I have been staying at the Park Lodge over Christmas'*.

As there is no verb form available for the backshifting of a past perfect form, a sentence like the following is – out of context – ambiguous too:

(10)   Peter told me that when the second half began Rush had scored two goals.

Here *had scored* may be either a backshifted version of *scored* or an unshifted past perfect, i.e. the direct speech counterpart may be either *When the second half began Rush scored two goals* or *When the second half began Rush had scored two goals*. In the former case the hearer is instructed to identify a past time situation and in the latter to think of a past time and then to look back.

In closing this section we should draw attention to *free indirect speech*. Free indirect speech is restricted to written language and furthermore differs from indirect speech in that reporting clauses are omitted or parenthesized, in that question and exclamation structures can be incorporated and in that unshifted deictic words like *here*, *this* and *now* can be included. It can be illustrated by examples like these:

(11)   Presently, he reflected, it would become necessary for him to make some excuse and steal quietly out of the other's life.

(12)   Would she be able to recognize this interpretation of herself, he wondered?

Note finally cases of *implicit* indirect speech like the following where the speaker enquires about the listener's conversation with a third party:

(13)   'So what time did the train leave tomorrow morning?'

9.6.14. Tense-aspect in literary narrative

In fiction it is typically only the *past verb forms* (past, past perfect, past future, past future perfect, progressive as well as non-progressive) which are used, even in stories about imaginary future events. In using the past, the writer instructs the reader to identify not a past time situation but an *imaginary* situation at the stage reached in the narration. What is common to both these types of situation, however, is remoteness from the (real) world as it is now. The difference between them can be perceived by comparing the following examples (cf. Bache 1986: 94)

(1)   'I *climbed* the steep dune yesterday, now it's your turn.'

(2)   He *climbed* the steep dune before him hurriedly, not taking the time to remove his shoes and socks. His panting under the effort of running uphill *seemed* delicious to him; it *was* the taste of his renewed youth.

In the spoken utterance in (1), the situation of 'climbing' is mentally distant for the hearer, who is instructed to identify a past situation. In the written piece of fiction in (2), the writer creates, or introduces, an imaginary situation of climbing at the stage reached in the narration, simply by writing it. The 'climbing' thus becomes mentally present for the reader, who is instructed to 'witness', or envisage, the situation at this particular point in the narration. More technically, the difference is that the past is deictic in (1) while it is non-deictic in (2): the interpretation of the form in (2) is not dependent on the reader's awareness of the moment of communication (the writing of the novel). Thus in (2) but not in (1), we can replace the past forms by present forms with little or no difference of meaning:

(2')   He *climbs* the steep dune before him hurriedly, not taking the time to remove his shoes and socks. His panting under the effort of running uphill *seems* delicious to him; it *is* the taste of his renewed youth.

The difference between the present and the past in literary narrative is this: the past establishes a fictional distance from reality (which, however, is more or less neutralized once the reader has entered the fictional universe, i.e. has started reading) whereas the present creates the illusion that there is no fictional distance from reality and thus has a more dramatic potential (cf. the dramatic present mentioned in section 9.6.2), representing a calculated stylistic choice on the part of the writer. In both present-form and past-form narration, however, the writer creates the situations of his fictional universe by writing them and the reader is mentally present at the 'occurrence' of the situations narrated when reading them.

Outside literary narrative, a change from past form to present, or vice versa, typically results in ungrammaticality (e.g. *I climb the steep dune yesterday, now it's your turn*) or in a change of temporal meaning (as in e.g. *I know/knew what I am/was doing*).

There is in narration often an imitation of deixis in *dialogues*:

(3)   Silas took another sip. 'I *sent* Fiona off to Berlin last week', he said.

There are also deictic-like uses of verb forms in narration even outside dialogues – not relative to the writing of the novel, but relative to the stage reached in the narration. Thus the *past perfect* and the *past future* forms instruct the reader to look back and ahead, respectively, from the stage reached in the narration (cf. Davidsen-Nielsen 1990: 70f):

(4)   He was sitting beside his radio set which he *had* just *switched* off. It was late at night. He *had listened* to a symphony concert ... Now all was silent.

(5)   Ready to weep he prepared himself for bed. He *would* not *sleep*.

In using the *past future perfect* the writer instructs the reader to look ahead in the narration and then to look back:

(6)   Five days later Mrs Blair *would have left* her husband.

Similarly, when the present verb forms are used throughout a narrative (or long stretches of it), the reader may be instructed by the use of other tense-aspect forms to look back or ahead from the stage reached in the narration:

(7)   A window smashes in one of the small bedrooms; the cause is Henry, who *has put* his left arm through and down, and *slashed* it savagely on the glass.

(8)   What is happening upstairs is something Howard *will hear* about later.

Note that the difference between the instructions for verb forms in literary narrative and those for verb forms elsewhere involves only the first choice of form (present vs. past), which is redefined semantically when applied to verb forms in narration (most importantly in terms of loss of deictic meaning). The choices involving 'posteriority', 'anteriority' and 'simultaneous progression' apply equally well to fiction and non-fiction.

Literary narrative is similar to *historical* and *biographical* narrative, but in these types of narrative it is a real past time situation the reader is instructed to identify. Furthermore, the writer may step outside the narration and in so doing select a present form (e.g. *The next day I was appointed chairman. I must now get down to work*). The same goes for ordinary *everyday* narrative. With respect to tense-aspect, historical, biographical and everyday narrative resemble non-narrative language in that the addressee is instructed to identify a situation in real time. But they resemble fictional narrative in their fairly consistent use of the so-called 'epic preterite', i.e. the past forms charac-teristically used in story-telling fiction.

The fact that the loss of temporal deixis has given way to other, mainly stylistic functions in narration has certain important repercussions for the choice of progressive and nonprogressive forms (cf. Bache 1986: 91ff). As we have seen, we cannot normally use the simple present form of a verb with dynamic meaning to instruct the hearer to identify a strictly present action (for exceptions, see section 9.6.2):

(9a)   *'He *opens* his packsack'.

(10a)   *'He *takes* off his shoes and socks'.

Here only the progressive is possible. But in fiction the simple present is not nearly as constrained. For the examples in (9a) and (10a) to become acceptable we only have to imagine a fictional context, such as a stage direction or simply a piece of narration:

(9b)   After a while David says 'Well children, time to break out the grass'. *He opens his packsack* and gropes around inside.

(10b)   The two little girls go with him, then slip out of their shoes. *Paul takes off his shoes and socks*, rolls up his trousers like an elderly tripper at the seaside.

Outside a fictional context, such simple forms have a more general habitual or iterative meaning:

(9c)   He *always opens* his packsack to check its contents.

(10c)   When going to bed, Paul *usually takes* off his shoes and socks.

9.7. Modal uses of tense-aspect forms

As shown in section 9.6.13, the English verb forms do not necessarily have the same temporal meaning in indirect speech as in direct speech. The same goes for tense-aspect forms when they are used *modally*. We return to modality in section 9.9, but for the time being we can say that it centrally involves non-factuality and concerns either degree of *probability* (logical possibility and necessity, hypothetical meaning, beliefs and predictability) or *desirability* (permission, obligation, volition). In section 9.5 this was illustrated by the modal verb MAY, which is used to judge the probability of a situation in *The economy may get worse* and to express permission in *May I come in?* The type of modality which concerns probability is termed *epistemic* (derived from the Greek word for knowledge *episteme*) while that which concerns desirability is termed *deontic* (derived from Greek *deont-*, participial stem of *dei* 'it is right').

In English all the tense-aspect forms except the simple present, the present progressive and the present perfect can be used modally. In the following account of these modal uses we shall disregard the use of the past forms in conditional sentences, for that has already been dealt with, cf. section 8.9.

Let us consider first the modal use of the *past* and the *past perfect* forms (progressive as well as nonprogressive). As in conditional clauses these forms can be used for the expression of hypothetical meaning, i.e. *epistemically*, in object clauses and adverbial comparative clauses. This can be illustrated by the following examples (which like most of the others in this section are quoted from Davidsen-Nielsen 1990: 159ff):

(1)   I wish I *knew* the answer to that.
(2)   I wish I *had known* the answer to that.
(3)   He talks as if he *was writing* a doctoral dissertation on the subject.
(4)   He talks as if he *had read* the entire literature on this subject.

In (1) and (3) the hearer is not instructed to identify a past time situation but is supposed to imagine a counterfactual situation in present time; and in (2) and (4) he is not instructed to look back from a past time but is supposed to imagine a counterfactual situation at a past time. What is common to this modal use of a past form and its temporal use, however, is remoteness from the world at the moment of speech, either in time or factuality (recall our discussion of the past future in literary narrative in section 9.6.14).

Factual remoteness is also involved in those cases where the past is used for the expression of (deontic) tentativeness and politeness:

(5)   *Could* you *do* me a favour?
(6)   We *were wondering* if we can expect to see you down here any time.

Here a situation is described as factually remote by means of a past form, and this makes the request less direct – and therefore easier to turn down – than if the present had been used.

In expressions like *It's time we left* and *It's time you went to bed*, the past is used deontically about that which is considered appropriate or necessary for the subject to do.

Future (perfect) (progressive) forms can be used both *epistemically* and *deontically*. The latter modal use can be exemplified by:

(7)   You *will do* as I say at once.
(8)   You *will drop* me by the cathedral in Léon.
(9)   You *will be studying* hard in your room when I return.

Here the present future and the present future progressive do not instruct the hearer simply to tag on to present time and then look ahead but express an *order*. This modal use of the two forms is also closely related to their temporal use. The order is presented in a non-negotiable way as a future fact, and this makes it impolite and condescending.

The future forms are used epistemically for the expression of nonfuture *predictability*. The following examples express *specific* predictability:

(10)   They *will be* home at this time of day.

(11)   They *will be watching* telly now.

(12)   It was 10 a. m. John *would be* in his office now.

(13)   It was nearly midnight. The President *would have written* his letter of resignation now.

Though modal tense-aspect usage is closely related to nonmodal usage here as well, there is at the same time a clear difference. In using a sentence like (10), for example, the speaker does not instruct the hearer to look ahead from present time but informs him that a certain situation is predictable at the moment of speech. In a sentence without a future time adverbial like *John will be in his office*, the present future can be used either temporally to instruct the hearer to look ahead or modally to express present time predictability. Here the speaker can specify which meaning he has in mind by adding a time adverbial, such as *soon* or *now*.

The future forms may also express *habitual predictability*:

(14)   She *will sit* there for hours doing nothing.

(15)   By four o'clock every afternoon he *will have finished* all his chores.

(16)   Occasionally a tradesman's cart *would rattle* round the corner.

(17)   Every afternoon between 4 and 6 he*'ll be preparing* dinner.

Finally, the present future – but not the complex present future forms – may be used to express *general predictability*:

(18)   Oil *will float* on water.

(19)   Sugar *will dissolve* in water.

Semantically, such present future sentences are closely related to sentences in the present expressing a universal statement, like *Water boils at 100 degrees centigrade* (see section 9.6.2). Nevertheless, there is a difference in meaning between e.g. *Sugar will dissolve in water* and *Sugar dissolves in water*, for unlike the latter the former sentence contains an element of aheadness that is a property of the temporal present future. This can be captured by the paraphrase 'If sugar is put into water, it will dissolve'.

Modally used future forms are also found in the passive voice:

(20)   This *will* certainly *be remembered* by most people. (specific predictability)

(21) $H_2 SO_4$ *will be revealed* as an acid by the litmus test. (general predictability)

(22)   Every morning she *will be let* in by the caretaker. (habitual predictability)

(23)   You *will be escorted* by your mother as I told you. (order)

In allowing the passive voice, modally used future forms — used future forms – differ from verb groups beginning wit WILL. This appears from the unacceptability of, for exar *be let in by the caretaker*. There are therefore strong re. that the use of WILL-forms described in this section represents not regu... modal verb usage but secondary modal usage of future forms.

9.8. Mood

9.8.1. Introduction

Mood in English is traditionally regarded as an inflectional verbal category with three members: the *indicative* (which has *-s* in the 3rd person singular of the present), the *imperative* (realized by Ø) and the *subjunctive* (also realized by Ø). These three moods can be illustrated by the following examples:

(1)   Somebody *opens* the door (all the time).
(2)   Somebody *open* the door (will you?).
(3)   (I suggest that) somebody *open* the door.

The indicative and the imperative typically indicate what status the situation referred to has, namely something which is real and something which needs to be made real respectively (as illustrated by (1) and (2)). The communicative functions statement and directive are thus typically implemented by sentences whose verb stands in the indicative mood and the imperative mood respectively (see section 4.4.3). The communicative function of the subjunctive mood is less homogeneous, however. In an example like (3) it appears to be directive like the imperative, in *God save the Queen* it expresses a wish and in *Lest anyone worry we're sinking, let me reassure you we're not* it describes a hypothetical situation. The subjunctive mood has been termed 'thought-mood' by Jespersen, who terms the indicative 'fact-mood' and the imperative 'will-mood' (1909-49, vol.7: 623). Though the subjunctive differs from the indicative and the imperative in being communicatively quite heterogeneous, the three moods are on a par grammatically in forming a morphological paradigm.

As pointed out in section 9.7, modality centrally involves non-factuality, so sentences in the indicative mood are here considered nonmodal (unless, of course, they contain other modal expressions, such as *She may join us later*). On the other hand, sentences in the imperative mood are modal (deontic) in referring to situations which are not yet real; and sentences in the subjunctive mood are non-factual and thus modal too (epistemic or deontic). Owing to its factual nature the indicative is usually regarded as the unmarked, or neutral, mber of the mood category. In the following discussion (which is based on Davidsen-Nielsen 1990: 98-111), we examine the two non-factual moods.

Grammatically, mood differs from modality expressed by auxiliaries in having its own paradigm and in being realized inflectionally, but semantically the two non-factual moods are closely related to the modal verbs. We shall therefore analyse the imperative and the subjunctive by means of the same concepts as the modals.

9.8.2. The imperative

In using the imperative the speaker typically issues a *directive* to the hearer to behave in a specific way. Directives may be divided into a number of different functional subtypes (see Huddleston 1984: 364f). The most important of these can be illustrated by the following examples:

(1)   Shut up. (command)

(2)   Sit down, please. (request)

(3)   Wash hair and rinse carefully. (instruction)

(4)   Don't buy that brand if you can get others. (advice)

(5)   Take as many sweets as you like. (permission)

(6)   Give us this day our daily bread. (prayer)

Which of these subtypes of directive a sentence in the imperative mood expresses is dependent on the linguistic and/or situational context. A marker like *please* informs the hearer that an imperative probably functions as a request, and if the speaker's relation to the hearer is that of a superior to his subordinate, an imperative is likely to be understood as a command.

While the function of an imperative is typically directive, this is not invariably the case. In sentences like *Sleep well* and *Have a good time* it is used for the expression of a wish, and here it is clearly non-directive. Nor is the imperative directive in a coordinated structure like the following:

(7)   Do that again and I'll strangle you.

Here the speaker expresses his intention to inflict injury on the hearer if a certain behaviour continues. The type of speech act performed is thus a conditional threat (cf. *If you do that again I'll strangle you*).

As illustrated by the next example, a coordinated structure may also express both a conditional threat and a directive:

(8)   Shut up or I'll strangle you.

Here the speaker orders the hearer to stop behaving in a certain way and at the same time expresses his intention to inflict injury on him in case this directive is ignored (*Unless you shut up I'll strangle you*).

The imperative shows no present/past distinction (and is therefore perhaps best considered nonfinite). Nor does it interact with the other choices in the tense-aspect system apart from the fact that its combination with the progressive cannot be ruled out entirely. But as it is not logical for the speaker to direct the hearer to perform an ongoing action (e.g. ?*Be studying* and ?*Don't be studying*), progressive imperatives are virtually never found. The imperative is also highly restricted with respect to voice. This is not surprising either, for in passive sentences the subject form never performs the participant role DOER but typically the role DONE-TO (see section 7.4.1). Nevertheless, it is possible to issue a directive that the hearer should avoid becoming the target (DONE-TO) of an action, and this is reflected in the occurrence of negative passive imperatives like the following:

(9)   Don't be taken in by that scoundrel.

While passive sentences of this type can be freely formed, an imperative like *Be seated* cannot be regarded as a productive passive construction.

A special type of imperative which is very common has LET as its verb followed by *us* (optionally contracted to *let's*):

(10)   Let's go to the theatre.
(11)   Let's not be petty-minded.

Here the directive is aimed not only at the hearer but simultaneously at the speaker, as it is also in an example like *Let you and me do the dishes*. Sometimes, however, we come across imperatives with LET which do not express such a mutual proposal:

(12)   Just let him try.
(13)   Let AB be equal to BA.

Prohibitive imperatives are expressed by *don't* + V:

(14)   Don't buy that brand if you can get others.

The auxiliary DO is also used in emphatic imperatives:

(15)   Do help yourself to some more wine.

Even BE gets DO-support in such constructions, cf. *Don't be late*, *Do be careful*. The negative of *let's* is *let's not* (e.g. *Let's not be petty-minded*), though in BrE *don't lets* is possible as well (*Don't let's waste more time*). When unaccompanied by *us*, LET requires DO-support (e.g. *Don't let him fool you*).

Imperatives are typically subjectless (cf. section 5.2.2), but where a contrast needs to be expressed, or emphatic displeasure, they contain the subject form *you*:

(16)   You take the wine and I'll take the hamper.

(17)   You mind your own business.

9.8.3. The subjunctive

Though the term 'thought-mood' would seem to indicate that the type of modality expressed by the subjunctive is purely epistemic, the subjunctive has not only epistemic but also deontic uses in English. What is common to these uses is non-factuality, i.e. they both involve "something existing in the speaker's mind only" (see Jespersen 1909-49, vol. 7: 624).

The *epistemic* subjunctive is used *hypothetically* in conditional, comparative and concessive clauses. Outside formal language the only instance of this is the use of *were* in combination with 1st or 3rd person singular subjects (this verb form being standardly analysed as subjunctive). The occurrence of this form in conditional clauses can be illustrated by:

(1)   The task would be difficult if the old party *were* suddenly to reappear.

(2)   Kinglake would have rung if the plane *were*n't on its way.

In BrE *was* is used in everyday language instead of subjunctive *were* in conditional clauses, except in the fixed expression *If I were you*. Subjunctive *were* is also found in the type of conditional clause signalled not by a subordinating conjunction but by inversion (see section 8.9) and in comparative and concessive clauses:

(3)   The total output would be much worse *were* it not for the winter crop.

(4)   It was as though no one else *were* there.

(5)   Even if it *were* expedient I couldn't say what came before what.

In those cases where the situation described by a concessive clause is not hypothetical but factual, *was* is naturally enough used instead of *were*, as in *Even if he was exceedingly well-off, I never considered marrying him.*

In formal style, subjunctive *were* is used in *that*-clauses (with or without *that*) for the expression of wishful or hypothetical speculation (thus typically in object clauses after the verbs WISH and SUPPOSE):

(6)   I wish I *were* famous.

(7)   Suppose a pretty high-school girl *were* to come forward with the solution.

In conditional and concessive clauses one occasionally also finds subjunctive *be*. This usage is formal (cf. Quirk et al. 1985: 1093):

(8)   If any vehicle *be* found parked on these premise, it shall be towed away at the expense of the vehicle's owner.

(9)   They did not approve of Atkinson who, *be* he a brewer in name, actually committed the indignity of conducting trial marshings and fermentations.

Subjunctive *be* is sometimes also found in certain types of *yes-no* interrogative and independent relative clauses:

(10)   Whether a solution to this problem *be* found or not, we have to go ahead.

(11)   Whatever *be* the reason, we cannot tolerate his disloyalty.

The subjunctive is used more frequently in AmE than in BrE. One example illustrating this is its use after the conjunction *lest*:

(12)   But lest it *appear* that I am always dishing it out, let me tell you, Miss Rose, that I have often been on the receiving end, put down by virtuosi, by artists greater than myself, in this line.

In BrE, *lest* is stylistically more marked (formal, old-fashioned) than in AmE, like the subjunctive; and when it is used, it selects not only the subjunctive but also *should* + V (e.g. *Lest it should appear that* ...).

The *deontic subjunctive* is used for the expression of *wishes* in set expressions like *God save the Queen*, *Long live Trotsky* and *Heaven forbid*. The use of MAY for this purpose, for example in *Please may it have been instantly*, will be dealt with in section 9.9.2.

The subjunctive is also used deontically for the expression of *compulsion* in *that*-clauses after verbs, adjectives or nouns expressing demand, resolution, recommendation or the like:

(13)

$$
I \begin{bmatrix} demand \\ insist \\ suggest \\ move \end{bmatrix} \text{that Smith} \begin{bmatrix} be\ fired \\ leave\ at\ once \end{bmatrix}
$$

(14)

$$
I\ support\ the \begin{bmatrix} demand \\ suggestion \\ proposal \end{bmatrix} \text{that Smith} \begin{bmatrix} be\ fired \\ leave\ at\ once \end{bmatrix}
$$

(15)

$$
It\ is \begin{bmatrix} essential \\ necessary \\ important \end{bmatrix} \text{that Smith} \begin{bmatrix} be\ fired \\ leave\ at\ once \end{bmatrix}
$$

In AmE this use of the so-called *mandative subjunctive* is standard practice:

(16)   Peg insisted that he *see* a psychiatrist in Providence.

(17)   Christian ministers demanded that the studio *destroy* all copies of the film.

..., on the other hand, compulsion may also be expressed by *should* + V in *that*-clauses, particularly in informal style (e.g. *I suggest that Smith should leave at once*).

With verbs other than BE there is no formal way of deciding whether the mandative subjunctive is used in an example of the following type:

(18)   One of the campus ladies suggested that I *urge* him to shave his ears.

As the subject pronoun in the subclause is not in the 3rd person singular, the absence of an *-s* inflection obviously does not demonstrate that *urge* is here in the subjunctive mood. But the fact that *urge* is here synonymous with *should urge* seems to indicate that this is the case, and so does the lack of temporal agreement between *urge* and *suggested*. With subjects not realized by 3rd person forms, lack of DO-support in negative *that*-clauses constitutes a non-inflectional criterion for identifying the mandative subjunctive: e.g. *I suggest that we not adopt this proposal*.

A third deontic use of the subjunctive, which we shall characterize as *concessive*, is found in frozen examples like these:

(19)   *Be* that as it may, we'll still finish on time.

(20)   *Come* what may, we'll proceed in the same way.

(21)   *Suffice* it to say that he's totally incompetent.

In some cases – where paraphrases with LET are synonymous – the concessive subjunctive comes close to expressing permission (compare e.g. *So be it* with *So let it be*).

9.9. Modality

9.9.1. Introduction

By modality we understand a *qualification* of an utterance whereby the speaker operates with alternatives to the actual world (see Davidsen-Nielsen 1990, on which this section is largely based, and from which examples are extensively quoted). Human beings often think as if things might be other than in point of fact they are, and for the expression of such conceptions they use *modal* rather than *categorical* utterances.

As pointed out in section 9.7, modality primarily involves two kinds of *non-factuality*: epistemic and *deontic*. In producing epistemically modalized utterances like *Perhaps Colonel Gaddafi is dead* and *Colonel Gaddafi may be dead* – which are qualified by *perhaps* and *may* respectively – the speaker expresses that a certain situation is conceivably real. And in producing a deontically modalized utterance like *She ought to be in bed* – qualified by OUGHT – he expresses that a certain situation is desirable. With *categorical* (non-modal) utterances like *Colonel Gaddafi is dead* and *She is in bed*, on the other hand, the speaker describes situations which he considers factual.

In English, modality may be expressed *lexically* in a number of different ways. This can be illustrated by examples like the following:

(1)   *Hopefully* this is enough. (deontic adverb)

(2)   She is *likely* to lose. (epistemic adjective)

(3)   I *permit* you to smoke. (deontic verb)

(4)   He's *alleged* to have resigned. (epistemic participle)

If modality is expressed *grammatically*, the qualifying element is either an *inflection* – as in the case of the subjunctive and imperative moods, both of which are realized by -Ø (see section 9.8) – or a *modal auxiliary*, i.e. a form of CAN, MAY, MUST, SHALL or WILL (see section 9.5). The expression of modality by modal auxiliaries can be illustrated by epistemic examples like the following:

(5)   She may/can't/must be right.

Here the finite verb forms signal a qualification whereby the speaker operates with alternatives to the actual world. And here the source of the modality is the speaker of the utterance: 'I consider it possible/impossible/necessary that she is right'.

As Hoye (1997) observes, modality is often expressed by highly regular *collocations* of modal verbs and certain adverbs:

(6)   They *can't possibly* be playing tennis.

(7)   It *may well* be a back-formation.

(8)   It *must certainly* result in a termination of the project.

Though the modal verb and the adverb in such combinations express the same kind of modality (e.g. epistemic modality), their combination is not a matter of pleonastic reiteration of the same modal meaning but rather a stylistically powerful, synergetic means of expression.

However, it is not always the case that modal auxiliaries are used for the expression of modality. This can be illustrated by the next examples:

(9)   Linford can run 100 yards in nine seconds.

(10)   He can touch the ceiling.

Here CAN is used in factual statements about ability. As it does not signal a qualification of an utterance whereby the speaker operates with alternatives to the actual world, examples like these are nonmodal. As pointed out by Palmer, CAN in the sense of ability "can be omitted from the strict typological classification of modality, although it is of interest that modal verbs have these meanings" (1986: 103). Notice also that CAN is here oriented not towards the speaker of the utterance (as in (5)) but towards the referent of the subject form: the source of ability is the person referred to by *Linford* in (9) and by *He* in (10).

In an important study on English modals by Klinge (1993), it has been shown that the distinction between epistemic and deontic modality, i.e. between expressions of probability and desirability, is not in fact a property of the modal verbs themselves but of other elements in the sentence or even outside it. For example, *Jones may join us* is likely to be understood as deontic (permission) if followed by *if he wants to* but as epistemic (possibility) if followed by *as far as I'm informed*. Whether *Jones may join us* is understood as epistemic or deontic may also depend on the situational context in which it is used. It thus seems that the distinction between epistemic and deontic modality is not related to the modal verbs themselves, i.e. is not a matter of lexical semantics, but is signalled by the context in which they are used, i.e. is a matter of utterance pragmatics. When we say that a modal is used epistemically or deontically, we thus imply that it occurs in an utterance which is intended and understood to be either epistemic or deontic. Similarly, a formulation like 'deontic CAN' is shorthand notation for 'CAN occurring in an utterance intended and understood to be deontic'.

As demonstrated in section 9.7, modality is closely related to tense-aspect in that most of the tense-aspect forms can be used modally. The interaction between these two categories also appears from the way the past forms of the modal auxiliaries are used. As illustrated by the following examples these forms are typically used not to instruct the hearer to tag on to world-before-now but to express a weaker degree of modality than the present forms:

(11)   She might be right.

(12)   Could she be right?

These differ from *She may be right* and *Can she be right?* only in that the degree of epistemic possibility expressed is relatively weak. Thus (11) can be paraphrased as 'I don't rule out the possibility entirely that she is right'.

In the course of history the past forms of the English modals have in some cases drifted away semantically from the corresponding present forms. This goes for *should*, for example, which is used neither for the expression of world-before-now nor as a weakened variant of *shall*. Examples illustrating such semantic drift are *You should be seeing them soon* (epistemic) and *These guys should be jailed* (deontic). In our discussion of the modals below, we use small capitals for both formal variants (e.g. SHALL/SHOULD) to stress their individual nature.

Finally we should mention that as they do not have nonfinite forms, the modal auxiliaries often alternate with semi-auxiliary replacement forms (see section 9.5). This can be illustrated by examples like the next ones:

(13) I *can* predict the result.

(14) *Being able* to predict the results is not enough.

(15) You *must* get up early.

(16) I hate *having to* get up early.

The expression of modality by means of tense-aspect forms (past, present future, etc.) was discussed in section 9.7 and will not be taken up again.

9.9.2. MAY/MIGHT

In modalizing an utterance *epistemically* by means of MAY the speaker indicates that a certain situation is *conceivably real*:

(1) That may be the best light I'll ever appear in, to them.

(2) She may have felt possessive about Gertrude.

MAY is used *deontically* to express *permission*:

(3) May I speak to you for a moment?

(4) As far as forgiveness is concerned, you may look for it in this household.

In everyday informal language the use of MAY for the expression of a personal permission is less frequent than that of CAN. An *impersonal* permission is typically signalled by CAN, but occasionally it is expressed by MAY. This usage is due to a prescriptive bias in favour of MAY (see Quirk et al. 1985: 224):

(5) You may pay by direct debit, by post, or by bank giro credit.

Whether MAY is used epistemically or deontically sometimes has to be determined on the basis of the extra-sentential or situational context (see section 9.9.1). For example, a sentence like *Jones may leave* can mean either that Jones's departure is conceivably real or that it is permitted. Note, however, that in either case MAY is used for the expression of *possibility*: presenting Jones's departure as conceivably real is the same as saying that it is possible; and in granting Jones permission to leave, the speaker also makes it possible for him to do so.

MAY (as well as MIGHT) is normally epistemic when followed by a perfect and/or progressive form: *Jones may be leaving / Jones may have left / Jones may have been leaving*.

Deontic MAY is sometimes followed by the adverbial (JUST) AS WELL:

(6) We may as well be straight with each other.

(7)   You may just as well hand in your resignation.

What the speaker typically indicates with this idiom is that a situation on reflection has to be accepted even if this is not the instinctively preferred reaction to it.

MAY is also used deontically for the expression of *wishes* and *maledictions* (in sentences with partial inversion, see section 5.3.3):

(8)   Please may it have been instantly.

(9)   May it choke him.

In *interrogative sentences*, epistemic MAY is virtually ruled out. Here epistemic possibility is expressed by CAN, as illustrated by *Can it be true?* and *Can spring be far behind?* (which should be compared with corresponding declarative sentences like *It may be true* and *Spring may be far behind*). Deontic MAY, on the other hand, is used as readily in interrogative sentences as in declarative sentences.

In *negative sentences*, the semantic scope of negation excludes epistemic MAY but normally includes deontic MAY (see section 7.5.8):

(10)   They may not have gone very far.
        [Possible [not [they have gone very far]]]

(11)   You may not borrow my car.
        [Not [permitted [you borrow my car]]]

If the speaker wishes to describe a situation as 'not conceivably real' rather than as 'conceivably not real', he can do so by means of epistemic CAN followed by NOT:

(12)   They can't have gone very far.
        [Not [possible [they have gone very far]]]

In *sentences in the past*, epistemic MIGHT is used to indicate that the speaker is relatively uncertain about the possibility of the situation described by the utterance. This use of MIGHT to convey a *tentative* attitude is illustrated by:

(13)   That woman might attack you.

(14)   What you suggest might be regarded as a recipe for folly and madness.

In examples like these, the past modal refers to *non-past time* and expresses *weak possibility* (see section 9.7 on past forms and factual remoteness). Epistemic MIGHT is also used without past time meaning in *hypothetical conditional sentences* and in *indirect speech* (see sections 8.9 and 9.6.13):

(15)   If I was a different person, it mightn't matter.

(16)   She said the time might come in my generation when the educational system itself was mixed.

Like epistemic MIGHT, *deontic* MIGHT is used with non-past meaning for the expression of weakened modality. In choosing the past form the speaker makes a permission tentative/hypothetical, and in interrogative sentences a request for it will therefore be felt to be polite:

(17)   Might I ask you to do me a favour?

MIGHT used as a tentative variant of deontic MAY is rare and is characteristically restricted to questions and wishes (e.g. *If only I might be allowed to see him*).

MIGHT is virtually never used to express past time permission. Exceptions to this rule are found in subclauses of sentences with main verbs of thinking, believing, feeling or knowing:

(18)   She expected that I might come in about nine o'clock, but then our meeting had to be cancelled.

9.9.3. CAN/COULD

Like MAY, CAN is used *epistemically* for the expression of what is *conceivably real* and *deontically* for the expression of permission:

(1)   Can spring be far behind?
(2)   Can I stay out as long as I wish, Mum?

Let us consider first the *epistemic* use of CAN. As pointed out in section 9.9.2, CAN is used to express possibility in *interrogative sentences*:

(3)   But can she be right?
(4)   How can this be irrelevance?
(5)   Whose beautiful antiques can these be?

Here CAN performs the same function as MAY in declarative sentences (compare e.g. (3) with *She may be right*).

CAN is used also in *negative declarative sentences*:

(6)   They can't have gone very far.
(7)   You can't be serious.

What sentences of this type express is that the situation described is 'not conceivably real', i.e. the semantic scope of NOT extends over the entire sentence and thus includes the possibility modal.

In *sentences in the past*, epistemic COULD is used like MIGHT to convey *tentativeness*, i.e. to indicate that the speaker is relatively uncertain about the possibility of the situation described:

(8)   He's not much here but he could arrive.
(9)   But could she be right?

In examples like these, the past modal refers to *non-past time* and expresses *weak possibility*. Epistemic COULD is also used without past time meaning in *conditional sentences* and in *indirect speech*:

(10)   If we instructed him carefully, Jones could be the right man for the job.

(11)   She asked me if it could be due to fear.

In *positive declarative sentences*, there are no restrictions on the epistemic use of COULD, as illustrated by (8). On the other hand, epistemic CAN in the sense of 'conceivable that' (or 'possible that') – which characterizes its use in interrogative and negative sentences – is ruled out in this sentence type. For example, **She can have felt possessive about Gertrude* is clearly ungrammatical. Here the speaker has to use MAY instead.

Like MAY, CAN (as well as COULD) is normally epistemic when followed by a perfect or progressive form: *Can she be staying at the Park Lodge? / They can't have left the hotel already / They could have left the stuff behind.*

Before turning to CAN used deontically for the expression of permission, we recapitulate that 'possible that' is expressed by CAN in interrogative sentences and in negative sentences where the semantic scope of NOT includes the modal (not-possible that) but that it is expressed by MAY in positive declarative sentences and in negative sentences where the semantic scope of NOT excludes the modal (possible-not that):

POSSIBLE THAT			
Declarative	Interrogative	Negative modal included	modal excluded
MAY	CAN	CAN	MAY

(12)   She may be right.

(13)   Can she be right?

(14)   She can't be right.

(15)   She may not be right.

If CAN is used *deontically*, the permission it expresses is often *impersonal*:

(16)   Make it clear that everyone can say anything.

(17)   You can smoke in here.

In using a sentence like (17), the speaker often does not personally grant permission to smoke but rather expresses permission indirectly by informing the hearer that the rules allow smoking (cf. *You can smoke in here, as far as I'm informed*). However, CAN is also widely used in informal style to signal permission given by the speaker – or requested from the hearer – exclusively:

(18) All right, sweetheart. We're going. You can go back in now.

(19) Can I stay out as long as I wish, Mum?

Deontic CAN is sometimes used for the expression of *compulsion*:

(20) 'Young man,' I say, 'you can just get up and leave this table. Leave the house while you are at it.'

This example is clearly directive and produced by a speaker in authority. As deontic CAN centrally serves the purpose of giving permission, the use of it to give orders is rather condescending (like the deontic use of the future form, see section 9.7). What it amounts to is approximately: You are 'permitted' to do something which I wish to see done. This directive effect, it should be added, can also be obtained by MAY, for example in *You may leave immediately, young man*.

The deontic use of CAN in *negative sentences* is illustrated by:

(21) You can't stay here.

Here – as in the case of epistemic *can't* – the semantic scope of NOT extends over the entire sentence: [Not [permitted [you stay here]]].

In sentences *in the past*, deontic COULD is used with *non-past meaning* for the expression of weakened modality:

(22) You could easily sleep here tonight.

(23) But couldn't we go to the cinema?

The past form makes a permission *tentative*, and in interrogative sentences like (23) a request for it will therefore be felt to be polite.

Unlike MIGHT, COULD is freely used to express *past time permission*:

(24) In the late sixties we could do pretty much as we pleased.

In section 9.9.1, we discussed the nonmodal ability meaning of CAN in positive declarative sentences like *Linford can run 100 yards in nine seconds*. Consider now positive declarative sentences like the following:

(25) It can be cold in Stockholm.

(26) The exit can be blocked.

Here CAN is used in the sense of *possible for*. Note that these examples are clearly different from 'possible that' examples like *It may be cold in Stockholm* and *The exit may be blocked*. While the sentences with MAY are synonymous with *Perhaps it is/will be cold in Stockholm* and *Perhaps the exit is blocked*, this is clearly not the case with the corresponding sentences with CAN.

While sentences like (25) and (26) do not express ability directly – but describe a *property* of the entity referred to (Stockholm, the exit) – it can be argued that they express ability in a more abstract way. Note that in both types of example the meaning of CAN can be captured by the formula *possible for*: in the same way that it is possible for Linford to run 100 yards in nine seconds, it is possible for Stockholm to be cold and for the exit to be blocked.

CAN used in the sense of 'possible for' differs from epistemic MAY in occurring freely in conditional sentences and in being ruled out before a perfect infinitive with past time meaning or in progressive verb groups:

(27)   If the exit can be blocked ...   (*If the exit may be blocked ...)

(28)   *It can be going either way.   (It may be going either way.)

CAN used in sentences like (25) and (26) is thus not only semantically similar to CAN of ability but also behaves like it syntactically (cf. *If Linford can run 100 yards in nine seconds ..., *Linford can have run 100 yards in nine seconds, *Linford can be running 100 yards in nine seconds*). Therefore it seems reasonable to group them together, and CAN is accordingly assumed to be *non-modal* not only when it is used directly for the expression of ability but also when it is used for the expression of what is a property of an entity. In our view, non-factuality is not involved in (25) and (26), and CAN does not in examples of this type constitute a qualification of an utterance whereby the speaker operates with alternatives to the actual world.

In generic contexts the meaning 'possible for' can in formal English be expressed not only by CAN but also by MAY (see Quirk et al. 1985: 223):

(29)   Vampires can/may kill.

(30)   Dogs can/may be snappish.

In examples of this type MAY is used non-modally, like CAN.

9.9.4. MUST

In modalizing an utterance *epistemically* by means of MUST, the speaker indicates that a certain situation is *necessarily real* and that this is something he *infers* from a set of facts. The modality involved here may therefore be termed not only *necessity* but also *deduction*:

(1)   I expect she hates me, why shouldn't she, she must be sore as hell.

(2)   You must have made her think we'd been together.

If MUST is used *deontically*, it expresses *compulsion*:

(3)   If the Labour Party disagrees with that assessment, it must give its reasons.

(4)   Your friends will be going and you must go with them.

As pointed out in section 9.9.1, the distinction between epistemic and deontic modality is a property not of the modal verbs themselves but is a matter of utterance pragmatics. For example, *Jones must be clever* can mean either that Jones's cleverness is inferred to be necessarily real or that it is compulsory (e.g. required in a certain situation). Note, however, that MUST is used for the expression of *necessity* not only when it is used epistemically but also when it is used deontically: in compelling Jones to be clever the speaker also makes it necessary for him to be so.

MUST is usually epistemic when followed by a perfect or progressive form: *She must be travelling with her brother again / They must have left separately / He must have been doing the dishes*. Strong contextualization may, however, secure a deontic meaning of MUST in combination with the progressive: *You must be studying when I return*.

Let us examine first the *epistemic* use of MUST in different sentence types. As illustrated by the next example we find it in *wh-interrogative sentences*:

(5)   What must it have been like in the Middle Ages, I wonder?

In *yes-no interrogative sentences*, on the other hand, MUST is very rare and restricted to those cases where a negative orientation has to be conveyed. For example, a speaker may pose a question like *Must he be on holiday?* if he challenges a claim that the person referred to is on holiday. Otherwise, epistemic necessity is expressed by the semi-auxiliary NEED in this sentence type (see section 9.5):

(6)   Need this suggestion have any party political implications?

(7)   Need it have happened that way?

In *negative declarative sentences*, epistemic MUST is not used. Here necessity is expressed by the semi-auxiliary NEED:

(8)   It needn't affect the incidence of local taxation.

(9)   Survival after death and unending improvement need not mean perfect happiness.

What sentences of this type express is that the situation described is 'not necessarily real', i.e. the semantic scope of NOT extends over the entire sentence and thus includes the necessity modal: [Not [necessary [it affect the incidence of local taxation]]].

The expression of epistemic necessity in positive declarative, interrogative and negative declarative sentences can be summarized and exemplified like this:

EPISTEMIC NECESSITY				
Declarative	Interrogative		Negative	
	yes-no	wh-	modal included	modal excluded
MUST	NEED	MUST	NEED	---

(10)   Boris must have committed this crime.

(11)   Need Boris have committed this crime?

(12)   Who must have committed this crime?

(13)   Boris needn't have committed this crime.

As appears, there is in English no negated modal form available for the expression of necessary-not. However, the speaker may obtain a comparable semantic effect by selecting the possibility modal *can't*. The meaning of a sentence like *Boris can't have committed this crime* can be captured by the notation [Not [possible [Boris commit this crime]]], and this is logically the equivalent of [Necessary [not [Boris commit this crime]]]. Note in this connection that example (13) is semantically close to *Boris may not have committed this crime*. This is due to the fact that [Not [necessary [Boris commit this crime]]] is logically the equivalent of [Possible [not [Boris commit this crime]]]. In this case, however, the speaker has a choice, and *Boris needn't have committed this crime* and *Boris may not have committed this crime* are not entirely synonymous, for there is a difference between making a judgement in terms of necessity and making it in terms of possibility. That epistemic MAY NOT and NEED NOT are not always interchangeable is apparent from an example like the following (see Palmer 1990: 61):

(14)   He may be there, but he needn't be.

In *sentences in the past*, weakened epistemic necessity can be expressed by SHOULD, as in *They should have reached their destination by now*. We return to this use of SHOULD in section 9.9.5.

Let us now turn to the *deontic* use of MUST. As pointed out above, sentences with deontic MUST express compulsion, and they are often used as directives (see e.g. example (4) above). In sentences where the subject is in the first person, compulsion is typically directed towards the speaker himself, either exclusively (singular) or inclusively (plural). In this way the speaker appeals to himself, i.e. *I/we must* has the meaning of self-admonishment (see Quirk et al. 1985: 225):

(15)   I must tell them that some other time, it's a separate story.

(16)   We must go round to Tim's place, at once, all of us.

The deontic use of MUST in *interrogative sentences* can be illustrated by the following examples:

(17)   Must I go back to school so soon?

(18)   But why must I sit here?

In *yes-no* interrogative sentences like (17), the speaker asks the hearer to decide a course of action for him. In *wh*-interrogative sentences like (18) the hearer is asked to explain the particular reason, place, time or identity of a directive. In some interrogative sentences with MUST where the subject is in the second person, the speaker indicates annoyance with the hearer:

(19)   Must you discuss all the time?

(20)   Why must you be so stubborn?

In interrogative sentences, compulsion may also be expressed by sentences with the semi-auxiliary NEED. In choosing NEED – which is rare in *wh*-questions except those beginning with WHY – the speaker also asks for a directive but at the same time asks the hearer whether the course of action described by the interrogative sentence is strictly necessary. NEED is therefore often accompanied by the adverbial *at all*:

(21)   Need she participate in the meeting at all?

(22)   Why need I stay at home at all?

In some interrogative sentences, NEED differs from MUST in that the latter implies that the hearer has the power personally to decide a course of action (see Palmer 1990: 78):

(23)   Need I stay at home tonight?

(24)   Must I stay at home tonight?

The deontic use of MUST in *negative declarative sentences* can be illustrated by examples like the next ones:

(25)   You mustn't think that I don't understand your feelings, my dear.

(26)   You mustn't take me for an old fool with his head in the clouds.

In sentences of this type, the semantic scope of negation excludes the modal: [Compulsory [not [you take me for an old fool]]]. If the speaker wishes to describe a situation that is not-compulsory, i.e. in such a way that the semantic scope of negation includes the modal, he must select the semi-auxiliary NEED:

(27)   And you needn't glare at me like that.

(28)   You needn't high-hat me.

The semantic contrast between deontic MUST and NEED in negative sentences can be illustrated by examples like *You mustn't reply* (compulsory-not) and *You needn't reply* (not-compulsory).

MUST NOT is also used with first person subjects for the expression of self-admonishment:

(29)   Anyway, I mustn't anticipate.

As compulsory-not is closely related to not-permitted, replacement of MUST by CAN or MAY would not result in any significant change of meaning in negative sentences, cf. an example like *You may not/can't (mustn't) park here*. As pointed out earlier in this section, however, there is a certain difference between making a statement in terms of possibility (permission) and making it in terms of necessity (compulsion).

In *sentences in the past*, weakened compulsion can be expressed by SHOULD, as in *These guys should be jailed*. We return to this use of SHOULD in section 9.9.5.

A frequent alternative to MUST for the expression of epistemic necessity or deontic compulsion is the semi-auxiliary HAVE TO (see section 9.5):

(30)   There must/has to be a way out. (epistemic)
(31)   You must/have to do it at once. (deontic)

9.9.5. SHALL/SHOULD

Though SHALL and SHOULD are historically different forms of the same lexical item, they are used for very different purposes, and we shall therefore discuss them separately.

Compared with the other modals SHALL is very rare, particularly in AmE. As illustrated by the following examples it is used *deontically* for the expression of *commitment* in declarative sentences with subjects in the second or third person (SHALL with first person subjects being a formal substitute for the future tense form WILL, see section 9.6.3):

(1)   You shall have your car back by Friday.
(2)   Our children shan't ever bother you again.
(3)   It shall be delivered tomorrow, sir.

According to Quirk et al. (1985: 230) this use of SHALL is archaic, and in by far the majority of cases the natural choice of modal here is WILL. Although this verb does not commit the speaker to the same degree as SHALL, the two verbs are nevertheless semantically close enough for the replacement of the latter by the former to be understandable.

SHALL is also used deontically for the expression of (relatively weak) *compulsion*, though only in *interrogative sentences* with first person subjects:

(4)   Shall we go to the theatre?

(5)   Where shall I put it?

The meaning signalled by *Shall I/we* is here 'Do you want me/us to ...?' As pointed out by Quirk et al. (1985: 231) this meaning is more commonly expressed by *Would you like (me/us) to* or *Should I/we*, particularly in AmE.

In *declarative sentences*, the use of SHALL for deontic *compulsion* is only found with third person subjects to denote what is legally mandatory, i.e. is restricted to ESP (see section 1.8):

(6)   It shall be unlawful to carry firearms.

(7)   The tenant shall quietly possess and enjoy the premises during the tenancy
        without any interruption from the Landlord.

SHALL is never used epistemically.

Let us now turn to the past form SHOULD. When this modal is used *epistemically*, the speaker expresses that he expects the situation described to be real but does not feel absolutely certain, for example because the facts upon which his deduction is made may not be complete. The use of SHOULD to indicate such tentative certainty can be illustrated by examples like:

(8)   They should have reached their destination by now.

(9)   You should be seeing my family tomorrow.

In sentences like these, SHOULD refers to *non-past time* (in fact, SHOULD never refers to past time) and expresses *weakened necessity*, which is the equivalent of high but not maximum probability.

The epistemic use of SHOULD in *negative sentences* is illustrated by:

(10)   It shouldn't be difficult to accomplish that.

Here the semantic scope of NOT excludes the necessity modal: [Weakly necessary [not [it be difficult to accomplish that]]].

The fact that SHOULD indicates *tentative* inference readily explains its common occurrence in *conditional sentences*:

(11)   If I remember right, this region should be just above the great face.

(12)   If you press that button, the engine should start.

Epistemic SHOULD is also common in the *subclause* (with inversion) of conditional sentences (see section 5.3.3):

(13)   Should you happen to be passing, do drop in.

A special use of epistemic SHOULD is found in examples like:

(14)   Well, it surprises me that Eileen should be surprised.

(15)   I can't think why he should have been angry.

According to Palmer, who quotes the first of these examples (1990: 189), the modal is here semantically empty, whereas Quirk et al., who cite the second (1985: 234) are of the opinion that it expresses 'putative' meaning. It might also be argued, though, that SHOULD is here used for the expression of *report*, i.e. to signal that the speaker passes on something he has heard about and the truth of which he is therefore not committed to. This use of SHOULD may be compared with the quotative use of German SOLLEN in e.g. *Er soll reich sein* 'He is said to be rich'.

Deontic SHOULD is used with *non-past meaning* for the expression of *weakened compulsion*. By this choice of modal a directive is made tentative and therefore less insistent. What is indicated in this way is often no more than a suggestion:

(16)   These guys should be jailed.

(17)   Perhaps we should draw a veil over the last year or so.

(18)   Etiquette demands that I should invite him.

As illustrated by (18), one context in which SHOULD of compulsion occurs is *that*-clauses after verbs, adjectives or nouns expressing demand, resolution, recommendation and the like (see the discussion in section 9.8.3 of the mandative subjunctive, which also occurs in this context).

The deontic use of SHOULD in *negative sentences* is illustrated by:

(19)   It shouldn't be supposed that Stone identifies with Socrates in any overt way.

Here the semantic scope of NOT excludes the modal: [Weakly compulsory [not [Stone identify with Socrates in any overt way]]].

Apart from the fact that it expresses compulsion tentatively, deontic SHOULD often differs from deontic MUST in indicating that the situation described is *morally desirable*:

(20)   A man shouldn't leave his home. Or he'll become a wanderer, a lost soul.

(21)   Fictional characters should, whenever possible, reflect the non-smoking majority of the population.

The meaning expressed by SHOULD – whether epistemic or deontic – can also be expressed by the semi-auxiliary OUGHT TO (see section 9.5):

(22)   They should/ought to have arrived by now.

(23)   We should/ought to have declared war on Hitler when he marched into the Rhineland.

Though SHOULD and OUGHT TO are not invariably interchangeable, and have different patterns of stylistic variation, they are normally synonymous.

9.9.6. WILL/WOULD

As the use of purely temporal WILL/WOULD in future forms has already been dealt with (in section 9.6.3), it is only the use of *volitional* WILL/WOULD which needs to be accounted for here. The use of the present form can be illustrated by examples like the following:

(1)   I think today I'll stick to cheese.
(2)   I will never leave you, father.
(3)   Will you come with me, Sancho?
(4)   If she'll wait in the study, I can see her in a minute.

Here WILL expresses volition, but at the same time it has futurity as a constant secondary meaning. In this way it differs from MAY, CAN and MUST (though not SHALL), for in some of their uses these modals do not describe future situations, cf. e.g. *This coat may be John's, How can this be irrelevance?* and *You must be tired.*

Like CAN of ability, volitional WILL is neither used epistemically nor deontically but in *factual statements* about willingness or intention. As it does not signal a qualification of an utterance whereby the speaker operates with alternatives to the actual world, the meaning of examples like (1) through (4) is *non-modal*. Like possible-for CAN, furthermore, volitional WILL is oriented not towards the speaker but towards the referent of the *subject* form. In an example like *Will you post this letter for me?* the source of volition is thus the person referred to by *you*, not the speaker of the utterance.

In *negative sentences*, the semantic scope of NOT usually includes WILL. For example, a sentence like *I won't put up with his behaviour any longer* clearly indicates that the person referred to by *I* is unwilling to accept the situation described. Sometimes, however, WILL is excluded from the semantic scope of negation. This is the case in *We won't bother you any more*, which indicates that the persons referred to by *we* are willing not to be a nuisance any longer.

Not surprisingly, volitional WILL is ruled out in passive and progressive sentences (see section 9.6.8 on temporal WILL + BE + V-*ing*) and before perfect infinitives. The finite auxiliary occurring in e.g. *You won't be bothered, They'll be leaving in half an hour* and *The committee will have finished its work soon* is thus not volitional but purely temporal.

WILL is occasionally used for what has been termed *strong volition* (see Leech 1987: 86):

(5)   He 'will go swimming in dangerous waters.

When used for this purpose, i.e. in the sense of 'insist on', WILL is obligatorily stressed and cannot be contracted to *'ll*.

The past form WOULD is used with *non-past meaning* for the expression of *weakened volition*, often in polite requests:

(6)   Would you pay us in cash, please?

(7)   You wouldn't have the time to do it now, would you?

(8)   We would like to sit down soon.

Volitional WOULD is also used without past time meaning in *hypothetical conditional sentences* and in *indirect speech* (see sections 8.9 and 9.6.13):

(9)   If you did that, I would bash in your brains.

(10)   My wife said she would phone us after dinner.

Here it seems clear that WOULD serves the purpose of expressing not only aheadness but also intention.

10. Nominals

While verbals typically express situations (cf. sections 7.2 and 9.1), nominals typically express the participants involved in situations, e.g. the agent, the affected or the instrument. The main communicative function of nominals is thus to code meaning as *things* (or 'entities') in a broad sense (concrete as well as abstract, animate as well as inanimate). This function is very composite, involving many different lower-level communicative functions, such as determination and modification. It can therefore be thought of in terms of a *functional domain*, by which we mean a general main function comprising a number of subfunctions. In this chapter we shall examine the ways in which nominals occupy this functional domain, i.e. how they enable the speaker to 'talk about things'.

10.1. Preliminaries

10.1.1. Nouns and noun groups

The present chapter deals with both types of nominal: single nouns and noun groups. As will be recalled, nouns constitute a major word class comprising items which typically express things (e.g. BOOK), and which are often combined with articles (e.g. *the book*) and inflected for the expression of number (e.g. *book/books*) and the genitive case (*book's*) (cf. section 3.1.4). A noun group is defined as a group with a noun as head (cf. section 3.3.1):

(1)   This must be *familiar scenery*.

(2)   Moira is smoking *a cigarette*. She takes *a drag*, passes it to *her husband*.

(3)   [*This time*] [*her eyes*] give him *a penetrating stare*.

However, we have to interpret this definition broadly to accommodate more complex cases involving *stacked* heads larger than the noun, as in the following examples (see section 4.1.1 on such stacks):

(4)   We were served *the big brimming jugs of cream you only see at farming functions*.

(5)   He was infinitely more interesting than *comparable apocalyptic zealots who were characteristic of that period of Jewish history*.

In a stack analysis, the nouns *jugs* and *zealots* are assigned head status, not at the primary group level but at a much lower constituent level.

10.1.2. The external relations of nominals

Nominals may assume the following functions:

S	*The restaurant* was crowded.
Od	I was drinking *vintage champagne*.
Oi	I finally told *Jack's wife* my little secret.
Cs	Most of the diners were *tourists*.
Co	We elected Irene *our first female director*.
A	*This time* the bastards won't get away with it.

In addition, nominals may serve as dependents (e.g. in noun, preposition and adjective groups) and as conjoints in compound units:

DEP	These *solar energy* schemes were proposed by *my boss*.
	The figure was *ten inches* tall.
CJT	*The organist* and *the photographer* were hired.

Note also that nominals may serve a number of communicative functions directly, e.g. EXC (*Christ!*) and QUE (*A book?*).

10.1.3. The internal structure of noun groups

By definition, nouns assume head function in noun groups. Dependents appear in either *pre-head* or *post-head* position. We can thus offer the following first approximation to the structural potential of noun groups:

pre-H dependents	H	post-H dependents

As pre-H dependents we typically find:

(i) articles (as in <u>*a*</u> bed / <u>*an*</u> honour / <u>*the*</u> boat);

(ii) possessive pronouns and nominals in the genitive (as in <u>*her*</u> book / <u>*my*</u> speech / <u>*John's*</u> pen / <u>*the old professor's*</u> office / <u>*my sister's*</u> new book);

(iii) demonstrative, interrogative and relative pronouns (as in <u>*this*</u> girl / <u>*those*</u> plays / <u>*which*</u> book / <u>*whose*</u> idea / <u>*what*</u> students);

(iv) indefinite pronouns and quantifiers (as in <u>*some*</u> sugar / <u>*any*</u> woman / <u>*no*</u> entry / <u>*every*</u> word / <u>*neither*</u> statement / <u>*many*</u> proposals / <u>*all*</u> the letters);

(v) adjectivals (as in <u>*excellent*</u> teachers / <u>*solar*</u> energy / a <u>*very interesting*</u> idea / a <u>*most original*</u> exhibition);

(vi) present and past participles (as in a <u>*dancing*</u> girl / <u>*rising*</u> prices / <u>*returned*</u> goods / a <u>*defeated*</u> enemy);

(vii) nominals (as in a <u>*development*</u> plan / <u>*university*</u> students / a <u>*civil rights*</u> movement / a fifth <u>*Middle East*</u> war).

Occasionally we find the following as pre-H dependents:

(viii) adverbs (as in *the then king / the above examples / the in thing*);

(ix) complex group- and clause-like structures, the unity of which is usually marked by means of hyphenation (as in *a two-year-old boy / the latest Humphrey-for-President movement / a small, what-else-can-you-expect nod*).

As can be seen, the relationships between pre-head dependent and head are typically determination (as in *a bed / her book*) and modification (as in *excellent teachers / university students*).

In post-head position we typically find:

(i) preposition groups (as in *a letter from my uncle / a rule of this kind / a town in Germany / a visit to my parents*);

(ii) relative clauses (as in *the letter which you wrote last night / John, who moved to Hove last year, / the film that you found so interesting*);

(iii) single or coordinated adjectivals (as in *the only stars visible / professors keen to take early retirement / the leaves, so soft and yellow*);

(iv) nominals (as in *the meeting last night / the match next week / Jack Parker, my neighbour, / our new manager, the tall guy who just left, / the number six / my dear friend Richard*);

(v) present and past participles and participial clauses (as in *all the guests leaving / the prisoners deported / the colleagues remaining behind / some of the cars tested last month*);

(vi) infinitive groups or infinitive clauses (as in *any attempt to move / the decision to break up the party*);

(vii) non-relative *that*-clauses (as in *the fact that she wants to leave / the idea that I should marry her / the hope that someone will step in and rescue her*);

(viii) adverbals (as in *the meeting inside / the book here / the road back*).

As these examples show, the most common relationships between head and post-head dependent are modification (as in *a letter from my uncle*) and complementation (as in *any attempt to move*), cf. section 6.3.3. But we also get what may be referred to as 'elaboratives', i.e. dependents which enter an identity relation to the head but at the same time elaborate on the content of the head: *Jack Parker, my neighbour,* → 'Jack Parker = my neighbour', *the number six* → 'the number = six'. In some constructions with clausal elaboratives, the head noun serves primarily as a means to nominalize the content of the dependent clause: *the fact that she wants to leave* → 'the fact = she wants to leave', *the idea that I should marry her* → 'the idea = I should marry her'. In such constructions the head noun is always abstract (other examples: ANSWER, BELIEF, CHANCE, CLAIM, NEWS, POSSIBILITY, PROPOSAL, SUGGESTION).

Post-head parenthetical dependents, i.e. dependents which are separated from the head by means of intonation or commas, are often referred to as *appositional* (e.g. *Jack Parker, my neighbour, / John, who moved to Hove last year,*). Some grammarians use the term 'apposition' to refer to elaboratives, whether parenthetical or not.

There are in general fewer post-head dependents in noun groups than pre-head dependents. On the other hand, post-head dependents are often realized by preposition groups or by clauses and thus tend to be longer than pre-head dependents, which are often realized by articles, pronouns and adjectives. While many post-head dependents are thus fairly complex, many pre-head dependents are fairly simple (being realized by single words or two- or three-word groups) but form more complex relationships with the head noun and each other. In order to describe these facts adequately it is important to relate the fairly automatic division of the noun group into pre-head, head and post-head to the functional domain of the noun group and to the fragmentation of this functional domain into subfunctions.

10.1.4. The functional domain of nominals

As mentioned in the introduction, the functional domain of nominals can be defined in traditional terms as the expression of meaning as 'things'. Nominals enable us to code what we want to talk about as things with the degree of specificity required for our communicative purposes: speakers encode meaning in nominals in the shape of things and listeners decode such constituents accordingly. Nominals are used for a variety of more specific communicative functions, such as to *identify* specific things:

(1)   *The restaurant* was crowded.

(2)   *The bastards* won't get away with it.

or to *mention* 'type of thing':

(3)   I told her I wanted *an apple*.

(4)   *Teachers who work overtime* must be very idealistic.

or to *describe* an already identified thing:

(5)   Most of the diners were *Japanese tourists*.

(6)   Rose is *a very good student*.

or to *specify* the 'situation' expressed by the verb in examples of syntactic and semantic fusion between predicator and object (cf. section 7.3.4 [I]):

(7)   The meeting took *place* yesterday. (*took place* = 'happened')

(8)   We caught *sight* of her. (*caught sight of* = 'saw', 'sighted')

In all these examples the italicized nominals code meaning as things, but the things coded are used for different purposes. To get a better understanding of the relationship between nominals and the things expressed, it is useful to examine examples like the following:

(9)   He found *the small yellow key* in *the kitchen sink*.

(10)   *A glass of orange juice* is just what I need now.

In the first example, the two noun groups *the small yellow key* and *the kitchen sink* can be understood to 'refer to' things in 'the real world' or in some 'fictional world' (e.g. in a novel), i.e. they identify a particular key and a particular sink, respectively. In such cases we can say that there is a relation between language and specific 'extra-linguistic' things, a relation in terms of *reference*. In the second example, the noun group *A glass of orange juice* can hardly be said to refer to a specific thing in this sense but to mention something that could become a specific thing of the world. For many linguists, 'reference' in connection with a nominal means 'reference to a specific thing'. Thus *the small yellow key* (as well as *the kitchen sink*) is usually regarded as a *referring expression*, whereas *A glass of orange juice* is not. In this grammar, however, we use the term 'reference' in a broader sense to include any link between a formal expression and our conception of the things expressed. There is thus a strong conceptual element in all reference, as we use the term. When we 'refer to' things, general or specific, we do so on the basis of how we conceive of them rather than on the basis of their objective reality. This is particularly clear when abstract 'things' (such as ideas, relations, conventions, etc.) and non-existent 'things' are involved (such as unicorns). Note also examples like (7) and (8) above, in which something that is not objectively 'a thing' is represented as 'a thing'. But even reference to, say, a key or a glass of orange juice has a conceptual, cognitive basis in the sense that we must share an understanding of 'key' and 'glass of orange juice' to be able to communicate about them. This understanding of a thing can be described as a *mental representation*. We use 'reference' about the link between expression and mental representation rather than the link between expression and things in the 'real world'.

The capacity of nominal reference (broadly defined as our capacity to express meaning in terms of things) is dependent on a number of communicative subfunctions. In the following, we shall take a closer look at these subfunctions.

Nominal reference normally relies on cognitively 'fat' lexical words (such as the head noun) as well as cognitively 'lean' function words (such as determiners), both contributing to a set of *contrasts*, some of which are context-dependent, others more context-independent. To describe the resulting delimitation (or 'singling out') of things, we use the term 'contrast-formation': nominals provide a set of *contrasts* with which to discriminate between things. Roughly, contrast-formation seems to work as follows. By using the definite article in a nominal like *the small yellow key*, the speaker signals that there will be enough information in the nominal for the listener to construe the referent (i.e. the thing expressed as we conceive it) as unique in the context. This functionally derived contrast between unique and non-unique is combined with three lexical contrasts, the first two of which are provided by the adjectives *small* and *yellow*. The meanings denoted by these ('smallness' and 'yellowness') must be considered in relation to the third and more context-independent contrast, the one provided by the head noun *key*. The particular combination of various contrasts evoked by *the small yellow key* enables the listener to construe the meaning intended by the speaker.

There is often more contrast-formation in nominals than we actually need in order to identify the intended referent in a particular context. In e.g.:

(11)   Have you met *my beautiful wife* yet?

we cannot say that the adjective *beautiful* is necessary to establish who the referent of the construction *my beautiful wife* is, unless of course the speaker has more than one wife and only one of them is beautiful. Instead it simply offers a description of the referent. Though this description clearly involves a (subjective) contrast (beautiful vs. non-beautiful), this contrast is, strictly speaking, redundant from the point of view of establishing the referent: an expression like *my wife* will usually do the job with sufficient precision. In general, whether or not contrast-formation is redundant may depend entirely on the context of the utterance. Consider:

(12)   *The unhappy mother* left at once.

If the context is such that there is only one mother present, the adjective *unhappy* is 'merely' intended as a description of that mother: it could be left out without making the noun group referentially unclear. If the context is such that there are several mothers present but only one of them is unhappy, *unhappy* provides information without which the listener cannot establish which mother left: without the adjective the noun group becomes referentially unclear. For the listener, the communicative status of the contrast provided by *unhappy* as either descriptive elaboration or identificatory clue must be worked out in context.

We may accordingly distinguish between *restrictive* and *non-restrictive* contrast-formation. This distinction is a fundamental, but also very general, subfunction of the functional domain of nominals. The following chart provides a first approximation to our description of the relationship between communicative function (shaded cells) and internal structure (white cells):

expression of meaning as things		
contrast-formation: restrictive/non-restrictive		
pre-H	H	post-H

One of the factors contributing to the pre-head complexity mentioned in section 10.1.3 above is the presence of two regular communicative sub-functions: *determination* and *modification* (cf. section 6.3.3). Determination and modification, as realized by pre-head dependents, can be thought of in terms of *zones* in the noun group arranged more specifically in the following order:

determination	modification	H	post-H

Determination is realized by articles, pronouns and genitive constructions, while modification is chiefly realized by adjectivals:

determination	modification	H	post-H
the	little	girl	with the shy smile
an	old	friend	from London
this	very dull	visit	to her parents
no	additional	staffing,	academic or secretarial,
my	best	student,	who left school early,
the	sudden	death	of my father
my neighbour's	thick fibrous	clothes	from Woolworth's

The communicative function performed by the head of a noun group is to provide a close lexical match for the referent of the construction. The head thus represents the referent as a member of a *category* of the things, persons,

Categorization

etc. In e.g. *the little girl with the shy smile*, the head noun *girl* categorizes the person referred to as a girl (rather than as e.g. a woman, a boy or a man). The functional nucleus of the noun group is thus *categorization*:

determination	modification	categorization	post-H

Post-head dependents are used for a variety of communicative functions: determination, modification, categorization and complementation (see section 6.3.3). Thus, for example, in *the sudden death of my father*, the post-head dependent *of my father* is determinative in conjunction with the definite article (cf. *my father's sudden death*, where *my father's* is pre-head determination). In *the little girl with the shy smile*, the post-head preposition group *with the shy smile* is clearly a modifier on a par with *little*, describing the head noun *girl*. In *no additional staffing, academic or secretarial,* the post-head compound unit *academic or secretarial* offers a subcategorization of the head noun *staff*. And finally, in *this very dull visit to her parents*, the post-head preposition group *to her parents* serves as complementation to the head noun *visit*. These many post-head functions do not often co-occur and therefore do not represent as well-established zones as the pre-head functions. Accordingly we shall simply operate with one post-head *multi-functional* zone:

determination	modification	categorization	(multi-functional)

One important communicative function – related mainly, but not exclusively, to the head and pre-head constituents – is *quantification*. Given the nature of the functional domain of nominals, it is natural for quantification to play a central role: when we talk about things it is often essential to signal their quantity. In any discussion of quantification, it is important to draw a distinction between *countable* and *non-countable* things. Countable things are things that we think of as something we can count: cars, houses, books, records, etc. Non-countable things are things that we think of as masses of some sort and which we do not usually count (though there are other ways of measuring them): water, flour, sand, sugar, etc. Countable things are indivisible while non-countable things are divisible in the following sense: we can divide water into parts, each part still being water, but we cannot divide a car into parts and regard each part as a car by itself. The singular/plural distinction in nouns referring to countable entities (e.g. *boy/boys*, *girl/girls*, *man/men*, *woman/women*, etc.) is at the very heart of quantification but by no means the only way of expressing this communicative subfunction, which also involves non-countable concepts: we can talk about more or less water, flour, sand, sugar, etc. Here are some examples:

(13)   *These ten books* are far too expensive.

(14)   *A short meeting* took place last night.

(15)   She complained about *my numerous girlfriends*.

(16)   *Some students* seem to think that life is a bowl of cherries.

(17)   It took *little effort* to finish the job.

(18)   *Students in great numbers* have cancelled their participation.

As these examples show, quantification is often expressed in connection with determination (*These, A, Some*) and categorization (singular *meeting* and plural *books, girlfriends, students*) but sometimes also in connection with modification (*short, numerous, ten, little, in great numbers*).

The following chart summarizes our discussion so far of the structure of the nominal in relation to its functional domain:

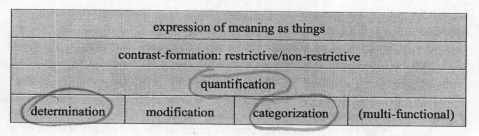

expression of meaning as things			
contrast-formation: restrictive/non-restrictive			
quantification			
determination	modification	categorization	(multi-functional)

To conclude, as this chart shows, nominals are used to express meaning in the shape of entities. The primary, but also most general means of serving this functional domain is contrast-formation (restrictive/non-restrictive). The functional domain of expressing meaning as entities is fragmented into contributing subfunctions, each more or less distinctly associated with the zones created within the pre-head, head and post-head structure of the noun group. The expression of entities often requires an interplay of two or more of these subfunctions. The rest of this chapter is devoted to a discussion of categorization (in section 10.2), determination (in section 10.3) and quantification (in section 10.4). Modification will be examined more closely in chapter 12 on adjectivals.

10.2. Categorization

10.2.1. What's in a head?

The central categorizing unit in the noun phrase is the head. The head typically consists of just a noun:

(1)   Sometimes the *boys* could entice the old *janitor* to time them with the official *clock*.

(2)   Reagan is proud of every *effort* he's made for the *contras*.

However, as pointed out in section 2.1, there are cases where two or more root forms that function independently in other circumstances seem to constitute a single lexical item as head, a *compound*:

(3)   We are now approaching the *airport*.

(4)   She simply adored her *mother-in-law*.

(5)   Have you met our new *dancing master*?

(6)   He takes a professional interest in the human *nervous system*.

In writing, the unitary status of these items is sometimes indicated by absence of an empty space or by hyphenation, as in (3) and (4). In speech, compounds consisting of two elements typically take main stress on their first element, i.e. they are pronounced with so-called *unitary stress*. Thus 'dancing ,master (= master of dancing) contrasts with the syntactic group ,dancing 'master (= master engaged in dancing), and the first element of 'nervous ,system contrasts with the first element in the group ,nervous 'girls. Sometimes, as in *French teacher*, stress is criterial for our classification of a word as either a noun or an adjective: with unitary stress on the first element ('French ,teacher), *French* is a noun forming a part of a compound with the meaning 'teacher of French'; with main stress on the second element (,French 'teacher), it is a premodifying adjective denoting the nationality of the referent of the head noun. Stress is sometimes a difficult criterion to work with, however. For example, some well established combinations like *headmaster* and *ginger ale* take main stress on their second element like syntactic groups such as *head waiter* and *ginger hair* and only differ prosodically from these groups in that their first element tends to be more weakly stressed. Our policy is to keep the head as simple as possible and only allow clear cases of compounding.

There are cases, however, where it is convenient to treat orthographically complex units as heads because they are fixed collocations, often resisting internal analysis, e.g. names, titles, and combinations of titles and names:

(7)   *Randi White*, our new headmaster, had also been busy.

(8)   Christie's *"Ten Little Niggers"* is a detective story with no detective.

(9)   My dear *Professor White*, what can I do for you?

Note also the following phrases, which, superficially, seem to consist of a noun plus a postmodifying adjective (typically of French origin): *court martial*, *heir apparent*, *Secretary General*, *devil incarnate*, *body politic*, *Poet Laureate*, *president elect*, etc. Unlike most other combinations of nouns and adjectives, these collocations are syntactically fixed and receive main stress on the adjective. It seems most appropriate to view them as compounds.

Disregarding the problem posed by compounds, heads in noun groups are fairly easy to identify. Thus when noun groups function as subject, the number of the head (singular or plural) governs subject-predicator concord:

(10a)   A *cup* of coffee *is* surely more expensive than a cup of tea.

(10b)   Two *cups* of coffee *are* surely more expensive than two cups of tea.

While this criterion is in general very reliable – even in cases where the head is not necessarily the most important word – there are occasionally factors (such as e.g. attraction, cf. section 7.6.5) which interfere with this neat regular pattern. One phenomenon in particular requires mention here: sometimes what looks like, and may well be analysed as, the *syntactic* head does not in fact determine subject-predicator concord directly. Consider the following examples (cf. Huddleston 1984: 236ff):

(11)   A *lot* of milk *was* needed.

(12)   A *lot* of eggs *were* needed.

In these examples concord seems to be governed by a part of the post-head constituent (*milk* and *eggs*, respectively). If we stick to the criterion of subject-predicator concord being governed by the head of the subject noun group, we are forced to analyse *a lot of* as a pre-head constituent (e.g. a quantifier on a par with *many* and *much*), which is syntactically awkward. A similar problem is posed by phrases like *plenty of, lots of, the rest of, the remainder of, a number of.* Huddleston (1993: 87) suggests the term *number-transparent* for these expressions: they let the number of the whole nominal be determined by what is syntactically part of a post-head constituent, thus in effect assuming number according to group-internal context.

Number-transparency sometimes affects determiner use in constructions with *kind of* or *sort of*: e.g. *these sort of theories*, *those sort of people*, etc.

The noun NUMBER itself is number-transparent when it has a quantifying meaning (typically with the indefinite article, as in e.g. *a number of students were present*). When it is used about a particular number *as a number* it behaves like other nouns (typically with the definite article as in e.g. *the number of students enrolled has gone up a bit since we last talked*).

10.2.2. The semantics of nouns

Nominal heads, as well as single nouns, can be classified in many different ways according to their meaning. In the introduction to this chapter we defined the main communicative function of nominals as that of coding meaning as *things*. But 'things' can be many, well, things! Nouns may be interpreted in terms of a variety of both concrete things and abstractions: physical objects (e.g. KNIFE, PIANO), persons (e.g. JOHN, PARENT), animals (e.g. HORSE, DUCK), ideas (e.g. DEMOCRACY, ROMANTICISM), relations (e.g. PARTNERSHIP, PARENTHOOD), emotions (e.g. LOVE, SUSPICION), situations (e.g. ARRIVAL, RECITAL), etc. We can even talk about things which do not exist in reality (e.g. ATLANTIS, UNICORN, FAIRY). For a 'thing' to be encoded in language, all it takes is that we have some mental representation of it. What is more, our understanding of a thing may depend not so much on any inherent, objective features it may have as on how we conceive of it. For example, 'a school' may be a 'physical object' (as in *They finished building the school last year*), it may be a 'place' (as in *We walked all the way to the school*), and it may be an 'institution' serving a certain function (as in *He went to school for 7 years only*). What is more, our subjective conception of 'school' in a particular context is sometimes grammatically relevant, cf. the distinction between *to the school* and *to school* in the examples above.

Another important distinction is that between human and non-human referents of nominals. This distinction is relevant for the use of pronouns in relation to nouns. Thus, when nouns with a human referent are postmodified by a relative clause, the relative pronoun *who* is often selected (e.g. *My father, who retired last year, has moved to Brighton*). By contrast, when nouns with a non-human referent are postmodifed by a relative clause, the relative pronoun *which* is often selected (e.g. *The bike, which my son got for his birthday, was stolen yesterday*), cf. section 11.3.3. Also the choice of a singular third person central pronoun (cf. section 11.1.2) relating to a nominal depends on the human/non-human distinction: if the (head) noun has a human referent, either the male term (*he/him/his/himself*) or the female term (*she/her/hers/herself*) is used; if the (head) noun has non-human reference, *it* is used:

(1)   *My neighbour* didn't find *his* car key.

(2)   *The girl* found *herself* in a bit of a mess.

(3)   I looked for *the dissertation*, but I couldn't actually find *it*.

Interestingly there is sometimes vacillation according to the speaker's disposition towards the referent: animals (especially domestic animals), ships, cars, countries, and other objects of human affection or concern may be referred to (often endearingly) with the male or female term (e.g. *Django, my old labrador, was wagging his tail* and *She is an old Dutch schooner*).

The following three sets of distinctions are examined in further detail below: a) those pertaining to *gender* reflecting the sex of the referent of the noun; b) those pertaining to what may be termed the *referential scope* of nouns; and c) those pertaining to *countability*.

10.2.3. Gender

In many languages (e.g. Latin and German) each noun is marked specifically for gender. The gender category typically comprises three members: the masculine, the feminine and the neuter (in German, gender is expressed by distinct determiners, e.g. *der Mann*, *die Frau* and *das Buch* (= 'the man', 'the woman' and 'the book', respectively). These three members sometimes bear some relation to the sex of the referent (male, female or inanimate), but in general this relation is very tenuous. In modern English there are no traces left of the gender system of Old English. But the semantic distinctions involved, especially between male and female, are occasionally expressed morphologically. Below we review some of the ways to reflect sex distinctions in nominals. Before we begin our presentation it is important to remember that most nouns having human or animate referents are 'common gender' or 'unisex': e.g. READER, NEIGHBOUR, DOCTOR, MUSICIAN, IN-MATE, STUDENT, FRIEND, TEACHER, HELPER, EDITOR, FOOL, DRIVER, PRISONER, EMPLOYEE, etc.

In some cases, English has one term for female referents, another for male referents and a third for referents of either sex:

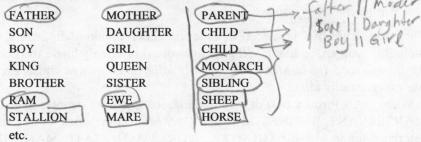

FATHER	MOTHER	PARENT
SON	DAUGHTER	CHILD
BOY	GIRL	CHILD
KING	QUEEN	MONARCH
BROTHER	SISTER	SIBLING
RAM	EWE	SHEEP
STALLION	MARE	HORSE
etc.		

The male/female distinction is often expressed by unrelated words, as in the trios above (cf. also UNCLE/AUNT, GENTLEMAN/LADY, MONK/NUN, BACHELOR/SPINSTER, etc.). Occasionally, however, the distinction is expressed morphologically (with -*ess* as the most common suffix):

HERO	HEROINE
ACTOR	ACTRESS
LION	LIONESS
MASTER	MISTRESS
GOD	GODDESS
etc.	

In these examples, the male term is basic and the female term derived. There are few exceptions to this dominant pattern:

WIDOWER	WIDOW
BRIDEGROOM	BRIDE

In some cases where we have related male and female terms, the male term may be used as a unisex term, especially in contexts where the male/female distinction is irrelevant:

LION	LIONESS
TIGER	TIGRESS
JEW	JEWESS

In such cases, the male term is actually semantically unmarked while the female term is semantically marked (positively female). This means that the male term is only explicitly masculine when there is an overt contrast involved (as in e.g. *I saw both a lion and a lioness*). Otherwise, the male term has unisex reference (as in e.g. *He shot three lions the other day*). In the following examples, the female is the unmarked term, having either feminine or unisex reference, while the male term is explicitly masculine:

DRAKE	DUCK
GANDER	GOOSE
DRONE	BEE

The male term MAN is special in denoting either 'mankind' in general (thus including women, as in e.g. *All men are equal*) or simply 'male members of the human race' (as in *Men are generally taller than women* and *These men are exceptionally tall*).

When MAN forms a part of a compound, it sometimes denotes male (as in MANSERVANT, BUSINESSMAN, DOORMAN), sometimes it has unisex reference (as in MANSLAUGHTER, SPOKESMAN, STATESMAN, CHAIRMAN). But there is a tendency to avoid using MAN compounds about women: CHAIRPERSON, STATESWOMAN, SPOKESWOMAN.

As Jespersen (1933: 192) points out: when assuming complement function, male terms are sometimes used more readily about women:

(1)   She was a *master* of the situation.

(2)   Ann was always a *lover* of beautiful art.

In addition to *man* and *woman*, *male* and *female* are often used to specify sex in neutral nouns: *male/female reader, male/female driver, etc. Note also: gentleman friend, lady friend, boy friend, girl friend, maid-servant.*

Note finally that special compounds are sometimes used of animals to specify sex: COCK-PHEASANT / HEN-PHEASANT, JACKASS / JENNY-ASS, BILLY-GOAT / NANNY-GOAT, TOM-CAT / TABBY-CAT.

10.2.4. Types of nouns and referents

Let us begin this section by offering a note on our use of the terms 'referent' and 'reference' in connection with nominals. Both terms are used in a fairly broad sense: 'referent' about our mental representation of a thing coded in an expression and 'reference' about the communicative function of establishing something as a referent. Thus, for example, when a speaker says *I bought a new car yesterday*, our conception of the car that he bought is the referent and *a new car* is a referring expression, and the link between them is one of reference. In other words, whenever we use 'referent' we emphasize the nature of the thing expressed and whenever we use 'reference' we emphasize the way we use language to code things.

Central to the notion of categorization are the following main kinds of referents: *unique, generic* and *class-member* referents. Though, from a strictly objective point of view, every thing in the world is unique in some sense, as human beings we tend to classify things sharing one or more similarities as belonging to the same *type* or *class*. Thus apart from persons or entities that we recognize as unique (such as Peter Schmeichel, Paris, Spain, etc.), we have cars, bikes, books, trees, etc. Every car is, strictly speaking, unique and yet the noun CAR can be used to refer to a fascinating range of vehicles. Any particular car is thus a member of the class of things which may be appropriately referred to by the noun CAR. Most of the examples offered so far in this chapter are examples of class-member referents in this sense: the (head) noun is used to refer to one or more particular things that may be conceived of as members of a class of things which may be appropriately referred to by using the noun. For example, in an expression like *I found the dissertation in the top drawer*, the referent of the direct object *the dissertation* may be understood as 'a (specific) member of the class of things appropriately termed *dissertation*'; and in an expression like *I want an apple, please*, the referent of *an apple* may be understood as 'a (non-specific) member of the class of things appropriately termed *apple*'. Whether specific or non-specific, the referent is viewed as an instance of a more general *kind* or *type* of thing (dissertations, apples).

Significantly, instead of referring to individual class members, we may choose to refer to the *kind* or *type* in question as such: e.g. *The funnel-web spider is very common in New South Wales* and *Young children need a lot of attention.* Here *The funnel-web spider* refers to a kind of spider (in contrast to an example like *Jack killed the funnel-web spider with his spade*, which refers to a particular member of the class of funnel-web spiders), and *Young children* refers to the whole class of young children (in contrast to *The young children missed their parents*, which refers to a group of particular young children). In both cases we have a so-called generic referent.

Corresponding to the semantic distinction between unique referents and non-unique (generic or class-member) referents there is the form distinction between *proper nouns* and *common nouns.* Proper nouns are capitalized, and with their central function – that of naming – they are fairly restricted with respect to determination and quantification: *Mary, Sweden, London, the Hebrides, *a Mary, *the Sweden, *some Londons, *these Hebrides.* Common nouns, by contrast, are fairly unrestricted with respect to determination and quantification: *a/the/these/some trains, a/the/these/some pencils,* etc. The distinction between generic and class-member referents is also grammatically relevant. It is not, however, reflected in different classes of nouns but, as we shall see, in the use of determiners.

There is no strict one-to-one correspondence between unique referents and proper nouns, on the one hand, and between non-unique referents and common nouns on the other. Following grammarians like Huddleston (1984 and 1988), we distinguish between *proper nouns* and *names.* Proper nouns are typically, though far from inevitably, used as names (e.g. *Jack, Germany,* etc.). But names may consist, wholly or partially, of common nouns: e.g. *High Street, Congress, the Copenhagen Business School, London Bridge, Mother, Uncle,* etc. And when not used simply for naming, proper nouns are far more unrestricted with respect to determination and quantification:

(1)   He can be a real *Sylvester Stallone* sometimes.

(2)   It was good fun to watch all the young *Peter Schmeichels* practising.

In these examples, the proper noun expressions *all the young Peter Schmeichels* and *a real Sylvester Stallone* have class-member referents rather than unique referents, assigning to their referents certain ambitions, qualities, status or behaviour that we associate with the bearer of the name.

10.2.5. Countability

The referents of common nouns are subject to a further distinction between countable and non-countable. Nouns whose referents are conceived of as something individualized we can count are called *count nouns* whereas nouns whose referents are conceived of as something *un*individualized we cannot count (or simply do not count) are called *mass nouns*. Here are some examples of count nouns: BOOK, WINDOW, CAR, PENCIL, HOUSE, BOAT, IDEA, FRIEND, etc. And here are some examples of mass nouns: WATER, SAND, BUTTER, MILK, RICE, MONEY, FURNITURE, ADVICE, NEWS, PERMISSION, etc. The possible referents of most of these are obviously non-countable but, strictly speaking, e.g. rice and money are countable. In English, however, the nouns RICE and MONEY are mass nouns by convention.

Count nouns allow of quantification in terms of the singular/plural distinction (e.g. *book/books*, *window/windows*, etc.) and are thus compatible with pronominal determiners and quantifiers like *some, more, many, few, several*, etc. and incompatible with *much* and *less*: *many ideas, few movements*, *much computers, *less schools (the not infrequent use of *less* in connection with count nouns, as in *less schools, less problems*, etc., is generally considered colloquial). Mass nouns, by contrast, allow of direct quantification only in terms of pronominal determiners and quantifiers: the singular/plural distinction does not apply to mass nouns. They are compatible with *much, less, little, some* and *more* but not with *many, several, few* and *one* or with the indefinite article *a(n)*: *much water, less wine, little sand,* **few furniture / ***a furniture / **many furnitures.

However, mass nouns, whether concrete or abstract, may be quantified more indirectly in partitive *of*-constructions preceded by a quantified count-noun: *two pints of bitter, a cup of coffee, many bottles of wine, few bowls of rice, several slices of bread, an acre of land, a word of advice, a fit of passion, an attack of pneumonia*, etc. In some such partitive expressions there is a very close relation between the head count noun and the quantified mass noun: *a suit of armour, a tankard of beer, a sheet of paper, a clove of garlic; a stroke of luck, a pang of remorse, a flash of lightning*. Note that count nouns may be quantified in a similar fashion: *a page of a book*, etc. Very similar to quantity partition is quality partition as in *a new kind of butter* and *a new generation of computers*.

It is important to note that the distinction between count nouns and mass nouns is somewhat blurred, grammatically speaking. Many nouns are used equally well as count nouns (for bounded entities) and mass nouns (for unbounded material or concept), e.g. STONE, COCONUT and CONVICTION:

(1a)   He found *three stones*.

(1b)   The figure was of *stone*.

(2a)   There were *coconuts* everywhere on the beach.

(2b)   The worshippers bought *coconut* and flowers for their offerings.

(3a)   He acted in accordance with his *convictions*.

(3b)   It appeared to be the result of blind *conviction*.

Many nouns that primarily behave like count nouns are sometimes used the way mass nouns are used, and vice versa:

(4)   Everything was grimy under a low ceiling of grey *cloud*.

(5)   One black sock had sagged to reveal a section of bare *leg*.

(6)   There was enough *moon* now to silver the minarets outside.

(7)   This is actually *an* excellent *wine*.

(8)   He imports *several coffees* from Africa.

(9)   Over the years she did me *many kindnesses*.

(10)   *Two coffees*, please.

When typical count nouns, such as CLOUD, LEG and MOON, are used like mass nouns (as in (4) to (6)), the speaker or writer emphasizes the *material*, *character* or *concept* of the referent rather than simply the referent as a bounded entity (thus e.g. *moon* in (6) gets very close in meaning to MOONLIGHT). Conversely, when typical mass nouns are used like count nouns, as in (7) to (10), the expression either has *sub-generic* reference, i.e. it denotes a subclass of a class, as in (7) and (8) (*an excellent wine = an excellent kind of wine, several coffees = several kinds of coffee*), or it denotes *instances* or *realizations* of the non-countable entity (*many kindnesses = e.g. many acts of kindness, two coffees = two cups of coffee*) as in (9) and (10).

The concept of countability does not usually apply to proper nouns functioning as *names*: they are neither count nouns nor mass nouns. Though names are either formally singular (e.g. *John Wilson, London, France*) or, less often, formally plural (e.g. *the Hebrides, General Motors*), we do not immediately conceive of their referents as countable, or even quantifiable. However, like count nouns, names typically have individualized referents. With a more extensive function than simply naming, proper nouns readily accept quantification: *all the young Peter Schmeichels, a real Sylvester Stallone*, etc. But there are also examples where proper nouns retain their status as names despite the association of countability:

(11)   Have you invited *the Wilsons* to stay with us?

(12)   Is there *a Sarah Mortimer* staying at this hotel?

Here *the Wilsons* means 'the Wilson family' and *a Sarah Mortimer* means 'a certain Sarah Mortimer or 'someone called Sarah Mortimer'. In both cases there is a clear sense of uniqueness despite the explicit quantification. Consider finally examples like:

(13)   *How many Peters* are there in this department?

(14)   Where does he spend *all his Christmases*?

(15)   We play badminton on *Mondays*.

Here the proper noun expressions *Peters, Christmases* and *Mondays* have referents actually called 'Peter', 'Christmas' and 'Monday', respectively (and thus differ from the proper noun expressions *Peter Schmeichels* and *a real Sylvester Stallone*). Such examples combine classmembership and uniqueness by referring to 'unique but recurring phenomena'. What these examples also show is that there is a grey zone between common nouns and proper nouns, and that this affects the question of countability.

10.2.6. Recapitulation

Let us briefly recapitulate the findings of the last few sections on categorization. As we have seen, there is no clear-cut definition of what exactly constitutes the head in a noun group. A practical working definition is that it is a single noun or syntactically fixed compound with unitary stress and a noun as the key element. The function of the head is to categorize the referent. This categorization can be described in terms of a number of general semantic distinctions (e.g. human/non-human, male/female/unisex/inanimate), the referential scope of nouns (unique, generic and specific/non-specific class-member referents) and countability (countable vs. non-countable). These distinctions are grammatically relevant in a number of ways: e.g. morphological derivation, choice of co-occurring pronouns, determiner usage and classification of nouns into subtypes (proper vs. common nouns; count vs. mass nouns, singular vs. plural nouns).

The following charts summarize the classification of referents and nouns:

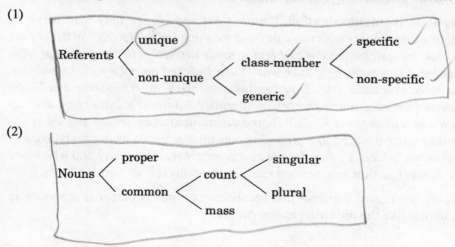

10.3. Determination

10.3.1. Types of determiner

Determiners are used to signal the kind of reference involved in the expression of a nominal. There are four main subcategories of determination:

(i) Definite determination. There are four form types realizing definite determination: a) the definite article *the* (as in *the* doctor, *the* bright girls); b) the demonstrative pronouns *this, that, these, those* (as in *this* bicycle, *those* bastards); c) the possessive pronouns *my, your, his, her, its, our* and *their* (as in *my* wedding, *his* student days); and d) genitive nominals (as in *Jack's* truck, *my old father's* idea). To these types of definite determination we may add *such*, which is a demonstrative-like qualitative pronoun with subgeneric meaning: *such* misery, *such* students.

(ii) Indefinite determination. There are three form types expressing indefinite determination: a) the indefinite article *a(n)* (as in *a* new hall, *an* arrogant journalist); b) zero (Ø) (as in _ professors, _ sugar); c) the indefinite pronouns *any, no, each, every, either, neither, some* (as in *any* suggestion, *no* joy, *either* way, *some* girl(s)). To these indefinite determiners we may add *one* as an emphatic alternative to the indefinite article and *another*, which combines the indefinite article *an* and the modifier *other* (cf. the definite counterpart, which is in two words: *the other*).

(iii) Interrogative determination. Interrogative determination, which is often indefinite in character, is used to form a question about the head. There are three interrogative pronouns which may serve a determinative function: *which, what* and *whose* (as in *Which* book do you prefer? / *What* solution did she come up with? / *Whose* key is this?).

(iv) Relative determination. *Which, what* and *whose* may also serve as relative determiners with more definite meaning (as in *Her visitor left at four o'clock, by which time the FBI had already arrived / He enjoyed what wine was left / The boy whose bike was stolen knocked on my door*). In addition we have emphatic *whichever* and *whatever* (as in *Whichever book you choose I am sure your parents will approve / Whatever solution he comes up with she will support him*). Relative determination by *which* and *whose* is used to relate the head to a preceding constituent. While *whose* is stylistically unmarked, *which* is rather formal as a determiner. *What(ever)* and *whichever* are in this function *independent* relative pronouns (cf. section 5.4.1).

We do not regard the first- and second-person plural personal pronouns in examples like the following as determiners:

(1)   What are *you* guys doing on Sunday?
(2)   *We* Americans believe in democracy.
(3)   They simply hate *us* Germans.

In such examples, the noun specifies the meaning of the pronoun and is thus best analysed as an elaborative dependent in a pronoun group.

Note that the noun could be replaced with a different form type without changing the overall construction type; compare e.g. (2) with (4):

(4)   We *in the English Department* believe in tough grammar exams.

This kind of construction should not be confused with the non-standard, colloquial use of *them* as an alternative to *those* in examples like:

(5)   We don't like *them bastards*.

We also exclude from our class of determiners indefinite pronouns like *all*, *both* and *one*. These pronouns, which are quantifiers rather than determiners, will be briefly dealt with in section 10.3.3.

Here is an overview of the determiners identified in this section:

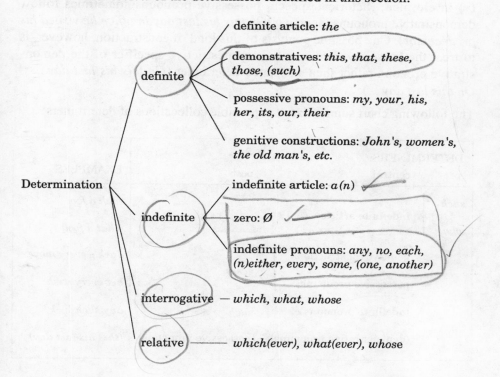

10.3.2. Co-occurring determiners: pre- and postdeterminers

Determiners are normally in a paradigmatic choice relation (cf. section 2.8) and thus in complementary distribution: if we select one, we cannot also select another. There are, however, certain exceptions to this restriction:

(i) *such* may precede the indefinite article plus singular count noun (as in *such a fool*, *such a good idea*);

(ii) *what*, too, may precede the indefinite article plus singular count noun to form an exclamative expression (as in *What a fool! / What a good idea*);

(iii) possessive pronouns and genitive constructions may be followed by *every* plus a singular count noun as an emphatic alternative to an expression with the quantifier *all* plus a plural count noun (compare *the old man's every move / all the old man's moves, her every wish / all her wishes*);

(iv) *such* occasionally follows a determinative indefinite pronoun (as in *no such luck, any such move, each such development, some such problem*);

(v) in elevated, rhetorical speech, possessive pronouns sometimes follow demonstrative pronouns (as in e.g. *On this his last day in office he visited his predecessor*). One possible analysis of this kind of construction, however, is to treat the possessive pronoun as a nonrestrictive specifier of the demonstrative pronoun rather than a separate determiner (*On this his last day ... = On this last day ...*).

The following chart summarizes the possible collocations of determiners:

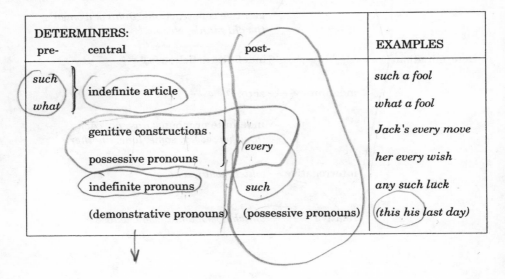

DETERMINERS: pre-	central	post-	EXAMPLES
such / what	indefinite article		such a fool / what a fool
	genitive constructions / possessive pronouns	every	Jack's every move / her every wish
	indefinite pronouns	such	any such luck
	(demonstrative pronouns)	(possessive pronouns)	(this his last day)

What and *such* are *predeterminers* when they precede the indefinite article and *every*, *such* and possessive pronouns are *postdeterminers* when they follow other determiners. All other determiners are *central determiners*. When *what*, *such* and *every* are the only determiners in noun groups (as in *such misery*, *every woman*, etc.) they, too, are called central determiners.

10.3.3. Determiners and quantifiers

Determiners are inextricably linked up with *quantifiers*. Thus, obviously, demonstrative pronouns are either singular (*this*, *that*) or plural (*these*, *those*) in concord with the head noun, and the indefinite article (as well as its emphatic alternative *one*) is used only with singular count nouns (in contrast to Ø, which is used with plural count nouns and with mass nouns). Also the indefinite determiners *any, no, each, every, either, neither, some* have a more or less clear association of quantification about them: in some of their central uses they add different nuances of quantifying meaning to the basic indefinite class-member or mass referents of the noun group as a whole. Of the indefinite determiners, *no* and *some* are the ones with the clearest association of quantification: *no* means 'absence of quantity' and *some* means 'indefinite, undefined amount or number of'. At the same time, however, *no* and *some* are clear determiners. When followed by e.g. a singular count noun, *no* is the negative form of the indefinite article (= *'not a(n)'*); compare:

(1)   There is *a pen* in the top drawer.
(2)   There is *no pen* in the top drawer.

When followed by e.g. a plural count noun, *some* is the plural equivalent of the indefinite article in noun groups with class-member reference; compare:

(3)   I met *a professor* in London.
(4)   I met *some professors* in London.

Some thus supplements Ø, which in connection with plural count nouns often signals generic reference; compare:

(5)   *Professors* like poetry.
(6)   *Some professors* like poetry.

While *any, no, each, every, either, neither* and *some* are primarily determiners with an association of quantification, other indefinite pronouns and numerals are primarily quantifiers with an association of determination: e.g. *both, all, half, one, many, five, second*, etc. Note that unlike the indefinite pronouns listed as determiners above, all these items are compatible with both definite and indefinite reference: *both girls / both the girls*; *all cars / all the cars*; *half a bottle / half the bottle*; *one case / the one case*; *many books /*

the many books; *five calls / the five calls*; *the second attempt / a second attempt*. While many of these items may occur in constructions without genuine determiners, they can all co-occur with central determiners. Like predeterminers, the following quantifiers may precede central determiners:

(i) *Both, all, half*: these three quantifiers may precede definite central determiners (the definite article, demonstrative pronouns and genitive/possessive constructions). They can also function as heads in pronoun groups with a very similar meaning; compare: *all the soldiers / all of the soldiers*; *half the money / half of the money*; *both these solutions / both of these solutions*. Unlike the two others, *half* may precede the indefinite article in connection with head nouns expressing quantity or measurement: *half a pound, half a mile, half a pint, half an inch*.

(ii) Multipliers: *double, twice, three times*, etc. may precede definite central determiners (just like *both, all* and *half*): *double the average, twice his income, three times this amount*. In expressions of frequency where the head noun expresses a standard against which the frequency is determined, *once, twice* and expressions with *times* (e.g. *three times*) may precede the indefinite article or the indefinite pronouns *every* or *each*: *once a week, twice each month, three times every fortnight*.

(iii) Fractions: *two-thirds, one-fifth*, etc. may precede the definite article (e.g. *two-thirds the amount*) or serve as group heads followed by an *of*-construction (e.g. *two-thirds of his salary*).

Like postdeterminers and modifiers, many quantifiers may follow central determiners:

(i) Cardinal numbers: *one, two, three, four*, etc. may follow definite central determiners (*his one objection, these two claims, the three pencils*, etc.). Cardinal numbers may also serve as group heads followed by an *of*-construction (*one of his objections, two of these claims, three of the pencils*).

(ii) Ordinal numbers and other ordinals: *first, second, third, fourth*, etc.; *next, last, other, further*. These items may follow definite central determiners (*the first attempt, his second car, this third meeting*, etc.). When ordinal numbers serve as classifiers, they may follow indefinite central determiners such as the indefinite article and *each*: *a first chapter, a second attempt; each first chapter, each second attempt* etc. In expressions of frequency, ordinal numbers follow *every*: *every second meeting, every third visitor*, etc.

(iii) Other quantifiers: *many, (a) few, several, various, more, most, (a) little, less* and others may follow central definite determiners: *the many problems, his few friends, John's several attempts, these various solutions,* etc. They also serve as group heads followed by an *of*-construction: *many of the problems, few of his friends*, etc. Only *many* may precede the indefinite article in cases like *many a kiss* (which is close in meaning to *many kisses* but has a singularizing effect).

Of the determiners identified in section 10.3.1 above, we shall now examine more closely the definite article (in section 10.3.5), the indefinite article (in section 10.3.6), zero (in section 10.3.7) and the genitive construction (in section 10.3.8). Pronominal determiners (demonstratives, indefinites, possessives, interrogatives) will be dealt with more thoroughly in chapter 11.

10.3.4. Referential orientation

There are two ways in which it is relevant to speak of types of *reference* (as distinct from types of *referents*, cf. section 10.2.4): a) types relating to the question of 'referential orientation' of referring expressions (i.e. the question of where to look for a referent), and b) types relating to the relationship between referring expression and type of referent (e.g. 'definite specific reference' = reference to a specific referent by means of a definite nominal). In this section we examine the former typology, leaving the latter to our discussion of the use of the articles in sections 10.3.5-7.

Let us begin by distinguishing two main referential orientations. There is reference to something mentioned elsewhere in the (spoken or written) text: this is called *textual (or endophoric) reference* (note that 'text' and 'textual' are to be understood to include not only written language but also spoken language). And there is reference to something in the extralinguistic, non-textual context, i.e. something in some real or fictional world: we call that *non-textual (or exophoric) reference*. Here are first some possible examples of non-textual reference:

(1)   Will you pass *the salt*, please.
(2)   There's *an apple* in the basket.
(3)   Hurry up, or you will run into *their security guard*.
(4)   *The sun* set about half an hour later.

These examples are perfectly well-formed even if there is no other mention of the referents in the preceding or following text. As we see, the context may be very *specific*, as in (1) to (3), where the referent is close by and can be manipulated in one way or another, or it may be very general, as in (4), where the referent is a natural phenomenon on which human existence depends, and thus actually part of any context if only very implicitly.

There are two main types of textual reference: *anaphoric* and *cataphoric* reference. Anaphoric reference is *backward* reference to a preceding textual unit (called the *antecedent*), whereas cataphoric reference is *forward* reference to a following unit (there is no appropriate traditional name for this unit, but let us call it 'postcedent'). Here are some examples of anaphoric reference (in which the antecedent/postcedent is indicated in curly brackets):

(5)   {A man} and a woman entered. *The man* was wearing a tie.

(6)   If *the movement* is to preserve its appeal, {radical feminism} must realize that the ideological climate has changed.

Textual reference, both anaphoric and cataphoric, may cut across the sentence boundary: in example (6) the relation is *intrasentential*, in example (5) it is *extrasentential*.

Anaphoric reference is *repetitive* if the head noun of the referring group is identical with the head noun of the antecedent, otherwise it is *non-repetitive*. Thus while (5) above is an example of repetitive anaphoric reference, the following sentences are examples of non-repetitive anaphoric reference:

(7)   {A man and a woman} were sitting on the bench; *the couple* seemed to be very much in love.

(8)   For several weeks I avoided {Roger}. I couldn't bear to see his gleeful face. God, how I hated *the bastard*.

Cataphoric reference is always non-repetitive (cf. example (6)).

Non-repetitive anaphoric reference is either *direct* or *indirect* (repetitive reference is always direct). The examples looked at so far are instances of direct reference in the sense that the expression under analysis establishes (repetitively or non-repetitively) exactly the same entity as the antecedent. With indirect reference, the expression establishes a referent which is related to, but not identical with, the antecedent. The antecedent provides a background against which the existence of the referent of the expression under analysis may be recognized or accepted, as in:

(9)   It was {a very wide ditch}, and when they crept up to *the edge* and looked into it they could see it was also very deep, and there were many rocks at *the bottom*. (for discussion of this example, see Kvistgaard Jakobsen 1994: 65f)

The italicized noun groups are examples of indirect anaphoric reference with *a very wide ditch* as the antecedent: *the edge* and *the bottom* are to be understood precisely as 'the edge of the ditch' and 'the bottom of the ditch', respectively.

The following chart summarizes the types of reference identified above in connection with referential orientation:

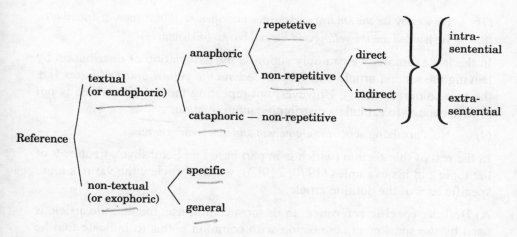

10.3.5. The definite article

Historically, the definite article *the* is a weakened demonstrative form. In many of its uses, this is semantically evident: the definite article typically singles out or delimits the referent of the noun group relative to the communicative context. Syntactically, the definite article is a central determiner and thus precedes any modifiers in the noun group:

(1)   He is *the right man for the job.*
(2)   He gave *the very same talk* last week.

However, certain degree adverbs and pronouns like QUITE and MUCH may intensify the noun group as a whole, especially in expressions involving comparison, in which case they precede the definite article:

(3)   He is not *quite the man* he used to be.
(4)   He gave *much the same talk* last week.

When nouns are coordinated, article usage varies:

(5)   The Danes and Swedes felt humiliated.
(6)   The Danes and the Swedes felt humiliated.

In (5) it is possible to interpret the two nouns as more closely connected (i.e. as referring to a group of Danes and Swedes). In (6) the repetition of the definite article secures a separate focus on the two nouns (i.e. there are two separate groups involved: a group of Danes and a group of Swedes).

When modifiers are coordinated, each receives a separate focus if the definite article is repeated. In noun groups with a plural noun, this repetition of the definite article sometimes results in distributive meaning with the modifiers relating to different referents of the noun; compare:

(7)   He was by far *the kindest and the most competent officer.* (non-distributive)

(8)   He handed me *the yellow and the red boxes.* (distributive)

In the last example, we can only suppress the association of distribution by leaving the second article out: *He handed me the yellow and red boxes* (i.e. the two-coloured boxes). However, not repeating the definite article is not always enough to exclude a distributive interpretation:

(9)   No, I'm talking about *the eighteenth and nineteenth centuries.*

In the rest of this section (which is in part based on Schibsbye's treatment of the topic and his examples (1970: 219ff)), we shall review the various more specific uses of the definite article:

A) Definite specific reference. In its most central use, the definite article is used by the speaker in connection with common nouns to indicate that he expects the listener to be able to single out a particular referent, typically on the basis of *a shared familiarity*. For example, if someone says: *Have you seen the kettle?*, the speaker signals that he expects the kettle in question to be familiar to the listener. If the speaker thinks that the listener may not know about the kettle, he will use the indefinite article: *Have you seen a kettle around here somewhere?* If the speaker thinks that the listener has some knowledge of the possible referents of the noun KETTLE but not enough to recognize the particular kettle in question, he will supply what information he deems necessary for the listener to do so. In other words, he will *establish* a shared familiarity, e.g.:

(10)   Have you seen the kettle *that I borrowed from Sally?*
(11)   Have you seen the kettle *with the broken handle?*
(12)   Have you seen the *new* kettle?

In example (10), the shared familiarity is provided by the restrictive relative clause. Put differently, the restrictive relative clause *warrants* the use of the definite article by expressing information which will enable the listener to recognize what the speaker is talking about. In example (11), the definite article is warranted in this sense by the postmodifying preposition group *with the broken handle*, and in example (12) it is warranted by the premodifying adjective *new*. In other words, by using the definite article the speaker signals that he will provide the listener with enough information to figure out what the speaker is talking about. Sometimes the speaker is wrong, in which case a dialogue like the following may take place:

(13)   Speaker A: Have you seen the kettle?
        Speaker B: What kettle?
        Speaker A: The one I borrowed from Sally.

Note here the interrogative determiner *What* in speaker B's question.

The degree of precision with which the listener is expected by the speaker to recognize the referent may vary contextually. In some cases, the definite article merely signals a plea for the listener's acceptance of the existence of a particular referent. For example, in a case like *It turned out that John had been to the same school as Max* (cf. Huddleston 1984: 249), the speaker expects no more of the listener than his or her ready acceptance of the existence of a particular school to which both John and Max used to go.

The kind of reference involved when the definite article is used by the speaker to indicate that he expects the listener to be able to single out a particular referent is called *definite specific reference.* Definite specific reference is possible with all four main kinds of nouns (common count singular, common count plural, common mass, proper):

(14)   Dan argued that Owen truly adored *the school.*

(15)   *The girls next door* were doing their homework.

(16)   She passed him *the sugar.*

(17)   I want *the two Peters* in this class to report to Mr Wilson.

Characteristically, definite specific reference picks the referent out as one or more particular members of a class (as in examples (14), (15) and (17)) or as particular, limited 'sub-mass' (as in example (16)). In each case, however, there is a clear implication that, *in context*, the referent is unique (if the noun is singular) or all-inclusive (if the noun is plural). Thus in the context of example (14) there is only one school to which the expression *the school* may apply and in the context of example (15), all and only the girls next door are included in the referent of *The girls next door*.

Reference to specific limitations or specific bounded instances of non-countable entities such as e.g. 'love', 'life', 'nature', 'goodness', 'tyranny', 'art', 'materialism', 'mud', 'water', 'rice' etc. requires the definite article; compare:

(18a)   He studied *architecture.*

(18b)   He studied *the architecture of the Roman Empire.*

(19a)   *Life* is sweet.

(19b)   *The new life she gave me* was so exciting.

Non-specific limitation of a generic referent is often possible without the definite article, as in:

(18c)   He studied *Roman architecture.*

The result of such limitation is sub-generic reference: in (18c) the referent 'Roman architecture' is a subtype of 'architecture'.

While definite specific reference is the central function of the definite article, there are other important uses:

B) Definite 'non-specific' reference. Sometimes the definite article is used in cases where there is no specific referent yet but simply an expectation or assumption that there will be a specific thing answering the description of the definite expression as a whole. Such cases of potential but unrealized specificness is sometimes called *definite non-specific reference* (despite the fact that the non-specific meaning is a result of contextualization rather than linguistic expression):

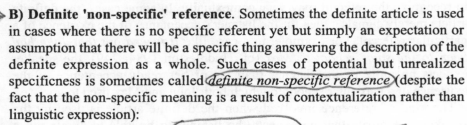

(20)   He is still looking for *the* right girl to marry.

(21)   I want you to reach *the* cheapest possible solution.

(22)   *The* winner of the final tomorrow morning will receive £2,000.

As these examples indicate, definite non-specific reference is especially common in constructions involving (implicit or explicit) comparison and/or future situational reference.

C) Generic reference. In the singular, generic expressions may take the definite article:

(23)   He took a professional interest in *the diesel engine*.

(24)   *The funnel-web spider* is common in New South Wales.

To use a singular count noun representatively for the whole class or kind in this way is often somewhat more formal than to use indefinite plural expressions (e.g. *diesel engines, funnel-web spiders*). With musical instruments and dances, however, the definite singular noun group is the usual expression:

(25)   She plays *the guitar* and *the lute*.

(26)   Jack absolutely hates to dance *the foxtrot*.

In the plural, generic reference is typically indefinite: *diesel engines* ('all engines'). Normally the definite article is used only when there is reference to national or ethnic groups (e.g. *the Russians, the Europeans, the Blacks*, etc.).

    For generic expressions with the definite article in adjective groups (like *the rich, the young*, etc.) cf. section 12.4.2.

D) Unique reference. Since names have unique referents, they usually lack the definite article (*Jack, London, France, Europe, Carlsberg*, etc.). There are, however, a number of exceptions to this rule:

(i) Some geographical names, especially plural names of regions, archipelagos and mountain ranges, take the definite article: e.g. *the Hague, the Tyrol, the Sahara, the Ukraine; the Americas, the Orkneys, the Alps*. The same applies to names of seas, rivers and canals: *the Pacific, the Atlantic, the Thames, the Nile, the Suez Canal*, etc. The article is dropped in a river name if it is part of the name of a town (as in *Newcastle-on-Tyne*) or if it is part of an enumeration (as in *a network of canals, connecting Humber, Severn, Mersey and Thames*, cf. Schibsbye 1970: 221f).

(ii) Names of hotels, restaurants, clubs, cinemas, theatres, major buildings, journals and ships often require the definite article: *the Imperial, the Hungry Monk, the Savoy, the Taj Mahal, The Times, the Estonia, the Mayflower*, etc.

(iii) Some titles of persons: *the Queen of Denmark, the Reverend Roger Smith, the President of the United States, the Marquess of Salisbury*, etc.

(iv) Proper nouns used as names may take the definite article if they are (restrictively or non-restrictively) modified to express a certain aspect or version of the referent: *the young Churchill* (= 'Churchill as a young man' / 'Churchill Junior' *or* 'Churchill, who was a young man', depending on *young* being restrictive or non-restrictive), *the real Spain, the famous Mick Jagger*, etc. Expression like *the young Churchill* and *the famous Mick Jagger* may also be interpreted to refer restrictively to particular bearers of these names in contrast to other bearers of the same name, e.g. someone called Churchill who is not young and someone called Mick Jagger who is not famous. The article may be dropped if the group assumes the status of a new name (as in *Merry Old England* and *Ancient Ireland*) or if the speaker or writer wishes to express what Schibsbye (1970: 227f.) calls "benevolent interest", as in:

(27)   The fall is that of *famed Niagara*, the roar awe-inspiring.

(28)   When Jess Conrad kissed *11-year-old Susan Pinkney, pretty Yvonne Kersting* broke down.

Such examples are particularly common in journalism.

(v) Proper nouns used for specific, limited (typically restrictively modified) class-member reference:

(29)   Mr Crossman is *the Burke of our day*.

(30)   Stockholm is *the Venice of the North*.

(31)   I would like to speak to *the two Peters in this class*.

In the first two examples, the names *Burke* and *Venice* are used qualitatively about referents with other names. In the last example, *Peters* is used quantitatively about specific members of the class of people called 'Peter'.

(vi) Note in particular the use of the definite article in connection with the names of weekdays, months, annual events, etc. Without the definite article, such nouns are used *deictically*, i.e. in relation to the 'here and now' of the speaker, whereas with the definite article, they are used in relation to some other point of time relevant in the context; compare:

(32)   I will see you on *(next) Monday*.

(33)   I will see you on *the (following) Monday*.

(34)   She fell in love with him *last August*.

(35)   She fell in love with him *the following August*.

Without the article, such nouns have unique referents, with the article they have definite specific class-member referents.

It is interesting to note that in many names the presence of the definite article is caused by the name being partially or fully derived from common nouns or constructions containing common nouns as the head of the group: *the Pacific (Ocean)*, *the (River) Thames*, *the Gulf (of Mexico)*, *the Tate (Gallery)*, *the Sahara (Desert)*, etc.

E) The emphatic definite article. Note finally the emphatic use of the definite article (pronounced /ðiː/) to denote that the referent deserves the description provided by the group in the highest degree:

(36)   He is *the* expert on computational linguistics.

(37)   She is *the* master of modern dance.

10.3.6. The indefinite article

We turn now to the indefinite article. As pointed out earlier, the indefinite article *a(n)* is used only in connection with singular nouns. Historically, it is a reduced form of *one* and in some examples it is close to having the meaning of a numeral (cf. Jespersen 1933: 174f.):

(1)   In *a word*, I don't like him.

(2)   Rome wasn't built in *a day*.

(3)   I would like two cheeseburgers and *a coke*, please.

The indefinite article is a central determiner and thus usually precedes any modifiers in the noun group:

(4)   Farrokh was *an unassimilated Canadian*.

There is, however, attraction of modifiers to pre-determiner position by HOW(EVER), AS and SO in examples like the following (cf. the use of *such* and *what* as predeterminers mentioned in section 10.3.2):

(5)   *However beautiful a woman* she is, she does not fool me.

(6)   He may not be *as competent a doctor* as Bill.

(7)   I cannot resist *so nice a proposition*.

Attraction is also possible (with little or no difference of meaning) when modifiers appear in conjunction with the degree adverbs TOO and NO LESS:

(8)   Sandra is *a too critical reader.*

(9)   Sandra is *too critical a reader.*

Adverbs like QUITE and RATHER are often found in pre-determiner position relating to all of what follows in the noun group rather than simply as a dependent of a modifier; compare:

(10)   Bill is *a quite/rather competent sailor.*

(11)   Bill is *quite/rather a competent sailor.*

In connection with coordinated nouns, the indefinite article is usually repeated if the two nouns refer to separate entities, qualities, aspects, etc. If there is felt to be a close relation between the two nouns, the indefinite article is used only before the first noun; compare:

(12)   I asked for *a knife and fork.*

(13)   Dr. Daruwalla was *an orthopedist and a Duckworthian.*

In connection with coordinated modifiers, the indefinite article is not repeated except to create emphasis on different aspects of the referent or if the modifiers relate distributively to different referents; compare:

(14)   She was *a stunningly beautiful and an intelligent woman.* (non-distributive)

(15)   This was *an acceptable, even an honourable, tradition.* (non-distributive)

(16)   I gave him *a red and yellow box.* (non-distributive)

(17)   I gave him *a red and a yellow box.* (distributive)

Like the definite article, the indefinite article is used for a number of determinative functions:

A) **Unmarked determination: class-member reference.** Basically, the indefinite article is used by the speaker in connection with singular count nouns with class-member referents to indicate that he or she does not expect the listener to be familiar with (and hence to be able to single out) a particular referent of the noun group. In this way, the indefinite article is used when the conditions for using the definite article are absent:

(18)   She was stuck between *a grim-looking American* and *a grim-looking Scandinavian.*

(19)   He was seated in the darkness in *a gazebo* by the lakeshore, quietly listening to *a recording of Kierkegaard's Either/Or.*

(20)   She was wearing *an enormous full-length kimono-style dress.*

(21)   You were stepped on by *an elephant* while your father was buying cigarettes?

In each case, the noun group containing the indefinite article refers to a member of the class of things potentially referred to by the head noun: for example, *an elephant* refers to a member of the class of elephants.

Once the speaker or writer has introduced a referent by an indefinite noun group, enough familiarity has been established to warrant the use of the definite article in subsequent noun groups with the same referent (anaphoric repetitive or non-repetitive reference):

(22)   'You were stepped on by *an elephant* while your father was buying cigarettes?', Farrokh asked ... The doctor didn't believe he could fix what *the elephant* had done.

(23)   *A badly limping boy* could occasionally be seen standing on his head at Chowpatty Beach. The doctor knew that this wasn't a trick of sufficient promise for Vinod and Deepa to offer *the urchin* a home at the circus. *The boy* had slept on the beach ...

B) Description in terms of class-membership. Noun groups containing the indefinite article are particularly frequent as complements, as well as after *as* or *for* and as appositional elaboratives, serving as descriptions of the referent of other constituents (e.g. the subject or the object):

(24)   Mr. Garg was *a regular customer.*
(25)   They called him *a damned fool.*
(26)   Vinod refused to see himself as *a "servant".*
(27)   I took him *for a criminal.*
(28)   She fell in love with Max Jones, *a real-estate agent from Minnesota.*

In these examples, the indefinite noun group provides a description of the referent of some other constituent by assigning to it membership of the class of potential referents of the head noun. It is interesting to compare such constructions with the following examples without the indefinite article:

(29)   Bill Clinton became *president of the United States.*
(30)   As *chief director of this firm* I disapprove of your 'useful contacts'.

Here the italicized noun groups without the indefinite article have unique reference rather than class-member reference.

The indefinite article is also sometimes left out to create an emphasis on different aspects or (changing) 'character' or 'quality' of the referent described rather than simply assigning class membership, especially in constructions with *as* or after the verb TURN (cf. Schibsbye 1970: 287):

(31)   As *American*, the writer has distrusted Europe; as *writer*, he has envied the riches available to his European counterpart.

(32)   He had turned *spy.*

This emphasis on 'character' or 'quality' is also found in connection with *kind of* and *sort of* expressions; compare:

(33)   What *sort of man/a man* would do such a thing!

Such examples are more frequently without the indefinite article.

Note finally examples involving *enough* (cf. Schibsbye 1970: 287):

(34)   I am still *optimist* enough to credit life with invincibility.

C) Indefinite specific vs. indefinite non-specific reference. As with groups containing the definite article, groups containing the indefinite article are susceptible to an analysis in terms of the distinction between specific and non-specific. Most of the examples offered so far in this section are examples of *indefinite specific reference*: in each case a particular referent answering the description of the noun group is picked out specifically. Thus in example (22) above, *an elephant* does not simply refer to a random member of the class of elephants, but to a particular member. When an indefinite noun group does not refer to a particular member but more loosely to potentially any member of the class, we speak of *indefinite non-specific reference*. Here are some examples of indefinite non-specific reference (with indefinite specific counterparts in parentheses):

(35)   I would like *an apple*, please. (cf. *He gave me an apple*)

(36)   Are we likely to see *a viper* in this region? (cf. *We saw a viper here yesterday*)

Here the indefinite article approaches the meaning of 'any': any entity answering the description of the head (plus modifiers) is a potential referent.

Some noun groups are ambiguous between a specific and a non-specific reading:

(37)   Sally wants to marry *a Norwegian who is rich*.

The noun group *a Norwegian who is rich* either refers to a particular person, a rich Norwegian (specific reference), or it marks anyone who is a rich Norwegian as a potential future husband (non-specific reference).

D) The indefinite article in generic-like expressions. Moving one step further away from indefinite specific reference, the indefinite article is used in general statements to denote 'typical class-member', cf. the following examples:

(38)   *An elephant* is a potentially very dangerous animal.

(39)   *A linguist* is someone who studies languages.

(40)   *A funnel-web spider* is poisonous.

The indefinite article here implies 'any' but differs from *any* in that it does not single out the members of the class individually but rather has a generic-like function. Such constructions are more restricted in general statements than truly generic plural expressions with zero article (e.g. *Elephants are potentially very dangerous animals*). Thus, as Greenbaum and Quirk point out (1990: 85), there are cases where we cannot use the indefinite singular expression:

(41a)   Elephants are becoming extinct.
(41b)   *An elephant is becoming extinct.

Example (41a) is a statement about the species as a whole and therefore cannot be replaced by example (41b) with its class-member association.

Generic-like expressions with the indefinite article also differ from generic expressions with the definite article (e.g. *The elephant is a potentially very dangerous animal*) in being less formal and less contrastive. Note here that generic singular expressions with the definite article express 'class as a whole' rather than 'typical class-member' and are not subject to the restriction mentioned above:

(41c)   The elephant is becoming extinct.

E) Count nouns with little association of class-membership. The indefinite article is sometimes used in idiomatic expressions where it does not really make sense to speak of class-member reference, (cf. Jespersen 1933: 175):

(42)   I have *a mind* to tell him exactly what I mean.
(43)   The child was in *a fever*.
(44)   I did it with *a view* to being useful.

Note especially constructions where there is fusion between the predicator and the direct object in S P O and S P O O constructions (creating semantically intransitive and monotransitive constructions, respectively, cf. our discussion of role suppression in section 7.3.4):

(45)   He gave *a nod*. (cf. *He nodded*)
(46)   They had *an argument*. (cf. *They argued*)

F) The indefinite article and mass nouns. As a general rule, mass nouns do not take the indefinite article. When unmodified, they typically appear without article (generic use) or with quantifiers like SOME:

(47)   *Sugar* is more expensive than *rice*.
(48)   Could I have *some water*, please.

However, as pointed out in section 10.2.5, the indefinite article is used in connection with mass nouns to denote 'subtype of the non-countable entity' (especially in noun groups containing restrictive modification as in example (49)) or 'instances' of the non-countable entity (as in example (50)):

(49)   This is actually *an excellent wine.*

(50)   He ordered *a beer* and *a coffee.*

If the referent is an abstract concept and this concept is restricted by the meaning of one or more modifiers, the indefinite article is used for indefinite expression (cf. our discussion of the use of the definite article in similar contexts in section 10.3.5); compare:

(51)   She showed *a loyalty* towards her master *which I could not match.*

(52)   This was Ranjit's condemning reference to Deepa, for whom he harboured *a forbidding disapproval* – the kind that only Mr. Sethna might have shared.

In these examples, the meaning expressed is 'kind of ...' ('kind of courage', 'kind of loyalty' and 'kind of disapproval'; note the appositional elaborative in the last example: *the kind that only* ...) and is thus similar to example (49), which expresses 'kind of wine'.

G) The indefinite article and proper nouns. The indefinite article is occasionally used with proper nouns to denote class-membership, as in:

(53)   Dr. Aziz said, 'Have you heard about Dr. Dev?' Farrokh wondered, Which Dr. Dev? There was *a Dr. Dev* who was a cardiologist, there was another Dev who was an anesthesiologist – there are a bunch of Devs, he thought.

(54)   I was struck by his dark eyes and small ears. There was no doubt about it: he was very much *a Staines.*

In these examples, the referents actually belong to a class of people bearing the name provided by the proper noun (cf. sections 10.2.4 and 10.2.5). But proper names may also be used with the indefinite article for members of a class of people simply sharing some quality with the bearer of the name or being of the same standard, as in:

(55)   This country has never produced *a Shakespeare* or *a Picasso.*

(56)   'That's it! That's absolutely it! Somebody like John Aubrey, who listens to everything, wonders about everything. This university needs *an Aubrey.*'

The indefinite article (as well as emphatic *one*) is sometimes used in connection with a proper name to indicate that the bearer of the name is unknown to the speaker or assumed by the speaker to be unknown by the listener:

(57)   Is there *a Sarah Mortimer* staying at this hotel?

(58)   In the cupboard I found a pretty volume, the work of *one William Canton.*

Groups containing a modified proper noun preceded by the indefinite article typically express that the bearer of the name is in a temporary (physical or mental) state:

(59)   "I hope it won't be another 50 years before we can celebrate like this again," joked *a high-spirited Bing Crosby*.

(60)   It was *a young Peter Simpson* that I saw in the picture.

H) The indefinite article as a basis of quantification. As a marker of singular meaning, the indefinite article lends itself to quantified expressions involving a standard against which something is measured or counted:

(61)   They made love twice *a day*.

(62)   It costs £45 *a pound*.

The indefinite article here approaches *each* (or *per*) in meaning.

10.3.7. Zero determination

The zero determiner must first of all be distinguished from cases where two or more nouns *share* a determiner (as in *I asked for a knife and fork, the Danes and Swedes felt humiliated*, etc., where the head of the group is realized by a compound unit). A distinction must also be drawn between 'zero determiner', which is associated with indefiniteness, and 'no determiner'. Names take *no* determiner rather than *zero* determiner because they have unique (and thus inherently definite) reference, as in the following examples:

(1)   *Farrokh* and *Julia* were sharing a bath together.

(2)   The view of *Back Bay* was stunning. *Martin Mills* could see *Malabar Hill* and *Nariman Point*.

Note in this connection the lack of determiner in connection with count nouns expressing family relations: *Uncle will join Mom and Dad in a moment*. This applies also to vocatives like the following: *How are you this morning, Professor? / Come on, Darling / See you there, mate*.

Let us turn now to the uses of zero determination:

A) Indefinite class-member reference. Zero is regularly used in connection with plural count nouns for indefinite specific or non-specific class-member reference (corresponding to the use of the indefinite article plus singular count noun):

(3)   I was going to buy *clothes*. (cf. *I was going to buy a hat*)

(4)   Madhu won't be working with *clowns* – or with *elephants*. (cf. *Madhu won't be working with a clown – or with an elephant*)

(5)   She wore *bells* on her ankles and wrists. (cf. *She wore a bell on her left ankle*)

This use of plural nouns with zero determiner is compatible with modification and/or quantification:

(6)   They wore *navy-blue shorts and kneesocks*, too – and *black shoes*.

(7)   Sai Baba was a patron saint of *many circus performers.*

(8)   She dances with *two beautiful peacocks*.

Indefinite class-member reference with zero determiner and quantification is found also in examples where what is basically a mass noun is used in the plural to denote 'instances or realizations of', as in *Over the years she did me many kindnesses*, *Two coffees, please*, etc. (cf. section 10.2.5 above).

B) Indefinite mass reference. Zero is also used in connection with mass nouns for indefinite specific or non-specific reference to non-countable entities and concepts:

(9)   Danny poured *hot water* over the peas.

(10)   It contained *some whitish stuff – curdled milk* or *flour* and *water*.

(11)   The cripple looked to Dr. Daruwalla for *help*.

(12)   Martin would be kept in *perpetual darkness*.

Non-specific reference to non-countable entities and concepts, as in the last two examples, have a generic potential (cf. subsection C below).

   Note that names for diseases are usually non-countable and take zero determiner: e.g. CANCER, PNEUMONIA, CLAMYDIA, etc.:

(13)   He suffers from *cancer*.

(14)   Her child had *pneumonia*.

C) Generic reference. As already noted, zero is used in connection with plural count nouns and with mass nouns for indefinite non-specific reference. In very general contexts, i.e. when there is no explicit or implicit limitation on the referents of the plural noun, or the mass noun, the construction may assume a generic meaning, referring to all the members of a class:

(15)   *Elephants* are dangerous animals.

(16)   *Professors* like *poetry*.

(17)   *Trachoma* is one of the leading causes of *blindness* in the world.

(18)   *Time* is still a mystery to *science*.

The generic quality of these examples is a result of the lack of restriction on the referent of the noun (the class-members or the mass) rather than the representative value of the noun. In other words, the referent is in principle 'all-inclusive' (e.g. *Elephants* actually means 'all elephants'). Restriction of the noun may however occur without this resulting in specific reference: *Indian elephants are dangerous animals, Polish professors like poetry*, etc. Such examples are subgeneric. Subgeneric reference without the article is found also when what is basically a mass noun is used in the plural to denote 'kinds of' as in *He imports several coffees from Africa* (= 'kinds of coffee').

Unlike other count nouns MAN and WOMAN take zero article in generic expressions, the former sometimes in the sense of 'mankind' (though this is often avoided to escape accusations of sexism):

(19)   The temperament of *man*, either male or female, cannot help falling down before and worshipping this sacrificial note.

(20)   It was *man* who ended the Cold War in case you didn't notice. It wasn't weaponry, or technology, or armies or campaigns.

(21)   The nineteenth century was an age where *woman*, not *man*, was sacred; and where you could buy a thirteen-year-old girl for a few shillings.

Count nouns occasionally serve as generic terms for academic subjects, sports and activities:

(22)   Mary studied *dance* as well as *film*. (Greenbaum & Quirk 1990: 85)

(23)   All he is interested in is playing *football*.

D) Generic-like expressions in specific contexts. Abstract and concrete mass nouns, as well as plural count nouns, are sometimes used in a generic-like way in contexts that are so specific that the meaning is close to definite specific expressions (see e.g. Vestergaard 1985: 113):

(24)   *(Our) sources* say he was once a paid informer for the FBI.

(25)   *(The) traffic* had to be diverted because *(the) roads* were flooded.

(26)   *(The) productivity* in most industries is lower than two years ago.

Note particularly the use of certain general count nouns like CONDITIONS, MATTERS, EVENTS, THINGS, etc., without determiner even in rather specific contexts:

(27)   *Conditions* were hopeless.

(28)   Don't make *matters* worse.

E) Other uses of zero. In our discussion of the definite and the indefinite article in sections 10.3.5 and 10.3.6, we have already noted a certain vacillation in the choice relation between the articles and zero determination. Let us look at some of the finer details of this choice relation:

(i) As pointed out in section 10.3.6, count nouns take zero article when they are used as complements, as appositional elaboratives, and after *as* and *for* for unique reference rather than class membership: *Bill Clinton became president of the United States / She was elected chairman of the Equal Rights*

Committee, etc. Note further fronted complements in concessive and conditional subclauses:

(29)   But *pious man* that Reverend Jackson was, he was also a father whose children needed a mother.

(30)   This fault – if *fault* it is – is an amiable one. (Vestergaard 1985: 30)

(ii) Count nouns are sometimes used like mass nouns to emphasize the material, character or concept of the referent rather than simply the referent as an individual entity (cf. also section 10.2.5), in which case they take zero article: *The scrapyard was full of smashed car / He is impervious to argument / The proposal was discussed in great detail* (cf. Vestergaard 1985: 91) / *She was incapable of plotting murder / Word got round that he had already resigned*. Note especially the frequent absence of determination after *kind of* and *sort of*: *What kind of car is this / Any sort of knife will do*, etc.

(iii) Count nouns of the following kind are used without determination in a great many standard expressions for typical recurring activities, events and conditions (cf. Greenbaum & Quirk 1990: 82f):

• locatives with an emphasis on the function of the place rather than its location: e.g. *be in* or *go to bed/church/school/prison/college*;

• transport and communication: e.g. *go/travel/come by bus/train /car, send by post/satellite*;

• meals: e.g. *When is dinner? Do come for lunch tomorrow*;

• time expressions: *summer, autumn, morning, evening*; *at dawn, by night, in winter*.

As many of the examples show, the lack of article is especially frequent in preposition groups.

(iv) Count nouns are often used without determiner in compound units even if the individual noun would require an article:

(31)   As he spoke, he cupped his hand near the bony fusion of *ankle* and *foot*, which the beggar awkwardly rested on the heel.

(32)   We could say that they are *brother* and *sister*, that one looks after the other.

A similar phenomenon is observed in fixed adverbial collocations and idiomatic expressions like: *hand in hand, side by side, mile after mile*, etc.

(v) Nominals serving as dependent modifiers typically take zero determination (though the superordinate noun is usually determined): *these onion choppers, other available child prostitutes, some guest workers*, etc.

(vi) Nouns with zero determination often occur in fixed expressions, especially verb + noun collocations (such as *catch sight of, take place, make use of, make contact with, take pains, take care, cast anchor*, etc.) and in preposition groups (such as *at ease, at pains, in mind, in proportion to, at first glance, off balance, for sale, in need of, in style, by hand, by surprise, on holiday, peace of mind, out of character, in writing, in support of, in fear that, at high speed, in case, by means of, in charge of*).

10.3.8. The genitive

The genitive construction is first and foremost a central definite determiner used to express a relation between two referents: that of *the genitive construction* itself and that of *the head of the group*. This relation is often but by no means always one of possession, as in e.g. *the old man's hat*. This example refers to a particular hat (and is thus much closer in meaning to *the hat* than to *a hat*). At the same time it indicates that the hat belongs in some sense to the referent of *the old man*. In its central function, the genitive construction is called *the specifying genitive*. Note that a noun group containing the specifying genitive is definite even if the genitive construction is indefinite: *a young man's desperate attempt* (= '*the* desperate attempt of a young man').

In writing, the genitive case is formed by adding *'s* to singular nouns or (certain indefinite) pronouns and to irregular plural nouns that do not end in *-s*: *father's, Jack's*; *somebody's, nobody's*; *women's, children's*. The genitive of plural nouns ending in *-s* is formed by simply adding the apostrophe: *boys', writers'*. In speech, the genitive marker is /ɪz/ after sibilants, /s/ after voiceless sounds other than sibilants and /z/ elsewhere, and: *witch's* /wɪtʃɪz/, *wife's* /waɪfs/, *boy's* /bɔɪz/. In speech, the regular plural is not marked for the genitive: *boys'* /bɔɪz/, *writers'* /raɪtəz/. There are few exceptions to these rules: foreign, especially Greek names of more than one syllable ending in *-es* take only the apostrophe: *Socrates', Xerxes'*. With names, English as well as foreign, ending in *-s* pronounced /z/, usage varies: *Lyons'* or *Lyons's*, /laɪənz/ or /laɪənzɪz/. The bare apostrophe is usual after a sibilant in *for ... sake* expressions: *for goodness' sake*.

Though the genitive marker is added simply to nouns (or certain pronouns), the genitive construction potentially contains a whole noun group or compound unit: cf. *women's (disinclination)* vs. *the old women's (disinclination)* and *Jack's (humour)* vs. *Jack and Jill's (humour)*.

Sometimes the genitive marker is not added to the head of the group contained in the genitive construction but to the postmodification, in which case we have what is traditionally referred to as a 'group genitive':

the King *of Sweden*'s (decision)

somebody *else*'s (friend)

the girl *who lives next door*'s (bike)

The term 'group genitive' is somewhat misleading if restricted to such examples: the genitive in cases like *the old women's disinclination* is also, strictly speaking, a group genitive (*the old women* being a noun group as much as *the King of Sweden*).

There is an obvious relationship between genitive constructions and possessive pronouns: compare *the old man's hat* and *his hat*. By and large possessive pronouns are used like genitive constructions. Thus much of what we have to say about the use of genitive constructions applies also to possessive pronouns (for some of the differences see section 11.2.2). Let us turn now to some of the important features of the genitive.

A) Syntactic functions of the genitive. Although the genitive construction is basically a central definite determiner (the specifying genitive), it has other important uses. It may serve as a premodifier, entering a compound-like relationship with the head of the group:

(1)   She lives in a quaint old *shepherd's* cottage. (not 'the cottage of a quaint old shepherd' but 'a quaint old cottage of a certain kind')

(2)   He took a *doctor's* degree. (i.e. 'a special kind of degree')

(3)   She bought some *children's* shoes. (i.e. 'some shoes for children')

Compare the two possible interpretations of *These children's shoes are very expensive* from a sentence analytic point of view. Here is first the interpretation of the example in terms of a specifying genitive ('shoes belonging to these children'):

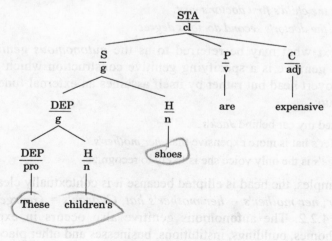

By contrast, the following tree diagram shows the interpretation of the
example in terms of a premodifying genitive ('these shoes for children'):

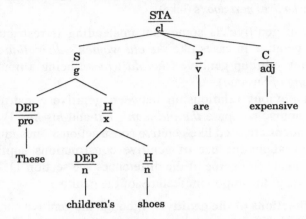

The premodifying genitive, which is called *the classifying genitive*, differs
from the specifying genitive phonologically in having unitary stress on its
first element and syntactically in being inseparable from the head of the
group. Semantically the classifying genitive denotes 'kind' or 'type'. Note that
we cannot insert e.g. an adjective between the genitive and the head and still
preserve the status of the genitive as a classifying genitive: cf. *some
children's expensive shoes / some expensive children's shoes*. And while
groups containing a specifying genitive always have definite reference,
groups containing a classifying genitive may have indefinite reference (as in
the examples above). A specifying and a classifying genitive may co-occur,
as in:

(4)   It was *the child's first doctor's visit.*

(5)   It was *the doctor's second doctor's degree.*

Consider next what may be referred to as the *autonomous genitive*. The
autonomous genitive is a specifying genitive construction which does not
relate to an overt head but rather by itself assumes an external function like
that of a group:

(6)   I parked my car behind *Jack's.*

(7)   Jennifer's hat is more expensive than *her mother's.*

(8)   *George's* is the only voice she is likely to recognize.

In these examples, the head is ellipted because it is contextually clear (*Jack's*
= *Jack's car, her mother's* = *her mother's hat, George's* = *George's voice*),
cf. section 4.2.2. The autonomous genitive also occurs in expressions
referring to homes, buildings, institutions, businesses and other places:

(9)   I met her at *my uncle's*.

(10)   I got these rolls at *the baker's*.

(11)   He has been to London often but never actually seen *St Paul's*.

In such examples of what is often referred to as the 'local genitive', the missing head may occasionally be uniquely retrievable (as in the case of St Paul's <u>Cathedral</u>); as a rule, however, the missing head could be any one of a number of nouns belonging to the same semantic type, viz. 'locations' (*my uncle's = my uncle's place/home/residence/ etc.*).

Finally the autonomous genitive may appear in a postmodifying *of*-construction with a quantifying, partitive meaning ('of several'). This genitive we call *the post-genitive*; examples:

(12)   He introduced me to some friends of *my neighbour's*.

(13)   Jack borrowed a picture of *my sister's*.

The post-genitive, which provides an indefinite alternative to the specifying genitive (cf. *my neighbour's friends, his sister's raincoat*), is compatible with a head noun determined by the definite article or a demonstrative pronoun when followed by a restrictive relative clause: *the/that/this unfortunate student of Otto Jespersen's who failed the grammar exam*. The partitive content becomes especially clear when we consider similar constructions with the uninflected noun:

(14)   Jack borrowed a picture of *my sister*.

(15)   He was a student of *Otto Jespersen*.

(16)   He introduced me to some friends of *my neighbour*.

There is in these examples no partitive meaning but rather a relation defined by the head of the group directed towards the complement of *of* (i.e. 'Jack borrowed a picture representing my sister', 'he studied Otto Jespersen', ' he introduced me to some people who consider themselves to be friends'). Nouns incapable of expressing such a unidirectional relation do not appear in this kind of construction: **He wore a raincoat of my sister*.

In examples containing demonstrative pronouns like:

(17)   Now tell me something about *that/this brother of Stephanie's*.

the partitive association is replaced by an association of the speaker's (approving or disapproving) interest in the referent.

Here is an overview of the syntactic functions of the genitive:

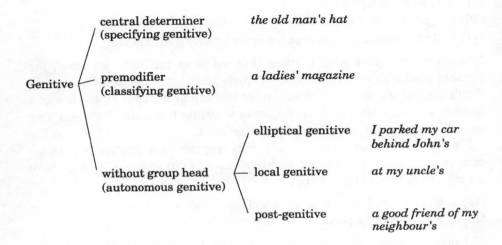

central determiner
(specifying genitive)   *the old man's hat*

Genitive

premodifier
(classifying genitive)   *a ladies' magazine*

                           elliptical genitive   *I parked my car
                                                 behind John's*

without group head   local genitive   *at my uncle's*
(autonomous genitive)

                           post-genitive   *a good friend of my
                                                 neighbour's*

The rest of this section is devoted to the specifying genitive.

B) The semantics of the specifying genitive. The specifying genitive is
traditionally said to express possession in a broad sense: *the doctor's right
hand, his wife's only other reading material, another family's mansion, My
son-in-law's cigarettes*. In an example like *the girl's bathtub at the Hotel
Bardez*, the bathtub is more likely to belong to the hotel than to the girl; and
in *John's bike*, John may or may not be the owner of the bike (for example,
the bike could simply be one that John is riding).

The fact is that in many cases, there is simply just *some unspecified
relation* between the referent of the genitive construction and the referent of
the group as a whole. This has led to various classifications of the specifying
genitive on a semantic basis. Apart from the possessive genitive, we get e.g.
the *genitive of origin* (as in *Jack's letter* 'the letter is from Jack'), the *genitive
of attribute* (as in *Nancy's irritation* 'Nancy is irritated'), etc. Two distinct
kinds of genitive have attracted special attention: the so-called *subjective
genitive* and the so-called *objective genitive*. These genitives are relevant in
connection with verbal nouns, such as ESTIMATION, DELIVERY, EM-
BRACE, RIDICULE, etc., to which we can assign potential participant roles
usually associated with syntactic 'subject' and/or 'object' function.

In the following examples, the specifying genitive is a subjective genitive
in the sense that the referent of the genitive construction is the DOER of an
(explicit or implicit) situational referent of the group as a whole:

(18)   In *Dr. Daruwalla's estimation*, the Jesuits were intellectually crafty and sly.

(19)   *Patel's cool delivery of the news* appalled me.

(20)   Dr. Daruwalla sat shivering in *Julia's embrace.*

(21)   Julia wasn't amused by *Farrokh's constant ridicule of St. Francis's violated remains.*

When the head of the group is a nonfinite clause, the referent of the subjective genitive is either the active DOER/SPECIFIED or the passive DONE-TO of the situation expressed by the clause:

(22)   *Jenny's neglecting to write that letter* upset John. (Jenny = DOER)

(23)   *Jack's being so considerate lately* made her suspicious. (Jack = SPECIFIED*)*

(24)   *Jenny's getting pushed over the edge* was an accident. (Jenny = DONE-TO)

While the subjective genitive is frequent, the objective genitive has rather restricted occurrence, the objective relation being often expressed more naturally by an *of*-construction:

(25)   Was there another clue to *Mr. Lal's murder*, or another threat to Dhar? (= 'the murder of Mr. Lal')

(26)   She relished the details of *old Jack's release.* (= 'the release of Jack')

(27)   Without this evidence *St. Francis's canonization* might never have occurred. (= 'the canonization of St. Francis')

In these examples, the referent of the genitive construction is semantically the DONE-TO.

Note that if both a subjective and an objective relation are to be expressed, we have a subjective genitive followed by an *of*-construction expressing the objective relation: *Jack's release of the prisoners* (= 'Jack released the prisoners'). Objective genitives may, however, be accompanied by a following *by*-phrase expressing the subjective relation: *Denmark's occupation by Germany* (cf. *the occupation of Denmark by Germany*).

In connection with head nouns derived from intransitive verbs, the *of*-construction unambiguously expresses the subjective relation: cf. *the king's arrival / the arrival of the king.*

C) The specifying genitive vs. the *of*-construction. The use of the genitive is somewhat restricted in the sense that many nouns do not normally occur in the genitive: it would be fairly unusual to say e.g. *the table's price, the house's roof, obedience's ramifications, his conversion's miracle*, etc. To express the intended meaning, we often use an entirely different syntactic construction: the definite article + head noun + an *of*-construction containing the referent to which the head is related (*the price of the table, the roof of the house, the ramifications of obedience, the miracle of his conversion*). In many cases, both expressions are possible with little or no difference of meaning: *Veronica Rose's offspring / the offspring of Veronica Rose, the girl's mutilated body / the mutilated body of the girl*, etc. For this reason, traditional grammar used the term '*of*-genitive' for this construction and provided rules for the use of the 'two competing genitives'. We do not use the term 'genitive' about the *of*-construction because, syntactically, it is completely unrelated to the genitive: the genitive is a determiner while the *of*-construction is a postmodifier. But since *semantically* the two kinds of construction are often choice-related, we do find it relevant to provide some guidelines for their use. Let us review some of the factors determining the choice of construction, keeping in mind that there are few absolute rules involved:

a) Semantic considerations. The greater an association of humanness, animacy and/or individuality, the more likely we are to be able to use a noun in the genitive. Thus names of persons and higher animals and count nouns referring to people usually take the genitive (e.g. *Jim's book, Fido's kennel; the girl's arm, the teacher's car*, etc.) while nouns referring to inanimate entities usually take the *of*-construction (e.g. *the colour of the wall, the other side of the coin, the result of this test*, etc.).

Geographical names, collective nouns, count nouns referring to institutions, regions, places, etc. are common in both constructions: *Goa's white beaches / the white beaches of Goa; my family's reputation / the reputation of my family, the clinic's name / the name of the clinic*; etc.

It is often claimed that more 'individuality' or 'focus of interest' is placed on an inanimate or non-human referent of a noun by using it in the genitive rather than in the *of*-construction in examples like *the bikini's bottom half, a lizard's eyes, the novel's title, the fire's friendly crackling, the envelope's shape and size*, etc. In practice such distinctions are hard to perceive.

Abstracts rarely take the genitive (*the significance of this concept, the beauty of this idea*, much rather than *this concept's significance, this idea's beauty*) unless personified or individualized (*nature's wonderful solution to that problem, life's many mysteries*).

As already noted above, the objective genitive is rarer than the possessive and the subjective genitive, being typical only in connection with names and nouns referring to persons (*John's defeat, the woman's release*).

Time and distance expressions often appear in the genitive: *within two or three weeks' time, at a yard's distance, a moment's reflection*, etc.

When a noun relates to one of the lexical items EDGE, END, SURFACE and SAKE as head of the noun group, we often get a genitive construction rather than an *of*-construction: *the water's edge, the journey's end, the lake's surface, for brevity's sake*, etc. In the case of WORTH only the genitive construction is possible: *his money's worth*.

Note finally idiomatic expressions like: *Not for the death of me / Not for the life of me / I don't like the look of that man.*

b) Formal considerations. Strings of genitives are often avoided (*Martin's heart's desire, my cousin's wife's first husband*). Strings of *of*-constructions are common even if somewhat clumsy (*many of the conclusions of the report*). Mixtures of the two constructions are often a happy compromise (*the first husband of my cousin's wife, many of the report's conclusions*), cf. Schibsbye 1970: 117.

Heavy genitive constructions are generally avoided in formal language, especially if the genitive marker can only be placed on a postmodifier (cf. *the man I met yesterday's wife / the wife of the man I met yesterday, the former division officer in this firm's secretary / the secretary of the former division officer in this firm*). Considerations of end-focus and end-weight are important in cases like *the former prime minister's daughter* vs. *the daughter of the former prime minister*.

Of-constructions are used in order to make it possible to attach a relative clause or participial construction directly to the head it modifies, cf. the following example from Vestergaard 1985: 107:

(28)　There is a characteristic 'double deprivation' in the lives of these children, who tend to deprive themselves further through ... (.. in these children's lives, who tend to ..)

Often we get a combination of considerations, e.g. heaviness, postmodification and avoidance of the plural genitive, as in the following example:

(29)　These were usually the houses of producers, directors or actors to whom Danny owed a finished screenplay.

Adjectives used with generic nominal referents, as in *the poor, the rich, the merely fanciful*, etc.) do not take the genitive case: **the poor's conditions / the conditions of the poor*, cf. section 12.4.1.

When the head of the group is realized by a nonfinite clause, only the genitive is possible: *Jenny's neglecting to write that letter / *the neglecting to write that letter of Jenny.*

In cases where the genitive singular and plural are identical in sound (*friend's/friends', girl's/girls'*, etc.), the *of*-construction is sometimes used instead of the genitive plural to avoid ambiguity: *his friend's opinion / the opinion of his friends*. In writing, such plural genitives are common:

(30)　He awakened to the sound of the *skiers'* boots tramping on the hard-packed snow.

(31)　It was at least partly the passion of such *writers'* convictions that gave their novels such value.

10.4. Quantification: the number category

As already pointed out in sections 10.1.3, 10.2.5 and 10.3.3, quantification is
one of the central subfunctions within the functional domain of nominals: we
rarely code specific things without quantifying them, either implicitly or
explicitly. One of the most explicit ways of quantifying something is by
using exact terms of measurement, e.g. cardinal numbers: *six apples*, *two
bottles of apple juice*, etc. But quantification is not limited to expression by
such lexical means. Nor is it tied down to one specific component in the
noun group (such as cardinal numbers). It rather involves a number of
different types of constituent: the head noun (with its singular/plural number
contrast: *girl/girls*, *car/cars*, etc.), certain determiners (which show number
concord with the head: the indefinite article (*a*), indefinite pronouns (such as
every, each, (n)either) and demonstratives (*that/those*, *this/these*)), and
quantifiers serving as predeterminers, postdeterminers or modifiers (such as
all, *both*, *many, five*, *numerous, few*, etc.). In the following subsections we
examine a central grammatical means of quantification: the singular/plural
number distinction in nouns.

10.4.1. The regular singular/plural distinction

Number is a morphological category in English with the singular as the
unmarked base form and the plural as the morphologically marked form. In
speech, the plural is formed by adding:

(i) /ɪz/ to nouns ending in sibilants: e.g. *noses, niches, fringes*

(ii) /s/ to nouns ending in voiceless non-sibilants: e.g. *cats, kicks, taps*

(iii) /z/ to other nouns: e.g. *dogs, clans, shows*

In writing, the plural is usually formed by adding 's' to the base form (as in
the examples above). Note however the following modifications to this
simple spelling rule:

(i) *-s or -es*. Nouns ending in a sibilant take *-es* instead of simply *-s* unless
they are written with a silent *-e*: *latch/latches*, *mass/masses*, etc. (but e.g.
bridge/bridges).

(ii) Consonant doubling. There is doubling of the final consonant in *fezzes*
and *quizzes*. Occasionally *bus* is pluralized as *busses* instead of the more
regular *buses*. Note also that a number of abbreviations are pluralized by
means of consonant doubling alone: e.g. *pp. 1-5* (= 'pages 1-5'), *exx.* (=
'examples'), *MSS* (= 'manuscripts').

(iii) -y → -ies or -ys. The plural form of nouns ending in written *-y* is *-ies* (as in *fly/flies, cry/cries, ally/allies,* etc.) except if *-y* is immediately preceded by another written vowel (as in *toys, delays, ways,* etc.). Exceptions to this rule are: most proper nouns (*Marys, Germanys, Julys;* but *the two Sicilies*) and members of other word classes (*stand-bys, the whys and wherefores*). Note also *soliloquies*, where *-qu-* is regarded as a consonant group.

(iv) -o → -oes or -os. Some nouns ending in *-o* take plural *-es: echoes, heroes, potatoes, tomatoes, vetoes.* Others (especially proper names, abbreviations and cases where *-o* is immediately preceded by another written vowel) take plural *-s* only: *Eskimos, Neros; kilos, photos, pianos; embryos, studios;* etc. There is vacillation in: *banjo(e)s, buffalo(e)s, cargo(e)s, commando(e)s, halo(e)s, motto(e)s, volcano(e)s,* and others. Note the difference between *bravos* (= applause) and *bravoes* (= bandits).

(v) -s or -'s. The plural form of letters is *-'s* rather than simply *-s:* e.g. *p's and q's*. With abbreviations and numerals written in figures there is vacillation with *-s* as the commoner form: *MP's* or *MPs, 1980's* or *1980s*. Quoted words usually take *-'s: There were too many but's in the passage.* Words which do not merely function as quotes but assume an integrated meaning in the sentence take *-s: Some of his whys are hard to answer* (Schibsbye 1970: 94).

Pluralization sometimes results in a sound change:

(i) /-θ/ → /-ðz/. This change is very common in nouns like *baths, mouths, paths, youths*. There is vacillation (/-θs/ or /-ðz/) in *oaths, sheaths, truths, wreaths*. If *-th* is preceded by a consonant, or a short vowel, or a written *-r-* we only get /-θs/: *healths, lengths; deaths; moths; births, hearths*.

(ii) /-s/ → /-zɪz/. This change affects only one word: *houses*.

(iii) /-f/ → /-vz/. This change affects both the pronunciation and the spelling of nouns like *calf/calves, half/halves, knife/knives, leaf/leaves, life/lives, loaf/loaves, self/selves, shelf/shelves, thief/thieves, wife/wives, wolf/wolves*. However, most nouns ending in /-f/ take plural /-fs/: *beliefs, chiefs, cliffs, coughs, cuffs, flagstaffs, laughs, paragraphs, roofs, sniffs*. There is vacillation in: *dwarfs/dwarves, hoofs/hooves, scarfs/scarves, wharf/wharves*. Note the difference between *staffs* (= groups of people working together) and *staves* (= sticks, rods). Note also the painting term *still lifes*.

10.4.2. Irregular plurals

By far the majority of English nouns follow the reasonably regular pattern of pluralization described in section 10.4.1 above. However, there are a number of important exceptions:

(i) Vowel change. This form of pluralization is found in the following nouns: *man/men, woman/women, foot/feet, goose/geese, louse/lice, mouse/mice, tooth/teeth*. Correspondingly, we find a vowel change in compounds containing these nouns (e.g. *dormouse/dormice, gentleman/gentlemen, chairwoman/chairwomen*). Note that there is normally no difference in pronunciation in compounds containing *-man*: both the singular and the plural is pronounced [mən]. Words containing *-man* which are not compounds take the regular plural: *Normans, Germans*.

(ii) *-en/-ren* plural. Only three nouns take the *-en/-ren* plural ending, two of them with additional vowel change: *child/children, ox/oxen* and *brother/brethren* (used only about the members of a religious community; *brothers* is the normal plural of *brother*).

(iii) /-s/ (-ce) after voiced sound. This plural ending is found in two words: *dice* (the corresponding singular *die* is used only in standard phrases like *The die is cast*) and *pence* (used about amounts and 'small change', in contrast to *pennies*, which is used about the individual coins).

(iv) Foreign plurals. Many nouns of foreign, especially Latin or Greek, origin take foreign plural forms rather than the regular English plural form, though in many cases there is vacillation with the regular form as the less formal. Here are some of the most common examples:

- *-us* → *-i* (/aɪ/) or *-a* (/ə/):

alumnus/alumni, stimulus/stimuli; cactus/cacti or *cactuses, octopus/octopi* or *octopuses*. Note regular examples like: *campus/campuses, genius/geniuses, virus/viruses*. *Corpus* and *genus* take the irregular plural form *corpora* and *genera* in formal, technical language.

- *-a* → *-ae* (/-iː/):

alumna/alumnae, larva/larvae, vertebra/vertebrae. Note regular examples like: *area/areas, villa/villas*. There is vacillation in *antenna/antennae* (of insects) or *antennas* (= aerials), *formula/formulae* (mathematical formulae) or *formulas* (more generally).

- *-um* → *-a* (/ə/):

addendum/addenda, bacterium/bacteria, erratum/errata and others. Note regular *album/albums, museum/museums, asylum/asylums*. Vacillation: *aquarium/aquariums* or *aquaria, symposium/symposiums* or *symposia*. Note that the plural form of *datum* is, strictly speaking, *data*, but *data* is increasingly used as a singular mass noun instead of *datum*, especially in scientific language, and especially about 'a collection of facts, examples, etc.'

- *-ex* or *-ix* → *-ices*:

codex/codices, index/indices (in science) or *indexes* (more generally), *appendix/appendices* (in books) or *appendixes* (in anatomy), *matrix/matrices* or *matrixes*.

- *-is* → *es* (/-iːz/):

analysis/analyses, axis/axes, basis/bases (the plural spelling thus coinciding with the spelling of *base/bases*), *crisis/crises, diagnosis/diagnoses, hypothesis/hypotheses*, etc. The regular English plural is rare: *metropolis/ metropolises*.

- *-on* → *-a* (/ə/):

criterion/criteria, phenomenon/phenomena but *demon/demons, electron/ electrons*, etc.

- Others:

portmanteau/portmanteaus or *portmanteaux, bureau/bureaus* or *bureaux, corps* (/kɔː/)/*corps* (/kɔːz/).

(v) Identity of form. With certain count nouns there is no formal difference between the singular and the plural. This applies to:

- some animal names (*deer, grouse, plaice, salmon, sheep, snipe, trout*); others vacillate (*buffalo(es), antelope(s)*);

- nationality names in *-ese* (*Chinese, Japanese, Portuguese*) and *Swiss*;

- *craft* (= 'boat') and compounds containing *-craft* (*aircraft, spacecraft*); *counsel*; *offspring*;

- the following special nouns denoting number, weight or measure: *head* (as in *five head of cattle*), *brace, yoke, gross, horsepower, hundredweight, stone*).

There is also no formal distinction between the singular and the plural of the following nouns ending in *-s*: *barracks, gallows, headquarters, innings, means* (= 'method(s)'), *series, species, works* (and compounds containing *-works*: *gasworks, waterworks*). When *means* means 'money' it is always plural. Unlike the nouns mentioned under a) to d), these *-s* nouns may be used as plurals (e.g. with respect to concord) even if they refer to a single entity (van Ek and Robat 1984: 101): *Our old headquarters were abandoned*.

.4.3. Number-invariable nouns

Some nouns are invariably either singular or plural, or at least restricted with respect to the singular/plural contrast. For example, as we have seen, mass nouns (like *remorse* and *mud*) are singular (unless they express 'instances' or 'kinds of' as in e.g. *kindnesses* and *wines*). The same applies to situation-referring *-ing* forms: cf. *Their dancing on the table is unlikely to please him* vs. *His writings have caused quite a scandal*. Names are either singular (such as *John, Denmark, the University of Sussex*) or, less often, plural (such as *the Hebrides, the Alps, General Motors*), but they are usually invariable with respect to quantification (for the use of proper nouns for class-member reference in examples like *the two Peters*, see sections 10.2.4 and 10.3.5). Let us look a some more specific cases involving number-invariable nouns:

(i) Nouns with 'plural form' used as singular nouns. Several kinds of noun ending in *-s* fall under this heading:

• Nouns ending in *-ics* denoting a science or a subject: *acoustics, athletics, mathematics* (also *maths*), *linguistics, pragmatics*, etc. (e.g. *Pragmatics is a fascinating new subbranch of linguistics*). Note that *politics* may be treated as a plural noun if it denotes an individual's views (*His politics were becoming an embarrassment to the government*). Similarly, *statistics* can be used more loosely about 'figures', in which case it contrasts with singular *statistic*.

• Nouns ending in *-s* denoting diseases are usually used as singular nouns: *mumps, shingles, rickets, measles*.

• Nouns ending in *-s* denoting games: *billiards, cards, darts, dominoes*, etc.

• *News* is always singular: *No news is good news, This news is very depressing*. The same applies to *shambles*: *The house is in a shambles*.

(ii) nouns with 'singular form' used as plural nouns. Under this heading we find aggregate nouns (i.e. nouns referring to composite entities) like *cattle, clergy, police, poultry, vermin, people, crew, staff*. These nouns behave differently with respect to quantification:

• *Cattle* is compatible with large and/or imprecise numbers: *There were fifty/some cattle in the field, He bought hundreds of/1,000 cattle* (but *?I saw three cattle* is unusual).

• *Clergy* and *police* accept precise quantification even in small numbers: *There were three clergy and 12 police present at the meeting*.

• *Poultry* and *vermin* do not usually allow of precise quantification: *a lot of poultry/vermin; *seven /*a hundred poultry/vermin*.

- *People*, *crew* and *staff* are 'internally countable' like *police*: *ten/several people/crew/staff*. Unlike *police*, however, they can be used as singular nouns with regular plural forms: e.g. *The Danes are a tough people/There are several English-speaking peoples*.

(iii) nouns with 'plural form' used as plural nouns. We here include the following:

- The so-called binary nouns (nouns referring to entities which consist of two equal parts, usually instruments or articles of dress): *binoculars, glasses, forceps, scissors, pliers, pincers, scales; jeans, pants, trousers, slacks, tights*. To indicate a number distinction, we here have to use partitive constructions like *a pair of/several pairs of glasses/scissors/ jeans/* etc.

- A number of nouns which regularly occur in the plural form with a meaning that has no obvious counterpart in the singular: *airs* (as in *to put on airs*), *brains* (*He has got brains*), *contents* (= that which is contained, as in *table of contents*), *colours* (as in e.g. *to join the colours*), *customs* (= import duties), *fireworks, funds, goods, greens, looks* (as in *his good looks*), *media, oats, odds, outskirts, pains* (= 'care', as in *to take pains*), *premises* (= building, location), *remains, riches, savings, spirits* (= strong liquour), *stairs, surroundings, thanks, wages*. Some of these are found in the singular but then usually with a different meaning: e.g. *content* (= 'that which is written or spoken', or about 'proportion', as in *the silver content of this spoon*), *custom* (= habit), *pain* (= physical suffering), *premise* (= hypothesis, part of a formal argument), *spirit* (= mind, soul); these singular nouns have regular plural forms which preserve the meaning of the singular form.

Obviously related to this last group are the so-called 'intensive plurals', i.e. plurals with a distinct meaning which is, however, related to the concept of the corresponding singular mass or count noun: *apologies* (as in *She sent her apologies*), *fears* (*She felt grave fears for him*), *gardens* (e.g. *the botanical gardens*), *orders* (*She was under orders to kill her boss*), *regrets* (e.g. *He expressed his regrets*), *sands* (area of sand), *skies* (*the sunny skies of Italy*), *waters* (*the waters of the lake, the stormy waters of the Atlantic*), etc.

10.4.4. Collective nouns

As pointed out in section 7.6.4, collective nouns are count nouns which in BrE may serve, in unchanged form, as either singular or plural depending on the speaker's view of the referent as either a unit (singular association) or a collection of individuals or individual entities making up a unit (plural association): *audience, board, committee, council, family, flock, government, party, team*, etc.:

(1)   My family disagree about almost everything.

(2)   My family disagrees with her family about almost everything.

(3)   The audience was definitely hostile. (cf. van Ek & Robat 1984: 108)

(4)   The audience were running to the emergency exits. (cf. van Ek & Robat 1984: 108)

Unlike aggregate nouns like *people, crew* and *staff* (see section 10.4.3), collective nouns are not 'internally countable': we cannot say **There were three family and four committee present at the meeting.* On the other hand, like *people, crew* and *staff,* singular collective nouns may be pluralized to denote more than one unit: *families, governments,* etc.

10.4.5. What is pluralized?

Usually there is no problem in identifying the relevant unit to pluralize in a noun group: it is, of course, the head noun. Thus we say e.g. *the two <u>chaps</u> from London,* not *the two <u>chap from Londons</u>.* In other words, there is normally no such thing as 'group plurals' (cf. our discussion of the group genitive in section 10.3.8). In compound units with nouns as conjoints, each noun is normally pluralized if plural meaning is intended: e.g. *knives and forks.*

With compounds and noun + noun combinations, the plural suffix is usually added to the last element if it is a noun: *headmasters, toothpicks, city halls, state universities,* etc. Even if the final element is not a noun, we pluralize the last element if the compound is felt to be a regular unit: *bucketfuls, breakdowns, stowaways, knock-outs, break-ins.*

The first element of a hyphenated compound is pluralized in the following cases:

(i) Noun + preposition + noun combinations: *fathers-in-law, men-of-war, commanders-in-chief,* etc.

(ii) Noun + adverb combinations if the noun expresses the agent: *lookers-on, passers-by, runners-up.* Note, however, also *goings-on.*

(iii) Noun + adjective combinations: *postmasters-general, poets-laureate,* etc. but there is often vacillation: *courts-martial/court-martials, attorneys-general/attorney-generals.*

Both elements in noun + noun combinations are pluralized in the following cases:

(i) Compounds where the first noun is *woman* or *man* (also *gentleman*) denoting the sex of the referent: *men-servants, women doctors, gentlemen thieves* (such examples contrast with *man-eaters, woman-haters,* etc.).

(ii) Certain formal titles: *Knights Templars, Lords Chancellors, Lords Justices*.

There is vacillation in combinations consisting of title + name (cf. Schibsbye 1970: 99): *the two Miss Smiths / the two Misses Smith*, the latter being the more formal variant.

10.4.6. The uses of the singular and the plural

The number category is primarily used to make a distinction between 'one' and 'more than one' with regard to the referent(s) of count nouns (or nouns used as count nouns). However, as we have already seen, matters are considerably more complex (see especially section 10.4.3). In this section we shall briefly mention a number of specific rules for the use of the singular and the plural, which do not follow automatically from any general characterization of the number distinction.

(i) The distributive plural. The distributive plural is common in constructions consisting of two or more premodifying adjectives and a head noun where the adjectives refer to separate entities, the head noun being often pluralized even if each adjective relates to a single entity only: *the sixteenth and seventeenth centuries, the English and French nations, the third and fourth chapters*, etc. (cf. Jespersen 1933: 204). The singular is sometimes used to avoid ambiguity, cf. *in this and the following chapter* vs. *in this and the following chapters*.

The distributive plural is also found in constructions consisting of head noun + *of* + compound unit, as in *the reigns of Elizabeth and James, the ages of 14 and 18*. Similarly in reciprocal expressions, especially with verbs like CHANGE, SWAP, etc.: *They changed seats, He changed trains at Reading, The two women swapped husbands, They shook hands*. For discussion of individualizing expressions like *Bob and John took their hats off* (i.e. 'each his own hat'), *They ought to be having their bottoms kicked and their noses tweaked* (Schibsbye 1970: 107), see section 7.6 on concord.

(ii) Noun groups as modifiers. When noun groups function as modifiers or as parts of modifiers, the head noun is singular even if it would have been plural in the corresponding independent noun group; compare: *three pieces / three-piece suits; four courses / a four-course dinner, eight hours / the eight-hour day; ten years / a ten-year-old boy; six feet / a six foot tall boy*, etc. There is occasionally vacillation with single nouns serving as modifiers or first elements of compounds (Schibsbye 1970: 106): *a wage(s) agreement, trouser(s) pocket*. The plural is used when it has a distinct meaning (cf.

section 10.4.3) and thus serves to avoid misunderstanding: *a customs officer, a goods train*.

(iii) Number and weight. The numbers *dozen, score, hundred, thousand, million* and *billion* are not pluralized when they are (part of) dependents or when, as heads, they are preceded by definite numerals (cardinal numbers):

(1)   two hundred bikes / *two hundreds bikes (but *hundreds of bikes / *two hundreds of bikes*)

(2)   a few thousand cars / *a few thousands cars (but *several thousands of cars / *four thousands of cars*)

(3)   How many bikes were there? – About two hundred / *two hundreds

(4)   Can you count to four thousand / *four thousands?

Foot and *pound* remain singular when followed by a numeral: *four foot two, five pound fifty*. Both the singular and the plural of *ton* is found when it serves as the head of the group: *two ton(s) of flour*.

(iv) Collectivizing. Many animal names have both singular and plural forms (e.g. *lion/lions, elephant/elephants, duck/ducks*, etc. When regarded as food or as prey, the singular is used with a collectivizing effect (Huddleston 1984: 240; van Ek & Robat 1984: 101f); compare: *They have shot several lion / We saw several lions in the park*; *We bagged three elephant that day / Three elephants came running towards us*.

11. Pronominals

Like nominals, pronominals (i.e. pronouns or pronoun ⸻
to express the participants involved in situations. ⸻
constituents serve this communicative function by mean⸻ ⸻rong lexical
element (the noun) categorizing some entity, pronominal constituents do it
without specific categorization, either deictically by determining the referent
directly in relation to the communicative situation (e.g. *I* and *you*, which
represent the speaker and hearer of the utterance, respectively) or more
indirectly by representing referents already established by nominals in the
linguistic context (e.g. *When Roger finally got hold of Rebecca, <u>he</u> did not
even tell <u>her</u> about the deal*). In addition, as we saw in section 10.3.1,
pronominals often serve as determiners (as in e.g. <u>*her*</u> *wish*). In this chapter
we examine the various types of pronominal with a view to establishing their
functional domain more precisely.

11.1. Preliminaries

11.1.1. Definition of the pronoun group

As will be recalled, a pronoun group is defined as a group with a pronoun as
head (cf. section 3.3.1). Examples:

(1)   This must be *someone* new.

(2)   *Which of them* called out?

Pronoun groups are relatively rare. One reason for this is that pronouns do
not specifically categorize referents but instead single them out directly in
the communicative context (i.e. deictically) or more indirectly in the
linguistic context (textually). In the latter case, they easily represent whole
noun groups (not just nouns, as the term 'pronoun' may lead one to believe),
and therefore do not often require group status themselves:

(3)   *My little sister* thinks *she* is the boss around here.

(4)   *The old gentleman staying in the room at the end of the corridor* hardly
         recognized *himself* in the mirror.

In these examples, *she* does not simply represent the head noun *sister* but the
whole subject group *My little sister*, and *himself* represents not only the head
noun *gentleman* but the whole subject group *The old gentleman staying in
the room at the end of the corridor*.

The main emphasis of this chapter is therefore on single pronouns.

Classification of pronouns

here are several distinct types of pronoun:

personal:	*I/me, you, he/him, she/her, it, we/us, they/them*;
possessive:	*my/mine, your/yours, his, her/hers, its, our/ours, their/theirs*;
reflexive:	*myself, yourself, himself, herself, itself, ourselves, themselves*;
demonstrative:	*this/these, that/those*;
interrogative:	*who/whom, which, what; whoever, whichever, whatever; where, when, how, why*;
relative:	*who/whom, which, what, that, Ø; whoever, whichever, whatever; where, when, why*;
indefinite:	*any/anybody/anyone/anything* *every/everybody/everyone/everything* *no/nobody/no one/none/nothing* *some/somebody/someone/something* *all, each, both, either/neither, one/ones, other(s)*.

Pronouns always have determinative force: definite (personal, possessive, reflexive, demonstrative), interrogative, relative or indefinite (cf. section 10.3.1).

Personal, possessive and reflexive pronouns are sometimes grouped together as 'central pronouns': they are special in showing person distinctions and in being formally related (e.g. possessive pronouns can be regarded as an inflectional case variant – the genitive – of personal pronouns).

Interrogative and relative *where*, *when* and *why*, and interrogative *how*, are traditionally classified as adverbs rather than pro*nouns*. However, as the term 'pronoun' is often used more generally about pro-forms, it seems reasonable to include them in this chapter. As pro-forms they typically represent preposition groups (e.g. 'at what place', 'for what reason', etc.).

Even on a strict delimitation of the class of pronouns, it would not be easy to define pronouns rigidly. A number of items seem to serve pronoun-like functions. Among them are quantifiers like *much, many, more, most, little, less, least, few, several, half, enough, other(s)* and *another*, ordinals (e.g. *first, second*, etc.), cardinals (e.g. *two, three*, etc.), *so, such, same,* demonstrative expressions like *the former* and *the latter*, the adverbial pro-forms *here, there, now* and *then* and the provisional subject *there*, which may all be used representatively like pronouns:

(1)   *Many* regard him as a genius.

(2)   The *two* never returned.

(3)   *Such* was her beauty that I was speechless, and *so* was my brother.

(4)   *There* were many students in the hall.

In these examples the representative function of the italicized constituents is fairly obvious (for example, in (1) *Many* represents e.g. 'many people'). But are they pronouns?

A possible way of distinguishing genuine pronouns from members of other word classes is to see if, as group heads, their determinative force is such that they are incompatible with the definite and indefinite article. According to this criterion, *Such* and *so* in (3) are pronominal while *two* in (2) is not. More generally, this criterion allows us to exclude ordinals, cardinals and adjectives used nominally (as in *the rich, the unthinkable*, etc., see section 12.4). Unfortunately, however, some items traditionally treated as pronouns are also excluded: *one* and *others* (cf. *She gave me a new one, The others may refuse*). *Few, many, more, most* and *less* are borderline cases: though they do not generally accept the definite or indefinite article, there are exceptions, such as the idiomatic or fixed expressions *the chosen few, a good many, the more the better, I like her the most*, etc. Note also the distinction between *few/little* and *a few/a little* (cf. section 7.5.5). *Many* and *few* only accept the definite article regularly if restrictively postmodified, as in *The many who wanted to leave* and *the few who are likely to support you*.

We conclude that it is difficult to delimit the class of pronouns rigidly from other word classes.

11.1.3. The external relations of pronominals

Initially it is convenient to distinguish two main syntactic uses of pronouns: *autonomous* and *determinative*. Some pronouns only have autonomous use (e.g. *he, somebody, there, who, it*, as in *He* called *somebody*). A few only have determinative use (*my, your, their, no*, as in *Their* boss paid *no* attention to *my* efforts). Many have both uses (e.g. *his, her, which, what, some, any, either*, as in *Some* like it hot vs. *Some* guys like it hot). Pronominal constituents may serve the following autonomous, external functions:

S	*We* tried eating out on the little balcony.
Sp	*There* was nothing we could do about it now.
Od	Jack shot *himself*.
Oi	*Whoever* did you give that book?
Op	I take *it* that you are going to resign.
Cs	Jane is *someone I regard very highly*.

Co	You can call me *that* again!
A	*Where* did you hide the doll?

In addition they may function autonomously as conjoints and as prepositional complements:

CJT	It was a row between *me* and *someone you don't know*.
DEP	The scheme was proposed by *those working in our department*.

In the following example, an autonomous pronoun group *somebody else* is down-ranked to determinative status by means of the genitive marker *'s*:

DEP	I borrowed *somebody else's* book.

Determinative use of pronominals is typically found in noun groups:

(1)   [*Her* smiles] lasted just a fraction of a second too long. (noun group)

(2)   [*No* teacher] likes [*all his* students]. (noun groups)

Occasionally pronouns serve as modifiers:

(3)   It cannot be [*that* bad]. (adjective group)

(4)   [He *himself*] cannot speak a word of French. (pronoun group)

The determinative function of pronouns exemplified by *Her smiles*, *No teacher* and *all his students* is of central importance to our understanding of the functional domain of pronouns, as we shall see in the next section.

11.1.4. The functional domain of pronominals

Superficially, pronominals seem to serve two main communicative functions: specification (as in e.g. *his decision*, *this mess*, *every step*, *what church*, etc.) and representation of 'things' (e.g. *they*, *mine*, *herself*, *who*, *whatever*, *everybody*, *none* in examples like *They ignored mine*, *She hated herself*, etc.). These two communicative functions are closely related to the determinative and autonomous uses mentioned in section 11.1.3 above and thus syntactically distinct. However, if we examine the two communicative functions more closely we find that they are inextricably related.

To see this, it is useful to recall the discussion of the functional domain of nominals in section 10.1.4. There the functional properties of nominals were described in terms of the subfunctions determination, modification, quantification, categorization, etc. For example, in a noun group like *the many poor artists*, the definite article *the* is a determiner, *many* is a quantifier, *poor* is a modifier and *artists* is a categorizer and the bearer of the properties expressed by the other subfunctions. The four subfunctions jointly establish the referent of the expression.

Significantly, English provides ways of referring to entities where one or more of the potential subfunctions is not employed, because it is either irrelevant or can be taken for granted. Thus, obviously, we can often leave out modification (e.g. *the many artists* without the adjective *poor*). Less obviously perhaps, we can leave out the type of constituent typically serving as a categorizer and focus primarily on modification: this is what we see in the nominal use of adjectives (e.g. *the poor* = 'poor people', *the inevitable* = 'that which is inevitable'). The modifiers *poor* and *inevitable* are here used as generic categorizers. To achieve more specific reference in expressions with focus on modification we can use ONE as a substitute for the head noun (as long as the referent is countable): *the poor one/ones*. The interpretation of *one* or *ones* is here dependent on e.g. the preceding linguistic context. We can also focus on quantification alone, as in e.g. <u>*Many*</u> *seem to cope with things after all*. Here, too, the expression relies heavily on the context for the correct interpretation of the referent.

Last, but not least important, we can focus primarily on determination, as in e.g. <u>*They*</u> *seem to cope with things after all*. The pronoun *They* may here represent a full noun group like *The many poor artists*. The difference between the two expressions is that while the full noun group establishes the referent by means of explicit categorization, modification, quantification and determination, the pronoun simply does so by means of determination and leaves categorization, modification and, to some extent, quantification implicit. *They* can be said to represent e.g. *The many poor artists*, but of the subfunctions involved in this noun group, *They* simply expresses definiteness (and general quantification by being a plural pronoun). It is important to note that the definite meaning of *They* is not a representationally derived value, but a value inherent in the pronoun. This becomes clear when we consider examples like the following:

(1)   An old woman and a young man entered the building just before noon. *They* were never seen again.

Here *They* is definite despite the fact that the antecedent *An old woman and a young man* is indefinite.

Similarly, the difference between expressions like *Look at this mess!* and *Look at this!* concerns the explicit categorization of the referent. In both cases we have definite determination.

The picture that emerges is that the speaker may rely on general context or on information already expressed explicitly and accordingly leave out subfunctions in a referring expression. In the case of pronouns, they are used with determinative function not only when they serve as actual determiners (as in *Look at this mess!*) but also when they serve a representational purpose more directly (as in *Look at this!*).

It is not surprising, therefore, that the notions of reference and referent (cf. section 10.3.4) are relevant in any discussion of pronouns. Consider e.g.:

(2)   I didn't know half the people *who* were there.

(3)   Not having a key to our new home in Mount Street, I had to knock at the door. Fiona opened *it*.

(4)   Before anyone could stop *her*, Zelda yelled out.

(5)   'Look at *this*!' [uttered by someone pointing at the mess in the kitchen]

(2) and (3) are examples of direct non-repetitive anaphoric textual reference: the antecedent of *who* is *people* and the antecedent of *it* is *door*. While there is intrasentential reference in (2) there is extrasentential reference in (3). In (4), *her* allows of an interpretation in terms of non-repetitive cataphoric textual (more specifically intrasentential) reference to *Zelda*. Finally, in (5) we have non-textual deictic reference to a specific referent (the mess).

11.2. Central pronouns

11.2.1. Personal pronouns

The table below offers an overview of personal pronouns and the categories which apply to them:

NUMBER	PERSON	GENDER	CASE	
			subjective	objective
singular	1	-	*I*	*me*
	2	-	*you*	*you*
	3	masculine	*he*	*him*
		feminine	*she*	*her*
		neuter	*it*	*it*
plural	1	-	*we*	*us*
	2	-	*you*	*you*
	3	-	*they*	*them*

Four categories are relevant to the discussion of personal pronouns: number, person, gender and case. The first three of these also apply to the derivatives of personal pronouns: possessive and reflexive pronouns.

A) Number. As with nominals, the pronominal number category comprises the members *singular* and *plural*. But while the number category is largely regular in connection with nouns, plural nouns being morphologically derived from singular nouns (e.g. *car/cars*), singular and plural personal pronouns are formally unrelated (except, of course, for the second-person pronoun *you*, which is both singular and plural). There is also an important semantic difference between the nominal and pronominal number category: while e.g. the plural noun *cars* is the plural of the singular noun *car* in the sense that it simply denotes a plurality of entities denoted by the singular form, the plural central pronouns do not necessarily denote a plurality of entities denoted by the singular pronouns. Thus, for example, *we* is not in any obvious sense the plural of *I* (the pronoun denoting the speaker of the utterance): the plural pronoun does not normally denote a plurality of 'speakers' of the utterance (though in principle it may, e.g. in chants or petitions involving several individuals). Rather, *we* typically includes the speaker plus others associated with the speaker (potentially including the hearer(s)). In passing we may also note that in formal language *we* is sometimes used authoritatively about a singular speaker (e.g. the 'royal *we*', as in *We are not amused* for 'I am not amused', spoken by e.g. the Queen; or the 'editorial *we*', as in *We therefore propose* ... for 'I therefore propose ...', used by e.g. an author or public speaker).

Singular *you* represents the hearer: here an ordinary plural interpretation is more normal. Plural *you* may represent a plurality of hearers. But it may also represent a single hearer (or a number of hearers) *plus* others associated with the hearer(s).

The third-person plural *they* differs from the third-person singular pronouns in being gender-neutral: *they* may refer to a plurality of persons or things, and if it refers to persons it may refer to male groups, female groups or mixed groups. Increasingly, *they* and its derivatives are also used as gender-neutral terms referring anaphorically to a singular concept, as in *Everybody took their children along* (see subsection C on gender below).

The pronominal number category affects subject-predicator concord, but this topic is best dealt with in connection with the person category, to which we now turn.

B) Person. In conjunction with the number category, the person category has formal repercussions for subject-predicator concord. In connection with BE (cf. section 7.6.2), each person is associated with a distinct form in the present tense: first person *am*, second person *are* (which is also used with all three plural pronouns), third person *is*. In the past tense, the first- and third-person singular pronouns take *was* while the others take *were*. With other verbs, person is marked only in the present tense, and only in the third person singular (e.g. *takes* vs. *take*). Referentially, the person category is a deictic category, the first person being defined in terms of the speaker of the expression (*I* referring to the speaker and *we* referring to the speaker plus others), the second person in terms of the hearer (either the hearer alone or the hearer plus others associated with him or her), and the third person in terms of referents not directly involved in the communicative act. Note the occasional use of *we* about the *hearer*, basically as an expression of solidarity but often with a humourous, ironic or condescending effect:

(1)   Good morning, Alma, how are *we* today?

(2)   What's this? Are *we* wearing an expensive new shirt this morning?

As we shall see in the paragraph below on the referential properties of personal pronouns, there are other extensions of the basic person system.

C) Gender. The gender category applies to the third-person singular personal pronouns only (plus derived possessive and reflexive forms). The basic system is as follows: masculine *he* is used for human males, feminine *she* for human females, and neuter (or non-personal) *it* elsewhere; there is no common gender term.

This basic system has a number of extensions. As noted in section 10.2.2, pronominal gender terms are not simply a question of objective sex distinctions but often reflect the speaker's attitude towards the referent: *he* and *she* may thus be used about animals (e.g. domestic animals, as in *He always barked fiercely at strangers*), and especially *she* is used about other objects of human affection or concern (ships, cars, countries, etc., as in *She's a fine ship*). More generally we can say that *he* and *she* are used stylistically as a means of personification (as in e.g. *History has revised her verdict*). Conversely, the neuter term *it* is occasionally used about a baby (typically as a marker of dissociation, e.g. *It kept screaming all night*). Note in this connection the use of *it* vs. *he* or *she* in examples like the following:

(3)   Someone opened the door and entered. *It/*She* was my mother.

(4)   Jack was standing at the top of the stairs. *He/*It* must be the captain.

While *it* is used in presentations of identity (as in the first example), *he* and *she* (and plural *they*) are used in sentences providing further information. Sometimes both expressions are possible with merely a stylistic difference:

(5)   We had invited our new neighbour for dinner. He/It was a young man with sporty looks.

The traditional use of *he* (and *him* as well as the derived possessive pronoun *his* and reflexive pronoun *himself*) as an unmarked, neutral common gender term when the sex of the referent is unknown, irrelevant or meant to include both sexes, is still not uncommon although, increasingly, there is a tendency to avoid the sexist bias, compare:

(6)   The reader who works *his* way through this exposition will be rewarded.
(7)   Practically everybody in the place had fallen into the habit nowadays of looking cautiously over *his or her* shoulder before *he or she* spoke.

As the second example shows, there is no simple solution to the problem: compound units like *he or she* and *his or her* are not only cumbersome but, alas, give linear priority to the male term. The third person plural pronoun *they* (plus derived forms) is increasingly used as a common gender pro-form for singular referents, especially when the antecedent is an indefinite pronoun:

(8)   Everybody/Somebody/Nobody cheered when *they* heard the news.

These indefinite pronouns are grammatically singular (cf. e.g. *Everybody calls me Jack*) but have plural associations, thus inviting representation by a plural pronoun. That this usage is not always possible or considered entirely appropriate is shown by the following examples:

(9)   ?Somebody just put *their* head round the door.
(10)   If someone thinks *he or she* hasn't got love-making completely mastered, then *he or she* is likely to try harder, isn't *he or she*?
(11)   'And almost one in two has a homosexual experience of a genital order at some time in *their* lives.' 'In *his* life,' Adam said. 'Even in the face of the unbelievable we can still try and be grammatical.'

D) Case. In English, case – apart from the genitive – applies only to pronouns. Within the class of central pronouns the basic case system is as follows: there are three cases, the subjective – traditionally referred to as the 'nominative' – the objective – traditionally referred to as the 'accusative' – and the possessive – traditionally referred to as the 'genitive'. Possessive pronouns will be treated separately in section 11.2.2. The two cases recognized in connection with the class of personal pronouns, the subjective and the objective, are assigned on a syntactic basis. Generally, the subjective form is used only when the pronoun functions as the subject of *finite* predicators, the objective form elsewhere (e.g. as direct object or as subject of nonfinite predicators), e.g.:

(12)   *She* had chosen Wednesday for their flight.
(13)   I want *him* to leave now.
(14)   Macon hadn't seen *her* since his son was born.

Note, however, that the subjective form is also used in the normal subject position in examples like *He was hard to beat*, which may be analysed in terms of a discontinuous subject clause (*he ...to beat* 'to beat him') with *he* as the direct object of the infinitive *to beat*. Note also the special use of the subjective form of pronominal subjects in absolute clauses (cf. section 8.8): e.g. *She moved forward, he remaining behind*.

As subject complement, the subjective case does occur but is generally felt to be (humourously) hypercorrect unless it is the antecedent of a following relative clause in which the relative pronoun serves as the subject of a finite predicator, compare:

(15a)   'Who's there?' he called out. 'It is *I*,' she whispered.

(15b)   'Who's there?' he called out. 'It is *me*,' she whispered.

(16)   Actually it is *she* who rings him.

Compound units pose special problems. A pronoun realizing a conjoint in a subject compound unit is often found in the objective case in very informal, spoken language, especially if it realizes the first conjoint:

(17)   'Meet us at noon tomorrow and *me* and my fat friend will take you to see whatever you want to see.'

Conversely there is a tendency to use *I* as the last conjoint (especially in *you and I*) irrespective of the function of the compound unit – no doubt as a result of hypercorrection (cf. Greenbaum & Quirk 1990: 112):

(18)   Between you and I, there was some cheating.

Sometimes, if subject function is implied, the subjective case is found even outside subject position, especially after the prepositions *except* and *but*:

(19)   No one but *he/him* laughed. (subject position)

(20)   No one laughed but/except *he/him*. (outside subject position)

(21)   Actually it is she who rings him, not *I*. (outside subject position)

After *as* and *than* there is also vacillation:

(22)   Lena is much richer than *I/me*.

The objective case is here the unmarked choice, the subjective case being slightly formal or affected. Alternatively the speaker may add an operator, thus explicitly making *as* or *than* a conjunction rather than a preposition:

(23)   Lena is much richer than *I am*.

This construction may be chosen to avoid ambiguity, compare:

(24)   I hate her more than *him*. (... *than I hate him* or *than he hates her?*)

(25)   I hate her more than *he does*. (... *than he hates her*)

Note finally that when postmodified by an elaborative nominal (cf. section 10.1.3), the objective form *us* is an informal alternative to the subjective form *we*:

(26)   'You know what *us* field agents are like,' I said.

E) Syntax. As light-weight constituents, personal pronominal subjects are not usually separated from the predicator by heavy adverbials (see also section 5.5.8):

(27)   Bob *a few minutes later* left the building.
(28)   *He *a few minutes later* left the building.
(29)   He left the building *a few minutes later*.

While nominals may precede or follow the adverb in a phrasal verb construction, unstressed pronouns always precede the adverb (cf. *I called him up / *I called up him*). There are also restrictions on pronouns in connection with full inversion (cf. sections 5.3.5-9), cf.:

(30)   'This is an outrage,' said John / *said he.
(31)   At his side sat a black Alsatian dog / *sat it.

And, as pointed out in section 3.2.6, while nominal indirect objects always precede nominal direct objects, pronominal indirect objects may occasionally follow pronominal direct objects in BrE (e.g. *I gave it them*).

In compound units, the first person is in polite language realized as the last conjoint and the second person as the first conjoint: *he and I, you and me, you and he*, etc. In the third person singular the masculine precedes the feminine: *he or she* rather than *she or he* – the obvious sexual bias of this ordering is normally present also in nominal compounds: *husband and wife / men and women / boys and girls / Adam and Eve* (but *Ladies and gentlemen*). If nominals and third person pronominals are conjoined, the principle of end-weight (within the compound unit) generally determines the order, compare:

(32)   *He and Rose* disappeared / *Rose and he* disappeared.
(33)   *She and an old friend of mine* were elected.
(34)   *Jack and she who was on the phone just before* had a brief affair last year.

Personal pronouns only take pre-head dependents in expressions like *Poor him, Clever you*, etc. and when used as nouns in examples like:

(35)   Is it *a he* or *a she*? (i.e. 'a male or female')
(36)   I didn't sell my virginity for a sable coat. I've just been me. On the other hand, *that me* isn't settled.

However, they do take a broad range of post-head dependents (other pronouns, elaborative nominals, preposition groups, relative clauses):

(37)   You *yourself* must have realized what was going on.

(38)   We *professors* must make a stand.

(39)   We *in the English Department* cannot support further cuts.

(40)   He *who stayed the longest* fell in love with my wife.

But there are many restrictions: **They professors must make a stand / *He professor must make a stand / *They who fought in the war oppose the motion.*

F) Reference. Generally first and second person singular and plural pronouns (*I, we, you* plus derivatives) have non-textual deictic reference to the participants of a communicative situation and others associated with them. Thus, as mentioned in our discussion of the person and number categories above, *I* refers to the speaker, not to another constituent in the linguistic context. *We* refers to the speaker plus others and *you* refers to the hearer or to the hearer plus others (strictly speaking, therefore, the term 'pronoun' is especially inappropriate for these pronouns). A possible exception to first and second pronominals being purely non-textual deictic referring expressions is found in cases where *we* and *you* have anaphoric reference to compound units with first and/or second person pronouns as conjoints:

(41)   {You and I} know what's best, don't *we*.

(42)   {You and Jack} will write to me, won't *you*.

By contrast, third person singular and plural pronouns (*he, she, it, they* plus derivatives) generally have textual anaphoric reference, as in:

(43)   'You heard what {Fiona} was saying. *She* was in East Berlin long enough to develop strong feelings of friendship.'

Occasionally we come across cataphoric textual reference in subordinate adverbial clauses optionally placed in sentence-initial position:

(44)   Before anyone could stop *her*, {Zelda} yelled out.

(45)   Apart from everything else *she*'d done to me, {Gillian} had put me off sex.

Only rarely do we come across third person pronouns with specific non-textual reference:

(46)   'I'm not going with *her*, if that's what you think.' [uttered by a child pointing at a nurse]

The number of people or things embraced by the plural pronouns *we, you* and *they* (plus derivatives) vary from expression to expression (<u>*We*</u> *raised our children in Birmingham* / <u>*We*</u> *Americans cherish our freedom of speech*).

Sometimes they are used in a very general sense, somewhat abstracted from specific referents:

(47)   In the twentieth century *we* have come to take too many things for granted.

(48)   I remember thinking as we stood in the baggage hall, this is a bit like the rest of life. Two of us in a great mass of strangers, and various things to do that *you*'ve got to get right, like follow signs and collect *your* luggage; then *you* get looked over by the customs, and no-one particularly cares who *you* are or what *you*'re doing there so the two of *you* have to keep one another cheerful.

(49)   I have stopped smoking altogether. *You* never know what cigarettes will do to *you* in the long run.

(50)   Somewhere beyond Amiens I had a memory of the car-ferry docks at Calais. First *they* send *you* all round the town and then *you* get processed into a system with thousands of other people.

(51)   Another thing this young chap does. He talks to himself in his room. I've heard him. *They* say these creative people can be a bit potty. But he's got bags of charm.

Despite the generic-like value of the pronouns in these examples of non-textual reference, *we* retains its basic speaker-inclusive meaning while *they* retains its speaker- and hearer-exclusive meaning ('those responsible or in the know'). In examples like (48) to (50), *you* is all-inclusive and not specifically hearer-oriented. In (49), the speaker uses *you* to avoid referring directly and bluntly to him- or herself. A more formal and impersonal alternative to general *you* is *one*:

(52)   *One* never knows what cigarettes will do to *one* in the long run.

Note finally that *he* followed by a restrictive relative clause is sometimes used generically in the sense 'anyone':

(53)   *He* who betrays our country must be punished.

Such expressions are formal and have an old-fashioned ring to them by comparison with e.g. *those who* ...

G) The uses of *it*. In this final paragraph we summarize the uses of *it* noted so far in this grammar (see especially sections 3.2.2 and 3.2.5):

It as provisional subject or object:

(54)   *It* is cruel to let her imagine she is suffering a terrible imitation of her mother.

(55)   I thought *it* unwise to tell my daughter about the affair.

It as a non-referential grammatical prop word, especially in expressions about weather conditions, time and distance:

(56)   Is *it* snowing again?

(57)   *It* was only two o'clock.

(58)   *It*'s a long way to Charlotte Pass.

– and in more or less fixed idiomatic expressions:

(59)   If they hit *it* off together, so be *it*.
(60)   This is *it*!

It in expressions of 'identity to be established':

(61)   Someone was crying. *It* was my wife.
(62)   'Come on, tell me, what is *it*?'

and thus also in cleft sentences:

(63)   *It* was my wife who was crying.

It as a referential pronoun:

(64)   'So what do you think of {my song}?' I asked.
       'I think that *it*'s riddled with nauseating self-pity.' (textual extrasentential, anaphoric reference)

With a collective noun as its antecedent *it* is in competition with *they* (cf. section 7.6.4 [A]).

As a referential pronoun, *it* may have (part of) a preceding sentence or, more vaguely, the condition(s) expressed by the preceding linguistic context as its antecedent:

(65)   Being in love makes you liable to fall in love. People think *it* has to do with sex, that someone is not doing his duty in bed, or her duty in bed, but I think this is not the case. *It* has to do with the heart.

Here *it* is in competition with the demonstrative pronouns *this* and *that*.

After *as* and *than*, non-referential *it* is not used as a subject in examples like:

(66)   I shall act *as seems best*.
(67)   It was a book more rewarding *than at first sight might appear*.

If, however, the clause contains an infinitive lacking its object or complement, the subject is not omitted:

(68)   The translation is as removed from plain prose *as it is possible to be*.
(69)   He got more *than it is possible to get today*.

11.2.2. Possessive pronouns

Possessive pronouns can be regarded as personal pronouns in the genitive case. There are two sets of possessive forms, determinative and autonomous, corresponding to the specifying and the autonomous nominal genitive (cf. section 10.3.8 [A]):

NUMBER	PERSON	GENDER	FUNCTION	
			DET	AUT
singular	1	-	*my*	*mine*
	2	-	*your*	*yours*
	3	masculine	*his*	*his*
		feminine	*her*	*hers*
		neuter	*its*	*(its)*
plural	1	-	*our*	*ours*
	2	-	*your*	*yours*
	3	-	*their*	*theirs*

Here are some examples showing the determinative and autonomous uses of possessive pronouns:

Determinative use:

(1)   He tacked a note on the door of *his* little yellow house.

(2)   Most of the women were fastening *their* corsets.

Autonomous use:

(3)   He learned that there was probably not another stomach like *hers* on earth.

(4)   He'd fucked up his own life, so he stole *mine*.

Except for *mine* and *his*, the autonomous items are formed by adding the suffix *-s* to the determinative form. This suffix should not be confused with the apostrophe *s* (*'s*) suffix used in connection with nominal genitives such as *John's* (thus while *its* in *its colour* is a possessive pronoun, *it's* is the contracted form of *it is*). Note in this connection that *its* is rarely, if ever, used with autonomous function without the emphasizer OWN to give it sufficient weight (cf. Greenbaum & Quirk 1990: 117):

(5)   The cat knows that this dish is *its own*.

A) Possessive pronouns vs. *of*-constructions. Though generally the determinative possessive forms correspond to specifying nominal genitives (both constructions expressing definiteness, as in e.g. *the old man's hat* and *his hat*), determinative possessive pronouns have a wider distribution, covering much of the ground occupied by the *of*-construction as well as the specifying genitive in noun groups. Thus while we would normally have to say *the roof of the house* rather than *the house's roof*, we can only say *its roof*, not *the roof of it*. Even objective relations and relations involving abstract nouns (cf. section 10.3.8 [C.a]) invite expression by possessive pronoun rather than *of*-construction – possibly as a result of the principle of end-weight, cf. *the significance of this idea / its significance; the formulation of the hypothesis / its formulation; the release of the prisoner* or *the prisoner's release / his release*, etc.

The *of*-construction with a personal pronoun in the objective form rather than a construction with a possessive pronoun is often used in connection with:

(i) expressions with little or no possessive meaning: *Let's stop this discussion – I quite frankly don't see the point of it / The kitchen was one big mess and in the middle of it was this young kid getting supper ready.*

(ii) fixed expressions: *the long and short of it / on the face of it / by the look of him / for the life of me / he soon got the knack of it*, etc.;

(iii) pronoun groups ending with a personal pronoun like *all of them / one of us / both of you / either of them*, etc.: *the feelings of either of them* rather than *either of their feelings*, which strictly speaking is ambiguous.

B) Possessive pronouns as post-genitives. Since determinative possessive pronouns are definite determiners like nominal genitives, indefinite reference can only be achieved by means of the post-genitive:

(6)   I met *a friend of his* the other day.

Like nominal post-genitives, pronominal post-genitives typically have partitive meaning (*a friend of his = one of his friends*). Pronominal post-genitives behave like nominal ones with respect to determiner usage (cf. section 10.3.8 [A]). Note in this connection the lack of partitive association in groups with a demonstrative determiner expressing the speaker's (approving or disapproving) interest:

(7)   Stuart married *that boring little goodie-goodie wife of his*.

(8)   No doubt she used some rather choice language about *this hypothesis of hers*.

C) Possessive pronouns vs. the definite article. Since both types of determiner are definite it is not surprising that there is some overlap. Generally the distinction is clear: the definite article signals definiteness only, possessive pronouns signal definiteness plus some relation between two referents involved (for example, *his wife* is not only definite but also expresses a relation between the referents of *wife* and *his*). In expressions referring to parts of the body or clothes associated with someone, possessive pronouns are used rather than the definite article: *He put his hand in his pocket*. The definite article is in such cases used:

(i) in detached, clinically objective expressions such as *How is the chest now?* and the rather unusual *He put the hand in the pocket* (i.e. somebody else's hand in a separate pocket).

(ii) in preposition groups if the 'possessor' is represented as DONE-TO or SPECIFIED elsewhere in the clause:

(9)   I gave [him]$^{DONE-TO}$ a little poke in *the* face with *my* head.

(10)   [Bob]$^{DONE-TO}$ was hit right on *the* nose by Jack.

(11)   [My sister]^{SPECIFIED} has a terrible pain in *the* chest.

But there are exceptions:

(12)   [Oliver]^{SPECIFIED} needed five stitches in *his* cheek.

D) Possessive pronouns vs. personal pronouns. As shown in section 8.3, there is sometimes vacillation between possessive pronouns and the objective form of personal pronouns when followed by a clause:

(13)   It happened without *him/his* realising what was going on.

E) Possessive pronouns emphasized by OWN. Possessive pronouns can be emphasized by OWN, as in the following examples:

(14)   He apologised for going on so much about *his own* life.

This combination of pronoun and OWN can also be used autonomously, even in post-genitive constructions without partitive association. In such cases, however, the determinative form of the pronoun is retained:

(15)   I realized that the husky voice was *my own*.

(16)   She hasn't even got a car of *her own*.

11.2.3. Reflexive pronouns

Below we offer an overview of the reflexive derivatives of personal pronouns in English. In the first and second persons the reflexive pronouns are formed by adding the singular suffix -*self* or the plural suffix -*selves* to the determinative possessive pronoun. In the third person the suffixes are added to the objective form of the personal pronoun.

In addition to the reflexive pronouns listed in the table, *oneself* is used as the counterpart to *one* in its generic sense, cf. examples like *One does not, on the whole, permit oneself to attend formal ceremonies to which one has not been invited.*

NUMBER	PERSON	GENDER	REFLEXIVE
singular	1	-	myself
	2	-	yourself
	3	masculine	himself
		feminine	herself
		neuter	itself
plural	1	-	ourselves
	2	-	yourselves
	3	-	themselves

There are three distinct uses of reflexive pronouns in English: a) reflexive, b) emphatic dependent, and c) emphatic autonomous.

A) Reflexive use. When used reflexively, the pronoun assumes one of the following functions: Od, Oi, Cs, S of nonfinite P, CJT or DEP of a preposition, as in the following examples, respectively:

(1)   Porter just perched *himself* up in the attic window. (Od)

(2)   She bought *herself* a new Ferrari. (Oi)

(3)   Liz and Roger were not quite *themselves*. (Cs)

(4)   'You get out now,' I heard *myself* saying. (S of nonfinite P)

(5)   She blamed me and *herself* for what happened. (CJT in O:cu)

(6)   You see, I used to have this joke with *myself*. (DEP of preposition)

A defining feature of pronouns used reflexively, apart from their functional potential, is the fact that they are *coreferential* with the subject of the clause within which they occur, as in examples (1) to (3), (5) and (6). If the pronoun occurs in a subordinate nonfinite clause it is coreferential with the subject of the matrix clause if it is the subject of the subclause, as in example (4). If in a nonfinite subclause the pronoun assumes one of the other functions, it is coreferential with the explicit or implied subject of the subclause, compare the following examples:

(7)   I wanted [her to improve *herself*].

(8)   I wanted [to improve *myself*].

Transitive constructions with reflexive pronouns as object do not allow passivization (cf. section 7.4.4 [B]): cf. *Jack loves only himself / *Himself is loved only by Jack.*

Some verbs always require reflexive objects. Such verbs are called reflexive verbs: e.g. ABSENT, BESTIR, INGRATIATE, PRIDE.

(9)   He obviously tried to ingratiate *himself* with his superiors.

Other verbs are used reflexively with a distinct meaning: e.g. APPLY, AVAIL, CONDUCT, EXERT.

(10)   I sometimes got better marks than him, but that was when he chose not to exert *himself.* (i.e. EXERT used in the sense 'make a great effort', not 'use' as in 'to exert one's influence')

Reflexivization is obligatory in most cases of coreferentiality. There are however notable exceptions. In examples like:

(11)   Jack loves only Jack.

the lack of reflexivization is a deliberate stylistic choice to emphasize the two participant roles of the person involved (DOER and DONE-TO) as distinct and independent.

With some verbs, such as BEHAVE, DRESS, SHAVE, WASH, there is a choice between strictly intransitive use and transitive reflexive use with only a slight difference of meaning:

(12)   She began to dress (*herself*).

In preposition groups, the objective form of a personal pronoun is occasionally used instead of the corresponding reflexive pronoun, thus commonly in constructions expressing space or location:

(13)   He didn't seem to notice the decoration above *him.*

(14)   She closed the door behind *her.*

(15)   I have no money on *me.*

In some cases, the reflexive pronoun is used idiomatically while the personal pronoun is used in a concrete locational sense, compare:

(16)   They were beside *me.* (concrete location)

(17)   They were beside *themselves* with rage. (figurative meaning)

B) Emphatic dependent use. When used as emphatic dependents, reflexive pronouns add contrastive meaning to a (pro)nominal constituent:

(18)   They didn't appreciate the astonishing privilege they were being granted of having their troubles treated by Miss Florence Nightingale *herself.*

(19)   He was seeing himself at twelve, standing in Milkman's shoes and feeling what he *himself* had felt for his own father.

As in these examples, reflexive pronouns with emphatic dependent use receive primary stress and often appear in post-head position. But, as pointed out in section 5.6.3, they also take up other positions, positions identified elsewhere as adverbial positions in the clause:

(20a)   Helen would *herself* tell me the bad news. (central-M)

(20b)   Helen would tell me the bad news *herself*. (T)

If interpreted as adverbials rather than dependent group constituents, the reflexive pronouns here look more like separate referring expressions with anaphoric, coreferential value.

C) Emphatic autonomous use. Finally, reflexive pronouns are used non-reflexively and autonomously as emphatic alternatives to the personal pronouns – typically after prepositions (especially *than, as, like, except* and *but*) or when serving as a CJT in a compound unit:

(21)   No one knew this better than *himself*.

(22)   She's about the same age as *myself*.

(23)   No one's to blame but *yourself*.

(24)   He's a pro, just like *yourself*.

(25)   Everybody except *herself* laughed at the joke.

(26)   That topic was connected with the terminal row between Sally and *myself*.

The reflexive pronoun is here often used to avoid having to choose between the subjective and objective form of the personal pronoun (*than he / than him, as I / as me*, etc.).

11.3. Pronouns without a person distinction

11.3.1. Demonstrative pronouns

The demonstrative pronouns in English can be presented in terms of the two categories applying to them, number and deixis:

DEIXIS \ NUMBER	singular	plural
near	*this*	*these*
distant	*that*	*those*

To these four central demonstratives we can add the two locative adverbial demonstratives *here* and *there*.

Demonstratives are emphatic in nature. They have both determinative and autonomous uses:

(1)   At *that* exact moment they were both indoors.
(2)   In *this* way, the name acquired a quasi-official status.
(3)   *These* couldn't be her children.
(4)   He counted *those* who were late.

Constructions like the following are ambiguous with respect to the distinction between determinative and autonomous use:

(5)   He preferred that chair to *this*.

Either we here have autonomous use of *this* referring deictically to some entity in the context or we have determinative use with suppressed repetition. The determinative status of *this* can be made clear by adding *one*:

(6)   He preferred *that* chair to *this one*.

Demonstratives assume the usual range of external functions:

(7)   *That*'s normal, isn't it? (S)
(8)   Why am I telling you *this*? (Od)
(9)   I'm going to give *those who failed me* a little surprise. (Oi)
(10)   And that's *that*. (Cs)
(11)   Did you really call her *that*? (Co)
(12)   I want *this* and a few other things. (CJT)
(13)   How did it ever come to *this*? (DEP of preposition)

Elsewhere, demonstratives normally serve as determiners (as in *that exact moment*, *this way*, etc.). But in connection with adjectives and quantifiers such as *much* and *many*, the singular demonstratives may serve also as degree adverbs, indicating a precise amount or measure:

(14)   I didn't give her *that much*.
(15)   Do we need *this many recommendations*?
(16)   The worm was *this long*.

More informally they serve as intensifiers without an association of precise degree:

(17)   The party wasn't *that bad*.
(18)   I was *that pleased*!

A) The number category. The singular pronouns *this* and *that* are used in connection with singular and uncountable concepts:

(19)   *This* is my favourite dish.

(20)   *That* may prove our worst case ever.

(21)   We have to use a little bit of *that* sugar.

(22)   Can you imagine, she didn't want to listen to *this* music.

These and *those* are used in connection with plural concepts:

(23)   They say *these* creative people can be a bit potty.

(24)   I want two of *these* and three of *those*.

Only the singular pronouns are used in connection with aggregate nouns like FAMILY, GOVERNMENT, TEAM, FIRM, etc.: *this family, that government*, etc., not **these family, *those government*, etc. However, collectives which are 'internally countable' (see section 10.4.3) allow of both singular and plural pronouns, depending on the intended meaning: *this people / these people*; *that crew / those crew*; *this staff / these staff*.

B) Reference to persons. When used determinatively, all four demonstratives are compatible with personal referents: *that girl, this woman, those neighbours, these composers*. When used autonomously, the singular forms are used only with personal referents in expressions serving as introductions or identification (in competition with *it*):

(25)   *This* is my wife.

(26)   *That* was my brother on the phone.

Elsewhere emphatic personal pronouns, not demonstrative pronouns, are used to refer deictically to singular personal referents:

(27a)   'I'm not going with *her*.'

(27b)   *'I'm not going with *that*.'

The plural forms are used in these contexts too: *These are my neighbours / Those were two of my colleagues*. But in addition, *these* is occasionally used anaphorically in competition with *they* (as in *All her best friends were there and these never dare criticize her*), and *those* is used freely with personal reference when restrictively modified (as in *Those who want to continue, please raise your hands / Those in the know will surely keep it a secret*).

C) Deixis. Like the definite article, the demonstrative pronouns are markers of definiteness. But unlike the definite article, the demonstratives specify the referent as near or distant in relation to the speaker, especially in cases of non-textual reference. The basically deictic nature of demonstrative pronouns is clear in examples of non-textual reference like the following:

(28)   I want *these gloves*, not *those*.

(29)   Non-native language teacher, holding a book in his hand: 'Repeat after me: *This is a book.*'
Learner at the back: '*That is a book.*'
Language teacher: 'I said: *This is a book.*'
Learner: 'Well, let's just say: *It's a book.*'

This last example is from an authentic classroom situation, where the learner had a better intuitive understanding of the deictic nature of the demonstrative pronouns than the teacher. In both examples, the near pronouns *this* and *these* are used about what is near at hand in relation to the speaker, and the distant pronouns *that* and *those* are used about more distant referents.

The deixis of demonstratives operates not only on a spatial dimension but also on a temporal one:

(30a)   *This/*That is* the News in English read by ...

(30b)   *That/*This was* the News in English read by ...

(31a)   How*'s* life *these days*?

(31b)   How *was* life back in *those days*?

As we see in these examples, *this* and *these* are used about present time and *that* and *those* about past time.

D) Related referential properties. When used with textual reference, the deictic nature of the demonstratives is often subdued. Only very rarely do we find examples like (32) (cf. Schibsbye 1970: 208-9), where the interpretation of the demonstratives rests exclusively on the near/distant distinction:

(32)   Work and play are both necessary to health: *this* gives us rest, and *that* gives us energy.

Instead expressions like the following are used: *the former ... the latter, the first ... the second.*

Normally, with the demonstratives the near/distant distinction is modified or extended to serve the requirements of textual reference. Both the near and the distant pronouns are used anaphorically in competition with the lighter pronoun *it*:

(33)   Oliver's {career}, if *that* isn't too grand a word for it, had made only a single movement, and that was downwards.

(34)   He's a friendly dog called Poulidor, but {he's now got so old that he's gone stone deaf}. Both Oliver and I find *this* terribly sad.

The difference between the near and the distant pronouns is in such cases very subtle. Often, as in (33) and (34), both variants are possible. The effect of using the distant pronouns is to direct the hearer's attention to something mentioned in the preceding linguistic context, while the effect of using the near pronouns is to 'update' something mentioned in what is technically the preceding linguistic context as part of the current linguistic context, with the immediacy of present relevance. In other words, with the distant pronouns, the hearer is guided backwards in the text, whereas with the near pronouns, the hearer is prompted to consider the antecedent as immediately present in the communicative situation. The distant pronouns imply a distinction between the here and now of the speaker and the preceding linguistic context. With the near pronouns this distinction is more blurred because the antecedent is presented as part of the current linguistic context.

In practice, though often interchangeable, the distant pronouns tend to be used with specific, clearly delimited antecedents while the near pronouns tend to be used with more general antecedents, often approaching a qualitative value like *such*, compare:

(35)   They sent me Linda. She cost {£100}. *That* was her price.

(36)   {Filthy old lecher, seducer of schoolgirls, abandoner of wife and child} ... A chap can't expect to get much of a hearing with *those* labels attached.

(37)   It was awful. It was a shouting match. I was just trying to be practical, trying to express something that I thought came out of my love for Oliver, and he got all jumpy and hostile. *These* things don't immediately go away, either.

(38)   ... I pass my favourite road sign: ROUTE INONDABLE. Such Gallic economy. In England it would be DANGER ROAD LIABLE TO FLOODING. Here, just ROUTE INONDABLE. Then carefully through the village, and into the welcoming arms of wife and child. How she hugs me, the iridescent bambino, Little Sal. She clings to me like a wet shower-curtain. Isn't *this* the life?

In the last example, it is difficult to identify the antecedent with precision: it covers in a general way all the good or charming things mentioned in the preceding context and goes even further back in the passage from which the example is extracted.

Not surprisingly, the near pronouns rather than the distant pronouns are used cataphorically, often in contrast to an anaphoric distant pronoun:

(39)   Anyway, the point is *this*: {I didn't go to university}.

(40)   Poor old Ollie, up to his mucous membrane in a tub of merde, how inspissated, how uncheerful ... No, actually *that*'s not what I think. What I think is *this*. {I love Gillian, she loves me}. *That*'s the starting-point ...

The distant pronouns can be used in a cataphoric-like way if what follows them picks up something from the preceding linguistic context:

(41)   Even when I got pregnant it didn't seem to concentrate Oliver's thoughts. I tried to explain my concerns to him, and he just said, in a rather pained way, 'But I'm happy, Gill, I'm so happy.' I loved him of course, for that, and we kissed, and he stroked my tummy which was still as flat as a pancake, and

made some silly joke about the tadpole, and everything was fine for the rest of the evening. *That*'s the thing about Oliver: {he's very good at making things fine for the rest of the evening}.

E) Uses without a deictic contrast. The deictic value of the demonstratives is sometimes replaced by an association of familiarity (plus approval or disapproval):

(42)   I wish him everything, *that* Stuart: health, hearth, happiness and herpes.

(43)   Perhaps he's ashamed of *this* girlfriend of his.

Idiomatically, demonstratives are used with little or no deictic value:

(44)   Oh, we talked about *this* and *that*.

(45)   *That*'s my big girl!

(46)   She finally left him, and *that*'s that.

(47)   I know the pedagogue is meant to enthuse his charges by an infectious zest for learning and all *that*.

The distant pronouns are used without a contrast to the near pronouns when followed by restrictive modification:

(48)   Let us agree upon the following generality: that *those* who have inflicted marriage upon themselves assume such rival guises alternately.

(49)   Roger was careful not to mention *that* which everybody had already guessed.

The construction *that which* is in competition with the more frequent independent relative pronoun *what* with a slightly less precise value (see section 11.3.3 [B.c] below):

(50)   There are various problems with *what* I'm doing.

When followed by restrictive modification, *that* and *those* are in competition with *the one* and *the ones* but not personal pronouns:

(51)   Sam changes his chair for *that* / *the one* / **it* in which his uncle had been sitting.

(52)   The issues in 1960 are no longer *those* / *the ones* / **them* / **they* that existed in 1935.

In the singular, the expression with *that* is more formal than *the one*, while in the plural *those* is normal in expressions implying 'established category', *the ones* being somewhat colloquial; cf. also the following example, where the explicit categorization would render *the ones* very odd:

(53)   The world divides into two categories: *those* who believe that the purpose of life is love and everything else is merely an etc.; and *those* unhappy many who believe primarily in the etc. of life.

In expressions with specific referents, *the ones* is normal:

(54)   Americans are very friendly, and *the ones* I know are nice to me.

Note that when referring to persons, only *the one* is possible in the singular:

(55)   I was *the one* who used to be so gloomy about things.

That and *those*, but not *this* and *these*, are used determinatively followed by a restrictively modified nominal head:

(56)   I even had time to give an ironic accent to *that* crappy bit of the service in which you promise to 'share' your worldly goods with your partner.

(57)   Oliver is one of *those* people who makes more sense in a context.

The difference between the definite article and demonstrative pronoun in such constructions is that the latter implies not only definiteness but also 'established category'.

11.3.2. Interrogative pronouns

The central interrogative pronouns in English are:

>   who, whom, whose
>   which
>   what

To this list we can add the following:

>   when, where, why, how

We retain the term 'pronoun' for these items despite the fact that they usually correspond to adverbial preposition groups (*at what time, in what place, for what reason, in what way*). The archaic items *whence* 'from where' and *whither* 'where' and the old-fashioned *whether* used of two possibilities instead of *which*, will not be considered here.

A) Syntax. Interrogative pronouns, whose primary function is to form *wh*-interrogative constructions, normally take up clause-initial position. In main clauses they trigger subject-operator inversion unless they serve as subjects (see section 5.3.3):

(1)   *Who* did you meet? (O)
(2)   *What* is this? (Cs)
(3)   *Where* do you live? (A)
(4)   *Who* wants to go? (S)

Interrogative pronouns may take up terminal position in 'double-barrelled questions' (*Who is who? / He does not know which is which* (cf. Jespersen 1933: 307)), as well as in echo-questions (*You said WHAT?*).

There is no partial inversion in interrogative subclauses:

(5)   I asked her *who you met / what this was / where you live / who wanted to go*.

Note that in corresponding *yes-no* interrogative subclauses, *if* and *whether* serve as interrogative conjunctions:

(6)   I asked her if/whether you met her.

Interrogative pronouns are rarely used as indirect objects, corresponding adverbial preposition groups being used instead:

(7a)   ?*Who/whom* did you give the book?

(7b)   *Who/whom* did you give the book *to*? (or more formally: *To whom* did you give the book?)

(8a)   *Which of them did you order this radio?

(8b)   *Which of them* did you order this radio *for*?

(But there is some vacillation: e.g. *Who/whom did you serve a four-course dinner?* is acceptable to some native speakers.) In cases of role suppression in constructions like 'GIVE someone a kiss/smack/nudge etc.', where the predicator is fused semantically with the direct object, turning a syntactic ditransitive S P O O pattern into a semantic monotransitive S P O pattern (cf. section 7.3.4 [I]), interrogatives may serve superficially as 'indirect' objects, as in *Which of them did you give a kiss?*

Autonomous interrogative pronouns are occasionally modified by specifying or intensifying expressions: *where in France, who on earth, why the hell*, etc. Intensification is often provided by adding *ever* to the pronoun: *whoever, whatever, wherever*, etc. *Which* is frequently followed by an *of*-construction: *Which of them did it? / Which of your friends are coming?* Similarly, *who* may be followed by *among*: *Who among them knew what was going on?* Rhetorically, *who* is also followed by an *of*-construction, or even by a relative clause: *Who of us would join the Republicans? / Who that has heard him can doubt his motives?*

The following interrogatives can serve not only autonomously but also as determiners: *whose, which* and *what*, as in e.g. *Whose car is this? / Which book do you prefer? / What strategies have you prepared?* Exclamatory *what* may serve as a predeterminer: *What a load of rubbish you are saying!* Only *how* can serve as a modifier: *How expensive is this car?*

B) Categories. Three categories are relevant to the description of interrogatives: case (*who* vs. *whom* vs. *whose*), gender (*who* vs. *what*) and what might be termed 'interrogative scope' (*who* and *what* vs. *which*).

a) Case applies to the series *who, whom* and *whose*, the two last being inflectional variants of the first. While *whom* is an objective form like e.g.

him, its distribution is different. It is obligatory only after a preposition in clause-initial position, a fairly formal construction: *To whom did you give the book?* Very colloquially, the subjective form does occur even after a preposition but only when the group appears as a complete utterance by itself (*To who?*) or in clause-final position (*Di shacked up with who?*). The reason we are unlikely to find *To who did you give the book* is that there is a stylistic clash: fronting of the whole preposition group is formal whilst the use of the subjective form *who* is informal.

The objective form is used also as prepositional complement in discontinuous adverbials and as object: *Whom did you give the book to? / Whom did you call last night?*, but such constructions are felt to be somewhat cumbersome and formal. The following sentences thus increase in degree of formality:

(9a)   *Who* did you give the book *to*?

(9b)   *Whom* did you give the book *to*?

(9c)   *To whom* did you give the book?

The genitive form *whose* is used determinatively and autonomously like possessive pronouns: *Whose shoes are these? / Whose are these shoes?*

b) Gender. The gender distinction between personal and non-personal is relevant to the description of all the three central pronouns *who*, *which* and *what*. While *who* (and its derivatives *whom* and *whose*) can be used only about personal referents, *which* is used about both personal and nonpersonal referents, cf. the following examples which show determinative and autonomous use, respectively:

(10)   *Which car/kid* had disappeared?

(11)   *Which of the cars/kids* had disappeared?

Determinative *what* is also used about both personal and non-personal referents:

(12)   *What cars/drivers* will make it in time?

Used autonomously, *what* is used about non-personal referents (but see subsection c below):

(13)   *What* did he say?

(14)   *What* went wrong?

c) Interrogative scope works on two dimensions: quantitative and qualitative selectivity. *Quantitative selectivity* affects the choice of pronoun in this way: if a question is general, not assuming a limited set of possible answers, *who* or *what* is chosen; if a question assumes a limited number of alternatives, *which* is chosen (with an implicit or explicit *of*-construction). Thus, for example, the difference between:

(15)   *Who* is Roger Wilkinson?

(16)   *Which (of them)* is Roger Wilkinson?

is that (16), unlike (15), requires a specific context with a limited number of potential bearers of the name Roger Wilkinson. Similarly, in:

(17)   *What books* do you like?

(18)   *Which (of these) books* do you like best?

the first question is completely open, while the second assumes discrimination within a limited set of books. One exception to the rule about *who* assuming general selectivity is when it is followed by *among*, resembling *which* followed by *of*:

(19a)   *Who among them* would think up such a plan?

(19b)   **Which among them* would think up such a plan?

Sometimes *who* and *what* are used in contexts where, superficially, there seems to be a limited choice:

(20)   *What* would you like to do: go for a walk or make love to me?

(21)   *Who* did you call, John or Roger?

However, even in such cases, *who* and *what* retain their association of general selectivity, the specified alternatives serving more as examples of possible answers than as an imposed limitation.

The second dimension of interrogative scope, *qualitative selectivity*, distinguishes *what* from *who/whom* and *which*. The difference between them is often that *what* is used to query 'kind of referent' whereas *who/whom* and *which* are used to query 'identity of referent', compare:

(22a)   *Who* is your best friend? (Roger!)

(22b)   *What* is your best friend? (A university professor)

(23a)   *Which years* are leap years? (1952, 1956, 1960 ...)

(23b)   *What years* are leap years? (e.g. years in which February has 29 days)

(for these last examples, see Schibsbye 1970: 238). In rhetorical questions, *who* is however used not so much about identity but about 'kind of referent':

(24)   *Who* would do such a thing? (i.e. 'What kind of person would do such a thing?')

11.3.3. Relative pronouns

The central interrogative pronouns serve also as the central relative pronouns:

> who, whom, whose
>
> which
>
> what

To these we can add the conjunction-like *that*, the 'zero relative' Ø, the relative adjuncts *when, where, why* and *how* and the intensive *-ever* forms: *whoever, whichever, whatever*. The archaic forms *whence* and *whither*, the very formal compounds of *where* and a preposition (*whereby, whereto*, etc.) and the rhetorical *-soever* forms (e.g. *whosoever*) will not be dealt with here.

A) Syntax. Relative pronouns, unlike interrogative pronouns, characteristically serve a double purpose: they signal clausal subordination like subordinating conjunctions and at the same time they take on a clause function other than SUB in the subclause (e.g. subject or object), referring anaphorically to a constituent in the matrix:

(1)   You remember the case of {the craftsman} *who* chipped out a priest's hole for himself on the ship? (S)

(2)   {The second story}, *which* I pass on without comment, touches on more delicate matters. (O)

Autonomous function only: *who, whom, that, Ø, whoever* (as well as *when, where, why* and *how*), as in:

(3)   They arrested Jeremy Soames, *who* was on his honeymoon.

Determinative function only: *whose*, as in:

(4)   Why did God preserve this species, *whose creation* did not reflect particularly well on its creator?

Either autonomous or determinative function: *which(ever)* and *what(ever)*; compare:

(5)   He used a gun *which* he had borrowed from a friend.

(6)   He used a gun, *which fact* bothered the rabbis.

Autonomous relatives may serve as S or Od (as in some of the examples above) or as Cs, Co, A or DEP in a preposition group, but usually not as Oi:

(7)   Roger wasn't quite the speaker *that* he used to be. (Cs)

(8)   He's a bit of a jerk, *which* some of the girls even call him to his face. (Co)

(9)   I met him in the gallery *where* we used to meet. (A)

(10)   Eventually came the day Ø we had been longing *for*. (DEP in preposition group)

(11)   *Jane called Roger, *whom* I wanted to give the book. (*Oi)

Relatives always appear in clause-initial position, as in the examples above, but note that they are sometimes embedded in larger clause-initial constituents *part of which* may precede the relative pronoun, as indeed in this sentence. Note in this connection the possibility of discontinuity (cf. Vestergaard 1985: 175 and Preisler 1992: 215-6); compare:

(12a)   We interviewed a great many applicants, *the majority of whom* we rejected. (continuous)

(12b)   We interviewed a great many applicants, *of whom* we rejected *the majority*. (discontinuous)

(12c)   We interviewed a great many applicants, *who* we rejected *the majority of*. (discontinuous, informal spoken language)

Apart from intensification in the form of the *-ever* suffix, relatives are modified only by the indefinite pronouns *both*, *each* and *all*, as in *She had invited her friends, who all seemed to enjoy the party*.

The distinction between restrictive relative clauses (which help establish the referent of the antecedent) and non-restrictive relative clauses (which offer additional information about the referent of the antecedent) is important syntactically as well as to the choice of relative pronoun (see below):

(13a)   The soldiers *who were brave* ran forward. (restrictive)

(13b)   The soldiers, *who were brave*, ran forward. (non-restrictive)

As far as syntax is concerned, restrictive relative clauses form a DEP closely tied to its antecedent in a group structure, whereas a non-restrictive clause, which is syntactically optional and always marked orthographically or intonationally as a separate information unit, is perhaps best analysed as an adverbial. For further discussion of the uses of restrictive and non-restrictive relative clauses, see Bache & Jakobsen 1980.

B) Categories. Relative pronouns are number- and person-transparent in the sense that it is the number and the person of the antecedent that determine subject-predicator concord in relative clauses with the relative pronoun as subject:

(14a)   The *soldiers* who *were* brave ran forward.

(14b)   The *soldier* who *was* brave ran forward.

(15)   *I* who *am* ... / *You* who *are* ... / *He* who *is* ..., etc.

a) The gender category accounts for the distinction between *who(m)* and *which*. As in the examples offered so far, *who(m)* is used with personal or personified antecedents (including e.g. pet animals, as in *Spotty, who was our first dog, followed little Jane everywhere*) while *which* is used with non-personal or depersonified antecedents (including sometimes small children, as in *She bore four children, one of which died in infancy*. With collective antecedents (such as FAMILY, GOVERNMENT, etc.), *who(m)* or *which* is used in BrE according to the speaker's view of the referent in terms of individuals or as a unit (see section 7.6.4 [A]). Determinative *which* with a personal antecedent is rare, even in formal language: *Mr Johnson, which gentleman was present, ...* (Schibsbye 1970: 247).

That and *Ø* are used with both personal and nonpersonal antecedents: *The woman that/Ø you met at my party is Jack's sister; The house that/Ø they built has never been insured.*

What is used with personal referents only in determinative use in examples like *She called what friends she had left* ('she called the friends that she had left') where the relative is used *independently* of an antecedent (on the so-called independent relatives, see the paragraph on reference below).

Though basically non-personal, *which* is used indirectly about 'type or kind of person' when serving as subject or object complement in non-restrictive relative clauses:

(16)   They considered him a frightful bore, *which* he is.

(17)   He's a bit of a jerk, *which* some of the girls even call him to his face.

Note finally that *whose* is used not only with personal antecedents (as in *I ran into Jack, whose car had just been stolen*) but also with non-personal antecedents (as in *This is the palace whose demolition has been ordered by the King*), though some speakers tend in such cases to prefer the more cumbersome and formal *of*-construction (as in *This is the palace the demolition of which has been ordered by the King*).

b) The case category accounts for the distinction between *who, whom* and *whose*. The genitive form *whose* is used determinatively like the possessive pronouns and therefore never overlaps with *who* and *whom*, which are always autonomous. The objective form *whom* is obligatory after a preposition and generally the preferred form as object and as discontinuous DEP of a preposition, especially in non-restrictive relative clauses; while the subjective form *who* is used as subject and informally as object and DEP in a discontinuous preposition group; cf. the following examples:

(18)   The agent *to whom/*to who* I transferred all the money has disappeared.

(19)   Ian, *whom/who* I trusted with the money, has disappeared.

(20)   Ian, *whom/who* I transferred all the money *to*, has disappeared.

(21)   The agent *who/*whom* transferred all the money to me has disappeared.

c) Reference. As already indicated, one of the central functions of relative pronouns is to refer anaphorically to (part of) a group realizing a clause function in the matrix, typically a (pro)noun group, as in most of the examples presented so far, or a preposition group, as in the case of the relative adjuncts: *I met her {at a time}* <u>*when*</u> *her parents were still alive; I found the book {in a place}* <u>*where*</u> *no one had thought to look.* However, relative pronouns may also have clausal referents (i.e. serve as *sentential* relatives, cf. section 8.10 [C]), *which* with anaphoric value and *what* with cataphoric value, as in the following classic example, in which the sentential relative clauses very clearly have the value of a disjunct:

(22)   {She was late}, *which* was bad, but *what* was worse, {she didn't apologize}.

As a parenthetical insertion after a coordinating conjunction *which* very occasionally has a cataphoric-like value:

(23)   X is reduced to virtually nothing, and, *which* shouldn't bother us unduly at this point, {Y is left unaffected}.

The relative clause can here be interpreted as a fronted anaphorically referring expression, cf. *X is reduced ..., and Y is left unaffected, which shouldn't bother us unduly at this point.* When fronted, the referent of the relative clause is delimited more precisely as the second conjoint clause only.

Sentential *which* is commonly used as a determiner, especially in preposition groups: *..., which fact led her to state ... / ..., for which reason she decided ... / ..., in which case we will have to ...*

The close relationship between relatives and conjunctions becomes apparent when we compare sentential relative clauses to clauses with AS as SUB:conj (see section 8.10 [C]):

(24a)   Being 'selected' was a mixed blessing, *as they soon realized.*
(24b)   Being 'selected' was a mixed blessing, *which they soon realized.*

A distinction must be drawn between relatives with the normal textual (anaphoric or cataphoric) reference and the so-called *independent relatives* (see section 8.3). Independent relatives have non-textual reference and can be interpreted as a fusion of a relative and an antecedent. The following items can be used in this way: *what(ever), whoever, whichever, where(ever), when(ever), why, how;* cf.:

(25)   I gave her *what* was left.
(26)   *Whoever* fails to attend the meeting will be fired.

Independent relatives thus approach the value of a demonstrative or an indefinite pronoun followed by an anaphoric relative (i.e. 'that which', 'anyone who', etc.). *What*, unlike *whoever*, is also used determinatively with personal or non-personal referent, often with an association of 'small quantity':

(27)   I gave her *what oranges* we found.

(28)   She called *what friends* she had left.

Who(m) was formerly used as an independent relative, especially in literary language: *Who steales my purse steales trash* (Jespersen 1933: 354). Today, independent *who(m)* is found only in similar idiomatic expressions like *Who delays pays* and with a very restricted set of verbs (CHOOSE, LIKE, PLEASE) as a very formal alternative to *whoever*: *You may marry whom/whoever you like*. The objective form *whomever* is rare, if not actually non-existent, even as a prepositional complement: *You may give this book to whoever you want.*

Which is used as an independent-like relative only in a clause following a coordinated clause with independent *what*:

(29)   She held up her hand to stop *what* she thought was clapping at the back, but *which* was two or three women trying to quiet their babies. (Schibsbye 1970: 246)

Arguably, *which* is here not independent but has anaphoric reference to *what*.

That is not used independently, except in rare expressions like *Handsome is that handsome does.*

The relative adjuncts *when, where* and *why* can be used independently:

(30)   8 p.m. is (the time/moment) *when* you leave.

(31)   This is (the place) *where* I was born.

(32)   That was (the reason) *why* he left.

Relative *how* is always used independently: *This is (*the manner) how you operate the machine.*

Relative *whoever, whatever,* and *whichever* are distinguished along the same lines as the corresponding interrogative pronouns, i.e. in terms of gender and selectivity:

(33)   You may choose *whoever* you like. (personal; general selectivity)

(34)   You may choose *whatever* you like. (non-personal; general selectivity)

(35)   You may choose *whatever books* you like. (non-personal; general selectivity)

(36)   You may invite *whatever guests* you like. (personal, general selectivity)

(37)   You may choose *whichever (book, partner)* you fancy the most. (personal or non-personal, limited selectivity)

C) The choice of relative pronoun. There are only few hard-and-fast rules applying to the choice of relative pronoun. But as a rough first approximation we can offer the following overview:

Restrictive clauses

Function of pronoun	Choice of pronoun	Examples
S	who/which/that	*The man who/that remained* *The table which/that remained*
O or DEP of preposition placed finally	that/Ø/which	*The man that/Ø I saw* *The man that/Ø I glanced at* *The table which/that/Ø I saw* *The table which/that/Ø I glanced at*
DEP of preceding preposition	whom/which	*The man at whom I glanced* *The table at which I glanced*
C	that/Ø	*He is not the lover that/Ø he used to be*

Non-restrictive clauses

Function of pronoun	Choice of pronoun	Examples
S	who/which	*Peter, who lives in Lancaster,* *Paris, which is the capital of France,*
O or DEP of preposition placed finally	who(m)/which	*Peter, who(m) I know well,* *Paris, which I know well,* *Peter, who(m) I glanced at,* *Paris, which I am fond of,*
DEP of preceding preposition	whom/which	*Peter, to whom I sent the contract,* *This room, from which the noise came,*
C	that/Ø	*They consider him a frightful bore,* *which he is*

Let us now look at some of the finer details in connection with the choice of relative pronoun:

a) After a preposition only *whom* and *which* are used. Continuous relativized preposition groups are fairly formal:

(38)   They chose the material according to the purpose *for which* it was intended.

(39)   She had lied to Charles, *to whom* her affair came as a nasty surprise.

b) As complement *which* is used in non-restrictive relative clauses and *that* or *Ø* in restrictive relative clauses, irrespective of the nature of the antecedent, as in *They consider him a frightful bore, which he is* and *He is not the lover that/Ø he used to be.*

In *other* functions, there is much more vacillation in the choice of pronoun, with the gender-neutral and light relatives *that* and *Ø* as common alternatives to *who(m)* and *which*, above all in restrictive relative clauses. In general, considerations of weight, rhythm, syntactic complexity and medium play an important role. Thus *that* and *Ø* are commoner a) when immediately following the head (pro)noun of the antecedent; b) when the relative clause is syntactically simple; and c) in informal, spoken language. For example, *that* is a more likely pronoun than *which* (or *who*) in:

(40)   You are right, by the way, to see the animals *that* fled as the nobler species.

By contrast we are not surprised to find *which* rather than *that* in:

(41)   They had mobile faces very similar to human beings *which* you could swear were about to utter speech.

c) As subject *who* and *which* are used in non-restrictive relative clauses. In restrictive relative clauses, *that* is sometimes chosen instead of *who* especially if the antecedent is modified/determined by a superlative or by *all, any, every, no* or *only*.

(42)   They were obliged to advertise, and then select *the best pair that* presented itself.

(43)   *Any student that* passes this exam will be admitted to the advanced phonology course.

As subject, *that* is a common choice instead of *which* in restrictive relative clauses. The difference between them is largely one of medium and style, the light pronoun being frequent in spoken, informal English, *which* in written, formal English:

(44)   Now, in the version *that* has come down to you, the raven has a very small part.

(45)   On the list were several books which could only be studied in the departmental library.

That is also a common alternative to *who* and *which* in cleft sentences (cf. section 8.4).

As a rule of thumb, *Ø* is not used as subject. Exceptions are a) constructions with zero for real subject in existential clauses with *there* as provisional subject; b) existential *there* sentences in colloquial speech; and c) very colloquial cleft sentences, as in the following examples respectively:

(46)   We quickly decided to lie about how many of us *Ø* there were.

(47)   There is someone here *Ø* wants to see you.

(48)   It was John Ø did it, not me!

d) As object or DEP in discontinuous preposition groups in non-restrictive relative clauses, we find *which* with non-personal antecedents and *whom* (or informal *who*) with personal antecedents. In restrictive relative clauses *that* and Ø are frequent alternatives to *who(m)* and *which*:

(49)   Here's the book *that/Ø* I got from my sister.
(50)   Here's the book *that/Ø* he keeps quoting *from*.
(51)   My sister helped the girl *that/Ø* we just met.
(52)   My sister helped the girl *that/Ø* I sent the book *to*.

With personal antecedents, *that* or Ø is often chosen to avoid the case problem of *who* vs. *whom*, both of which are also often felt to be somewhat cumbersome and, in the case of *whom*, formal. Thus the first example is clearly preferred to the second:

(53)   The man *that/Ø* I saw said it was all right to visit you this afternoon.
(54)   The man *who(m)* I saw said it was all right to visit you this afternoon.

e) As adverbials relative *when* and *where* may occur in both restrictive and non-restrictive clauses, relative dependent *why* only in restrictive clauses with REASON as antecedent. *How* is only used independently. In restrictive relative clauses, *when* and *why* are often replaced by Ø or *that*, *where* only occasionally so:

(55)   I am thinking of the time/morning *Ø/that* he had the ass keel-hauled.
(56)   The only reason *Ø/that* he didn't come was that he didn't want to be elected.
(57)   The place *Ø/that* we used to meet was unknown to my boss.
(58)   *The village *Ø/that* I was born lies in the Blue Mountains.

The relative adjuncts are normally avoided in cleft sentences:

(59)   It was in London *Ø/that/?where* I met her.
(60)   It was in the afternoon *Ø/that/?when* I met her.

Relativized prepositional groups are often used instead of the proadverbials *when* and *where*:

(61)   My secretary noted the exact time *at which* the first meeting started.
(62)   The room *in which* the negotiations took place was next to my office.

Note in this connection formal expressions with determinative use of *which*:

(63)   I met her at 10 o'clock, *at which time* it was too late to warn her.
(64)   My boss was late, *for which reason* we had to cancel the meeting.

f) A few extra points: Nonpersonal *all*, *everything* and *anything* are virtually always followed by *that* (or Ø outside subject function):

(65)   All *that* matters is that you get well.

(66)   Everything Ø/*that* he said made her very angry.

In subject function, *who* is normal after personal *all, everyone, anyone* and *someone*:

(67)   Anyone *who* knows anything about wood could have told him that it was a hopeless idea.

(68)   I am looking for someone *who* can write up the report for us.

With gender-neutral *those, the one* and *the ones*, gender may be signalled by *who* and *which* but of course not by *that* and Ø: *those which* vs. *those who*. Demonstrative autonomous *that* is nearly always followed by *which*: *I exchanged my hat for that which he found in the closet.*

    That instead of *which* is rare in non-restrictive relative clauses:

(69)   The ash trees retain their long and melancholy-looking seeds, *that* are sometimes called ash-keys. (Schibsbye 1970: 250)

Outside subject function Ø is often used in restrictive relative clauses if the subject is a personal pronoun (cf. van Ek & Robat 1989: 169):

(70)   The soldier you killed was only a boy.

(71)   This is the dictionary I bought yesterday.

11.3.4. Indefinite pronouns

The following four series of pronouns constitute the central system of indefinites in English:

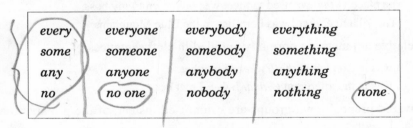

every	*everyone*	*everybody*	*everything*	
some	*someone*	*somebody*	*something*	
any	*anyone*	*anybody*	*anything*	
no	*no one*	*nobody*	*nothing*	*none*

In addition there are *each* and *all*, the *dual* pronouns *both, (n)either* and *other(s)* and the marginal pronoun *one(s)*. Other marginal items such as the quantifiers *many, more, few, little, enough*, etc. and the indefinite pro-adjuncts (e.g. *everywhere, sometimes, somehow*) will be touched on in passing. The *-one* forms should not be confused with basic items followed by emphatic *one* with strong individualizing force as in *Every 'one of them objected to my proposal.*

A) The central system. The four basic items *every, some, any* and *no* and their derivatives are distinguished syntactically and semantically in a number of ways.

a) Syntax. The derived forms function autonomously only (i.e. as group heads, S, Oi, Od, Cs, Co and prepositional complement); *every* and *no* serve as determiners only, and *some* and *any* have both functions:

(1) *Everyone* laughed at *anything* he said.

(2) *No* director has time to consider *every* script that comes his way.

(3) *Some* projects did not get *any* funding at all.

(4) While I got *some* of the money, my brothers hardly got *any*.

The more marginal items expressing place (*some-, any-, no-, else-, every-where*), time (*sometimes*) and manner (*somehow, anyhow,* AmE *someway*) typically (but not exclusively) serve as adverbials:

(5) We couldn't find the flute *anywhere*. (A)

(6) They *sometimes* let her down. (A)

(7) Jack *somehow* managed to finish the manuscript. (A)

(8) *Nowhere* is as well suited for the project as Brighton. (S)

(9) I comforted the *sometimes* unhappy sister. (DEP)

The form *anyway* serves as a conjunct (as in *I couldn't find the flute, anyway*).

When used autonomously, indefinite pronouns allow of postmodification (e.g. adjectives, preposition groups, relative clauses, *else, but*-constructions) but not premodification or determination:

(10) He was toying with *something dangerous*.

(11) *Someone in Paris* leaked information to *some of his agents*.

(12) I don't think we should do *anything which might upset them*.

(13) I'll give the copy to *someone else*.

(14) The petitioners were too trepid of this court to let *anything but the clear fountain of truth* flow from their mouths.

But note that pre-head dependents qualifying the qualitative meaning are sometimes possible: *hardly anything, nearly everyone, virtually everyone,* etc.

Derived indefinites are occasionally used as nouns and thus allow of pre-H dependents:

(15) She's *a mere nobody*.

(16) Bond remarked on *the cute little nothing she was wearing*.

The *of*-construction is particularly frequent with *some, any* and *none* in partitive expressions:

(17)   I gave her *some of the money/books*.

(18)   Have you read *any of John Irving's novels*?

(19)   *None of his students* applied for the instructorship.

With *something* and *nothing* the *of*-construction has qualitative meaning rather than partitive meaning:

(20)   There is *something of the mad scientist* about him.

(21)   She had *nothing of her brother's charm*.

No and *any* may serve as dependents in comparative or comparative-like adjective and adverb groups:

(22)   He is *no longer* my supervisor.

(23)   Is her behaviour *any better* now?

(24)   In my view this is *no different*.

Note in this connection expressions with the positive form *good* (e.g. *Is he any good? / They are no good*) and *all/any/none* in comparative expressions with the definite article: *We didn't feel any the better for it / We felt none the wiser*.

None is used in connection with *too* + adjective/adverb and in expressions with *other*: *I was none too proud of what we had done / He was none other than the king himself*.

Something, nothing and *anything* approach adverb-like status in expressions like *He is something/nothing/not anything like his father*.

In colloquial AmE *some* and *any* may serve as degree adverbials: *Then she cried some, but that did not bother me any* (Preisler 1992: 235).

b) Gender. Among the derivatives, the *-one* and *-body* forms are distinguished from the *-thing* forms in terms of the gender category (personal vs. non-personal). The basic forms *some* and *any*, as well as the derived form *none*, are used autonomously about both personal and non-personal referents: *Some/None of his cars/friends impressed me*. All four basic forms are used determinatively in expressions with either personal or non-personal referents: e.g. *no sugar / no friend, some cars / some people*.

c) Case. The *-body* and *-one* forms behave like nouns with respect to case: they appear in the subjective case (as in the examples examined so far) and in the genitive case:

(25)   It is *nobody's* fault.

The 'group genitive' (see section 10.3.8) is frequent with *else*:

(26)   It is always *somebody else's* fault.

d) Number. All the derived forms except *none* are singular in relation to the predicator (e.g. *Everybody is happy for you*) but often enter concord with plural central pronouns (*Everyone gave their consent*; cf. section 11.2.1 [C]). *None* takes a singular predicator when referring to something non-countable (*I was looking for some food but there was none left*) and a singular or plural predicator when referring to countable entities (*He gave me many suggestions but none was/were good enough*), see also section 7.6.3 [D]. Autonomous *some* and *any* are singular when referring to non-countable referents (e.g. *I was looking for some sugar but there wasn't any*); with countable referents they are plural (*I was looking for some students but there weren't any*).

e) General/restricted. There is no well-established category for the distinction between the *-one* forms and the *-body* forms. Often the two are felt to be interchangeable: *Everybody/Everyone laughed when he fell*. The difference between them is subtle: the *-body* forms often imply a general context (as in e.g. *Nobody loves me*), whereas the *-one* forms imply a restricted context (e.g. *No one [i.e. no one in the English Department] agreed with me*).

f) Universal/partitive. Moving on to the difference between the four series of central indefinite pronouns, we operate with the following classification:

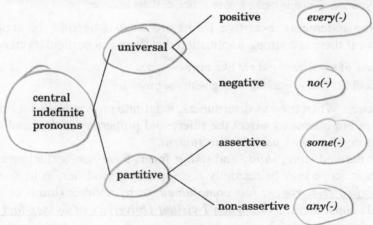

While the positive/negative distinction of universal pronouns is intuitively obvious, the assertive/non-assertive distinction of partitive pronouns requires some explanation. The assertive forms imply the existence of a referent whereas non-assertive forms do not. Thus, in positive statements, assertive forms are normal:

(27)   I found *some/*any* magazines in the drawer.

(28)   There was *someone/*anyone* in the kitchen.

By contrast, non-assertive forms are normal in questions and negative statements:

(29)   I didn't find *any* magazines in the drawer.

(30)   Was there *anyone* in the kitchen?

Non-assertive forms are frequent also in conditional clauses:

(31)   If you find *anything* in the drawer, please tell me at once.

However, non-assertive forms are sometimes used in positive statements with the implication that within the bounds specified there is *no limit* on the possible referent. In such cases the non-assertive forms typically occur in modal contexts and/or are restrictively postmodified; semantically they are close to the universal, generic *every(-)* items:

(32)   *Anyone* can beat him in chess.

(33)   He did absolutely *anything* he could think of.

(34)   He would tell her *anything* to discourage her.

Assertive forms are used in questions and conditional clauses with the implication that there is, or is likely to be, a particular referent:

(35)   Did *somebody* mess up your life?

(36)   If you see *someone* make a pass at her, call me at once.

In negative statements, assertive forms are used if outside the scope of negation or if there is a strong implication that there is a particular referent:

(37)   *Some* of my friends did not like my new wife.

(38)   I couldn't find *something* wrong with the camera.

g) Reference. When used as determiners, indefinite pronouns do not refer by themselves but obviously affect the referential properties of the head of the construction; cf. *every student* vs. *no student*.

All the derived *-one*, *-body* and *-thing* forms have non-textual reference though their scope may be textually restricted by a modifier, as in *Someone in the English Department has complained*, or by another (intra- or extra-sentential) constituent, as in *When I visited University of Sussex last year, everyone was very helpful*.

With autonomous *some*, *any* and *none*, textual restriction by means of an *of*-construction is particularly frequent:

(39)   *Some of my students* didn't want to attend *any of the courses*.

(40)   *None of my friends* could accept the proposal.

The *of*-construction is occasionally fronted:

(41)   *Of the many callings that comprise the over-world of intelligence, none* requires as much devotion as that of the sisterhood of listeners.

Despite the strong textual restriction such expressions have strictly non-textual reference. In practice, the pronouns here function in a determiner-like way (cf. *Some of my students = Some students of mine)*, letting the prepositional complement serve as a semantic nucleus in the referring expression as a whole. With plural meaning *some* and *none* are occasionally used for non-textual reference without any form of textual restriction:

(42)   *None* are so deaf as those that will not hear. (Schibsbye 1970: 260)

(43)   *Some* will say that he did it for the money.

Autonomous *some*, *any* and *none* have textual, anaphoric reference in constructions like:

(44)   I offered them {some peanuts}. He didn't want *any* but she took *some*. She then asked for {some milk}, but there was *none* left in the fridge.

Having reviewed the four basic series of indefinite pronouns, we now go on to briefly examine *all*, *each*, the dual pronouns and *one*.

B) All. Like *every(-)* and *no(-)*, *all* is a universal pronoun. It is used autonomously (with or without postmodification) and (pre)determinatively about both personal and non-personal, singular and plural referents:

(45)   I hope *all* is well with you and your family.

(46)   *All* of us agreed to join him for dinner.

(47)   Why not take *all* of me?

(48)   Did not Adam give the names to *all* the cattle?

(49)   I shall, in *all* humility, remain silent on the matter.

With non-textual reference, *all* is used idiomatically with a general meaning about non-personal referents (i.e. 'conditions'), as in the first example. With personal or non-personal plural referents, non-textual *all* is normally replaced by *everyone/everybody* or *everything* unless there is clear textual restriction on the potential referents, as e.g. in the second example, where *all* is followed by an *of*-construction. In such cases, autonomous *all* is close in meaning to determinative *all*, cf. *all of the children* vs. *all the children*, *all of the books* vs. *all the books*. With singular referents, *all* is used with non-countable meaning: *all humility*, *all milk*, *all life*, etc. *All* is used determinatively with geographical names conceived as collectives in constructions like *All Brighton were down at the beach.*

   All is also used as a postmodifier:

(50)   I am tired of it *all*.

When the group functions as subject, postmodifying *all* is in the adverbial central-M position and thus potentially detached from its head (see section 5.6.3)

(51)   They (have) *all* betrayed her.

All serves as an adverb-like modifier of some adjectives, prepositions and adverbs:

(52)   Jack was *all* upset about the news.
(53)   She was *all* against my proposal.
(54)   A happy solution is now *all* but ruled out.
(55)   He knows that *all* too well.
(56)   The job was done *all* wrong.

Note finally the use of *all* in an expression like *She was all smiles* and fixed idiomatic collocations: *above all, after all, all in all, at all.*

C) Each is an individualizing universal pronoun used autonomously (if there is sufficient textual restriction) or determinatively about both personal and non-personal singular referents:

(57)   The two sisters smiled, *each* handing me a small envelope.
(58)   *Each* of the books was signed by the author.
(59)   I gave *each* car a thorough examination.
(60)   He talked to *each* member of the department.

Unlike *all*, *each* is not used autonomously with non-textual reference unless there is some textual restriction, as in the first two examples above. When followed by an *of*-construction, autonomous *each* approaches determinative *each* in communicative function: cf. *each of the books* vs. *each book*.

Like *all* and *every(-)*, *each* refers to all members of a group. But there is a difference: *all* focuses on the group as a whole while *each* picks out the members of the group individually; *every(-)* shares some of the value of both *all* and *each*, referring to the individual members of the group collectively: *He told all of us / everyone / each of us the truth. Each* is thus near-synonymous with emphatic *every 'one* (which has the association of 'without exception'). *He told every 'one of us the truth.* Unlike *all* and *every(-)*, *each* is capable of referring to groups containing two members only (as in the first example above).

Like *all*, *each* is also used as a postmodifier:

(61)   We gave them *each* a big apple.

When the group serves as subject, postmodifying *each* is in the adverbial central-M position and thus potentially detached from its head (see section 5.6.3):

(62)   They *each* took a big apple / They have *each* taken a big apple.

Unlike *all*, postmodifying *each* may appear also in terminal position:

(63)   We gave them a big apple *each*.

(64)   They took a big apple *each*.

D) The dual pronouns, which include *both*, *(n)either* and marginally *other*, presuppose the existence of a class consisting of only two members.

a) Both is the dual counterpart to universal *all*. It is used autonomously (if there is sufficient textual restriction) or (pre)determinatively about both personal and non-personal referents:

(65)   My parents turned up later in the evening. *Both* wanted to see Ann about the funeral.

(66)   *Both* of the books were signed by the author.

(67)   Jack broke down on *both* occasions.

(68)   The referee warned *both* players.

When followed by an *of*-construction, autonomous *both* approaches (pre)determinative *both* in communicative function, cf. *Both of the boys disappeared / Both (the) boys disappeared.*

Like *all* and *each*, *both* is also used as a postmodifier:

(69)   We gave them *both* a big apple.

When the group serves as subject, postmodifying *both* is in the adverbial central-M position and thus potentially detached from its head (see section 5.6.3):

(70)   They (have) *both* understood what you are driving at.

b) (N)either. Positive *either* is the dual counterpart to *any*, while negative *neither* is the dual counterpart to *no/none*. The two pronouns are used autonomously (if there is sufficient textual restriction) or determinatively about both personal and non-personal referents:

(71)   Ann and Joan both played, but *neither* made a good impression.

(72)   He was quite happy to sign *either* of the books.

(73)   *Either* player can make the first move.

(74)   *Neither* painting fetched the expected price.

Either normally means 'one *or* the other of two group members', as in the examples above. In connection with nouns like SIDE and END however, it is sometimes used in an inclusive sense 'one *and* the other', approaching the meaning of *both* or *each*:

(75)   People were waiting at *either* side of the street.

(76)   There was a little candle at *either* end of the table.

c) Other is a marginal indefinite pronoun indicating a definite or indefinite specific alternative. It is used as a (post)determiner or premodifier with or without determiner: *other people, his other daughter, any other suggestions, all the other neighbours,* etc. It is fused with the indefinite article in singular expressions like *another car, another solution,* etc. Singular *another/the other* and plural *others* are autonomous with textual or non-textual reference in constructions like *Would you like another? / I put one book in the bag and the other back on the shelf / Others disapproved of his departure.*
In the singular, *the other* is used as a contrast to *one,* in the plural *others* is used as a contrast to *some: I told him it was one or the other / Some like it hot, others like it cold.*

Other is found in the two reciprocal constructions: *each other* and (the more formal) *one another: They promised each other / one another to keep in touch.*

E) One has a number of distinct functions:

(i) It is used determinatively or autonomously as a kind of emphatic indefinite article with singular numerical value in contrast to plural *some,* other cardinal numbers (*two, three* ...) and quantifiers like *several, many,* etc.:

(77)   The terrorists were going to execute *one* hostage an hour.

Its affinity with the indefinite article is obvious also in connection with proper names; compare: *I am looking for a/one Sarah Mortimer* (cf. also section 10.2.5). With contrastive stress it combines with the basic indefinite pronouns constituting an individualizing alternative to the *-one* compounds: *Everyone objected / Every `one of them objected.*

(ii) As noted in section 11.2.1 [F], generic *one* (as well as its derivatives *one's* and *oneself*) is used as a formal alternative to *you*:

(78)   *One* never knows what cigarettes will do to *one* in the long run.

In AmE, this *one* may be referred anaphorically to by central pronouns:

(79)   *One* can't always trust *himself,* now can *he*?

In tags *you* is a frequent alternative in colloquial AmE:

(80)   *One* cannot trust anyone anymore, can *you*?

(iii) *One* without determination refers in (somewhat formal) expressions to persons; here *one* approaches the meaning of 'someone':

(81)   She was never *one* to help her friends out of trouble.

(82)   He was *one* who would never forgive but who might forget.

(83)   He told her about it, in the casual tone of *one* commenting on the weather.

One(s) is perfectly normal in definite singular or plural expressions about persons:

(84)   John was the *one* to consult on sentence analysis.

(85)   They are the *ones* who wouldn't let my sister alone last night.

Note in this connection the more or less fixed expressions: *the Holy One, the Evil One, the little/young ones*.

(iv) *One* is used anaphorically as a pro-form for a whole singular (pro)noun group ('g-replacive *one*'):

(86)   When she asked for {a cigarette}, I gave her *one*.

(87)   Have you got {another film for this camera}? – Yes, there's *one* in the drawer.

(v) Singular *one* and plural *ones* are used as a pro-form for a singular or plural count noun rather than a whole group ('n-replacive *one*'):

(88)   There were three armed {visitors}. The tall *one* with the glasses had an almost scholarly air as he tapped the microphone in the manner of lecturers everywhere.

(89)   There were countries in the world which didn't welcome {journalists}, and who thought that white-skinned *ones* pretending interest in archaeological sites were obviously British spies.

Note that n-replacive *one(s)* serves as a group head, allowing both pre- and postmodification, as well as determination.

N-replacive *one(s)* is naturally avoided when the antecedent is non-countable: *Old furniture is sometimes more expensive than new/*new one(s)*. It is also normally left out:

(i) after autonomous genitives/possessive pronouns and after *own*: *I much prefer her car to his / my own / my brother's*.

(ii) after numerals and quantifiers like *many, several, a few*, etc.: *They offered me five books of my own choice but I only took <u>two</u> / There were plenty of coins in the bag but he only gave her <u>a few</u>*.

There is vacillation in the following cases:

(i) in indefinite plural or definite singular or plural constructions with two parallel adjectives, *one* is often left out, especially in literary language, and especially if the adjectives express a natural contrast: *There were many Dutch politicians at the meeting but very few German (ones) / He curiously preferred poor women to rich (ones) / Everyone likes the old manager better than the new (one).*

(ii) after a comparative adjective *one* is often left out: *Two men entered the saloon. The younger ordered a drink / This is not a good solution but can you think of a better?*

(iii) after a superlative form *one* is often avoided outside distinctly colloquial speech: *Having examined the many bottles very carefully, he selected the cheapest.*

(iv) after *another*, *other*, *last* and *next*, and after ordinals, *one* is optional but often avoided in formal language: *If you miss the first news broadcast you can always watch the next one / I liked the first proposal better than the second.*

With some of the examples with the definite article, it is difficult to decide whether the adjective is used substantivally (cf. section 12.4) or is part of an elliptic construction.

N-replacive *one* is normally used:

(i) after the indefinite article + adjective in the positive form: *Having examined the many bottles very carefully, she selected a cheap one.* In distinctly literary language *one* is here sometimes dropped if the construction expresses a natural contrast.

(ii) to avoid syntactic ambiguity in cases where the modifier is a potential nominal head: *They were clearly human trails, not just the usual animal ones.*

(iii) after *only*: *Having examined the bottles very carefully, she selected the only one from Barossa Valley.*

12. Adjectivals and adverbals

Adjectivals and adverbals are closely related in a number of ways, the most important of which are: a) both types of constituent typically express *properties*, though in relation to different types of concept; b) the category of comparison applies to them both; and c) adverbs are often 'de-adjectival', being derived morphologically from adjectives (e.g. *blunt* → *bluntly*). In the following we deal first with adjectivals, focussing on three major problem areas: positional ordering (section 12.2), comparison (section 12.3) and the substantival use of adjectives (section 12.4). Much of what we say about adjectivals prepares the ground for the discussion of adverbals in the final section 12.5.

12.1. Preliminary discussion of adjectivals

Adjectivals typically express *properties* in relation to the things or entities expressed by (pro)nominals. For example, in a sentence like *The movie was very boring*, the property 'very boring' expressed by the complement group is assigned to the subject group *The movie*. The same property may be expressed as an integrated part of the subject group, as in e.g. *The boring movie (took three hours)*. In this chapter we shall examine the ways in which adjectivals serve the communicative function of assigning properties.

12.1.1. Adjectives and adjective groups

As will be recalled, adjectivals are either single adjectives or groups with an adjective as head. Examples:

(1)   The *bitter* rivals spent a *long* time developing *very different* systems.
(2)   *French* women are *famous for their sensuality*.
(3)   He was *too frightened to tell her the truth*.
(4)   She is a *much more beautiful* dancer.
(5)   They are clearly *taller than she is*.

In adjective groups the head adjective accepts a pre-head dependent (as in *very different* and *much more beautiful*) or a post-head dependent (as in *famous for their sensuality* and *taller than she is*) or both (as in *too frightened to tell her the truth*). We can thus offer the following description of the structural potential of adjective groups:

pre-H dependents	H	post-H dependents

Pre-head dependents are predominantly adverbals (adverbs or adverb groups) modifying the adjective with respect to *degree,* as in the examples above. Frequent degree adverbs found in this position are: VERY, MUCH, QUITE, EXTREMELY, RATHER, HIGHLY, REALLY, AS, SO, TOO, MORE, MOST, LESS, LEAST. But we also find pre-head nominals expressing quantity: *two years old / five feet tall / several miles long / a little reluctant.*

Post-head dependents take the following forms: finite clauses (*certain that she will be there*), *to*-infinitive clauses (*eager to try it out*), *than*-clauses (*taller than she is*) and preposition groups (*capable of anything / keen on playing soccer / better than me*). In addition we find the adverb *enough* in post-head position (*clever enough / fast enough*). After WORTH we find post-head nominals and *-ing* clauses (*worth millions/a fortune/my while/ doing again*). Post-head preposition groups and clauses usually express complementation rather than modification (cf. section 6.3.3). In some cases the presence of a post-head dependent is obligatory: *fond of her / bent on doing it / bound to accept / tantamount to a confession* (cf. e.g. **He was fond*). In others the dependent is syntactically optional but if there is one, and if it is realized by a preposition group, the adjective often selects a certain preposition to the exclusion of others: *keen on, afraid of, similar to,* etc.

We often find discontinuous dependents in adjective groups, especially in connection with comparison:

(6)   Sally is *more* beautiful *than Jane.*

(7)   Sally is *as* calm *as she was yesterday.*

(8)   Sally is *too* frightened *to tell him the truth.*

Here the post-head dependent is, strictly speaking, a post-head dependent of the adverb (*more/as/too*) rather than of the adjective. For discussion of such cases, see section 5.6.5.

The definite article is used as a pre-head dependent in connection with comparatives in correlative constructions like the following:

(9)   *The calmer* Sally appeared, *the angrier* Jack became.

(10)   *The more important* it is to her, *the more tongue-tied* she becomes.

Such constructions express a systematic relation between two changing properties. Strictly speaking, the definite article is here associated with the comparative element (*-er, more*) rather than with the adjective. The same is true of constructions with the indefinite pronouns *all, any* or *none* followed by the definite article and a comparative adjective or adverb, e.g. *His explanation left me none the wiser / I hated her all the more because she told her parents about me.*

Adjectives also take the definite article as a pre-head dependent when used 'substantively' to express entities directly rather than to assign properties to them: *the rich / the inevitable / the stronger / the smallest* (for discussion of this use of adjectives, see section 12.4).

12.1.2. Semantics

Semantically, adjectives express a large range of properties, such as subjective or emotional evaluation (NICE, GOOD, BAD, BEAUTIFUL), size (BIG, SMALL, HUGE, LITTLE), shape (ROUND, SQUARE, FLAT, OBLONG), colour (RED, GREEN, YELLOW, GOLDEN, DARK, LIGHT), nationality (ENGLISH, CHINESE, FRENCH), age (OLD, YOUNG, ANCIENT), material (WOODEN, SILVER, SILKY), category (REPUBLICAN, CONGRESSIONAL, POLITICAL, SOLAR), etc. Many adjectives form pairs of opposites (antonyms, binary relations): GOOD-BAD, TALL-SHORT, HEAVY-LIGHT, etc. Some pairs consisting of a positive and a negative member are formed morphologically by means of affixation (cf. section 7.5.6): HAPPY-UNHAPPY, CAPABLE-INCAPABLE, SATISFIED-DISSATISFIED, etc. A large number of adjectives do not enter a binary system but are systemically more complex (e.g. colour terms and nationality terms) or systemically indeterminate (such as ECONOMIC, RELIGIOUS, LINGUISTIC, INDUSTRIAL, etc). (see further section 12.1.6).

A number of terms have proved useful for the description of the semantics of adjectives:

(i) Gradable vs. non-gradable. Gradable adjectives (e.g. NICE, SENSIBLE, BAD, BEAUTIFUL, etc.) denote scalar properties and thus take degree adverbs like VERY and EXTREMELY and allow of comparison (e.g. *very beautiful, nicer*). Non-gradable adjectives (e.g. ATOMIC, LINGUISTIC, MEDICAL, OWN, OTHER) denote categorial or determinative properties and are not normally compatible with intensification or comparison (**very linguistic, *more atomic, *owner, *very other*). Some adjectives are gradable in one sense and non-gradable in another, cf. *a (very) popular politician / popular culture* and *a (more) civil young man / civil rights*.

(ii) Inherent vs. non-inherent. Inherent adjectives directly ascribe a property to the *referent* of the head they modify and may be used equally well as pre-head modifiers and as subject complements, e.g. *a beautiful girl / the girl is beautiful*; *a very angry man / the man is very angry*. Non-inherent adjectives relate by way of association to the meaning of the *head noun* rather than ascribing a property to the referent as such. Generally, non-inherent adjectives cannot be used as subject complements. Thus, for example, *an old friend* is not necessarily a friend who is old but someone with whom one has had a friendship of long standing, and *a heavy sleeper* is someone who sleeps heavily, not a sleeping person who is heavy. Other examples of non-inherent adjectives are: *a complete idiot / sheer nonsense / a functional grammarian / foreign policy / young clothes / animate nouns / a royal hatmaker*. Note that non-inherent adjectives sometimes relate to something rather less than the full head noun (*a functional grammarian / a royal hatmaker*), sometimes to more than the head noun (*an old friend →* 'old friendship'), sometimes to something that is only very indirectly expressed by the head noun (*young clothes* = 'clothes for young people'). As can be seen, many adjectives can be used both inherently and non-inherently, cf. *an old horse* vs. *an old friend* and *a heavy box* vs. *a heavy sleeper*. In examples where it is syntactically possible to change a pre-head non-inherent adjective to subject complement position, it becomes inherent: *my old friend → my friend is old*. For further discussion of this distinction, see Ferris 1993: 19ff.

(iii) Temporary vs. permanent. This distinction is sometimes used to describe the difference between examples like *the only stars visible* and *the only visible stars*. In the first construction, *visible* denotes a temporary property (i.e. 'visible at the moment'), in the second a more permanent property (i.e. 'normally within sight'). Similarly, *a written statement* is a certain kind of statement whereas *the statement written* is a statement composed in writing on a particular occasion. In the first instance, *written* denotes a standard, enduring property, in the second it has more verbal character, modifying *statement* in terms of a situation taking place at a particular time.

(iv) Stative vs. dynamic. This actional distinction (cf. section 7.2.1) arguably also applies to adjectives. For example, CAREFUL expresses a property which presupposes activity while TALL expresses a physical property independent of activity. Note in this connection that dynamic adjectives, unlike stative adjectives, may serve as complements in imperative clauses: *Be careful / *Be tall*. The fact that both verbs and adjectives can be described in terms of the distinction between stative and dynamic has led some linguists to claim that verbs and adjectives belong to the same category of constituents.

(v) Restrictive vs. nonrestrictive. Dependent adjectives denoting properties which help the listener establish the referent of the head are called restrictive adjectives. Whether an adjective is restrictive or nonrestrictive usually depends on the context. Thus, for example, *brave* is restrictive in *The brave soldiers ran forward* if it singles out a subclass of soldiers in the context (i.e.

if only some of the soldiers, those who were brave, ran forward). If it describes a property of all the soldiers present in that particular context, it is nonrestrictive (i.e. 'the soldiers, who were all brave, ran forward'). For further discussion, see section 10.1.4.

At a later point (section 12.1.6), we examine the classification of adjectives into *descriptive*, *specifying* and *classifying* adjectives.

12.1.3. Morphology

Adjectives can be divided into several fairly distinct morphological classes. There are, first of all, a number of simple lexical stems: GOOD, BAD, NICE, BIG, LONG, OLD, YOUNG, FAIR, CLEVER, NOBLE, MELLOW, etc. But many adjectives are morphologically more complex in that they are derived from other word classes, or from other adjectives, by means of affixation. The two major types are:

(i) denominal adjectives (e.g. BEAUTIFUL, RESTLESS, FRIENDLY, BOORISH, POETIC, HISTORICAL, HUMOROUS, CONSTITUTIONAL)

(ii) deverbal adjectives (e.g. CHARMING, DERIVED, DRUNKEN, REMARKABLE, RESISTIBLE, RESTRICTIVE, DOMINANT).

In some cases, there is more than one derivation from a noun or verb depending on the intended meaning: FRIENDLY / FRIENDLESS, WORRIED / WORRYING, etc. In the case of denominal adjectives ending in *-ic* or *-ical*, there is often little or no perceptible difference of meaning, e.g. POETIC/POETICAL. There is a tendency for the adjective ending in *-ic* to denote 'category' and for the one ending in *-ical* to be gradable and more descriptive in meaning. A good example of this is ECONOMIC ('of economics') vs. ECONOMICAL ('careful in spending money, time, etc.'). An important exception, where the relation is exactly the opposite, is HISTORIC ('notable or memorable in history') vs. HISTORICAL ('pertaining or belonging to history').

Many deverbal adjectives are present or past participles. Some of these are fully adjectivalized (e.g. *a worried man / a fascinating event*) in the sense that they behave like other typical adjectives (e.g. may be intensified by VERY). Others preserve more of their verbal character: *a rarely/*very heard opera*; *rapidly/*very falling share prices* (for discussion, see Huddleston 1984: 301ff and 1988: 111ff; see also section 7.4.6 on passives vs. adjectival non-passives).

Usually adjectival past participles are passive in meaning: *the deported prisoners* (i.e. the prisoners were deported), *the invited relatives* (i.e. the relatives were invited), etc. Occasionally adjectival past participles have active meaning if they are derived from an intransitive verb denoting a change of state, e.g. *the escaped prisoners* (i.e. the prisoners had escaped), *the departed relatives* (i.e. the relatives had departed). Some participles allow of both a passive and an active reading, depending on the nature of the head, e.g. *a returned letter* (i.e. the letter has been returned) and *a returned soldier* (i.e. the soldier has returned). Often past participles with passive meaning appear in post-head position: *the relatives invited / the prisoners deported*. In such cases, the past participle retains more of its verbal character and can be interpreted as a reduced relative construction (cf. *the relatives who were invited / the prisoners who were deported*) (see also our mention of the distinction between permanent and temporary properties in section 12.1.2).

Special mention should be made of denominal adjectives ending in the 'verbal suffix' *-ed*: WINGED (*a winged animal*), WALLED (*a walled garden*), etc. Such adjectives have little verbal character. Instead they imply a prepositional *with*-group: 'an animal with wings', 'a garden with a wall', etc., cf. also:

(1) These expressions were addressed to a *long-legged, short-bodied, small-headed, white-haired, hog-eyed*, funny sort of genius.

A number of adjectives and adverbs contain the prefix *a-*: AFLOAT, AFRAID, ALERT, ALONE, ASLEEP, ABROAD, AWAY, etc. One way of distinguishing between the *a*-adjectives and *a*-adverbs is to see whether they can follow the copula verb SEEM. If they can, they are adjectives (e.g. *the patient seemed afraid/asleep/*abroad/*away*). Conversely, if they can follow intransitive verbs of motion, they are adverbs (e.g. *She went *afraid/*asleep/abroad/ away*), cf. Greenbaum & Quirk 1990: 131.

We also come across adjectives derived from other adjectives: U̲NHAPPY, A̲TYPICAL, DI̲SHONEST, I̲NCOMPETENT, U̲NDER-SEXED, HY̲PERSENSIT-IVE, PO̲ST-COLONIAL, PR̲E-LINGUISTIC, KINDL̲Y̲, SMALL̲I̲SH̲, etc. In some of these the prefix locally negates the basic adjective, as in the first four examples mentioned (see sections 7.5.6 and 12.1.2).

Compounding is also an important factor: MUCH-DEBATED, GOOD-LOOKING, HAND-MADE, etc. Note in this connection the frequent use of hyphens to signal adjectival status of nominal compounds and other complex constituents: *a remarkable last-ditch effort / other Soviet-bloc countries / the latest Clinton-for-President movement / a three-year-old girl / a small, what-else-can-you-expect nod*.

12.1.4. The external relations of adjectivals

Adjectivals typically take on one of the following functions:

DEP	The *clever* girls told their *anxious* mother nothing.
Cs	Jane is *exceptionally intelligent*.
Co	They drove him *mad*.

Naturally, adjectivals also frequently function as conjoints in compound units with these three functions, e.g.:

CJT	She sent him a *long* and *rather boring* letter.
	Jack is *small* and *rather cute*.
	They painted the boat *yellow* and *blue*.

Adjectivals are often used as complements in verbless adverbial clauses:

Cs	They considered Jane (to be) *exceptionally intelligent*.
	If *necessary*, I can help her.
	However disagreeable their presence, you have to let them in.

Adjectives serving as dependents in (pro)noun groups are called *attributive adjectives* while adjectives with subject or object complement function are called *predicative adjectives*.

In addition to attributive and predicative uses, adjectivals may assume adverbial function:

A	*Unhappy with the result*, he decided to resign.
	I didn't ask him if he liked jazz or, *more important*, what wine he preferred.
	Dicky hurried in *breathless*, wearing his new trenchcoat.
	Expressionless he drew his head back in again.
	He brought his gun *loaded*.
	I was the last person to see her *alive*.

Adjectivals in this last category are sometimes referred to as 'independent' or 'free' complements rather than adverbials. They are borderline cases: on the one hand they assign a property to the subject or object, like genuine subject or object complements; on the other they are independent optional units providing supplementary background information, typically about the *state* of the entity involved, like many rather more typical adverbials.

In constructions like:

(1)   He was out walking this *great* big dog of his.
(2)   She was rather enjoying the *nice* warm water.

the italicized adjective seems to modify the following adjective rather than the head noun of the construction and thus assumes adverb-like, dependent status in relation to the following adjective (i.e. *great big = very big; nice warm = warm in a nice way*), see also section 12.2.5 [B] below.

Predicative adjectives (which normally take on subject complement function after copula verbs) are sometimes used in connection with verbs that are normally classified as *intransitive* rather than as copula:

(3)   The moon shone *bright*.

(4)   Hope springs *eternal* in the young man's breast.

(5)   The wind blew *strong*.

In these examples, the italicized adjectives alternate with the adverbs *brightly*, *eternally* and *strongly*. The effect of using a complement adjective instead of an adverbial adverb is to change the status of the verb from intransitive to copula with a corresponding bleaching of the content. Alternation between complement adjective (describing the subject) and adverbial adverb (describing the situation) is especially common in connection with the verbs HANG, LIE, SIT and STAND:

(6)   The clouds hung *heavy /heavily*.

(7)   The guests stood *silent/silently*.

For further discussion of the delimitation of adverbs from adjectives, see Schibsbye 1970: 160ff.

Like other constituent types, adjectivals may independently assume communicative functions such as EXC (e.g. *Beautiful! / So true! / How sad!*). As the following example shows, adjectivals may also serve as QUE in heavily context-dependent elliptical constructions:

(8)   I was wondering what sort of a gathering it will be. *Big? Small? Very formal?* Dinner suit? Sit-down? What's he planning?

Adjectives are sometimes dislocated (cf. section 4.5 on dislocation):

(9)   *Tricky*, that's what writers are!

Note also that adjectives occasionally appear after *as* and *than*:

(10)   They regarded him *as very competent*.

(11)   She was more hard-working *than clever*.

An analysis of such construction in terms of preposition groups with dependent adjectives is possible. But since the adjectives in such constructions are very predicative-like (cf. *They considered him to be very competent / She was more hard-working than she was clever*), an attractive alternative is to analyse them as C:adj in verbless clauses on a par with expressions like *If necessary, I can help her.*

When used attributively, adjectivals typically serve as pre-head dependents: *a friendly doctor / a competent teacher / a very promising career*. Occasionally, however, they appear in post-head position: *things*

Italian / rivers navigable at this time of year. We therefore draw a distinction between 'attributive pre-head' and 'attributive post-head' adjectivals.

A further distinction should be drawn between those attributive post-head adjectivals which are restrictive and those which are non-restrictive (often referred to as *appositional*). While restrictive attributive post-head adjectivals (e.g. *the stars visible*) are directly attached to the head they modify, like most attributive pre-head adjectivals, appositional adjectivals provide parenthetical elaboration (cf. section 12.1.7):

(12) Problems, *political, environmental and moral*, were dealt with very casually by the new government.

(13) In the distance he heard a laugh, *musical but malicious*.

12.1.5. Parataxis and hypotaxis

As noted in the previous sections, adjectivals may realize conjoints in compound units. The analysis of strings of adjectives is fairly straightforward in examples like the following:

(1) In the distance he heard a laugh, *musical but malicious*.

(2) The letter was *long and rather boring*.

In these examples, we clearly have linked coordination (cf. section 6.2.3) requiring an analysis in terms of conjoints and coordinators. Unlinked coordination in post-head and predicative positions is possible but fairly marked, signalling a 'lingering' literary style:

(3) In the distance he heard a laugh, *loud, shrill, malicious*.

(4) The letter was *long, pathetic, boring*.

Again an analysis in terms of compound units seems appropriate but this time without coordinator conjunctions. In (3) and (4) an alternative is to analyse the adjectives separately as dependent adjectives directly in relation to the head noun *laugh*. But no matter how we analyse them, the adjectives are *paratactically* related, i.e. they are at the same level of analysis. Whenever there are two or more adjectives in attributive post-head or predicative position, they are always paratactically related.

Parataxis is found also in attributive pre-head position:

(5) He rather enjoyed her *dry and light* stage kisses.

(6) What she saw was a *big, brutal, sweaty* boxer.

But in this position, matters are somewhat more complex. Consider the following examples:

(7) She was visited by a *tall dark handsome* stranger.

(8)   The *envious Republican* senators complained.

In these examples there is no overt marker of parataxis (coordinators, commas). The question therefore arises how precisely to interpret the relation between the adjectives as well as the relation of the adjectives to the head noun. One possible approach to this problem is to supply the examples with overt markers of parataxis and see what happens:

(7')   She was visited by a *tall, dark and handsome* stranger.

(8')   The *envious, Republican* senators complained.

What happens here is that we change the meaning somewhat in (8') but not perceptibly in (7'). This is evidence of parataxis in (7). What we have in (8) is *hypotaxis*, i.e. a relation between elements at different levels of analysis. Without the commas, *envious* either offers a (non-restrictive) description of the Republican senators present in the context or it restricts the Republican senators: some but not all the Republican senators in the context are envious. In either case, *envious* assigns a property to *Republican senators* as a unit rather than just to *senators*. As argued in section 4.1.1, a closeness relation like that between *Republican* and *senators* can be captured by analysing the collocation as a head form stack. By contrast, when *envious* and *Republican* are separated by a comma, as in (8'), the two adjectives relate individually to the head noun *senators* or form a compound unit. The implication of this instance of parataxis is that the envious senators present in the context happen to be also Republicans. We conclude that in attributive pre-head position, unlike the attributive post-head and predicative positions, both hypotaxis and parataxis are possible relations between adjectives.

Note finally that *distributive* sequences of adjectives, i.e. adjectives expressing properties in relation to different referents of the same head noun are always paratactically related and overtly linked: e.g. *French and Italian supporters / professional or non-professional advice.*

12.1.6. Descriptive, classifying and specifying adjectives

As a first approximation to the description of adjectives as a word class, we subclassify them into *central* and *peripheral* members. Central adjectives share the following characteristics:

(i) They are gradable and therefore allow of comparison and intensification by means of adverbs like VERY and EXTREMELY: *these (very) funny plays / a(n extremely) proud woman / the cold(er) weather / (very) angry teachers / the (most) beautiful song.*

(ii) They occur freely in both attributive pre-head position (as in the examples above) and in predicative position: *these plays are <u>funny</u> / the woman was <u>proud</u> / the weather was <u>cold</u> / some of the teachers were <u>angry</u>.*

(iii) They often serve as conjoints in linked coordination (or separated by comma), expressing different properties of the same referent: *his ugly and fat opponent / a high, tinny echo / those Indians are tough and mean-looking.*

(iv) They *describe* rather than classify or define the referent to which they assign a property.

(v) They typically though not inevitably enter a binary semantic system, e.g. BIG-SMALL, TALL-SHORT, GOOD-BAD, BROAD-NARROW, SOFT-HARD, PRETTY-UGLY, CLEAN-DIRTY, STRONG-WEAK, COLD-HOT, HIGH-LOW, PLEASANT-UNPLEASANT, SIGNIFICANT-INSIGNIFICANT, etc.

Because of their typical semantics, we shall refer to central adjectives as *descriptive adjectives*: by assigning a property to a thing they *describe* the thing.

Peripheral adjectives do not conform to (some or all of) the criteria mentioned above:

(i) They are ungradable and therefore do not allow of comparison and intensification by means of adverbs like VERY and EXTREMELY: **very <u>utter</u> madness / *extremely <u>solar</u> energy / *the <u>onlier</u> solution / *a most <u>medical</u> dictionary / *a more <u>native</u> speaker.*

(ii) They do not occur freely in predicative position: **The bed is <u>wooden</u> / *This mess is <u>entire</u> / *That nomination was <u>presidential</u> / *The student is <u>former</u>.*

(iii) They do not normally enter overtly linked coordination with descriptive adjectives (or with each other) for the expression of different properties of the same referent: **their mere and monetary opponent / *my only and American friend / *those interesting and primary elections.* However, we do find linked coordination distributively assigning properties to *different* referents: *Danish and Swedish officials / nuclear and solar energy.* Note also that peripheral adjectives may be separated by comma: *central, descriptive adjectives / semantic, interpretational rules.* In such cases the property expressed by the second adjective is presented as reformulation or further specification of the property expressed by the first.

(iv) They classify or define rather than describe the referent to which they assign a property.

(v) A few peripheral adjectives enter binary semantic systems like descriptive adjectives: NATIVE-FOREIGN, NATIONAL-INTERNATIONAL. However, most peripheral adjectives do not enter binary systems but are systemically complex (like *medical dictionary* / *political science* / *solar energy*) or do not seem to enter a subsystem at all (*sheer ignorance* / *his usual excuse* / *our main reason* / *the very person*).

There are two main types of peripheral adjectives: *classifying* adjectives and *specifying* adjectives. Classifying adjectives subcategorize the head they modify. For example, a *medical dictionary* is a special kind of dictionary and *solar energy* is a special kind of energy. Classifying adjectives thus help establish precisely what sort of thing is involved in the expression. By contrast specifying adjectives help single out or quantify the referent of the construction in relation to some context. For example, in *his main reason* and *my former colleague*, the specifying adjectives *main* and *former* have determiner-like properties.

It is important to note that the division of adjectives into descriptive, classifying and specifying adjectives is function-based. This means that it is often difficult to determine the precise subclass membership of adjectives examined out of context. In each case we have to consider the functional relationship between the adjective and the head it modifies. For example, in *an English university*, *English* is a categorizing adjective whereas in *a very English response* it is a descriptive adjective. Compare also *civil behaviour* vs. *a civil court* and *popular culture* vs. *a popular actress*.

12.1.7. Positional restrictions

Many descriptive adjectives freely allow of both attributive pre-head and predicative position, but not attributive post-head position in noun groups, compare:

(1)   the new car / the car is new / *the car new

(2)   the happy children / the children are happy / *the children happy

Classifying and specifying adjectives normally appear only in attributive pre-head position:

(3)   the medical dictionary / *the dictionary is medical / *the dictionary medical

(4)   his main reason / *his reason is main / *his reason main

However, there is a lot of variation with respect to adjectival positions.

In formal language, attributive adjectives may appear in post-head position and thereby receive *end-focus*:

(5)   He had no patience with *problems hypothetical*.

(6)   His German had the flavour of years *long past*.

(7)   We have other tasks *more urgent*.

This constituent order is found in indefinite noun groups if the meaning of the noun is highly general and the adjective subclassifies it, for in such cases it is natural to give prominence to the constituent with more specific meaning:

(8)   Her weakness for *things Italian* is quite ludicrous.

Constructions with *so* + adjective or *as* + adjective invite post-head position in connection with indefinite constructions as an alternative to a position before the indefinite article (cf. section 10.3.6), cf. e.g. *so ill a man / a man so ill* and *as clever a boy as Jack / a boy as clever as Jack.*

In indefinite *pronoun groups*, the head is so light and general that an attributive adjective is obligatorily placed in post-head position:

(9)   I am looking for *something different*.

(10)   Is there *anything interesting* on the front page?

Post-head position motivated by the principle of end-focus is also found in noun groups, definite as well as indefinite, containing dependent *deverbal* adjectives:

(11)   Some agent *unnamed* had reached Schlema and gained access to the reports.

As pointed out in our discussion in section 12.1.3 of examples like *the invited guests* vs. *the guests invited* and *the deported prisoners* vs. *the prisoners deported*, post-head position of participial adjectives emphasizes their verbal character and invites an interpretation in terms of a reduced relative clause. The same is true of deverbal adjectives ending in *-able* or *-ible*, such as e.g. *the navigable rivers* vs. *the rivers navigable*. It is here tempting to view *the rivers navigable* as a short version of *the rivers that are navigable*. In support of this analysis it may be argued that *the rivers navigable* can be expanded into e.g. *the rivers navigable by oil tankers at this time of year*, while *the navigable rivers* cannot be expanded in this way. It thus appears that many attributive post-head adjectives have clausal characteristics (see van Ek & Robat 1984: 75). An additional implication in connection with attributive post-head adjectives is that the property they express may have temporary application. This can be illustrated by comparing *problems soluble* and *stars visible* with *soluble problems* and *visible stars*. In the former cases, the adjective describes a temporary property (e.g. 'right now', 'tonight'), in the latter a more permanent, generally valid property of the head; for discussion see Bolinger 1967.

Adjectives ending in *-able* or *-ible* are particularly frequent in post-head position in noun groups premodified by a superlative or with a semantically related word such as ONLY:

(12)   They had the greatest *difficulty imaginable* getting there in time.

(13)   We must make the best *use possible* of this attractive offer.

(14)   The only *room suitable* is the one on the third floor.

Sometimes more distinct meanings come to be associated with the position of the adjective relative to the head noun, compare:

(15a)   The headmaster wrote a letter to the *parents concerned*.

(15b)   The headmaster wrote a letter to the *concerned parents*.

(16a)   He thanked all the *members present*.

(16b)   He thanked all the *present members*.

We leave it to the reader to sort out the different meanings of these examples.

Adjectives with the prefix *a-* (such as AFLOAT, AFRAID, ALIKE, ALIVE, ALONE, ASLEEP, AWAKE, AWARE) tend to occur in predicative or attributive post-head position only:

(17)   The children were asleep.
        (*the asleep children)

(18)   Parents *aware* of such problems should seek medical advice.
        (*aware parents)

ALERT and ALOOF are exceptions to this rule (e.g. *He had always shown aloof hostility to me*). Occasionally we find the other *a-*adjectives in attributive pre-head position if they are premodified and/or used in a descriptive sense: *the barely afloat oil tanker / a most alive mind*.

We often find coordinated classifying or descriptive adjectives in post-head position for the distributive expression of different entities by the head:

(19)   All sorts of problems, *political, environmental and moral*, would have to be solved if this bill is passed.

(20)   If I'm not allowed to make a profit on popular books, *good or bad*, I can't afford to publish less popular books for the discerning minority.

This constituent order, whereby the adjectives are added as an apposition, serves the purpose of highlighting the adjectives. Discontinuity, separating the adjectives even further from the head noun, is not uncommon:

(21)   If this bill is passed, all sorts of *problems* would have to be solved: *political, environmental and moral*.

Post-head position of coordinated descriptive adjectives is common in literary style narration:

(22)   He was a big man, *square-shouldered and virile*.

(23)   The leaves, *so soft and yellow*, gave way to the gentle breeze.

(24)   There were many sounds, *sinister and unidentified*, sounds of movement.

Such constructions too are sometimes regarded as reduced relative clauses (e.g. *The leaves, which were so soft and yellow, gave way to the gentle breeze*).

On the whole there is a tendency to avoid heavy pre-head modifiers in English noun groups. Thus a slight preference is given to constructions like *It was an essay far more interesting than well-written* rather than to constructions like *It was a far more interesting than well-written essay*. In general, adjective groups containing dependent complementation or postmodifiers are placed in post-head position or in predicative position, or in discontinuous pre- and post-head position (cf. section 5.6.5), as in the following examples:

(25)   Professors *keen to take early retirement* should contact me immediately.

(26)   Further back in the train there were old women with baskets *heavy with home-made vodka and smoked pork sausage*.

(27)   He was *afraid of his sisters*.

(28)   It falls into a *different* category *from the rest*.

When appositional, such modifiers are occasionally separated from their heads to observe the principle of end-weight:

(29)   The lamb had arrived, pink and succulent and tender enough to be eaten with a spoon.

In contrast to other Germanic languages like Danish and German, constructions of the following type are hardly ever found:

(30)   *A *by the judge highly valued* painting was reported missing.
       (or: *A *highly valued by the judge* painting was ...)

(31)   *This resulted in a *for Wilson unpleasant* experience.
       (or: *This resulted in an *unpleasant for Wilson* experience)

Perhaps the best general characterization of the attributive post-head adjective is to say (with Ferris 1993: 43ff) that it is a mixture of the attributive pre-head adjective and the predicative adjective. Like the attributive pre-head adjective it is a dependent in the noun group. But like the predicative adjective it assigns a property to a thing already fully established. At the same time, attributive post-head adjectives share a number of characteristics with the predicative adjective:

(i) We do not find uncoordinated *strings* of adjectives in these positions (cf. Ferris 1993: 53f):

(32)   *The only book *readable missing* is one by Twyford.

(33)   *The story was *long sad.*

(ii) Only in attributive post-head and predicative position do adjectives freely take postmodifiers and post-head complementation, e.g.:

(34a)   The experience was unpleasant for Wilson.

(34b)   The only experience unpleasant for Wilson was meeting her again.

(34c)   *The only unpleasant for Wilson experience was meeting her again.

(iii) Certain adjectives appear only in attributive post-head or predicative position: *the girl is asleep / the only girl asleep / *the asleep girl.*

(iv) Attributive post-head and predicative position are not normally taken up by specifying and (uncoordinated) classifying adjectives:

(35)   the former student / *the only student former / *the student is former

(36)   the medical student / *the only student medical / *the student is medical

Note finally expressions like *court martial, heir apparent, Secretary General, devil incarnate, body politic, Poet Laureate, president elect,* etc., which superficially seem to consist of a noun plus a restrictive attributive post-head adjective. As pointed out in section 10.2.1, such constructions are best viewed as compound heads.

12.2.   Adjectival modification and positional ordering

12.2.1.   The functional domain of adjectivals

As we have seen, adjectivals are typically used to express properties in relation to things or entities. Precisely how they do this depends on their syntactic realization. As subject and object complements, they denote an ATTRIBUTE or a RESULT, e.g. *The children were unhappy / She got pretty mad at me / Tyson knocked Bruno unconscious,* cf. section 7.3.4. In such cases the assignment of a property to a thing or entity is the primary communicative purpose of the sentence. As dependents, adjectivals serve a secondary communicative role, as in e.g. *The happy children returned to the kindergarten,* which primarily reports on the situation of 'returning', with *happy* merely describing one of the two participants of this situation. But the function of such adjectives is basically the same: to assign a property.

The general term used to describe the functional domain of dependent adjectivals is *modification* – one of the subfunctions in the functional domain of nominals, cf. section 10.1.4. Let us look once again at the relevant part of the chart offered there for the description of the functional domain of nominals:

determination	modification	categorization	(multi-functional)

As this chart shows, the subfunctions of determination, modification and categorization are arranged in certain specific syntactic zones. In the following, we shall examine the way in which attributive adjectives occupy the modificational zone *between* determination and categorization.

12.2.2. Modificational zones

In section 12.1.6 we recognized three different kinds of adjective: specifying, descriptive and classifying. As pointed out, these three kinds of adjective are not (sub)classes in an ordinary sense: an adjective cannot be identified unambiguously as one or the other in isolation. In each case the relationship between the adjective and the head noun in a particular noun group must be carefully examined and interpreted. Rather than speaking of three subclasses of adjectives, it is more appropriate to operate with three *subfunctions* of modification which adjectives may assume in relation to a noun: specification, description or classification. This approach is supported by such data as:

CIVIL:	*civil reply*	(description)
	civil rights	(classification)
BLACK:	*black cloud*	(description)
	black coffee	(classification)
PRIMARY:	*my primary concern*	(specification)
	this primary election	(classification)
WILD:	*a wild party*	(description)
	Australian wild birds	(classification)
DANISH:	*Danish cheese*	(classification)
	a very Danish approach	(description)
SECRET	*a secret plan*	(description)
	the Polish secret service	(classification)
WOODEN:	*wooden bed*	(classification)
	wooden methods	(description)
ONLY:	*an only child*	(classification)
	the only child	(specification)
etc.		

In these constructions, one and the same adjective functions in two of the three different ways depending on how it relates to the head noun.

The three subfunctions of modification (specification, description and classification) are arranged in different syntactic zones between determination and categorization in noun groups. In other words, they impose a certain positional order on attributive pre-head adjectives: when two or more such premodifying adjectives appear together in a noun group, specifying adjectives precede descriptive adjectives, which in turn precede classifying adjectives, as shown in the table below. To emphasize the positional characteristics of the three subfunctions, we refer to specification as Mod. I (= 'modificational zone I'), description as Mod. II and classification as Mod. III. Each of these zones may accommodate zero, one, or more than one adjective.

Determination	Modification			Categorization
	Specification (Mod. I)	Description (Mod. II)	Classification (Mod. III)	
the	usual	sound	English	stock
her	own	handsome	naval	officer
the	same	beautiful	French	actress
the	next	interesting	congressional	procedure
	certain	serious	organic	diseases
the	last	mighty	German	attack
the	earliest	important	Aboriginal	carvings
	many	eager	medical	students
this	particular	informal	linguistic	rule
	other	horrid	psychological	tricks

In strings of premodifying adjectives belonging to different Mod. zones, it appears that those adjectives which are closest in function to determination, viz. specifying adjectives, are placed closest to the determiner and those adjectives which are closest in function to categorization, viz. classifying adjectives, are placed closest to the head of the noun group. This means that there is no strict separation between determination, modification and categorization but rather a continuum of values from determination to categorization: from the left determination fades into modification via specification and from the right categorization fades into modification via classification. In the middle we have modification at its purest: description. The term 'central adjective' (which was replaced by 'descriptive adjective') thus acquires new functional and syntactic significance: a central adjective appears in central position in the modificational zone and is functionally pure (i.e. left untainted by determination and categorization).

Adjective order is thus first and foremost a question of the functional characteristics of adjectives in relation to the head noun. It follows that the same adjective may appear in different positions depending on its sub-function. That this is indeed the case is shown in the following data:

(1a)	Scottish *popular* ballads	(III + III)
(1b)	*popular* Scottish ballads	(II + III)
(2a)	the *first* brilliant chapter	(I + II)
(2b)	the brilliant *first* chapter	(II + III)
(3a)	the antique *occasional* table	(III + III)
(3b)	the *occasional* antique table	(I + III)
(4a)	this *good* international turn	(II + III)
(4b)	this international *good* turn	(III + III)
(5a)	English *dirty* books	(III + III)
(5b)	*dirty* English books	(II + III)

In each of these constructions, the italicized adjective changes its modificational subfunction in relation to the noun (e.g. *popular*, which subclassifies *ballads* with respect to genre in (1a) and describes it in (1b) – we leave it to the reader to work out the interpretations of the other examples). (For a full presentation of this theory of adjective order, see Bache 1978.)

12.2.3. Inherent Mod. I, Mod. II and Mod. III adjectives

Despite the fact that we have defined specifying, descriptive and classifying adjectives in functional terms rather than as subclasses of adjectives seen in isolation, it is convenient to regard adjectives as *inherent* Mod. I, Mod. II or Mod. III adjectives, according to their typical usage. Thus, for example, GOOD, DIRTY and BRILLIANT are inherent Mod. II adjectives, ENGLISH, INTERNATIONAL and MEDICAL are inherent Mod. III adjectives, and SAME, FIRST and OTHER are inherent Mod. I adjectives. The point of treating adjectives as inherent members of Mod. zones is to be able to offer a description of some of the mechanisms in English for affecting the subfunc-tion of an adjective apart from changing its position in a string of adjectives.

One effective way of changing an inherent Mod. II or Mod. III adjective to a Mod. I adjective is to give it contrastive stress (`):

(1)   I'm taking about the `big girl not the `small one.

As the specifying force of the adjectives is made clear by prosodic means, it is possible to keep the normal position of the unstressed, classifying adjective rather than the one associated with the derived, specifying function:

(2a)   I'm talking about the good yellow chair. (II + III)

(2b)   I'm talking about the good `yellow chair. (II + I)

But in some cases, the order is made to conform with the derived function (cf. Martin 1968: 37-46):

(2c)   I'm talking about the `yellow good chair. (I + II)

Another way of changing inherent Mod. II adjectives, which are typically gradable (cf. section 12.1.6), to Mod. I adjectives is to subject them to comparison:

(3)   The *smarter* kids quickly learned how to avoid grounding.

This too may affect the positional order, compare:

(4)   The other great achievement was to beat Celtic. (I + II)

(5)   The *greatest* other achievement was to beat Celtic. (I + I)

Inherent Mod. III adjectives are occasionally changed to Mod. II adjectives by means of adverbs of degree superimposing gradability on the originally classifying meaning of the adjective:

(6)   That was a *very English* remark.

(7)   He gave a *fairly political* lecture.

Using these techniques of varying the modificational subfunction of adjectives, as well as positional order, we can offer examples in which the same adjective appears in all the three Mod. zones:

(8a)   the `black new car   (*I* + II)

(8b)   a small, thin, *very black* figure   (II + II + *II*)

(8c)   strong, sweet *black* coffee   (II + II + *III*)

(9a)   the *more popular* Scottish ballads   (*I* + III)

(9b)   *popular* Scottish ballads   (*II* + III)

(9c)   Scottish *popular* ballads   (III + *III*)

12.2.4. Structure in and across Mod. zones

There are often more than one adjective in the same Mod. zone:

(1a)   the first few primaries   (I + I)

(1b)   the greatest subsequent numbers   (I + I)

(1c)   the only other solution   (I + I)

(2a)	a new, strange way	(II + II)
(2b)	the sweet warm stale air	(II + II + II)
(2c)	a healthy and virtuous girl	(II + II)
(3a)	one Republican congressional leader	(III + III)
(3b)	classical Greek drama	(III + III)
(3c)	tactical nuclear weapons	(III + III)

If one wants to ascertain that the analysis of strings of non-central adjectives (such as (1a) to (1c) and (3a) to (3c)) is correct, one can always try inserting an inherent Mod. II adjective (such as e.g. INTERESTING or INFLUENTIAL): if the original adjectives are to the left of the inherent Mod. II adjective in its most appropriate position (as in *the first few interesting primaries*) then they are Mod. I adjectives; if the original adjectives are to the right of the inherent Mod. II adjective, then they are Mod. III adjectives (as in *one influential Republican congressional leader*); and if the inherent Mod. II adjective squeezes in between the original adjectives we have a Mod. I and a Mod. III adjective (as in e.g. *the only interesting Greek drama*).

Adjectives in Mod. I, in Mod. III and in combinations of Mod. I, Mod. II and Mod. III are *hypotactically* related, while adjectives in Mod. II are *paratactically* related. In Mod. II, many adjectives are separated by comma and/or conjunction (cf. (2a) and (2c) above). If they are not, it is always possible to separate them by such means without changing the meaning of the construction:

(4)   the sweet warm stale air
        = the sweet, warm, stale air
        = the sweet, warm and stale air

Furthermore, in many strings of Mod. II adjectives, the order can be reversed with little or no semantic change:

(5)   its dark soft eyes
        = its soft dark eyes
(6)   a new, strange way
        = a strange, new way
(7)   equally mindless and vicious types
        = equally vicious and mindless types

By contrast, within Mod. I or Mod. III, adjectives are not separated by comma and/or conjunction except to express *alternative specification* (in Mod. I) or *alternative classification* (in Mod. III):

(8)   the third and smallest class
        ≠ the third smallest class

(9)   white, Protestant women
≠ white Protestant women

In *the third and smallest class*, the class referred to could be specified precisely by *third* alone or by *smallest* alone. The construction thus provides alternative specification of the third class but, in addition, we get the information that the third class is also the smallest class. By contrast, in the unbroken sequence *the third smallest class*, there is complex, progressive specification. In *white, Protestant women*, the head noun *women* is subclassified by both *white* and *Protestant*. The two ways of classifying *women* are viewed as parallel, *Protestant* being an alternative to *white*. The implication is 'if white, then Protestant'. By contrast, in the unbroken sequence *white Protestant women*, there is complex, regressive classification: *Protestant* classifies *women*, and *white* subclassifies *Protestant women*.

Adjectives from different Mod. zones are not normally separated:

(10)   an interesting economic strategy   (II + III)
(11)   the same beautiful girl   (I + II)
(12)   the first medical dictionary   (I + III)

When separation does occur, it is usually semantically significant, as in the following examples:

(13a)   a second context-sensitive rule   (I + III)
(13b)   a second, context-sensitive rule
(14a)   the helpful local dealers   (II + III)
(14b)   the helpful, local dealers

Here (13b) and (14b) with the broken sequences differ in meaning from (13a) and (14a) with the unbroken sequences. (13a), unlike (14b), implies the existence of a 'first context-sensitive rule'. In (14a) *helpful* restrictively or non-restrictively describes *local dealers*, while in (14b) the description provided by *helpful* and the classification provided by *local* are viewed as separate, parallel properties of *dealers*, with the implication that there is some notional relationship between them (cf. our discussion of *the envious(,) Republican senators* in section 12.1.5).

Separation of adjectives is carried one step further in cases where parenthetical adjectival insertions elaborate or rephrase a preceding adjective:

(15)   a less central, or peripheral, position
(16)   purely abstract, but in some sense objective, entities
(17)   a further, and much more complex, question

In such cases there are few limitations on the separation of adjectives.

12.2.5. Zone-internal order

In this section we shall comment on the internal order in each Mod. zone:

A) Mod. I: In this zone we can distinguish four major groups of adjectivals which prove reasonably order sensitive:

(i) Precise and fuzzy ordinal numbers, like FIRST, SECOND, SEVENTH, NEXT, FINAL, etc.

(ii) Precise and fuzzy cardinal numbers, like TWO, FOUR, FEW, MANY, COUNTLESS, NUMEROUS, etc.

(iii) Compared forms like *older, smaller, better-known, finest, most beautiful*, etc.

(iv) Others, like ONLY, OWN, SAME, OTHER, SUBSEQUENT, FORMER, MAJOR, SIMILAR, DIFFERENT, MAIN, CHIEF, GENERAL, SPECIFIC, PRIMARY, CERTAIN, etc.

A string of two or more Mod. I adjectives provides increasing specification. There is a *tendency* for the adjectives in the four groups to appear in the order in which they have just been presented, i.e. 'ordinals *before* cardinals *before* compared forms *before* others':

(1)   the first five primaries
(2)   the two major categories
(3)   six smaller children
(4)   the greatest subsequent importance

It is important to note, however, that some Mod. I adjectives may contract more closely with the definite article for the expression of definite specific reference, in which case they precede other Mod. I adjectives, irrespective of their membership of the four groups presented above:

(5)   the same particular phenomena
(6)   the other six more positive roles
         (cf. *the six other more positive roles*)
(7)   the only two utterances
         (cf. *the two only utterances*)
(8)   the most beautiful two young ladies
         (cf. *the two most beautiful young ladies*)

Not surprisingly, therefore, positional order is occasionally dependent on the presence or absence of the definite article, compare:

(9a)   three other Nixon associates
(9b)   *other three Nixon associates

(9c)   the other three Nixon associates

B) Mod. II: In this paratactic, descriptive zone there are few hard and fast rules for adjective order. Often, as we have seen (cf. section 12.2.4), the order seems random and can be reversed with little or no change of meaning (e.g. *a harsh thin light* vs. *a thin harsh light*). There are, however, certain *tendencies* or *preferences*:

(i) Short adjectives tend to precede long adjectives (therefore underived adjectives typically precede derived adjectives):

(10)   a deep quiet sleep
(11)   a charming, hard-working child
(12)   a slight disdainful smile

(ii) Deverbal adjectives tend to precede denominal adjectives:

(13)   undulating hilly slopes
(14)   predictable wishful distortions
(15)   quivering dusky maidens

(iii) Adjectives denoting size, height and length tend to precede other Mod. II adjectives:

(16)   that big, tough guy
(17)   a tall, thin creature
(18)   long blank periods

(iv) Adjectives denoting size, length and height tend to appear in just that order:

(19)   big, long things
(20)   big, high cheek bones
(21)   long, low sheds

(v) Emotionally loaded adjectives like BEAUTIFUL, WONDERFUL, LOVELY, HORRIBLE, DREADFUL, NASTY, etc. tend to precede other Mod. II adjectives, even those denoting size, length and height:

(22)   lovely soft hands
(23)   a horrible ghoulish enjoyment
(24)   a nasty cold wind
(25)   a fine big fellow
(26)   a terrible small room

Note in this connection that emotionally loaded adjectives occasionally enter a close relation to the following adjective and assume an almost adverb-like status:

(27)   a great big dog
       (= 'a very big dog')

(28)   a tiny little tumour
       (= 'a very little tumour')

(29)   an awful long trip
       (= 'a very long trip')

It is important, finally, to emphasize the fact that adjective order in Mod. II is extremely variable and cannot be captured by any strict rules.

C) Mod. III: In this zone hypotaxis prevails, each adjective (sub)classifying the following adjective(s) and the head noun. Like the order in Mod. I, the order in Mod. III is relatively fixed. When variation does occur, it affects the way in which the head noun is (sub)classified, cf. e.g.:

(30a)   classical Greek drama

(30b)   Greek classical drama

(31a)   the paramilitary Protestant organizations

(31b)   the Protestant paramilitary organizations

(32a)   some therapeutic non-hypnotic technique

(32b)   some non-hypnotic therapeutic technique

But usually the order is fixed and can be described in terms of certain well-defined groups of adjectives:

(i) deverbal adjectives, like LEADING, SLEEPING, INTERNALIZED, RECOGNIZED, SUSCEPTIBLE, HYPNOTIZABLE, etc.

(ii) adjectives denoting colour, like GREEN, RED, YELLOW, BLACK, etc.

(iii) adjectives denoting nationality, like ENGLISH, FRENCH, CHINESE, etc.

(iv) (other) denominal adjectives, like INDUSTRIAL, PRESIDENTIAL, NUCLEAR, WOOLLEN, MEDICAL, CULTURAL, POLITICAL, AUTOMATIC, FISCAL, etc.

(v) nominals serving as premodifiers, like METAL, SILK, FOREIGN POLICY, TOURIST, AIRLINE, etc.

The linear order is 'deverbal *before* colour *before* nationality *before* denominal *before* nominal':

(33)   handwritten green pages

(34)   a retired Indian Judge

(35)   internalized linguistic representation

(36)   Mao's supposed deathbed benediction

(37)   white American men and women

(38)   her pink woollen Dior
(39)   a yellow silk handkerchief
(40)   the American political system
(41)   the increasing Russian military strength
(42)   the Democratic foreign policy establishment
(43)   an electronic metal detector

Mod. III adjectives which denote 'locality' or 'time' often precede (other) denominal or nominal modifiers but follow deverbal adjectives and adjectives denoting colour and nationality:

(44)   *local* economic independence
(45)   the giant *Memphis* grain-export firm
(46)   *daily* physical evaluation form
(47)   the *annual* aquatic contest
(48)   a mostly white *Atlanta* district
(49)   a growing American *national* concern
(50)   patched-up *nineteenth-century* houses

Non-inherent Mod. III adjectives (i.e. inherent Mod. I or II adjectives) always immediately precede the nominal head, forming a compound-like relationship with it:

(51)   South-African *wild* birds
(52)   Australian *fast* bowler Jeff Thomson
(53)   the various French *secret* services
(54)   unreconstructed *cold* warriors
(55)   this international *good* turn
(56)   key *primary* states
(57)   the five-times-wed *former* actress

The same place is occupied by one of the inherent determiners when serving as a modifier: the classifying genitive (cf. section 10.3.8 [A]):

(58)   a muggy London *summer's* day
(59)   a standard *tourist's* guide
(60)   black *Indian's* hair
(61)   artificial silk *women's* underwear

Finally it should be noted that LITTLE, OLD and YOUNG, which are inherent Mod. II adjectives, often occur immediately before the head noun with no intervening Mod. III adjectives and seem to enter a kind of compound-like relation with the head (e.g. *little girl*, *old man*, *young people*). But in strings of adjectives from both Mod. zones, they usually follow (other) Mod. II adjectives and precede Mod. III adjectives:

(62)   a very attractive little American girl
(63)   a handsome young Italian doctor
(64)   funny old driven snow

12.3. Comparison of adjectives

12.3.1. The basic system of comparison

In section 5.6.5 we introduced the basic system of comparison in English in order to describe discontinuities in adjective and adverb groups expressing comparison. Let us begin this section by recapitulating the essential terminology employed for the description of comparison:

(i) We distinguish three members of the category:

positive	tall / beautiful
comparative	taller / more beautiful
superlative	tallest / most beautiful

(ii) There are two types of formal expression: a) *morphological* comparison with the suffixes *-er* and *-est*:

tall / taller / tallest

and b) *syntactic* comparison with *more* and *most*

beautiful / more beautiful / most beautiful

(iii) A maximal comparative construction consists of three things:

comparative element	-er / -est / more / most
adjective (or adverb)	tall / beautiful
comparative basis	than I am / than me / of them all

Here are some examples:

(1)   The *younger* man was about twenty, with wavy hair and long sideburns.
(2)   I liked public phones, they were *more private than private ones*.
(3)   This was our *oldest* suitcase.

Using the terminology suggested above we can describe the instances of comparison in examples (1) to (3) in this way:

– in (1) we have morphological comparison; the comparative form *younger* consists of the adjective YOUNG and the comparative element *-er*; there is no explicit comparative basis.

– in (2) we have syntactic comparison; the comparative form *more private than private ones* consists of the adjective PRIVATE, the comparative element the adverb *more* and the comparative basis the preposition group *than private ones.*

– in (3) we have morphological comparison; the superlative form *oldest* consists of the adjective OLD and the comparative element *-est*; there is no explicit comparative basis.

Note that in these descriptions we use the term 'comparative' in two different ways: it is used specifically to refer to the second member of the category (*taller/more beautiful*) but it is also used more generally as the adjective corresponding to 'comparison' in the terms *comparative element* ('the element which marks the comparison formally') and *comparative basis* ('the standard on the basis of which the comparison is expressed'), which are used in connection with both comparative and superlative constructions.

Comparison involves the *ranking* of entities on the basis of the *degree* to which they possess some property. The kind of comparison dealt with so far, comparison assigning a 'higher rank' or 'the highest rank', constitutes the central formal system of comparison in English (in the sense that we here have regular cases of morphologically marked comparison). It is important to realize, however, that there are also ways of expressing comparison assigning the 'same rank' and a 'lower rank' to an entity.

Assignment of the *same* rank is expressed by *as ... as* (or sometimes *so ... as*).

(4)   All right, we'll give you a typing test. Let's see if you are *as good as you claim.*

(5)   She wouldn't be *so mean as him.*

In such constructions the first *as* (or *so*) is a degree adverb, the second *as* a conjunction (as in example (4)) or a preposition (as in example (5)), cf. section 5.6.5.

Assignment of a *lower* rank is expressed by means of the irregularly compared forms of LITTLE, *less* and *least* (cf. section 12.3.3 below), plus the positive form of the adjective (i.e. on analogy with syntactic comparison assigning a higher rank by means of *more* and *most*):

(6)   This was a *less agreeable* place *than the railway station.*

(7)   She is the *least pretentious* professor I know.

(8)   Further away there was a smaller, *less ostentatious* house.

Note in this last example that though the two comparatives in example (8), *smaller* and *less ostentatious*, are paratactically related and semantically compatible, the former is comparison assigning a higher rank (albeit of 'smallness') whereas the latter is comparison assigning a lower rank.

In addition to the three ways of indicating rank on a property scale ('higher rank', 'same rank', 'lower rank'), there is a wealth of degree adverbs used in connection with adjectives to modify the property expressed in terms of degree but without explicit comparison being involved:

(9)   It wasn't *very pleasant* for Ruth, but she took it so coolly.

(10)   The room was *rather dark* and *extremely noisy*.

(11)   The carving was *too asymmetrical for his taste*, and the resemblance not *good enough*.

12.3.2. Spelling and pronunciation

Certain orthographical changes (very similar to those described in connection with verbal inflections in section 9.2) occur in connection with morphological comparison:

(i) adjectives ending in written *e* require only additional *-r* and *-st* in the comparative and superlative, respectively:

fine	finer	finest
free	freer	freest

(ii) single final written consonants (except *w*) are doubled before *-er* and *-est* when the preceding vowel is stressed and spelled with a single letter, compare:

big	bigger	biggest
narrow	narrower	narrowest
neat	neater	neatest

Especially in BrE we get doubling of final consonant also in:

cruel	crueller	cruellest

(iii) final written *-y* is normally changed to *-i-* when following a consonant but remains unchanged after a vowel, compare:

dry	drier	driest
grey	greyer	greyest

Especially in BrE, SHY, SLY, SPRY and WRY keep the *y*:

shy	shyer	shyest

Turning now to the spoken language, we begin by noting that the pronunciation of the suffixes *-er* and *-est* are [ə(r)] and [ɪst]. A number of phonetic changes occur when these suffixes are added to adjectival stems:

(i) final written *-r* is always pronounced when the suffixes are added:

      dear: [dɪə]   [dɪərə]   [dɪərɪst]

(ii) [ŋ] in *long, strong* and *young* becomes [ŋg] when the suffixes are added:

      long: [lɒŋ]   [lɒŋgə]   [lɒŋgɪst]

(iii) final syllabic dark *l* [ɫ] becomes non-syllabic clear l [l] when the suffixes are added:

      ample: [æmpɫ]   [æmplə]   [æmplɪst]

In such words morphological comparison thus does not increase the number of syllables.

12.3.3. Irregular comparison

There are a few irregularly compared forms:

bad/ill	worse	worst
good/well	better	best
much/many	more	most

In some cases there are competing comparatives and/or superlatives:

far	farther	farthest
	further	furthest
late	later	latest
	latter	last
little	less	least
	lesser	
near	nearer	nearest
		next
old	older	oldest
	elder	eldest

As adjectives and adverbs both *farther/farthest* and *further/furthest* are used about 'distance' (e.g. *The village is further/farther than the border*), though the *-a-* forms are not frequent in BrE. Only the *-u-* forms are used in the 'additional' sense (e.g. *further evidence / without further delay*).

The regular forms of LATE (*later* and *latest*) are used about 'time' (e.g. *a later bus / his latest novel*) whereas the irregular ones (*latter* and *last*) are more specialized: in formal language *latter* is used in contrast to *former* about the second of two entities already mentioned (e.g. *Joan and Ruth were both dedicated to the cause: the former offered to take night shifts at the local hospital, the latter joined our first aid unit*). But it is also used to denote a 'period towards the end' (e.g. *In the latter part of the century / her latter years*). While *latest* means 'most recent', *last* is used to describe the final entity in a sequence (cf. *her latest/last novel*). But *last* is also used deictically in contrast to *next* (cf. *last/next week*) and with the meaning 'the one earlier than the one we are talking about' in contrast to demonstrative *this* (cf. *This meeting is more boring than the last one*).

The distinction between *nearest* and *next* is similar to the distinction between *latest* and *last*: the regular form *nearest* is used in the locational sense whereas *next* is used with sequential meaning.

The two comparatives of LITTLE typically differ in that *less* is used quantitatively, *lesser* qualitatively and in certain idiomatic expressions:

(1)   They gave me *less* money than I needed.
(2)   This is one of his *lesser* works.
(3)   To invite him along would certainly be *the lesser of two evils*.

As we saw in section 12.3.1, *less* and *least* are furthermore used in connection with comparison assigning a lower rank.

The compared *o-* forms of OLD are used generally in comparative expressions involving the age of entities (e.g. *My car is much older than yours / my sister is much older than she looks / Roger is my oldest colleague / my much older sisters*). In predicative position only the *o-* forms are used. And only the *o-* forms can be modified, as in *much older* and *the very oldest*. The *e-* forms are used in attributive pre-head position (as well as 'substantivally', cf. section 12.4 below) as an alternative to the *o-* forms in expressions involving family relations (e.g. *My elder brother is now her eldest relative*). But as the following example shows, the *e-* forms are sometimes also used in connection with looser relations:

(4)   Two men – dressed in leather jackets and jeans – had followed me. Both
       looked like manual workers, but there was a marked age disparity. The *elder*
       man was about thirty-five.

Note finally the occasional use of *elder* in connection with proper names, e.g. *the Elder Matlock* and *Pliny the Elder*, and in the expression *an elder statesman*.

In addition to the irregularly compared forms presented above, there are in English a number of items that do not enter the normal, three-member system but which serve as comparative-like or superlative-like forms. Among such unpaired forms we find adjectives which inherently express comparison, such as e.g. OTHER, FIRST, SAME, DIFFERENT, SIMILAR, IDENTICAL:

(5)   They don't want anyone to know that they are still doing the *same* nasty
things *they did in the bad old days*.

There are also a number of items with comparative-like formal characteristics: INNER, OUTER, UPPER, NETHER, LATTER and FORMER. Unlike
genuine comparatives, these express contrast rather than rank within a
property scale. To indicate superlative meaning in connection with 'locality',
the suffix *-most* is used in a number of derivations from different kinds of
root: INNERMOST, OUTERMOST, UPPERMOST, FOREMOST, HINDMOST,
INMOST, TOPMOST, etc.

12.3.4. The choice between morphological and syntactic comparison

Most adjectives require or permit syntactic comparison with *more* and *most*.
But some adjectives require morphological comparison and a not insignificant number permit morphological comparison. Here are the rules:

(i) Monosyllabic adjectives (e.g. BIG, CLEAN, FAST, GREAT, HARD, HIGH,
LOW, QUICK, SMALL, THICK, YOUNG) normally require morphological
comparison:

kind	kinder	kindest
fine	finer	finest

Exceptions: JUST, LIKE, REAL, RIGHT, WORTH, WRONG and adjectives
denoting nationality like FRENCH, DUTCH, SWISS, etc. All these require
syntactic comparison.

(ii) Disyllabic adjectives with the stress on the final syllable often but not
invariably take morphological comparison:

polite	politer	politest
	(more polite)	(most polite)
profound	profounder	profoundest
	(more profound)	(most profound)

However, the following disyllabic adjectives almost always take syntactic
comparison: ANTIQUE, BIZARRE, CONTENT, DEVOUT, ORNATE, those
ending in *-esque* (e.g. BURLESQUE, GROTESQUE) and those with the prefix
a- (AFRAID, ASLEEP, ALOOF, etc.).

(iii) Disyllabic adjectives ending in an unstressed vowel or syllabic [ł]
(written *-er*, *-ow*, *-y*, *-le*) often but not invariably take morphological
comparison:

clever	cleverer	cleverest
	(more clever)	(most clever)

mellow	mellower	mellowest
	(more mellow)	(most mellow)
happy	happier	happiest
	(more happy)	(most happy)
simple	simpler	simplest
	(more simple)	(most simple)

The same applies to COMMON, CRUEL, HANDSOME, PLEASANT, QUIET and STUPID:

common	commoner	commonest
	(more common)	(most common)

Other disyllabic adjectives normally require syntactic comparison:

urgent	more urgent	most urgent
careful	more careful	most careful
anxious	more anxious	most anxious

(iv) Adjectives in three or more syllables require syntactic comparison:

creative	more creative	most creative
melancholy	more melancholy	most melancholy
impressionistic	more impressionistic	most impressionistic

(v) Participles serving as adjectives such as MARKED, DETACHED, FELT, PLEASED, PRONOUNCED, SHAKEN, MESMERIZED, BORING, DYING, INTERESTING, SOOTHING, WORRYING, etc. are always syntactically compared:

pleased	more pleased	most pleased
boring	more boring	most boring

(vi) Derived adjectives consisting of an adjectival stem which is normally compared morphologically and a negative prefix take morphological comparison but also permit syntactic comparison:

unkind	unkinder	unkindest
	(more unkind)	(most unkind)
untidy	untidier	untidiest
	(more untidy)	(most untidy)

(vii) The syntactic comparative of adjectives which permit both morphological and syntactic comparison is especially frequent in predicative position and when followed by a *than*-construction:

(1)   She was *more happy* than I thought.

The syntactic comparative is normally required in constructions comparing two properties in relation to the same entity:

(2)   She was *more happy /*happier* than *worried*.

Exceptions to this are HIGH, LONG, THICK and WIDE (and their antonyms), which are followed by a full *than*-clause (cf. Schibsbye 1970: 136):

(3)   The wall was *thicker than it was high*.

Morphological comparison is occasionally used for emotional effect in connection with adjectives normally requiring syntactic comparison:

(4)   She would give herself violently; then yawn at the *wrongest* moment.

(5)   He was shy and *awkwarder* than ever.

(6)   '*Curiouser* and *curiouser*!' cried Alice.

Note finally that when compared adjectives are coordinated, morphologically compared adjectives usually precede syntactically compared adjectives:

(7)   He wanted to head the *largest* and *most successful* publishing house in England.

(8)   The second option was a *longer* and *more tedious* route.

Interestingly this order normally coincides with the order that the corresponding positive forms would have (e.g. typically short before long), whether or not explicitly coordinated: *a large successful publishing house / a long tedious route* (cf. section 12.2.5 [B]).

For a string of adjectives some of which require, others permit syntactic comparison, this form of comparison is sometimes extended to the whole string (cf. e.g. Vestergaard 1985: 209):

(9)   A solution that is at once *more simple, economical and realistic* would be to return to the earlier practice.

12.3.5. The use of compared forms

The positive form of adjectives are used in an *absolute sense* (i.e. simply to express a property in relation to an entity with no inherent association of comparison). By contrast, the comparative form is used in a comparison to assign to some entity a *higher rank* on the property scale defined by the adjective, and the superlative form is used in a comparison to assign the *highest rank* to some entity. The term 'property scale' is here used to emphasize the fact that comparison applies only to gradable adjectives, i.e. adjectives with scalar meaning. With both comparative and superlative forms it is important to notice that what is expressed is ranking on the property scale defined by the adjective rather than the presence of the property denoted by the positive form of the adjective. For example, in an expression like *Jack is bigger and older than Joan*, the speaker ranks Jack higher than Joan on the property scales of 'bigness' and 'oldness'. This, however, does not necessarily mean that the speaker ascribes the properties of 'big' and 'old' to Jack. Jack can in fact be quite small and young even if he is bigger and older than Joan.

The comparative is found in expressions of 'comparison between two'. More specifically it is used:

(i) to assign a higher rank on the property scale defined by an adjective to one entity (or set of entities) than to another:

(1)   He suspected that Henry was *cleverer* than David.

(2)   The incident amused some of the *older* members.

The comparative basis is either explicit, as in (1), or implicit, as in (2).

(ii) to indicate that an entity ranks higher on a property scale on one occasion than on another:

(3)   She did not look a day *older* than when they had first met.

(4)   Once darkness had fallen the house became *more mysterious and sinister*.

(iii) to assign a higher rank to an entity on one property scale than on another:

(5)   His eccentricities were *more repugnant than amusing*.

(6)   The letter was *more mischievous than threatening*.

The comparative form in English is not infrequently used in an absolute sense with an association of '(fairly) high degree' rather than 'higher rank'. In some examples inviting this analysis, the comparison signalled by the comparative form is left unspecified in the context and therefore implies a very general comparative basis: e.g. *This company produces larger tents* (i.e. 'larger than most') and *Our dog seems to like older people* ('older than average'). In such examples the distinction between 'fairly high degree' and 'higher rank' is difficult to draw precisely. In other examples we have comparative forms expressing a more genuine absolute meaning, namely 'contrast', as in *the lower classes, an upper lip, the outer walls*, etc.

A gradually increasing degree of a property is expressed by repeating the comparative form (or marker) in a compound unit:

(7)   She sounded *angrier and angrier*.

(8)   He became *more and more irritating*.

482	*Adjectivals and adverbals*

Turning now to the superlative we note first of all that this form is found in expressions of 'comparison between more than two'. More specifically it is used:

(i) to assign a higher rank on the property scale defined by the adjective to one entity (or set of entities) than to *any* other (sets of) entities in a comparison, thus in effect ranking the entity as 'number one':

(9)   This is the *oldest* publishing firm in the country.

(10)   He bought the house on the *highest* mortgage obtainable.

(11)   She was the *youngest* actress of them all.

(ii) to indicate that an entity (or set of entities) ranks higher on the property scale on one occasion than on *any* other occasion:

(12)   Children are *happiest* when they know from the start who is boss.

(13)   Do you have any political enemies, using that word in the *widest* sense?

Several comments are pertinent in connection with the uses of the superlative. First of all, it is important to draw a distinction between 'comparative basis' and *'scope* of comparison'. In examples (9) and (10), unlike example (11), the comparative basis is merely implied (because there is no reference to the other entities involved in the comparison), but both examples contain a specification of the scope within which the other entities are to be found (*in the country / obtainable*). Secondly, examples like (11), where we find an explicit comparative basis (*of them all*) in connection with a pre-head superlative, are not frequent. More often one comes across examples where the superlative assumes head function (cf. section 12.4 below) with an explicit or implied *of*-construction as the comparative basis:

(14)   The incident brought back to mind unbidden *the greatest of all Thames tragedies*.

(15)   She was by far *the youngest*.

In both head and pre-head position the superlative requires a definite determiner.

The morphological superlative is occasionally used in an absolute sense, i.e. with an association of 'exceptionally high degree' rather than the usual association of 'highest rank':

(16)   Her face expressed the *liveliest* gratification.

The syntactic collocation of *most* and an adjective (or adverb) is often used for such purposes, especially in connection with the indefinite article:

(17)   It was a *most indecent* proposal.

(18)   I had a *most interesting* conversation with her the other night.

Note in this connection also standard expressions like: *With best wishes, at last, at least, my dearest Sarah*, etc.

The superlative is often informally used instead of the comparative in expressions of 'comparison between two' when there is an explicit or implied *of*-construction as the comparative basis:

(19)   Joan is the *more/most considerate* of the (two) sisters.

(20)   He accepted the *smaller/smallest* sum.

12.4. The substantival use of adjectives

12.4.1. What is meant by 'substantival use'?

Traditionally, adjectives are said to be used substantivally when they serve as heads in entity-expressing constructions like the following:

(1)   The new images were frightening. They ranged from *the grotesque* to *the obscene* to *the simply horrible*.

(2)   Pina was a formidable Italian matron who welcomed *the rich and famous* while ruthlessly pruning from her clientele those of lesser appeal.

(3)   Pauline is mildly piqued at the film's suggestion that it was Astrid rather than Stu who was *the more influential* of the pair.

(4)   James hadn't told us *the worst* yet.

We have retained the term 'substantival use' because it aptly reflects the fact that when adjectives are used in this fashion, 'substance' is in some (concrete or abstract) sense added to the normal adjectival expression of a property: a property becomes an entity. In example (1), the three italicized constructions express general abstract properties *as if they were entities* (e.g. *the grotesque* = 'something grotesque' or 'that which is grotesque'). In example (2), *the rich and famous* refers to 'rich and famous people' as a general kind, and in example (3), *the more influential* refers to a particular person. Finally in example (4), *the worst* expresses a specific entity (e.g. 'the worst information', 'the worst aspect of the case'). In each of these instances, the adjective expresses a property (like adjectives used non-substantivally) but the property is not related to an entity expressed by a separate constituent but is itself used to establish an entity.

Substantivally used adjectives are a mixture of adjectives and nouns. Like nouns they are used to express entities, and they normally take the definite article, as we have seen. Like adjectives they can be modified by adverbs (cf. *the simply horrible*) and permit comparison (*the more influential / the worst*).

Substantivally used adjectives should be delimited from:

(i) Lexical items that serve as both adjectives and nouns, such as CRIMINAL, GERMAN, IMBECILE, PRIMARY and SAVAGE. Unlike these, substantivally used adjectives do not normally accept the indefinite article, nor do they accept the plural *-s* form or the genitive, e.g. *a criminal / criminals / this criminal's* vs. **a more influential / *more influentials / *this influential's*.

(ii) Elliptical constructions with adjectives missing their head nouns:

(5)   This is not a good solution but can you think of *a better* (one)?

(6)   There were many Dutch politicians at the meeting but very few *German* (ones).

(7)   Old furniture is sometimes more expensive than *new*.

In these examples we have anaphoric ellipsis (cf. section 4.2.2). Unlike substantivally used adjectives, *better, German* and *new* are here used as parallels to premodifying adjectives (*good/Dutch/old*) and invite the use of N-replacive *one* if the entities involved are countable, as in examples (5) and (6), cf. section 11.3.4 [E].

(iii) Pronoun groups with a demonstrative pronoun as head, cf. *the injured* vs. *those injured*. The former is an example of substantival use of INJURED expressing a category of people, the latter is a pronoun group with *those* as head having specific reference.

12.4.2. Generic and specific reference

Substantivally used adjectives may have either generic or specific reference. Generic reference is typically found in connection with:

(i) Descriptive (i.e. inherent Mod. II) adjectives expressing an abstract entity:

(1)   Having put up with Mrs Thatcher for 10 years he clearly felt he could no longer defend *the indefensible*.

(2)   'Look,' she retorted angrily, 'I know I'm good, but even I can't manage *the impossible* at such short notice!'

(3)   Dale didn't look well for this interview; his waxy pallor had slid over into *the sickly*.

(ii) Descriptive (i.e. inherent Mod. II) adjectives expressing a category of people:

(4)   He accepts opponents without distinction – *the stupid, the wily, the vain, the cautious, the desperate, the hopeless*.

(5)   If the police waste time suspecting *the innocent* they'll have less chance of catching *the guilty*.

(6)   They know how to change the way people look. They make *the pretty* beautiful, *the passable* pretty, and *the ugly* interesting.

There is normally a clear association of plurality involved in such expressions, and as subjects they enter plural concord with the predicator (e.g. *The rich <u>tend</u> to prefer this area*).

Certain nationality terms and participles typically appearing in Mod. III may also be used substantivally to refer to a category of people: *the English / the French / the Irish / the Welsh /the Dutch / the Swiss / the Chinese / the Indonese / the Japanese / the Portuguese / the living / the dying / the injured.*

Specific singular or plural reference is typically found in connection with:

(i) Comparatives and superlatives (i.e. forms usually appearing in Mod. I):

(7)   *The older* of the two men turned out to be the poetry editor and *the younger* the accountant.

(8)   She would be *the less regarded* of the two, *the less popular*, the poor relation.

(9)   These clubs were by far *the most convenient* in London.

(10)   The incident brought back to memory *the greatest* of all Thames tragedies.

The use is particularly frequent in connection with an explicit or implied *of-* construction as the comparative basis.

(ii) Certain other adjectives typically appearing as Mod. I adjectives:

(11)   She promised to give me a call some time, but I knew that it would never be quite *the same*.

(12)   I went up to him and asked for *the usual*.

(13)   In *the following* we shall offer the rules for comparison in English.

(14)   Of the two wars it was *the first*, not *the second*, which had produced the greater poetry.

(iii) Certain fixed expressions: *the Almighty / the accused / the deceased / the condemned / the departed*:

(15)   The *accused* was/were greeted by many supporters.

As we have seen, substantivally used adjectives normally require the definite article. There are, however, exceptions to this, especially in the area of fixed expressions, e.g.: *to do one's best / at last / at least / my beloved / my intended / our poor / a bird feeding its young / a new class of rich* (cf. Schibsbye 1970: 123f). Note that in several of these a possessive pronoun functions similarly to a definite article.

The distinction between substantival use of adjectives with specific and with (sub)generic reference is not always clear-cut. Thus, we occasionally come across examples with superlative forms with generic reference and, conversely, examples of positive forms with rather specific meaning:

(16)   Equally hard to handle were the aggressively overconfident. But *the worst*,
         Maggie confided, were the conceited.

(17)   Oh, come on, Leo, don't play *the innocent* with me!

In this last example, *the innocent* still denotes 'type' but clearly does not have
general plural meaning.

12.5. Adverbals

12.5.1. Preliminaries

We begin our treatment of adverbals with some remarks on *adverbs as a
word class*. As indicated by its name, an adverb is a word which is closely
connected with a verb. In this way adverbs differ from adjectives, which
normally attach themselves to nouns. This difference can be illustrated by an
S P A sentence like *Numerous Danes drink immoderately*, in which
immoderately is closely connected with *drink* and *numerous* is attached to
Danes. Now to a large extent the words that are closely connected with verbs
are the same as those that modify adjectives and different from the ones that
modify nouns (see Huddleston 1984: 330). This can be illustrated by the
following examples:

(1)   She admires him *excessively*.

(2)   The debate was *excessively* long.

(3)   She drank an *excessive* amount of whisky.

The words that are closely connected with verbs and which modify
adjectives also modify words like themselves, i.e. other adverbs:

(4)   She spoke *excessively* quickly.

The fact that words like *excessively* share these three properties essentially
"provides the rationale for the very broad definition of adverb given in
traditional grammar" (Huddleston 1984: 330). Some words normally
classified as adverbs, it should be added, do not have all three relational
properties (for example, NOT, ACROSS and UPSTAIRS cannot modify an
adjective or another adverb). Others modify not just the verb but the rest of
the clause:

(5)   Surprisingly/Unfortunately/Sadly, no one turned up.

As compared with the other open word classes (nouns, verbs, adjectives)
adverbs are highly *heterogeneous*, particularly semantically. This can be
illustrated by words like NOT, WELL, ACROSS, ELEGANTLY and CLOCK-
WISE. It is therefore not surprising that they have been defined negatively as
those words that belong to an open class other than the noun class, the verb

class or the adjective class (i.e. as the *default* open word class). In positive terms, adverbs can be characterized as words whose functional domain is to express properties in relation to situations (as expressed by a verbal or a whole clause) or in relation to other properties (as expressed by adjectivals or other adverbals).

Morphologically, a large number of adverbs can be identified by the suffix *-ly* (for example SLOWLY, FAINTLY, REMARKABLY, BLATANTLY, CARE-FULLY, NICELY). We return to the morphology of adverbs in section 12.5.2.

Let us now consider *adverbals*. As pointed out in section 3.3.1, an adverbal is either a single adverb or a group with an adverb as head. This can be illustrated by the following examples:

(6) Please contact us *directly* for brochures or subscription information.
(7) The boys are playing *very nicely*.
(8) She was so surprised she stopped *right there*.
(9) They may arrive *sooner than you expect*.
(10) You just didn't look *carefully enough*.
(11) Lack of money is wiping out Russia's armed forces *more efficiently than any nuclear bomb*.
(12) She jerked her head *so violently she woke the baby*.

As appears, the head adverb of an adverb group accepts a pre-head dependent (7, 8), a post-head dependent (9, 10) or a discontinuously realized dependent which envelops the head adverb (11, 12). Occasionally an adverb may have two dependents, as in e.g. *very fortunately for me* in which there is not discontinuity but two separate dependents.

Pre-head dependents in adverbals are adverbs or adverb groups which typically modify a gradable adverb with respect to *degree*. This is the case in e.g. (7) and can be further illustrated by

(13) The rain smelled *ever so* slightly of home.

In both these sentences the pre-head dependent (*very*, *ever so*) intensifies the meaning of the head adverb, and so it does in an example like (8) in spite of the fact that THERE is not a gradable adverb, i.e. *right there* signals exact location and in that sense a high degree of 'thereness'. It should be noted that a pre-head dependent may also signal a *lower* degree of the quality expressed by the head adverb, cf. e.g. *She behaved less politely last week*. Frequent degree adverbs found in pre-head position are the ones which also premodify adjectives (see section 12.1.1): VERY, MUCH, QUITE, EXTREMELY, RATHER, HIGHLY, REALLY, SO, AS, TOO, MORE, MOST, LESS, LEAST. Pre-head adverbals may also occasionally express 'viewpoint', i.e. the respect in which something is done, as in the *(She reacted) politically correctly*.

Post-head dependents are realized by *than*-clauses (in cases of morphological comparison) or by the adverb ENOUGH, as in (9) and (10), respectively. They may also be realized by preposition groups:

(14)   Fortunately *for me*, they've already left.

Discontinuous dependents are found in cases of syntactic comparison:

(15)   Pundits were hedging *even more* blatantly *than usual.*

(16)   Mary danced *the most* elegantly *of them all.*

They may also be realized by constructions with *as ... as ..., so ... as ..., so ... that*-clause, *less ... than* and *too* + *to*-infinitive clause:

(17)   Mary dances *as* elegantly *as Joan.*

(18)   She has never danced *so* elegantly *as tonight.*

(19)   Kemp and Gore got along *so* famously *that it looked like a fraternity picnic.*

(20)   Mary dances *less* confidently *than she did last night.*

(21)   He is speaking *too* eloquently *to be entirely trusted.*

Adverbals express a variety of meanings (see also sections 3.2.9, 7.3.2 and 8.8 on the semantics of adverbials more generally). Some of these are illustrated in the following examples:

(22)   She was so surprised she stopped *right there.* (place)

(23)   The economy has *only now* begun to emerge from four years of stagnation. (time)

(24)   You just didn't look *carefully enough.* (manner)

(25)   I love you *very much.* (degree)

(26)   These items are rare and *therefore* very expensive. (reason)

(27)   *Even so*, what would you do? (concession)

(28)   *Politically*, he is quite mad. (viewpoint)

As mentioned in section 9.9.1, adverbals may also express *modal* meanings, cf. e.g. *Evidently they have slept here* (epistemic) and *Hopefully this is enough* (deontic).

12.5.2. Morphology

Adverbs are morphologically simple (YET, ENOUGH, etc.), complex (BACKWARDS, BLATANTLY, etc.) or compound (FURTHERMORE, THEREABOUTS, etc.). *Complex adverbs* constitute by far the largest of these subclasses, and most of them are formed by adding *-ly* to an adjective. This adverb-forming suffix is highly productive and much more so than the adjective-forming suffix *-ly* (FRIENDLY, COWARDLY, etc.). Adverbs in *-ly* frequently express *manner*. For example, the meaning of BLATANTLY is 'in a blatant way', and words like QUIETLY, RAPIDLY, FAINTLY, VIOLENTLY, SILENTLY, EASILY and NICELY can also be glossed 'in an [adjective] way'. In many other cases, however, and as demonstrated by the following examples, the meaning of an adverb in *-ly* is different:

(1)   He's occasionally late. (time-frequency)
(2)   I haven't heard from her recently. (time-duration)
(3)   There's a lot of crime locally. (place)
(4)   Theoretically, this is a good solution. (viewpoint)

Note that an adverb in *-ly* may express manner if it functions as a pre-head dependent in an adjective group but have another meaning if it realizes an adverbial:

(5)   The room is barely [= sparsely] furnished. S P C (manner)
(6)   The room is barely [= scarcely] furnished. S P A C (degree)
(7)   They can barely [= scarcely] read. S P- A -P (degree)

Complex adverbs may also be formed by adding *-ly* to an *-ing* or *-ed* participle form, as in JOKINGLY and HEATEDLY, or to a noun, as in MONTHLY and YEARLY (which are matched by identical adjectives). On the other hand, they cannot normally be formed by adding *-ly* to an adjective ending in *-ly*, i.e. from an adjective like FRIENDLY one cannot freely derive *FRIENDLILY. An example like *Jeremy sat in a misery of embarrassment, sicklily smiling* (quoted from Schibsbye 1970: 151) is thus exceptional.

As regards *spelling*, it should be mentioned that the final *-y* of an adjective in more than one syllable is changed to *-i-* in a derived *-ly* adverb, as in PRETTILY (PRETTY). Furthermore, the final *-e* of the adjectives DUE and TRUE is dropped in the derived adverbs DULY, TRULY (but note that it is retained in e.g. PALELY and SOLELY). The letter *-e* is also omitted in adverbs derived from adjectives ending in *-le*, though here an *l* is dropped as well (except in WHOLLY): SUBTLY (SUBTLE), NOBLY (NOBLE), etc. Adverbs derived from adjectives in *-ic* end in *-ically*, as in PROBLEM-ATICALLY (PROBLEMATIC), except for PUBLICLY and POLITICLY. Note finally an adverb like OFFHANDEDLY, derived from the adjective OFFHAND. In this case, it should be added, the form without a suffix may also be an adverb, as in *I can't say offhand whether it's route 66 or 69*.

A large number of complex adverbs in *-ly* are matched by adverbs without this suffix, for example LOUDLY by LOUD:

(8)   A dog was barking loudly.
(9)   Read the letter out loud.

Other examples of such adverb pairs are CLOSE/CLOSELY, DEEP/DEEPLY, DIRECT/DIRECTLY, FLAT/FLATLY, HARD/HARDLY and HIGH/HIGHLY. While the variants in -*ly* in many of these pairs are usually unmarked and the commoner ones, the short forms are largely restricted to idiomatic usage. Examples illustrating such usage are *hold me close, deep down, due east, take it easy, your memory is playing you false, aim high, pretty stupid, come as quick as you can, it serves you right, live rough* (i.e. without the usual facilities), *sleep tight* and *open your mouth wide*. A detailed account of adverbs in -*ly* which have matching forms without a suffix is given by van Ek & Robat (1984: 361ff) and by Schibsbye (1970: 152ff). In order to make sure to choose correctly between the two forms, the reader is also advised to consult a good dictionary.

Some adverbs in -*ly* expressing time are matched by formally identical adjectives, for example EARLY, HOURLY, DAILY, WEEKLY, MONTHLY and YEARLY. While it is an adverb which occurs in a sentence like *I got up early today*, the -*ly* form in a sentence like *She's in her early thirties* is an adjective.

Complex adverbs may also consist of a noun followed by the suffix -*wise*. In examples like CRABWISE and CLOCKWISE, which express manner and direction respectively, this type of derivation is unproductive. However, adverbs may be freely formed – particularly in AmE – by adding -*wise* to a noun for the expression of viewpoint, i.e. in the sense of 'so far as [noun] is concerned'. Examples illustrating this type of formation are FOODWISE, DRINKWISE, MONEYWISE, BUSINESSWISE and WEATHERWISE. Some complex adverbs end in the suffix -*ward(s)* (the forms without -*s* being typical of AmE). As illustrated by WESTWARD(S), HOMEWARD(S), BACK-WARD(S) and FORWARD(S) such adverbs express direction. Finally, a small group of complex adverbs begin with the prefix *a*-: ABROAD, APART, ASHORE, ASIDE, ASUNDER (see Huddleston 1984: 333). This type of adverb formation is completely unproductive.

In comparison with simple nouns, verbs and adjectives, *simple adverbs* (VERY, SOON, TOO, YET, etc.) constitute a fairly small class. Some simple adverbs, for example FAR, FAST, LITTLE, LONG, LOW, ONLY, STRAIGHT and WELL, are matched by formally identical *adjectives*. This can be illustrated by examples like the following:

(10)   Let's buy low and sell high. (adverbs)

(11)   Though in a low state of health, she's in high spirits. (adjectives)

As pointed out by e.g. Huddleston (1984: 333), the justification for saying that *low* and *high* are adverbs in (10) and adjectives in (11) is that it is usually contrasting forms we find in these two types of environment, as in *buy badly* and *a bad state of health*. Another group of simple adverbs, for example AFTER, BY, IN, NEAR, ON, OVER, THROUGH, UNDER and UP, are matched by formally identical *prepositions*:

(12) Our relationship is over. (adverb)

(13) She put her hand over my mouth. (preposition)

As illustrated by e.g. ABOARD, BENEATH, INSIDE, OUTSIDE and UNDERNEATH, such 'prepositional adverbs' may also be complex. Finally, attention should be drawn to simple words like WHEN, WHERE, WHY and HOW. Though often termed 'pro-adverbs' because they represent adverbial preposition groups (*at what time / at what place / for what reason / in what manner*), these are here classified as pronouns and have therefore already been dealt with (in sections 11.3.2 and 11.3.3).

Compound adverbs constitute a relatively small class. A number of these have HERE or THERE as their first element and a preposition as their last, for example AFTER, BY, IN, OF, TO or UPON. Compounds ending in these prepositions may also begin with WHERE, but as mentioned in section 11.3.2 WHERE is in this book analysed as a pronoun. Apart from HEREABOUTS, THEREABOUTS and THEREFORE adverbs beginning with HERE or THERE are formal, and so are compound adverbs like EVERMORE, FORTHWITH, HENCEFORTH, THENCEFORTH and WELLNIGH. Other examples illustrating this morphological subclass of adverbs are HALFWAY, NEARBY, OUTRIGHT, STRAIGHTFORWARD and words composed of a preposition followed by a noun such as DOWNHILL, DOWNSTAIRS, INDOORS, OFF-HAND and OUTDOORS. Note that apart from INDOORS and OUTDOORS these words can only be classified as adverbs rather than adjectives by looking at the context in which they occur (see section 3.1.4).

12.5.3. VERY vs. MUCH

Among the simple adverbs VERY and MUCH are particularly common, and as these two words usually present difficulty to foreign learners of English, their distribution will briefly be dealt with. MUCH is used if the adverb functions as an adverbial, i.e. if it is closely connected with the verb. This use of MUCH is almost always restricted to non-assertive sentences:

(1) We didn't enjoy the play much.

(2) It doesn't much matter what you say.

VERY is used before positive adjectives and adverbs:

(3) This is very useful.

(4) You'll hear from me very soon.

MUCH, however, is used in constructions with *too* followed by a positive form and is sometimes preferred before positive forms with the prefix *a-*:

(5)   I was much too fond of her.
(6)   Her little brother was much afraid.

VERY is used as a pre-head dependent before an adjective or adverb in the superlative form while MUCH is used before the combination of the definite article and the superlative form:

(7)   This is our very lowest price.
(8)   Friday is the very soonest I can have it ready.
(9)   This is much the noisiest place.

If the head of an adjective or adverb group is in the comparative form, however, it is MUCH which is required:

(10)   This is much better.
(11)   You'll notice much sooner than you expect.

Latinate 'comparatives' like SENIOR, JUNIOR, SUPERIOR, INFERIOR, etc. take MUCH if comparative meaning is expressed but otherwise VERY, cf.:

(12)   This paper is much superior to the last one you submitted.
(13)   This is very inferior stuff.

Note also that in accordance with the above rules an *-ed* participle form combines with MUCH if it is passive and with VERY if it is an adjectival non-passive (see section 7.4.6):

(14)   Your attitude is much disliked by your colleagues. (S P- A -P A)
(15)   The case is very complicated. (S P C)

Before preposition groups we only find MUCH:

(16)   He was much in love.
(17)   She decided to meet with him again, much to my annoyance.

Finally it should be mentioned that MUCH is often premodified by VERY and in some idiomatic cases obligatorily so:

(18)   I like it very much.

12.5.4. The external relations of adverbals

Adverbals typically function as *adverbials* or as *dependents*. When they take on the former function, they may realize adjuncts, disjuncts or conjuncts (cf. section 3.2.9):

(1)   She couldn't bring herself to go *any closer*. (adjunct)

(2)   Chi's arrival went *smoothly*. (adjunct)

(3)   *Unfortunately*, there has been strain over China's arms and nuclear transfers to Iran and Pakistan. (disjunct)

(4)   *Quite frankly*, relations are no longer entirely satisfactory. (disjunct)

(5)   Your book has its flaws. *Nevertheless*, we're going to publish it. (conjunct)

(6)   My first reaction was to say no. Since then, *however*, I've changed my mind. (conjunct)

When functioning as a dependent, an adverbal most often modifies an adjective:

(7)   U.S. officials find it *almost* inconceivable that Beijing would jeopardize its interests.

(8)   Moscow is having *unseasonably* warm weather.

(9)   He just isn't careful *enough*. (postmodification)

However, an adverbal may also modify an adverb, a nominal or a pro-nominal:

(10)   The rain smelled *ever so* faintly of home.

(11)   *Only* afterward did I consider the irony of the situation.

(12)   Vice President Al Gore intends to visit China *early* next year.

(13)   He's totally dedicated to his work and will do *virtually* anything to kill the rest of us.

Adverbal premodification of (pro)nominals is often performed by degree adverbs like QUITE, RATHER, ALMOST and NEARLY, as in *quite a blow, rather a pity, almost/nearly everybody* (see sections 10.3.5-6 and 11.3.4).

Adverbals may also function as dependents in preposition groups:

(14)   She's just returned from *abroad*.

(15)   Do you see anything up *there*?

Note finally examples like *She went straight to bed* and *We finished well within time* where *straight* and *well* may be regarded as premodifiers in relation to a preposition.

In compound units realizing an adverbal or a dependent, adverbals may function as *conjoints*:

(16)   Candido had heard *over and over* how they had clinics and housing and food slips for poor Americans. (A)

(17)   He'd stared *so long and so hard* at that strip of road that it wasn't a real place any more. (A)

(18)   The weather is *unexpectedly and unseasonably* warm. (DEP)

In non-clausal utterances adverbals may directly realize different speech act functions, such as STA (e.g. *Very badly* said in reply to *Has she been hurt?*),

QUE (e.g. *Very badly?* said in reaction to *She's been hurt*) and DIR (e.g. *Down* said to a dog).

Finally it should be mentioned that adverbals may function as *subjects* or *objects* in sentences like the following where locative or temporal conditions are referred to:

(19)   *Indoors* is recommendable at this time of day.

(20)   I prefer *outdoors.*

(21)   *Later* is not good enough, it has to be done now.

(22)   I prefer *tomorrow.*

12.5.5. Comparison

Adverbs which have – or which can be interpreted as having – scalar meaning, such as EARLY, NEAR, QUIETLY and SOON (but not e.g. YET, NOW, CLOCKWISE), are capable of being compared. The type of comparison they select is usually syntactic, but a number of *monosyllabic* adverbs – all of which are matched by identical adjectives – take morphological comparison:

(1)   She couldn't bring herself to go any *closer*.

(2)   Jane stayed the *longest* of them all.

(3)   Speak *louder* but don't come any *nearer*.

(4)   Let's see who can think of an answer *quickest*.

(5)   You'll see me *sooner* than you expect.

Among the derived adverbs in *-ly*, EARLY is compared morphologically while a couple of others, also matched by formally identical adjectives, vacillate between morphological and syntactic comparison:

(6)   Cole was injured *earlier* this season.

(7)   He speaks *kindlier / more kindly* to his children than he used to.

(8)   She is playing it *poorlier / more poorly* than she did yesterday.

Vacillation between morphological and syntactic comparison is also found in the case of a simple adverb like OFTEN:

(9)   I hope you'll come and see us *oftener/more often* next year.

For spelling and pronunciation of morphologically compared forms see section 12.3.2.

In the large majority of cases – including virtually all the numerous adverbs formed by adding *-ly* to an adjective – adverbs are compared *syntactically*:

(10)   That's what prominent Republicans said, on the airwaves and *more vehemently* in private.

(11)   Mary danced the *most elegantly* of them all.

The compared forms *quicker/quickest* and *louder/loudest* are often found whether or not the positive forms of the adverbs would have lacked the *-ly* suffix:

(12)   You'll probably get a cab *quicker* by walking to Waterloo Road.

When compared forms are coordinated, morphologically compared adverbs usually precede syntactically compared adverbs:

(13)   Gore spoke longer and more eloquently than Kemp.

Comparison to a lower and to the same rank on a property scale can be illustrated by examples such as:

(14)   I come here *less often* than I used to.

(15)   Let's hear if you can play it *as convincingly* as you claim.

A small group of adverbs have *irregular* comparison (see section 12.3.3 on irregularly compared adjectives):

badly	worse	worst
far	farther	farthest
	further	furthest
little	less	least
much	more	most
well	better	best

This manner of comparison can be illustrated by the following examples:

(16)   All this happened when we *least* expected it.

(17)   I know their secrets *better* than anyone else.

For the *use* of compared forms see section 12.3.5.

References

Aarts, Bas – Charles F. Meyer (eds.)
   1995   *The verb in contemporary English* Cambridge: Cambridge University Press.
Bache, Carl
   1978   *The order of premodifying adjectives in present-day English.* Odense: Odense University Press.
Bache, Carl
   1985a *Verbal aspect: a general theory and its application to present-day English.* Odense: Odense University Press.
Bache, Carl
   1985b "The semantics of grammatical categories: a dialectical approach", *Journal of Linguistics* 21: 51-77.
Bache, Carl
   1986   "Tense and aspect in fiction", *Journal of Literary Semantics* 15: 66-70.
Bache, Carl
   1994   "Verbal categories, form-meaning relationships and the perfect", in: Carl Bache – Hans Basbøll – Carl-Erik Lindberg (eds.), 43-60.
Bache, Carl
   1995   *The study of aspect, tense and action.* Frankfurt am Main: Peter Lang.
Bache, Carl – Hans Basbøll – Carl-Erik Lindberg (eds.)
   1994   *Tense, aspect and action: empirical and theoretical contributions to language typology.* Berlin and New York: Mouton de Gruyter.
Bache, Carl – Mike Davenport – John Dienhart – Fritz Larsen
   1993   *An introduction to English sentence analysis.* Copenhagen: Munksgaard.
Bache, Carl – Leif Kvistgaard Jakobsen
   1980   "On the distinction between restrictive and nonrestrictive relative clauses in modern English", *Lingua* 52: 243-267.
Bolinger, Dwight
   1952   "Linear modification", *Publications of the Modern Language Association of America* 67: 1117-1141.
Bolinger, Dwight
   1967   "Adjectives in English: attribution and predication", *Lingua* 18: 1-34.
Bolinger, Dwight
   1975   *Aspects of Language* (2nd edition). New York: Harcourt Brace Jovanovich, Inc.
Chomsky, Noam
   1957   *Syntactic structures.* The Hague: Mouton & Co.

Collins Cobuild English grammar:
  see John Sinclair 1990.
Davidsen-Nielsen, Niels
  1985   "Has English a future?", *Acta Linguistica Hafniensia* 21, 1: 5-20.
Davidsen-Nielsen, Niels
  1990   *Tense and mood in English: a comparison with Danish.* Berlin and New
          York: Mouton de Gruyter.
Davidsen-Nielsen, Niels (ed.)
  1991   *LSP: nine studies on language for special purposes.* Copenhagen: Handels-
          højskolens Forlag.
Dienhart, John
  1992   "Adverbials, direct objects and the style of Carson McCullers", *The Twain
          Shall Meet,* POET 18, Department of English, University of Copenhagen:
          121-134.
Dik, Simon
  1989   *The theory of functional grammar.* Dordrecht: Foris Publications.
Dirven, René (ed.)
  1989   *A user's grammar of English: word, sentence, text, interaction.* Frankfurt
          am Main: Peter Lang.
Downing, Angela – Philip Locke
  1992   *A university course in English grammar.* New York and London: Prentice
          Hall.
Elsness, Johan
  1997   *The perfect and the preterite in contemporary and earlier English.* Berlin
          and New York: Mouton de Gruyter.
Ferris, Connor
  1993   *The meaning of syntax: a study in the adjectives of English.* London: Long-
          man.
Fodor, Jerry A. – Jerrold J. Katz (eds.)
  1964   *The structure of language.* Englewood Cliffs, N. J.: Prentice-Hall.
Granger, Sylviane
  1983   *The be + past participle construction in spoken English with special em-
          phasis on the passive.* Amsterdam: North Holland.
Greenbaum, Sidney – Randolph Quirk
  1990   *A student's grammar of the English language.* London: Longman.
Halliday, Michael A. K.
  1985   *Spoken and written language.* Victoria: Deakin University Press.
Halliday, Michael A. K.
  1994   *An introduction to functional grammar.* London, New York, Sydney and
          Auckland: Edward Arnold.

Hansen, Erik
   ms. *"Det*-kløvning".
Harder, Peter
   1989 "The instructional semantics of conditionals", *Working Papers in Functional Grammar* 30: 1-42.
Harder, Peter
   1996 *Functional semantics: a theory of meaning, structure and tense in English.* Berlin and New York: Mouton de Gruyter.
Hartvigson, Hans – Leif Kvistgaard Jakobsen
   1974 *Inversion in present-day English.* Odense: Odense University Press.
Hopper, Paul J. – Elizabeth C. Traugott
   1993 *Grammaticalization.* Cambridge: Cambridge University Press.
Hoye, Leo
   1997 *Adverbs and modality in English.* London: Longman.
Huddleston, Rodney
   1976 "Some theoretical issues in the description of the English verb", *Lingua* 40: 331-383.
Huddleston, Rodney
   1984 *Introduction to the grammar of English.* Cambridge: Cambridge University Press.
Huddleston, Rodney
   1988 *English grammar: an outline.* Cambridge: Cambridge University Press.
Huddleston, Rodney
   1995 "The English perfect as a secondary past time", in Bas Aarts – Charles F. Meyer (eds.), 102-122.
Jakobsen, Leif Kvistgaard
   1994 "Variation in the use of the definite article and the demonstratives as cohesive devices", RASK 1 (Odense University Press): 63-82.
Jespersen, Otto
   1909-49 *A modern English grammar on historical principles.* Copenhagen: Munksgaard, and London: Allen & Unwin.
Jespersen, Otto
   1929 *The philosophy of grammar.* London: Allen & Unwin.
Jespersen, Otto
   1933 *Essentials of English grammar.* London, Boston and Sydney: George Allen & Unwin.
Johansson, Stig – Per Lysvåg
   1986 *Understanding English Grammar* 1. Oslo: Universitetsforlaget.
Johansson, Stig – Per Lysvåg
   1987 *Understanding English Grammar* 2. Oslo: Universitetsforlaget.

Juul, Arne
   1975   *On concord of number in modern English*. Copenhagen: Nova.

Juul, Arne – Knud Sørensen
   1978   *Numerus i moderne engelsk.* Copenhagen: Schønberg.

Klima, Edward
   1964   "Negation in English", in: Jerry A. Fodor – Jerrold J. Katz (eds.), 246-323.

Klinge, Alex
   1993   "The English modal auxiliaries: from lexical semantics to utterance inter-
          pretation", *Journal of Linguistics* 29: 315-357.

Kragh, Bodil
   1991   "LSP, science and technology: a sociological approach", in: Niels David-
          sen-Nielsen (ed.), 39-52.

Lakoff, George – Mark Johnson
   1980   *Metaphors we live by*. Chicago and London: University of Chicago Press.

Lauridsen, Karen
   1986   *Øvelser til engelsk grammatik.* Copenhagen: Schønberg.

Leech, Geoffrey
   1981   *Semantics* (2nd edition). Harmondsworth: Penguin.

Lyons, John
   1968   *Introduction to theoretical linguistics*. Cambridge: Cambridge University
          Press.

Lyons, John
   1981   *Language and linguistics*. Cambridge: Cambridge University Press.

Lyons, John
   1995   *Linguistic semantics: an introduction*. Cambridge: Cambridge University
          Press.

Martin, James Edward
   1968   *A study of the determinants of preferred adjective order in English*. Un-
          published doctoral dissertation, Urbana, Illinois: University of Illinois.

Matthews, Peter
   1981   *Syntax.* Cambridge: Cambridge University Press.

McArthur, Tom (ed.)
   1992   *The Oxford companion to the English language.* Oxford: Oxford University
          Press.

Munck, Lena
   1991   "Les textes techniques: leurs éléments constitutifs et leur réalisation en da-
          nois", in: Niels Davidsen-Nielsen (ed.), 53-66.

Nässlin, Siv
   1984   *The English tag question.* Stockholm: Almquist & Wiksell.

Nølke, Henning
  1984 "Clefting in Danish", *Nydanske Studier & Almen Kommunikationsteori* 14 (Copenhagen: Akademisk Forlag): 72-111.
Palmer, Frank
  1986 *Mood and modality.* Cambridge: Cambridge University Press.
Palmer, Frank
  1987 *The English verb* (2nd edition). London: Longman.
Palmer, Frank
  1990 *Modality and the English modals* (2nd edition). London: Longman.
Payne, John
  1985 "Negation", in Timothy Shopen (ed.), 197-242.
Preisler, Bent
  1992 *A handbook of English grammar.* Aarhus: Aarhus University Press.
Quirk, Randolph – Sidney Greenbaum – Geoffrey Leech – Jan Svartvik
  1985 *A comprehensive grammar of the English language.* London: Longman.
Radden, Günter
  1989 "Semantic roles", in: René Dirven (ed.), 421-472.
Schibsbye, Knud
  1970 *A modern English grammar* (2nd edition). Oxford: Oxford University Press.
Shopen, Timothy (ed.)
  1985 *Language typology and syntactic description I: clause structure.* Cambridge: Cambridge University Press.
Sinclair, John (ed.)
  1990 *Collins Cobuild English grammar.* London and Glasgow: Collins.
Steller, Poul – Knud Sørensen
  1974 *Engelsk grammatik* (2nd edition). Copenhagen: Munksgaard.
Swan, Michael
  1995 *Practical English usage.* (2nd edition). Oxford: Oxford University Press.
Twaddell, W. Freeman
  1965 *The English verb auxiliaries.* Providence: Brown University Press.
van Ek, Jan A. – Nico J. Robat
  1984 *The student's grammar of English.* Oxford: Basil Blackwell.
Vestergaard, Torben
  1985 *Engelsk grammatik.* Copenhagen. Schønberg.
Vikner, Carl
  1973 "Quelques réflexions sur les phrases clivées en français moderne", *Actes du 5ème Congrès des romanistes scandinaves,* Turku, 221-235.
Wells, Rulon S.
  1947 "Immediate constituents", *Language* 23: 81-117.

Subject index

Word index

a/an 180, 246, 360-1, 390
aboard 491
about 86
above all 442
abroad 452, 490
absent (v) 417
acclaim 211
according to 182
(the) accused 485
acoustics 394
across 86, 486
actor 354
actress 354
addendum 392
advise 254
afloat 452, 460
aforementioned 4
aforesaid 4, 11
afraid 448, 450, 452, 478
after 63, 184, 491
after all 442
ain't 221
airline 471
airs 395
alert 452, 460
alike 460
alive 460
all 182, 224, 244, 361-4, 390, 400,
    434-6, 441, 443, 448
all in all 442
allow 153
almost 493
(the) Almighty 485
alone 452, 460
aloof 460, 478
(the) Alps 241, 247, 370, 394
already 218, 229
although 134, 184
alumna 392
alumnus 392
always 140, 294
am 221, 239, 406
among 427
ample 476

analysis 393
ancient 449
and 166, 172-6, 178, 213, 241,
    248-9
(the) Andes 241, 247
anger 241
animate 450
another 180, 360-1, 400, 446
answer 264, 344
antelope 393
antenna 392
antique 478
any 165, 180, 228, 360-1 363, 400-1,
    434, 436-40, 443, 448
(the) Americas 370
anybody 228, 243, 400, 436
anyhow 260, 437
anyone 228, 260, 400, 436, 440
anything 228, 243, 435, 438, 440
anyway 437
anywhere 229, 260, 437
apart 490
apart from 156
apologies 395
appear 43, 53, 153, 276
appendix 393
apply 417
aquarium 392
are 239, 406
aren't 221
as 272, 275, 372, 374, 408, 412, 418,
    448, 459, 487
as … as 474
as if 64, 188
as soon as 188
as though 188
as well as 175, 327
ashore 490
aside 490
asleep 452, 460, 462, 478
assume 195
assuming 119, 270
at all 335, 442
athletics 394

Lyons 382

main 458
major 469
majority 245
make 204
make do with 95
man 354, 380, 392
man-of-war 396
man-servant 397
many 182, 224, 357, 363-5, 390, 400-
    2, 419, 436, 444-5, 469, 476
mare 353
marked 479
marry 213
master 354
mathematics 241, 394
matrix 393
matters 380
may 6, 39, 119, 220, 232, 269, 283-5,
    290, 316, 323, 325, 327-8, 332,
    334, 336, 339
the Mayflower 371
me 360, 400, 404, 408-9, 414, 417
mean 248, 298
means 240, 393
measles 241, 394
media 395
meet 168, 213
medical 449, 457-8, 465, 471
meet 164, 213
mellow 451, 479
mesmerized 479
metal 471
metropolis 393
the Midlands 248
might 39, 269-70, 328-9
million 398
mine 400, 402, 413
mistress 354
monarch 353
money 357
moneywise 490
monk 353
monthly 489-90
moon 358
more 161, 218, 357, 364, 400-1, 436,
    448, 473-4, 476, 479, 487

morning 381
most 161, 218, 364, 400-1, 448, 473-
    4, 476, 482, 487
motto 391
mouse 392
much 224, 367, 400, 419, 448, 476,
    487, 491-2
much-debated 452
mumps 241, 394
music 241
must 6, 39, 283, 285, 325, 332-6,
    338-9
my 180, 246, 361, 400-1, 413
myself 400, 415-6, 418

nanny-goat 355
narrow 457, 475
nasty 470
national 458
native 457-8
navigable 455, 459
near 491, 476, 494
nearer 476
nearest 476-7
nearby 491
nearly 493
neat 475
need 6, 214, 284, 333-6
negotiable 284
neither 121, 180, 222- 4, 226, 244,
    246, 249, 360-1, 363, 390, 436,
    443
neither ... nor 176-7, 188, 242
nether 478
the Netherlands 240
never 140, 227, 260, 294-5
nevertheless 260
Newcastle-on-Tyne 371
news 241, 344, 394
next 364, 446, 469, 476-7
nice 449, 451
nicely 487, 489
night 381
the Nile 371
no 180, 224, 360-1, 363, 400-1, 434,
    436-40, 443
no less 373
no one 224, 249, 400, 436, 439